Information Systems
for
Modern Management

ROBERT G. MURDICK

*Professor of Management
College of Business and Public Administration
Florida Atlantic University
Registered Professional Engineer, N. Y.*

JOEL E. ROSS

*Director, Graduate Studies
College of Business and Public Administration
Florida Atlantic University*

Information Systems for Modern Management

PRENTICE-HALL, INC., *Englewood Cliffs, New Jersey*

© 1971 by Prentice-Hall, Inc., Englewood Cliffs, New Jersey

All rights reserved. No part of this book may be reproduced in any form or by any means without permission in writing from the publisher.

13-464503-0
Library of Congress Catalog Card Number 70-130842

Current printing (last digit)
10 9 8 7 6 5 4 3

PRINTED IN THE UNITED STATES OF AMERICA

PRENTICE-HALL INTERNATIONAL, INC., *London*
PRENTICE-HALL OF AUSTRALIA PTY. LTD., *Sydney*
PRENTICE-HALL OF CANADA, LTD., *Toronto*
PRENTICE-HALL OF INDIA PRIVATE LIMITED, *New Delhi*
PRENTICE-HALL OF JAPAN, INC., *Tokyo*

To Emily and Carol

foreword

The accelerating complexities of modern organizations demand new dimensions in modern management. Perhaps the most profound and promising of these dimensions is the emerging utilization of more advanced information systems. These systems are changing the process of management in several ways.

First, the basic functions of planning and control now depend to an increasingly greater extent on access to computer-based information systems as decision making becomes more structured and relies more and more on the flow of information to and between decision centers. Second, the organization is changing to accommodate information technology. The structure and composition of organizational resources are beginning to reflect a new approach to organizational design caused by the systems approach. A third major change is the manner in which the technical functions of the business are managed. Marketing, finance, manufacturing, and the other functional areas are largely controlled by the design of information systems to facilitate decision making and operations within and between these subsystems of the firm.

Professors Murdick and Ross have put together a stimulating and challenging approach to information systems and modern management. They have synergistically combined the related disciplines of management, information systems design, and decision making into a gestalt of modern management. It becomes increasingly necessary in the 1970's that the manager and the student of management keep abreast of these developments.

BILLY E. GOETZ

Visiting Professor
Department of Accounting and Finance
Florida Atlantic University

preface

Management theory and practice have undergone radical changes in the past two decades; these changes are certain to continue and indeed to accelerate. It is no longer enough that the manager be skilled in a functional specialty such as engineering or marketing and that he understand the traditional functions of planning, organizing, and controlling. Something more is needed: the systems approach to management, coupled with the ability to participate in the design and utilization of computer-based information systems. Indeed, the systems approach is the new philosophy of managerial life. The 1970's are ushering in the "age of systems."

There are a number of books available on the individual topics of (a) management and organization, (b) computers, (c) information, and (d) the systems approach. However, none have combined and blended these topics into a set of related concepts, a unified body of knowledge and practice. This is the ambitious aim of our book. We hope it will provide a more up-to-date and integrated treatment of organization and management, as well as emphasizing the utilization of management information systems to improve the art of managing.

One objective is to get the practicing manager and the student of management to "think systems." If we can take the mystery out of computer-based information systems for them, they should be better prepared to become involved in the effective design and use of those systems. Such involvement is essential for the manager of the 1970's!

For the computer specialist, the information-systems specialist, or the student of computer systems, the objective is to improve the utility of the systems they design. We make the unequivocal point that such systems must always be designed from the point of view of the manager–user and not that of the specialist. In order to achieve this perspective, the information-systems specialist must understand management, management decision making, and the role of systems design in improving the management process.

An additional objective of the book is to help close the communication gap that separates the manager from the computer specialist. This gap undeniably exists and is the direct cause of the gross underutilization of the vast majority of computer installations. The reasons are readily apparent. The manager either is too busy, is uninterested, or will not take the time to raise his understanding to a level necessary for direct involvement. This book should bring him to that minimum level. The information-systems specialist, on the other hand, is more often engrossed in the hardware and techniques of computer operation and frequently overlooks the special nature of the system—that it should be designed for the requirements of the manager–user. In other words, if he is left to his own devices, he designs a system that ignores reality. This book can direct him to new and vastly more profitable areas of application.

The organization of the book is straightforward in structure. Part I presents first an overview of management and systems so that the following chapters in this part have a focal point. The basic structure of organizations is introduced as a point of departure for the important behavioral aspects of organizations. The management information system as both a binding system and a basis for decision making is then discussed in Part II, along with the power of the computer for increasing decision-making and organizational effectiveness.

Part III concentrates on conceptual aspects of information and decision problems. Without a grounding in these concepts, the manager can only grope for improved information systems through trial and error. The systems designer without such understanding can be at best a mechanic, and at worst a hack.

Part IV proceeds from the organizational and information-decision concepts of the first three Parts to present the methods of application to real-world systems design. The description of what a completed system ought to be like, presented so commonly by writers, is of little value to the manager and system designer. We have taken a bold approach in our attempt to guide the manager and designer step by step along the major routes leading to the installed system. We have supplied the managerial event-paths rather than the nuts-and-bolts details that are the province of every skilled designer.

Part V differs from the conceptual and operational Parts to present a view of the future.

References will be found grouped at the ends of chapters, and case studies are provided at the ends of each of the first four Parts.

Probably any attempt to cover all aspects of MIS in less than several dozen volumes will lead to criticisms of superficiality, misplaced emphasis, and omissions. We acknowledge the criticisms in advance, but we believe there is a great need for a good first text of the scope of this one. We wish to express our appreciation to the many companies and executives who gave so freely of their time and ideas toward this end. In particular, we appreciate the valuable and detailed review and comments of Dr. Billy Goetz. We relieve him of responsibility for errors and our own viewpoints, of course. Professor Ronald Zoll provided us with several helpful suggestions. Dr. John Sullivan furnished us many stimulating ideas during free-for-all luncheon discussions. We also acknowledge gratefully the valuable assistance of Mr. Ned Heinbach of the General Electric Company and Professor Donald Holmes of Union College, who supplied us with information concerning their joint MIS educational programs.

We are grateful also to the reviewers who examined our manuscript and offered many helpful suggestions—Professors Leonard J. Garrett of Temple University, Charles H. Kriebel of Carnegie-Mellon University, and Christopher E. Nugent of the Harvard Business School; Assistant Professor John P. Seagle of the State University of New York at Buffalo; and Mr. Stanford L. Optner, President of Stanford L. Optner & Associates, Inc., Los Angeles.

Finally, there were three of the fair sex in the background without whose effort this book would never have materialized. Mrs. Irene Sherbini transcribed the rough manuscript into finished form. Emily Murdick sustained one of the authors by numerous typings of rough drafts. And Carol Ross provided continued encouragement to the other author during many periods of frustration.

ROBERT G. MURDICK
JOEL E. ROSS

Boca Raton, Florida

contents

I Management and Systems

1 management and systems — 3

THE AGE OF SYSTEMS. WHAT IS A "SYSTEM"? THE SYSTEMS APPROACH: Characteristics of the Systems Approach. Systems versus Inductive Approach. REASONS FOR THE SYSTEMS APPROACH: Complexity in Modern Organizations. Advances in Management. THE SYSTEMS APPROACH AND THE MANAGER OF THE FUTURE: The Organization of the Future. The Manager of Tomorrow.

2 development of management and organization theory — 31

MILESTONES IN THE DEVELOPMENT OF ORGANIZATION AND MANAGEMENT THEORY: Frederick W. Taylor. Henri Fayol. The Hawthorne Experiments. The Electronic Computer. Modern Organization Theory. The Systems Age—The Age of Synthesis. SCHOOLS OF MANAGEMENT ANALYSIS: The Behavioral School. The Empirical School. The Decision Theory School. The Quantitative School. The Management Process School. Summary. APPROACHES TO ORGANIZATION THEORY: Classical Theory of Organization. Neoclassical Theory of Organization. MANAGEMENT—ART, SCIENCE, OR PROFESSION?

3 modern organization theory: behavioral aspects 67

ORGANIZATION SYSTEMS. RELATIONSHIP OF ORGANIZATION THEORY TO MANAGING. WHOM DOES THE ORGANIZATION SERVE? BEHAVIOR AND MOTIVATION: Differentiation. Needs. Basic Needs or Motivations. Theory X and Theory Y in Motivating Workers. Organizational Control and Motivation Assumptions. Motivation and Hygiene Factors. Frustration and Adjustment. Economic and Noneconomic Incentives. THE INFORMAL ORGANIZATION AS A SOCIAL SYSTEM: Nature and Formation of Informal Groups. Communication. Group Standards and Norms. Nature and Sources of Power and Authority. Conflict and Cooperation. LEADERSHIP FOR MANAGERS: Nature of Leadership. Situational Approach to Leadership. Leadership Styles.

4 the systems approach to organization and management 103

MODERN ORGANIZATION THEORY: A SYSTEMS VIEW: System Parts and Their Interdependency. Integrating Processes. Summary. INTEGRATING BASIC MANAGEMENT FUNCTIONS: PLANNING, ORGANIZING, CONTROLLING: Planning. Organizing. Controlling. Integration of Managerial Functions. MANAGEMENT AND SYSTEMS CONCEPTS: Planning and Systems Concepts. Organizing and Systems Concepts. Control and Systems Concepts. THE SYSTEM OF ORGANIZATION AND MANAGEMENT.

CASE STUDY:

AMERICAN SCIENTIFIC PRODUCTS COMPANY, INC. (A), 145

II Computer-Based Management Information Systems

5 information systems and management 153

EVOLUTION OF AN INFORMATION SYSTEM. ELEMENTS AND OPERATION OF THE MANAGEMENT INFORMATION SYSTEM (MIS): Prerequisites of an Information System. Elements of a Management Information System. Operation of a Management Information System. INFORMATION AND MANAGEMENT: Information and Planning. Information and Organizing. Information and Control. Summary. BASIC INFORMATION SYSTEMS: Financial Information. Production/Operations. Marketing Information. Personnel Information. Other Information Systems. AUTOMATION, COMPUTERS, AND MANAGEMENT: Information Automation. Automation and Decision Making.

6 what the manager should know about the computer 193

DATA PROCESSING AND THE COMPUTER: Components and Operation of a Data Processing System. OPERATION OF A MANUAL INFORMATION SYSTEM: Input. Processor. Storage. Program/Procedure. Output. COMPONENTS OF A COMPUTER SYSTEM: Input. The Central Processor. Storage. Output. Summary. CONVERSION OF MANUAL TO COMPUTER-BASED SYSTEMS: System Description. Input Documents. Output Documents. File Design. The Program Flowchart. Computer Assembly. Computer Program. Program Operation. Summary. THE DATA-BANK CONCEPT: Information Storage—Manual Systems. Information Storage and Retrieval—Data Bank. TYPES OF COMPUTER-BASED APPLICATIONS: Batch Processing Applications. Real-Time Applications. Decision Applications.

7 computer-based information systems for decision making 237

AUTOMATION OF INFORMATION: The Programmed Decision System. Decision-Assisting Information Systems. DECISION SYSTEMS AND LEVELS OF MANAGEMENT: Clerical and Supervisory Level. Middle-Management Level. Top-Management Level. INTEGRATION: THE OBJECTIVE OF COMPUTER-BASED SYSTEMS FOR DECISION MAKING: Integration of Information Systems. Integration of the Functions of Management. Integration of Resources. Integration of Management Levels. CLASSIFICATION OF SYSTEMS: Task or Function. Resource. Network Flows. Levels of Systems. Environment.

8 systems theory and management information systems 277

SYSTEMS CLASSIFICATIONS: Conceptual and Empirical. Natural and Man-Made. Social, Man–Machine, and Machine. Open and Closed. Permanent and Temporary. Stationary and Nonstationary. Subsystems and Supersystems. Classification of Organizational Systems and of MIS. SOME SYSTEM CONCEPTS: Principal System Quantities or Variables. System Parameters. Components. Attributes of Components. Structure. Process. Boundaries. Characteristics of Systems. NEED FOR A GENERAL SYSTEMS THEORY: The Aims of General Systems Theory. Fundamental Approaches. INFORMATION FEEDBACK SYSTEMS: The Elements and Operation of a System. THE BUSINESS ORGANIZATION AS A SYSTEM.

CASE STUDY:

AMERICAN SCIENTIFIC PRODUCTS COMPANY, INC. (B), 306

III Information, Decision Making, and Management Science

9 data, information, and communication   313

MEANING OF INFORMATION AND DATA. THE DATA LIFE CYCLE. CHARACTERISTICS OF INFORMATION. INFORMATION, MANAGEMENT, AND THE COMPUTER. INFORMATION SEARCH, STORAGE, AND RETRIEVAL. COMMUNICATION: Interpersonal Communication. Communication Network in Organizations.

10 problem solving and decision making   341

PROBLEMS, MANAGEMENT, AND SYSTEMS. THE NATURE OF PROBLEMS. FORMULATION OF THE PROBLEM. THE PROBLEM-SOLVING PROCESS: A Pragmatic Approach. A Procedure for Solving Ill-Structured Problems. Organizational and Individual Problem Solving. DECISION MAKING AND MIS: Programmed and Nonprogrammed Decisions. Making Nonprogrammed Decisions. Making Programmed Decisions. MIS as a Technique for Making Programmed Decisions. THE DECISION PROCESS: Decision Making and Information. Factors That Shape the Decision Process. Management and the Decision Process. ANATOMY OF CHOOSING: Simplifying the Choice Process for Complex Decision Problems.

11 management science and systems modeling   375

WHAT IS MANAGEMENT SCIENCE? WHAT ARE MODELS? KINDS OF MODELS. USE OF MODELS FOR ANALYSIS OF SYSTEMS CHARACTERISTICS: Block Diagram and "Black Box" Concepts. Feedback and Control. State-Descriptive Models of Systems. SIMULATION. CONSTRUCTION OF MODELS.

CASE STUDIES:

AN INFORMATION PROBLEM, 408

THE DEVELOPMENT OF A MANAGEMENT INFORMATION SYSTEM FOR FIELD OFFICE MANAGERS OF THE NORTHWESTERN INSURANCE COMPANY, 410

IV Planning, Design, and Implementation of MIS

12 planning and programming management information systems — 421

THE NEED FOR SYSTEMS PLANNING. OBJECTIVES OF MANAGEMENT INFORMATION SYSTEMS PLANNING. PROJECT PLANNING AND MIS. NEEDS RESEARCH. SETTING PROJECT OBJECTIVES. PROJECT PROPOSAL. PLANNING TECHNIQUES: Work Breakdown Structure. Sequence Planning. Master Program Schedule. Budgeting. REPORTING AND CONTROLLING: Reporting Techniques. Reporting Problems. Control Through "Completed Action."

13 MIS design: gross design concepts — 445

DEFINE THE PROBLEMS. SET SYSTEM OBJECTIVES. ESTABLISH SYSTEM CONSTRAINTS: Internal Constraints. External Constraints. DETERMINE INFORMATION NEEDS. DETERMINE INFORMATION SOURCES: Analysis and Integration. Information Sources—Summary. DEVELOP ALTERNATIVE GROSS DESIGNS AND SELECT ONE. DOCUMENT THE SYSTEM CONCEPT: General System Flow. System Inputs. System Outputs. Other Documentation. PREPARE THE GROSS DESIGN REPORT.

14 detailed systems design — 473

INFORM THE ORGANIZATION OF THE PURPOSE AND NATURE OF THE SYSTEMS DESIGN EFFORT. AIM OF DETAILED DESIGN. PROJECT MANAGEMENT OF MIS DETAILED DESIGN: Project Planning. Project Control. IDENTIFY DOMINANT AND PRINCIPAL TRADE-OFF PERFORMANCE CRITERIA FOR THE SYSTEM. DEFINE THE SUBSYSTEMS: Information for Defining Subsystems. Obtaining Information. SKETCH THE DETAILED OPERATING SUBSYSTEMS AND INFORMATION FLOWS. DETERMINE THE DEGREE OF AUTOMATION OF EACH OPERATION. DEVELOP THE DATA BASE. MODEL THE SYSTEM QUANTITATIVELY. DEVELOP THE SOFTWARE. ESTABLISH THE INFORMATION OUTPUT FORMATS FOR MANAGEMENT. TEST THE SYSTEM BY SIMULATION. PROPOSE AN ORGANIZATION TO OPERATE THE SYSTEM. DOCUMENT THE DETAILED DESIGN.

15 implementation of the new MIS — 505

PLAN THE IMPLEMENTATION: Identify the Implementation Tasks. Establish Relationships Among Tasks. Establish a Schedule. Prepare a Cost Schedule Tied to Tasks and Time. Establish a Reporting and Control System. ACQUIRE FLOOR SPACE AND PLAN SPACE LAYOUTS. ORGANIZE FOR IMPLEMENTATION. DEVELOP PROCEDURES FOR IMPLEMENTATION. TRAIN THE OPERATING PERSONNEL. DEVELOP THE SOFTWARE; ACQUIRE THE HARDWARE. DEVELOP FORMS FOR DATA COLLECTION AND INFORMATION DISSEMINATION. DEVELOP THE FILES. TEST THE SYSTEM. CUT OVER. DOCUMENT THE SYSTEM: Documenting a Manual Information System. Documenting a Computer-Based MIS. EVALUATE THE MIS. CONTROL AND MAINTAIN THE SYSTEM.

CASE STUDIES:
THE ARTCRAFT COMPANY, 527
QUANTUM ENGINEERING ASSOCIATES, INC., 529

V The Future of MIS

16 management information systems: the future — 547

THE FUTURE: AN OVERVIEW. FUTURE TRENDS IN MANAGEMENT INFORMATION SYSTEMS: The Changing Nature of MIS. The Growth of Real Time. Time Sharing. Service Systems. Improved Technology. The People Problem. MIS: Impact on the Manager and the Management Process. THE NEED FOR MANAGERIAL INVOLVEMENT IN SYSTEMS DESIGN: Causes of Systems Difficulties. Prerequisites for Useful Management Information Systems. Managerial Involvement—Conclusion.

index — 565

Information Systems
for
Modern Management

Management and Systems

The accomplishment of complex tasks—such as producing millions of automobiles, operating airlines, running hospitals, or directing governments—is achieved by organizing human effort. Management is both a part of such organizational systems and the guiding influence in them. If, in a more complex future, greater tasks are to be accomplished and the vast unused potential of people at work is to be released, we will need far greater insights into management, organizational behavior, and systems than we now possess.

Part I introduces the nature of management from a systems viewpoint. It covers the powerful roles of information systems and computers in the management process. At the same time, the motivations, responses, and roles of those who actually perform the work are examined. The need for greater understanding of the "people-components" of systems is made clear. Although basic organizational structures are presented, the dynamic process of people at work within living systems is also brought out, with management style and worker motivation related in these systems by modern organizational behavior theory.

In essence, Part I is an examination of the nature of managed organizational systems.

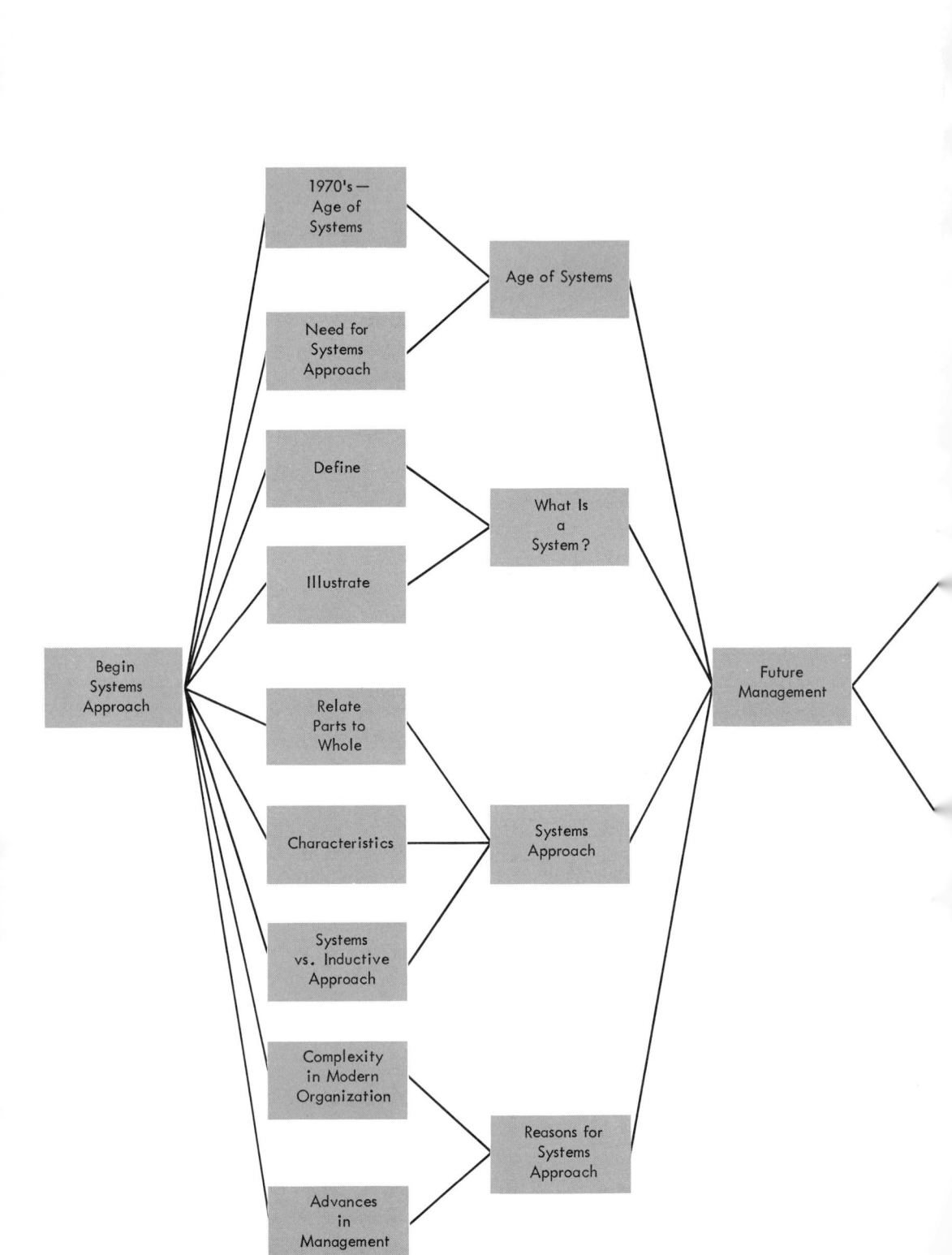

```
Begin Systems Approach
├── 1970's — Age of Systems ──┐
├── Need for Systems Approach ─┴── Age of Systems ──┐
├── Define ──┐                                      │
├── Illustrate ─┴── What Is a System? ──┐           │
├── Relate Parts to Whole ──┐           │           │
├── Characteristics ────────┼── Systems Approach ──┼── Future Management
├── Systems vs. Inductive Approach ─┘              │
├── Complexity in Modern Organization ──┐          │
└── Advances in Management ─────────────┴── Reasons for Systems Approach ─┘
```

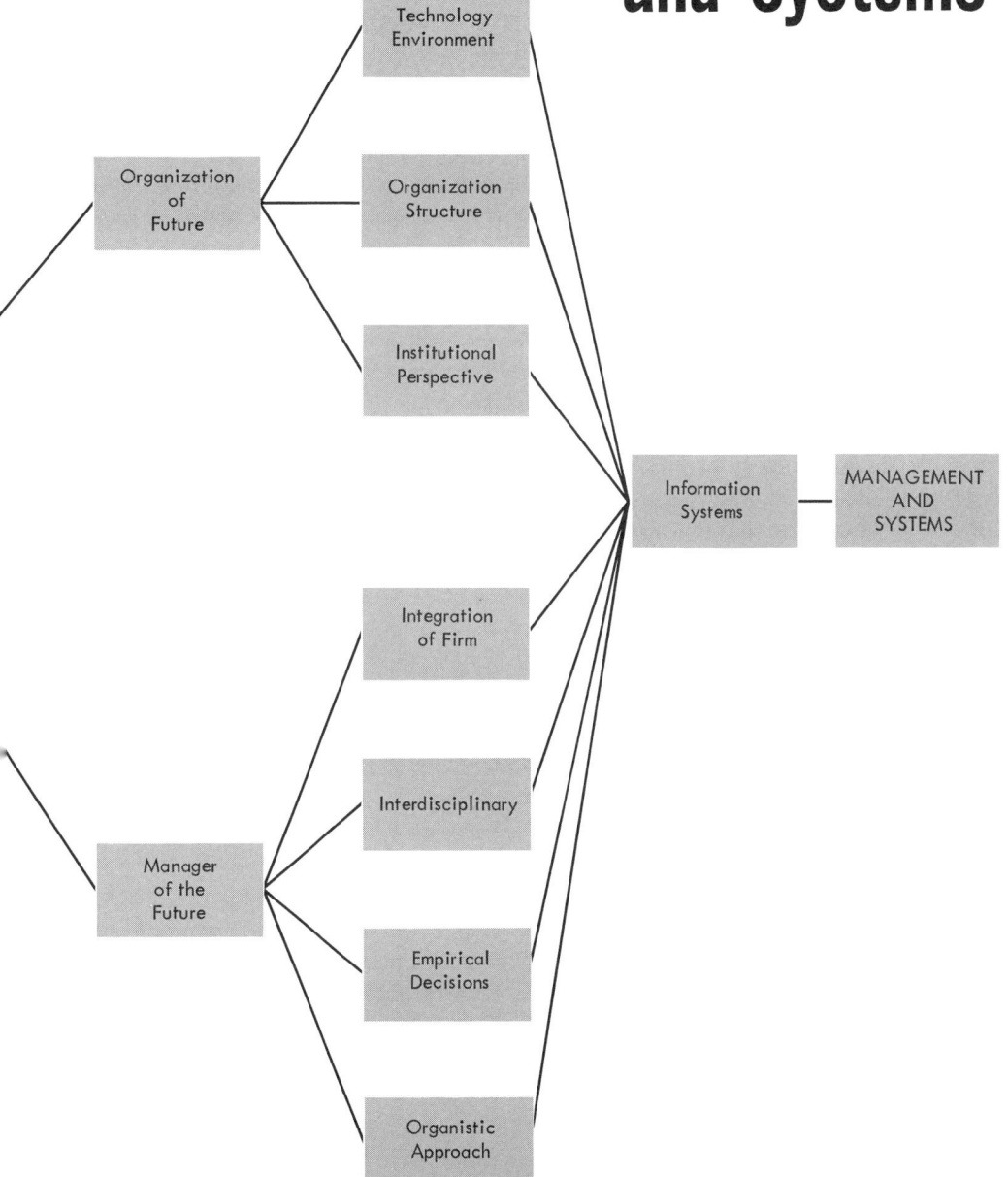

1
management and systems

- Technology Environment
- Organization Structure
- Institutional Perspective
- Integration of Firm
- Interdisciplinary
- Empirical Decisions
- Organistic Approach

Organization of Future

Manager of the Future

Information Systems — MANAGEMENT AND SYSTEMS

1

Systems era . . . age of synthesis . . . open systems . . . cybernetics . . . homeostatic systems . . . decision rules . . . information feedback . . . automatic control . . . systems design . . . management information systems . . .

These and similar phrases are part of the jargon and vocabulary of the new science of management information systems—the science that holds great promise for coping with the vast growth in size, complexity, and diversity in operations of the modern organization. This increasing size and complexity characterizing the modern large-scale organization has made the classic managerial functions of planning, organizing, and controlling more difficult to perform, yet increasingly essential to the stability and growth of today's enterprise.

Whether evolutionary or revolutionary, the systems era is upon us. For more than a hundred years—since the Industrial Revolution—management has been considered an art, which has been advanced by the acquisition and recording of human experience. From a discussion of management situations and an examination of past experiences recorded in the literature, the manager and the student have been expected to gain an intuitive insight into the principles underlying the problems they are expected to face. However, the manager of today needs more help than he is likely to find in studying the experiences of others. What is needed is an underlying science, or at the very least a more structured approach to decision making.

The systems approach provides the process for accommodating the complexity in the modern firm. The tools are provided by management information systems, computer-based or manual. Taken together, the framework of the systems approach and the tools of management information systems provide the manager with modern techniques and methods for planning, organizing, integrating, and controlling his operations more effectively.

THE AGE OF SYSTEMS

Although the adoption of the systems approach as a philosophy of management and the use of management information systems as a vital tool of management are fairly recent developments, this trend is certain to accelerate. The growing impatience with the "classical" guides for organizing the work of managers is accompanied by an awareness that neither the traditional, the technical, nor the "experience" approach to organizational administration is sufficient for the complex operations of today. Along with the wider acceptance of the manager's role as primarily a decision maker, the growing use of the computer and associated analytical tools also assists in the decision-making process. This approach implies more emphasis on systems analysis and a realization that the customary methods of arranging the work of managers are inadequate, although they may have been satisfactory when the organization was smaller or when it operated in a less complex environment.

More and more firms are beginning to realize the importance of the systems approach and the need to redesign their information systems around decision requirements. Systems personnel and managers who "think systems" are exercising broader influence in the planning and operations of organizations. In short, we are witnessing a fundamental change in the administration of organizations. The process of management is rapidly making the transition from decades of "seat-of-the-pants" techniques based on experience or intuition to an era of management problem solving through systems analysis, an era during which the problems of management are approached as identifiable, observable, measurable, and solvable through the new methodology of systems. Indeed, the decade of the 1970's promises to be the "systems age."

The pre-World War I era might be characterized in scientific and economic history as the period of analysis. Scientists were breaking down knowledge to study its parts. Chemists analyzed matter to find new elements; biologists looked for new species; economists studied primarily the characteristics of the individual firm; engineers designed new products without consideration of technical or economic integration with related products.

Between the two World Wars, there was a gradual transition from breaking things down to putting them together. Einstein produced his general theory of relativity; economists turned to national income accounting and aggregative economics; technologists designed network systems such as the Bell telephone system.

Aggregative and systems concepts and applications developed rapidly after World War II. We hear of "defense systems," "water resource systems," "economic systems," and "management systems." Indeed, if pre-World War I was the Age of Analysis, post–World War II has become the Age of Synthesis. It is not that analysis has disappeared; on the contrary, it has grown more powerful with constantly developing techniques and tools. It is the emphasis on combining the results of analysis into a *whole* that has changed so drastically, and it is this emphasis that makes the concept of systems synthesis so dramatic.

With each decade, in fact each year, accelerating scientific progress has produced such vast amounts of information that increased specialization by scientists has become necessary. Yet there is also a growing need for people who can relate the parts to the whole. These "generalists" or "systems designers" are people who can synthesize complexity. They are needed not only to provide structures or frameworks for scientific disciplines but also to formulate approaches to practical problems of mankind. The building of a dam or the polluting of a river in the United States is now recognized as more than a local concern; these are actions that should be viewed in relation to the total water resource system of the country. Shipping lines, airlines, rail systems, and trucking companies should be viewed not as separate private enterprises, but rather as subsystems of the country's transportation system. A business organization itself is more than a collection of separate activities such as marketing, manufacturing, and finance. The various functions, divisions, products, markets, and the internal and external environments of the firm must be synthesized. The firm must be considered as more than mere components tied together in static fashion by a hierarchical structure of management; it must be viewed as a system of closely related parts with a dynamic fluidity.

The synthesis of large, complex systems and the development of the concept of systems have also focused attention on the need for a systems approach to science and to man's problems. The term "large and complex" does not necessarily refer to size alone, but rather to the number of parts that make up the system and to their multiple interrelationships. The human organism and the microbiological systems are not large in physical size, but they are very complex when measured by number of parts and by processes in which the parts engage.

If we are to understand the complexities of nature and if we must design complex systems such as the modern management information system, we must develop the science of systems. That is, we must look more closely at what constitutes a system, at what the characteristics of systems are, what distinguishes classes of systems, and what comprises the systems approach. The methods of science require more precision than commonsense, intuitive methods. Science requires a thorough study of structure and processes. Therefore, although such careful inquiry may seem dry to the practice-minded reader, it is necessary for the design of effective, complex, practical systems.

A major element of this type of inquiry is careful definition for purposes of communication. Now that we have introduced the terms *systems* and *systems approach,* we shall sharpen our focus and capture these terms in more detail.

WHAT IS A "SYSTEM"?

In an elementary way, a system may be described as a set of elements joined in some way for the purpose of attaining common, mutual goals. This definition is illustrated by examples of some very diverse types of systems:

System	Elements	Basic Goal
Human body	Organs, connective tissue, bone structure, nerve network	Homeostasis
Social club	Members	Recreation for members
Factory	Man, machines, buildings, materials	Production of goods
Missile system	Man, missiles and launch sites, detection and communication networks	Counterattack
Police	Men, equipment, buildings, communication networks	Control of crime
Computer	Physical components and connections	Processing of data
Galaxy	Stars, planets, energy	Unknown
Philosophy	Ideas	Understanding
Accounting	Journals, ledgers, computers, people	Report of financial operations and value of the firm and document transactions

This list of examples shows that systems vary greatly in elements, apperance, size, attributes, and basic goals. A carefully worded definition is therefore needed to identify their common features. In Chapter 8 we will provide a system of classification to distinguish differences among systems.

A study of definitions formulated by many scholars[1] leads us to adopt the following comprehensive one:

> *A system is a set of elements forming an activity or a processing procedure/scheme seeking a common goal or goals by operating on data and/or energy and/or matter in a time reference to yield information and/or energy and/or matter.*

Some specific cases illustrate the somewhat abstract definition:

1. *Manufacturing system.* A group of people, machines, and facilities (*a set of elements*) work to produce a specified number and type of products (*seek a common goal*) by operating on product specifications, schedules, raw materials, subassemblies, and electrical power converted to mechanical power (*operate on data, matter, and energy*) to yield the specified products and information by the date the customer wants them (*to yield matter in a time reference*).

2. *Management information system.* A group of people, a set of manuals, and data processing equipment (*a set of elements*) select, store, pro-

cess, and retrieve data (*operate on data and matter*) to reduce the uncertainty in decision making (*seek a common goal*) by yielding information for managers at the time they can most efficiently use it (*yield information in a time reference*).

3. *Business organization system.* A group of people (*set of elements*) gather and process material and informational resources (*form an activity*) toward a set of multiple common goals including an economic profit for the business (*seek common goals*) by performing financing, design, production, and marketing (*operate on data, energy, and matter*) to achieve finished products and their sale at a specified minimum rate per year (*yield matter in a time reference*).

From the foregoing definitions and what we know about systems, several common characteristics of *organizations* and *information systems* emerge:

1. An information system and an organization are systems and can be analyzed, designed, and managed as such by the general principles of systems design.

2. Both are ongoing processes. This implies that they are dynamic rather than static and that account must be taken of their changing nature.

3. The elements of each are functionally and operationally united. Here we see the necessity to design an information system in a way that will permit the integration of the parts of the organization it serves. This integration is known as the "total systems" approach.

4. Both the organization and the information system have outputs. In both cases the output is an objective, but the information system's output is a decision resulting from data furnished through the system. A major part of information system design effort is devoted to programming these decisions.

THE SYSTEMS APPROACH

Essentially, the systems approach to management is designed to utilize scientific analysis in complex organizations for: (a) developing and managing operating systems (e.g., money flows, manpower systems), and (b) designing information systems for decision making. The link between these two processes is obvious: the reason for *information* systems design is to assist in making decisions regarding the management of *operating* systems.

A fundamental concept of the systems approach to organization and management is the interrelationship of the parts or subsystems of the organization. The approach begins with a set of objectives, and it focuses on the design of the whole as distinct from the design of components or subsystems. The *synergistic* characteristic of the systems approach is all-important.

Organizational and information systems are designed to achieve *synergism*—the simultaneous action of separate but interrelated parts producing a total effect greater than the sum of the effects taken independently. The results obtained by a team or a "system" of eleven football players is greater than that achieved by eleven individual players performing without integrated effort. The analogy for a business organization is clear.

In the past, business organizations fell short of optimum effectiveness because they failed to relate the parts or functions (subsystems) to each other and to the whole. The sales function was sometimes performed without adequate regard for the manufacturing function; production control was not coordinated with financial or personnel planning; and the classic management information system consisted of the chart of accounts. The traditional accounting system was concerned largely with the production of ex post facto information for financial statements, not with forward-looking management decision making.

This focus on separate functions and failure to interrelate the parts into a unified whole can be attributed to a variety of causes, primarily the narrow view of the specialist (i.e., engineer, accountant, inventory clerk) who cannot or will not relate his specialty or his "box" on the organization chart to the remainder of the organization. Other causes are improper organization, poor planning, or failure to integrate the organizational components through the systems approach. Focus on the design of the whole as distinct from the design of components and subsystems—a fundamental premise of the systems approach—is illustrated in Figure 1–1. The heavy solid line indicates the authority relationships and hierarchical structure of the classical organization; concern is with formal authority relationships and the chain of command rather than with the interrelationship of the parts. The dotted lines show the same organizational structure with the parts joined in a system by means of information flow and the systems approach to organization and management.

The reader should not conclude from Figure 1–1 that the distinction between the "classical" and "systems" approaches is clear and absolute. Indeed, the classical approach has always provided for the routine exchange of information across the chain of command. Copies of sales orders have gone to the credit, production scheduling, shipping, and accounts receivable departments. Budgets have looked to the future and have included the separate parts of the organization. However, these devices, while providing a measure of integration and coordination, were not *synergistic* and did not achieve the degree of decision-making sophistication that we want to obtain from the systems approach.

We will be concerned in this book with solving *practical* problems by means of the *systems approach*, particularly with problems requiring decision making by management. The systems approach to problem solving embodies (1) a philosophy of approach, and (2) a method for design of

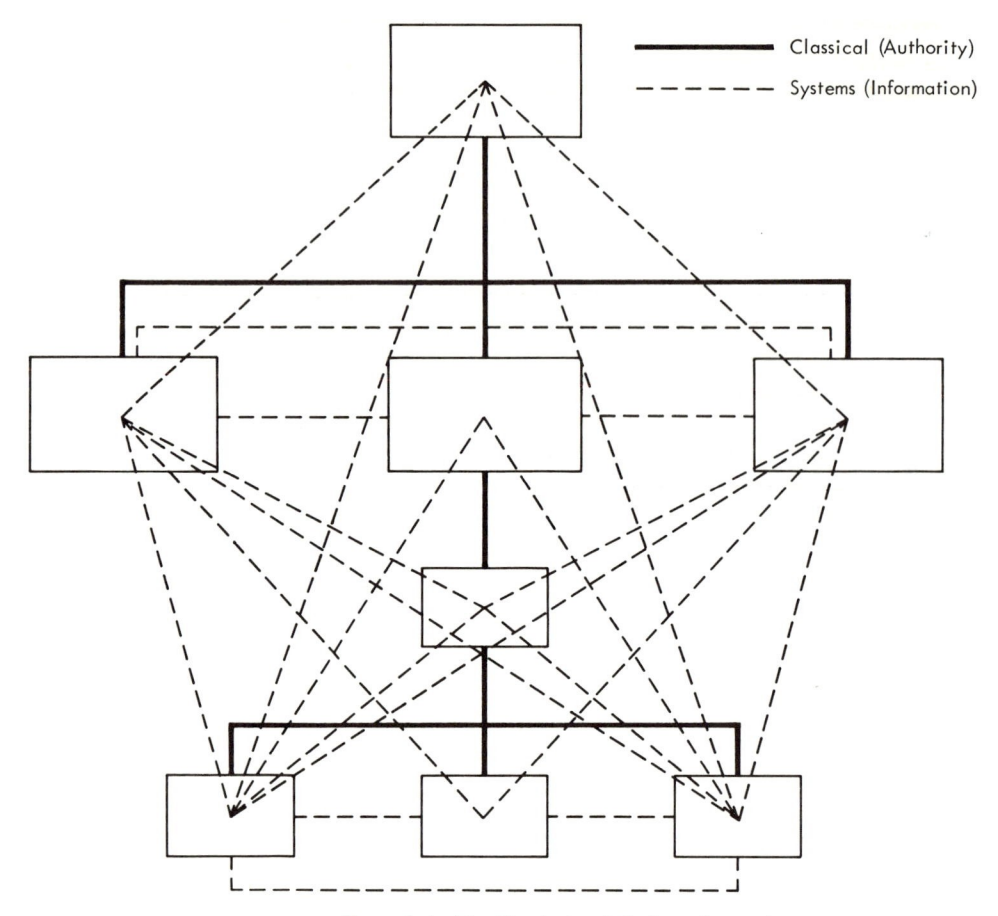

Figure 1–1 The Classical and Systems Approach to Organization and Information Flow

problem-solving systems. The philosophy consists of always viewing the problem and its components in their related entirety instead of as pieces. This approach has been described by Thome and Willard:[2]

> The Systems Approach is an orderly way of appraising a human need of a complex nature, in a let's-stand-back-and-look-at-this-situation-from-all-its-angles frame of mind, asking oneself:
>
> How many distinguishable elements are there in this seeming problem?
>
> What cause-and-effect relationships exist among these elements?
>
> What functions need to be performed in each case?
>
> What trade-offs may be required among resources once they are defined?

Because the systems approach focuses on the design of the whole, it deals with relationships before perfecting components. To illustrate this point, consider the "Sizzling Steak House." In the old, component approach, the management sought to:

1. Optimize the cooking area and process
2. Optimize the serving process
3. Optimize the dining area and money-collecting process

The cooking arrangement could thus be superb, but it might be very inconvenient and inefficient for serving customers. The serving process might be excellent but the dining area so arranged for customers and billing that service could not easily be adapted or integrated with the dining area.

In this case, what did management do? It stated its systems objectives of giving the customer well-prepared food to eat in a pleasant layout. By surveying the whole system, management decided that the customer should place his cold-food order first and then his hot-food order, both at a cafeteria counter. As the meat is cooked to order, he pays his bill and gets a numbered receipt. He brings his cold food to the dining area and picks up his hot plate when his number is called. Efficiency of the total production system and low cost to the customer are achieved by this system design. Note the trade-off between material handling of food by the restaurant and economy to the customer. Also, the arrangement for order taking, billing, and cooking are very closely integrated in the setup.

It is not possible to give exact instructions for designing a system such as the one cited. Instead, a generalized procedure and a set of guidelines may be developed. The systems designer develops the art of tackling systems problems largely through experience, and his methods may range from simple common-sense reasoning to sophisticated operations research techniques. Basically, though, the systems approach is a systematic application of intellect, techniques, and tools in order to achieve an integration of components for a specified purpose.

Characteristics of the Systems Approach

The systems approach is also organized, creative, theoretical, empirical, and pragmatic.[3] Although the same may be said of past management practice, there are differences of degree and procedure. These characteristics of the systems approach are as follows:

1. *Organized.* The systems approach is a means for solving large, amorphous problems whose solutions involve the application of large amounts of resources in an organized fashion. Usually a team of skilled professional generalists (systems designers) and specialists (technique and

component experts) examine the problem domain for a specified period of time in order to formulate the problem. The problem formulation is critical to the entire design project because the objectives of the system are derived from the problem statement on needs. Management plays a large part in the identification and formulation of problems. Although the development of the system in later stages may not provide the best component design, the system may still function to provide an adequate solution. If the problem is incorrectly diagnosed, however, and incorrect objectives are established, the system fails, regardless of how well the detailed design is carried out.

The organized approach requires that the systems team members, despite diverse specialized backgrounds, understand the systems approach. The language of systems design is the basis for their communicating.

2. *Creative.* Despite the generalized procedures developed for systems design, the systems approach must be a creative one that focuses on goals first and methods second. The ultimate system is greatly dependent on the originality and creativeness of the individuals contributing to its design.

The systems approach must be creative because:

a. The problems are so complex and ill-structured that there is no unique formulation or solution.

b. Much of the available data are so incomplete, uncertain, or ambiguous that imagination of a high order must be used to form a theoretical framework for the problem.

c. Alternative solutions must be generated for subsystem problems, and from among many solutions, selections must be made that yield an approximation of an optimal total system.

d. Traditional functional and disciplinary barriers must be subordinated to the synthesis of the solution.

3. *Theoretical.* Underlying the systems approach are the methods of science. Science provides theoretical structures (their validation increasing with time) upon which we can construct practical solutions to problems. The structure is the skeleton, and the data provide the flesh that fills out the form. Different data may yield different forms, but the theory provides the mold. Relevant theory for the systems approach may be drawn from any discipline as required, and systems theory itself is based on many disciplines.

4. *Empirical.* The search for empirical data is an essential part of the approach. Relevant data must be distinguished from irrelevant, and true data from false. Pertinent data generally include not only facts on the technical aspects but also facts on the practices, functions, interactions, attitudes, and other characteristics of organization in man–machine systems.

5. *Pragmatic.* For empirical or real systems, a crucial characteristic of the systems approach is that it yields an action-oriented result. The system must be feasible, producible, and operable. Systems activities are di-

rected toward fulfilling a set of actual purposes or of real needs. The systems designers must therefore gain a good understanding of the organization for which the work is being done. Further, the personnel of the organization must become involved in the process of diagnosis, development, and design.

Systems versus Inductive Approach

We can distinguish further between the systems approach and the component or inductive approach by comparing Figure 1-2 and Figure 1-3. In the inductive approach, observations of data yield objectives for the development of components (or subsystems). The focus is on the parts rather than the whole, on the data rather than on total system objectives. The process is one of *synthesis* of bits to plaster together the whole system.

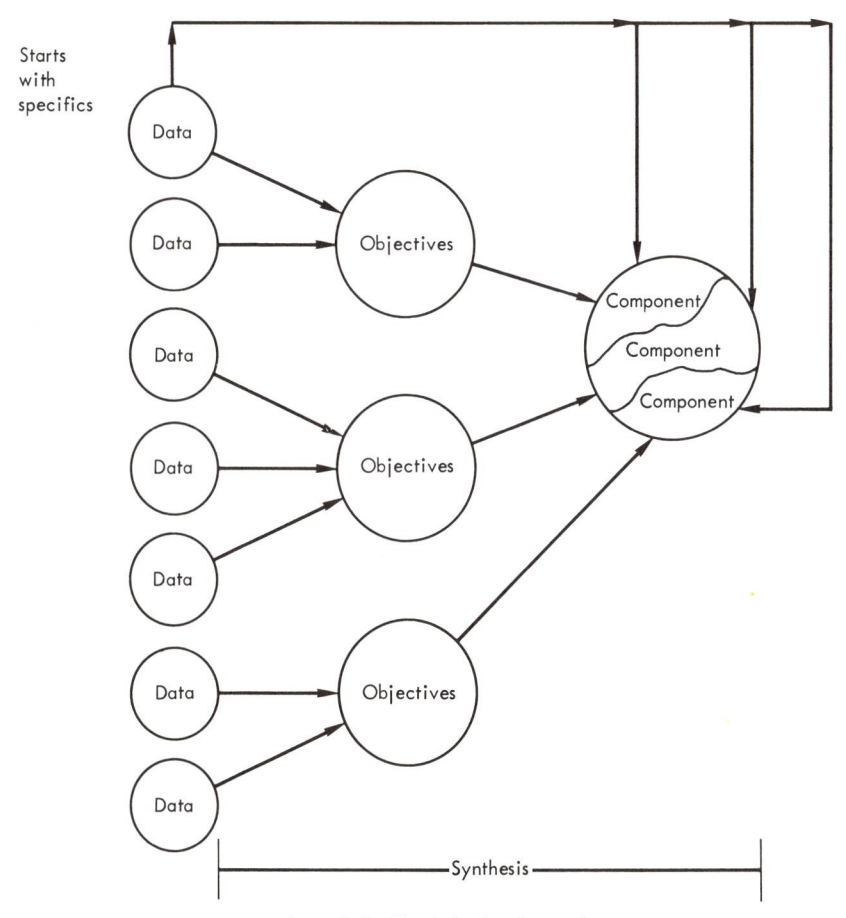

Figure 1-2 The Inductive Approach

14   Management and Systems

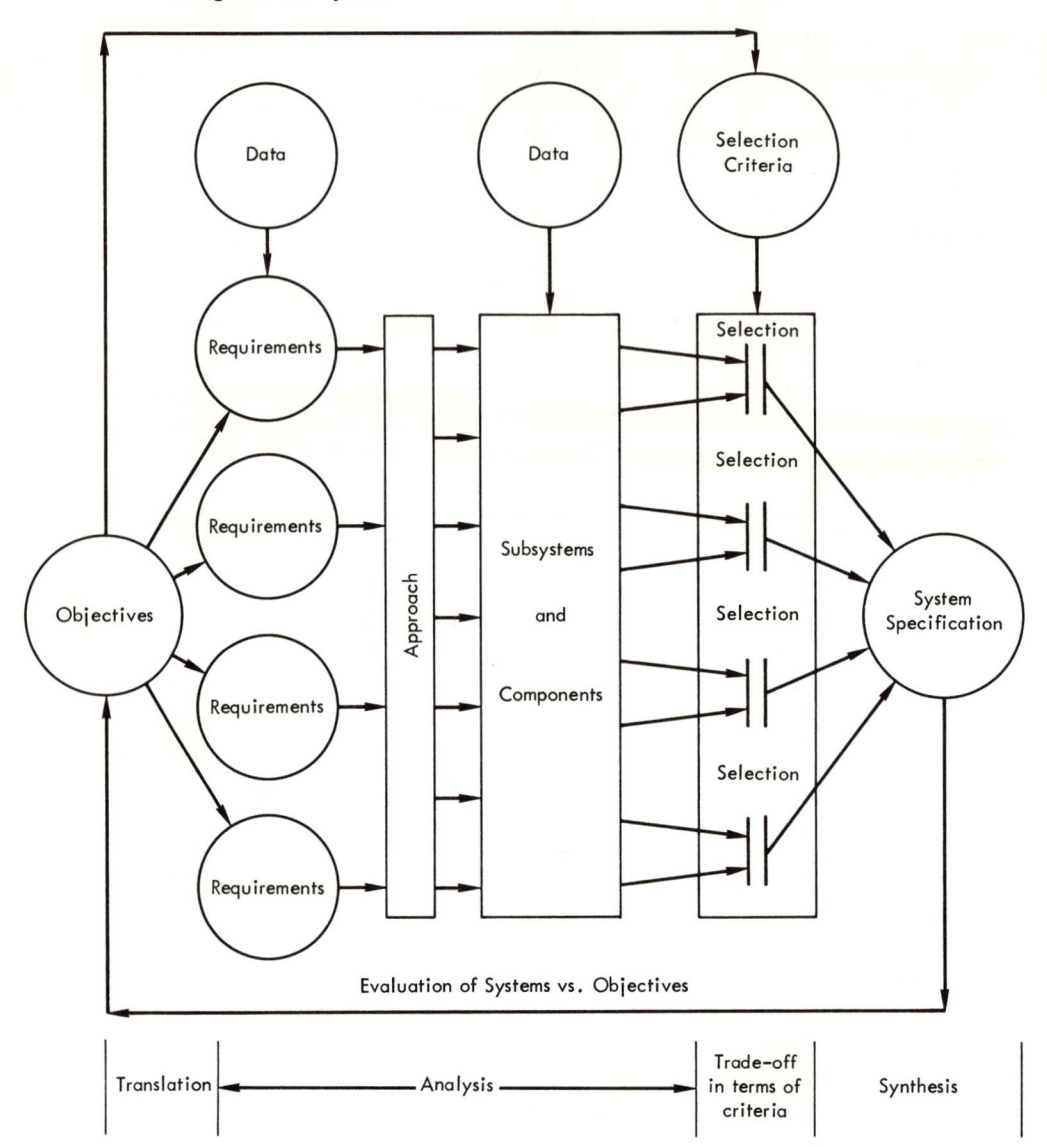

Figure 1–3   The Systems Approach (deductive and inductive)

Figure 1–3 shows that the systems approach begins with objectives for the system as a whole. Requirements for the entire system are established by combining data or knowledge of natural phenomena. Various configurations and components are developed that possibly fit together in the system. Criteria for selection of a set of components provide the basis for trade-offs in selection. The final best fit is synthesized into the final system. We can see, therefore, that the systems approach has two major stages. One is an expanding stage (the analysis), and the other is the contracting stage (the synthesis).

Let us translate these two different conceptual approaches into a very simplified business situation. Suppose a new small firm, Systems Incorporated, notes that similar firms have certain capital requirements, certain amounts of working capital, and certain amounts of cash. The firm also gathers further data about the amount of capital it can raise and then sets facility and operating objectives. It decides simultaneously that a financial component will be needed to handle this part of the business.

At the same time, Systems Incorporated sets up a production component, which decides to establish facilities for manufacturing 100,000 midget-widgets per year to gain economies of scale.

The company also forms a marketing organization, which proceeds to make a market study. The study convinces this group that sales will start with about 20,000 units per year and grow to 50,000 per year in about five years. The firm begins to contract for advertising and warehousing on this basis.

When all these plans have been prepared and initial steps at implementation have just begun, the company president calls a meeting of his three managers to discuss company plans. It is immediately evident that a synthesis of these plans is urgently needed; some major decisions are required and the plans must be revised for compatibility. There is also a question as to whether all major objectives for the company as a whole have been defined and taken into account by the three functional components of the firm.

Now consider a systems approach to the start-up of the firm. A preliminary study identifies a basic need for midget-widgets by a clearly definable market segment of a certain size. The president sets objectives for product profit, general growth, and return on investment. He appoints the managers for finance, production, and marketing to start off the analysis phase, shown on the scale at the bottom of Figure 1–3. Each manager hires one or two key people to assist him. Data are gathered on which to base requirements for these functional groups to achieve the company's objectives. The management then gets together to develop the general approach to the establishment of facilities, marketing policies, and fund raising. The approaches to establishing *subsystems* in the business are developed and evaluated, and a specific *set of subsystems* is selected with the hope that a nearly optimum total system will result. A few subsystems are likely to be: (1) manufacturing planning and control, (2) materials control, (3) master financial planning and control, (4) selling–pricing–advertising, (5) warehousing–transportation–channels of distribution, (6) personnel, and (7) a total management information system for planning, operating, and controlling at the top decision level.

In the systems approach, Systems Incorporated started with objectives and translated them into integrated requirements. Marketing requirements and manufacturing requirements were established to accomplish identical *company* objectives, not component objectives. As the plans for the company developed, the emphasis was put on company subsystems that cut across functional lines to tie together activities that must be carried out in unison. Alternative subsystem approaches were considered, and combinations of these were evaluated for ability to achieve company objectives. Finally, a specification of the total business is formulated in order to achieve continuing integration of operations.

REASONS FOR THE SYSTEMS APPROACH

Why does the systems approach come to the forefront of management at this particular moment in history? The answer lies, on the one hand, in our original premise of complexity in modern organizations, and on the other, in the emergence of several fundamental changes in the management process over the past twenty years. These two factors—increased complexity and managerial change—will continue to accelerate during the 1970's. The focus will be on the management of change.

Complexity in Modern Organizations

Accelerating complexity is undoubtedly a characteristic of modern large-scale organizations. Although the causes are many and varied, the nonhuman causes that affect the management process and result in the need for better information systems are generally attributed to: (1) the technological revolution, (2) the effects of research and development, (3) product changes and the decreasing life cycle of products, and (4) the information explosion. Table 1–1 gives some dramatic examples of the magnitude of these changes, to show how they may affect the nature of managing in the 1970's.

The Technological Revolution

We need only look around the home and workplace to witness the fantastic changes wrought by the technological revolution of the past twenty to twenty-five years. Man has walked on the moon and returned. Time and space have been dwarfed. Transportation, communications, agriculture, and manufacturing are among the many industries undergoing vast changes in products, techniques, output, and productivity. This technological revolution is not a continuation of the Industrial Revolution; it is a vast and fundamental change in its own right, as advanced mechanization and automation

Table 1-1

Some Factors Causing Increased Complexity
in Modern Organizations

Factor	Example
TECHNOLOGICAL REVOLUTION	Speed of computation in the electronic computer has gone from 16,000 additions per second to one and one-half million per second.
RESEARCH AND DEVELOPMENT	The index of industrial research and development has climbed from 100 in the base year of 1953 to over 400 in 1965.
PRODUCT CHANGE	The C-141 StarLifter aircraft, in production for four years, requires about 250 engineering design changes per week.
INFORMATION EXPLOSION	Papers published on Maser/Laser grew from 10 in 1950 to 300 in 1960.

techniques are adopted and improved across a broad range of industries. The future of this revolution is not entirely clear, but two things are quite certain: change will continue at an accelerated pace, and this change will demand giant steps in improved management. It is fundamental that in order to cope with these changes, the manager of the future will require large amounts of selective information for the complex tasks and decisions ahead. Thus *the technological revolution will require a managerial revolution.*

Research and Development

The breathtaking rate of the technological change racing through all types of industry is due in large part to increasing expenditures for research and development. Despite the fact that relatively few firms engage in R&D and that these concentrate in a few areas,[4] the impact of these expenditures is felt by all. Not only are products and supporting operations becoming more complex but the life cycle of products is being shortened. For example, consider how the DC-6, a reciprocating engine airplane, was made obsolete in less than five years by the pure jets.

Charles Kettering once commented: "By its very nature research is a gamble . . . but the only risk that is greater than doing research is not doing it." This comment was not intended to imply that all companies should perform research. However, all should be aware of its impact on their operations and provide for better planning, better management, and better information to accommodate the effects.

Product Changes

Technological advances resulting partly from research and development, partly from growing customer sophistication, have resulted in the third cause of complexity—product changes. Whereas the manager of the past could depend upon a high percentage of his product ideas becoming marketable, today's manager must deal with an enormously high product mortality rate. Moreover, the modern organization is faced with the necessity to optimize return from a given product in a much shorter time. The Model T Ford may have been good for a product life span of ten years, but today's automobile manufacturer must offer more than a thousand combinations of model, color, and power selections. Du Pont's nylon, invented in the 1930's, had no competition for many years. Today the head start of many chemical fabrics is measured in months. It is a point of pride with many companies that over half their income today is derived from products that did not exist five to ten years ago. New industries are being born overnight. The computer and electronics industries provide dramatic examples.

These factors contributing to complexity combine to form another element that calls for better management and the systems approach—the lengthening time span required between decisions and realization of commitments. These commitments are for such large amounts of money and for such long periods of time that the manager cannot afford to make mistakes. Major oil companies plan twenty years ahead for acquisition sources. Consider also the complexity of decisions required by airlines, heavy equipment, manufacturing, and other industries that cannot afford to guess wrong.

The implication emerges that today's manager must keep abreast of the factors influencing his products and his future operations. This requirement demonstrates once again the need for a properly designed management information system, particularly with regard to the environment—an environment that includes competitors who are themselves using up-to-date methods.

The Information Explosion

Finally, the information explosion has profound impacts upon the complexity of management and organizations. As a decision maker, the manager is essentially a processor of information. The modern manager knows that the ability to obtain, store, process, retrieve, and display the right information for the right decision is vital. This is, after all, the basic reason for an information system—better decisions.

Various estimates have been made concerning the information explosion. It is said, for example, that man's knowledge is doubling in each five-to-ten-year period and that this rate of knowledge accumulation is accelerating. It is estimated that 85 to 90 percent of the scientists of all time are now living, an indication of the accelerated growth of knowledge and information in recent years. Here we are interested not so much in the precise degree to which information is expanding as in the knowledge that information available to and required by today's manager is expanding enormously. In order to remain ahead of his competitors and to keep pace with the technological revolution and its impact on his products or services, he must keep abreast of selected information and organize it for decision making.

Advances in Management

Thus far, we have argued that the systems approach is needed to deal with complexity. We now turn our attention to developments in the process of management itself and ask, What new techniques or theories have become available that make the 1970's the era of the systems approach? The answer lies partly in four recent and fundamental developments that, when integrated into what we already know about management, may give us a breakthrough for improving the management process. Essentially, these four developments are: (1) the theory of information-feedback systems, (2) a better understanding of the decision-making process, (3) operations research or management science techniques that permit an experimental or simulation approach to complex problems, and (4) the electronic computer.

Information-Feedback Systems

Basic to the understanding of the systems approach and to the design of management information systems is the concept of information-feedback systems. This concept or theory is something more than our old exception principle. It explains the goal-seeking, self-correcting interplay between the parts of a system, whether the system is business, mechanical, or otherwise. Essentially, feedback systems are concerned with the way information is used for the purpose of control, and they apply not only to business or management systems but to engineering, biological, and many other types of systems. Examples of information-feedback systems would include the thermostat–furnace–temperature, as well as the subsystems comprising the missile, the automobile, the body, the economic system, the inventory control system, and countless others. All have a vital trait in common: *the output of the system leads to a decision resulting in some type of action that corrects the output, which in turn leads to another decision.* Although the theory of information-feedback systems is not entirely new (the speed governor for steam engines dates back to about 1780), it has only recently become available to and applied in business applications. Later chapters will explore this theory more fully.

Decision Making

A development of extraordinary importance to building a foundation for the systems approach is the recent notion of *automatizing* or *programming* decisions. Indeed, this concept is at the very core of systems design, as we shall discover later.

Forrester attributes this improved understanding of automatic decisions and the decision-making process to the military.[5] Prior to 1950, the commander, using "tactical judgment and experience," made such on-the-spot decisions as threat evaluation, weapon selection, enemy identification, alerting of forces, and target assignment. Subsequently, these and similar decisions were "automated" by formal rule and procedure, thus leading to the proposition that formal rules may yield better decisions for routine problems than those based solely on human judgment, given the constraints under which humans must make decisions.

The notion of *programming* decisions by *decision rule* is now a basic consideration of management and information systems design. If decisions can be based upon a policy, a procedure, or a rule, they are likely to be made better and more economically. Moreover, if the decision rule can be programmed for computer application, the potential exists for faster, more accurate, and more economical operations. Examples of common decision rules that have been programmed for computer solution are payroll, inventory control, customer billing, and purchasing.

Later chapters will explain in detail decision rules in information systems design and the use of management science in designing these rules.

Management Science

Closely allied to programmed decisions and decision rules are the techniques of management science. Indeed, one of the primary purposes of these techniques is the design of programmed decision rules. Another purpose, often overlooked, is that of assisting managers to make complex decisions. The techniques of management science combine with the computational ability of the computer to provide problem solutions that were not practical heretofore.

Linear programming, system simulation, Monte Carlo, queuing, gaming, probability theory, and other quantitative techniques are available to the management scientist. However, we are interested not so much in specific tools or techniques as in the management science approach to problem solving.

A powerful tool of management science is *simulation*.[6] Although this technique was used relatively infrequently prior to 1970, it offers great potential breakthroughs for applications of the systems approach. The technique involves construction of a mathematical model of the system (e.g., business or function) under study. The behavior of the model under manipulation simulates the behavior of the real system to the extent that the consequences of different management policies, marketing assumptions, or resource alternatives can be forecast prior to final decision.

The Electronic Computer

The fourth major development making the systems approach to management possible is the electronic digital computer. Without it, the vast amount of data handling connected with the storage, processing, and retrieval of information would not be possible, nor could the arithmetic computations required in many problem-solving situations be economically undertaken.

Despite the fact that the computer is nothing more than a tool for processing data or making computations, many managers view it as *the* central element in an information system. This attitude tends to overrate and distort the role of the computer. The vital element in an information system is the human one; it is the managerial talent that designs and operates the system!

The computer's capability to process and store information has outraced man's ability to design systems that adequately utilize this capability. "Brainware" has fallen woefully behind "hardware." Unfortunately, it appears that the human talent available for the design of managerial applications will lag behind the technology of the computer for many years to come.

THE SYSTEMS APPROACH AND THE MANAGER OF THE FUTURE

A major understatement was made in 1949 by *Popular Mechanics* magazine when it predicted: "Computers in the future may have only 1000 vacuum tubes and perhaps weigh only one and one-half tons." Another prediction was made ten years later by Leavitt and Whisler in their landmark article, "Management in the 1980's."[7] Their prognosis was that the forthcoming age of computer technology and information systems would "dehumanize" the firm, reduce the number of managers through automation, and centralize decision making.

These two examples illustrate the difficulty of accurately forecasting the future. Both were correct regarding trends, but each failed to hit the mark on the extent of the trend and the time schedule. And although the decade of the 1980's is not yet upon us, we can probably say that the prediction of Leavitt and Whisler was somewhat pessimistic regarding the dehumanizing effect of the computer.

Despite the difficulty of predicting the shape of the firm and the attributes of the manager of tomorrow, sufficient speculation and study have been undertaken so that we can arrive at a prognostication.[8] We start from a premise about which there is no disagreement: tomorrow's firm and tomorrow's manager will be different from today's. Moreover, the difference can be attributed to the accelerated rate of change and the implications of this change on the management process. These implications are indicated by a statement from former Secretary of Defense Robert McNamara: "What, in the end, is management's most fundamental task? It is to deal with change. Management is the gate through which social, political, economic, and technological change—indeed, change in every dimension—is rationally and effectively spread through society."

We want to examine first the impact of these changes on the organization and then turn our attention to what they mean for the manager of the future. The question will be: What, if anything, will be the impact of the systems approach on the organization and the manager?

The Organization of the Future

If the events of the past and the needs of the future are any indication, we can expect that the firm of the future will have undergone several important changes. The most significant of these are the expanding technological environment, organizational changes within the firm, and increasing interaction between the firm and its outside environment.

The advancing technological intensity of the resources of the firm will continue. Rate of investment in plant and equipment, due largely to technological advances, continues to grow steadily. More spectacular are the expenditures in research and development, which, in turn, account for the breakthroughs in technology. Also significant is the increasing proportion of expenditures devoted to computers and related equipment.[9]

A curious dichotomy is presented by this increasing technological complexity. As it increases, the manager is required to devote more and more resources to advances about which he understands less and less. This paradox suggests that decision making surrounding these important matters may require the participation of technologists in a group decision-making process.

The firm of the future will also be subjected to increasing pressures to modify classical organization structure. Two trends in this direction are already evident. First, there is the growing use of the task-force type of organization,[10] owing largely to the need to cut across the established structural lines in order to coordinate company-wide effort. A second development, designed to ease the increasing pressures of management overload, is the creation of a corporate office containing several chief executive offices.[11] These are two of several innovations in organizational structure that seem to herald a movement away from insistence on classical structure and toward a systems approach that will accommodate change.

A third major trend providing a clue to the nature of the future firm is the increasing institutional perspective within which the firm must operate. The expanding interaction between the firm and society has been attributed to "the growing importance of business as a social force on the one hand and expanding governmental concern with social welfare on the other. . . ."[12] Two implications for the manager are seen in this trend. First, the manager of tomorrow will be equipped to handle these broader problems of society and may be called upon to put his skills to work. Second, his firm will very likely be part of the new government–industry combinations that will be formed to carry out the work of society.[13]

The Manager of Tomorrow

What will be the nature and skills of the manager in the future? Will he be a superman, as Uris predicts,[14] or will he be a modification of today's model, brought up to date to meet the changes of the future? What effect will the systems approach have on the process of management?

The future environment in which a manager operates will be a systems environment. We have emphasized that the systems approach is identified by several distinctive qualities: (1) integrative—characterized by *synergism*, productive of a total effect greater than the sum of individual parts; (2) interdisciplinary—utilizing techniques and methods of several disciplines; (3) empirical—subject to experimentation and scientific verification; (4) organistic—viewing the organization as composed of human individuals and groups reacting in a formal structure to achieve human and organizational goals; (5) decision-oriented—directed to decision making for optimum resource allocation, a major purpose of the systems approach in business applications; and (6) informational—since the catalyst, the physiology of the systems approach, is information and the structure is an information system. A prediction concerning the requirements and nature of the manager of tomorrow can be constructed around these qualities.

The future manager will be deeply involved in *integrating the firm as a system*. He will be skilled in creating among the people *and* the physical resources a structure of relationships that maximizes the firm's performance potential within the constraints of the goals of its members. This view is different from that of past practice, which tended to emphasize the parts of the structure rather than their interrelationships. Consequently, organizational systems tended to develop over time through a combination of chance and the necessities of the moment, rather than in accordance with a plan. In the future, the systems approach to management will encourage the deliberate design of business systems, design that will allow for all the many variables of complex organizations and their interaction. This scientific approach to management will be facilitated by systems design competence on the part of tomorrow's manager.

Business systems of the future will be far too complex to be managed by the experience, insights, and skills of any single individual, regardless of his ability. The manager will be required to operate in an *interdisciplinary* environment; he will find it a great challenge, indeed a necessity, to absorb and utilize the methods of mathematics and the physical and natural sciences and the findings of the social and behavioral sciences. All these are needed in the systems approach to management. The manager will be able to think organizationally in terms of human response—the interfacing of parts designed to interact compatibly for the achievement of goals.

Basically, this interdisciplinary education of the manager will move in three directions. First, decision making in an increasingly complex environment will demand that better use be made of physical resources. The scientific approach of the physical and natural sciences combined with the quantitative methods of mathematics will become increasingly important in achieving this improved utilization. Second, a knowledge of the human themes and experiences contained in the humanities will better enable the manager to design and administer the organization as a system of human response. The methods of the social and behavioral sciences are also important in this respect. Third, as more and more firms go multinational and become involved in the social environment at home, the manager will become *extracultural* as he operates in urbanized and international environments.[15] He will be required to understand new values, beliefs, customs, and patterns of action.

A third requirement of the systems approach is that the manager will have to rely more and more on *empirical* and *factual* information for decisions. The "old" way of doing things will be nearly always suspect and frequently unacceptable.[16] Extrapolation of past experience as a basis for future decisions will give way to the new techniques for rational, scientific decision making. The necessity for the empirical approach will grow out of the increasing number of new, poorly structured decisions involving not only problems not previously encountered but problems that do not lend themselves to solutions based on historical experience. This is not to say that imaginative analysis and judgment will not be valuable. Indeed, these attributes will become more important as advancing technology moves the manager further from the point of decision and the managerial job becomes increasingly one of "management of technical experts."

The *organistic* approach to management means simply that the manager must view the company as an organism—a system of human relationships and interactions operating within the framework of a formal structure. The classical view of organizing maintains that if you know what you want to achieve, the work can be grouped into positions that can be defined in terms of duties to be performed. These can be assigned, and the assumption is that individuals will perform as instructed. This mechanistic approach will no longer be acceptable in the future. The firm of tomorrow will be viewed as a total behavioral system, suggesting the need for less face-to-face and person-to-person leadership skills and more ability to design an organizational environment in which groups of people, each with different knowledge and skills, interact with all levels of management for joint contributions to the achievement of organizational and individual objectives.[17] This approach takes account of the holistic nature of a system—anything that affects one component will affect all other units.

The future manager will be highly skilled in the process of rational *decision making*. Decisions will become not only more numerous but more difficult as well. Upper management will deal increasingly with the formulation of policies and strategies, as well as with the design of systems to implement these important plans. Operating decisions, the major concern of today's middle-management group, will be increasingly automated, thus permitting the application of more time to the important area of planning for the future.

The increasing use of man–machine interactive systems will demand more and more design effort. The future manager must be able to participate in the design and use of responsive, adaptive decision systems. An essential component of these systems will be formal simulation models of the firm, which will permit the manager to evaluate possible outcomes of decisions for which no precedent exists. As decisions become increasingly complex and therefore subject to inputs from a wide variety of specialists, an important attribute of the manager will be the ability to evaluate these inputs and to manage these technical specialists.

Information will be the means and *information systems* the structure for implementing the systems approach for the manager of tomorrow. A major trend of the future will be the continuation and acceleration of the current information explosion, coupled with the need for more and better information for decision making. Vastly improved equipment and techniques will be available to handle this information, but the critical element in the future will remain the same as it is today: *information management*. The management of information requires the proper blending of the remaining elements of the organization into an information systems design. Tomorrow's manager must, above all else, take an active part in the design and implementation of information systems. This is the essence of the systems approach.

SUMMARY

This chapter has introduced the systems approach to management and established a framework of concepts that will be expanded throughout the book.

The systems approach, a basic change in the philosophy of management, is required in the complex organizational life of the 1970's. It views the organization as the sum of interrelated parts, and management's task is to relate these parts into a coordinated whole. This approach is increasingly necessary because of the complexity of modern large-scale organizations and the advances in management that make the systems approach inevitable.

Both the organization and the manager of the future will undergo several important changes. The increasing technological environment of the firm will require organic changes in structure as well as greater interaction with the firm's external environment. The manager of the future will be more concerned with integrating the parts of the organization into an organistic whole. In order to do this he will rely more and more upon empirical decision making and an interdisciplinary approach.

Both the organization and the manager of the future will rely increasingly on the systems approach, fundamental to which is the design of management information systems.

DISCUSSION QUESTIONS AND PROBLEMS

1. What are the political and social consequences of implementing the systems approach? For example, how can we implement government planning of airport facilities when unbridled competition is permitted? Is it reasonable for five different airlines to fly only half-filled planes to the same destination at about the same time?

2. What impact would (a) the technological revolution, (b) research and development, (c) product changes, and (d) the information explosion have on the need for information by management in an automobile manufacturing company? A hospital? A university?

3. Four advances in management development have been described: (a) the theory of information-feedback systems, (b) a better understanding of the decision-making process, (c) management science, and (d) the electronic computer. Compare the use of these developments, by an organization of your choice, in the 1930's and in the 1970's. Possible selections are a manufacturing firm, a retail chain, a railroad system, and airlines company, a bank, and an insurance firm.

4. The president of one of the nation's largest food manufacturers and packagers recently declared, "Our information system gives us the edge we need over our competitors." Describe ways in which an information system could provide a competitive edge for this company.

5. Show how the systems approach would be useful in attacking the ecology problems of a large city. How might an industrial organization cooperate with the government in these problems?

6. The organizational components in a manufacturing company usually include sales, production, finance, accounting, and so on. Do we need to integrate these organizational components into a system? If so, how do we do it?

7. In the 1960's and early 1970's, there was an upsurge in the growth of light electronic manufacturing in the South Florida area. Among the major firms that established plants there were United Aircraft, International Telephone and Telegraph, Radio Corporation of America, Westinghouse, and International Business Machines. Because transportation costs in these industries were such a small part of total costs, and because jet travel made sales and service available nationwide, plant location was largely independent of transportation factors. Additional arguments for selecting this area for plant location included availability of unskilled labor and lack of militant unions. However, the major advantage was the climate. For example, it was much easier to recruit urgently needed engineers and scientists for relocation to South Florida than to the northeastern states.

In 1971, the executive committee of the Computer Components Corporation (CCC) decided that expansion to an additional plant was necessary and tentatively agreed to examine the West Palm Beach area for a location site. CCC, headquartered in Boston, was a manufacturer of custom computer components.

Questions:
(1) In a systems approach to the plant location project, what would be the major parts of the system and how would these interact?
(2) How would information problems be compounded by location of the additional plant?
(3) If you were put in charge of the move, what information would you need?
(4) What "people" problems might arise from such a move?

REFERENCES

1. See particularly R. C. Hopkins, "A Systematic Procedure for System Development," *IRE Transactions, on Engineering Management,* June 1961, p. 85, and Davis O. Ellis and Fred J. Ludwig, *Systems Philosophy* (Englewood Cliffs, N.J.: Prentice-Hall, Inc., 1962).
2. P. G. Thome and R. G. Willard, "The Systems Approach, A Useful Concept of Planning," *Aerospace Management* (General Electric Company), Fall/Winter 1966, p. 25.
3. The authors are indebted to Professor Ronald Zoll for providing the basis of the discussion of these ideas.
4. George A. Steiner, *Top Management Planning* (Toronto: Collier-Macmillan Canada, Ltd., 1969), pp. 659–60. For example, in 1966, 87 percent of R&D funds were spent by manufacturing firms having more than 5000 employees. Eighty-five percent of all expenditures went to five areas: aircraft and missiles, electrical equipment and communications, chemicals and allied products, motor vehicles and transportation equipment, and machinery.
5. Jay W. Forrester, *Industrial Dynamics* (Cambridge: The M.I.T. Press, 1961), p. 17.
6. For readers interested in further information on simulation and gaming, a comprehensive bibliography of 439 entries is contained in Thomas H. Naylor, "Bibliography 19. Simulation and Gaming," *Computing Reviews,* January 1969, pp. 61–69.
7. Harold J. Leavitt and Thomas L. Whisler, "Management in the 1980's," *Harvard Business Review,* November–December 1958, pp. 41–48.
8. For example, see M. Anshen and G. L. Bach, *Management and Corporations 1985* (New York: McGraw-Hill Book Company, 1960); H. I. Ansoff, "The Firm of the Future," *Harvard Business Review,* September–October 1965, pp. 163–78; Max Ways, "Tomorrow's Management," *Fortune,* July 1966, pp. 84–87.
9. Robert G. Murdick and Joel E. Ross, "The Need for Systems Education," *Journal of Systems Management,* July 1969, pp. 8–12. The annual shipment of computers and related equipment in the U.S. is estimated to reach $9–10 billion by 1973—about 12 percent of total investment in new plant and equipment.
10. Wilbur M. McFeely, "The Manager of the Future," *Columbia Journal of World Business,* May–June 1969, p. 89.
11. H. Igor Ansoff and R. G. Brandenburg, "The General Manager of the Future," *California Management Review,* Spring 1967, p. 65.
12. *Ibid.,* p. 66.
13. *Ibid.*
14. Auren Uris, "Executives of the Future," *Nation's Business,* January 1969, p. 71.

15. McFeely, "The Manager of the Future," p. 89.
16. Uris, "Executives of the Future," p. 71.
17. Ansoff and Brandenburg, "The General Manager of the Future," p. 67.

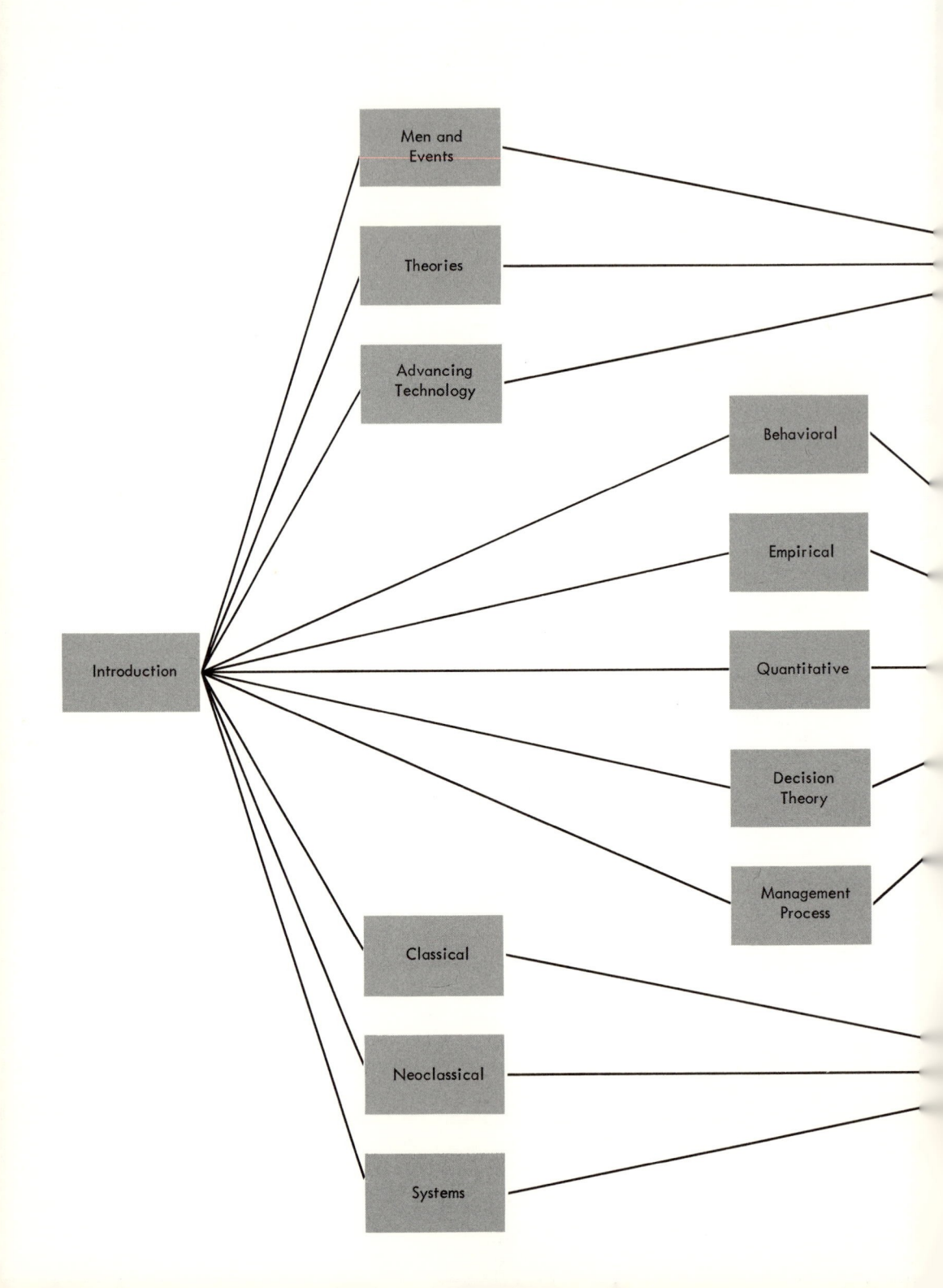

```
Introduction
├── Men and Events
├── Theories
├── Advancing Technology
├── Behavioral
├── Empirical
├── Quantitative
├── Decision Theory
├── Management Process
├── Classical
├── Neoclassical
└── Systems
```

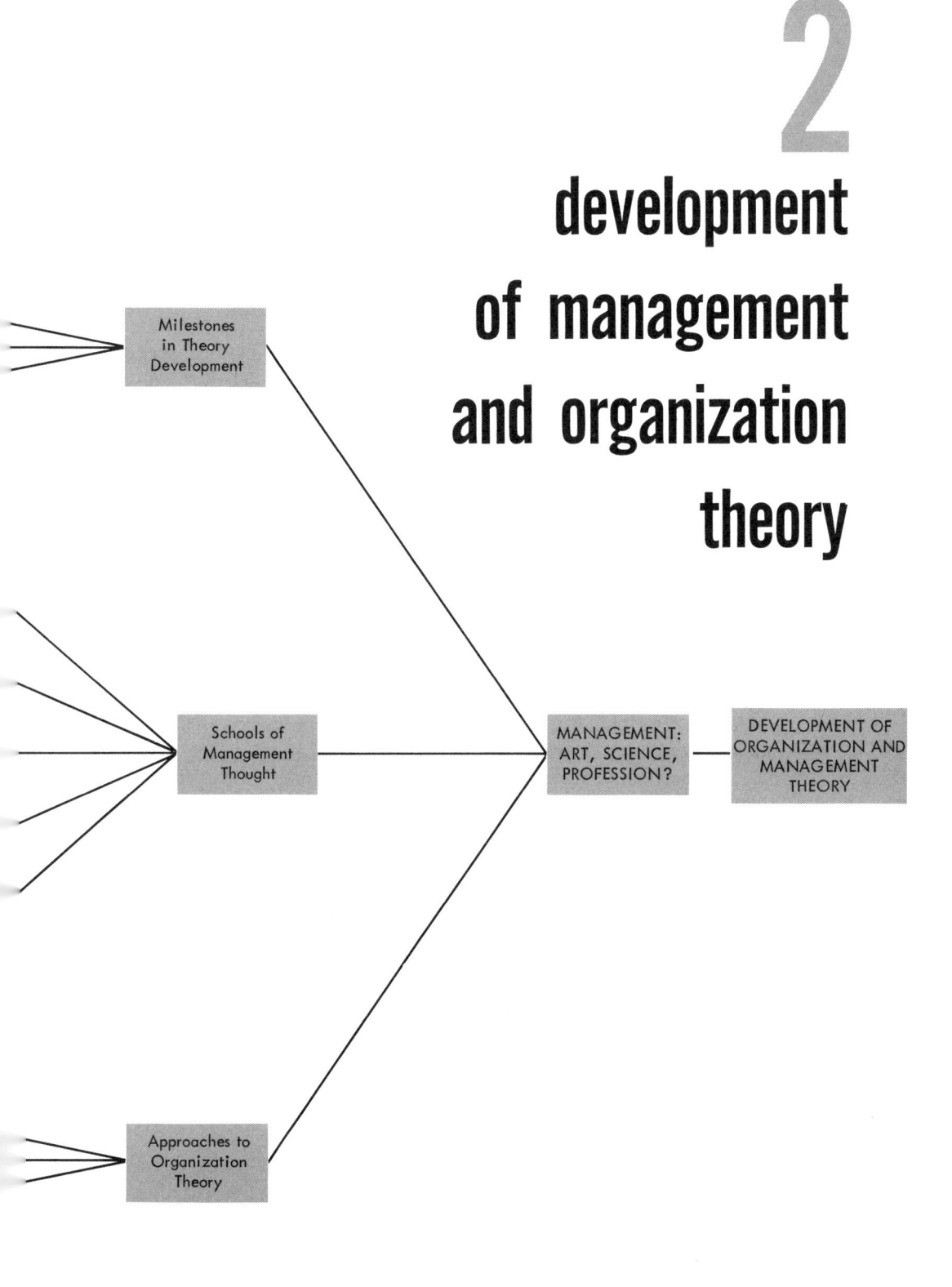

2
development of management of organization and theory

- Milestones in Theory Development
- Schools of Management Thought
- Approaches to Organization Theory
- MANAGEMENT: ART, SCIENCE, PROFESSION?
- DEVELOPMENT OF ORGANIZATION AND MANAGEMENT THEORY

2

The statements and writings of managers and scholars diverge widely on what constitutes the process of mangement and how it is carried on in practice. Despite the fact that management of some type has existed since man first learned that cooperative society was necessary to accomplish goals, the extraordinary interest now shown in the topic has been a phenomenon of recent years. As a result of this accelerating interest, a number of theories of management and organization have developed. Many different viewpoints and beliefs have been advanced to explain the nature and behavior of organizations and the practice of management. The numbers and variety of these points of view have caused some confusion and controversy as to what management is, how it should be practiced, and how it should be taught. Indeed, the confusion has been aptly labeled "the management theory jungle."[1]

It is understandable that such an important topic as management, which involves so many fundamental issues affecting people, would attract the attention of university scholars, practitioners, and the public at large. The growing pervasiveness of management and organization theory in our society and in the world was well stated by Max Ways: "What industrialization was to the nineteenth century, management is to the twentieth. Almost unrecognized in 1900, management has become the central activity of our civilization."[2] Peter Drucker has called it the most important activity in our society.[3]

Our purpose in this chapter is to take a panoramic view of the major events in the history of management and then to review some of the major classifications of thought concerning organization and management theory, in order that a springboard for management in the 1970's can be constructed. In later chapters we will synthesize the potpourri. For now it will be enough to recognize various patterns of management thought, to classify these patterns, and to understand how to use them.

MILESTONES IN THE DEVELOPMENT OF ORGANIZATION AND MANAGEMENT THEORY

James G. March has pointed out that the study of organizations has a history but not a pedigree. The distinction is simple: "A pedigree suggests a series of causally connected events in time; history (in the present sense, at least) consists in a temporal ordering of events."[4] This suggestion that the development of organization and management theory has been a series of unconnected "islands of discovery" indicates how we happened to arrive where we are, at least until fairly recent decades. Hence, we have chosen the term "milestones" to describe a few major developments in our necessarily cursory examination of events preceding the 1970's.

Although management as we know it today is largely a development of recent years, it has been of great concern to organized society throughout civilized history. The antecedents to modern organization and management theory are numerous and impressive. There is hardly a major philosopher, historian, or biographer who has not written of the management of organizations; among the more notable were Aristotle, Thucydides, Caesar, and Aquinas. Writings of the Egyptians extending as far back as 1300 B.C. indicate a relatively sophisticated knowledge of management and its use in the administration of the bureaucratic states of that time. It is also evident that the affairs of the Greek and Roman empires could not have been conducted in such efficient fashion without an understanding and use of some principles of administration. The church, the army, and the state had to be managed.

The history of Western civilization is replete with evidence that organizations like the military and the Roman Catholic Church have pioneered in such innovations as line and staff, formal organizational authority relationships, and similar managerial innovations that still exist today. About the middle of the eighteenth century, the Industrial Revolution brought about the centralization of factories, resulting in the greater utilization of machinery vis-à-vis human labor and prompting the era of employer–employee relations. It was during the eighteenth and nineteenth centuries also that such economists as Adam Smith and Alfred G. Marshall became the harbingers of much of today's organization and management thought. Smith popularized the notion of specialization of labor, the classical view of the competitive economy, and "economic man."[5] Marshall was among those economists who were concerned with the operation of the firm and how it should be managed.[6] These innovations led to developments in management practice that by today's standards might be termed elementary but were revolutionary for that time. However, not until the twentieth century did anything resembling a modern theory of management develop.

When compared to progress and developments in the natural and physical sciences, progress made in the development of organization and management theory has been meager indeed. Some relative measure of the diverse progress made in the two areas can be seen in Figure 2–1. No degree of precision of measurement is intended in the figure, but rather a general view of comparative progress and the "management gap" caused by failure to advance the science of management as rapidly as the technical sciences.

Despite this relatively small progress, several major steps forward have been taken along the road to a modern theory of organization and management and to the improved practice of management. At the risk of over-

34 Management and Systems

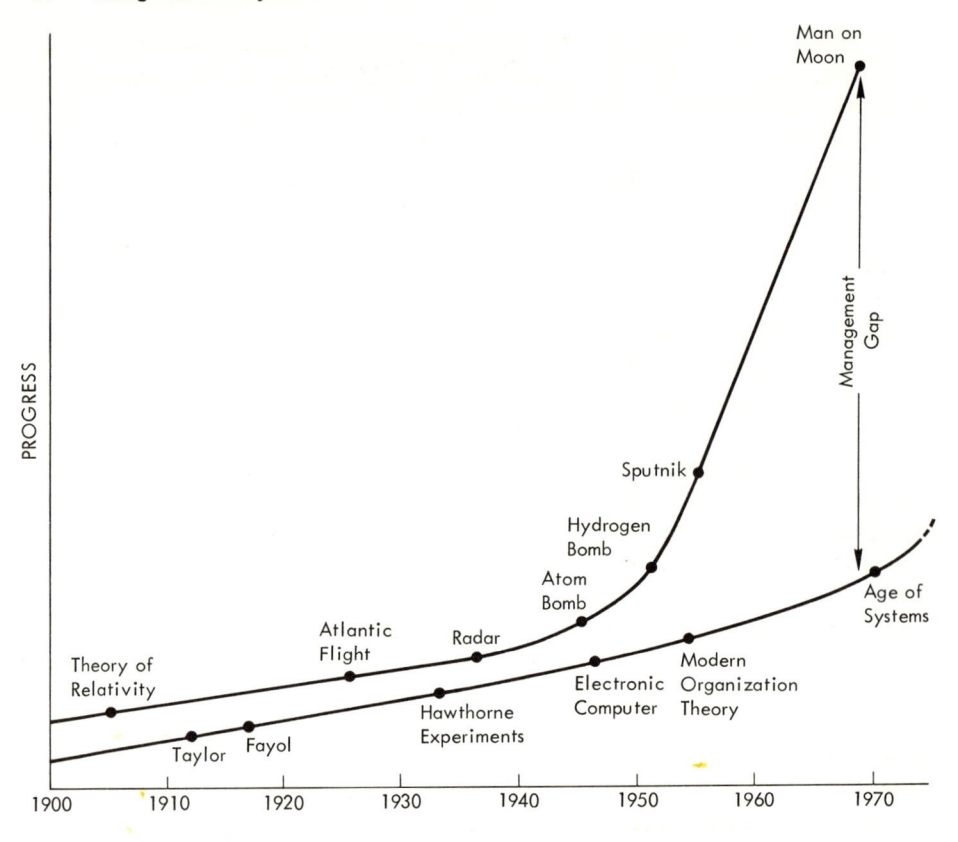

Figure 2–1 A Comparison of Progress in Science with Progress in Management

looking many significant persons and events along the progress route, for purposes of this book the following milestones are chosen:

1. *Frederick W. Taylor*, who was largely responsible for "scientific management" and for beginning the modern management movement.
2. *Henri Fayol*, the "universalist" whose universal managerial functions became the forerunner of the management process school, the most prevalent among today's managers.
3. *The Hawthorne Experiments*, which ushered in a new era of concern for people in organizations. This extraordinary event resulted in the neoclassical theory of organizations and the "human relations" approach to management.
4. *The electronic computer*, which is profoundly affecting the manner in which firms are managed and organized. It is also accelerating the systems approach.
5. *Modern organization theory*, a development of very recent years characterized by the behavioral movement, an interest in interdisci-

plinary approaches to organizations, and a conceptual–analytical–empirical approach embodied in the behavioral sciences.
6. *The systems age—the age of synthesis.* The time has finally arrived when we can take a systems approach to management, an approach that can synthesize all prior developments.

These milestones will be discussed individually because all are important for an understanding of organization and management theory as well as in the design and implementation of management information systems.

Frederick W. Taylor (1856–1950)

Frederick W. Taylor, frequently called the "father of modern scientific management," is probably responsible more than any other single individual for the development of modern management thought. Although the roots of his principles are found in earlier writings, it was Taylor who published and popularized these principles initially in his book, *The Principles of Scientific Management,* first published in 1911.[7] His great contribution to management thought and practice was due not only to his research and writings on the subject but also to the fact that he was in the vanguard of a movement made inevitable by economic and social changes.

Although Taylor's *Principles* were intended for application throughout an entire industrial organization, he emphasized the use of scientific management at the shop level. He was concerned mainly with the efficiency of workers and managers in the manufacturing and production processes. He believed that a major difficulty was the lack of expression by managers of what they expected, coupled with the resultant lack of understanding by the employees regarding expectancies. Among the first to undertake detailed examination of the steps in the work process with a view toward scientific improvement of it, he was constantly in search of the answer to the question: What constitutes an honest day's work? Time-and-motion study and other modern-day industrial engineering methods originated with Taylor and were popularized by him.

Taylor's approach to management appears rather elementary today, but it was revolutionary for his time. He saw the functions of managers as these:

1. Scientific determination of each element of a man's job
2. Scientific selection and training of workmen
3. Collaboration of management and labor to accomplish work in accordance with the scientific method
4. Equal division of responsibility between managers and workers, with managers planning and organizing the work

Taylor provided many of the individual ideas for the conceptual framework later adopted by management theorists, such as (1) the use of standards in control, (2) the separation of planning from execution, (3) the functional organization, and (4) the exception principle. His underlying assumption that workers were motivated by money accounted for his belief that greater productivity could be obtained primarily through wage incentives. Taylor's emphasis was on the lower levels of management and the use of scientific techniques at the shop level.

Henri Fayol (1841–1925)

A contemporary of Taylor's and not unknown to him was the French industrialist, Henri Fayol, who may be called the "father of classical management theory." For the first time in the development of management thought, Fayol provided an explicit and broad framework of general principles of management that explained the nature of the process. His observations first appeared in 1916 in French, under the title of *Administration Industrielle et Générale*. The fact that this book was not widely available in English in the United States until 1949[8] indicates the delay in the development of a modern management theory.

Fayol's observations fit remarkably well into what is generally conceded to be the basis of classical management theory, much of which is contained in modern management. Although he addressed himself to a broad range of management topics, his major contribution was to define the basic *elements of administration* and to list his *general principles of management*.

Fayol maintained that management is "universal" and that all managers, regardless of their level in the organization or the kind of organization they manage, perform essentially the same tasks or elements of administration. These are: (1) planning (*prévoyance*), (2) organizing, (3) commanding, (4) coordinating, and (5) controlling. These elements of administration generally referred to what were later called duties or functions of management. A large part of his book is devoted to an examination of these functions, and on the whole his observations are still valid in the 1970's. Other writers have added to the functions or renamed them, but current practice in management universally recognizes planning, organization, and control as descriptive of the manager's job and a useful classification for studying management. Indeed, planning theory, organization theory, and control theory have developed into substantial bodies of knowledge in their own right.

Throughout Fayol's treatment of management is an understanding of the universality of principles. He maintained, as do most management writers, that principles of management apply not only to business but also to military, institutional, political, religious, and other undertakings.[9] Thus, Fayol has come to be known as a "universalist," a term describing those who believe that administration is essentially the same in any environment and is subject to a common set of principles.

Fayol noted that principles of management are flexible, not absolute, and are capable of adaptation to every need. His fourteen principles are summarized:

1. *Division of work.* This is the "specialization of labor" principle of economics that Fayol extended to individuals and groups of people and to all kinds of work, whether managerial or technical.

2. *Authority and responsibility.* Authority is the right to give orders and the power to exact obedience. Responsibility is the corollary to authority and arises from it; wherever authority is exercised, there is responsibility.

3. *Discipline.* According to Fayol, "Discipline is in essence obedience, application, energy, behavior, and outward marks of respect observed in accordance with the standing agreement between the firm and its employees." Good superiors, fair agreements, and judicious sanctions are means of maintaining discipline.

4. *Unity of command.* No person should receive orders from more than one superior.

5. *Unity of direction.* This principle requires "one head and one plan for a group of activities having the same objective." Taken together, Principles 4 and 5 relate to both personnel and corporate entities.

6. *Subordination of individual interest to general interest.* The interest of any one employee or group of employees should not prevail over the interest of the whole firm.

7. *Remuneration of personnel.* Pay should be fair and afford maximum satisfaction to both employer and employee consistent with conditions over which the employer has control.

8. *Centralization.* Individual degree of centralization of authority is a matter of proportion and of finding the optimum degree for the specific organization.

9. *Scalar chain.* This refers to what we know as the "chain of command," and is called the "chain of superiors" by Fayol. This authority relationship should not be departed from unless superiors have authorized their subordinates to communicate directly across authority lines.

10. *Order.* The old adage, "A place for everything and everything in its place," is the essence of this principle, and it applies to material as well as to people. Human arrangement is made easier with a chart or a plan.

11. *Equity.* In dealing with people, the manager should take account of their desire for equity and equality of treatment. A combination of kindliness and justice will elicit loyalty and devotion.

12. *Stability of tenure of personnel.* Unnecessary turnover is both the cause and the effect of bad management, and therefore, in common with all other principles, stability of tenure is a question of proportion.

13. *Initiative*. Subordinates should be allowed to exercise initiative within the limits imposed by respect for authority and discipline. Initiative is thinking out and executing a plan.

14. *Esprit de corps*. This principle points out the need for teamwork and the importance of communication in obtaining it. "Harmony, union among the personnel of a concern, is great strength in that concern." The abuse of written communications and a misguided notion of the motto "divide and rule" are dangers to be avoided.

Fayol's impact on the theory and practice of management cannot be overemphasized. His conceptual framework is still widely in use today; it provided a platform upon which modern management theory has developed. Henri Fayol can truly be called the father of modern management.

The Hawthorne Experiments

Prior to the 1930's and 1940's, managers were generally more concerned with the process of production itself than with the production worker. The concept of "economic man" pervaded management thought and the worker was believed to be motivated by considerations of pay and the sanctions that the employer could bring to bear upon him. Although management writers such as Taylor and Fayol recognized the importance of the human element, the mechanistic aspects of management and the formal structure of organizations were emphasized instead. Loyalty and devotion on the part of the employee were assumed because of the system of rewards and sanctions available to the employer.

These notions about how workers were motivated were dispelled by the now-famous experiments at Western Electric's Hawthorne plant in Chicago. The results of these experiments were to usher in a new era, concerned with human relations, motivational research, and inquiry into the relationship between productivity and motivation.

The Hawthorne studies, designed to measure the effect on output of changes in physical working conditions, proved that worker productivity is affected much more by human factors—the way that workers feel about their interaction with others in the group, their attitudes, and their sense of recognition by peers and superiors.[10] Conversely, lack of productivity is not so much a function of working conditions, sanctions, or incentives as of the isolation of the worker and his feeling of anonymity resulting from insignificant jobs that contribute negligibly to the final product.[11]

These studies are generally considered to indicate the new beginning in management thought. The focus of attention for the first time became the worker, his work environment, and his interpersonal relations with work groups. The importance of human relations, worker motivation, and managerial leadership began to be emphasized. Moreover, the belief began to develop that the contributions of the behavioral sciences, such as sociology and psychology, were valuable adjuncts to the body of knowledge in management. We shall return to the Hawthorne studies later in this chapter and see how they contributed to the development of organization and management theory.

The Electronic Computer

What the Industrial Revolution was to the nineteenth century, the computer will be to the twentieth, which may very well come to be known as the century of the computer revolution.

One of the most remarkable advances in decades has been the electronic computer. As George Terry says, "It is no exaggeration to state that the computer has probably contributed more to our current management development than has any other single entity."[12] It has served to hasten the development of management thought and has been the catalyst for enlarging the scope of organization and management theory.[13] Consider the advances made in the quantitative approach to management and the many techniques (linear programming, modeling, simulation, and the like) now available because of the computer's availability to perform the necessary calculations. Consider also the *systems approach* to organization and management theory, an approach whose development can largely be traced to the computer. The importance now placed upon information as an integrative device and the move to structuring or *programming* decisions provide more evidence of the impact of the computer—not only upon managerial techniques but also upon the development of a theory of organization and management.

With regard to the computer's effect on the *practice* of management, three fundamental trends are evident. First, the computer has eliminated the practical computational barrier from complex management problems. It has become a device for exploring by numerical analysis the properties of mathematical problems and systems too large or too complex to be treated by known analytic methods. And the capacity of computers to perform low-cost computations continues to grow fantastically—in the past ten years by a factor of 100,000 or more when measured by the cost to perform a calculation. This ability to perform enormous amounts of calculations cheaply and efficiently has extended the application of mathematical techniques to problems that humans could not process in a lifetime.

Second, the computer is rapidly bringing a high level of automation to routine, programmed decisions that were formerly the province of clerks and lower-level managers; moreover, the frontiers of these programmed decisions are being rapidly moved forward to areas that have up to now been regarded as judgmental. Indeed, as programmed decision-making concepts are applied to more and more levels and areas of managerial operations, the extension of these frontiers has become the current challenge to both management and technical information systems design.

Finally, there are the bread-and-butter applications of the computer to business decision making and record keeping: the automation of paperwork, payrolls, and accounts receivable—the repetitive data-processing activities that had for years been highly programmed but not automated. Today there is a host of applications in which large-scale data processing is a "factory" operation—automation of the processes of handling, storing, and retrieving routine repetitive paperwork operations.

Modern Organization Theory

The origins of modern organization theory cannot be identified with any specific time or attributed to any individual. The transition from the traditional fuctional approach to management to a concern with organization structure and human behavior is hardly perceptible in the literature.

During the late 1940's and early 1950's, there began a trend away from the management approach based solely on the entrepreneurial functions of planning, organizing, and controlling, to a consideration of the processes of coordinated activity and the techniques of decision making. In addition, modern organization theory began to study the effect of different social systems, goals, and environmental factors on the administrative process. Study is directed to: (a) identifying the individuals and groups who achieve the power to give direction to the organization, and (b) the conditions under which power can be made effective. In other words, the managerial functions of planning, organizing, and controlling cannot be carried on without regard to the social system of the organization. Hence an inextricable relationship exists between organizational (not necessarily managerial) goals and the social system. This attention to the human interactions in an organizational setting is pointed up by a definition: "Organization is defined as a system of structural interpersonal relations. . . . individuals are differentiated in terms of authority, status, and role with the result that personal interaction is prescribed. . . ."[14] Another view of an organization is given by Scott: ". . . a mechanism having the ultimate purpose of offsetting those forces which undermine human collaboration."[15]

In contrast to the "classical" or "functional" approach to management, which was frequently descriptive and based largely on experience or observation, modern organization theory is conceptual, analytical, and empirical. This last characteristic requires the theorist to utilize a number of disciplines, reflecting the second characteristic of the approach—it is *interdisciplinary* and *cross-disciplinary*.[16] The representative academic areas involved in organization theory include anthropology, biology, geography, economics, mathematics, philosophy, political science, psychology, and sociology.

The third major characteristic distinguishing modern organization is increased awareness of the behavioral sciences. Indeed, the major contributors to an understanding of the social anatomy of organizations have been sociologists and psychologists. Among the more widely quoted sociologists represented are Weber,[17] Homans,[18] Dubin,[19] and Dalton.[20] Leadership, the sources of motivation, and greater understanding of the aspects of rational behavior and influence are among the areas of individual and social psychology that have become very important to organization theory. Some of the major contributors, in order of their publications, are March and Simon,[21] McGregor,[22] Likert,[23] Argyris,[24] and Bennis.[25]

The Systems Age—The Age of Synthesis

It is quite possible that the emerging systems approach to management may become the greatest milestone of all. We use the phrase "may become" because the approach is so embryonic that it is difficult to assess its true impact.

All systems definitions are similar; they describe a system as an assemblage of complex parts that go to make up a whole in order to achieve an objective. The essence of the approach is that when the parts are combined effectively, the whole is greater than the sum of its parts. The problem in the development of organization and management theory is to coalesce, make a "system" of, the varying approaches, principles, and techniques of existing theory. Properly integrated, this system of management will achieve the objective more effectively than examining the individual parts in isolation.

The systems approach and systems analysis had their roots in the development of operations research during World War II and the evolution of the weapons systems management concept following the war. Since that time, the approach has been increasingly used in business, economic, and social problems, although the name has only recently been applied to problems of this last type.

The remainder of this book is essentially an attempt to develop a systems approach to management and then to utilize the development and design of management information systems as the common ingredient by which the organizational system is integrated. We shall go into the details of the systems approach in subsequent chapters.

SCHOOLS OF MANAGEMENT ANALYSIS

Because of the expanding frontiers of management thought and because of the extraordinary interest in the study of management and its related disciplines in recent years, a number of approaches to its study have developed. What was formerly the province of the practitioner, later to be shared with management scholars, has now become fair game for a variety of persons interested in quite a number of related disciplines. The psychologist, the sociologist, the anthropologist, the statistician, the mathematician, the economist, and the political scientist are just a few of those who espouse particular and specific approaches to the study of management. Consequently, there has been some confusion about what management theory is and how to go about studying it.

As a result of this proliferation and the large number of persons, particularly from universities, who support different approaches to management, a number of "schools" have developed.[26] In essence, these schools represent the varying academic disciplines and subjects emphasized by different researchers.

In this book it is argued that the systems approach is the logical one to integrate the various ways of looking at management and also to provide a method for combining the research results of other viewpoints into a total theory of organization and management. This view is taken because: (a) the systems approach will accommodate the subsystems of management, the interrelated variables, constraints, and parameters; (b) it is compatible with all "schools" because it embraces all approaches either as tools or subsystems; and (c) it is pervasive and all-inclusive in that all theories can be explained in terms of its framework. This argument will be developed in subsequent chapters.

We shall discuss here five significant schools of management theory: (1) behavioral, (2) empirical, (3) decision theory, (4) quantitative, and (5) management process. The historical development of these approaches is shown in Figure 2–2. Some but by no means all of the proponents of each school are listed chronologically. In the brief sketches to follow it is impossible to deal with the nuances of each school because all lie along a continuum and shade into each other. The schema is at times oversimplified for ease of understanding.

The reader should not assume that these "schools" or approaches to management are mutually exclusive, because most of them are compatible, at least to the extent that they become subsystems in a system of organization and management theory. Nor should the existence of a "management theory jungle" concern us. Speaking of this "jungle" while he was president of the Academy of Management, Ernest Dale concluded, "Our real problem is not to clear it away by developing one grand all-inclusive theory but to be aware of the many paths through it. . . ."[27] Dale also advised business schools to "avoid giving the impression that any of our theories have been proved to be applicable in all circumstances and at all times. The best they can do is make the students aware of the appropriate mix of major factors that may be inherent within a given situation. . . ."[28] The task is to avoid adoption of any one approach as the total conception of management and to view each as a partial answer that might be useful at a particular time for a given problem.

development of management and organization theory   43

	BEHAVIORAL					
	Human Relations	Social System	Empirical	Decision Theory	Quantitative	Management Process
1900		Weber			A. Marshall	
1905						
1910			Practitioners		Taylor	
1915					Gilbreths	Fayol
1920					Gantt	
1925						
1930	Hawthorne Studies					Mooney
1935	Mayo					Urwick
1940	Roethlisberger		Am. Mgmt. Assn.	Barnard		
1945						
1950		Homans	Harvard "B" School	Armed Forces	J. Dean Von Neumann	Practitioners
1955		Maslow Argyris				
1960	K Davis McGregor	Simon Herzberg	Dale	March & Simon	Schlaifer Hitch	Koontz Terry
1965		Likert	Learned	Cyert & March Simon		Newman etc.
1970						

Present-Day Organization and Management Theory

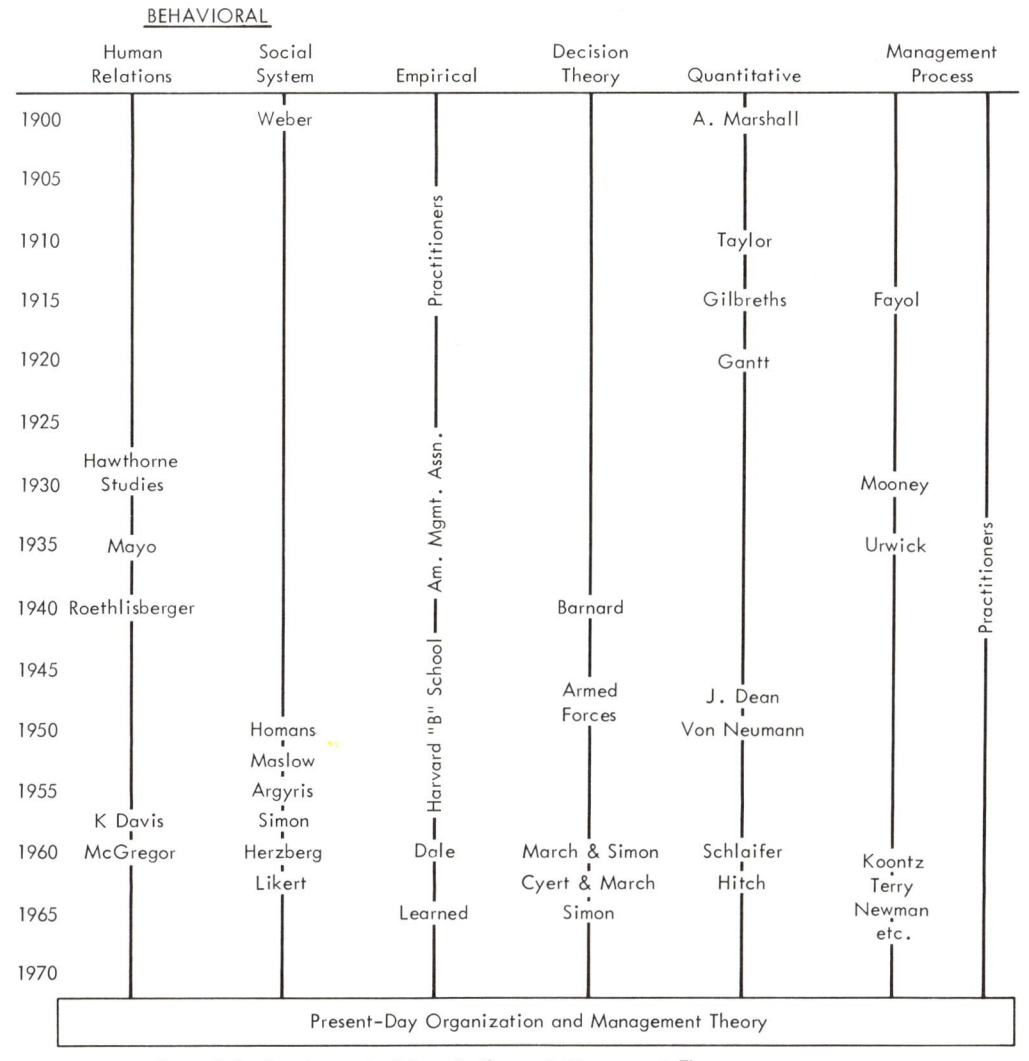

Figure 2–2 **Development of Organization and Management Theory**

The Behavioral School

Those who subscribe to the behavioral school of management can generally be divided thus: (1) the human behavior group, and (2) the social system group. The former approach is based on the notion that management consists of getting things done through people, and therefore, if the manager is to succeed, he should understand human relations, leadership, and the other behavioral science approaches to describing interpersonal relations among people. People are viewed as the important component of management, and study is devoted to determining how greater productivity and motivation can be gained by the use of good human relations. Motivation, leadership, training, and communications are among the common topics of this school and it has spawned such popular movements as "bottoms-up management" and "management by participation."

Practitioners and scholars of the *human behavior school* are oriented generally toward individual and social psychology. Many of them equate good management with leadership; others see management as being performed through the study of group dynamics. This school of management and the human relations movement had their beginnings in the Hawthorne studies and were followed by the writings of Elton Mayo[29] and Fritz Roethlisberger,[30] Harvard professors who were responsible for the studies. In more recent years, this approach has been popularized by such writers as Keith Davis[31] and Douglas McGregor,[32] the latter of whom advanced the notion of Theory X and Theory Y. The classical approach to management was represented by Theory X, which maintains that there is no satisfaction in work, that humans avoid work as much as possible, that positive direction of workers is required, and that workers possess little ambition. The human relations approach of Theory Y is the antithesis of Theory X, holding that workers have much greater potential than is realized and will exercise self-direction and seek responsibility if motivated. Theory Y is a *participative* approach.

The *social system group* is closely related to the human behavior group but different in that it looks upon management as a social system, a system of cultural interrelationships. The sociologists and others who subscribe to this school of organization theory see the formal organization in terms of cultural relationships of various social groups rather than as a system of authority relationships, as has been the custom in the classical approach.

Fundamental to the social system notion of an organization is the need to surmount the various limitations through cooperation of members of the group. The interaction and cooperation of people making up the organizational system are stressed and there is a constant search for a method of making the goals of the organization and the goals of the group compatible. Thus, the approach has been called *ecological* because it attempts to deal with the parts and relationships among (1) the organization, (2) the environment, both external and internal, and (3) the forces bringing about change and adjustment.

The social system approach to organizational behavior was an outgrowth of the neoclassical approach begun with the Hawthorne studies, but the movement has taken a direction all its own. It has become quite large and influential. Among its pioneers have been Maslow, Argyris, Simon, and Herzberg. More than fifteen years ago Maslow[33] developed his now-famous "hierarchy of needs," which maintains that human needs range from those that are physiological to those involving love and esteem. This classification of needs from "lowest" to "highest" and his proposition that workers could be motivated by appealing to their esteem and self-actualization needs changed the direction of the classical view, which held that workers were motivated by monetary rewards.

A popular contemporary writer is Chris Argyris, whose basic thesis is that the classical approach to organizing (authority relationships, formal structure, position descriptions, and the like) tends to stifle the adult need for self-actualization and that greater productivity could be gained by an organizational design that facilitates this need.[34] The amazingly brilliant and productive Herbert Simon is probably responsible more than any other individual for modern organization theory. His *Organizations* (with J. G. March)[35] and *Administrative Behavior*[36] are landmarks. Frederick Herzberg's up-to-date studies on job enrichment are opening up exciting new frontiers in motivation research and organizational design.[37]

Notwithstanding the overwhelming importance of human behavior and leadership in management, to equate the field of human behavior or the behavioral school to the field of management would be quite erroneous. The disciplines in the body of knowledge surrounding the behavioral science approach to management provide the manager very valuable tools, but we must look to other contributions to find a "system of management."

The Empirical School

The empirical method of managing, sometimes called the "experience" or "custom" approach, attempts to analyze management by a study of experience. It is probable that a large proportion of practitioners and businessmen belong to this school and hold the view that experience is the single greatest determinant of managerial success. In their approach to the problems of management decision making and problem solving, they make a study of the successes and mistakes made by other managers in similar cases, in the hope of being able to come up with generalizations about similar problems or at least the answer to a specific problem. The subscriber to this school might ask, "How would my predecessor have solved such a problem?" or, "What are the managers in a competitive situation doing about this problem?" It is more an approach to developing problem-solving skills than an attempt to develop a science.

The empirical school is typified by the American Management Association,[38] which has its roots in the top management group of the nation and views its primary function as providing a forum where practicing managers can trade experiences. The bulk of the association's publications report the experiences of various managers and companies. In the academic world this empirical school is represented by schools of business that teach by the "case method," the Harvard Graduate School of Business having been the forerunner in this movement. Among the more widely used texts in this approach is that of Learned.[39] Ernest Dale's comparative approach to management may also be called empirical.[40] His *Great Organizers* studied the experience of successful managers, presumably in an attempt to draw generalizations from it.

Although few deny that knowledge of successful management of yesterday's problems may help in handling similar problems of today's management, there is the danger that yesterday's answer will not be good enough for today's problem and will not apply to tomorrow's. What fits one organization might not fit another at all, and comparing past issues with those of the present and future is hazardous for the novice.

The Decision Theory School

Decision making is the most important task of managers; many scholars believe that decision making and the process leading up to it account for most of what executives do.[41] Among those who place great importance on the process is Herbert Simon, who states, "I shall find it convenient to take mild liberties with the English language by using 'decision making' as though it were synonymous with 'managing.'" Decision making in its broadest context includes among the activities preceding the decision: (1) finding occasions for making a decision, (2) finding possible courses of action, and (3) choosing among courses of action.[42]

Viewed in the foregoing context, decision making becomes the "keyhole" look at management. Moreover, if we accept the thesis of the pure decision theorists, the entire process of management can be explained in terms of decision making. We take the position in this book that decision making is a fundamental aspect of management. Indeed, the systems approach to management would use the decision as its central focus. However, to say, as some decision theorists do, that the entire body of management theory can be based on the structure of decision making is to oversimplify the matter. Although decisions may be the end result of managing, other approaches, schools, disciplines, and processes provide the manager with the total body of knowledge he requires.

An additional doubt about whether decision theory has the total answer is raised by the question: Does the decision complete the action sought or commence the action? In other words, once the decision is made it must be implemented, and the process of implementation may require more than the answers provided by decision theory—particularly if we are concerned with only the quantitative aspects of decision theory.

According to Forrester, "Investigation of the nature of decision making in the context of modern military tactics forms a basis for understanding the place of decision making in industry."[43] At any rate, the armed forces were largely responsible for promoting a structured approach to decision making. Cyert, March, and Simon[44] are among those who have advanced the notion of adapting these decision-making methodologies to administration and opening a new era in which organization members are viewed as "decision makers and problem solvers." This idea is one of the key concepts of organization and management theory and a vital one in the design of management information systems.

The Quantitative School

The quantitative approach to the solution of management problems, sometimes called the mathematical school, includes practitioners and scholars who seek to describe management in terms of mathematical symbols, relationships, and measurable data. They hope that eventually the variables in the problem-solving situation can be quantified and related in an equation so that a quantitative solution will result. In this respect, the school is primarily concerned with decision making and systems analysis. Some applications have been made to organizational behavior.

Included among the proponents of this approach are operations researchers, management scientists, and mathematicians. Methodologies of the school include simulation and modeling; techniques include operations research, mathematical programming, Monte Carlo methods, queuing theory, gaming, and heuristics.

Although the quantitative school of management is comparatively new, those who practice it have made some spectacular breakthroughs in specific problem areas that lend themselves to this treatment. The use of its techniques forces the manager to define his problem precisely and encourages careful thinking, logical methodology, and recognition of definite constraints. Generally speaking, the usefulness of this school is limited by its ability to define the variables in a management equation as well as to quantify them. The complexity of human behavior makes it difficult to describe in quantitative terms at this stage; this appears to be one of the major restrictions of these methods at this time. However, to the extent that quantitative methods can be used in the design of decision rules and in systems analysis, they are essential both to the theory and to the practical use of management information systems. More of this topic will be covered in subsequent chapters.

If they were alive today, Frederick Taylor,[45] the Gilbreths,[46] and Gantt[47] would surely be called "operations researchers." Although we do not normally think of these pioneers in terms of the quantitative school of management, they were among the first to take a scientific management approach and therefore can be considered forerunners of this school. Later, Joel Dean[48] was to abandon the descriptive macro approach to economics and attempt a quantification of those variables important to allocation of resources. Von Neumann[49] extended the frontiers of mathematics and computers. Later Charles Hitch[50] was to set the pace of applying mathematical and systems analysis to large-scale problems with his applications in the U.S. Department of Defense. Ackoff[51] and Schlaifer[52] are among current scholars expanding the use of mathematical techniques to an ever-increasing array of problems.

The Management Process School

The most widespread approach to management is the so-called process school, which defines what managers *do*. This school, frequently called the "traditional," "universalist," or "functional" approach to management, had its beginnings in the writings of Henri Fayol. We recall that Fayol defined the functions of management in terms of what the manager does. The management process school regards the job of the manager as universal, regardless of the type of organization or the manager's level in it. The process is analyzed, principles identified, and a conceptual framework constructed.

Fundamental to the approach is the description and analysis of the functions of management: planning, organizing, staffing, directing, and controlling. Each of these functions has its body of knowledge and its techniques, and each utilizes knowledge from other fields of science. The process school not only does not deny the validity of other approaches to management, it attempts to absorb or utilize the methodology and techniques of these other schools in performing the five functions of management.

The Functions of Management

No matter to which approach or "school" the manager subscribes, an understanding of the fundamental functions of management is essential. These five functions—planning, organizing, staffing, directing, and controlling—constitute the process by which a manager manages, by which he does his job. Each function is defined below. Shortly we will examine each of these in depth as it relates to the systems concept of management.

Planning is the thought that precedes the action; it involves development and selection from alternatives as the necessary course of action to achieve an objective. Planning is the primary function of management; every manager performs it prior to the other functions.

Organizing involves definition of the tasks necessary to perform the objective, distribution of these tasks among subordinates, and assignment of authority to get the job done. This involves the manager's grouping the activities for which he is responsible, assigning them to subordinates, and providing for the necessary coordination of efforts.

Staffing is the process by which personnel requirements are defined and necessary staffing action (recruiting, selecting, hiring, placing, training) is taken to man the positions provided for by the organization's structure. Staffing implies, therefore, the forecasting of manpower requirements and

development of management and organization theory

includes inventorying, appraising, and selecting personnel for positions.

Directing involves the guiding and supervising of subordinates. It is the essential leadership function in the management process and involves the motivation and coordination of subordinates. Direction deals exclusively with people. It includes the capacity to enlist, through communication and persuasion, the efforts of subordinates in working toward a given objective.

Control compels events to conform to plans. Thus, control (1) sets standards of performance in order to reach the objective, (2) measures actual performance against these standards, and (3) corrects deviations to insure that actions remain on course. Plans are not self-achieving or decisions self-implementing; carrying them out means prescribing the activities of personnel at designated times.

After Fayol's initial definition of the conceptual framework for the process school, a second attempt was made by two executives of General Motors, James D. Mooney and Allan C. Reiley.[53] Their conclusions are generally consistent with Fayol's and are built around four principles: (a) coordinative; (b) scalar, which defines the hierarchical flow of authority; (c) functional, which stresses the need for specialization in organizing; and (d) staff. Urwick[54] and Gulick[55] are also among the pioneers who modified and expanded upon Fayol's work. In 1937 Gulick codified the work of the executive under the acronym POSDCORB, which identifies seven elements: planning, organizing, staffing, directing, coordinating, reporting, and budgeting. This classification of management functions and the management process has remained generally intact to this time, with some minor differences in number and definitions of the elements of management.

Despite frequent assaults upon it, the management process school, with its liturgy of planning, organizing, staffing, directing, and controlling, has withstood the test of time and use and seems to be growing stronger each year. As we enter the decade of the 1970's the functional approach to management remains the most popular and widespread. Authors like Terry,[56] Koontz and O'Donnell,[57] Newman,[58] Moore,[59] and McFarland[60] continue to dominate the management scene in schools of business. Moreover, the process approach to management is far and away the most frequently used framework for practicing administrators in both industry and government. Perhaps, as Koontz suggests, the reason is that the functional approach analyzes management ". . . in a way most useful to the manager, reflecting the way he sees his job."[61]

Schools of Management Analysis—Summary

Because the empirical and decision theory schools of management are so closely allied with the management process and quantitative schools, we can combine the five schools into three: (a) behavioral, (b) quantitative, and (c) process or functional. And, since both the behavioral and process schools admit the logic and usefulness of the quantitative techniques, we are left with two schools for which a philosophical conflict remains. Therefore, the "management jungle" consists of our functional, or process of management, approach and the behavioral approach, which can be equated to organization theory. The problem is to integrate these two major approaches to management.

The clash between the management process school and the behaviorists is easy to detect. The former views subordinates as limited in ability and motivation (Theory X of McGregor) and sees the goals of the organization as technical output—productivity. The behaviorists, by contrast, hold that the basic nature of man is one of goodness, creativeness, responsibility, and energy (Theory Y of McGregor). Although both schools admit the *technical* superiority of the formal approach in business organizations, the behaviorists contend that this effectiveness is obtained at the cost of human sacrifice. Their basic tenet is that there is a conflict between the needs of organization members and the formal structure of the process school of management. How do we reconcile these two conflicting approaches?

Several concepts have been developed over the years to integrate the opposing values pursued by the management process approach and the behaviorists of modern organization theory. Among these is the *Managerial Grid* of Blake and Mouton,[62] a two-dimensional grid portraying the relationship between organization demands (production) and human demands. Bakke's *fusion process* is a conceptual scheme in which the organization adapts to the individual's needs and the individual to the needs of the organization.[63] Rensis Likert's notion is that organizational and human needs reflect two sets of values and hence two sets of books should be maintained to reflect these conflicting values.[64]

All these schemes apply the notion of trade-off—because neither the individual's nor the organization's needs can be given full rein, one must be balanced against the other until an optimum point is reached. Flippo's concept of the continuum is useful for illustrating various degrees of trade-off (integration) that might be achieved.[65] For example, a continuum for a selected number of commonly held characteristics of each approach is established in Figure 2–3. The behavioral extreme on the left represents some of the collegial, permissive, democratic attributes advanced by modern organization theory. On the right are similar characteristics attributed to the classical school of management. Both approaches are slightly exaggerated to make the point.

As indicated in Figure 2–3, neither extreme of such a continuum yields maximum effectiveness for the organization or the individual; maximum effectiveness lies somewhere in the intermediate range. No degree of preciseness is implied by this illustration. Rather, the point is made that the solution to integrating the two conflicting views lies not in total acceptance or rejection of either but in accommodation of both.

development of management and organization theory 51

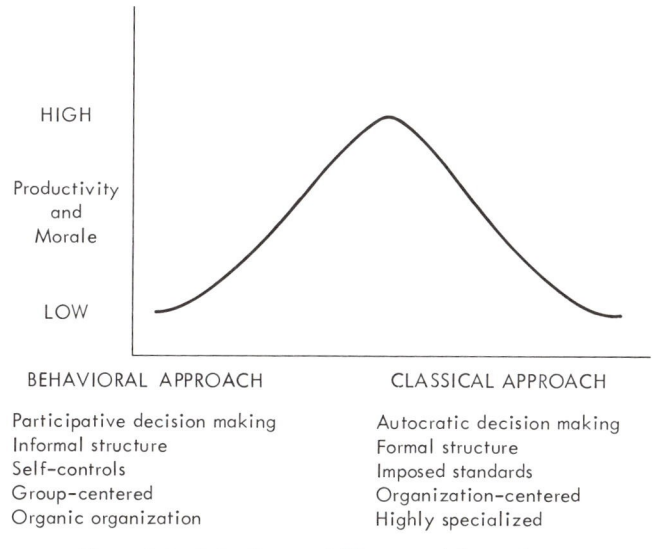

Figure 2–3 A Continuum of Management Approaches

BEHAVIORAL APPROACH
Participative decision making
Informal structure
Self-controls
Group-centered
Organic organization

CLASSICAL APPROACH
Autocratic decision making
Formal structure
Imposed standards
Organization-centered
Highly specialized

In summary, good management practice can utilize *all* schools of management. It is natural to expect that the productivity goals of the organization will frequently be in conflict with those of its human members. Productivity and human goals can be balanced in an environment of good management and an accommodation at less than the maximum level for each.

Finally, it is necessary to integrate the behavioral and management process approaches and utilize the best elements of each. The degree to which either is emphasized in any given situation is a function of the situation, the managers involved, the industry, and the particular set of circumstances in which the manager finds himself.

It is important at this point to state that a theory of organization and management draws upon all disciplines and recognizes that no single approach or theory holds the total answer to management, despite the several "schools" that attempt to explain it. In a subsequent chapter we will attempt to make a "system" of these individual approaches.

APPROACHES TO ORGANIZATION THEORY

Organization theory and management theory differ in two ways. First, the former is concerned with the structure of interpersonal relations and the organization as a mechanism for promoting human collaboration. Management, on the other hand, sees the organization largely as a vehicle for achieving an output or an objective, not the development of a structure for its own sake. If the organization facilitates interpersonal relations, fine!

However, this is not the reason for structuring an organization. The primary goal is to get a job done. Second, modern organization theory is a relatively new discipline, a development of the past few years.[66]

Despite the "management theory jungle" and the emergence of sometimes divergent "schools" of management, the state-of-the-art in management theory is probably more advanced and certainly more synthesized than that of pure organization theory. The latter is far from a homogeneous science based on generally accepted principles. The major area common to the different approaches to organization theory is the convergence of interest in the sphere of organization that is "administered, bureaucratic, formal, complex, large-scale."[67]

Among the more prevalent schools or models of organization theory are the decision-making, bureaucracy, social systems, and systems models. The foremost proponent of the decision-making approach is Herbert Simon, who views organization members as "decision makers and problem solvers" and concludes that "administrative processes are decisional processes."[68] The bureaucracy model had its beginnings in the remarkable and prophetic writings of Max Weber and is still an interesting and valuable approach to organizations despite the widespread popularity of such satirical, antibureaucratic books as *Parkinson's Law*[69] and *The Peter Principle*.[70] Weber's delineation of the structural and procedural characteristics of bureaucracy, the hierarchical structure of authority, and the notion of discipline based on formal positions are all concepts widely in use today and characteristic of a theory that provided a foundation for construction of subsequent theories. The social systems model is primarily identified with sociology, and its basic idea is that organizations are social systems.[71] A major proponent of this model is Talcott Parsons, who maintains that today's bureaucratic organizations came into existence as a result of complex modern society and its functional specialization and differentiation.[72] Moreover, it is the "primacy of orientation to the attainment of a specific goal" that is the "defining characteristic of an organization which distinguishes it from other types of social systems."[73]

Two additional theories of organization have so influenced the development of modern organization and management theories that they deserve special treatment. We shall examine the classical and neoclassical approaches in some detail, which will bring us naturally to the systems approach to organization theory. A fundamental premise of this book is that the systems approach better fits the needs of a manager in today's organizations.

Classical Theory of Organization

Classical (i.e., traditional, orthodox), the original theory of organization, refers to the type that can be traced back to Frederick Taylor and his concept of functional foremanship and planning staffs. The classical approach is concerned almost solely with the *anatomy of formal organization,* its structure, and how orders are transmitted through it and results achieved.

Classical theory achieved its momentum in the 1930's when the popular formal approach was developed by Gulick and Urwick,[74] and by Mooney when his book *Principles of Organization* was first published.[75] In addition to popularizing the acronym POSDCORB (planning, organizing, staffing, directing, coordinating, reporting, budgeting) for the work of a manager, Mooney identified four methods of organizing: by major purpose, by process, by clientele, and by place. Mooney and his contemporaries discussed organization in terms of the coordinative, scalar, functional, and line-and-staff principles.

The basic premise of the classical school is that organizing is a logical, rational process. Given the objective, what you want accomplished, you determine the work to be done, group this work into logical units, and define positions within these units in terms of a structure of accountability. Out of this comes the chart of organization and the position description of duties —a symmetrical picture of design. Emotional, illogical behavior is pathological; the work will be done if everyone follows the organization structure. The classical theory assumed that workers were rational, logical, and would perform as expected. Moreover, workers prefer to have their job limits clearly defined. The activities of a group should be viewed on an objective and impersonal basis without regard to personal problems and characteristics. To the classicist, organizing relates to formal relationships between jobs to be done and positions; behavioral characteristics are treated, but as a separate matter. Hence, organization has a more limited meaning to classicists than to some of the more modern theorists.

Classical organization is constructed around four key tenets: the scalar principle, unity of command, span of control, and organizational specialization. The basis of most classical theory can be derived from these concepts.

1. *The scalar principle* refers to the idea of hierarchy, that authority and responsibility should flow in an unbroken line from the chief executive to the lowest operator. This is frequently called the "chain of command" of superior–subordinate relationships, and leads to delegation of authority and responsibility.

2. *Unity of command* follows from the scalar principle and says in effect that no member of an organization should receive orders from more than one superior. As organizations increased in size and complexity, the classicist was forced to prescribe a simple line structure that was supplemented by staff advisors. Failure to clarify specifically the duties of staff personnel has led to constant controversy on the place of line vis-à-vis staff.

3. *Span of control* refers to the number of subordinates a manager can effectively supervise, and it has been universally accepted that the number

should be limited. In most instances, the classical theorists have specified the number as five or six, but others have suggested three at the top of the hierarchy and about six at the bottom.[76]

4. *Organizational specialization* is probably the cornerstone of the classical theory; the notion of division of labor, basic to this concept, goes back to Adam Smith and the functionalization of Taylor. This concept assumes that division of labor results in increased efficiency. The classical theorist assumes that it is possible to break down the tasks necessary to achieve the organization's objective. These tasks can then be grouped into like departments and assigned to a manager. Bases for departmentation include numbers, place, customer, function, and process.

In summary, the classical theory is valuable and is widely used today. However, it is limited by its concentration on the *formal anatomy* and structure of organizations and its insistence that human problems will take care of themselves if tasks are assigned and duties organized. This somewhat narrow view overlooks such important factors as the informal organization, human interactions within work groups, and the contributions of the behavioral sciences. However, classical theory is still very much alive, is widely utilized, and is probably the approach taken by the preponderance of practicing managers.

Neoclassical Theory of Organization

The inspiration and origins of neoclassical theory are generally conceded to be the Hawthorne studies[77] and the subsequent writings of Elton Mayo.[78] The school is commonly associated with the "human relations" movement.

The primary advance made by the neoclassical school over the classical was the introduction of behavioral sciences into organization theory. The basic tenets of the classical approach were regarded as given and were modified by the behavioral view as follows:

1. *The scalar principle* breaks down in practice because of "human failings," says the neoclassical theory, and "human tools" are suggested to make the principle operational. Problems encountered in the scalar principle include failure to delegate authority and responsibility equally, overlapping of authority causing personality clashes, and gaps in authority resulting in failure to complete the total job.

2. *The unity of command principle* leads to conflict and structural friction, according to the neoclassicists. Human behavior thwarts the best-laid plans for structure. The causes and remedies for friction between line and staff are treated and various devices invented to achieve harmony and

communications. These devices include committees, job rotation, junior boards, and various formulas for participation in decision making.

3. *Span of control* for a manager is determined by human factors and by the nature of the job, and cannot be reduced to a precise number or ratio. Existing degree of planning, communications, training, and the nature of the work are some of the determinants of span of control.

4. *Organizational specialization* is also of major concern to neoclassical theory. In contrast to the classicist, whose concern is mainly the work itself, the neoclassicist wants to know the impact of work on the worker—isolation, the feeling of anonymity, monotony, and human engineering considerations. These bad effects increase as size and increased specialization increase, resulting in the need for better motivation, coordination, and leadership.

Another major change was the introduction into neoclassical theory of the notion of the *informal organization*. As opposed to the structured formal organization, the informal organization consists of a natural grouping of people in a work situation—a group that appears in response to the social need of people to associate with others.

The neoclassical or "human relations" approach to organizations gained extraordinary acceptance and is in widespread use today. We have only to review current management literature or popular management development programs and supervisory training films to find the lore of the "human relations" approach still very much in evidence. Typical subjects include "the grapevine," "overcoming resistance to change," "participative decision making," "bottoms-up management," "democratic leadership," and "management by participation."

Scott has described the state of the neoclassical approach to organization: "The neoclassical school of organization theory has been called bankrupt. Criticisms range from 'Human relations is a tool for cynical puppeteering of people' to 'Human relations is nothing more than a trifling body of empirical and descriptive information.' "[79] If this assessment is correct, what are the reasons? It appears that one essential oversight on the part of the neoclassical school is emphasis on the wrong factors of the work environment. Despite the appointment of "vice-presidents for human relations"; despite the bowling leagues, credit unions, and other fringe benefits; despite the establishment of "better communications" programs, "happy workers" have not always been productive workers. Moreover, the human relations approach maintains that job satisfaction, and hence productivity, is a function of working conditions, the nature of supervision, and the relationship between worker and supervisor. Recent research indicates that these factors are less important in job satisfaction and productivity than the nature of the work and whether it yields achievement and recognition.[80]

These factors are either overlooked or regarded as less important by the neoclassicists.

In summary, the major weakness of the neoclassical approach is its failure to integrate the many facets of human behavior that it studied into the framework of classical management. Further, it has a rather shortsighted perspective and is incomplete in many respects.[81]

The description of organization theory thus far has been largely concerned with classical and neoclassical theories because these are the antecedents of modern theory and provide the springboard for examining modern theory in more detail. Despite the murkiness of the waters of modern organization theory, in subsequent chapters we will try to bring some clarity to it. Our objectives will be to examine the major contributions of the behavioral sciences, to construct a modern systems approach to organization theory, and to design an integrated framework for both organization and management.

MANAGEMENT—ART, SCIENCE, OR PROFESSION?

The field of management is generally considered to fall within the area of social sciences, as opposed to the natural or physical sciences such as biology or physics. It is also an applied science, like medicine or engineering. The social sciences are generally conceded to be "inexact" compared to the "exact" physical sciences, and management may be described as perhaps the most inexact of all.

In practice, management can probably be characterized as both an art and a science. As in the case of engineering or medicine, in which basic sciences are applied to the solution of practical problems, management is the artful application of techniques, rules of thumb, principles, and theory. The art of management has to do with the bringing about of a desired result through the application of skill and general principles; that is, art is the applying of knowledge, or science, or expertness of performance. Artistry is extremely important in management, where the complexity of people and the human equation are such an important part of successful operations. Consideration for people, creativeness and adroitness in applying managerial efforts, on the one hand, and the application of scientific principles, on the other, must be balanced in the "art of management."

Despite the clear case that there is much art in the process of managing, there is a growing recognition of science in management as well. This concept implies that there is a body of knowledge about the subject, that this knowledge is objective, and that it is free from prejudice. Moreover, the subject is open to critical examination and testing. As in the case of the natural and physical sciences, the body of knowledge surrounding management is becoming codified and classified within the structure of theory in

development of management and organization theory

order to expedite the understanding of it. It is important to point out, however, that the development, application, and stratification of the body of knowledge pertaining to management are incomplete, and will continue to be so, owing to the three factors that distinguish it from other sciences.

These factors would include, first, the very extensiveness of the subject and the fact that it pervades almost every activity of man. Unlike the other social or natural sciences, whose boundaries are relatively clearly defined, management concerns everyone and has implications for all social, political, and economic activity. Second, management problems are extraordinarily complex because of the enormous number of variables involved. Whereas problems in many other sciences (e.g., engineering, physics, economics) lend themselves to a degree of preciseness in solution, management problems are ill-structured, composed of innumerable variables whose values cannot be defined, and further complicated by the unpredictable behavior of humans. And finally, the relative "newness" of management compared to the other sciences is a complicating factor. Indeed, significant attempts to reduce management knowledge to a structured body of principles and theories resembling a science have been attempted only in recent years.

The conclusion emerges then that in spite of the great strides being made by both practitioners and scholars, the area of management cannot yet be labeled a science in the sense of the physical and natural sciences. We must say that the *practice of management* consists of the artful application of scientific principles to problem solving in order to select courses of action that optimize the utilization of scarce resources in achieving the chosen objective.

Is management a profession? Despite attempts by some professional groups to advance the "profession of management,"[82] the answer to this question is complicated and is largely a matter of definitions and semantics. If we classify the American economy today as industrial, governmental, and institutional, it is clear that the operation of this economy is in the hands of persons who consider their vocation to be management. As further evidence of "professionalization," consider the growth of management-consulting firms and the fact that the operation of an overwhelming proportion of industry has passed from owners to "professional" managers.

In an excellent comprehensive survey prepared by Professor Kenneth Andrews of the Harvard Graduate School of Business, the topic of professionalism in management was examined in some depth. The most representative criteria of professionalism were chosen and management was evaluated against them. Although it was found that management falls short of meeting the criteria in some technical respects, it qualifies surprisingly well in others. There is much evidence to support the notion that management will ultimately gain full recognition as a profession. The results of the evaluation of management against the selected criteria are summarized:[83]

Criteria of Professionalism	*Management Evaluation*
1. *Knowledge* that has been subjected to disciplined analysis, has produced and been tested by concepts extending its usefulness and determining its possible meanings, and is capable of being extended further by systematic research.	The practice of management rests upon a body of knowledge that meets this criterion. Moreover, the curriculum, methods, and research of most business schools are directed to extending and furthering this effort.
2. *Competent application.* The knowledge described is applied to problems of complexity and concern to organized society by persons taking responsibility for what they know these problems to be. This usually implies certification or licensing.	Managers are not required to study the business curriculum or to be licensed. However, like other professionals (e.g., doctors, lawyers), managers learn more in practice than in academic preparation. Moreover, trial by experience in business establishes a presumption of competence.
3. *Social responsibility* means that the professional is motivated less by his own self-interest than he is by the desire to satisfy needs, solve problems, or accomplish goals appropriate to the field. Monetary reward is not valued primarily for its own sake.	The persistence of classic economic theory, the inability of managers to express their intents and actions, and the tendency to regard pursuit of profit as the sole objective are among the factors making it difficult to appraise social responsibility. However, the strong current in today's business practice is to undertake the reconciliation of conflicting responsibilities and to realize that the interests of the corporation and of the system of which it is a part can be combined.
4. *Self-control.* The membership of a profession should have the power to discipline its members, set standards of conduct, and influence behavior in order to ensure the technical validity of criticism.	Unlike the case with doctors or lawyers, it has not been necessary to examine or supervise managers by a public agency or have their practice or behavior supervised by a business group. Internal checks by trade associations are growing. Group norms inside the industry and firm are powerful self-controls, and in the final analysis, incompetence will be punished by failure or other pressures.
5. *Community sanction.* As a consequence of the four criteria listed, the persons served by a profession grant its members respect, authority, and considerable freedom in which to pursue their profession.	Despite the reserve with which the public views some operators, confidence in corporate management has never been higher.

In summary, we can conclude that management is most certainly an art and that the artful application of knowledge will probably remain a manager's greatest skill. And while the state of science in management may be called inexact, it is also a science, although not in the exact sense of physical or natural sciences. Finally, we cannot technically call management a profession according to established criteria, although its professionalism and hence its acceptance will surely grow in the future. The rate at which progress toward professionalization moves will depend on the adoption of the scientific or systems approach to management and organization theory, on the clarification of the purposes of business, on the degree to which managers and organizations become involved in the systems of which they are a part, and on the desirability of professionalism among managers. This view is little different from that held by Mary Parker Follet many years ago: ". . . for most people the word 'profession' connotes a foundation of science and a motive of service."

SUMMARY

In this chapter we have reviewed the major chronological events leading up to today's state-of-the-art in organization and management theory. Although we have labeled the modern era the "age of synthesis," there still remains a bewildering choice among coexisting approaches, theories, views, and "schools." A major objective of subsequent chapters is the synthesis of these approaches.

Major milestones leading to the systems age include men (Taylor and Fayol), events (Hawthorne studies), and technology (the computer). To a great extent these men and events shaped the development of the approaches to organization and management.

Schools of management tend to polarize around different academic disciplines and what past experience has shown to be workable. Major differences can be summarized as those existing between the behaviorists and the management process school. The latter approach views the goals of the organization in terms of productivity and believes that subordinates are limited in ability and motivation. The behavioral school, on the other hand, believes that the technical superiority of the process approach is obtained at the expense of human sacrifice. Various schemes are advanced for integrating these views.

Approaches to organization theory are as numerous as those to management. In both organization and management theory, the answer appears to be the systems approach.

DISCUSSION QUESTIONS AND PROBLEMS

1. Is management an art? A science? A profession? Will the increasing complexity of management advance its professionalism? If so, how?

2. In view of the fact that the world made progress for thousands of years prior to the advent of management as we know it today, what justification is there in Peter Drucker's statement that management is the most important activity in our society?

3. List the major milestones in the development of modern organization and management theory and illustrate the contribution of each.

4. Contrast the behavioral school of management with the management process school, with the decision theory school, and with the quantitative school.

5. To which theory of organization do you think most practicing managers subscribe? Why?

6. Draw a model of a systems approach to management that includes the various schools as well as the technical functions (e.g., accounting, marketing, engineering).

7. What is a specialist? A generalist? How do each of these fit into the systems approach to management?

8. A recent symposium of corporate presidents identified some of the major problems facing American business as: complexity of manufacturing and distribution processes, adequate financing at reasonable cost, accelerating technology and the information explosion, motivation of workers, and acquisition of managerial manpower. Show how each of the schools of management might solve these problems. How would the computer help? Does solution of all these problems have implications for the systems approach? Discuss.

9. "We must find out what we are in business for and concentrate on a limited line of products." This statement indicated the growing confusion that John Bishop felt about the operation of the Midwest Stationery Company. His expanding line of office-supplies (paper, carbon paper, typewriter ribbons) had grown to more than 2,000 varieties and sizes of products. Mr. Bishop, until then a typewriter salesman, had founded the company in 1940 in Waukegan, Illinois. Although the plant remained in Waukegan, all sales and office work were performed in Chicago.

Mr. Bishop personally accounted for about 40 percent of company sales and was personally responsible for government and major corporate accounts. Four other salesmen accounted for the remainder of sales, which were organized as "East of Chicago" and "West of Chicago." Salesmen were permitted to quote prices for both standard and custom-made products. About 50 percent of sales were for custom-made.

The plant in Waukegan had extraordinarily good labor relations; the average tenure of the workers was 14 years. Mr. Bishop's son was superintendent and also acted as quality control supervisor, production control manager, and maintenance officer. His major complaints included the impossibility of production planning because of the large variety of orders he received, and his inability to produce many of these orders for the prices quoted by salesmen.

Although Mr. Bishop held the title of treasurer, financial planning and control was the responsibility of an outside CPA, who visited both plant and office once a quarter to prepare financial statements. At the end of the fiscal year and during the preparation of the annual statement, the CPA realized that the Midwest Stationery Company was in serious financial difficulty. Accounts payable, including payroll, amounted to substantially more than available working capital and bank credit limit combined.

What does Mr. Bishop do now? Justify your answers.

REFERENCES

1. Harold Koontz, "The Management Theory Jungle," *Journal of the Academy of Management*, Vol. 4 (December 1961), 174–88.
2. Max Ways, "Tomorrow's Management," *Fortune,* July 1966, p. 85.
3. Peter Drucker, *The Practice of Management* (New York: Harper & Row, Publishers, 1954).
4. James G. March, ed., *Handbook of Organizations* (Chicago: Rand McNally & Co., 1965), p. ix.
5. Adam Smith, *An Inquiry Into the Nature and Causes of the Wealth of Nations,* edited by Edwin Cannan (New York: Modern Library, Inc., 1937).
6. Alfred Marshall, *Principles of Economics* (New York: The Macmillan Company, 1890).
7. Frederick W. Taylor, *The Principles of Scientific Management* (New York: Harper & Row, Publishers, 1911).
8. Henri Fayol, *General and Industrial Management* (London: Sir Isaac Pitman & Sons Ltd., 1949). The book has experienced a revival in the English language, with six printings since 1949.
9. It is interesting to note that in 1968 *Fortune* reported that "the M.I.T. faculty [of the Alfred P. Sloan School of Management], like a growing number of others, believes there is a core of knowledge applicable to management problems in education, health, and public affairs as well as in business." Sheldon Zalaznick, "The M.B.A.—The Man, the Myth, and the Method," *Fortune,* May 1968, p. 206.

62 Management and Systems

10. Reported in F. J. Roethlisberger and William J. Dickson, *Management and the Worker* (Cambridge: Harvard University Press, 1939).
11. Elton Mayo, *The Human Problems of an Industrial Civilization* (Cambridge: Harvard University Press, 1933).
12. George Terry, *Principles of Management,* 5th ed. (Homewood: Richard D. Irwin, Inc., 1968), p. 11.
13. For an evaluation of the impact of the computer and quantitative techniques on education for management, see Zalaznick, "The M.B.A.—The Man, the Myth, and the Method," pp. 168–206.
14. Robert V. Presthus, "Toward a Theory of Organizational Behavior," *Administrative Science Quarterly,* June 1958, p. 50.
15. William G. Scott, "Organization Theory: An Overview and an Appraisal," *Journal of the Academy of Management,* April 1961, p. 7.
16. Among the contributors to his monumental *Handbook of Organizations,* March lists five economists, four political scientists, five psychologists, six students of business or industrial administration, and ten sociologists. March, *Handbook of Organizations,* p. xiv.
17. Max Weber, *The Theory of Social and Economic Organizations* (New York and London: Oxford University Press, 1947).
18. G. C. Homans, *The Human Group* (New York: Harcourt, Brace & World, Inc., 1950).
19. R. Dubin, *The World of Work* (Englewood Cliffs, N.J.: Prentice-Hall, Inc., 1958).
20. M. Dalton, *Men Who Manage* (New York: John Wiley & Sons, Inc., 1959).
21. James G. March and Herbert A. Simon, *Organizations* (New York: John Wiley & Sons, Inc., 1958).
22. Douglas McGregor, *The Human Side of Enterprise* (New York: McGraw-Hill Book Company, 1961).
23. Rensis Likert, *New Patterns of Management* (New York: McGraw-Hill Book Company, 1961).
24. Chris Argyris, *Personality and Organization* (New York: Harper & Row, Publishers, 1957).
25. Warren Bennis, *Changing Organizations* (New York: McGraw-Hill Book Company, 1966).
26. Among these schools are: custom, experience, scientific, human behavior, social system, systems, decision making, quantitative, process, empirical, rational qualitative, management science, decision theory, social psychology, group behavior, individual behavior, mathematical, and operations.
27. Ernest Dale, "A Plea for Coalition of the Quantifiable and the Non-Quantifiable Approaches to Management," *Journal of the Academy of Management, Academy of Management Proceedings,* December 26–28, 1968, p. 9.
28. *Ibid.,* p. 7.
29. Mayo, *The Human Problems of an Industrial Civilization.*

development of management and organization theory 63

30. Roethlisberger and Dickson, *Management and the Worker*.
31. Keith Davis, *Human Relations in Business* (New York: McGraw-Hill Book Company, 1957).
32. McGregor, *The Human Side of Enterprise*.
33. A. H. Maslow, *Motivation and Personality* (New York: Harper & Row, Publishers, 1954).
34. Argyris, *Personality and Organization*.
35. March and Simon, *Organizations*.
36. Herbert A. Simon, *Administrative Behavior* (New York: The Macmillan Company, 1950).
37. Frederick Herzberg, "One More Time: How Do You Motivate Employees?" *Harvard Business Review*, January–February 1968, p. 53. See also Frederick Herzberg, "Job Enrichment Pays Off," *Harvard Business Review*, March–April 1969, p. 61.
38. See, for example, S. Blickstein, "How Good is the AMA?" *Dun's Review*, March 1969, pp. 44–47.
39. Edward P. Learned, C. R. Christensen, and K. R. Andrews, *Business Policy* (Homewood, Ill.: Richard D. Irwin, Inc., 1965).
40. Ernest Dale, *The Great Organizers* (New York: McGraw-Hill Book Company, 1961).
41. Herbert A. Simon, *The New Science of Decision Making* (New York: Harper & Row, Publishers, 1960), p. 1.
42. *Ibid.*, p. 1.
43. Jay W. Forrester, *Industrial Dynamics* (Cambridge: The M.I.T. Press, 1961), p. vii.
44. Richard M. Cyert and James G. March, *A Behavioral Theory of the Firm* (Englewood Cliffs, N.J.: Prentice-Hall, Inc., 1963). See also Simon, *The New Science of Decision Making*.
45. Taylor, *Principles of Scientific Management*.
46. Lillian M. Gilbreth, *The Psychology of Management* (New York: The Macmillan Company, 1914).
47. See A. W. Rathe, ed., *Gantt on Management* (New York: American Management Association, 1961).
48. Joel Dean, *Managerial Economics* (Englewood Cliffs, N.J.: Prentice-Hall, Inc., 1951).
49. John Von Neumann, "The General and Logical Theory of Automata," *Cerebral Mechanisms in Behavior* (New York: John Wiley & Sons, Inc., 1951).
50. Charles J. Hitch, *Decision Making for Defense* (Berkeley: University of California Press, 1966). Also, C. J. Hitch and Roland N. McKean, *The Economics of Defense in the Nuclear Age* (Cambridge: Harvard University Press, 1960).
51. Russell Ackoff, "Management Misinformation System," *Management*

Science, Vol. 14 (December 1967). Also, C. W. Churchman and R. L. Ackoff, *Introduction to Operations Research* (New York: John Wiley & Sons, Inc., 1957).

52. Robert O. Schlaifer, *Analysis of Decisions Under Uncertainty* (New York: McGraw-Hill Book Company, 1967).
53. J. D. Mooney and A. C. Reiley, *The Principles of Organization* (New York: Harper & Row, Publishers, 1939).
54. Lyndall Urwick, *The Elements of Administration* (New York: Harper & Row, Publishers, 1943).
55. L. Gulick and Lyndall Urwick, eds., *Papers on the Science of Administration* (New York: Institute of Public Administration, 1937).
56. Terry, *Principles of Management.*
57. Harold Koontz and Cyril O'Donnell, *Principles of Management,* 4th ed. (New York: McGraw-Hill Book Company, 1968).
58. William H. Newman and Charles E. Summer, Jr., *The Process of Management* (Englewood Cliffs, N.J.: Prentice-Hall, Inc., 1961).
59. Franklin G. Moore, *Manufacturing Management* (Homewood, Ill.: Richard D. Irwin, Inc.).
60. Dalton E. McFarland, *Management Principles and Practices* (New York: The Macmillan Company, 1958).
61. Koontz and O'Donnel, *Principles of Management,* p. 34.
62. R. R. Blake and J. S. Mouton, *The Managerial Grid* (Houston: Gulf Publishing Company, 1964).
63. E. Wright Bakke, *The Fusion Process* (New Haven: Labor and Management Center, Yale University, 1953).
64. Likert, *New Patterns of Management.*
65. Edwin B. Flippo, "Integrative Schemes in Management Theory," *Journal of the Academy of Management,* March 1968, pp. 91–98.
66. Although modern organization theory is a development of the past few years, the brilliant Max Weber designed his bureaucratic model around the turn of the century, and it is largely unchanged today. Weber's analysis of bureaucracy is contained in Chapter VIII, "Bureaucracy," in H. H. Gerth and C. Wright Mills, ed. & trans., *From Max Weber: Essays in Sociology* (New York: Oxford University Press, 1946).
67. Dwight Waldo and Martin Landau, *The Study of Organizational Behavior: Status, Problems, and Trends* (Washington: The American Society for Public Administration, 1966), p. 3.
68. Simon, *The New Science of Decision Making,* p. 66.
69. C. N. Parkinson, *Parkinson's Law* (Boston: Houghton Mifflin Company, 1957). Among Parkinson's anti-bureaucratic statements are, "Work expands to fill the time available," and, "An official wants to multiply subordinates, not rivals."
70. Laurence J. Peter and Raymond Hull, *The Peter Principle—Why Things*

Always Go Wrong (New York: William Morrow & Co., Inc., 1969). Peter's principle asserts that "in a hierarchy every employee tends to rise to his level of incompetence."

71. Waldo and Landau, *The Study of Organizational Behavior,* p. 11.
72. Talcott Parsons, *Structure and Process in Modern Societies* (New York: The Free Press, 1963), pp. 16–58.
73. *Ibid.,* p. 17.
74. Gulick and Urwick, eds., *Papers on the Science of Administration.*
75. Mooney and Reiley, *Principles of Organization.*
76. Joseph Massie, "Management Theory," in March, ed., *Handbook of Organizations,* p. 398.
77. Roethlisberger and Dickson, *Management and the Worker.*
78. Mayo, *The Human Problems of an Industrial Civilization.*
79. Scott, "Organization Theory: An Overview and an Appraisal," p. 7.
80. Herzberg, "One More Time: How Do You Motivate Employees?" p. 57.
81. Scott, "Organization Theory: An Overview and An Appraisal," p. 10.
82. For example, the Administrative Management Society requires its members to adhere to the principles of the "profession of management." For a detailed discussion of the characteristics of a profession, see Robert G. Murdick, "The Meaning of Management as a Profession," *Advanced Management,* April 1960.
83. Kenneth R. Andrews, "Toward Professionalism in Business Management," *Harvard Business Review,* March–April 1969, pp. 49–60.

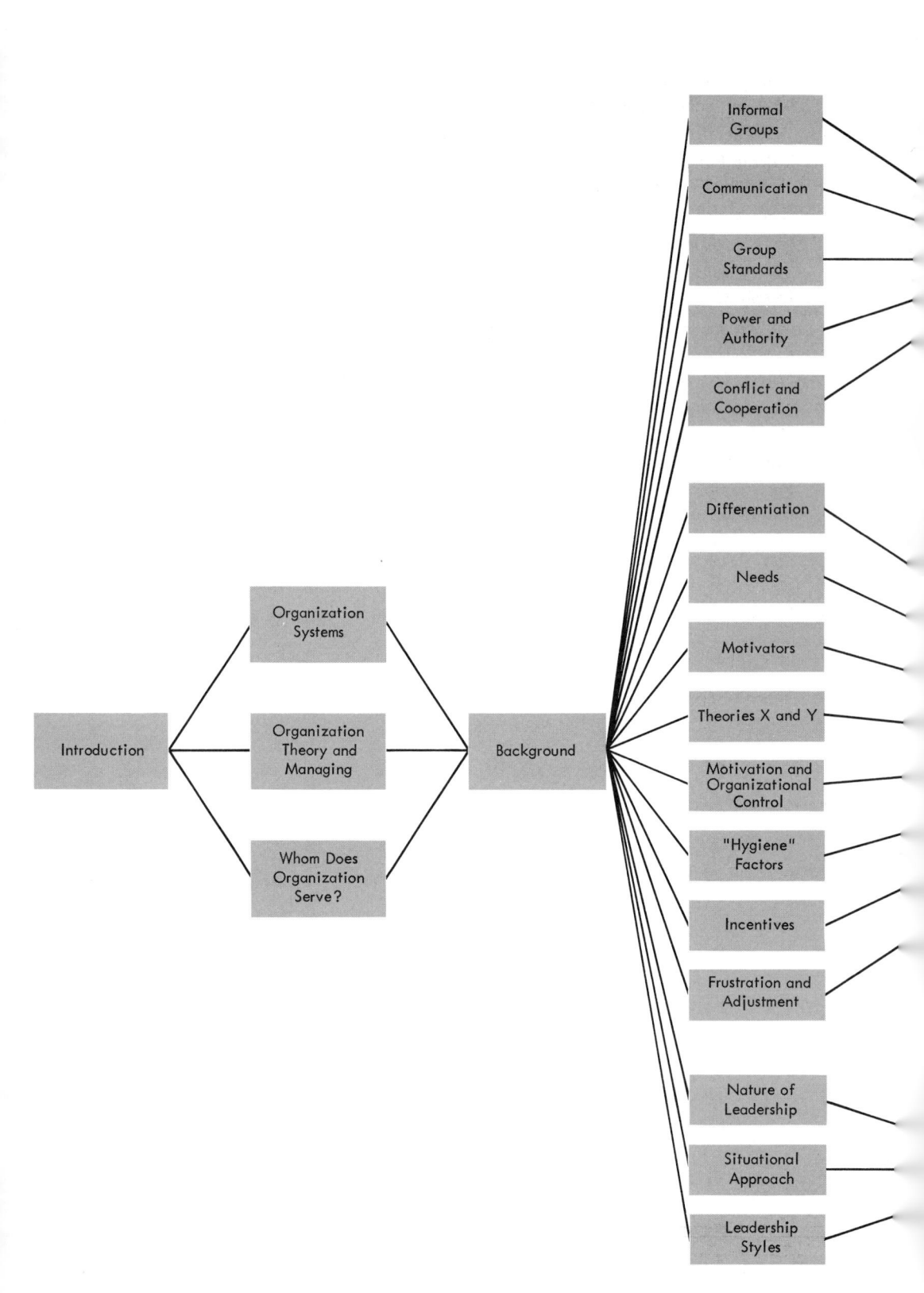

```
Introduction ──┬── Organization Systems ──┐
               ├── Organization Theory and Managing ──┼── Background ──┬── Informal Groups
               └── Whom Does Organization Serve? ─────┘                ├── Communication
                                                                       ├── Group Standards
                                                                       ├── Power and Authority
                                                                       ├── Conflict and Cooperation
                                                                       │
                                                                       ├── Differentiation
                                                                       ├── Needs
                                                                       ├── Motivators
                                                                       ├── Theories X and Y
                                                                       ├── Motivation and Organizational Control
                                                                       ├── "Hygiene" Factors
                                                                       ├── Incentives
                                                                       ├── Frustration and Adjustment
                                                                       │
                                                                       ├── Nature of Leadership
                                                                       ├── Situational Approach
                                                                       └── Leadership Styles
```

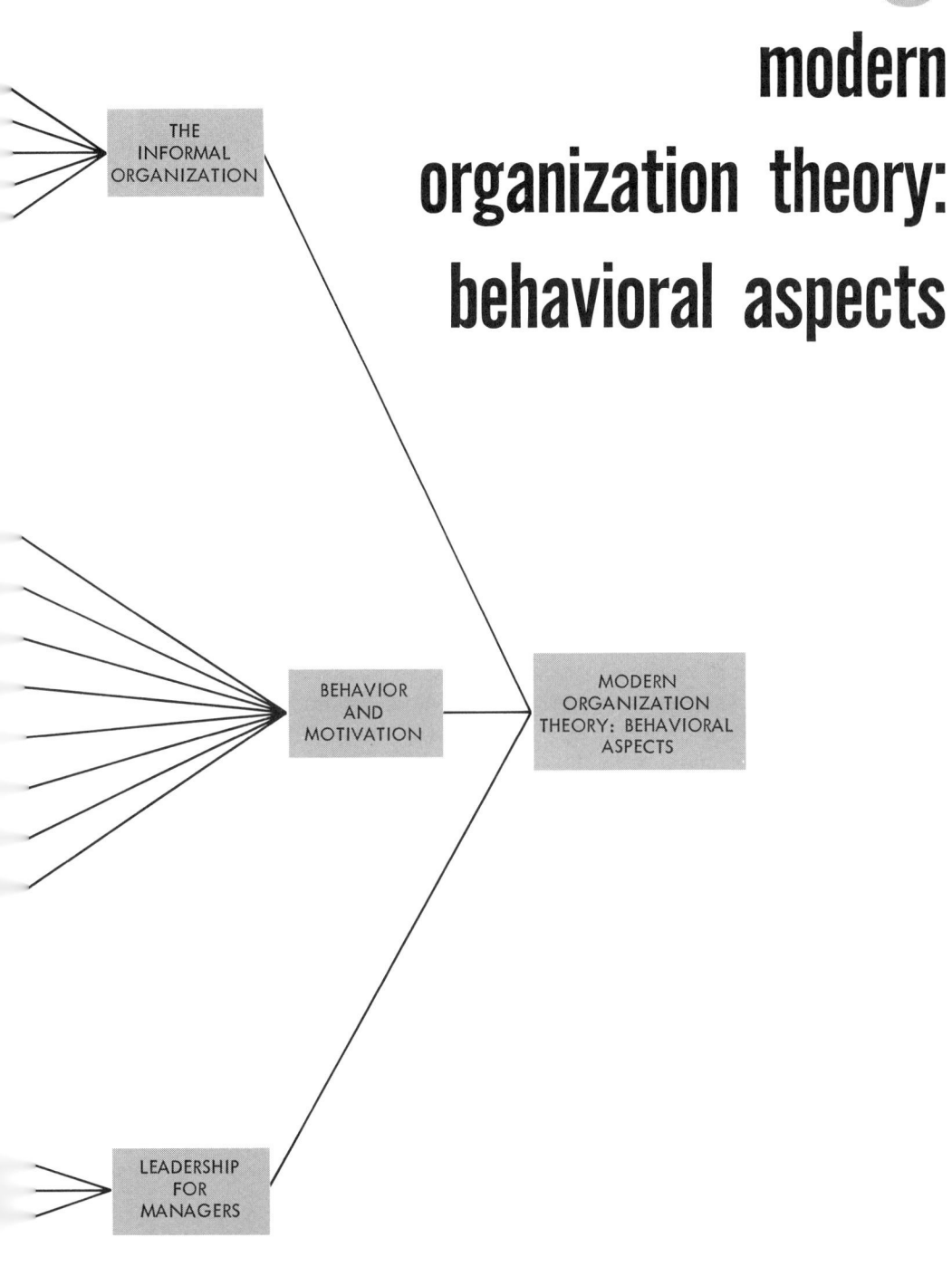

3
modern organization theory: behavioral aspects

THE INFORMAL ORGANIZATION

BEHAVIOR AND MOTIVATION

MODERN ORGANIZATION THEORY: BEHAVIORAL ASPECTS

LEADERSHIP FOR MANAGERS

3

Chapter 2 traced the development of classical concepts of managing organizations and showed how these concepts are based upon the observations and experiences of pioneers in management thought. Although some conclusions of these early writers were derived from empirical research (e.g., the Hawthorne studies), most assertions were developed from reasoning about organizations and managing and from what was observed over time from first-hand experience. The classical model of the organization that resulted was therefore an approximation of reality. It still provides a useful first approximation today, once its limitations are known and modern organization theory is integrated with it. Moreover, it did provide the foundation or beginnings from which modern organization theory was later constructed.

The milestone represented by the Hawthorne studies advanced organization theory by two steps. First, it took an empirical approach to determine the factors that affect human behavior and hence productivity, and second, it hypothesized for the first time that these factors are not economic rewards and sanctions, as the commonly held view espoused. Notwithstanding the somewhat crude experimental approach of these studies, they did hasten the time when a truly modern theory of organizational behavior could be examined and advanced.

Chapter 2 also examined and provided the classical and neoclassical framework for the analysis of organizations. The framework of modern organization theory will be developed in more detail in this and subsequent chapters. As we pointed out in Chapter 2, the distinctive characteristics of modern organization theory are: (1) its conceptual–empirical–analytical base, and (2) the systems viewpoint of the organization. The confusion about the systems view of the organization arises because students do not recognize that there are many systems and subsystems that make up the organization. Various scholars have selected specific systems as *the* approach to the representation of the organization. Let us identify just a few of these systems and subsystems.

ORGANIZATION SYSTEMS

1. *The formal organizational system as described in charts, policies, and procedures.* This is the "legal" structural system, which defines levels of authority and responsibility. It is the mechanistic system for relating tasks, positions, and methods of operation. It is the system that is most visi-

ble, because of its basis in logic (apart from behavioral considerations) and because of its thorough documentation. Its main weakness is that it is a static system model representing a dynamic system.

2. *The informal organization.* The informal organization is a dynamic social system model. If it were properly set down on paper, it would show attachment relationships among individuals, communications networks as they actually exist, and numerous factors that affect the operation of this social system. A disadvantage of studying this system alone is that it is difficult to set down the relationships and behavior of people and groups, particularly because they are constantly changing.

3. *The individual as a system.* The psychological makeup of people as individuals describes the individual person as a subsystem. The total business system comprises the aggregate of these subsystems. The weakness of this model is that the needs and behavior of people in cooperative groups extend beyond those of each individual by himself. The interactions and the behavior of those around him affect the values, attitudes, and behavior of the individual.

4. *The management information system.* Every organization must have means for gathering and transmitting information to the major decision makers to control present and future activities. The information system and the management group are similar to the nervous system and brain of the human being. If sensing or reporting is faulty, incomplete, or cut at some major juncture, the entire organism will become disoriented. The study of the management information system of a business organization requires consideration of every behavioral and mechanistic aspect of the organization, and therefore this is an excellent system to study.

5. *The organizational communications system.* Communication within a company depends upon the formal and informal organizations that have been established and upon the framework imposed by the management information system. Communication is a function of the behavior of people, of the formal procedures established by management, and of the equipment available. Communication is a vital system, but only a part of other, larger systems.

6. *The power system.* Besides the "legal" power system set forth by the formal organization, there is a network of sponsor–protégé relationships and informal conversions of activities into control over other people in the organizations. For example, either individuals in the accounting area or secretaries to managers may exert and develop power through the blocking or delaying of communications. A production manager may achieve power by gaining the support of the sales manager, who cannot afford to have shipments delayed. Managers who socialize together outside of work may form a power group or clique. The power system is difficult to define and describe, although the sociologist Melville Dalton has presented excellent

studies of it in three plants. The power system is an important part of organization processes.

7. *The functional systems.* The processing of a customer need from its identification through conversion of raw materials into finished goods and the distribution of these goods is carried out by a sequence of fairly distinct activities. These activities, sometimes known as the technical subsystems, consist of marketing, engineering, production, finance, logistics, and sometimes others. Many people visualize the entire business system as the integration of these subsystems. Information needs with respect to the operation of all the systems represent one approach to the construction of a management information system.

8. *The management process systems.* The system for management planning, the system for organizing, the system for initiating, and the system for measuring and controlling may, taken together, represent the organizational system. As indicated in Chapter 2, these systems are not independent. They are so closely interwoven that their study on an individual basis does not offer a good "systems" approach to the study of organization and management.

9. *The material logistics system.* It may be considered that the entire firm is essentially a logistics system, a processor of materials into finished goods that are shipped to customers. In such a case, the focus is on the operational aspects and systems. Little attention is given to the behavioral and managerial subsystems.

It is apparent that, for some purposes, all these systems comprise the entire managerial/organizational system. However, we want to utilize the limited framework developed in Chapter 1 for the initial stages of our systems approach. To summarize our definition: The systems approach to management and organization theory views the organization as a *system* composed of subsystems integrated by proper systems design. Moreover, a system is characterized by synergism, which is the simultaneous action of separate but interrelated parts that together produce an effect greater than the sum of the effects of its individual parts. The subsystems that we want to integrate include: (1) operating systems (resource flows of money, manpower, materials, etc.), (2) the organization that transforms these resource flows, and (3) the management process—the means by which the transformation is performed.

To repeat our basic definitional tenet: organization theory focuses on human organization; the management process focuses on acquisition and utilization of resources. The fusion of organization theory and management into a systems approach will therefore advance the optimum arrangement of the parts of the system. This fusion is a major objective of Part I of this book.

The systems approach to management and the integration processes of balanced design and decision making will be discussed at length in subsequent chapters. Our task in this chapter is to explore the vital concepts of modern organization theory and how its behavioral aspects serve to link the parts of the organizational system.

RELATIONSHIP OF ORGANIZATION THEORY TO MANAGING

If Captain Bligh had known more about modern organization theory, he might still be sailing the *Bounty* in the Great Beyond. It is not enough for those who have management responsibilities to understand the technical aspects of production systems; they must understand the human aspects as well. Although we are a long way from predicting the response and behavior of individuals in all situations, we *can* describe some key factors that influence individual and group behavior in an organizational setting. We can also describe some important activities of organizations, such as communications (Chapter 9) and problem solving and decision making (Part III). Finally, we can point out to managers various styles of leadership, methods of motivating people, and the impact of leadership style on motivation and productivity.

In our culture, organizations have a formal system of accountability, as indicated by this classical system model. Occupying vital positions within this system are the formal leaders, or managers. Regardless of who influences or makes decisions in an organization, it is the managers who are held accountable. Sanctions may be applied against them for poor major decisions or chronic operating problems to the extent of demotion or release from the company. Their success rests largely upon obtaining the maximum performance from all the talent in their organization. It is for these reasons that organization theory is so important to managers.

WHOM DOES THE ORGANIZATION SERVE?

The question of whom the organization serves may seem an odd place to start discussing the behavior of people in organizations. If an organization were a closed system, there would be no need to ask this question. The fact is, however, that a business organization is somewhat like a loose football in a football game. Many are trying to get hold of it to move it in the direction they prefer. But in business, instead of just two teams, there are many teams and many individuals, such as:

1. *The stockholders and directors.* The stockholders have the "legitimate" property claim to the corporation, which they presumably exercise through the board of directors that represents them. However, the directors

are often far removed from the dispersed stockholders; besides, different stockholders want different things—such as dividends versus reinvestment, safety versus risk, or stability versus growth.

2. *The government.* The federal government affects the direction of a business through legislation and taxation. As a partner who takes about 50 percent of the profits, it is often at odds with the interests of other claimants. State and local governments also regulate, tax, and influence the direction of a company.

3. *The public.* The public feels that corporations should not exist just for profit, that they should also act in the public interest. Noise, pollution, and beautification of factory sites are considered subjects for public action.

4. *Customers and vendors.* The customers are tugging on the firm for better service, better products, and lower costs. At the other end, the vendors are trying to obtain higher prices and to sell more standardized supplies.

5. *Special interest groups.* The trade associations, consumer groups, conservationists, and individuals owning large blocks of stock in the company all pursue their own special and different interests.

6. *The management of the company.* Different managements of similar companies in an industry may pursue different ends. It is also natural that management wishes to avoid taking large risks for large profits and prefers to simply do well enough to stay in power. The management seeks special remuneration that may or may not exceed its contribution.

7. *The employees of the company.* Both as individuals and as a group, employees frequently find that their goals do not jibe with those of management. Worse yet, employees may engage in a constant struggle against management without regard to their own long-term interests. Some companies, in the face of this, have simply liquidated.

The problems that confront managers are how to identify the objectives and goals of the company and how to manage its resources in such a way as to integrate these varied interests, many of which are in apparent conflict. For example, stockholders may believe that salaries of managers and key employees are too high and are resulting in low dividends. At the same time, the managers and employees may feel that salaries are too low, so that they are not motivated to perform to their utmost. The problem might be resolved by convincing stockholders that profits will decline if managers leave to be replaced by less capable people. At the same time, managers may be given some status rewards that are not as costly as large salary increases, i.e., company cars or country club memberships. Although this hypothetical example is extremely simplified and is based upon an assumption about motivation that is often suspect, it does indicate the process of integrating apparently diverse interests.

We recognize that the business firm is an open system. We observe that the fundamental problem of managers is to develop and achieve goals that integrate the often conflicting interests of those outside the firm and those inside. We now must ask what it is that people within the firm seek. What are their interests and goals? How can we integrate the employees' needs with the typical organizational goals of survival, growth, profitability, and increased effectiveness and efficiency? As scientists we note that we are starting our inquiry with some major assumptions about the identity of organizational goals. At any rate, we have given here some clues as to why the typical manager's notion that profit maximization is the sole objective of the firm is a mistaken view. Objectives of the firm and of the individual manager are in fact far more complex than this simple notion indicates.

BEHAVIOR AND MOTIVATION

If we could utilize as much as half of the potential of human beings for productive work, productivity would far exceed that which all the mechanical improvements of modern technology can provide. An indication of this tremendous potential is visible if we look at just a few historic events, such as the construction of the Pyramids, the struggle of Great Britain during World War II, and the rebirth of West Germany after the war. Try to imagine what a company could do if every worker put his heart and soul into the life of the company!

Why do people behave the way they do? What inner mechanism motivates people to give their all? It is well worth a great effort by management to seek the answers to these questions. Without such knowledge, management systems remain primarily paper systems.

Social scientists have provided some hypotheses with prescriptive as well as descriptive value. Several of these, expressed in a simplified fashion, follow.

Differentiation

The one law about human behavior that we can be certain of is that all people are different. The often-heard phrase, "All people are equal but some are more equal than others," has tremendous implications for the busy manager who tends to treat all his subordinates alike, or for the more sophisticated manager who attempts to structure them into two or three classes.

Behavior differences between individuals are produced by physical differences, mental capabilities, life experiences, culture, and perceptions of a situation. With age often comes a reinforcement of experiences and interpretations, which leads to resistance to new methods and concepts. Not only do patterns of behavior vary among individuals, the behavior of an individual changes over time.

We point out this important fact of *differences* among individuals at this early stage because we are now going to present some characteristics of human behavior that appear to be shared by most people. We first wished to sweep out of the way the fallacy of stereotypes that entraps the insensitive leader.

Needs

A need is a tension within an individual produced by a desire for achievement of some goal. Sometimes, "need," "want," and "desire" are used synonymously. A motive is a response selector of action (behavior) to achieve the goal. A simple example is pictured in Figure 3–1.

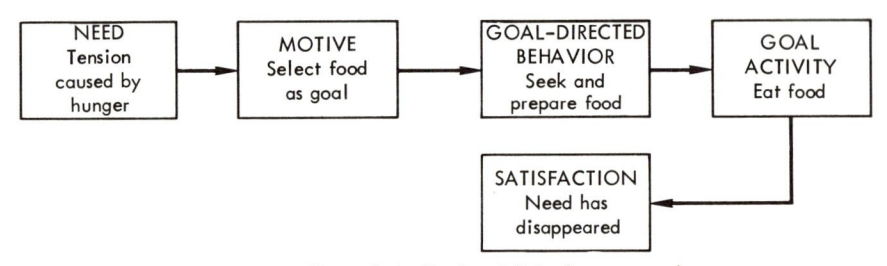

NEED Tension caused by hunger	→	MOTIVE Select food as goal	→	GOAL-DIRECTED BEHAVIOR Seek and prepare food	→	GOAL ACTIVITY Eat food
				SATISFACTION Need has disappeared	←	

Figure 3–1 Need and Behavior

Needs are internal to the individual, and managers cannot impose them in the minds of their subordinates by edict, policy, or regulation. Managers may, however, provide *incentives* with the hope that needs will arise. The incentive pay system in the factory shows that incentives are often blocked by other factors in an individual's environment. Relatively few workers are motivated to become "rate-busters" by externally offered rewards. A second important implication for managers derived from Figure 3–1 is that *a satisfied need is not a motivator.* The "human relations" concept of organizational behavior floundered on the assumption that the happy worker would be a highly productive worker. The proponents of this earlier theory failed to recognize that dissatisfaction (tension) is the cause of goal-directed activity.

Needs may generally be categorized as biological needs for maintenance of life and acquired (or learned) needs arising from experience. The strength of a need depends upon expectancy and availability. Expectancy is the degree of belief that a need can be satisfied. The proposition for the manager is, "Set goals and rewards within the capabilities of each individual." Availability of need satisfaction is also under the control of the manager in many cases. The management may make possible such goals as increased income, security through vesting in a pension plan, vacation time, personal fulfillment in work, or status achievement.

Basic Needs or Motivations

Because humans may be considered as goal-directed subsystems within the total organizational system, it is important for systems designers and managers to know the source of human goals and how these goals affect the performance of the organization. Attempts have been made to generalize on the needs of all people, leading to considerable research directed toward refinement and verification of the generalities. As a result, a few operational rules appear to be developing that have at least some scientific substance and practicality.

The psychologist A. H. Maslow developed a classification he called the "hierarchy of needs,"[1] which has stood the test of later research, although the ranking of the three psychological (higher) needs appears to be indeterminate or variable. The five categories, from first priority to subsequent needs, are:

1. Physiological needs
2. Safety, stability, and security
3. Affiliation, belonging to a group, love
4. Self-esteem (ego need) and the esteem of others (social recognition)
5. Self-actualization—fulfillment of the person's potential and interests

This classification with specific illustrations is shown in Figure 3–2.

In our society, the basic physiological needs are usually satisfied through the medium of money. We might expect therefore, as managers, that constant increments of money decrease in importance once the physiological needs are satisfied. Money remains important only to the extent that it can contribute to social or ego-need fulfillment, and then we may begin to substitute specific rewards or sanctions of the social or ego-need type.

In the case of people with whom security is a high-priority need, we can place them in stable organizations, provide security against layoffs and firing, offer steady growth, and provide comfortable medical, health, and pension benefits. Affiliation need may be closely associated with security. The individual desiring security feels safer in a group to which he belongs and in which his role and the roles of the others are clearly defined—that is, where he is "accepted."

The affiliation need develops just as strongly, or more so, in groups under pressure, in groups dissatisfied with working conditions, or in groups who find the work boring and trivial. This is discussed further in the section on informal organization.

76 Management and Systems

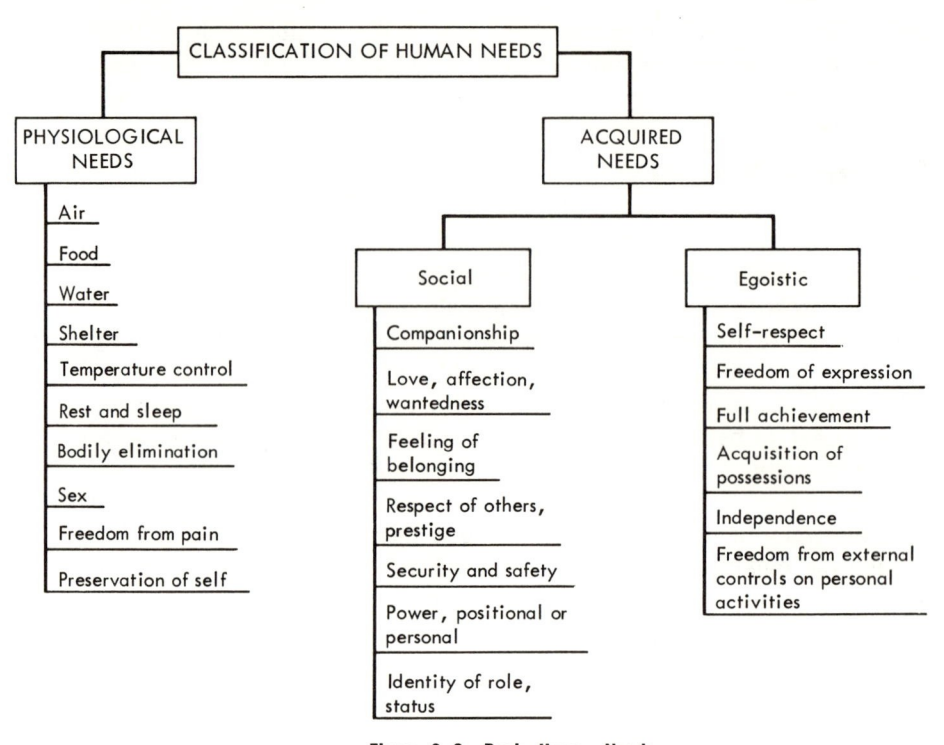

```
                    CLASSIFICATION OF HUMAN NEEDS
                    ┌──────────────┴──────────────┐
              PHYSIOLOGICAL                  ACQUIRED
                 NEEDS                         NEEDS
                                         ┌───────┴───────┐
                                       Social         Egoistic
```

PHYSIOLOGICAL NEEDS
- Air
- Food
- Water
- Shelter
- Temperature control
- Rest and sleep
- Bodily elimination
- Sex
- Freedom from pain
- Preservation of self

Social
- Companionship
- Love, affection, wantedness
- Feeling of belonging
- Respect of others, prestige
- Security and safety
- Power, positional or personal
- Identity of role, status

Egoistic
- Self-respect
- Freedom of expression
- Full achievement
- Acquisition of possessions
- Independence
- Freedom from external controls on personal activities

Figure 3–2 Basic Human Needs

    The need for the esteem of others can be a very strong motivator in many instances. People who have an unconscious feeling of inadequacy may overcompensate by striving hard and by repeatedly seeking new successes. This need often appears characteristic of successful managers who seek prestige, status, power, and symbolically large salaries.

    Self-esteem may be fulfilled in many ways, making it difficult for management to develop incentives based on this need. Suppose, for example, that possibly illegal price-fixing is being conducted by many officials throughout a large company in working with competitors and customers. One individual may find self-esteem because he can outperform other managers in this activity. Another finds that self-esteem is lost if he participates, and he seeks a transfer or quits. Self-esteem is essentially a matching of a person's performance with his values. The lesson for management is to learn the nature of values and of those values held by the individuals in the organization. Each manager or supervisor is best prepared to use this motivator on an individual basis with his immediate subordinates.

    The highest need in the hierarchy is the need for self-fulfillment, the need to achieve all that the individual is capable of, and to achieve it in a kind of work that he enjoys. One of the authors overheard a man on a bus, riding to his government job in Washington, say to his companion, "Do you know, I hate my job. It's just eight hours to kill every day until I can get out of there and back home." It is apparent from this and other observations within companies that many people attain a greater measure of self-fulfillment off the job than on it. Many people do not find enough independence of action and breadth of responsibility within the confines of the division of work developed through classical organizational precepts. Modern managements are now taking this learned need into account and are attempting to turn loose the vast unused potential of their people. Job enrichment through vertical and horizontal expansion of duties, increased participation of individuals in setting their own goals and in decision making, and a more careful search for the interests and capabilities of each employee are being carried out by the more progressive companies. In other words, the potential for performance, good and bad, of the individual in any system or subsystem of the organization must be recognized by managers and systems designers.

Theory X and Theory Y in Motivating Workers

Douglas McGregor has distinguished between the "non-people" assumptions of the rational, classical model and the behavior considerations of modern organization theory.[2] Theory Y is essentially a development of the self-fulfillment need in the modern business firm. It should be pointed out that culture, level of economy, and point in time have all contributed to placing the American worker in a position where self-fulfillment is both available and attainable. In our early history, men worked long, arduous hours to satisfy basic, minimum physical needs.

Theory X and Theory Y are contrasting models of human motivation and behavior. Theory X actually represents the lack of behavioral theory in the early classical theory, although many writers use it as a reason for discarding all contributions of the rationalistic aspect of organization and work design. The two sets of assumptions and implications are shown in Table 3–1. Modern organization theorists believe that Theory Y is the means by which the tremendous capacity of each individual may be released for productive achievement.

Organizational Control and Motivation Assumptions

Chris Argyris of Yale University has published some controversial hypotheses and conclusions.[3] Argyris believes that the formal structure and emphasis on control set forth by classical organizational theory are in conflict with the needs of healthy, mature individuals. Classical theory (and the majority of managers) assumes that employees are apathetic, lazy, or dependent, and that all the trappings of an "engineered" organization are

Table 3–1
Theory X and Theory Y

Theory X indicates that efficiency will be high when:

1. Authority flows down a hierarchical chain in which each subordinate has but one supervisor or manager.
2. Work is divided into the smallest number of sets of similar functions.
3. Span of management is kept small, but balanced against the number of levels of management.
4. Work is carefully specified and the worker is hired to fit the job.

Theory X assumes that:

1. Most people prefer to be directed and have little desire for responsibility and creativity.
2. Motivation occurs only at an economic level. The worker is resistant to change.
3. People must be closely supervised. They have a short time span of responsibility. Men are by nature indolent.
4. People can be considered alike as units of production. No differentiation of jobs to utilize different interests and capacities is desirable. The worker is self-centered, indifferent to organizational needs.

Theory Y implies that efficiency will be high when:

1. Authority and communication flow in both formal and informal systems.
2. Work is varied and enriched.
3. Span of management is as broad as possible as long as major objectives can be achieved.
4. Tasks are grouped into different, meaningful jobs to accommodate individual talents and capacities.

Theory Y assumes that:

1. Workers are social beings who can work together for organizational and personal goals.
2. Capacity for creativity is present to some degree in everybody. Needs at the level above the economic level are powerful motivators.
3. People desire self-fulfillment through directing their own activities and participating in setting their own objectives.
4. Workers achieve their fullest potential when their aspirations and job challenges are matched to their capabilities.

necessary, including manuals, organization charts, position descriptions, incentive systems, procedures, reports, inspections, and numerous control systems to achieve efficiency. These assumptions and related corollaries, as shown in Table 3–2, imply that workers are like children, who need and like to be told what to do, and who must be watched carefully.

Argyris concluded from his study that, contrary to these managerial assumptions, mature people resent the constrictive control of the typical business organization. They react to it in such a way that management seeks tighter controls on their actions. Tighter controls produce further reactions, such as aggression against company property or individuals, frustration expressed by absenteeism or quitting the company, or relapse into docile, immature behavior.

Relaxation of controls and job enlargement for employees who desire it would produce considerable gains in productivity and organizational morale, Argyris believes. He points out that leadership must be reality-oriented; some workers require more direction than others, and workers do not gain maturity immediately by the lifting of controls.

The immaturity–maturity concept once more deals with managers' assumptions regarding the motivation of workers. Argyris essentially indicates that greater organizational effectiveness will be achieved if management's assumptions are based upon self-fulfillment needs of workers instead of low-level, physiological needs.

Table 3–2

Immaturity Assumptions

Managers believe that efficiency will be high if:	*Managers assume that:*
1. The only relations between people in organizations are those defined by the organization manuals and charts.	1. Employees are uninterested, apathetic, and passive.
2. Logical incentive systems and clear specific directions are provided.	2. Employees are lazy, money-crazy, and have a short time-perspective.
3. Employees are subjected to persuasion, education about the economic objectives of business, and even compulsion.	3. Employees create errors and waste. They have shallow interests and behave pretty much alike.
4. Control is increased as deviant activities increase.	4. The manager knows best how problems should be solved. Employees lack awareness of and control over themselves.

Motivation and Hygiene Factors

As the United States has become more affluent, its citizens in general have become better educated, more mature, and secure from worry about satisfying their needs at the lower levels of Maslow's hierarchy. Self-esteem, social esteem, and self-actualization have become the motivators. Frederick Herzberg has refined the concepts of Maslow, McGregor, and Argyris to the extent of identifying specific factors under the control of management that are important in motivation.

Herzberg's studies led him to conclude that there are two different categories of motivating factors. He discovered that poor *environmental* factors—such as working conditions, policies and administration, money, and reshuffling of tasks—may make workers dissatisfied, but improving these conditions—that he calls *hygienic* factors—does not motivate workers to greater productivity. Management's imposition of such external influences he refers to as "KITA" (kick in the pants). This approach has resulted in total failure. On the other hand, the *positive* motivators, Herzberg says, are stimulated by:

1. Removing controls over the worker but holding him accountable for results
2. Giving a person a complete, natural module of work, not just adding and subtracting tasks
3. Granting the worker additional authority and job freedom
4. Making periodic reports available to the employee so that he may initiate corrective action instead of being directed to take it
5. Introducing new and more difficult assignments so that the employee may learn and grow

Factors characterizing 1,844 events on the job that led to extreme dissatisfaction

Factors characterizing 1,753 events on the job that led to extreme satisfaction

Percentage frequency

- Achievement
- Recognition
- Work itself
- Responsibility
- Advancement
- Growth
- Company policy and administration
- Supervision
- Relationship with supervisor
- Work conditions
- Salary
- Relationship with peers
- Personal life
- Relationship with subordinates
- Status
- Security

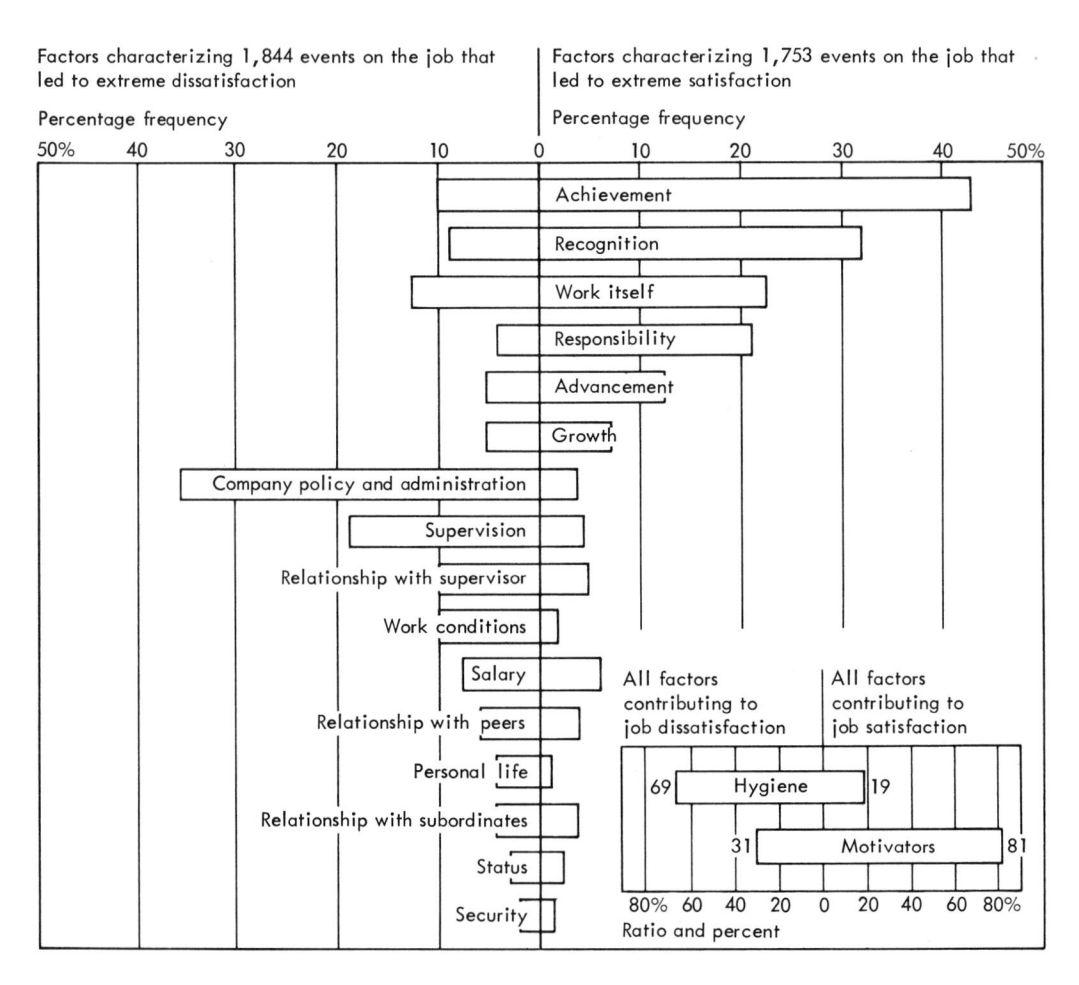

All factors contributing to job dissatisfaction: Hygiene 69 | 31 Motivators

All factors contributing to job satisfaction: Hygiene 19 | 81 Motivators

Ratio and percent

Figure 3–3 Factors Affecting Job Attitudes

SOURCE Frederick Herzberg, "One More Time: How Do You Motivate Employees?" *Harvard Business Review*, January–February 1968, p. 57

modern organization theory: behavioral aspects 81

Schaffer Professional Men	Herzberg, et al. Engineers and Accountants	Myers Engineers	Scientists	Manufacturing Supervisors	Technicians	Female Assemblers	
1. Creativity and challenge	Achievement +	Work itself +	Responsibility −	Advancement +	Responsibility +	Competence of supervision	1.
2. Achievement	Recognition +	Responsibility −	Work itself +	Responsibility	Advancement +	⎛ Recognition ⎞ −	2.
3. Social welfare ("need to help others")	Work itself +	Company policy and administration −	Company policy and administration +	Pay −	⎛ Pay ⎞ −	⎝ Security ⎠ −	3.
4. Moral value scheme (need to have behavior agree with this scheme)	Responsibility +	Pay −	Recognition +	Achievement −	⎝ Work itself ⎠ −	Friendliness of supervision +	4.
5. Interpersonal relationships	Advancement +	Advancement +	⎛ Competence of supervision ⎞	Possibility of growth +	Company policy and administration +	Pay +	5.
6. Self-expression	Salary	Recognition −	⎝ Advancement ⎠ +	Friendliness of supervision −	Achievement	Achievement +	6.
7. Dominance	Possibility of growth	⎛ Achievement ⎞	Achievement	Company policy and administration	Competence of supervision −	Work itself	7.
8. Recognition	Interpersonal relations (subordinates)	⎛ Competence of supervision ⎞		⎛ Competence of supervision ⎞	Recognition	⎛ Company policy and administration ⎞ −	8.
9. Economic security	Status	⎝ Friendliness of supervision ⎠ −		⎝ Peer relations ⎠		⎝ Peer relations ⎠ −	9.
10. Independence	Interpersonal relations (superior) −			Recognition +			10.
11. Socio-economic status	Interpersonal relations (peers)						11.
12. Dependence	Supervision-technical −						12.
13.	Company policy and administration −						13.
14.	Working conditions −						14.
15.	Factors in personal life						15.
16.	Job security						16.

KEY: those in parentheses are nearly equal in rank;
+ lead to satisfaction (primarily);
− lead to dissatisfaction (primarily);
those unmarked are bipolar (primarily).

Figure 3–4 Employee Needs

SOURCE Philip B. Applewhite, *Organizational Behavior,* © 1965. By permission of Prentice-Hall, Inc.

Other investigators using Herzberg's research methods have confirmed his results for various types of workers. Positive motivators have been found to be the needs for achievement, recognition, the work itself, responsibility, advancement, and growth. A summary of hygiene factors and positive motivators is given in Figure 3–3, and a comparison of hygiene and motivating factors for several different occupations in Figure 3–4.

The implications of Herzberg's research are clear. Management must provide a satisfactory level for work factors such as salary, work conditions, and others indicated in Figure 3–3. Paying very large salaries will not motivate workers, however. Management must seek the positive work motivators, such as opportunity for growth and recognition. These factors appear to be different for different classes of workers, as indicated in Figure 3–4.

One of the most fascinating cases of the application of Herzberg's principles is found in a study of Robert Townsend's management of Avis Rent A Car Corporation. Townsend has expressed in detail, and with humor, guidelines for managing in his classic book, *Up the Organization*.[4]

Frustration and Adjustment

The systems designer and the manager should also be aware of the hazards to organizational performance when employees are frustrated—that is, blocked from goals. When an individual is strongly motivated toward attaining a specific goal, he will search hard for ways of reaching the goal. Considerable tension is present within him. If he is blocked from reaching the goal, the mature individual will adapt to the situation and revise his goals. This may mean a lowering of aspirations, which will affect his work on other projects.

More often, the employee is likely to adapt by some form of aggression against other people, objects, or himself. Aggression may appear as:

1. *Displacement.* In a company manufacturing refrigerators, the employees vented their frustration with company policies on the product, by mixing sand in the enamel for painting the refrigerators. In another instance, an employee may react to a reprimand by venting his aggression on a subordinate or fellow worker.

2. *Projection.* The individual attributes his own shortcomings to others. He may blame the company or some individual for his failure on a job or his failure to be promoted.

3. *Rationalization.* When the Lockheed Aircraft Corporation exceeded estimated costs by up to $2 billion on the C5A aircraft, a Navy procurement specialist "justified" presentation of misleading cost estimates to Congress by stating that Congress knew the true cost and was just playing games. He thus "rationalized" what Senator Proxmire characterized as lying. Within organizations, such behavior by employees leads to executive isolation from the activities of the company.

4. *Compensation.* To compensate for frustration on his job, an employee might compensate by transferring his interests and his energy to outside activities.

5. *Passivity and apathy.* As Argyris points out, tight control over individuals produces immature behavior, such as dependence on supervisors and company procedures. Employees lose their desire for independent action and become passive and even apathetic.

Economic and Noneconomic Incentives

Although we have indicated that the strongest positive motivation arises from the freedom and responsibility given the individual in his work, some important hygiene factors must be satisfied as well. The amount of salary may provide both economic and noneconomic satisfaction, since status is affected by salary rank within a company. Companies, particularly those that are not so affluent, may make use of status symbols as satisfiers. These may consist of artifacts or of special privileges. Table 3–3 (page 84) suggests a few types of status symbols for different executive levels.

THE INFORMAL ORGANIZATION AS A SOCIAL SYSTEM

The formal organization and the informal organization within a company are inseparable, even though each may be discussed separately in the way that doctors discuss various systems and organs of the body—for reasons of convenience rather than fact. Here we focus on the informal relationships so that their influence and impact on formally designed management systems may be taken into account. Without such informal relationships, the organization would "self-destruct" from literal adherence to formal rules and procedures of the business.

Nature and Formation of Informal Groups

Social organizations arise and persist because of man's need for interaction with other humans. (See Figure 3–2.) Two or more people who share activities, sentiments, or interactions form a social system. People gather into groups to satisfy needs of affiliation, security, identity, and power. The term *group dynamics* was popularized by Kurt Lewin, a social psychologist, to designate the forces and behavior that occur within a group. The linking groups and subgroups of members of a business organization form the *informal organization*. "The informal organization is the total of member-initiated institutions existing without the sanction of formal authority."[5] The informal and the formal organizations modify, supplement, and reinforce or weaken each other.

Sociologists have identified six types of informal groups:

1. The *total organization* consists of all the many interlocking groups or subsystems in the entire organization.

2. *Large groups* form over some issue of internal politics. Typical of these groups might be production versus marketing factions, one aggressive young executive and his followers versus an old-line executive and his followers, or nonunion groups versus union groups.

3. *Primary cliques* form when workers are located together for work

Table 3-3

Status Symbols

STATUS SYMBOL	COMMANDER-IN-CHIEF	VIP'S	MINOR BUREAUCRATS	STRAW BOSS	HUSTLERS	THE TROOPS
OFFICE LOCATION	60th floor penthouse	59th floor with panoramic view	Smaller office on any floor below 50th, window on courtyard	Cubbyhole next to machinery	Closet	What office?
OFFICE FURNITURE	Antiques and custom-designed desk	Deep brown mahogany furniture with leather upholstery	Modern oak furniture with Naugahyde trim	Metal furniture with vinyl—new	Metal furniture with vinyl—used	Oak—circa 1910
FLOOR COVERING	Parquet wood floor with antique Oriental rug	2-inch-thick, high-quality carpet	1-inch-thick, high-quality carpet	Wool rug—new	Wool rug—used	Vinyl tile
WASTEPAPER BASKET	Gold leaf—antique	Silver	Chromium	Stainless steel	Brought from home—son made in woodwork shop	Plastic
PARKING SPACE	Private space in company garage	Company garage	"Reserved" employee parking lot	Employee parking lot	Gets there early enough to find a place on the street	Rides the bus
HEALTH BENEFITS	Annual executive health examination at luxury resort (1 week)	Annual executive health examination at nearby clinic (1 day)	Nearby first-class restaurant	Annual visit to company doctor	No time	Can't afford to be sick
DINING FACILITIES	Penthouse, executive dining room	Penthouse, executive dining room	Nearby first-class restaurant	"Management" cafeteria	Sandwich sent in	Hot dog stand
SECRETARY	2 admin. assts. 1 exec. sec. 1 receptionist	1 exec. sec.	1 senior-level secretary	1/2 junior-level secretary	1 stenographer shared by 4 others	Gives work to a pool of clerk-typists
MORNING COFFEE BREAK	None—hasn't come into office yet	None—"too busy"	Sips coffee all morning while working	30-minute break with other supervisors	Brings in Thermos bottle with black coffee	Coffee cart arrives promptly at 10:15 A.M.

SOURCE Contributed by Fred Schuster, Florida Atlantic University

purposes or when employees have similar jobs and hence common interests. The workmen in a maintenance crew, the top executives who work together and dine together in the executive dining room, and the professional accountants dispersed throughout the company are examples of primary cliques.

4. *Cliques* include any small group that forms to gain some special power or social advantage.

5. *Friendship–kinship groups* form in many companies in which generation after generation of the same families become employees. Kinship groups form from relatives. Friendship groups form because of close social and neighborhood ties.

6. *Isolates* are the individuals who are loners and do not attach themselves to any group, or shift from group to group.

Cliques are composed of people who share the same values or norms. Acceptance in the clique is achieved only through acceptance by all members of the clique, not by just a single individual. Subcliques are linked partially to cliques in certain activities or by some common members. Isolates, not actually groups, are the "loners" who have weak connections with other people and groups. They do interact with other people and thus have some effect on the total social organization.

Determinants underlying the appearance of informal groups are:

1. *Location*—the physical location in plant or office that provides face-to-face contact.
2. *Occupation*—the tendency for people performing similar jobs to group together.
3. *Interests*—people with like interests form small, informal groups.
4. *Special issues*—the joining together for a common cause to form an informal group that usually disbands when the issue is resolved.

Informal organizations assume certain characteristics that are different from those of formal, structured organizations; these must be taken into account when managing in a climate of informal groups.

1. *Informal organizations* act as agents of *social control,* generating a culture that demands conformity from group members.
2. *Human interactions* are quite different from those in the formal organization and different techniques of analysis are required.
3. *Status and communication* systems exist quite apart from the formal structure.
4. Informal organizations *resist change.*
5. The group has an *informal leader* who is not necessarily the formally appointed one.

Since organizations are made up of people, not boxes on organization charts, managers and systems designers must not isolate themselves from the

Figure 3–5 Organization Structure

SOURCE   Reproduced from the Professional Systems Course, copyrighted by Leslie H. Matthies. Published by Systemation, Inc., P.O. Box 730, Colorado Springs, Colo.

actual organizational dynamics. Management must utilize information about social groups in the design of systems and must acknowledge the realities of organization as indicated in Figure 3–5.

Communication

One of the major functions of the informal organization is to provide for communication outside of the lengthy, rigid, formal chain of responsibility. Employees communicate with each other both laterally and vertically as necessary to get their jobs done, but this occurs according to the informal contacts they have in different parts of the organization. Such communication makes possible much more rapid response to job and situation requirements.

Communication also serves to relieve the monotony on boring, repetitive jobs. It may not be in the form of conversation only, but in behavior and role activities. Donald F. Roy describes how such communication and social interaction kept the four workers isolated in the clicking room from "going nuts" in his classic article, "Banana Time."[6]

When official channels fail to provide full information about events, the informal organization often constructs its own messages. These messages, called "rumors," appear to spread through the informal organization with the speed of light. When a leak of official information occurs or when official information begins to work its way through the formal channels, the informal "grapevine" takes over in the same way.

Theodore Caplow gives an illustration of rumor during war:

> It is hard to account for the speed with which a rumor can leap a 300-mile gap in the course of an afternoon. In one case, the rumor of an impending operation appeared in a detached, isolated island without radio communication approximately one day after it was introduced to the main body of the regiment.[7]

In Chapter 9 we discuss more extensively the nature of communications and information, particularly from the standpoint of the formal organization.

Group Standards and Norms

The informal organization exerts strong pressures for conformity through social control methods. Implicitly, a new member in a social group accepts the norms and standards of the group, which are communicated to him by example, anecdote, expressions of attitude, and other behavior. Pressure for conformity of attitude and of action are brought to bear upon group initiates.

Group norms may restrict work output or increase it. If management wishes to change group norms, it must find people who are accepted by the group or who are influential within the group and change their attitudes. Obviously, this is not easy.

Group discipline can be very severe. The first signs of individual deviation from group norms may be greeted by kidding or sarcastic remarks. Refusal to provide work assistance and to communicate may follow. Heated arguments, physical violence, or covert damage to the person's property, such as tools, lunch, automobile, or home, may occur.

Within an informal group, each member achieves identity through his role, a role determined by the behavior expectations of others in the group. Informal leadership is assumed by those who exert more influence on the group than other individuals do, since role and status within the organization are closely related. Further on, we will discuss these topics in terms of power and accommodation.

Nature and Sources of Power and Authority

Power and authority are derived from both the formal and informal organizations in complex ways. In order to understand how these influences are related, we will discuss some basic concepts, admitting at the start that scholars are in disagreement among themselves with respect to the meaning of authority and power and their relationship to acceptance, responsibility, accountability, and control.

Authority may be considered, roughly, the "legitimate" right to command and to apply sanctions. Thus authority is derived from the formal organization. But how much authority does a person have if his subordinates refuse to obey? There are a number of explanations concerning the source of authority. Some of the most commonly accepted are:

1. Institutional approach
2. Subordinate approach
3. Organizational relationship
4. Legal decree
5. Personal acceptance or consultative authority
6. Identification
7. Sanctions
8. Authority of the situation

In the institutional theory, authority is derived from accepted cultural institutions—traditional, legal, or theological. Thus the concept of private ownership of property bestows upon the owners the authority to use the property as they see fit within general constraints imposed by society.

The subordinate acceptance school of thought states that a manager has authority to the degree that his subordinates accept his decisions. Authority thus flows from the bottom of the organization upward and is gained by the manager through his leadership and ability to win support from his subordinates.

Authority is often considered to be based upon the organizational position or organizational relationships that have been established. Here the individual receives his authority by virtue of the authority of the position.

Authority by legal decree is commonly found in the government. The law grants authority so that enforcement of the statutes may be carried out.

Personal acceptance or consultative authority arises because of recognition of the leader. Recognition may be due to the leader's popularity, his past achievements, his integrity, or his skill and knowledge. In an organization, such a man may not have any formal authority (authority by position), but his recommendations may carry such weight that he appears to have extensive authority. Max Weber's charisma classification of authority would fall under this heading. Charismatic legitimacy is based upon irrational faith in the values and goals of the leaders.

One view holds that authority is derived from group "belongingness." According to this view, people will accept decisions that have been agreed upon by the group to which they belong, thereby delegating authority to the group. People who are strongly associated with the group making the decision will more readily accept the authority of the group. Therefore, the society in which we live is a source of authority, and society may thus be defined as the most comprehensive group to which an individual feels he "belongs." At the other end of the scale is the *ad hoc* committee that a manager appoints to develop a recommendation or make a decision where there is likely to be considerable resistance to any recommendation or decision. The committee participants, by taking part in the decision making, identify themselves with this group and accept its authority.

Authority is often identified with possession of sanctions, the rewards or punishment that one person may mete out to another. In almost all types of organizations, those with authority possess some sanctions that they can apply, such as slowdowns in work, carelessness in treating the organization's property, or starting unfavorable rumors.

The concept of the "authority of the situation" represents an attempt to integrate the goals of the organization with the goals of the individuals involved. Mary Parker Follett describes it thus:

> True authority springs from only the intrinsic competence, worthiness, and strength of one in a place of authority. To be called authority, it must be spontaneously and tacitly acquiesced in by the workers. Authority does not leap forth from the commands of those at the top simply because the organization charts say so. It arises out of "the law of the situation."
>
> Institutional situations demand action to be taken by those whom commonsense and general agreement indicate as the ones to take such action, regardless of what the hierarchic lines might be.

In application, the manager and his subordinate get together, assemble the facts of the situation, discuss alternate solutions to the problem at hand, and weigh the pros and cons. Through full discussion and mutual understanding, it is believed, one preferable course of action will be seen to be called for by the situation. The views of the manager (organization's goals) and of the subordinate (individual's goals) are thus integrated into a single course of action.

In all the situations except the last, authority is limited. Application of authority may lead to direct rebellion, reluctant acceptance, eager participation, or habitual acceptance such as occurs for routine instructions.

Power and authority are considered by many theorists to be closely allied but frequently distant. Power implies the capacity to exercise coercion —the hangman's rope, the policeman's club, the threat of firing from the job, or the threat of demotion. To the extent that authority involves some degree of sanctions, the ability to hurt the other person or group, it contains some element of power. Authority is separate from power when members of a group accept willingly the leadership of various members.

Table 3-4 gives an excellent comparison of the technical, social, and power subsystems of the organization. Note how the technical subsystem reflects the classical theory concepts. Also note that the power subsystem appears to grow out of the social subsystem.

Table 3–4
Technical, Social, and Power Subsystems

Characteristics	Technical Subsystem	Social Subsystem	Power Subsystem
1. Origin	Deliberate employment and arrangement of men and capital to perform tasks required by formal objectives.	Arises spontaneously from social interactions and shared values of men placed in contact with each other.	Arises as people use the various sources of power to acquire things that are judged valuable by others and successfully implement decisions.
2. Processes	Decision, communication, and action	Interaction, sentiments, and activity.	Politics, decision implementation, and maintenance of order.
3. Structure	Arrangement of jobs in relation to each other. Process and authority relations.	Differentiation based on expressions of sentiments of members for each other. Friendship relations.	Differentiation based on the number of behavior areas controlled.
4. Status	Man holds status because of his ability to meet the job requirements. Status is same as job in importance in the technical structure.	Man holds status because of the sentiments of others in the system. For example, the leader is liked most in the group.	Man holds status because of degree of success attained in implementing his decisions.
5. Roles	Man plays role according to job requirements.	Man plays role according to sentiments, beliefs, attitudes, and social mores.	Man plays opportunistic role.
6. Sources of authority and power	Directly related to the job and is delegated from those who have higher authority.	Informal authority is derived from those who are its subjects. Based on sentiments.	Official position, location, job importance, expertise, interest and tenure, personal characteristics, and coalitions.
7. Norms	Job descriptions, written policies, procedures, and rules.	Values and accepted norms of behavior. Unwritten tacit agreements.	Expediency. That behavior which sustains power. People who are objects of power follow orders of power holder to obtain desired values.

SOURCE Rocco Carzo, Jr., and John N. Yanouzas, *Formal Organization—A Systems Approach* (Homewood, Ill.: The Dorsey Press, 1967), p. 240

Conflict and Cooperation

Conflict occurs within groups and between groups in both the formal and informal organization. Conflict is related to both power and cooperation: conflict brings shifts in power and is often resolved by power (influence); cooperation is often the end result of conflict.

Cooperation is a stronger need for individuals with greater needs for affiliation and stability. However, for those who covertly seek power, cooperation is necessitated by mutual goals.

In the past, conflict was often considered harmful and destructive of organizational goals. Modern administrative thought takes the view that there is much constructive potential in conflict. In business, this is achieved through "controlled competition" among individuals and groups.

Solutions of conflict, other than integration and cooperation, are: (1) victory/defeat, (2) compromise, (3) avoidance of the subject, and (4) deadlock with varying ultimate consequences. Because the design and implementation of new systems often face group pressures against change, the designer and manager should be aware of methods for handling constructively the conflict of organizational and informal group goals.

An excellent insight into the nature of the stresses, conflict, and accommodation of opposing needs is provided by the sociologist Melville Dalton in his in-depth study of three firms.[8] He presents the backgrounds and activities of key individuals and some problem situations they face. Dalton shows how fully committed and partially committed personnel deal with various moral concerns of the firm. He describes how people in formal organizational roles accommodate to the needs of workers by participation in informal organizational roles. Dalton concludes that conflict is typical, that it is often hidden because of its danger to the organization, and that it is usually intermingled with all advances of a creative nature.

LEADERSHIP FOR MANAGERS

The essence of managing is effective and efficient utilization of resources, including human resources. In the organizational system, management must endeavor to stimulate the human components to achieve as much of their potential as possible. What behavior patterns should managers learn so that they may lead their subordinates toward achievement on basic organizational goals? This section will discuss such managerial behavior in the light of the motivation and organizational behavior factors that we have just covered.

Nature of Leadership

Leading means providing the values and focus of action for other members of a group. Some leaders are concerned with changing the status quo, with supplying and implementing new ideas, and with changing the attitudes of their groups or organizations. At the other extreme are the leaders who resist change and are fearful of new situations. In either case, leaders are those who seek to influence and control the behavior of others.

We can now relate this important type of behavior—leadership—to the two previous major topics, motivation and informal organization. In order to influence the behavior of other people, the leader must have a basic understanding of the needs of people. Although some gain this understanding from experience and intuition, formal study of scientific results, summarized briefly in this chapter, can be of help to many. To be most effective, leadership must take place within the informal organization as well as the formal. It may require a combination of the kinds of sources of authority discussed earlier.

Many writers divide leadership into two categories, informal and formal, because of the importance of each within an organization. Amitai Etzioni carries this further and makes the following distinction:

1. *Official*—One whose power (influence) is derived chiefly from his organizational position.
2. *Informal leader*—One whose ability to control others is due chiefly to his personal attributes, such as knowledge, personality, persuasiveness, identification with the informal group, charisma, or courage to speak out.
3. *Formal leader*—One who commands both positional power and personal influence.[9]

This last classification actually represents the ideal leadership style of a *manager*. The problem of systems design is to recognize all three types of leadership and their limitations so that the system becomes workable in terms of the current human components and susceptible to revision as these human components change.

Situational Approach to Leadership

For many years, companies sought stereotypes of leaders and potential leaders in terms of personality traits. The research literature, as well as experience, have proved this to be a sterile approach. It has been found rather that successful leadership is a function of (1) the forces in the leader, (2) the characteristics and types of needs of the subordinates, and (3) the situation.

Tannenbaum and Schmidt describe the forces within the manager that influence his style of leadership. These forces, readily observable, are the manager's value system, his confidence in the capabilities of his subordinates, his own leadership inclinations in terms of style, and his need for security obtained by the amount of control over decisions that he retains.[10]

The style of leadership that will be successful will vary with the nature of the subordinates. Argyris has pointed out the immaturity–maturity extremes that interact with leadership style. At the same time, other specific factors that are influential include education and training of the employees, tolerance for ambiguity versus need for security, interest in the work and the current problems (note the glamour fields of aerospace and nuclear power), understanding and sharing of goals of the organization, and group values.

The situation is a third function of leadership. It is not unusual to see a former successful executive of a large company take over the presidency of a smaller company and fail miserably. The reverse case is the freewheeling entrepreneur who moves to an executive position in a large company and is completely ineffectual in its large political bureaucracy. The situation is also a function of the problems to be solved. At one time, General Electric was in need of marketing and organization strength at the top and turned away from technical leadership. Later on, the need was for greater control, and the company turned to financial leadership. Similar turns toward marketing and then manufacturing may be observed in the Ford Motor Company.

The pressure of time is also a situational factor. Some men react and thrive under the challenge of urgency. Others fall apart in such situations, but perform outstandingly where time for careful thought and planning are the most important needs.

Another situational factor is the level of management. It is one thing to manage managers and another to manage the people who actually perform operational tasks. Consider the wide variety of forces that act upon the foreman in the shop. Line management, staff specialists, union officials, and sometimes even salesmen and customers get into the act. Figure 3–6 shows these situational forces. Note that the strong forces acting upon the foreman consist not only of line direction but also staff and even nonorganizational, such as union representatives.

Leadership Styles

One of the most important functions of good leadership is to set the direction for the organization by identifying basic purposes. Once these have been set, a long period of time is usually required for the organization to work towards these purposes. Leadership is then measured by the effectiveness and efficiency of the organization. Effectiveness is the degree to which the organization achieves its goals. For example, if a goal has been set to gain a 20 percent market share within two years and the market share

Figure 3–6 Forces Impinging Upon the Foreman

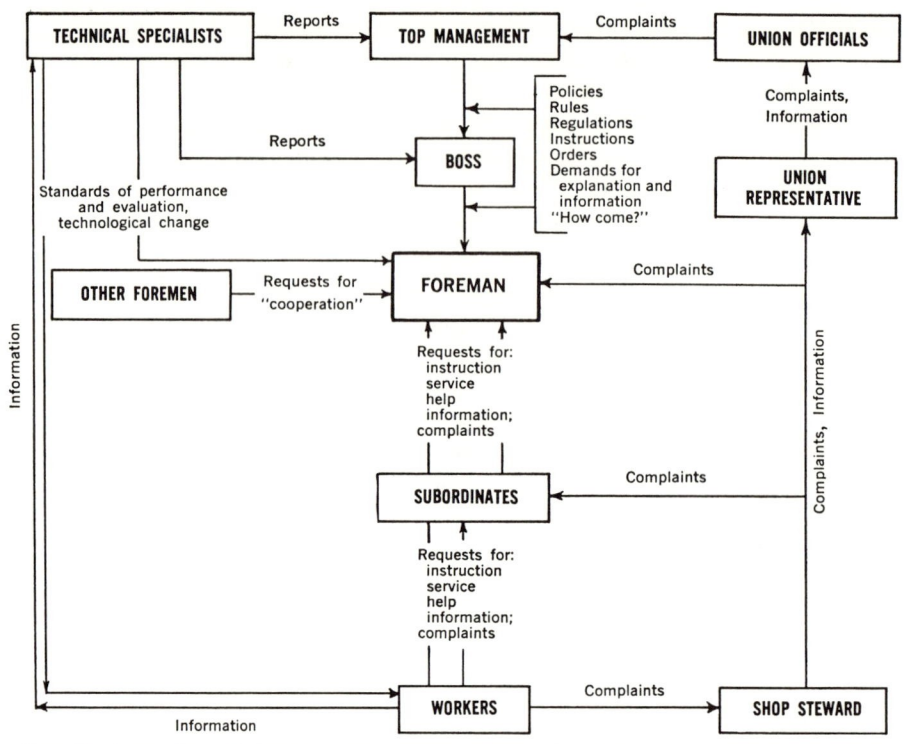

NOTE: This diagram shows only those forces impinging upon the foreman through the actions of other people. It is not designed to show the reaction of the foreman to these actions, in terms of either feelings or overt behavior; or to show the reactions of the workers to management's actions, which in turn become one of the chief forces acting upon the foreman.

SOURCE   F. J. Roethlisberger, "The Foreman: Master and Victim of Double Talk," *Harvard Business Review,* September–October 1965, p. 26

is 15 percent at the end of this period, the effectiveness of the effort was 75 percent. Efficiency, on the other hand, is concerned with the number of people (amount of resources) required to achieve the goal. In Chapter 11, it is defined as the ratio of output to input.

Ideally, the leader would adopt a style to fit his subordinates and the situation so that he would achieve optimum effectiveness and efficiency. *The effectiveness or efficiency of leadership is not dependent on the particular style of the leader, but whether it is appropriate to the situation in which it is used.* This should be kept in mind as we discuss leadership style apart from the situation.

In the past, research has concentrated on leadership style in terms of its impact on organizational behavior. Style was considered to vary along a continuum from task-centered (authoritarian) at one extreme to democratic (supportive) at the other. Keith Davis introduced a further development of "collegial" style, as shown in Table 3–5 (page 96). Note that the supportive and collegial models reflect the goals of Herzberg's positive motivators. Notice also how the continuum of leadership styles affects the vital variables of employee need, performance, and morale measure. We can speculate on which of the particular styles would best promote our goal of *subsystem integration* in a given work situation.

There are two implications of the task–subordinate continuum. The first is that it is not possible to be both task-oriented and person-oriented. The second is that by concentrating on people rather than on tasks, task achievement would be high. Recent research has indicated that task relationships and people relationships are not mutually exclusive. In fact, in some cases they may be closely related. Consider, for instance, that tasks correspond primarily to the goals of management. People relationships are concerned with satisfying the needs of workers. If these two are very closely related, then a combined task–people leadership style will yield a highly effective result, and vice versa, as shown schematically in Figure 3–7. Either (1) the goals of management must be changed, (2) new employees with

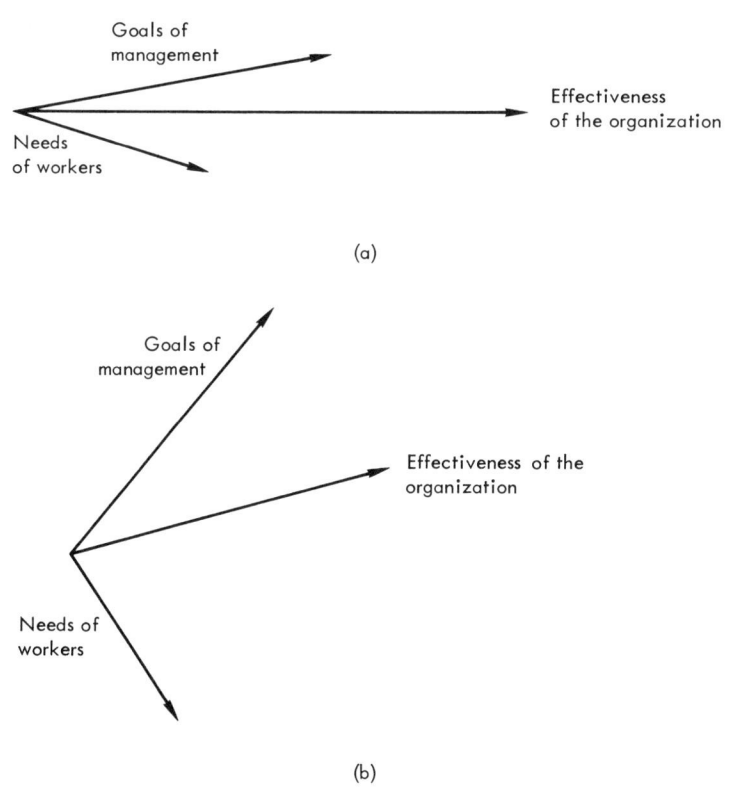

Figure 3–7 Organizational Effectiveness, Management Goals, and Workers' Needs

Table 3–5
Four Models of Organizational Behavior

	Autocratic	Custodial	Supportive	Collegial
Depends on:	Power	Economic resources	Leadership	Mutual contribution
Managerial orientation:	Authority	Material rewards	Support	Integration and teamwork
Employee orientation:	Obedience	Security	Performance	Responsibility
Employee psychological result:	Personal dependence	Organizational dependence	Participation	Self-discipline
Employee needs met:	Subsistence	Maintenance	Higher-order	Self-realization
Performance result:	Minimum	Passive cooperation	Awakened drives	Enthusiasm
Morale measure:	Compliance	Satisfaction	Motivation	Commitment to task and team

SOURCE Keith Davis, "Evolving Models of Organizational Behavior," *Academy of Management Journal*, March 1968, p. 29

different needs must be hired to replace the present ones, or (3) the present employees must receive education and training to change their attitudes and values.

Robert R. Blake and Jane S. Mouton developed and tested the concept that organizational goals and satisfaction of workers' needs are not incompatible.[11] They have been successful in analyzing or evaluating managers' styles in terms of these concepts. To do this, they developed a managerial grid for rating, as indicated in Figure 3–8. A manager may be evaluated and his style located on the grid. Then he may be retrained to move him toward the ideal (9,9) position.

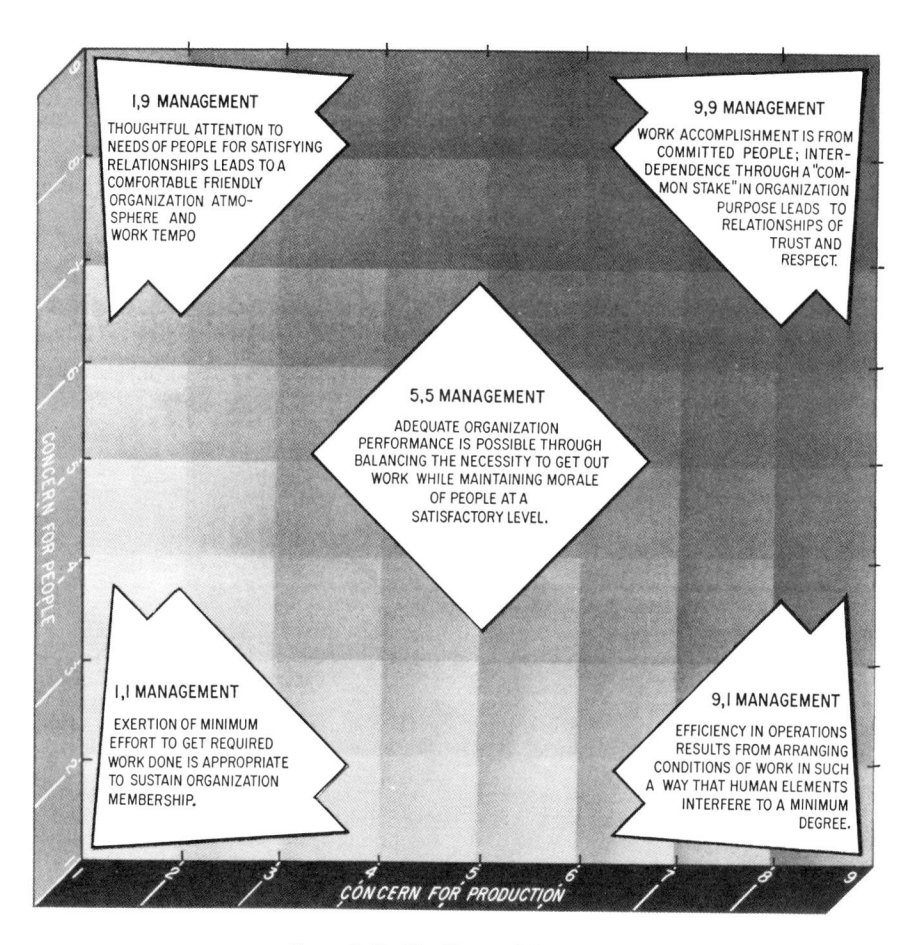

1,9 MANAGEMENT
THOUGHTFUL ATTENTION TO NEEDS OF PEOPLE FOR SATISFYING RELATIONSHIPS LEADS TO A COMFORTABLE FRIENDLY ORGANIZATION ATMOSPHERE AND WORK TEMPO

9,9 MANAGEMENT
WORK ACCOMPLISHMENT IS FROM COMMITTED PEOPLE; INTERDEPENDENCE THROUGH A "COMMON STAKE" IN ORGANIZATION PURPOSE LEADS TO RELATIONSHIPS OF TRUST AND RESPECT.

5,5 MANAGEMENT
ADEQUATE ORGANIZATION PERFORMANCE IS POSSIBLE THROUGH BALANCING THE NECESSITY TO GET OUT WORK WHILE MAINTAINING MORALE OF PEOPLE AT A SATISFACTORY LEVEL.

1,1 MANAGEMENT
EXERTION OF MINIMUM EFFORT TO GET REQUIRED WORK DONE IS APPROPRIATE TO SUSTAIN ORGANIZATION MEMBERSHIP.

9,1 MANAGEMENT
EFFICIENCY IN OPERATIONS RESULTS FROM ARRANGING CONDITIONS OF WORK IN SUCH A WAY THAT HUMAN ELEMENTS INTERFERE TO A MINIMUM DEGREE.

CONCERN FOR PEOPLE

CONCERN FOR PRODUCTION

Figure 3–8 The Managerial Grid

SOURCE Robert R. Blake *et al.*, "Breakthrough in Organizational Development," *Harvard Business Review*, November–December 1964, p. 136

SUMMARY

Modern organization theory is concerned with the positive (descriptive) science of how people in organizations behave and why. Managers and systems designers need to know how to put this knowledge to work. Therefore, we have developed in this chapter the concepts of:

1. The motivation of people and the implications for managers
2. Organizational behavior and characteristics with implications for leadership
3. Leadership styles as related to motivation and organizational factors

DISCUSSION QUESTIONS AND PROBLEMS

1. How would you relate the formal organization, the informal organization, and the management information system in a systems description of business organizations? Draw a block diagram, using solid and dotted lines to indicate relationships and information flows.

2. Some authorities consider an organization to be a problem-solving, decision-making system. Discuss this concept in terms of organizational behavior and company objectives and problems.

3. Are managers necessary in organizational systems? Justify your position.

4. Should systems be designed to fit the people in the organization or should the people be required to adapt to the systems? What inferences can you draw from your conclusion?

5. Assign a set of weights to represent the relative degree to which the business firm should serve the seven groups listed in the text. (See pages 71–72.)

6. Imagine a system that would call forth most of the potential for achievement of each individual in it. Can you conceive how this might be done within the present framework of company organization? Can you think up a completely new type of productive organization, arrangement, or system that might accomplish this?

7. Discuss in specific terms the needs of managers as opposed to the needs of functional individual workers.

8. Can you think of two or more specific needs an individual might have, drawn from Maslow's hierarchical classification, that might be in conflict? Consider both a manager and an individual worker.

9. Search the literature and report on other listings of needs. What evidence based upon research substantiates or refutes any or all of these?

10. Robert Townsend, former president of Avis, converted his car rental company from a loser to a winner. In his book, *Up the Organization* (Alfred A. Knopf, 1970), he stated, "Anyone who makes over $150 a week should be allowed to set his own office hours." Relate the underlying concept of this idea to Theory Y and to Argyris's theory of the behavior of people in organizations.

11. Distinguish between "incentive" and "motivation."

12. Search the literature and describe the effect of group cohesion on organizational behavior and as a system factor.

13. How would you relate the power structure to the organizational system? Draw a block diagram of a specific organization and show how

lines of authority, channels of communication, and flow of power might exist.

14. Discuss how Herzberg's conclusions about motivators could contribute to a total systems theory of organizational behavior.

15. Is conflict a necessary condition in a Theory Y type of organization? Justify your answer.

16. Contrast the concept of the "Protestant Ethic" (the survival of the fittest) with the bureaucratic style of leadership. (See William H. Whyte, Jr., *The Organization Man* [New York: Simon and Schuster, Inc., 1956], and the works of Max Weber.)

17. A national airline hired several hundred mechanics when its union mechanics went on strike. It negotiated with the union and agreed to reinstate all previous employees without loss of seniority. Evaluate this action in terms of theories of leadership.

18. A spokesman for a fairly large and successful company said his firm deliberately avoids preparing organization charts. Discuss the impact of this on leadership within the company.

19. A certain division of a large company employs about 2000 people, of whom approximately 800 are engineers and scientists. It follows an unwritten policy of dropping off (by transfer or squeezing out) approximately 10 percent of its lowest-performance people each year. They are usually given assistance in relocating and about six months notice in which to find new jobs. Analyze the effect of this policy on employee motivation and leadership style.

REFERENCES

1. A. H. Maslow, *Motivation and Personality* (New York: Harper & Row, Publishers, 1954).
2. Douglas McGregor, *The Human Side of Enterprise* (New York: McGraw-Hill Book Company, 1960).
3. Chris Argyris, *Personality and Organization* (New York: Harper & Row, Publishers, 1957).
4. Robert Townsend, *Up the Organization* (New York: Alfred A. Knopf, Inc., 1970).
5. Albert H. Rubenstein and Chadwick J. Haberstroh, eds., *Some Theories of Organization* (Homewood, Ill.: The Dorsey Press, Inc., 1960), p. 63.
6. Donald F. Roy, "Banana Time—Job Satisfaction and Informal Interaction," *Human Organizations*, Vol. 18 (1960), 158–68. Reprinted in a number of books of readings.
7. Theodore Caplow, "Rumors in War," *Social Forces*, Vol. XXV (October 1946–May 1947), 298–302.
8. Melville Dalton, *Men Who Manage* (New York: John Wiley & Sons, Inc., 1959).
9. Amitai Etzioni, *Modern Organizations* (Englewood Cliffs, N.J.: Prentice-Hall, Inc., 1964), p. 61.
10. Robert Tannenbaum and Warren H. Schmidt, "How to Choose a Leadership Pattern," *Harvard Business Review*, March–April 1958.
11. Robert R. Blake *et al.,* "Breakthrough in Organization Development," *Harvard Business Review*, November–December 1964.

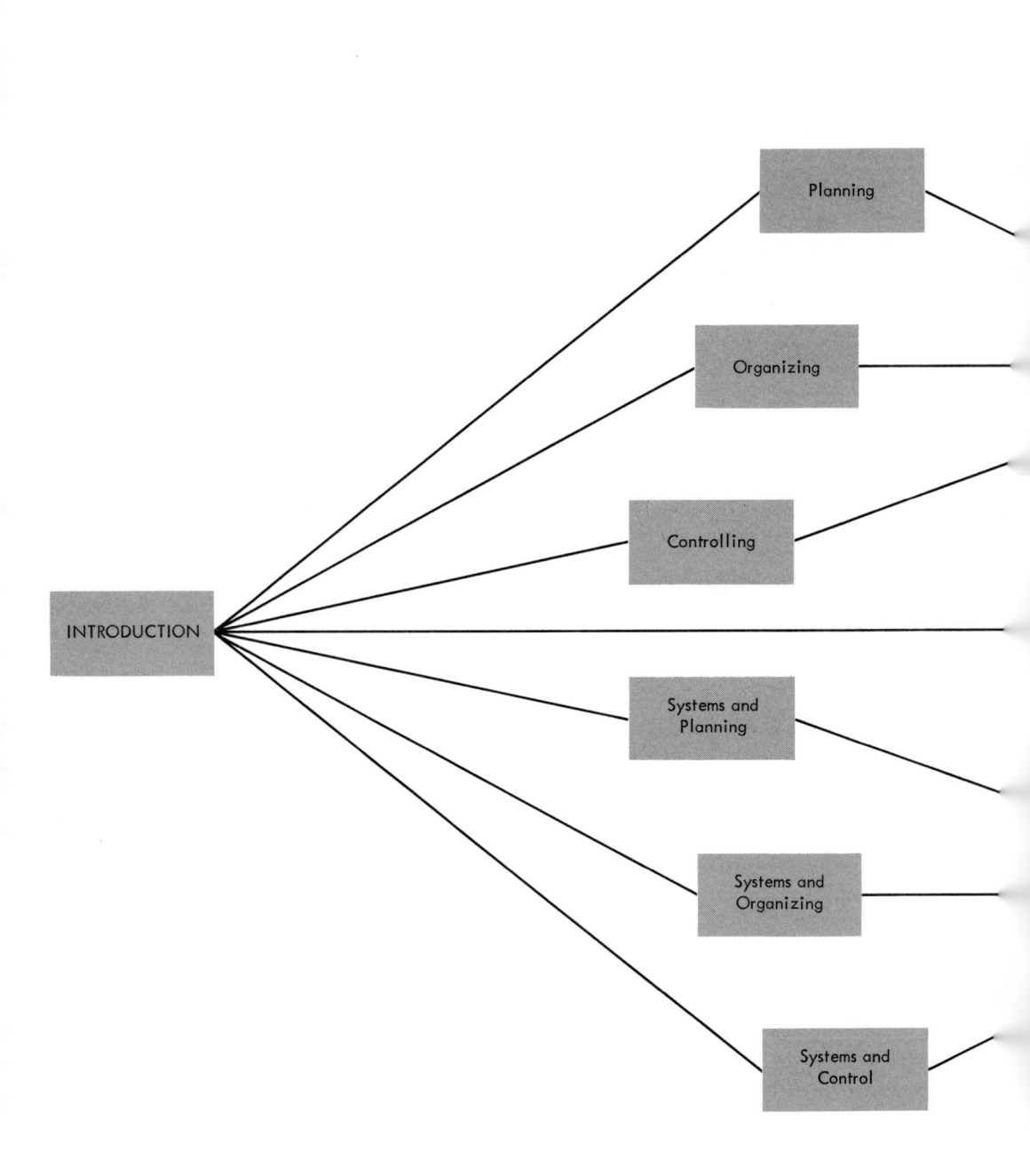

```
INTRODUCTION
    ├── Planning
    ├── Organizing
    ├── Controlling
    ├──
    ├── Systems and Planning
    ├── Systems and Organizing
    └── Systems and Control
```

4

the systems approach to organization and management

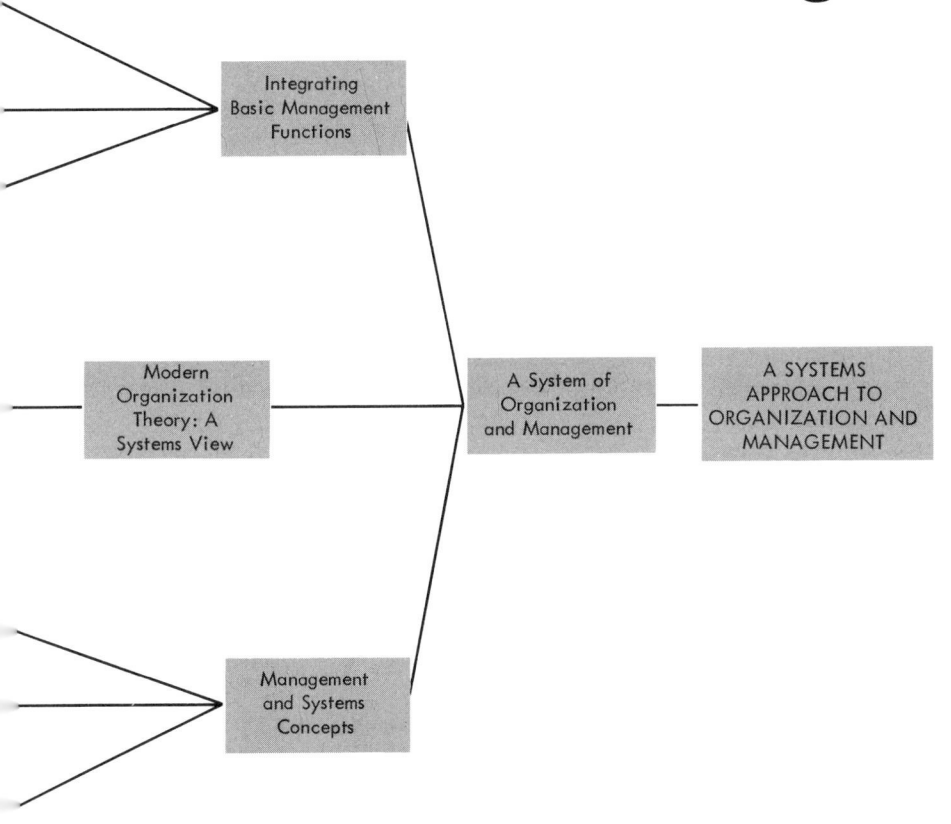

- Integrating Basic Management Functions
- Modern Organization Theory: A Systems View
- Management and Systems Concepts
- A System of Organization and Management
- A SYSTEMS APPROACH TO ORGANIZATION AND MANAGEMENT

4

Managerial activities have meaning only when the organization is in a dynamic state—when it is in the act of processing resource inputs into outputs of useful products or services. The firm may then be viewed as an *organism*—a dynamic system that requires management of its subsystems for transforming resource inputs. Given this concept, the questions arise: (1) What are the resources of the firm? (2) What is the nature of the organism that performs the transformation process? (3) What is the nature of the management process? (4) How do we manage this organism in order to create the outputs of products or services?

The answers to these questions form the framework for this chapter and the basic foundation for the systems approach to organization and management. The questions can be answered briefly:

1. The *resources* of the firm include information, materials, money, manpower, and machines and facilities. These are transformed into outputs. Under the dynamic *systems* concept of the firm, these resources are viewed as *flowing* through the transformation process. Therefore, the subsystems of the firm can be constructed around these *flow networks*. Thus we have the materials flow network, the manpower network, the money flow network, and the facilities and machines flow network. In order for these four systems to function effectively it is necessary to design an *information flow system* that integrates the other four and also serves as the nerve center for the entire firm.

2. The vehicle through which the inputs are transformed into outputs is the *organization*. Because the organization is composed of people, the manager is concerned with the behavior and interaction of the people within the structure, as well as with the structure itself. This is explained by modern organization theory.

3. The transformation of network flows into output through the vehicle of a dynamic organization can be explained in terms of a systems approach to organization and management. The three subsystems of this approach are: (a) a modern organization theory, (b) functions of management, and (c) the schools of management—empirical, behavioral, decision theory, management process, and quantitative. These schools provide the techniques.

4. A fourth subsystem makes the operation of the others possible. This is the integrating element provided by the management information system.

The objective of this chapter is to construct a systems approach to organization and management that will permit the implementation of the classic *functions* of management (planning, organizing, controlling) within the framework of behavioral knowledge developed by modern organization theory and the techniques of quantitative methods. We want to construct an umbrella—a system if you will—that will accommodate and incorporate the various approaches to management and to organization theory.

MODERN ORGANIZATION THEORY: A SYSTEMS VIEW

Systems analysis has been defined as a point of view plus a few key ideas, integrated into a logical pattern.[1] This is essentially the approach that is taken to the systems view of organization theory: the point of view is that an organization is a system—defined by McGregor as "a set of subsystems whose interaction determines its survival"[2]—and the few key ideas include the definition of the parts and interactions of the system and the process by which these are integrated.

The key questions to be asked of the systems approach to organization theory were defined in a landmark article by Scott: "(1) What are the strategic parts of the system? (2) What is the nature of their mutual dependency? (3) What are the main processes in the system that link the parts together and facilitate their adjustments to each other? (4) What are the goals sought by systems?"[3] The answers to these questions provide the framework for a systems approach to organization theory. Figure 4–1 (page 106) presents a simple conceptual model of the major elements of this framework and the processes by which they are integrated.

Systems Parts and Their Interdependency

The basic parts of the organization system are the individual, the formal organization, the informal organization, status and role patterns, and the physical setting. These parts and their interdependencies can be described thus:

1. *The individual.* The basic part of the system is the individual—his personality, motives, and attitudes. The concern here is not so much what the individual can contribute to the organization but how he perceives the fulfillment of his goals from participation in it.

2. *The formal organization.* The structure of the organization is composed of the assignment and interrelated pattern of tasks. In modern organization theory, basic incongruities result from the expectancies and interactions of organization and individual demands. Recent theories point out the conflict between the mature, normal personality and the demands made by the formal organizational structure.[4] In other words, the needs of the

106 Management and Systems

Diagram: A circular figure with outer ring segments labeled "The Physical Setting", "The Individual", "The Formal Organization", "The Informal Organization", and "Leadership Style". The inner circle contains "INTEGRATING PROCESSES" with three items: 1. Communications, 2. Balance, 3. Decision Making.

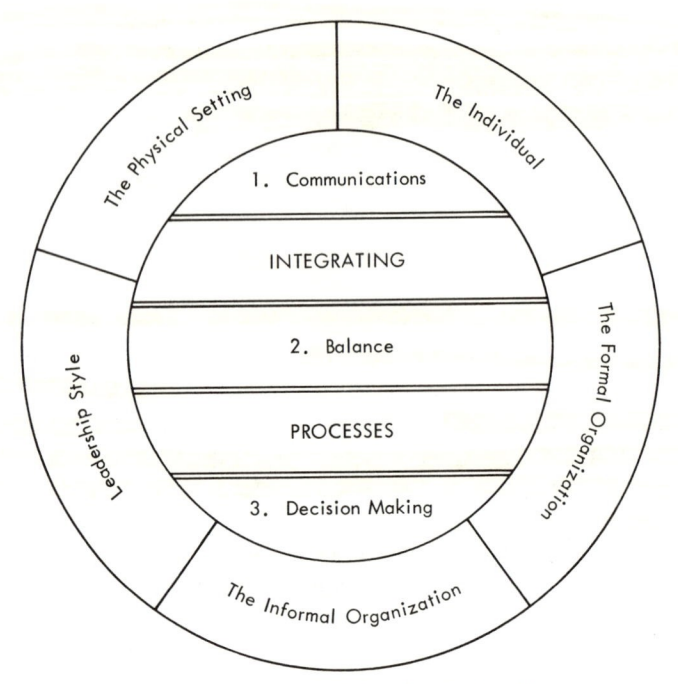

Figure 4–1 Elements of Modern Organization Theory

individual are not served by the trappings (formal chart, position descriptions, specialization of labor, tight controls, etc.) of the bureaucratic organization.

3. *The informal organization.* This is the subterranean organization of neoclassical theory. It interacts with the formal organization as well as with the individual. Each of these entities has expectancies from and makes demands upon the other two. For example, the informal organization makes demands of conformity upon the individual, and the individual in turn has expectancies of satisfaction from his membership in the group. The formal organization must accommodate—or at least take account of—these interactions.

4. *Managerial leadership styles.* (See Chapter 3.) Similar to considerations surrounding the informal organization are those concerned with individual leadership styles of managers and with patterns of behavior that result from role demands generated by the formal structure and the informal organization. Seldom are role perceptions the same as those proposed by the organizational system, formal or informal. The concern of the systems approach to organization theory is the modification and integration of role expectancies to the extent that the individual, the group, and the organization can operate within perceived patterns.

5. *The physical setting.* Interactions between individuals, groups, and the organization in the physical surroundings of complex man–machine systems are certain to be more complex in the future, and the technical or engineering approach to this problem will not be sufficient. The systems approach takes account of psychological, social, and physiological characteristics of people who interact with the machine. The machine should be designed to fit the man—not the man to fit the machine.

Integrating Processes

Figure 4–1 shows conceptually how the foregoing parts of the system are integrated by three processes: communication, balance, and decision making. Note that these three integrating concepts are useful in any kind of system, organizational or otherwise.

1. *Communication.* This linking process is a network that ties together the various parts of the system into a connected pattern. To use an analogy: if the formal structure (organization) is viewed as the anatomy of the system, then communication is the physiology. Later we will see how information systems provide the essential link that permits the parts of the system to communicate with each other and with their external environment. Indeed, the system can be represented by its communication functions.

2. *Balance.* Growth, stability, and interaction are the goals of a system; balance is the major means by which these goals are achieved. The concept of balance involves a complex cybernetic property of systems called *homeostasis*—the tendency of a system to operate between desired limits or to maintain a steady state.[5] The classic example is the homeostasis of blood temperature, which varies very little even when the body passes from deep freeze to sauna bath. In the case of an organizational system, the homeostat would be the equilibrating action or mechanism whereby the various parts of the system are maintained in a harmoniously structured relationship to each other. Management is the *process* by which this balance is maintained. Although the notion of maintaining balance is a complex one, it appears in two varieties—quasi-automatic (control and regulatory processes) and innovative (new programs to maintain internal harmony).[6] These concepts will be expanded in Chapter 8.

3. *Decision making.* As opposed to our normal concept of managerial decision making, the discussion of decision making in the systems approach to organization theory surrounds what March and Simon call decisions to produce and decisions to participate in the system.[7] According to Scott:

> Decisions to produce are largely a result of an interaction between individual attitudes and the demands of the organization. Motivation analysis becomes central to studying the nature and results of the

108   Management and Systems

interaction. Individual decisions to participate in the organization reflect on such issues as the relationship between organizational rewards versus the demands made by the organization. Participation decisions also focus attention on the reasons why individuals remain in or leave organizations.[8]

The integrative nature of decision making can be appreciated if we take the view that decisions are variables that depend on jobs, individual expectations, motivations, and organizational structure.

Summary

As organization theory advanced from classical to modern, we saw the emphasis change from the formal anatomy of structure in the classical school to include considerations surrounding "human relations" and the informal organization in the neoclassical approach. Modern organization theory includes a variety of approaches or models, but there is no unified body of principles. We have chosen to examine the systems approach because it is open-ended and able to include new variables as they arise. Moreover, the systems approach is the only school of organization theory purporting to *integrate* the major *subsystems* by means of a *linking* process.

INTEGRATING BASIC MANAGEMENT FUNCTIONS: PLANNING, ORGANIZING, CONTROLLING

The overall job of a manager is to "create with the enterprise the environment which will facilitate the accomplishment of its objective."[9] In doing this, the manager *plans* the work of his subordinates and his own activity, selects and trains subordinates by *staffing* his operations, *organizes* the work and task relationships, *directs* the work, and *controls* results by measuring performance against plan. These are the traditional *functions* of the manager. Although there are slight differences among writers in the number and names of these functions, the most common and useful method of classifying managerial functions is grouping them around the activities of planning, organizing, staffing, directing, and controlling.[10] As distinguished from operational functions (manufacturing, engineering, accounting, selling, and so on), which differ among the various types of organizations, *managerial* functions are common to all.

Despite attempts by other schools of management to preempt or modify this functional view of the management process, it still provides the basic action framework for the systems approach. Its continuing popularity and widespread use are probably due to its approach to the topic—the explanation of the process of management in terms of what managers do. Hence it reflects the way the manager sees his job, and it is therefore most useful to

the systems approach to organization and management 109

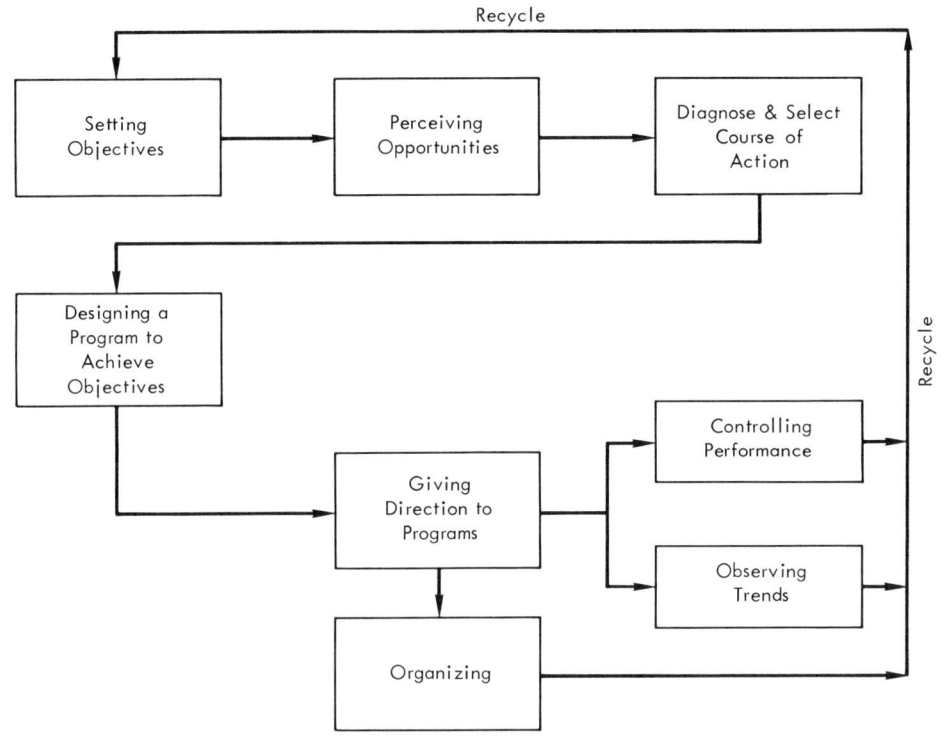

Figure 4–2 A Concept of Management

him. Moreover, it appears that the functional approach to management will be with us for some time in the future. One forecast of the future nature of management concludes:

> We can safely assume that there will continue to be a need for managers with a high degree of functional skill. As new knowledge and new tools are developed, we can expect continued refinement in the traditional skills of management. These are the essential skills of planning, of organizing, of decision making, and of measuring and controlling processes and operations. These are also the skills of leadership and the use of the general concepts governing organization performance and employee relations.[11]

The foregoing functions of management are not performed sequentially, nor is there any special time sequence involved. Planning is involved in organizing, directing, and controlling. Likewise, the process of organizing is involved in planning, directing, and controlling. Each function affects the others and all are interrelated to form the management process. The general nature by which these processes operate is demonstrated in Figure 4–2 and can be described thus:

Planning
1. Setting of objectives for the manager's area of activity
2. Perception of opportunities, problems, and alternatives surrounding the achievement of the objective
3. Diagnosis of opportunities, analysis of objectives, and selection of a course of action
4. Design of a program of action to achieve the objective

Direction
5. Leadership in the necessary organizational action required to achieve the program, including communication and motivation of subordinates

Organizing
6. Supervision of the action plan through an organization whose task relationships are defined and understood

Control
7. Observation and measurement of performance against standards for achieving the plan and correction of performance deviations if required
8. Observation of significant trends within and without the manager's activity so that goals and programs may be modified as necessary

Feedback
9. Recycling of information concerning plans, actions, and progress at different stages of the management process to insure that proper programming to achieve the objective is being accomplished

Thus, the management process is *iterative*.

Figure 4-3 shows the concept of the management cycle as it is practiced at the International Minerals and Chemical Corporation. This model does not show all the processes of management, but it serves to illustrate the iterative nature of planning and control and shows these functions work together for achievement of objectives.

Planning

The most basic and pervasive management function is planning. All managers at all levels plan, and the success of the performance of the other management functions depends upon this activity. Planning is deciding in advance what has to be done, who has to do it, when it has to be done, and how it is to be done. It bridges the gap from where we are to where we want to go. Managers plan for the allocation of resources and the work of other people, in contrast to the nonmanager, who plans only his own activities.

The past decade has witnessed a tremendous upsurge in formal planning by all types of organizations, both government and industrial.[12] Various causes have been advanced to explain this phenomenon. Steiner[13] attributes the growth in planning to six basic factors:

1. A changing philosophy, which insists that an organization can initiate trends and set its own course rather than merely sail on the tide of market conditions and business changes

Figure 4–3 The Management Cycle

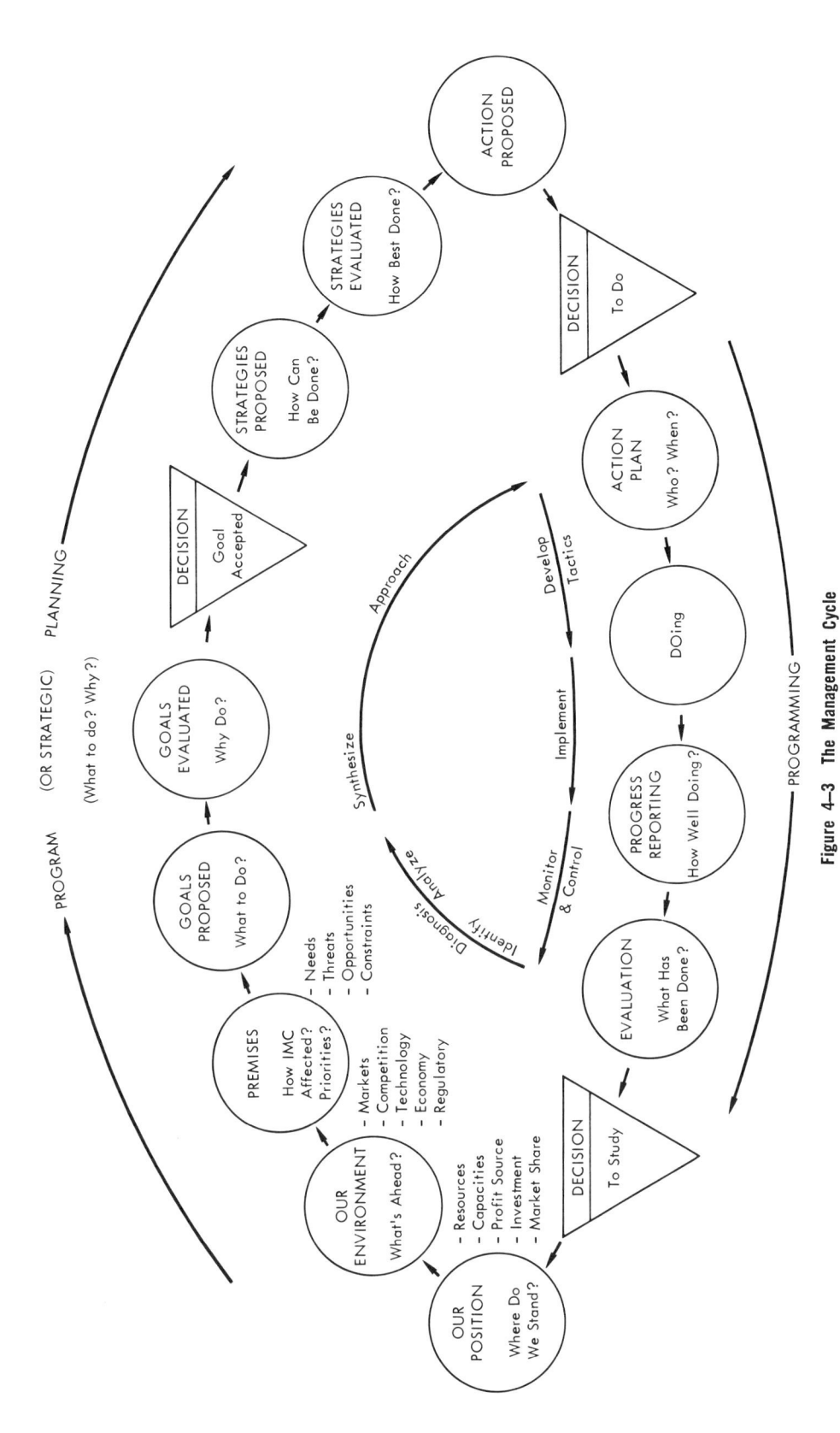

SOURCE International Minerals and Chemical Corporation

112 Management and Systems

2. The rapid rate of technological change
3. Increased complexity of management, owing to the growth in size and diversity of businesses
4. Growing competition, resulting partly from product obsolescence and growth of new industries
5. The increasingly complex environment of business
6. The lengthening span of time for which commitments must be made and the resultant need to forecast for longer periods of time in making today's decisions

Types of plans

Table 4–1 shows five classification schemes for business planning, to demonstrate that planning can be discussed from a variety of points of view and classifications, among which are time, function, level, purpose, and element. However, it should be remembered that any given plan includes more than one of the characteristics or dimensions shown in the table. For example, the statement "Growth will be financed from retained earnings" reflects a plan that represents a policy because of its breadth. It can be classified by level as corporate because of the level at which it was developed, or as financial owing to the specific business involved. Finally, the statement represents a long-range plan because of the time dimensions.

Table 4–1

Dimensions of Planning—Selected Classifications

Classification	Illustration			
TIME	Short range	Medium range	Long range	Etc.
FUNCTION	Inventory	Manpower	Marketing	Etc.
LEVEL	Corporate	Managerial	Operational	Etc.
PURPOSE	Merger	New product	Capital	Etc.
ELEMENT	Strategy	Policy	Procedure	Etc.

None of these classification schemes alone gives a comprehensive system for classifying plans, a scheme that integrates the dimensions of time, function, level, purpose, and breadth. The authors believe that the broad classification *strategic versus tactical* will provide this integration, because as we go along the continuum of the extremes represented by these two types, all the foregoing characteristics and dimensions are encompassed. Moreover, the extremes of this classification serve to highlight: (1) different methodologies of planning, (2) the sources of conflict that develop within an organization as a result of planning, (3) the differences between line and staff in the planning process, and (4) the differences in pace at which strategic and tactical planning are carried on.[14]

Steiner defines *strategic planning* as "the process of determining the major objectives of an organization and the policies and strategies that will govern the acquisition, use, and disposition of resources to achieve those objectives."[15] At the other end of the spectrum lies *tactical* planning, which refers to the process whereby detailed plans are developed for the deployment of company resources to achieve strategic plans. Between the two extremes of strategic and tactical planning we include: (1) long-range plans, (2) medium-range plans, and (3) short-range plans. The matrix of Table 4–2 serves to demonstrate how this classification integrates the dimensions and characteristics of the classification of time, function, level, purpose, and breadth (see Table 4–1).

Table 4–2

Integration of Planning by Classification

Classification	Strategic Planning	Medium-Range Planning	Short-Range Planning
TIME	Long range	Medium range	Short range
FUNCTION	Manpower Marketing	Inventory Manpower	Inventory
LEVEL	Corporate	Managerial	Operational
PURPOSE	Merger	New product	Capital
ELEMENT	Strategy	Policy	Procedure

An understanding of this classification and of how each type of plan is developed through the planning process can be better understood by referring to Figure 4–4, which is a conceptual model of the planning process at the International Minerals and Chemical Corporation.[16] Note how the categories of plans in this operational model equate to those we have chosen for discussion.

Strategic vs. Tactical	*IMC Model (Fig. 4–4)*
Long-range plans	Strategic plans
Medium-range plans	Corporate development plans
Short-range plans	Operations plans

Strategic Plans. As defined, these include objectives, policies, and strategies, and in general terms the characteristics and accomplishments that the firm can, and wants to, achieve.

The *objectives* of an organization are the fundamental purposes and lines of business that it wishes to pursue. As in the case of planning, objective setting itself has become more complex in recent decades. There was a time when the businessman had only to say, "My objective is return on investment, or percent of sales, or profit." Now it is generally realized that to state the total purposes of the organization in these terms is at best a short-sighted view. Other areas vital to the firm and in which objectives can be set include: market standing, innovation, productivity, physical and financial resources, profitability, manager performance and development, worker performance and attitude, and public responsibility.[17] Here we are defining the overall objectives of the organization and not the divisions, departments,

```
                                                                    ▲
┌──────────────┐                                                    │
│STRATEGIC PLAN│                                                    │
└──────────────┘                                                    │
  │││ │   ┌──────────────────────┐                                  │
  │││ └──▶│ CORPORATE DEVELOPMENT│                                  │
  │││     │         PLAN         │                                  │ JURISDICTION OF
  │││     └──────────────────────┘                                  │ CORPORATION MANAGEMENT
  │││       │  ┌─────────────────┐                                  │
  │││       ├─▶│ Divestment Plan │                                  │
  │││       │  └─────────────────┘                                  │
  │││       │  ┌───────────────────┐                                │
  │││       └─▶│Diversification Plan│                               │
  │││          └───────────────────┘                                │
  │││                │  ┌──────────────────────┐                    │
  │││                ├─▶│Acquisition and Merger│                    │
  │││                │  │        Plan          │                    │
  │││                │  └──────────────────────┘                    │
  │││  Broken Lines                                                 │
  │││  Reflect Multiple    Decision to Diversify by                 │
  │││  Semi-Autonomous     Research and Development                 │
  │││  Divisions                                                    ▼
─┼┼┼─────────────────────│──────────────────────────────────────────
  │││                    ▼                                          ▲
  │││              ┌──────────────────────┐                         │
  │└┼────────────▶│ Research and Development│                       │
  │ │              │      (R&D) Plan      │                         │
  │ │              └──────────────────────┘                         │
  │ │                 │   ┌────────────────────┐                    │
  │ │                 ├──▶│ Basic Research Plan│                    │
  │ │                 │   └────────────────────┘                    │
  │ │                 │   ┌────────────────────┐                    │
  │ │                 ├──▶│  Product R&D Plan  │                    │
  │ │                 │   └────────────────────┘                    │
  │ │                 │   ┌────────────────────┐                    │ JURISDICTION OF OPERATING MANAGEMENT
  │ │                 ├──▶│  Market R&D Plan   │                    │
  │ │                 │   └────────────────────┘                    │
  │ │                 │   ┌────────────────────┐                    │
  │ │                 ├──▶│ R&D Financial Plan │                    │
  │ │                 │   └────────────────────┘                    │
  │ │                 │   ┌─────────────────────┐                   │
  │ │                 └──▶│R&D Administration Plan│                 │
  │ │                     └─────────────────────┘                   │
  │ │   ┌────────────────┐                                          │
  └─┴──▶│ OPERATIONS PLAN│                                          │
        └────────────────┘                                          │
             │    ┌ ─ ─ ─ ─ ─ ─ ┐                                   │
             └───▶ Project Plans                                    │
                  └ ─ ─ ─ ─ ─ ─ ┘   ┌──────────────────┐            │
                       │       ├───▶│ Production Plan  │            │
                       │       │    └──────────────────┘            │
                       │       │    ┌──────────────────┐            │
                       │       ├───▶│  Marketing Plan  │            │
                       │       │    └──────────────────┘            │
                       │       │    ┌──────────────────┐            │
                       │       ├───▶│  Financial Plan  │            │
                       │       │    └──────────────────┘            │
                       │       │    ┌──────────────────┐            │
                       │       └───▶│Administration Plan│           │
                       │            └──────────────────┘            ▼
```

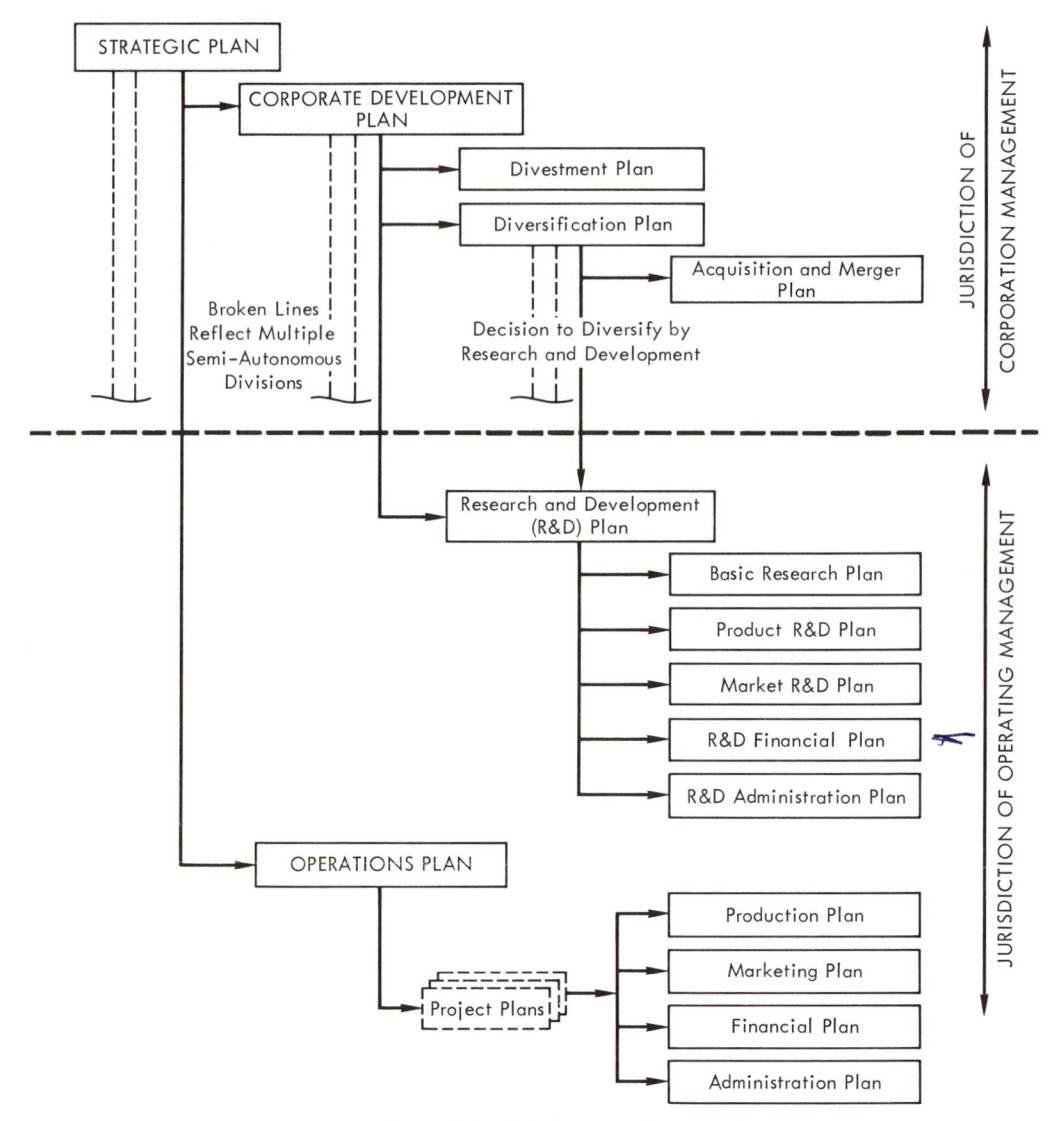

Figure 4–4 IMC System of Strategic Plans

SOURCE   International Minerals and Chemical Corporation

or other subsystems. Later in this chapter we will discuss how organizational objectives integrate the firm through a hierarchy of objectives.

Policies are statements that outline the boundaries and general guides to decision making. They reflect objectives and therefore establish frameworks for subsequent plans. To illustrate, a policy of "promotion from within" would have a definite effect on development of a management development program, and a "cash only" sales policy would affect other financial plans. Policies are usually classified along the lines of the functions of the organization and in a manufacturing firm might follow this framework:

114

Function	Policy	Example
Marketing	Advertising and promotion	Advertising budget will be 2% of sales
	Channels of distribution	Distribute through manufacturer's representatives
	Pricing	10% discount for carload lots
	Sales	Do not sell direct
Production	Inventory	Do not exceed thirty days' finished goods
	Make or buy	Make when price difference exceeds cost of capital
	Product stabilization	Operate within 70–90% of capacity
	Size of run	Economic lot size
Financial	Capital distributions	Quarterly dividend is 50% of net
	Capital procurement	Finance growth from retained earnings
	Depreciation	Use method with greatest tax benefit
	Working capital	Maintain 2:1 "acid test" ratio
Personnel	Compensation	Meet local rates
	Benefits	All benefits recommended by industry association
	Selection and training	Subsidize tuition reimbursement plan

It is becoming more difficult to distinguish between the strategic plan of the organization and the *strategies* for achieving it, because both refer to the overall "grand plan" for reaching objectives. Thus Steiner defines a strategy as "a specific action, usually but not always the deployment of resources, to achieve an objective decided upon in strategic planning."[18] Strategies are frequently related to the competition. For example, the strategic plan of a national newspaper may have the objective of increasing advertising revenues by x percent. The strategy chosen to achieve this objective may be the publication of separate geographic editions with regional advertising.

The purpose of strategies, then, is to determine a system of major objectives and policies for achieving the kind of organization that is envisioned. A few classifications of strategies are listed and illustrated below.[19]

Strategy Classification	Strategy Type	Example
Scope	Master	Growth through diversification and acquisition
	Pure	Counteract competitor's price reduction by introduction of new models
	Mixed	Use best "mix" of advertising, pricing, and product improvement to gain share of market
Organizational	Corporate	Encourage divisional competition
Level	Divisional (e.g.)	Base divisional product advertising on corporate image
Overall	Growth	Expand into foreign markets
	Overall company	Establish service organizations throughout market area
	Functional	Finance basic research by federal contracts

Medium-Range Plans. These plans, typically of five years' duration, flow naturally from the objectives, policies, and strategies established in the strategic plan. Indeed, the medium-range plans (or program) may have subobjectives, subpolicies, and substrategies of their own, and these are likely to be in more detail than the strategic plan from which they came.

Detailed plans are most often made in the functional areas, such as marketing, manufacturing, finance, personnel, and so on. Notice that in Figure 4–4 the strategic plan of the International Minerals and Chemical Corporation provides the input for the medium-range plan entitled Corporate Development Plan. This in turn is subdivided into Development Plans and Operations Plans.

By its very nature, the medium-range plan provides a systems approach to the organization. Because each function or major subdivision of the company must develop a detailed plan—one that *intermeshes* with other functions and subdivisions—coordination is obtained. Since pro forma financial statements are usually a part of the documentation of the plan, additional coordination is achieved through the integration of financial resources.

Short-Term Plans. Because the details of the medium-range plan are not sufficient for current and short-term operations, more detailed plans are necessary. The short-term plans are usually for one year or less and contain details and supporting schedules of the type normally found in the annual budget or financial plan. Thus the production plan will be supported by inventory schedules, purchasing plans, and labor schedules. The marketing and distribution plan will include sales quotas, distribution budgets, and sales expense estimates.

Figure 4–4 shows how the planning cycle has worked itself down the hierarchy to the operating divisions and how short-term plans are made in the functional areas of production, marketing, finance, administration, and technical support.

The Planning Process

The steps in planning are basically the same as those in decision making and problem solving. The basic concepts can be expanded to provide a logical sequence of steps for operations research and for systems design as well. We shall explore the commonality of the planning process, decision making, and systems design in a later chapter.

Most planning is conducted in an environment that lends itself to certain basic steps. The iterative nature of these steps is shown in Figure 4–5 and discussed briefly here.

1. *Recognize an opportunity.* A cardinal purpose of planning is to discover future opportunities and make plans to exploit them.[20] Part of management's job is to seek and identify problems and opportunities. Be-

the systems approach to organization and management 117

THE PLANNING PROCESS

- Awareness of Opportunity
- Setting Objectives
- Establishing Planning Premises
- Determination of Alternative Courses
- Evaluation of Alternative Courses
- Choice of an Alternative
- Implement the Plan
- Review and Revise

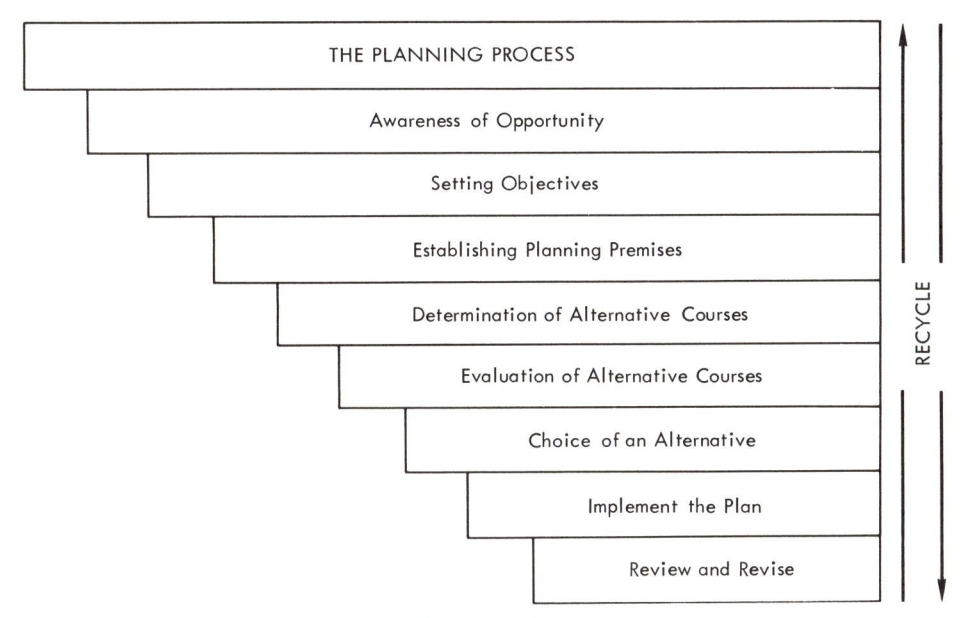

RECYCLE

Figure 4–5 The Planning Process

coming aware of opportunities must precede planning because the most profitable plans are those that identify and exploit opportunities.

2. *Set objectives.* This step involves establishing planning objectives as opposed to enterprise objectives, although if the latter have not been set, planning cannot proceed. Koontz and O'Donnell say that planning objectives "indicate the end points of what is to be done, where the primary emphasis is to be placed, and what is to be accomplished by the network of policies, procedures, rules, budgets, programs, and strategies."[21]

3. *Establish planning premises.* Premises are the data, facts, and information that influence alternative courses of action to reach objectives. They may be classified and illustrated thus:

External to the firm	*Internal to the firm*
Opportunities and problems	Organizational purpose
Business conditions	Values of top management
Population growth	Strengths and weaknesses of firm
Price levels	Financial position
Business cycles	Employment level
Etc.	Etc.
Noncontrollable (External)	*Controllable (Internal)*
Political environment	Production level
Economic conditions	Strategies
Price levels	Policies and procedures
Etc.	Etc.

A special type of premise is a *constraint*. It does little good, for example, to plan for a particular market share if capital investment, plant, or other constraints prohibit the realization of the forecast. Constraints are also internal and external to the firm.

As planning goes from strategic to tactical and moves down the hierarchy of the organization, the importance of internal planning premises becomes more evident. The premises of policies, budgets, and objectives are likely to weigh more heavily in short-range plans than in strategic plans at the corporate level.

4. *Determine alternative courses of action.* This involves the search for and determination of alternative ways to achieve the objective of the plan. In formal planning this process almost involves the quantification and documentation of alternatives to permit analysis.

5. *Evaluate alternative courses.* Evaluation involves the weighing of the desirability of each alternative in light of planning premises and goals. A few choices are reduced to mathematical selection because all variables can be quantified, and in these cases the new management science techniques are valuable. However, most planning problems are replete with intangibles and uncertainties, and a careful evaluation is very important.

6. *Choose an alternative.* This is the point at which a decision is made and a course of action selected. It is taken after a consideration of premises, constraints, and enterprise goals, plus the factors of expediency, adaptability, and cost.

7. *Arrange implementation of the plan.* After selection of an alternative, the plan is translated into derivative plans and its relation to all activities affected by it is worked out. This includes the details of where the action should be done, by whom, and in what order. The planning process does not stop with the choice of an alternative, because there are almost invariably derivative plans to be constructed to support and implement the basic plan.

Organizing

Organizing is required of managers because it is the method by which effective group action is obtained. A structure of roles must be designed and maintained in order for people to work together in carrying out plans and accomplishing objectives. This is the task of organizing. It involves the grouping of tasks necessary to accomplish plans, the assignment of activities to departments, and the provision for coordination through authority delegation.

"Organizing" as a distinct function of the management process should be distinguished from "organization" as we have used it in discussing organization theory. In the first case, organizing is a basic function of managers, concerned primarily with the formal structure as a means of gaining effective group action. This is the point of view of the most immediate value to the manager and is the approach that incorporates both structure and interaction. "Organization," as normally associated with organization theory, usually refers to the human relationships in group activity that, when taken together, are equated to the social structure.

Organizing, as a process of management, addresses itself to the structural system for achieving coordination and authority delegation. This is not in conflict with the systems model of organization theory described earlier in this chapter. Indeed, we can argue convincingly that the structure provided by the function of organizing facilitates the operation of the organization as a system. This concept is shown in Figure 4–6.

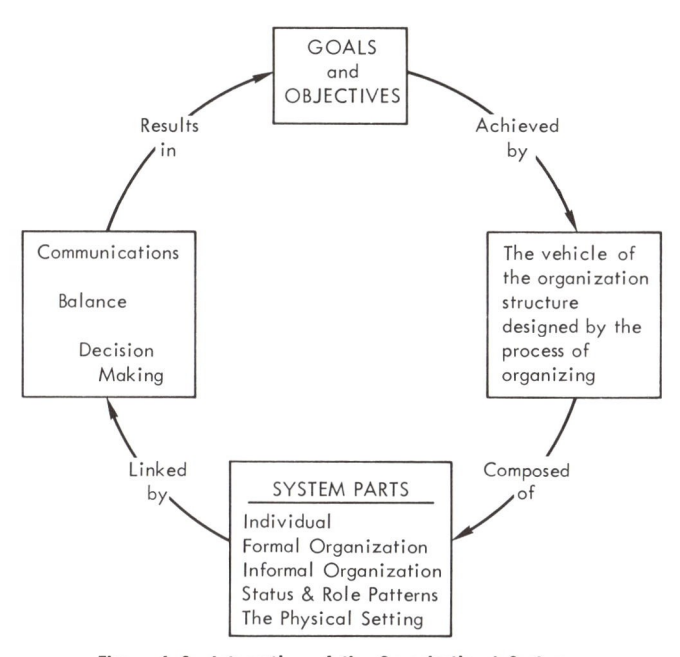

```
                    GOALS
                     and
                  OBJECTIVES
       Results                    Achieved
        in                           by

  Communications                The vehicle of
                                the organization
      Balance                   structure
                                designed by the
      Decision                  process of
      Making                    organizing

       Linked                    Composed
         by      SYSTEM PARTS       of
                 Individual
                 Formal Organization
                 Informal Organization
                 Status & Role Patterns
                 The Physical Setting
```

Figure 4–6 Integration of the Organizational System Through the Organizing Process

The design of an organization structure is largely concerned with the coordination of tasks and people. Some of the major considerations involved in this design—departmentation, span of management, and authority relationships—have their antecedents in the classical theory of organization. The cornerstone of that theory, and the reason we need organizations, is *specialization of labor*. It is probably a safe prediction that this specialization, and hence the need for organizational structure, will increase in the future.

Departmentation

Departmentation deals with the formation of organizational units. Among the first components of an organization structure is the manner in which work is divided into homogeneous groups of activities. The activities form departments. Methods of departmentation that experience has proved logical and useful are: by function, by product, by territory, by customer, by process, and by project. An example of each of these methods of departmentation is illustrated in Figure 4–7. For example, departmentation by *function* is shown at the top level by the common functions of marketing, personnel, operations, R&D, and finance. The breakdown of operations into the furniture division, the metal products division, and the floor-covering division is an example of *product* organization. The sales department is organized into eastern and western districts to establish a *territory* departmentation, and these territories are further departmented by the *customer* breakdown of retail, government, institutions, and manufacturer's representatives. The manufacturing operation in the metal products division depicts both *process* (assembly, welding, stamping) and *function* (maintenance, power, shipping). Finally, a special *project* team, organized for new-product development, reports to the president.

Functional departmentation is by far the oldest and most widely used form of grouping activities. In almost every organization there are three fundamental activities of producing, selling, and financing to be performed. These are the basic functions. As organizations grow, additional staff or service functions are added. Almost all organizations show some functional division of labor.

Product departmentation is common for enterprises with several products or services. The method is easily understood and takes advantage of specialized knowledge. Common examples are department stores (e.g., appliances, furniture, cosmetics) and banks (commercial, personnel).

Territory departmentation is frequently used by organizations that are physically dispersed. The rationale is that activities in a given area should be grouped and assigned to a manager. Such an approach takes advantage of economies of localized operation. The most frequent use of this method is in the sales force, where division by geographical region favors recruitment and training. Manufacturing and distribution may be organized by territory for similar reasons.

Customer departmentation may be used when the major emphasis is upon service to the customer or where it permits taking advantage of specialized knowledge. Sex, age, and income are common yardsticks for identifying customers. Examples of this type of organization include banks (loans to retailers, wholesalers, manufacturers), department stores (men's shop, teen shop, bridal salon), and aircraft manufacturers (government, foreign, domestic).

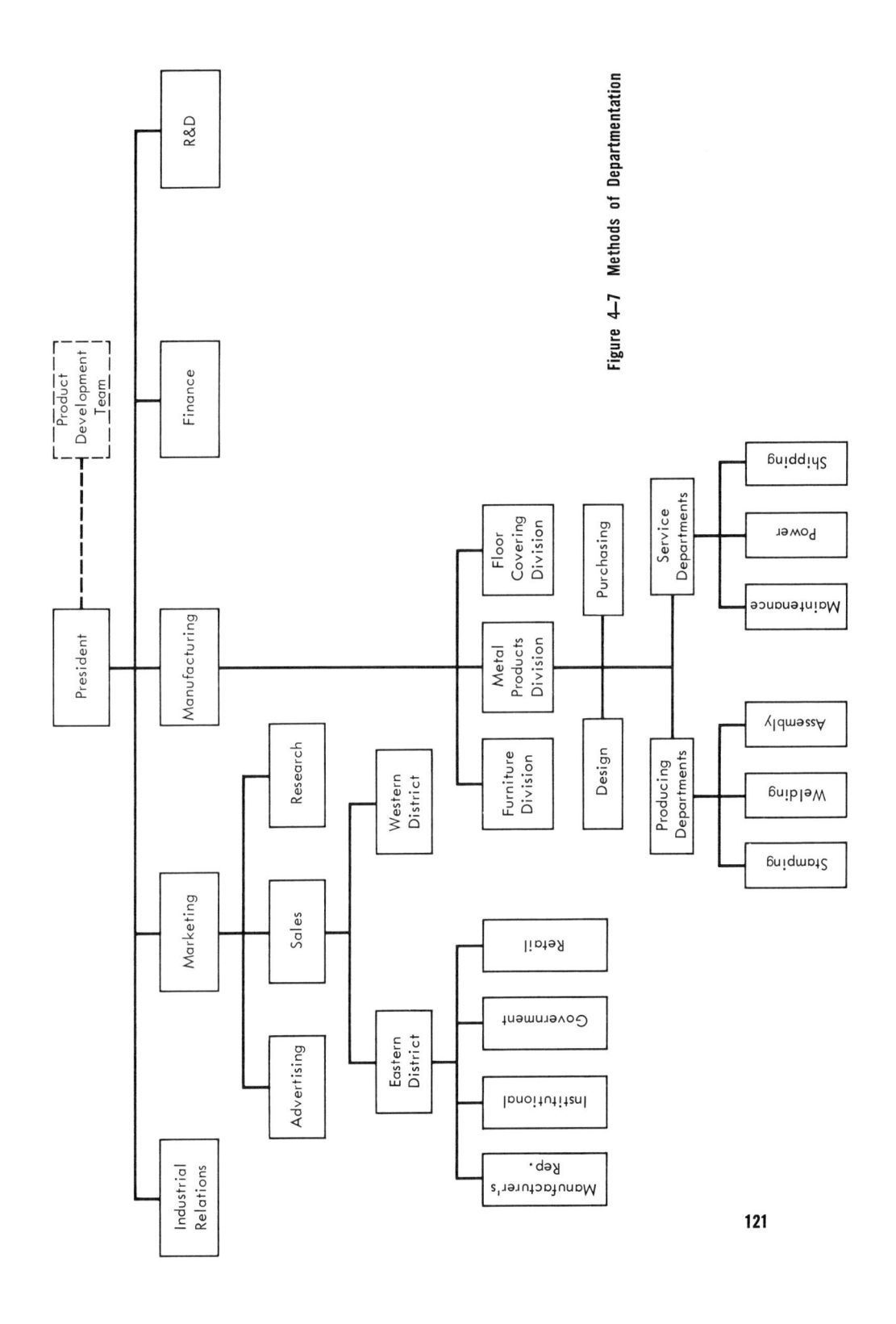

Figure 4–7 Methods of Departmentation

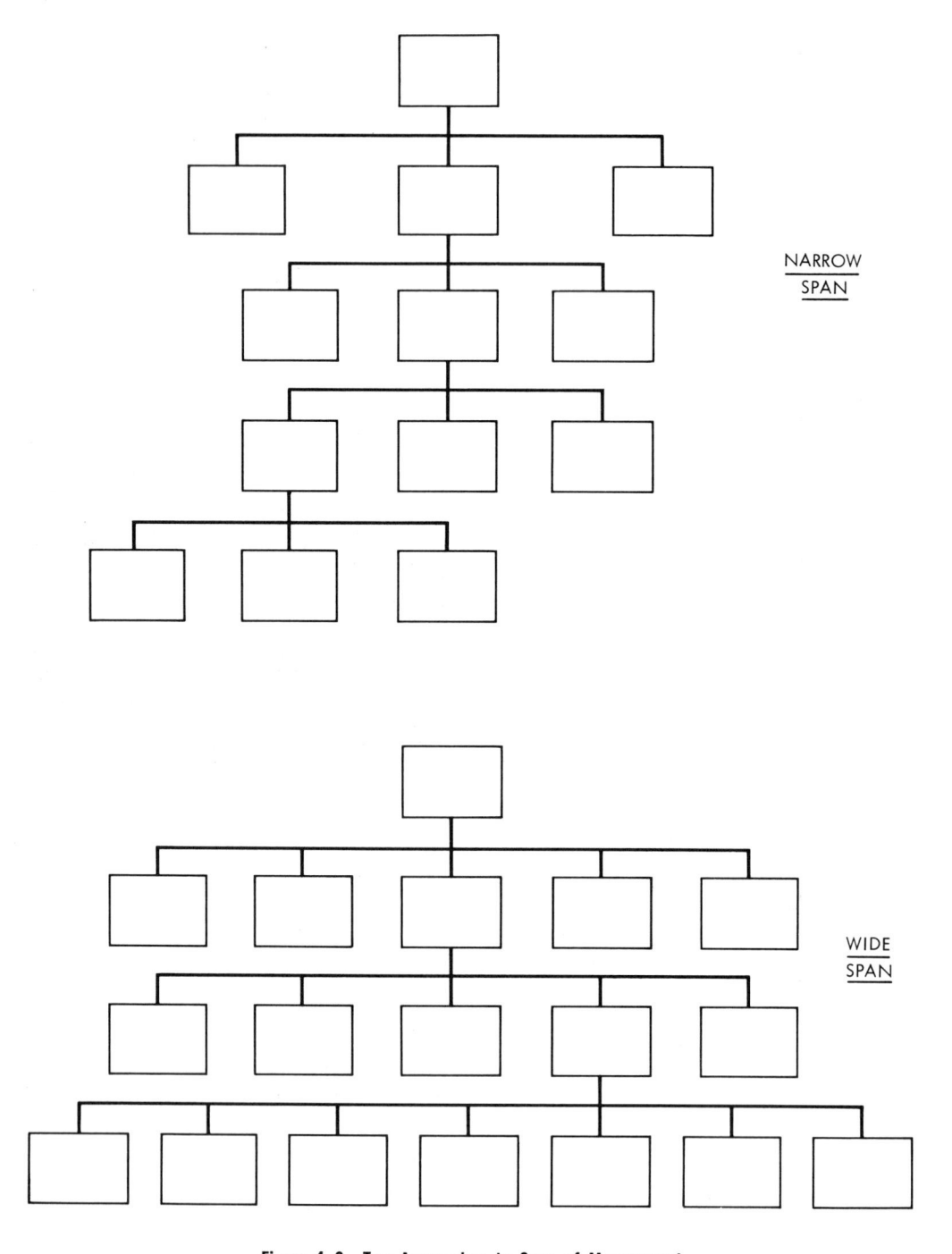

Figure 4–8 Two Approaches to Span of Management

Process departmentation, most frequently used in manufacturing enterprises and at the lowest level of organization, is a logical method whereby maximum use can be obtained from equipment and special skills. Frequently the process matches an occupational classification, such as welding, painting, or plumbing.

Project departmentation, sometimes referred to as team or task force, is relatively new and growing in importance. This approach has gained much favor in defense-related industries because the work involved in research and development lends itself to identification in natural blocks or events. A major advantage of the project organization is the feeling of identification it gives its members.

Span of Management

If it were not necessary to coordinate the activities of an organization, departmentation would permit its expansion to an indefinite degree. However, this coordinative need requires a structure composed of levels of supervision, a structure achieved by establishing these levels of supervision within the confines of the span of management—the number of subordinates that a manager can supervise. The importance of this factor can be appreciated if we consider that were it not for a supervisory limit, there would be no need to organize, since everyone in the organization would report to the president. Hence, the reason for organizing is to overcome the limitations of both human ability and time. Additionally, assignment of duties is clarified and control is facilitated.

The basic question surrounding the span of management—stated two ways—is: (1) How many subordinates should be assigned to a superior? and (2) Should the organization structure be "wide" or "narrow"? Figure 4–8 depicts the types of organizational structures involved in each instance.

Span of management has been a popular subject of debate since the beginnings of classical management theory. Several attempts have been made to quantify it. In 1933 the French management consultant Graicunas developed a mathematical formula[22] that showed the exponential increase in communication complexities as the number of subordinates increased. For example, where the number of subordinates is 5, the number of relationships is 100. If the subordinates are doubled to 10, the number of relationships becomes 5,210.

Generally speaking, the effort to identify a specific number or range of subordinates has not been productive. In practice the number varies widely. For example, former President Eisenhower was noted for his span of management of one—his chief of staff. To take another extreme, 750 Roman Catholic bishops report directly to the pope. In a survey conducted by Ernest Dale, only 13 of 47 large companies report that the president's span of control was six or less.[23] For the others, the figures were:

Span of control	Number of companies
7–10	22
11–13	6
14 and over	6

Span of management appears to be a function of the manager's ability to reduce the time and frequency of subordinate relationships. These factors, in turn, are determined by: (1) how well the subordinate is trained to do his job, (2) the extent of planning involved in the activity, (3) the degree to which authority is delegated and understood, (4) whether standards of performance have been set, (5) the environment for good communications, and (6) the nature of the job and the rate at which it changes.

Research indicates that the "wide" or "flat" type of organization structure with a wide span of control is preferable, *provided* that positive values exist for the six determinants of relationships listed in the preceding paragraph. In other words, adopt a wide span of management and organization structure *if* subordinates are well trained, if work is planned, if authority is delegated and understood, if standards exist, if there is good communication, and if the work does not change frequently. Given this situation, the "wide" organizational structure will yield these benefits: (1) it is economical in that extra layers of supervision are not required, (2) morale is improved because of better identification with top management and less restriction of close supervision, (3) subordinates are developed because they are required to accept more responsibility, and (4) authority is necessarily delegated more clearly.

Authority Relationships

Without the delegation of authority an organization would cease to exist; there would be only one department because the chief executive would be the only manager. It does no good to set up a structure of activities unless authority is delegated to the units within the structure to accomplish particular assignments.

Absolute centralization in one person and absolute decentralization of authority are the two extremes of delegation. Obviously, the tendency is to settle somewhere along the continuum. The major determinant of a manager's ability to delegate authority is his temperament and personality, but other determinants are beyond his control. Some of these are: (1) cost—the more costly the decision, the more likely it is to be centralized: (2) uniformity of policy—the more uniform and centralized a policy (price, personnel) the less need there is to delegate authority surrounding it; (3) complexity of the organization—the more complex, the greater the need for coordination and centralization of authority; (4) custom of the business—frequently the delegation philosophy and character of top management determine authority delegation; and (5) environment for good management—

the availability in the company of managers and good management practices (including control techniques) that would encourage delegation.

Among the tools and techniques for communicating the delegation of authority and organization structure are the organization manual, organization charts, position descriptions, activity charts, and procedural flowcharts. Others are plans, policies, programs, budgets, and procedures.

Controlling

If the manager could depend upon the flawless execution of plans by a perfectly balanced organization, there would be no need for control because results would invariably be as expected. However, plans and operations rarely remain on course, and control is needed to obtain desired results. The real test of a manager's ability is the result he achieves.

Control is a basic process and remains essentially the same regardless of the activity involved or the area of the organization. The fundamental process consists of three steps: (1) setting standards of performance, (2) measuring performance against these standards, and (3) correcting deviations from standards and plans.

Standards of Performance

Setting standards of performance involves defining for personnel in all levels of the organization what is expected of them in terms of job performance. Hence, standards are criteria against which results can be measured. These criteria can be quantitative (e.g., 10 percent increase in sales) or qualitative (e.g., maintain high level of morale). A frequently used definition of standards of performance is *a statement of conditions existing when a job is performed satisfactorily.*

A discussion of standards can be better understood when related to actual examples. Table 4–3 illustrates the basic components of a very important operation plan—the financial plan. Note that a standard of performance is indicated for each of these major items. (See page 126.)

The usual standards of performance for an activity are related to: cost, time, quantity, and quality. For example, in Table 4–3 the *cost* of raw materials for manufacturing a product can be controlled in terms of cost per unit, and this standard would apply in the purchasing operation. *Time* is a standard for the sales force when performance is measured in terms of meeting sales quotas during established time periods (e.g., weeks, months). In manufacturing, the direct labor hours per unit of output in a process operation is a common *quantity* measure. *Quality* is a common measure in judging the acceptability of such factors as product specification, grades of products sold, and reject rates in quality control.

Table 4-3

Standards of Performance for Controlling the Financial Plan

FINANCIAL PLAN	Cost	Time	Quantity	Quality	ILLUSTRATION OF STANDARD
Sales	x	x	x		Sales quota during time period at standard cost
Cost of goods sold					
Raw materials	x		x		Unit usage rate at standard cost
Direct labor			x		Hours per unit of output
Manufacturing expense	x	x		x	Maintenance cost per machine-hour
Total					
Gross margin on sales	x		x		Percent of sales
Less:					
Distribution expense	x				Percent of sales
Administrative expense	x	x		x	Budgeted amount
Total					
Operating income	x		x		Percent of sales
Federal income tax					
Net income		x	x		Return on investment

The foregoing are yardsticks, not areas of activity to be measured. Ideally, everyone in the organization should have some standard so that he understands what is expected of him.

Types of critical standards have been identified as:[24]

1. *Physical.* The fundamental nonmonetary measurements so common at the operating level. They may reflect quantitative performance (units per man-hour, raw material usage rate) or quality (color, hardness).
2. *Cost.* Monetary measurements that attach value to the cost of operations. These are usually cost ratios as, for example, overhead cost per unit of output.
3. *Revenue.* Monetary values that are attached to sales, expressed in ratios such as average sale per customer.
4. *Program.* Unlike ongoing operations, programs are one-time processes and performance is measured in terms of time to complete events, meeting program specifications, or cost.
5. *Intangible.* These are standards that are not ordinarily expressed in quantitative terms because they are hard to measure. Examples are advertising, employee morale, industrial relations, and public relations.

In addition to operating standards, there are critical areas of overall company performance that are the concern of top management. Is the company achieving its objectives? Are its strategies paying off? Indeed, by appraising overall company performance in these areas, the company evaluates its progress toward its basic purposes and objectives. These areas include:

1. Profitability
2. Market standing
3. Productivity
4. Innovation and product leadership
5. Employee and managerial attitudes and development
6. Public responsibility
7. Use of resources
8. Balance between short-range and long-range objectives

Measuring Performance

Once standards have been established, it is necessary to measure performance against the expectation of the standards. The statement of measurement, and of any differences, is usually in the form of a personal observation or some type of report—oral or written.

The oldest and most prevalent means of measuring performance is by personal observation. The shop supervisor is on the scene and can personally check the time, cost, and quality of product. Sales managers visit sales offices or make calls with their salesmen to observe performance personally. Advantages include the benefits of immediacy, personal direct contact, and firsthand observation of intangibles such as morale, personnel development, or customer reaction. Disadvantages are those associated with the time-consuming nature of the method and the lack of precision in measurement.

Oral reports of performance may take the form of interviews, informal reports, or group and committee meetings. Measuring performance in this way has many of the advantages and drawbacks of the personal observation method. Additionally, oral reporting usually does not result in any permanent record of performance.

Increasingly, control and performance reporting is in written form, owing in part to the accelerating use of computer-based information systems and related reporting. The written report has the advantage of providing a permanent record, subject to periodic review by the manager and subordinates. This method of measuring performance may take a variety of forms. Among the most common is the statistical report, which presents statistical analysis of performance versus standard, either in tabular or chart form. Special or one-time reports are frequently made in problem areas as they arise. A significant portion of written reports are operational in nature and concern performance against standards for the financial plan.

Correcting Deviations

It does little good to set standards of performance and measure deviations from standard unless corrections are made to get the plan back on course to achieve the objective. Methods and techniques for correcting deviations can be described in terms of the functions of management:

> Plan—Recycle the management process: review the plan, modify the goal, or change the standard.
> Organize—Examine the organization structure to determine whether it is reflected in standards, make sure that duties are well understood, reassign people if necessary.
> Staff—Improve selection of subordinates, improve training, reassign duties.
> Direct—Provide better leadership, improve motivation, explain the job better, manage by objective, make sure that there is manager-subordinate agreement on standard.

Integration of Managerial Functions

Thus far in our examination of planning, organizing, and controlling we have not advanced a very important concept—the integration of these functions. To treat each function as a separate management activity is to overlook the integration of all three under the systems approach. There is no question about the inextricable interconnection between planning, organizing, and controlling.

First, let us argue the need for viewing planning and controlling together. Control is multidimensional in the same manner as planning. The dimensions of each fit together to form an integrated model of these two vital activities. Just as we defined three levels of planning (strategic, medium-range, and short-range), we can define three equivalent levels of control. *Overall control* is directed to measuring progress and modifying strategic plans for achievement of major purposes and strategies and organizational objectives. It is performed by top management. The second level is *management control*, which flows from overall control. At this level the process is designed to measure performance in the efficient use of resources to accomplish the organization's objectives. At the third level, *operational control* is the process of assuring that "operational" tasks are carried out effectively. These tasks are the day-to-day operations that are measured in terms of specific performance standards (e.g., monthly sales quota, maintenance cost per machine-hour).

The integration of planning and control is shown conceptually in Figure 4–9, which illustrates how the three levels of plans are linked to three levels of control. Note also that information systems are an important element of both planning and control—indeed, information is their common denominator. Moreover, as indicated in Figure 4–9, the planning and control processes are not static but dynamic. Hence, their actual operation in

the systems approach to organization and management 129

PLANNING LEVELS   **CONTROL LEVELS**

```
                    STRATEGIC
                    PLANNING
                                        OVERALL
                                        CONTROL
    INFORMATION
    SYSTEM          MEDIUM-RANGE
    (Recycle)       PLANNING
                                        MANAGERIAL
                                        CONTROL
                    SHORT-RANGE
                    PLANNING
                                        OPERATIONAL
                                        CONTROL
```

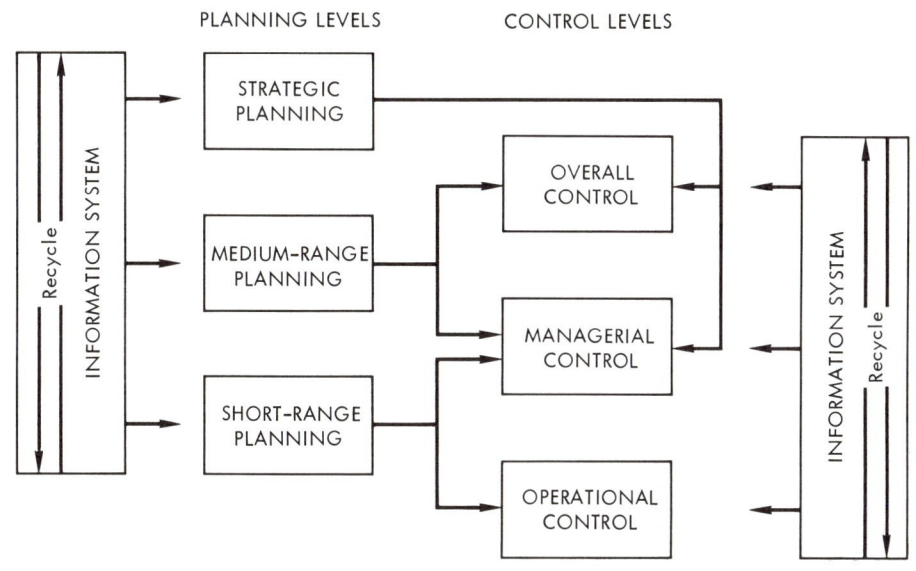

Figure 4–9 Integration of Planning and Control

practice is iterative, as shown in the recycling process. Planning is done in the light of control, performance takes place as a result of plans, deviations are corrected, new plans are made to meet the needs of deviations, and so on.

An additional integrative characteristic of these two activities is the frequent practice of designing control standards during the planning process. The best example of this is the financial plan of Table 4–3. When this plan is developed, standards become an integral part of it because the plan is phrased in terms of results expected. For example, sales plans are stated in terms of performance quotas, manufacturing plans in terms of labor standards and unit usage of raw materials. Any plan would be poor indeed if it did not take into consideration its subsequent control over management activities and performance.

An additional integrating concept is the growing tendency to involve the persons responsible for results in the planning for them. Various popular phrases have been devised to describe participation in planning and setting standards. Frequently called "management by objective,"[25] "management by participation,"[26] or "management by results,"[27] the approach is based on the principle that "human beings will direct their effort, exercise self-control and responsibility, use their creativity in the service of goals to which they are committed."[28]

We have shown that planning and control are inextricably interconnected, but what part does *organizing* play in the systems approach to these managerial functions? The answer lies in the nature of the organization and the organizing process.

130 Management and Systems

First, the organization is obviously the vehicle through which the plans must be achieved. Meaning must be given to plans, and the organization (people and structure) is the vehicle for converting plans to action. Hence the ability of the organization to activate plans and maintain subsequent control must be taken into account in the planning and controlling processes. Likewise, control must be exercised through the organization. A second argument for the integrative nature of organizing is that the manager must design a structure that facilitates planning and control. Because the action in the organization takes place around planning levels, decision centers, and critical control points, structure and communications should be organized around these elements. In short, the manager organizes to facilitate planning and control.

The systems nature of the basic managerial functions of planning, organizing, and control is shown in Figure 4–10. From the concept depicted here we see that these three basic functions form a *process* that is integrated, iterative, and dynamic.

MANAGEMENT AND SYSTEMS CONCEPTS

We have now completed our initial examination of the three basic functions of management. Each was treated separately before being combined into a system that is integrated, dynamic, and iterative. Now we want to determine how each of these major functions is influenced by the systems approach and how the performance of each is changed thereby.

In this "age of synthesis" in which we find ourselves, the systems approach cannot be overemphasized. By looking at a business as a pattern of flows throughout the organization rather than as a collection of parts, the manager will avoid suboptimization of the parts at the expense of the whole.

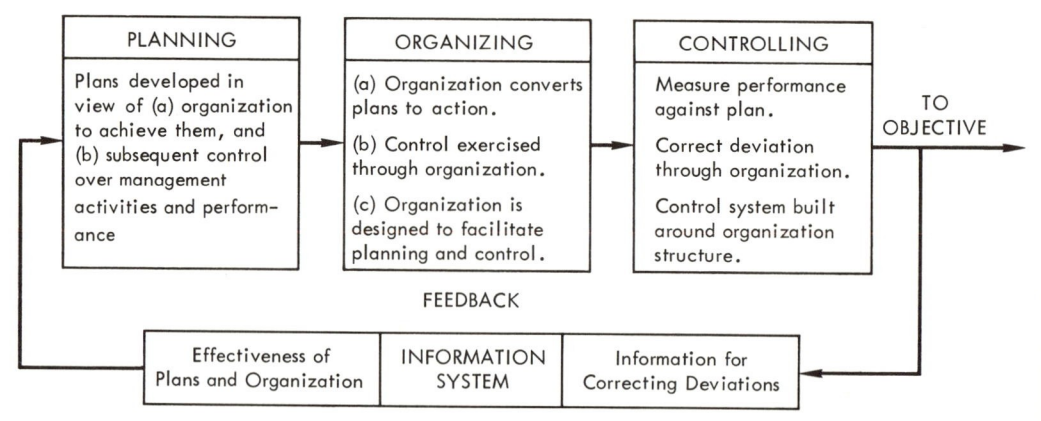

Figure 4–10 A System of Planning, Organizing, and Controlling

Engineers will not overdesign products that are noncompetitive from a cost standpoint, sales managers will not demand product variety and deliveries without regard to finished goods inventories, and short-range operational planning will not be emphasized at the expense of strategic top-management planning. The systems approach increases top management's understanding that it is running a business, a system composed of parts that interact with other subsystems within and without organizational boundaries.

Planning and Systems Concepts

A popular text in systems management asserts: "The systems concept in business planning should start with the awareness of the need to think of several levels and the integration of these levels into a hierarchy."[29] Studies of past company practices show that this integrative role of planning has not been achieved in many business firms. Planning, when done, was viewed as a function of top management and one that was performed in the rarified atmosphere of Cloud Nine. Moreover, if planning was done at a functional level (sales, finance, manufacturing, and the like), these functions were usually not integrated either horizontally or vertically.

Most planning has been short range in nature, and in many cases it was designed to react to changes as they occur. The systems approach to planning means planning for change. This view requires that the company be considered in the context of the greater system of which it is a part. Moreover, thinking must be in terms of how the subsystems of this greater system affect and interact with the organization itself. Integration therefore assumes that planning takes place after the receipt of inputs from the following three major subsystems:

1. *Environmental.* The broad, noncompetitive set of political, cultural, and social factors with which the firm must interact.
2. *Competitive.* Governmental, industry, economic, business environment, and producer–consumer relationships in the industry in which the firm operates or plans to operate.
3. *Internal organization.* The organizational structure, strategies, objectives, policies, and relationships that constrain or otherwise affect the planning process.

Figure 4–11 diagrams the systems approach to planning. Regardless of whether these levels are defined structurally, by type of planning conducted, or by hierarchical level, each can be integrated by the systems approach to planning. Each level, when participating in the planning process or devising its own plans, receives as information input the output from a higher order of plan in the organizational structure. Similarly, each level's output is utilized as input in a lower level of the organization. This concept not only facilitates integrated planning on a systems basis in manufacturing

132 Management and Systems

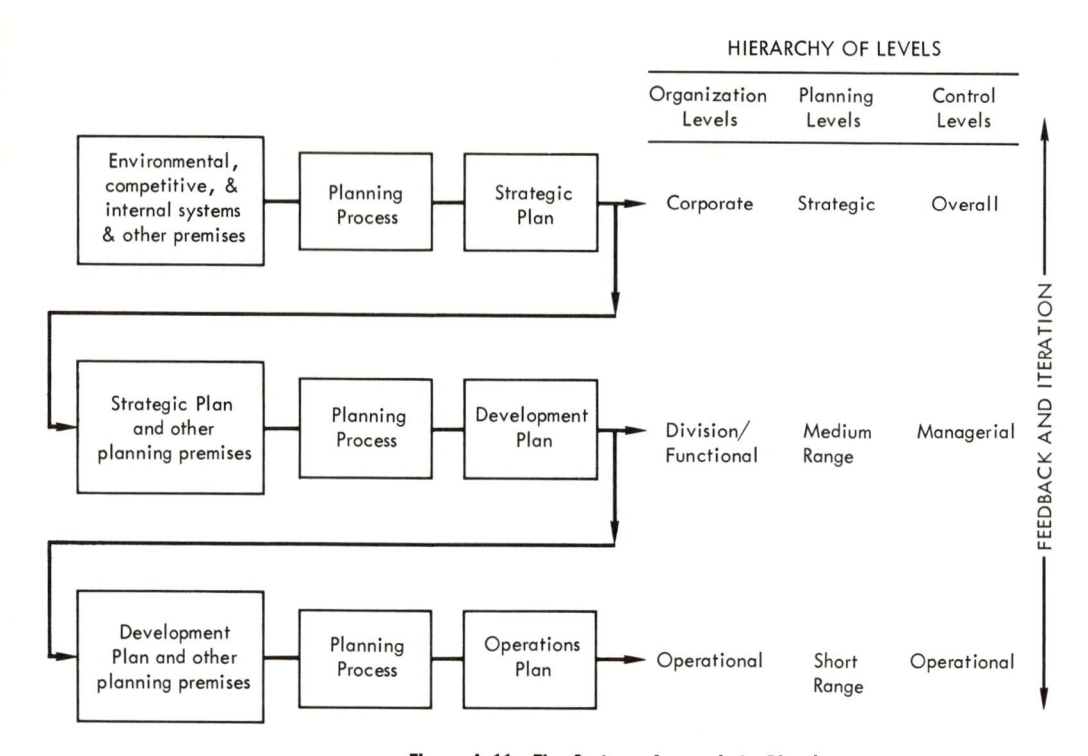

Figure 4-11 The Systems Approach to Planning

and other process-type operations, it is also most notably suited for the program or project type of organization to be discussed later.

In very recent years, planning (particularly long-range planning) and decision making have been greatly enhanced by the accelerating use of *systems analysis,* a process that interrelates the systems approach and the planning process. In a broad sense, systems analysis can be defined as a systematic way of looking at complex problems to assure that an objective is achieved more efficiently than if the individual parts were examined in isolation.[30] The approach includes:

1. Systematic development and comparison of alternatives relating to the accomplishment of an objective.
2. Utilization of cost–benefit analysis for comparison of each alternative.
3. Considerations of uncertainty surrounding alternatives.
4. Blending of a variety of areas of knowledge for ill-structured problems.
5. Emphasis of the scientific method—systematic and objective examination of each hypothesis that can be tested and verified. Information is quantified where practicable.
6. Development of a model to represent the system.
7. Application to problems that are broad and complex.

Program Planning and Budgeting Systems (PPBS), Program Evaluation Review Technique (PERT), simulation, and modeling are among the better-known techniques of systems analysis. The systems approach to planning not only integrates the hierarchical levels as desired but also gives the manager a powerful new approach to the solution of complex problems surrounding the management of organizations. It provides the framework for participation by various individuals and groups throughout the enterprise.

Organizing and Systems Concepts

By its very nature, the systems philosophy of organizing creates several basic and valuable by-products. The first of these is integration of the many subsystems making up the total organization. We have seen how planning tends to put managers in the frame of mind for thinking of the organization as a system. This approach to organizing will accomplish similar results. Further, people will begin to understand how their jobs interact with others in the company. A second benefit is the enhancement of decentralization. Advantages of decentralization include greater economies of supervision, improved morale, better development of managers, and in general more awareness of the contribution that decentralized units make to the whole. The systems approach and computer-based information systems give us many new and different capabilities for organization and management of a business, especially more centralized and more automated control of major portions of operations.[31] It is this *centralized control* that permits *decentralized operations*.

The greatest impact will come in the organization structure itself. Traditional organizational practice and theory have emphasized structure and authority. Under the systems approach the concept of the organization is changing from one of structure to one of process.[32]

Advanced technology, the information explosion, increasing complexity—these require an organization structure that will accommodate change. We are fitting increasingly sophisticated techniques to a primitive vehicle, the bureaucratic structure. By adopting the systems approach to organizing, we emphasize integration of the parts as well as design of a vehicle that will accommodate accelerating change.

Equally important is the emphasis that the systems approach places upon the *systems* as opposed to the *functions* of organizations. The typical business has been organized along functional lines (sales, finance, production) at the top, and by other methods (customer, process, territory, etc.) at lower hierarchical levels. This emphasis on organization structure has frequently overlooked the interrelationship of the parts and the programs, projects, and processes that the parts were designed to produce.

134   Management and Systems

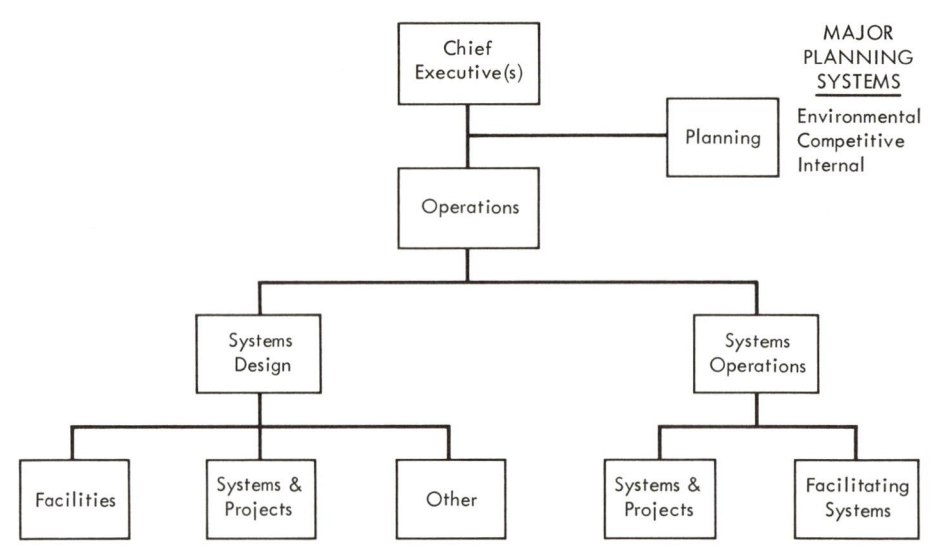

```
                    ┌──────────────┐
                    │    Chief     │                      MAJOR
                    │ Executive(s) │                    PLANNING
                    └──────┬───────┘                     SYSTEMS
                           ├──────────────┬─────────┐
                           │              │Planning │  Environmental
                    ┌──────┴──────┐       └─────────┘  Competitive
                    │  Operations │                    Internal
                    └──────┬──────┘
                ┌──────────┴──────────┐
         ┌──────┴──────┐        ┌─────┴──────┐
         │   Systems   │        │  Systems   │
         │   Design    │        │ Operations │
         └──────┬──────┘        └─────┬──────┘
      ┌────────┼────────┐         ┌───┴────┐
  ┌───┴──┐ ┌───┴───┐ ┌──┴──┐  ┌───┴───┐ ┌──┴────────┐
  │Facil-│ │Systems│ │Other│  │Systems│ │Facilitating│
  │ities │ │   &   │ │     │  │   &   │ │  Systems   │
  │      │ │Project│ │     │  │Project│ │            │
  └──────┘ └───────┘ └─────┘  └───────┘ └────────────┘
```

Figure 4–12   A Systems Approach to Organizing

An alternative method of organizing along systems lines is shown in Figure 4–12. The planning group would assume the functions now performed by the planning department except that these functions would be expanded to provide additional scope. The group relates the business to its environmental systems, both external and internal, in order to make all decisions and policies concerning strategies, objectives, products, and limits of operating programs. With the planning information as input, the systems design group provides facilities and manpower for the new project or staffs it to the point of preoperational readiness. At this point the system would commence operations either as a service system or as another new, major project system.

Warren Bennis sees the key word describing tomorrow's organization as "temporary."[33] He says, "There will be adaptive, rapidly changing *temporary* systems. These will be task forces organized around problems to be solved. . . ."[34] Whatever the form of tomorrow's organization, it will be influenced by the systems approach and management information systems. Because these systems call for new work flows and new types of operational relationships, they will become the source of new organizational relationships as well.[35]

Control and Systems Concepts

The concept of control lies at the very heart of the systems approach. Indeed, no system could exist for very long without control. Unlike our classical notion of control as a process of coercion, or "compelling events to

the systems approach to organization and management 135

conform to plan," control in a *cybernetic* sense or systems sense views the organization or subsystem as a "homeostatic machine for regulating itself."[36] The key idea underlying control is *feedback*.

The notion of the organization as a cybernetic system includes the thermostat, which maintains the temperature at a predetermined level by making or breaking an electrical circuit that starts or stops the heating system. The rotating arms of the steam engine governor rise and fall with changes in centrifugal force, controlling the input of steam and hence the speed of the engine. The turnover rate of raw materials inventory exceeds the accepted standard, causing a reduction in orders until the inventory level is within standard level. These examples illustrate the major characteristics of cybernetic systems: (1) a predetermined equilibrium to be maintained, (2) a feedback of changes in environment to the system, causing changes in its state, (3) a transfer of information from the external environment to within the system, (4) a device that prompts corrective action when the output of the system oscillates beyond desired limits.

The concept of control in a system is shown in Figure 4–13, which demonstrates how major functions of a business system may be self-correcting based on feedback of information from the external environment.

The objective of control is to maintain the output that will satisfy the system requirements. This necessitates the engineering of control into the system. In the case of information systems, control is a major consideration of systems design and may take the form of a programmed decision rule. The steady state of the system (organization) is maintained by feedback

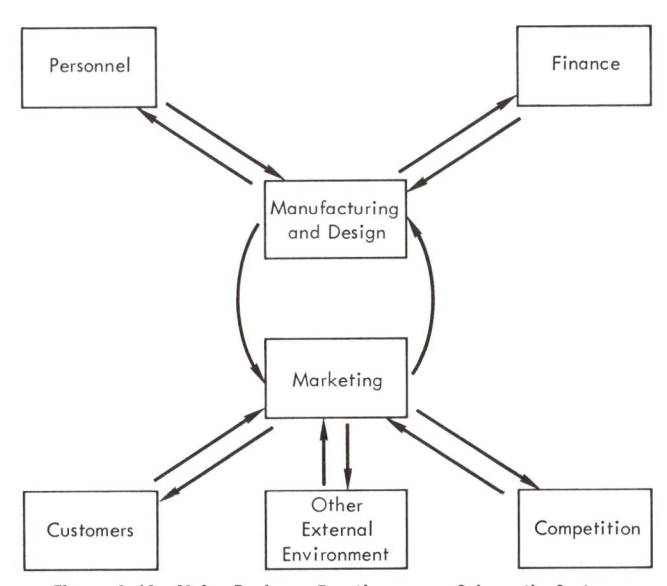

Figure 4–13 Major Business Functions as a Cybernetic System

of information concerning the functioning of the system within allowable limits.

Control systems are best regarded as information systems, because the rapidity and appropriateness of corrective action—the end result of the control process—depend on the kind of information received.

THE SYSTEM OF ORGANIZATION AND MANAGEMENT

At this point let us synthesize the separate parts of organization and management theory with which we have been dealing and design a *system* of organization and management. The task is to construct a conceptual model through which we can understand how to *manage* the transformation of *resource flows* through the *organization* by means of a systems approach. Such an approach must also include as essential components the functions of the management process, modern organization theory, and the techniques of the various "schools" of management.

Because our model will utilize the basic functions of management and the techniques of other approaches as the foundation, it is first desirable to indicate how these can be integrated. Figure 4–14 shows these interrelationships for selected illustrations. We have added an additional systems technique to show how this approach might also be useful in combining functions and techniques. The purpose of Figure 4–14 is to demonstrate how the functions of management utilize the techniques and approaches of other disciplines and that these approaches are of little value unless used to perform a function of management.

In actual practice the functions of management are interwoven and interrelated; the performance of one does not cease before the next commences, nor are the functions carried out in sequence. For example, a manager may perform controlling at the same time that he is planning and directing. Although there are times when some functions must be performed before others can be put into action (e.g., directing requires that persons have been assigned activities), generally speaking, there is no sequence to the operation of these functions nor to the utilization of the techniques of management. However, none of them can be performed in a vacuum. As a matter of fact, planning is involved in the work of organizing, controlling is performed in the work of staffing, decision theory is used in the function of organizing, and management information systems are utilized in all functions and all disciplines. Each function and technique affects the others, and all are intimately interrelated in a system to form the major components of the system of management.

Given the foregoing integration of functions and techniques, we can now construct a conceptual model (Figure 4–15) of the system of organization and management—*a system that integrates the parts: resource flows,*

		PLAN	ORGANIZE	STAFF	DIRECT	CONTROL	SYSTEMS
FUNCTIONS	PLAN	M	Implement plan through organization	Train for planning	Gain acceptance of plans	Plan is standard for achievement	Integrates planning
FUNCTIONS	ORGANIZE	Plan developed through organization	A	Assign tasks per organization	Communicate through organization	Organization is control vehicle	Organization structured for performance
FUNCTIONS	STAFF	Recruit and place for plans	Personnel requirements a function of organization	N	Delegate by job description	Performance standard for recruiting	Facilitates staffing process
FUNCTIONS	DIRECT	Direct with policies	Organization structure for direction	Motivate through training	A	Participation in setting standards	Enhances job satisfaction
FUNCTIONS	CONTROL	Plan must be controlled	Control depends on organization	Requirements a function of standards	Acceptance of controls	G	Minimizes output variation
TOOLS	Behavioral	Predicting organization acceptance	Human needs in organizing	Group participation in job standards	Motivation of employees	Gaining acceptance of standards	E
TOOLS	Quantitative	Forecasting	Organizing for project management	Forecast of skill requirements	Leadership research	Simulation for control	Design of decision rules
TOOLS	Decision Theory	Weighing alternatives	Organization modeling	Promotion policy	Alternatives in labor relations	Decision rules for control	Management science
TOOLS	Empirical	Judgment of sales forecast	Organizing alternatives	Experience of past	Experience in employee turnover	Historical standards	Assimilates historical data
TOOLS	Systems	Planning premises	Organize around info centers	Data bank of skills	Data for morale decisions	Decision rules for automatic control	Info is medium of management

Figure 4–14 Selected Illustrations Showing Interrelationship Between Tools and Functions of Management

138 Management and Systems

functions of management, organization theory, and the various techniques. Notice that a vital additional component has been added, *a management information system.* This is the component of the system that provides information for planning, activates plans, and furnishes the essential feedback information necessary to achieve stability through control.

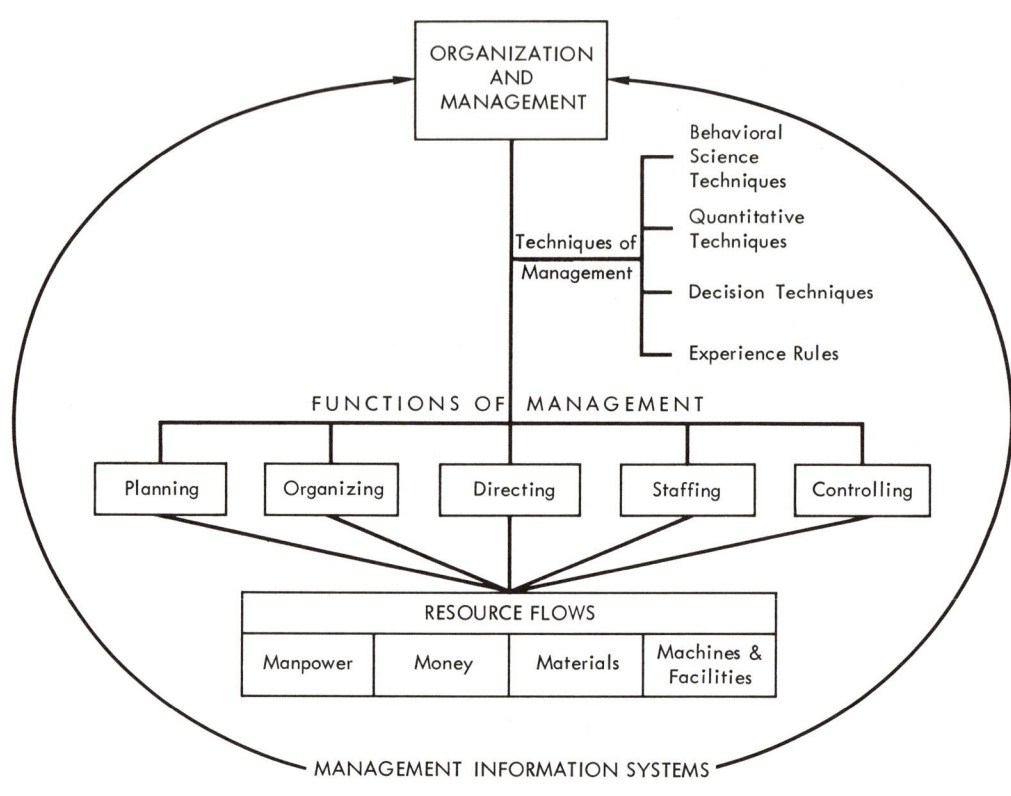

Figure 4–15 Organization and Management—A System

Figure 4–15 has taken the functions of management as the basic platform from which the system is constructed. These functions explain what the manager does, how he manages resources in order to accomplish objectives. In doing this he depends upon the behavioral science knowledge of organization theory and the techniques of the other approaches to management. In performing the functions of management, he calls upon these techniques for use in the systems approach to management. To illustrate, we can examine the function of planning and its relationship to other functions and techniques. It is clear that in developing a plan, the manager would want to utilize one or more of the techniques available to him. For example, the disciplines of the decision theorists as well as the techniques of mathematics would be most helpful if applicable to the particular situation. The past experience of the firm as well as that of other firms might also be of assistance. The behavioral science knowledge of modern organization theory is invaluable in implementing the plan.

The final component of the system is the envelope called *management information systems*, which encloses the entire model. This system collects, analyzes, stores, and displays data to management decision makers at all levels for the management of the resource flows of materials, manpower, money, and facilities and machines. This component is also vital to the practice of the functions of management.

Finally, if we want to manage the firm in a cybernetic sense as a "homeostatic machine for regulating itself," it is necessary to integrate our model of the systems approach to management with the notion of automatic control through feedback. This integration is demonstrated conceptually in Figure 4–16. No matter how the organization or subsystem outputs are stated (here we state them in terms of user's needs and desires), the inputs (resource flows) are managed during the transformation process in order to meet the output objectives. Control over the processing organization is maintained by our system of management, which maintains output within set limits. Periodic feedback of information concerning the achievement of objectives is furnished by means of the management information system, and deviations are fed as additional inputs to the planning system.

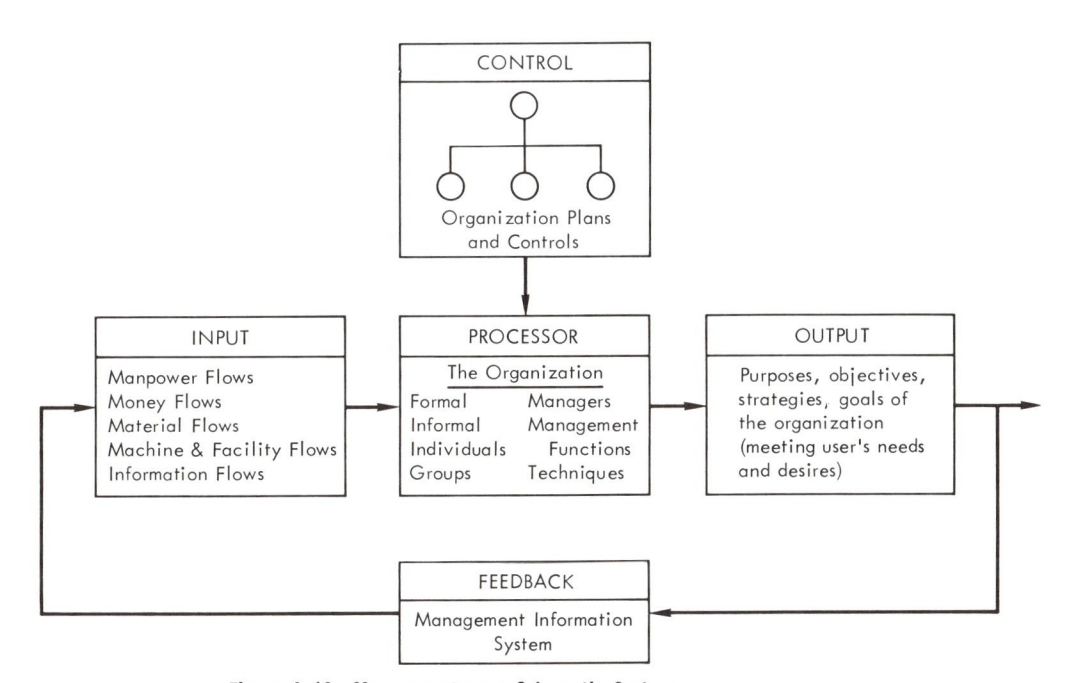

Figure 4–16 Management as a Cybernetic System

This closed-loop communication system should operate continuously if the organization is to optimize its resources and reach its objectives as determined in the planning process. Changes in objectives and needs should be fed back as quickly as possible to management so that plans can be revised and operations altered. This concept of information feedback is basic to the operation of the organization as a system. Thus, from the standpoint of the manager and from his approach to practicing management as a system, the organization can be viewed as a network of feedback systems. The notion of self-correction through information feedback will be examined in subsequent chapters.

SUMMARY

In this chapter we have attempted to build a system of organization and management—a system that accommodates all techniques, approaches, disciplines, and "schools." The objective is to explain how, by the process of management, resource inputs are transformed through the vehicle of the organization into outputs that reflect an objective. The organization is viewed as an organism. The approach encompasses: (1) resource flows, (2) modern organization theory, (3) the management process and the functions of management, (4) the techniques (e.g., quantitative, behavioral) of the various "schools" of management, and (5) management information systems.

Modern organization theory had its antecedents in the classical approach, which stressed formal structure and hierarchical authority, and in neoclassical theory, which added the informal organization and the "human relations" approach. Modern theory views the parts of the organizational system as: the individual, the formal organization, the informal organization, status and role patterns, and the physical setting. These parts are linked through the integrating processes of communications, balance, and decision making.

The three most basic functions of management are planning, organizing, and controlling. Under the systems concept, planning is viewed as the activity that integrates the organization by means of the hierarchy of plans: strategic, development, and operational. These plans also interrelate with the three basic systems affecting the organization: the environmental, the competitive, and the internal organization systems. The accelerating use of systems analysis will provide a systems approach to planning in the future.

Under the systems approach, the concept of the organization is changing from one of structure to one of process. Moreover, the emphasis in organizing is increasingly being placed upon the systems involved rather than upon the functions. Tomorrow's organization will be characterized by its temporary nature and its flexible structure that conforms to a problem to be solved or a system to be managed.

Control, under a systems concept, is a cybernetic approach to management that views the organization as a "homeostatic machine for regulating itself," with control as the function that coalesces all others. The fundamental notion behind the systems approach to control is the automatic feedback of information for self-correction.

Finally, we constructed a conceptual model embracing all the approaches to management and organization. Such a model provides an umbrella under which all past and evolving concepts of organization and management will fit.

DISCUSSION QUESTIONS AND PROBLEMS

1. Select a manufacturing firm with which you are familiar and illustrate how the following resources "flow" through the firm: raw materials, manpower, money, machines, and information.

2. Using the example of the Ford Motor Company, or a firm of your choice, show how the developments of the past ten years have caused an upsurge in the need for better planning.

3. Name the several classifications of plans and show how they integrate the organization structure both vertically and horizontally.

4. A manufacturer of farm equipment recently announced that its 100-year policy of distribution through independent dealers would be changed; henceforth distribution would be through company-owned outlets in 320 locations. How do you think this policy might reflect upon the development and adoption of a new company strategy? How would it affect policies in other areas, such as finance, production, marketing, personnel, and organizational structure? Show how such a change in policy decision might have been made by utilizing the steps in the planning process.

5. Contrast the motivational and managerial development implications of a wide span of control versus a narrow span of control. Does the new systems approach to organization hold any implications for span of control? Discuss.

6. Show how the control process relates to the other functions of management.

7. How would the notion of "cybernetics" relate to the management of an organization? Relate the elements of a cybernetic system of management to the operation of a retail store.

8. Professor Johnson was the instructor in a continuing seminar in organization and management for the Young President's Organization.

After several months of instructing in the seminar, he commented, "Most of these men are intelligent, vigorous, successful presidents of small and medium-size corporations. Yet many of them either have never heard of the basic principles of planning, organizing, and controlling or do not relate their jobs to these functions of management." How can these men be successful managers if they do not know the basic principles of management? Could other qualities or attributes be more important than specific knowledge of management functions? If so, what are they?

9. Encouraged by Secretary of Defense McNamara and the lead of the U.S. Air Force, the armed forces changed substantially from a *functional* type of organization in the 1960's to a *systems* type, with headquarters and subordinate commands organized around "weapons systems" (e.g., Polaris, Nike, Apollo, Strategic Air Command). This concept provided for the design and development of a weapons system as well as for its ultimate operation and evaluation in the field over its life. A similar type of organization, providing for *product managers*, has been developed in recent years by several multiproduct companies.

Following the lead of the armed forces, most defense contractors have moved to the weapons system or project type of organization, partly to accommodate the interface between the contractor and the particular defense organization for which the system is being produced, and partly because experience has shown that such an organization is preferable to the old-style functional approach.

Questions:
(1) Construct an organization chart showing how a functional type of organization might adapt to the weapons system or product approach.
(2) How might the functions (e.g., finance, personnel, marketing, production) be affected by such an organizational change?
(3) How might the functions of management (e.g., planning, organizing, controlling) be affected by such an organizational change?
(4) Which type of organization would be preferable in Sears, Roebuck? In General Electric? In IBM? In the Bell Telephone System? Support your answers.

REFERENCES

1. Chadwick J. Haberstroh, "Organization Design and Systems Analysis," in James G. March, ed., *Handbook of Organizations* (Chicago: Rand McNally & Co., 1965), p. 1172.
2. Douglas McGregor, in Warren G. Bennis and Caroline McGregor, eds., *The Professional Manager* (New York: McGraw-Hill Book Company, 1967), p. 39.
3. William G. Scott, "Organization Theory: An Overview and an Appraisal," *Journal of the Academy of Management*, April 1961, p. 10.
4. Chris Argyris, *Personality and Organization* (New York: Harper & Row, Publishers, 1957).
5. Stafford Beer, *Cybernetics and Management* (New York: John Wiley & Sons, Inc., 1964), p. 22.
6. Scott, "Organization Theory," p. 12.
7. James G. March and Herbert A. Simon, *Organizations* (New York: John Wiley & Sons, Inc., 1958), Chaps. 3 and 4.
8. Scott, "Organization Theory," p. 12.
9. Harold Koontz and Cyril O'Donnell, *Principles of Management,* 4th ed. (New York: McGraw-Hill Book Company, 1968), p. 47.
10. For example, George Terry, in *Principles of Management,* identifies: planning, organizing, actuating, and controlling. Ernest Dale, in *Management Theory and Practice,* classifies: planning, organizing, staffing, direction, control, innovation, and representation.
11. Wilbur M. McFeely, "The Manager of the Future," *Columbia Journal of World Business*, May–June 1969, p. 87.
12. In 1956, the National Industrial Conference Board reported that only 8 percent of the companies in a survey had one or more persons engaged in full-time planning. Yet in 1966 a National Planning Association study found that of 420 companies studied, 85 percent prepared long-term plans. For further data see George A. Steiner, *Top Management Planning* (Toronto: Collier-Macmillan Canada, Ltd., 1969), pp. 14–16.
13. *Ibid.,* pp. 16–17.
14. *Ibid.,* p. 40.
15. *Ibid.,* p. 34.
16. This is an adaptation of a planning model developed by the Stanford Research Institute. See Robert F. Stewart and Marian Doscher, *The Complete Development Plan* (Menlo Park, Calif.: Industrial Economics Division, Stanford Research Institute, September 1963), p. 21.
17. Peter F. Drucker, *The Practice of Management* (New York: Harper & Row, Publishers, 1954), p. 63.
18. Steiner, *Top Management Planning,* p. 238.
19. Adapted from Steiner, *Top Management Planning,* pp. 239–40.
20. *Ibid.,* p. 40.

144 Management and Systems

21. Koontz and O'Donnell, *Principles of Management*, p. 84.
22. V. A. Graicunas, "Relationship in Organization," *Bulletin of the International Management Institute* (Geneva: International Labour Office, 1933), in L. Gulick and L. Urwick, eds., *Papers on the Science of Administration*, (New York: Institute of Public Administration, 1937), pp. 181–87. The formula is: where n equals the number of subordinates, the number of all kinds of relationships will be represented by
$$n[(2^n/2) + (n-1)] \quad \text{or} \quad n[2^{n-1} + (n-1)]$$
23. Ernest Dale, *Management Theory and Practice* (New York: McGraw-Hill Book Company, 1965), p. 289.
24. Adapted from Koontz and O'Donnell, *Principles of Management*, pp. 649–50.
25. George S. Odiorne, *Management by Objectives* (New York: Pitman Publishing Corp., 1965).
26. Alfred J. Morrow, David G. Bowers, and Stanley E. Seashore, *Management by Participation* (New York: Harper & Row, Publishers, 1967).
27. Edward C. Schleh, *Management by Results* (New York: McGraw-Hill Book Company, 1961).
28. McGregor, *The Professional Manager*, p. 127.
29. Richard Johnson, Fremont Kast, and James Rosenzweig, *The Theory and Management of Systems* (New York: McGraw-Hill Book Company, 1967) p. 34.
30. Steiner, *Top Management Planning*, p. 394.
31. Victor Z. Brink, "Top Management Looks at the Computer," *Columbia Journal of World Business*, January–February 1969, p. 78.
32. Stanley Young, "Organization as a Total System," *California Management Review*, Vol. X, No. 3 (Spring 1968), 1.
33. Warren G. Bennis, "The Coming Death of Bureaucracy," in David I. Cleland and William R. King, eds., *Systems, Organizations, Analysis, Management: A Book of Readings* (New York: McGraw-Hill Book Company, 1969), p. 11.
34. *Ibid.*
35. Brink, "Top Management Looks at the Computer," p. 81.
36. Beer, *Cybernetics and Management*, p. 28.

CASE STUDY

AMERICAN SCIENTIFIC PRODUCTS COMPANY, INC. (A)

"We've got to develop a corporate strategy for achieving our objective and get organized to do it," declared Dr. Robert F. Dobrynski, M.D., president of American Scientific Products Company. Continuing his summary at an executive committee meeting in the fall of 1970, Dr. Dobrynski said, "Although very significant gains have been made in the sale of our superior product line, our income has not kept pace. Perhaps it is because our top-management physicians and engineers are too much oriented to product development and have overlooked such important considerations as control of production and distribution costs. Perhaps the company has outgrown our capacity to manage informally. It seems to me that what we need is a management information system."

Background

The American Scientific Products Company was founded in 1949 in Stoughton, Massachusetts, by a small group of physicians and engineers. These men had a great deal of interest in the research and development of hospital and laboratory equipment and enjoyed a personal relationship dating back to their college and medical school days. The original objective of the firm was to develop research and laboratory equipment, to produce the most modern microscopes available, and in general to improve significantly the quality of the laboratory research devices available to clinics, laboratories, hospitals, and universities.

During the first decade of its existence, the company enjoyed growth and prosperity, due in large measure to the absence of significant competition. However, beginning in the early 1960's, competition grew as additional firms entered the industry. Among these were Beckman Optical Equipment Corporation, Littman Medical Supply Company, Perkins and Elmer Laboratory Equipment Company, and Bausch & Lomb Optical Company.

In 1966 the Company acquired (through an exchange of stock) the Medical Science Instrument Corporation of Stoughton, Massachusetts, whose principal products are disposable laboratory and hospital supplies. In addition to providing new products and distribution outlets, this acquisition allows Scientific Products to concentrate additional engineering and production efforts in the new products area.

Recognizing that (1) industry sales will grow at a slower rate than in the past, and (2) competition in the industry will increase, the management of American Scientific Products feels that they should concentrate on locating and developing both new products and new markets. Accordingly, a "New Products and Market Analysis Committee" was formed in 1967 for the purpose of planning future growth and directing the efforts of research and development toward this growth. In 1967 the company also established a research and development center at Woods Hole, Massachusetts.

Although the rate of growth slowed somewhat, gross sales continued to increase, and in 1968 the company established foreign branch offices in Latin America. Sales volume during 1969 exceeded $17.8 million, but net earnings after taxes had been reduced to a figure that was called "alarming" by Dr. Dobrynski. Tables 1 and 2 show information concerning major milestones in the growth of the company and selected income statement data.

Table 1

Recent Major Milestones in Company Growth

Year	Sales in $000	No. of Employees	Major Accomplishments
1960	$753	111	Became major producer and distributor of precision electron microscopes.
1961	1,265	208	Became major producer and distributor of electroencephalographs.
1962	2,174	336	Significant increase in sales.
1963	4,261	431	Sales doubled, and market share increased substantially. Developed additional products.
1964	4,570	551	Opened additional sales offices in Miami, New Orleans, and San Francisco.
1965	6,037	748	Significant increase in sales due to new products being developed and introduced. Started enlargement and modernization of production facilities at Stoughton.
1966	9,745	753	Acquired the Medical Science Instrument Corporation. Added disposable laboratory and hospital supply equipment to their existing product lines. Completed modernization and enlargement of Stoughton plant. Established a major distribution center at Boston for the purpose of distributing products to branch offices.
1967	12,944	851	Established a research and development center at Woods Hole for the purpose of R&D for new products. Organized the New Products and Market Analysis Committee for the purpose of planning future growth and to direct the R&D efforts toward the development of new products.
1968	15,670	867	Established foreign branch offices in Latin America (Caracas, Mexico City, San Juan, Lima).
1969	17,845	971	Increased net sales from $753,000 in 1960 to $17,845,000 in 1969.

Table 2

American Scientific Products Company
Income Report and Stockholder Data
Years Ending December 31
(dollars in thousands)

	1969	1968	1967	1966	1965	1964	1963	1962	1961	1960
Net sales	$17,845	$15,670	$12,944	$9,745	$6,037	$4,570	$4,261	$2,174	$1,265	$753
Net earnings before taxes	1,163	709	2,226	2,184	1,138	547	258	268	175	49
Net earnings after taxes	587	355	1,075	1,070	561	258	129	138	89	27
Working capital	6,154	5,691	4,938	3,612	1,733	1,030	726	568	284	150
Long-term debt	610	1,658	1,276	975	25	25	65	40	40	40
Net worth	7,548	5,277	4,206	3,046	2,057	1,452	909	685	427	261
Number of common stockholders	3,143	2,170	1,485	921	717	527	418	314	151	77
Earnings per share	$ .98	$ .80	$ 2.48	$ 2.61	$ 3.00	$ 1.58	$ .79	$ .83	$ .42	$ .11
Dividends on common	100% Stk.	3% Stk.	3% Stk. +50¢	100% Stk. +50¢	.25	.25	.10			

Operations

The company is organized (see Figure 3) along typical functional lines. The facility at Stoughton, where all products are manufactured and assembled, is a modern production plant of 185,000 square feet. It could readily be increased to 225,000 square feet if demand for products created the need for additional capacity.

The company has four basic sources of revenue. The first is the established line of electron microscopes and standard inventory products like electroencephalographs, blood reagent equipment, and flame photometers. The second source is products of Medical Science Instrument Corporation. These are high-volume items with high demand, owing to their disposable features (syringes, laboratory glasswares, specimen containers, etc.). The third source is the sale of spare and replacement parts to existing customers. This market will continue to grow in proportion to the sale of major equipment. The fourth source of revenue, the design and manufacture of specially engineered products in response to requests from customers, has been rising at a rate of approximately 20 percent annually in recent years. Profits real-

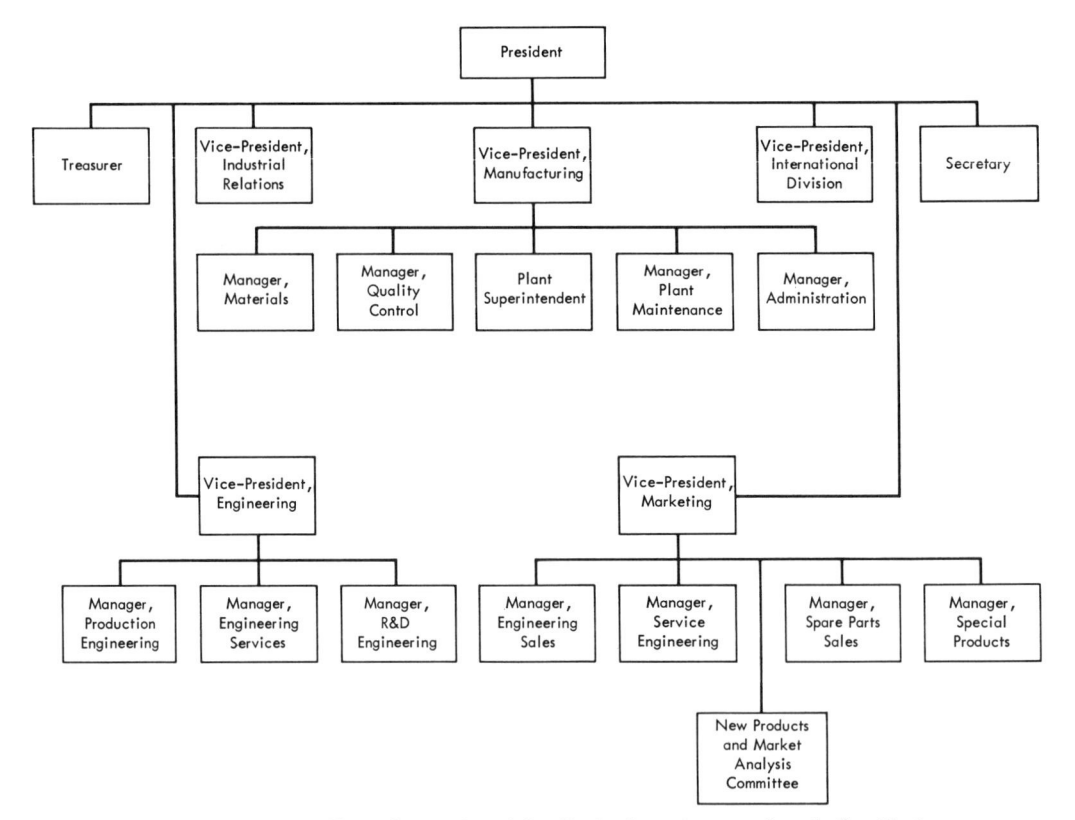

Figure 1 American Scientific Products Company Organization Chart

ized on these custom-designed units are presumed to be substantially lower than on production-line products and spare or replacement parts; therefore, marketing efforts are not concentrated on products of this type.

American Scientific Products Company merchandises its products through its own sales force, having one main and three branch offices in the United States and four in Latin America. The company also uses its research and development center at Woods Hole and main manufacturing plant at Stoughton to good advantage in the sales effort. Prospective customers visiting these locations gain a better appreciation of the products and are better able to verify for themselves their quality. Very often, purchasing agents, pathologists, clinical laboratory technicians, and pharmacologists visit the factory and the R&D center for the purpose of investigating innovative technology in the field of medical or medically related research devices. Moreover, ideas for new products are frequently obtained from these visitors.

A.S.P. has diversified its product line to include a number of new devices, so that it can successfully compete with other manufacturers; but this diversification has presented additional distribution problems. The demand for the newer products is increasing daily, but the distribution method within the present organization has not been too effective. A.S.P. has attempted to merchandise the newer high-demand products through its own sales force as it has done in the past (see below).

Branch Offices—Domestic	No. of Salesmen	Dollar Sales 1969
Boston	69	
Miami	18	
New Orleans	14	
San Francisco	21	
	122	$11.3 million

Branch offices—Foreign	No. of Salesmen	Dollar Sales 1969
Caracas	12	
Mexico City	11	
San Juan	10	
Lima	18	
	51	$6.2 million

Research and Development

Expenses for R&D are considered general engineering expense and are arbitrarily distributed among all company products, a method viewed by management as an equitable system of cost allocation.

The New Products and Market Analysis Committee has as its specific purpose the planning and introduction of new products and the direction of engineering efforts toward the development of these products. Industry statistical analyses by marketing areas are developed in order to concentrate effort in the proper product areas. When the committee locates or uncovers new markets or needs for new products, their findings are coordinated with the Research and Development Department. The R&D engineers then develop the prototype device required by a certain segment of the medical field. As the newly developed product gains acceptance, the sales force is familiarized with the product and its features, and the product is introduced through the salesmen to the medical research field as an A.S.P. innovation.

II

Computer-Based Management Information Systems

Formal structure, motivation, and leadership are not in themselves sufficient to solve the problems of large complex organizations. It is information—both substance and flow—necessary to produce dynamic response to rapidly shifting problems in the modern company that is the life-giving ingredient.

In Part II we will discuss the role of information systems in the management process and then examine management information systems from their bases in computerization and in systems theory. Every modern manager must have an understanding of the functions and capabilities of the digital electronic computer, to enable him to implement complex information systems for planning and control. At the same time, he must understand the elements and characteristics of systems, both informational and operational. Without such understanding on the part of management, the computer will always be a toy instead of a tool.

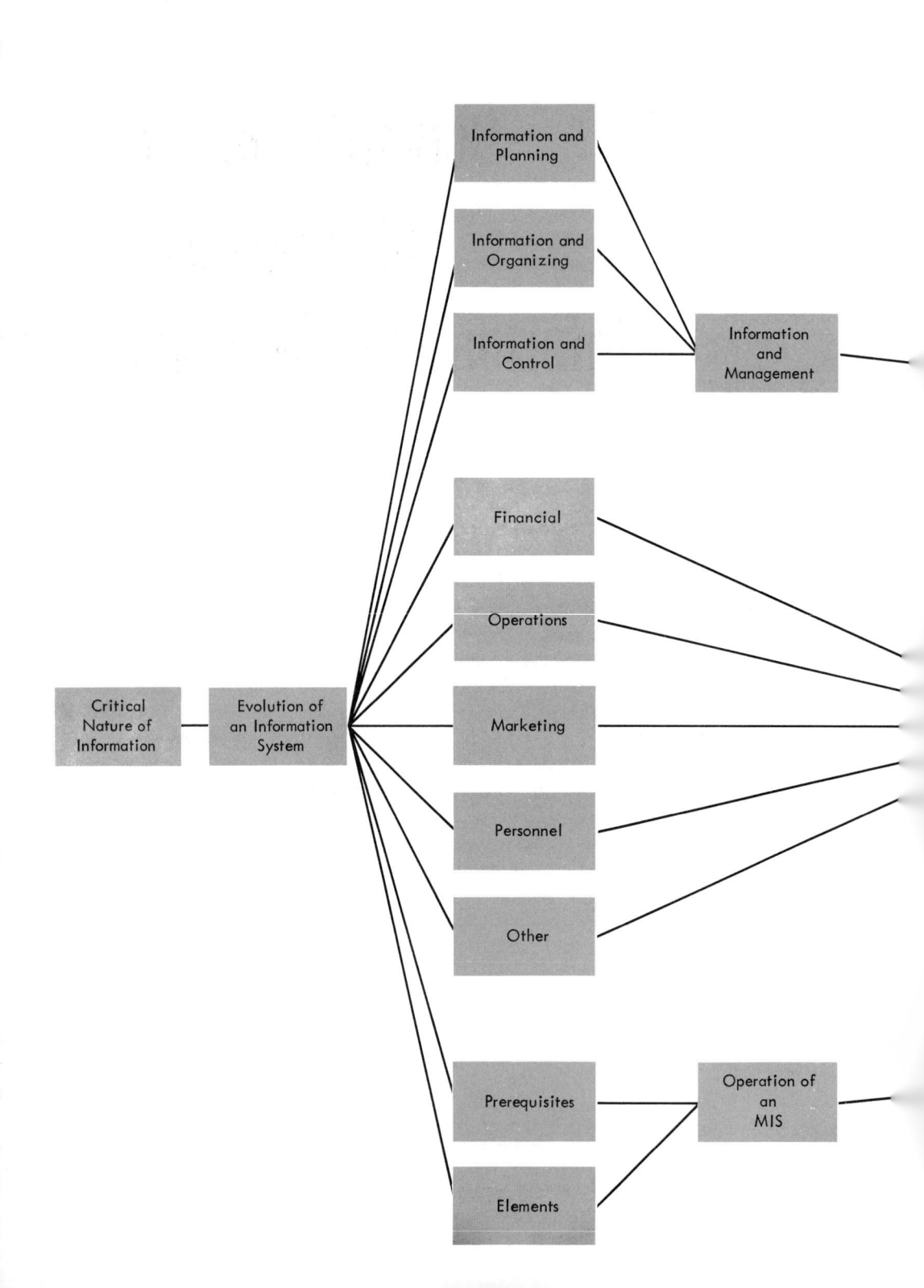

```
                                          ┌─────────────────┐
                                          │  Information and│
                                          │     Planning    │
                                          └─────────────────┘
                                          ┌─────────────────┐
                                          │  Information and│
                                          │    Organizing   │
                                          └─────────────────┘                ┌─────────────┐
                                          ┌─────────────────┐                │ Information │
                                          │  Information and│                │     and     │
                                          │     Control     │                │  Management │
                                          └─────────────────┘                └─────────────┘

                                          ┌─────────────────┐
                                          │    Financial    │
                                          └─────────────────┘
                                          ┌─────────────────┐
┌───────────┐   ┌───────────────┐         │    Operations   │
│ Critical  │   │  Evolution of │         └─────────────────┘
│ Nature of │───│ an Information│─────────┌─────────────────┐
│Information│   │    System     │         │    Marketing    │
└───────────┘   └───────────────┘         └─────────────────┘
                                          ┌─────────────────┐
                                          │    Personnel    │
                                          └─────────────────┘
                                          ┌─────────────────┐
                                          │      Other      │
                                          └─────────────────┘

                                          ┌─────────────────┐                ┌─────────────┐
                                          │  Prerequisites  │                │Operation of │
                                          └─────────────────┘                │     an      │
                                          ┌─────────────────┐                │     MIS     │
                                          │    Elements     │                └─────────────┘
                                          └─────────────────┘
```

5
information systems and management

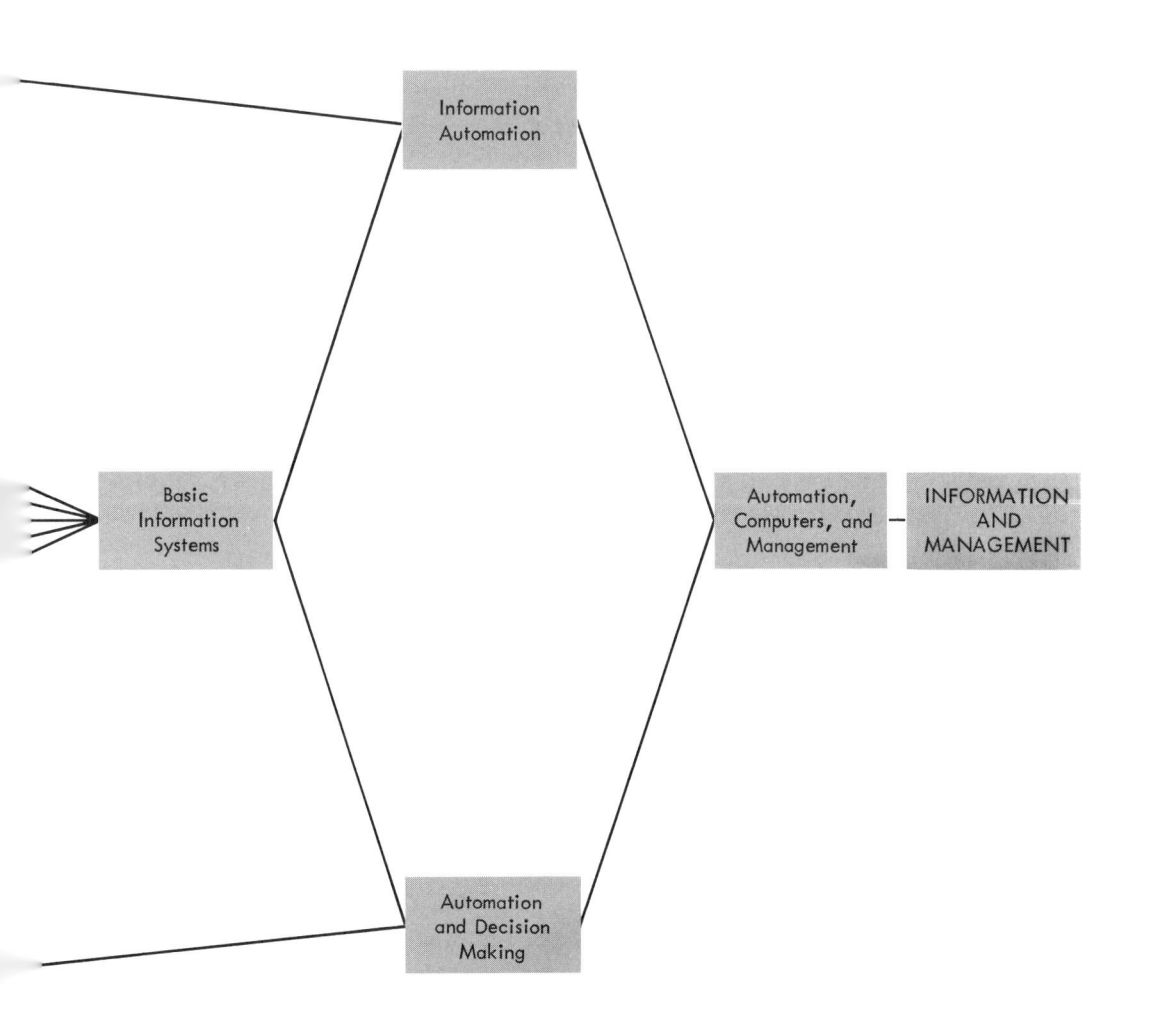

- Basic Information Systems
  - Information Automation
  - Automation and Decision Making
- Automation, Computers, and Management — INFORMATION AND MANAGEMENT

5

"I can't find out what our operating costs are." . . . "We don't know the relative profitability of our product lines." . . . "What would be the impact elsewhere in the company if our sales fell off by 10 percent?" These and similar questions reflect the dependence that managers have upon information, and also the most common complaint of managers—inadequate data for decision making. If there is a problem in the organization, the chances are that no one determined what kind of information was needed to prevent the trouble or took the time to organize a system to provide the information. Although data and information are frequently abundant, they are sometimes not enough of the right kind for setting objectives, evaluating alternatives, making decisions, anticipating problems, and measuring results against plans.

Although the great need for information systems should appear obvious to most managers, it is necessary to underscore their importance. Without information, a business simply cannot survive. This importance has been stated by Steiner: "Information flows are as important to the life and health of a business as the flow of blood is to the life and health of an individual."[1] This applies to small organizations as well as to large ones. Indeed, superior information systems have enabled many small companies to more than offset the economies of scale enjoyed by their bigger competitors.[2]

It has been said that the recipe for a good decision is "90 percent information and 10 percent inspiration." Information is the catalyst of management and the ingredient that coalesces the managerial functions of planning, operating, and controlling. The manager depends on one specific tool, *information,* and although he "gets things done through people," his tool for achieving this is the spoken or written word or the language of numbers. As Norbert Wiener remarked, ". . . any organism is held together by the possession of means for the acquisition, use, retention, and transmission of information."[3]

EVOLUTION OF AN INFORMATION SYSTEM

By examining the basic information needs of a company (large or small) and what constitutes a satisfactory management information system, we can gain a better understanding of how information needs become more complex as organization operations expand and of how information systems may be developed or improved through modification of a manual system or design of a computer-based system.

information systems and management 155

INFORMATION NEEDS
(Internal)

- Accounting control
- Plans and budgets
- Payroll by hourly and salaried groups
- Inventories of materials, in-process and finished goods
- Sales by product, salesman, customer, area
- Purchasing records, vendors, commitments
- Distribution—transportation and warehousing
- Production by product, customer, cost, overruns, backlog
- Engineering—new products, schedules, equipment, costs
- R&D
- etc...etc...etc...

Small Company

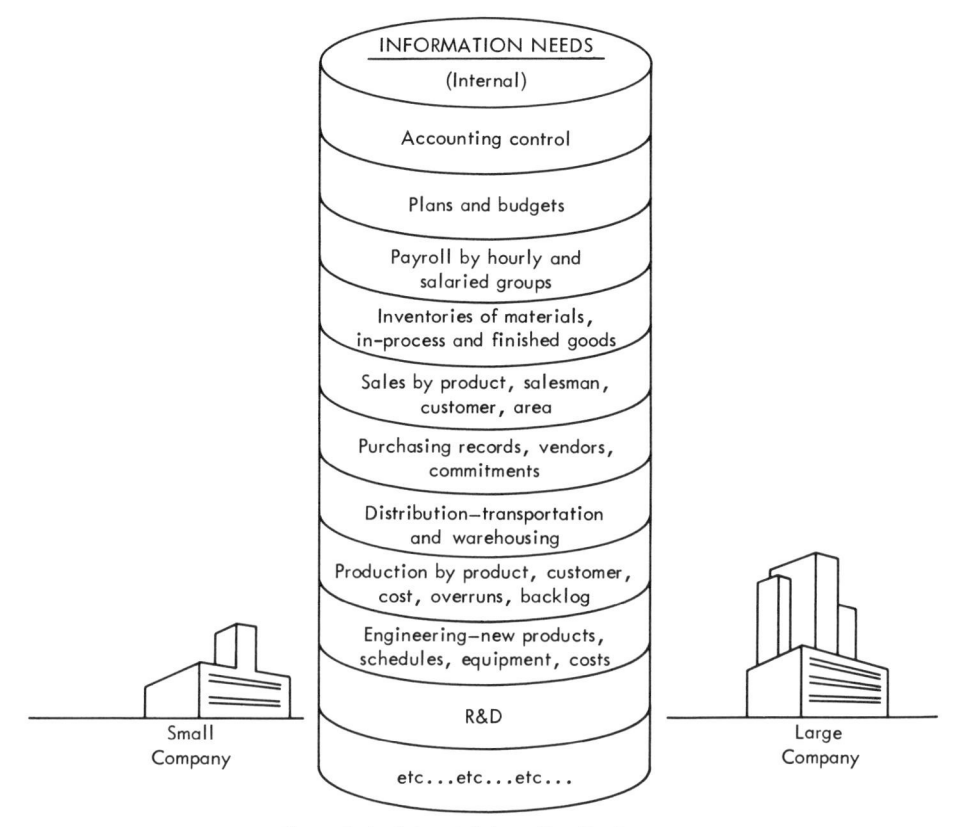

Large Company

Figure 5–1 Internal Information Needs— Large or Small Company

Figure 5–1 portrays some of the basic functions and some of the basic information needs that occur in almost any company, large or small. However, as we shall see, the nature of information required to perform these functions varies with the size and complexity of the company. Figure 5–2 portrays a small company (Owner and Sons) not so many years ago. Mr. Owner is president, proprietor, chief executive, and chairman of the board. Mr. Owner, Jr., is vice-president of sales, director of market research, controller, treasurer, and director of research and development. Their entire work force consists of two helpers.

Figure 5–2 also demonstrates Mr. Owner's complete information processing system. His transaction tickets are skewered on the spindle as the transactions occur. Historical information is contained in storage books on top of Mr. Owner's desk. With this system, upper management has on-line entry into the basic resource records of the company and immediate access to its entire data bank. Cash flow and balance information are within sight in the safe in the corner of the office. There is even an advanced system

Figure 5–2 Owner and Sons Information System

of exception reporting on the blackboard on the washroom door. What Mr. Owner has developed is a *real-time* information system—all information required to run the business is within reaching distance of the president and is available within seconds.*

Times change, however, and Mr. Owner's business has grown into the larger company depicted in Figure 5–3. The functions have remained basically the same, but the volume and complexity of information needs have increased enormously. As with all growing companies, new products are developed, sales volume grows, number of employees increases, factors outside the company become increasingly important, and generally the complexities of the operation expand more rapidly than company size.

---

*As opposed to batch processing, a real-time information system provides response to information inquiries in a time frame short enough to permit the user to shape an ongoing situation or make an immediate decision. The best known illustrations are telephone systems (communications), aerospace systems (command and control), and airline reservation systems (logistics).

This increase in company size results in an increase in information collecting, processing, and distribution. It now becomes necessary to handle many customer accounts and many production records with many more interrelationships. In addition to the increased records, information needs, and associated difficulties, there are now the problems connected with delegation of authority and responsibility. It is now necessary to assign people to supervise other people, and this development expands communication lines and compounds these problems.

As the need for information grows, additional people and equipment must be added to handle the information. Typewriters and calculators are purchased and additional clerks are hired. The next step is to procure tabulating and punched-card equipment. Finally, the first-, second-, and third-generation electronic computers are acquired one after the other in order to take advantage of the latest information-processing technology.

Meanwhile, what has happened to management? Like the other basic functions of the company (production, sales, finance, etc.), management functions have not changed and will not. Management still plans, organizes,

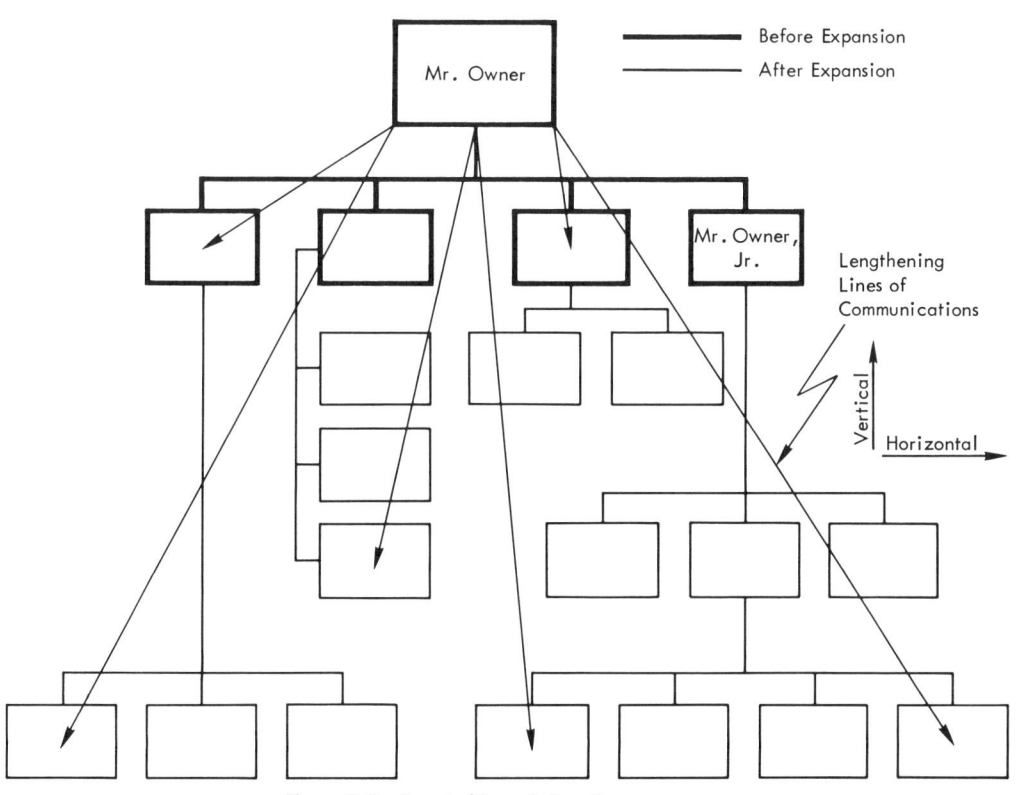

Figure 5–3 Complexities of Growth
(Communication, Delegation, Information)

staffs, directs, and controls. However, the communication network for information has increased fantastically.[4] A succession of delegations of duties and authority has lengthened the lines of communications and increased the complexity of the communication network of Mr. Owner's business a thousandfold. The functions of the company and of its management are essentially the same regardless of size, but the complexities associated with size have vastly increased the need for information in order to manage the organization.

Despite these complexities, the management of the now-larger company would like to be able to operate in the same fashion and with the same information requirements that old Mr. Owner enjoyed. The objective of developing or improving a management information system can be explained largely in terms of the new Mr. Owner's problems: (a) to provide the type of information environment that will integrate the basic operating functions, and (b) to provide management with access to information relative to complex activities in decentralized organizations. Both (a) and (b) need to be done with approximately the same ease that Mr. Owner enjoyed in his small operation with four persons and the information system contained in his rolltop desk.

It is apparent that change will continue to take place in management and in the operation of organizations. To handle the changes properly, the manager of the 1970's must learn what to do with information in order to deal with the resultant increased complexity. In other words, the manager must be prepared to take an active part in the design and installation of management information systems. This is worth repeating: *the manager must be prepared to take an active part in the design and installation of management information systems.*

ELEMENTS AND OPERATION OF THE MANAGEMENT INFORMATION SYSTEM (MIS)

It should be clear at this point that the management information system is the catalyst and the nerve center of the organization. Moreover, it is the common system that permits the four other resource systems (money, manpower, materials, machines and facilities) to function as an integrated whole. It performs this integrative role in four ways: (1) it provides information among all four systems regarding the impact of each on the whole; (2) it establishes sensors and control measures for data acquisition required by the other four systems; (3) it maintains central data banks relative to the decision processes of the other four systems; and (4) it generates output information on demand and on an exception basis that reflects the operation of all systems, including the management information system.

The four other systems controlled by the information system are physical; they control real phenomena of money, manpower, materials, and machines and facilities. Conversely, the information system is artificial in the sense that it controls the real world through artificial means—information developed through symbol manipulation. Therefore, to the extent that decision makers rely on the information system to control the real inputs of the organizational system, the information system itself must be properly planned and controlled so that its symbolic representation does not vary from the real activities and events themselves. In other words, the elements and operation of an information system should be planned and designed in the same way as the real systems it represents or controls.

Prerequisites of an Information System

What are the prerequisites of a modern, effective information system, and what must exist before it can be put together? The most fundamental prerequisite, of course, is *knowledge*. The word *managing* implies that knowledge (information) exists about an organization's objectives, its environment, its operations, its resources, its policies, and its procedures. This type of information represents the why, what, where, and how of the company's managerial operations and processes.

All companies have information stored in one form or another, whether it is in the mind of the manager, in accounting records, in filing cabinets, or on a computer. But in order to have a management information system, these data must be organized in a manner appropriate to the problem at hand, and they must be able to be recorded, stored, retrieved, and displayed as required for purposes of decision making.

The second element required for a modern management information system is the necessary *hardware* for storage, processing, and retrieval of information. This requirement is satisfied by: (1) the capability for economical, rapid access to large-scale storage of retrievable data, (2) economical, high-speed processors for this data, and (3) communications devices for entering and displaying information.

These two prerequisites, hardware and information, are available to all companies. There is no question but that computer technology provides the capabilities for information handling and that all companies have information of one sort or another. However, not all have the third basic prerequisite—*information management*.

Men, money, materials, and machines and facilities have always been considered the basic resources of production and the basic factors with which management is concerned. Each of these has a body of knowledge surrounding it and a set of principles devoted to its management. A fifth resource, now recognized as equally important, is *information*. The effective use of information has become as important as the effective use of any resource in the company. Indeed, the extent to which the classic resources are well managed is a function of how well information is managed. It also becomes clear that since information must be treated as a vital resource, then the corporate-wide acquisition, protection, dissemination, and utilization of this vital resource must be managed and controlled. This is *information management*.

Elements of a Management Information System (MIS)

We have previously defined a system in terms of a process comprising a set of elements that are functionally and operationally united in the pursuit of an objective. In the case of the MIS the objective is the design of a flow of information for decision making. The system elements are: procedures, equipment, information methods, people, organization, and money (as a yardstick of operational efficiency and information value). Major considerations surrounding each of these elements are discussed below.

Methods and Procedures. This term refers to the detailed instructions for delineating duties, responsibilities, and operations. These are also the formal instructions for operating the system. Among the most important procedures are those concerning the integration of individual subsystems that are related and comparable. Such integration should not overlook the flexibility required to assimilate new systems that arise as a result of new problems.

Procedures and instructions should also cover the tasks to be performed and the general instructions necessary for performance. Included here would be such important tasks as preparation of input/output documents, detailing of program flowcharts and computer programs, and the operation of the system once it is installed.

Equipment. The most notable catalyst for improved management information systems in the future will be the computer and related equipment. Design of the modern information system must take account of the economical utilization of this equipment. This is not to imply that computers alone make a system or that the company with up-to-date equipment necessarily has a good information system. Equipment is by no means the whole story. Management involvement in systems design and the application of computers in higher-level managerial problems are among the other considerations that go to make up a good environment for information systems. However, the computer is the catalyst, and planning for its use is essential.

Information. Information is the single most important consideration in the design and operation of an MIS. The system should provide information rather than facts. It should provide the relevant and omit the irrelevant data. Relevant data are those concerned with the environment and operational elements of the organization that contribute most to its success or failure. These elements should be identified and built into the system. Moreover, the futuristic nature of planning information should be distinguished from the more immediate need for control data. Finally, the system should be designed and operated to provide information that is timely and complete. Information is complete if it relates to critical areas of decision making and if it covers the financial as well as nonfinancial considerations. Additionally, it should relate to the long- as well as short-run considerations.

Organization. The design and operation of an MIS should relate not only to the organization of its own processes but to the overall organization of the total system (company) of which it is a part. With regard to the information system, it should be organized on an integrated basis so that levels of information and subsystems tie together into a consistent body of information. Moreover, the structure of the system should conform to the structure of the organization of the firm. Two requirements are implied by this structure. First, the system should match the delegation of authority of the organization, so that planning and control information is related to the organizational units responsible for performance. Second, the information in the system should be structured in such a way that it reflects *levels* of management and hence of detail. The timing, degree of detail, and purpose of systems design may change as the system is organized to serve different levels in the organizational hierarchy. This should be reflected in design.

Money. The financial plan and the accounting system attest to the fact that most of the information in a firm has the dollar as the common denominator. However, we are concerned here with money as a measure of the value of information in order that costs can be taken into account in MIS design and operation. Despite the growing importance of information, there is today no set of principles available that will permit us to balance the cost of getting information against the value of using it. Neither is there available a method for comparing the cost of information against the value received from considering additional courses of action as a result of the information.[5] In fact, we are spending more and more money on computers and information systems with the apparent result that most executives realize they are not getting their money's worth from these investments.[6]

Relevance, timeliness, and accuracy are often listed as desirable attributes of information. However, these are difficult to "cost." It appears that the best measure of performance in MIS operations lies in the organization of the function itself. A growing number of companies are establishing information systems operations (including EDP) as centralized, independent, and profit-oriented units of the regular organization. In this way the outputs from their service can be measured in terms similar to other producing units of the company.[7] As we move the boundaries of systems design from the simple (e.g., batch processing) to the more complex (e.g., real time), the expense increases rather severely. The design of better systems as well as the operation of existing ones should be compared with their effectiveness in use. If necessary, trade-offs must be made between cost and benefits.[8]

Organization on a profit-center basis will improve the identification of costs and benefits.

People. The people element is the least predictable, the least subject to control, but the most important of all the elements in a management information system. Although the human problems and the behavioral aspects of adapting to change are monumental, we must forego these considerations at this time.[9] We are most concerned here with two groups and their participation in design and operation. These groups are (1) those who design and operate the information systems—the analysts and computer technicians; and (2) the manager–users of these systems.

Steiner has identified what is perhaps the single most important principle surrounding people and information systems: "... in the development of information systems the technical interest of staff experts must be submerged to the interest of managers, but the two must cooperate in developing systems."[10] This implies, first, that managers should not abdicate their responsibility for systems design to technical operators, and second, that it is incumbent upon computer people to learn something about the functions of management and the manager's need for information for planning and control. Management must learn to control the computer or the computer will control it.[11]

There is little doubt that the single greatest hurdle to overcome in obtaining better information systems is the people involved, users and computer technicians. The serious "communication gap" existing between the two groups is due in large part to the fact that neither understands the needs of the other. Part of the solution lies in education. The manager needs to have a greater knowledge of the capabilities of computers and the improved management results that computer systems can offer.[12] On the other hand, the technician should learn more about the management process and the needs of the manager–user so that he can design and operate systems that fulfill these needs.[13]

Operation of a Management Information System

The design of a system involves the arrangement of its elements and components in some combination to produce a desired objective. To illustrate, take the elementary inventory accounting system of Figure 5–4. This system is designed to update master inventory records and to prepare inventory status reports. The elements include procedures, equipment, information, and people. Components of the system are input, processor, output, and control.

After its elements are arranged in a design, the system is ready to operate. Inputs of information (both data and planning information) are processed according to plan into an output. The output represents the ob-

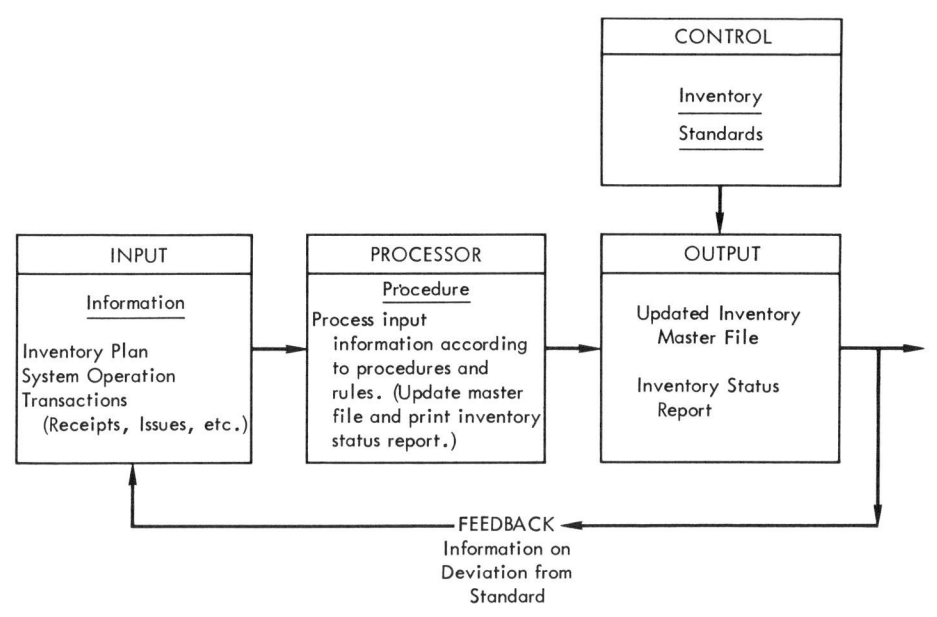

Figure 5-4 Components of an Inventory Accounting System

```
                              ┌─────────────────┐
                              │    CONTROL      │
                              │    Inventory    │
                              │    Standards    │
                              └────────┬────────┘
                                       │
                                       ▼
┌──────────────┐   ┌──────────────────┐   ┌──────────────────┐
│    INPUT     │   │   PROCESSOR      │   │     OUTPUT       │
│  Information │   │   Procedure      │   │ Updated Inventory│
│Inventory Plan│──▶│ Process input    │──▶│   Master File    │──▶
│System Oper.  │   │ information acc. │   │                  │
│Transactions  │   │ to procedures and│   │ Inventory Status │
│(Receipts,    │   │ rules. (Update   │   │      Report      │
│ Issues, etc.)│   │ master file and  │   │                  │
└──────▲───────┘   │ print inventory  │   └────────┬─────────┘
       │           │ status report.)  │            │
       │           └──────────────────┘            │
       │                                           │
       └─────────────── FEEDBACK ◀─────────────────┘
                       Information on
                       Deviation from
                       Standard
```

jective and the achievement for which the system was designed. In the inventory accounting system, there will be inputs of information regarding the plan for the system (e.g., maintain inventory levels), data concerning the operation of the system (deliveries, issues, prices, quantities), and transactions. The inputs are processed according to the plan and the procedure of the operation. For example, the supervisor of inventory control may determine the type of format for the input transaction, the output report format, the periods during which inventory will be updated, and the number of transactions to be posted daily.

Another essential component of the MIS is some means of *control*. Should the output of the system exceed the established control limits, a sensor is necessary to compare output with a standard and take the necessary action to adjust inputs to correct the deficiency. Stabilization of systems output within desired limits can be achieved only (1) if output can be measured against a standard, and (2) if some feedback mechanism is provided for furnishing this corrective information, either as input to the system or directly to the processor for deficiency correction. In complex systems involving exchange of information among subsystems, sensory devices are placed at strategic decision points in the system flow in order to measure output against standard.

The concept of how a management information system operates in the context of the "total system" of the organization is depicted in Figure 5–5. *Notice that the information flow for the information system is inte-*

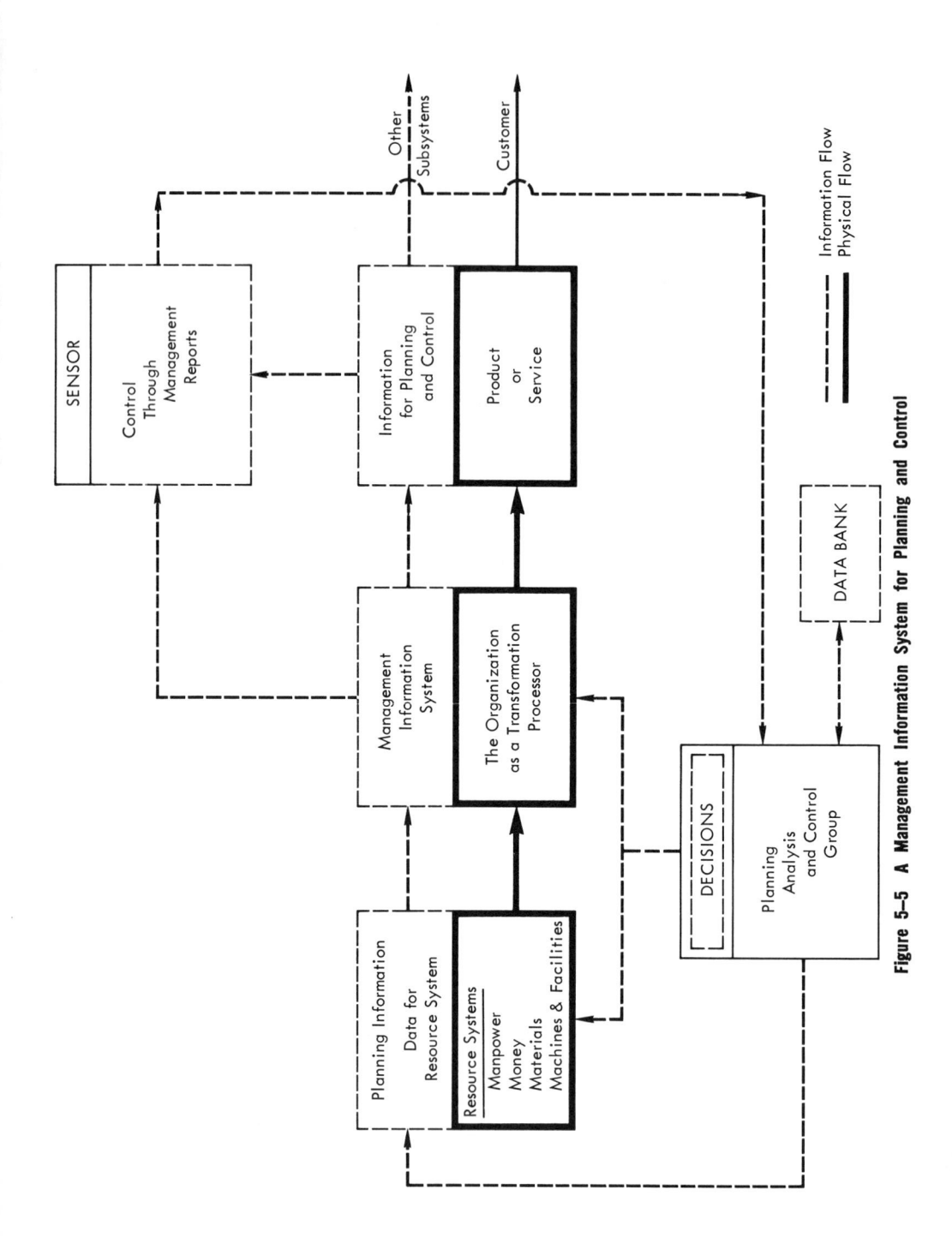

Figure 5–5 A Management Information System for Planning and Control

grated with the four other resource flows (money, manpower, materials, and machines and facilities) to provide a system of planning and control for the entire organization. Both the planning information and the data for the specific system provide inputs that are transformed by the processor into an output whose objective is to provide information for planning and control.

Sensors must be developed to measure the attributes of the output as well as the attributes of the transformation process. We will call these sensors *control*. A part of the control component contains management reports that track the status of the output relative to a predetermined standard of performance for the transformation process.

If the results being achieved in the organizational system (as opposed to the information system) do not conform to standard, this information is fed to the *planning analysis and control* component, which makes decisions regarding one or both of two actions: (1) alternative resource allocations are made as system input changes, or (2) modifications are made in the transformation process. Either or both of these decisions may be taken, based upon decision rules or data stored in the central data base.

If the inventory accounting illustration of Figure 5–4 represented the system of Figure 5–5, its operation could be outlined as follows:

1. The *objectives* of the system are: (a) inventory levels should not vary from established limits, and (b) sufficient inventory should be on hand to meet customer demand.
2. The *planning information* of the system includes inventory policies, levels, and procedures for the design and operation of the system.
3. The *input* to the system is information regarding the transactions that take place.
4. *System design* includes the organization of people, equipment, money, and procedures to process the information.
5. The *processing* of the system involves the processing of the transactions with programs and procedures.
6. *Control* consists of measuring inventory levels as reported by the *output* of inventory status reports against the *standards* of inventory policies and predetermined decision rules regarding inventory levels. Note that under this system as presently designed there is no output of the information system that provides a measure of performance against the objective of meeting customer demand.
7. Information concerning deviations from standards that are outside control limits is provided to the planning analysis and control component through *feedback*—an essential element of the *control* component.

The fundamental notion behind the operation of any system is the concept of feedback and control. Essentially, control monitors the resource flows through the system and signals the need for action when output does not conform to the original plan. The feedback loop operation of control provides correction of resource inputs or transformation process; in sophisticated systems this loop may be automatic and capable of providing self-correction. Although all management information systems ultimately require human intervention in the control and correction process, design efforts should be devoted to reducing this intervention to a minimum.

INFORMATION AND MANAGEMENT

Many organizations and managers make the basic mistake of believing that a management *information* system can be designed or made operational without the backup of an adequate *management* system. An adequate management system includes organizational arrangements, structure and procedures for adequate planning and control, clear establishment of objectives, and all the other manifestations of good organization and management. Given this management structure, this framework of good management practices, an information system can be designed upon its foundation. Only then can the information system provide the manager with the information he needs in the form, place, and time that he needs it in order to perform his job according to the specifications of the *management* system.

The purpose of the management system is to develop plans for achieving objectives, to organize for implementing plans, and to control performance so that plans and actions occur on schedule. The place of information in performing these three basic processes is shown in Figure 5–6. The first step, recognition of a problem or an opportunity, is usually prompted by information from the control process concerning a deviation from standard or by search and evaluation of those systems (environmental, competitive, internal) affecting the planning process. Definition of the problem, determination and evaluation of alternative courses of action, and selection of a course of action are fundamentally steps in the planning and decision-making process. Information needs for this process are those indicated in Figure 5–6. Finally, once a decision is made or a plan developed, it is necessary to *implement* and *control* the solution. Implementation becomes a matter of organizing the necessary resources and directing them in the performance of the plan. Control involves the measurement of performance and correction of deviations. The process starts over again either by a recognition of the need for planning or by the appearance of a new problem arising from the control process.

Information and Planning

Planning is the most basic of all the management functions because it involves the selection of organizational and departmental objectives and the determination of the means to achieve these objectives. Essentially, planning

information systems and management

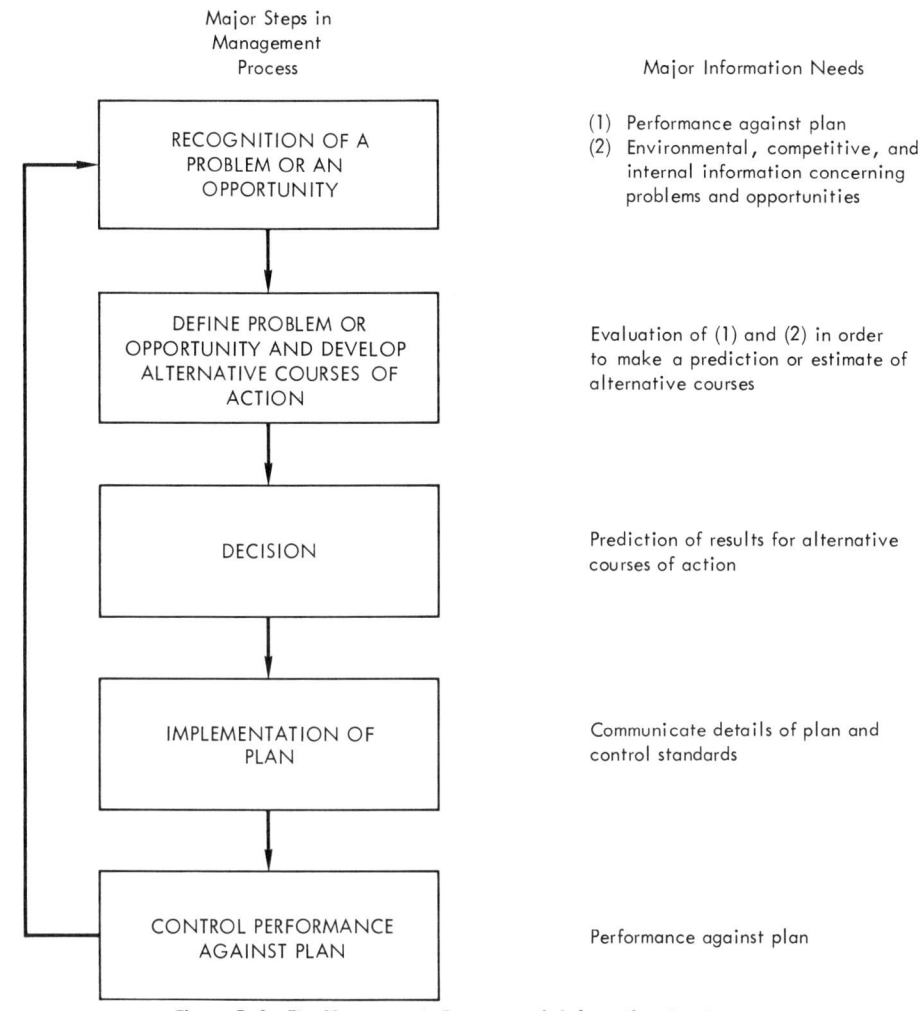

Major Steps in Management Process	Major Information Needs
RECOGNITION OF A PROBLEM OR AN OPPORTUNITY	(1) Performance against plan (2) Environmental, competitive, and internal information concerning problems and opportunities
DEFINE PROBLEM OR OPPORTUNITY AND DEVELOP ALTERNATIVE COURSES OF ACTION	Evaluation of (1) and (2) in order to make a prediction or estimate of alternative courses
DECISION	Prediction of results for alternative courses of action
IMPLEMENTATION OF PLAN	Communicate details of plan and control standards
CONTROL PERFORMANCE AGAINST PLAN	Performance against plan

Figure 5–6 The Management Process and Information Needs

is the same whether applied to an entire organization or to any hierarchical level in it. Planning generally involves five steps or processes:

1. Establishing objectives for the entire organization and each unit in it.
2. Developing planning premises—facts, data, and information that provide the critical planning assumptions surrounding alternatives.
3. Determining alternative courses of action for achieving the objective. There are always two or more alternatives, or there is no planning or decision making involved.
4. Evaluating alternative courses of action.
5. Choosing the course of action that is best in terms of the planning criteria that will achieve the objective.

It is evident that the second step in the planning process—developing planning premises—and all subsequent steps depend entirely upon the availablity and utilization of critical planning information. It is hard to imagine the manager trying to develop any of the major types of plans by function, level, purpose, or time element, without first gathering the necessary planning premises that permit adequate evaluation of alternative courses of action to achieve the plan.

The planning information needs of an organization can be classified into three broad types: (1) environmental, (2) competitive, and (3) internal. Because these are so important in the planning process and in the design of an information system for planning, it is desirable that each category be considered in some detail. Conceptually, planning premises can be viewed as shown in Figure 5–7.

Environmental Information

Environmental information needs can be classified and described as follows:[14]

1. *Political and governmental considerations.* Some information on political stability, at whatever level of government, is important for forecasting plans. Additionally, the nature and extent of government controls and their effect on the organization must be taken into account. A third factor is the important role played by government financial and tax policies; they have a very significant effect on many planning decisions.

2. *Demographic and social trends.* The products, services, or outputs

ENVIRONMENTAL INFORMATION
    Politics and government
    Demographic and social trends
    Economic trends
    Technological environment
    Factors of production

COMPETITIVE INFORMATION
    Industry demand
    Firm demand
    Competition
        Past performance
        Present activity
        Future plans

INTERNAL INFORMATION

Sales Forecast

Supply Factors

Financial Plan

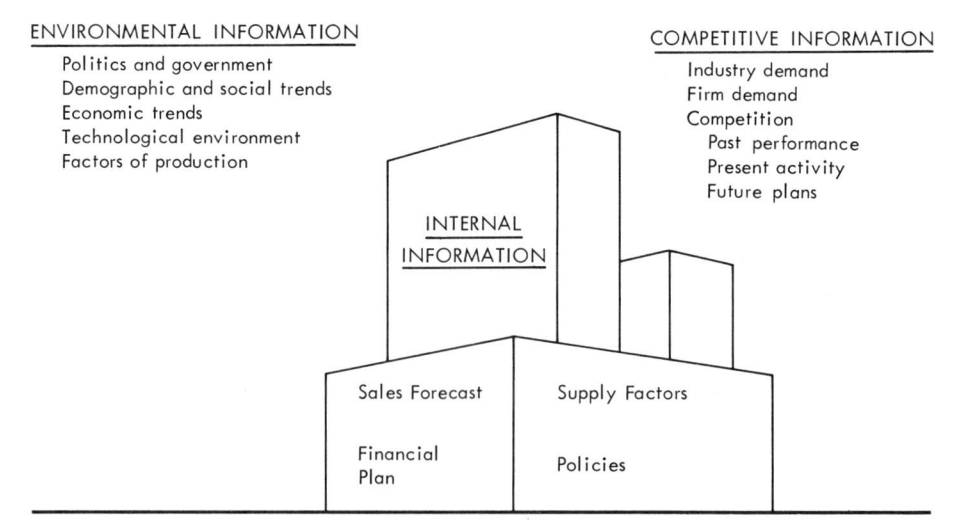

Policies

Figure 5–7 Planning Premises

of most firms and organizations are affected by the totals, composition, or location of the population. Social trends and consumer buying behavior are important. It is necessary therefore to forecast trends for both the short and long run in this critical area.

3. *Economic trends.* Included herein would be (a) the GNP level and trend, and consumer disposable income, which are significant for almost all organizations; (b) employment, productivity, capital investment, and numerous other economic indicators that provide valuable planning information for those firms whose output is a function of these important variables; and (c) price and wage levels, whose effects are vital to almost all organizations regardless of product or service.

4. *Technological environment.* Because of accelerating technical changes and their effect on new products and processes, it becomes necessary or desirable for many firms to forecast the technological changes in their industry and the probable effect on the firm. Firms like TRW, Inc., forecast key technological advances in all fields for a period of twenty years.

5. *Factors of production.* These include source, cost, location, availability, accessibility, and productivity of the major production factors of: (a) labor, (b) materials and parts, and (c) capital.

Competitive Information

Information concerning factors that affect the operation of the firm within an industry includes data concerning industry and firm demand as well as data on the competitors. Three types to consider are:

1. *Industry demand.* Because the sales and the corresponding level of operations for any single firm are largely a function of the level of demand for the given industry it is a part of, the firm must forecast the demand for that area or industry.

2. *Firm demand.* The demand for products of an individual firm is a function of the industry demand and the capabilities and activities of the individual firm relative to the capabilities and actions of competing firms.

3. *The competition.* Data on competing firms are very important for forecasting individual demands and making decisions and plans to achieve the forecast. This information generally falls into three types: (a) *Past performance*—profitability, return on investment, share of the market and similar data help to identify competitors and may also provide a yardstick for setting performance objectives for the individual firm. (b) *Present activity*—developments concerning the competition that will affect the planning process. Such developments may include price strategy, advertising campaigns, new product introductions, changes in distribution channels, and so on. (c) *Future plans*—information concerning new products, acquisitions, R&D efforts, and other plans that affect the individual firm's future.

Internal Information

Because internal premises affect the planning decisions of so many levels in the organization, in some respects they are more important than the external information. Though the business environment and premises surrounding competition are no doubt very important, these categories of information are, after all, considered necessary for decision making by relatively few managers in a firm, mainly top managers and marketing managers. However, internal planning premises are vital for subsidiary planning at all levels in the organization. A budget or a sales forecast, once adopted, becomes essential planning data for a variety of subsequent and connecting plans.

As they relate to the total planning process, internal data are aimed at an identification of the organization's strengths and weaknesses—the external constraints that, when viewed in the perspective of external information, are vital decision-making premises that help managers shape future plans. It is useful to think of internal premises as being of the following types:

1. *Sales forecast.* This is perhaps the single most important planning document in the organization, because the allocation of the entire company's resources is a function of the sales plan. It sets the framework on which most other internal plans are constructed and can therefore be regarded as the dominant planning premise internal to the firm.

2. *The financial plan.* This plan, frequently called the budget, is second only to the sales forecast in importance. In many ways, the financial plan preempts the sales forecast because it represents a quantitative and time commitment of the allocation of the *total resources* of the company (manpower, plant, capital, materials, overhead, and general and administrative expenses). Properly constructed, the financial plan involves the entire organization and, when completed, provides subsidiary planning information for a variety of subplans throughout the company. It is a system that links all activities of the company together.

3. *Supply factors.* Manpower, capital, plant and equipment, organization, and other supply factors are vital planning premises that provide constraints or boundaries within which planning takes place. These factors are controllable to a large extent by the firm, but their availability and limitations must be taken into account in developing the financial plan and subsidiary plans for achieving objectives.

4. *Policies.* Basic policies are relatively fixed for long-run purposes and cannot readily be changed to permit flexibility in developing alternative courses of action in the short run. To the extent that product, marketing, financial, personnel, and other basic policies are unchangeable in the short run, they provide constraints to planning in much the same way as do supply factors.

The Planning Information System

In order to have a system of information to support its planning process, the organization needs a set of management reports that regularly cover the classification of planning premises outlined: environmental, competitive, and internal. This need calls for the design of a planning information system that formalizes and makes regular reports of planning information.

In that vital first step of designing a planning information system—determination of information needs—it is essential to relate the types of planning data listed (or whatever the classification scheme adopted) to the steps in the planning process. The raison d'être of the information system is to facilitate this process, so it is only natural to design the system around the steps of: establishing objectives, determining alternative courses of action, evaluating alternative courses of action, and choosing the course of action that will achieve the objective. This is illustrated by the management cycle as shown in Figure 4–3. The complexity of the planning process and the supportive information system may also be inferred from the strategic planning concept shown in Figure 4–4.

Information and Organizing

Organization structure and information needs are inextricably interwoven. In an analogy between an organization and the human body, the organization *structure* can be compared to the human anatomy and the *information* to the nervous system.

The systems view of the organization takes into account the integrative nature of information flows. This concept is demonstrated in Figure 5–8, where each organizational entity is seen as an information system with the components of input, processor, and output. Each is connected to the others through information and communication channels and each organizational entity becomes a decision point.

Information also affects organizing by the manner in which information systems are designed. These should conform to the organizational structure and the delegation of authority within the company. Only then can each organizational unit's objective be established and its contribution to company-wide goals be measured. This means that organizations must be designed around information flow and those factors of information chosen to plan and control performance. Frequently organizational structure and performance reporting do not coincide. In these cases information systems cannot truly reflect plans and results of operations.

Another major cause of organizational and information mismatch is the lag between organizational changes and information systems to facilitate them. As needs, structure, and managers change, the information system should be changed to support them. Rarely does one find a change in informational systems matching a change in organizational responsibilities and the needs of managers. The result is often an "information lag."

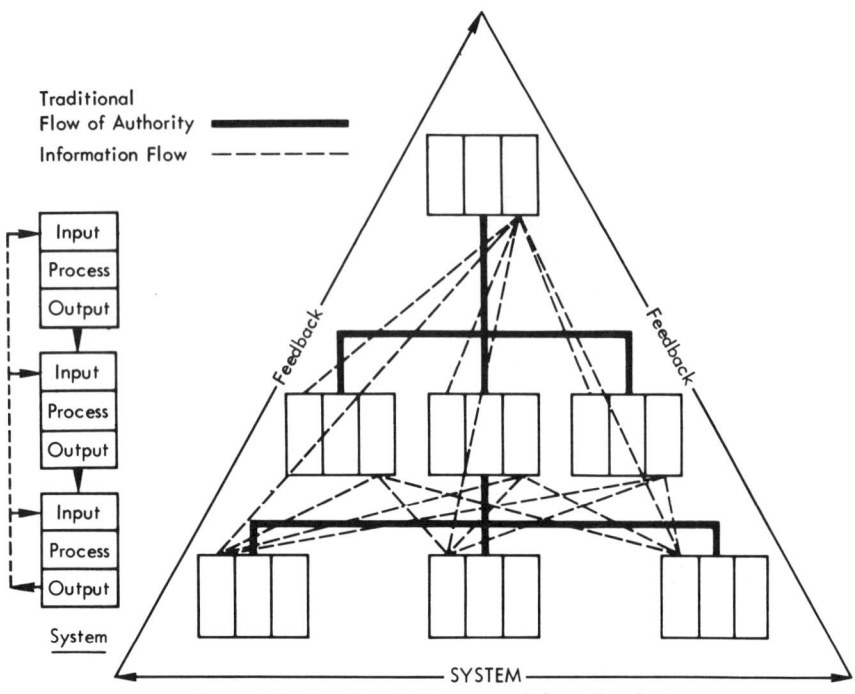

Figure 5–8 The Organization as an Information System

Information and Control

If we accept the definition that control is (a) setting standards of performance, (b) measuring performance against the standard, and (c) correcting deviations, then by definition the control process cannot be performed without information. Standards of performance are a part of any good plan, and hence determination of standards, like other aspects of the planning process, depends on obtaining relevant information. It is obvious that performance against standard cannot be measured unless some type of communication, report, or information on actual performance is supplied to the controlling individual.

Information required to perform control is different in both type and characteristic from information needed for planning. Planning places greater emphasis on structuring the future; control is based more on the immediate past and specific trends. Generally, *control* information can be classified into the following types:

1. *Market.* Information concerning the progress of the sales plan: quotas, territories, pricing, and the like. In other words, market information is basically that required to measure performance against the sales forecast. In addition, control information may be obtained in other areas of the marketing plan, such as product acceptance, advertising, market research, and distribution costs.
2. *Manufacturing.* Control information that measures performance against the manufacturing financial plan. This category covers control

of quantity and quality of direct labor, materials, overhead, and inventories. Control is also concerned greatly with the time aspect in the production system.
3. *Personnel* and various control reports concerning performance of personnel as well as the personnel function (staffing, recruiting, training, etc.).
4. *Financial.* This comprehensive category of control information concerns performance against the financial plan (profitability, costs, etc.) and information surrounding cash flow (credits and collections, tax, cash budget, etc.).
5. *Research, development, and engineering.*

The different characteristics of planning and control data reflect the difference in the nature of the two functions—time, futurity, comprehensiveness, and so on.

Information Systems and Management—Summary

Although we have attempted to examine information as it affects each of the major management functions of planning, organizing, and controlling, these functions cannot be separated; they are inextricably linked both functionally and by a common system of information. These systems characteristics of integration and linkage are shown in Figure 5–9. It can be seen that

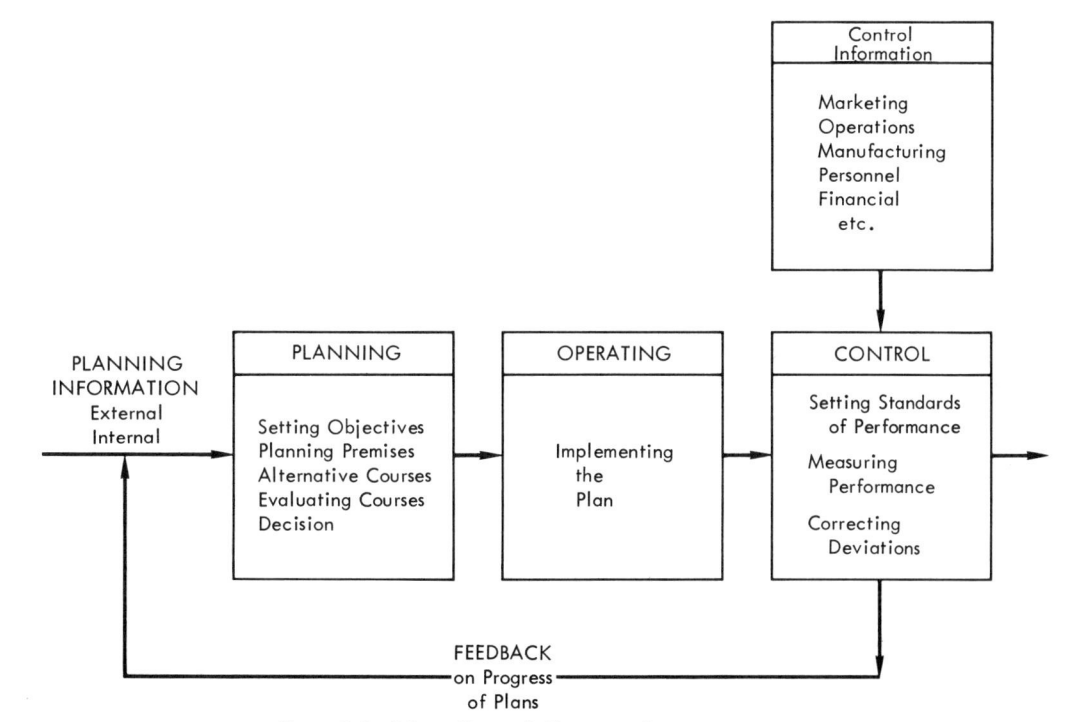

Figure 5–9 Information and Management

although the inputs of planning and of control information are basically different, the planning that results affects subsequent control, and the action and information processing resulting from control provide in turn a feedback that affects the planning process.

Figure 5–10 represents the three subsystems of planning, operating, and controlling integrated into the system of management. Shown also is the basic flow of information for operation of the integrated system. The planning system receives as input the planning premises and objectives, from which we get the output of management plans. These plans in turn provide the input to the operating system, which utilizes them as premises for the organization that attempts to achieve the plans. A basic output of the operating system is performance against plan, and information concerning this performance is in turn provided as input to the control system.

Feedback on performance is obtained through the control system, which monitors the operating system and furnishes feedback information to it as well as to the planning system. Decisions are made within each system based upon information, and within each system there is a flow of information to implement changes and correct deviations based on feedback from

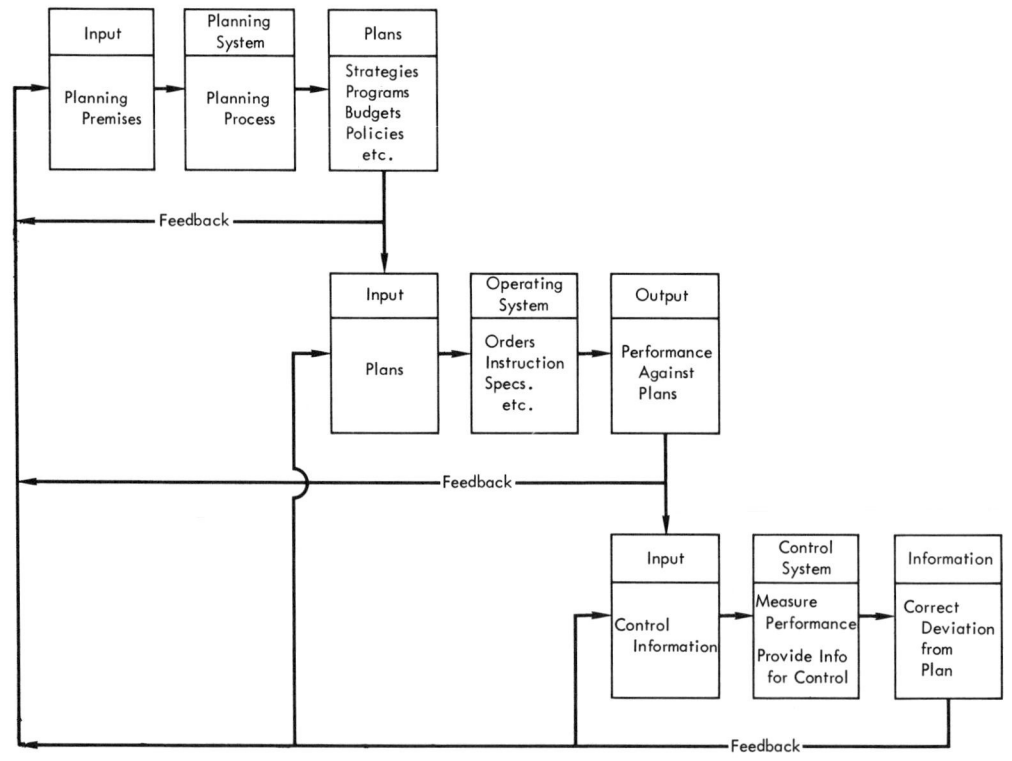

Figure 5–10 Information Flow in the Management Process (Planning System, Operating System, Control System)

other systems. It is evident that the key to success in planning, organizing, and controlling lies in the information–decision system. It follows that success in achieving the goals and objectives of the organization lies similarly in performing these managerial functions through the vehicle of properly designed management information systems.

BASIC INFORMATION SYSTEMS

Although many companies and organizations are making valiant efforts to extend computer applications from areas now considered proven and routine, nevertheless the bulk of information systems (manual or computer based) remain in the categories discussed in this chapter. The gathering and dissemination of information is usually the company's most difficult problem. Information is voluminous, scattered, and often difficult to obtain. If managers become embroiled in paperwork, they have no time for evaluation, planning, or decision making. Their workday is fraught with searches for information to handle the various crises that arise in addition to the normal work flow.

Over time the typical company has developed the major information systems shown in Table 5–1 to provide planning, operating, and control information to decision makers throughout the organization. These major systems are: (1) financial, (2) production or operations, (3) marketing, (4) personnel, (5) project control, and (6) other minor systems. As we will show, these systems are not separate and distinct; they connect, interact, and otherwise tie the subsystems of the organization together through the medium of information. Note also in Table 5–1 that although these major systems serve to integrate the basic functions of planning, operating, and controlling, most are designed and utilized primarily for one or two of these functions. Although virtually all planning information can be used for subsequent control, we are concerned here with major uses.

Financial Information[15]

All companies have some kind of financial information system; this category of information is the most common in use today. The basis of the system is the flow of dollars throughout the organization, and if they are designed correctly, the profitability and responsibility accounting systems follow the organization structure. These systems involve large amounts of data concerned primarily with historical and internal information, although in some areas of financial planning, the system provides the futuristic look associated with planning. Budgeting is wholly futuristic.

By and large, the conversion of a *manual* financial system to a *computer-based* system is subject to less improvement as a managerial device than are other types of information systems. From a data-handling and cost

Table 5–1

Major Information Systems and Subsystems

SUBSYSTEM	Planning	Operating	Control
FINANCIAL			
Cash budgeting	x	x	
Capital budgeting	x		x
Cost accounting	x		x
Profit planning	x	x	x
Responsibility accounting	x	x	x
Profitability accounting	x	x	
PRODUCTION/OPERATIONS			
Production planning	x	x	x
Inventory	x	x	x
Purchasing	x	x	x
Distribution	x	x	x
MARKETING			
Sales planning	x		
Sales and invoicing		x	
Sales analysis	x		x
Credit control			x
Market research	x		
PERSONNEL			
Personnel records	x	x	
Payroll		x	
Employment		x	
Placement		x	
Training		x	
Material and maintenance		x	
PROJECT CONTROL			
PERT/CPM, cost, time, etc.	x	x	x
OTHER			
R&D	x		
Strategic planning	x		x
Simulation	x		

point of view, financial systems are usually the first candidates for conversion, but there is less opportunity to improve the quality of the information system because of the nature of its operations, which are usually concerned primarily with budgetary control. Improvement is obtained in promptness and accuracy of reporting.

Periodically, management approves some type of financial plan (the master budget) that assigns responsibility for maintaining incomes, investments, and costs within standard limits. This plan then becomes the basis for periodic reports on performance against plan, and these reports become the device by which control is exercised. Major problems in such a system involve: (1) determining equitable standards for control, (2) determining when action is required, and (3) obtaining rapid, up-to-date information on variances. It is unlikely that the automation of financial records will decrease the problems associated with the first two attributes. It will, however, materially assist in speeding up reporting.

The financial system is probably the most important single management information system in the company, and in most companies it is the oldest and best developed. The major concern associated with this system is the necessary design actions to make it a vital tool for operating and planning.

Production/Operations

The production/operations system is concerned with information about the physical flow of goods or the production of goods and services. It covers such activities as production planning and control, inventory control and management, purchasing, distribution, and transportation.

Because the quantities of data are so large and the timing of information so essential, the production/operations system is the most adaptable to automation and yields the largest benefits in terms of immediate solution of critical and costly problems. Although other applications (e.g., decision making, total system simulation) may offer greater potential, this functional area usually offers immediate payoffs.

Dearden and McFarlan have identified six characteristics of the type of information that lends itself best to computer use:

1. *A number of interacting variables.* The computer has the ability to solve rapidly problems with multi-interacting variables, and hence its value is high in this type of usage.
2. *Reasonably accurate values.* Coefficients of equations should have reasonably accurate values, and equations should express accurately the relationships among the variables. The computer has an infinite capacity for compounding errors of inaccurate values and relationships.
3. *Speed an important factor.* The value of a computer in an information system is a function of the requirement of speed in processing data.
4. *Repetitive operations.* Operations of this type offer the most profitable area of applications.
5. *Accuracy as a requirement.* The greater degree of accuracy required in the output, the more likely it is that a computer will be helpful.
6. *Large amounts of information.* Because computers can handle large amounts of data quickly, applications with this attribute offer profitable employment.[16]

Because the information needed for effective management of productions/operations has all these characteristics, these systems are probably the most adaptable to automation of any in the company. Moreover, because of the requirement for timeliness in handling large quantities of data, the greatest advances in improvements and economy are likely to be made in the production/operations area.

The production/operations system, particularly in a manufacturing company, is unquestionably the most important from an operating standpoint. It crosses all subsystem boundaries and has an effect throughout the company. Yet despite this importance, the production/operations system has had less management involvement and consequently less development than the financial system. This is unfortunate, because in most companies this area offers more opportunity for development, cost saving, and management improvement than any other. Indeed, much of the "total systems" activity in recent years has begun because of problems in the production/operations area and because once begun, an examination of this area leads to the design of related and integrated subsystems throughout the company. This attribute and the importance of the production/operations system and its impact on systems elsewhere in the organization can be seen in Figure 5–11, which demonstrates how the production subsystem interacts with all major functions of a manufacturing company (pages 180–81). Note that the critical input to this system is the customer order.

Marketing Information

The basic areas of the marketing function that lend themselves to improvement through information systems include: (1) forecasting/sales planning, (2) market research, (3) advertising, and (4) operating and control information required to manage the marketing function.[17] Examples of the last include such information as sales reports and distribution cost reports.[18]

Marketing information is one of the most important information systems to most businesses, yet it is most often the one overlooked. Few marketing executives use information effectively on their jobs; most of them rely on intuition as a basis for decisions.[19] The vast majority of firms tend to maintain information only about sales records or orders and shipments. What is needed is a system that will give marketing managers information to help them make better decisions about pricing, advertising, product promotion policy, sales force effort, and other vital marketing matters. Such a system should also take account of the necessity elsewhere in the organization for information concerning marketing, sales, and other internal information that affects decisions in other subsystems of the company.

The effectiveness of marketing information systems depends to a large extent on feedback from the marketplace to the firm, so that the firm can judge the adequacy of its past performance as well as appraise the opportunities for new activity. Despite this feedback need, many firms consider their marketing information system to be some type of "sales analysis" activity that has been superimposed onto an accounting system. Yet there is no reason why this vital area of management activity should not take an approach similar to that of other areas of the firm whose information needs are designed around the managerial functions of planning, operating, and controlling.

Table 5–2 summarizes some of the more important types of information systems applications in the marketing area and indicates selected outputs that are useful for market planning, market research, and marketing control. These three types of marketing systems are summarized:

1. *Control systems.* Provide monitoring and review of performance against plan. Also provide information concerning trends, problems and possible marketing opportunities.
2. *Planning systems.* Provide information needed for planning the marketing and sales program. A good system furnishes information to permit the marketing manager to weigh the effects of alternate plans in trade promotion, pricing, and other variables in the forecasting equation.
3. *Market research systems.* Used to develop, test, and predict the effects of actions taken or planned in the basic subsystems of marketing (pricing, advertising, design, etc.).

Table 5–2

Selected Applications and Outputs of a Marketing Information System

Application	*Output*
MARKET PLANNING	
Forecasting	Parts requirements and production schedule based on demand for industrial goods
Purchasing	Automatic optimization of purchasing function and inventory control based on decision rules
Credit management	Automatic computer processing of credit decisions
MARKET RESEARCH	
Pricing policy	Policy based on historical analysis of past
Advertising strategy	Strategy based on sales analysis of a variety of market segment breakdowns
Advertising expenditure	Correlation by numerous market segments of sales and advertising expenditures
MARKETING CONTROL	
Marketing costs	Current reports of deviation from standard and undesirable trends
Sales performance	A variety of data to help discover reasons for sales performance and correct deviations
Territorial control of sales, distribution, costs, etc.	Timely reports of performance on territorial basis to permit reallocation of resources to substandard areas

Personnel Information

The personnel information system deals with the flow of information about people working in the organization as well as future personnel needs.

① ② ③ ④

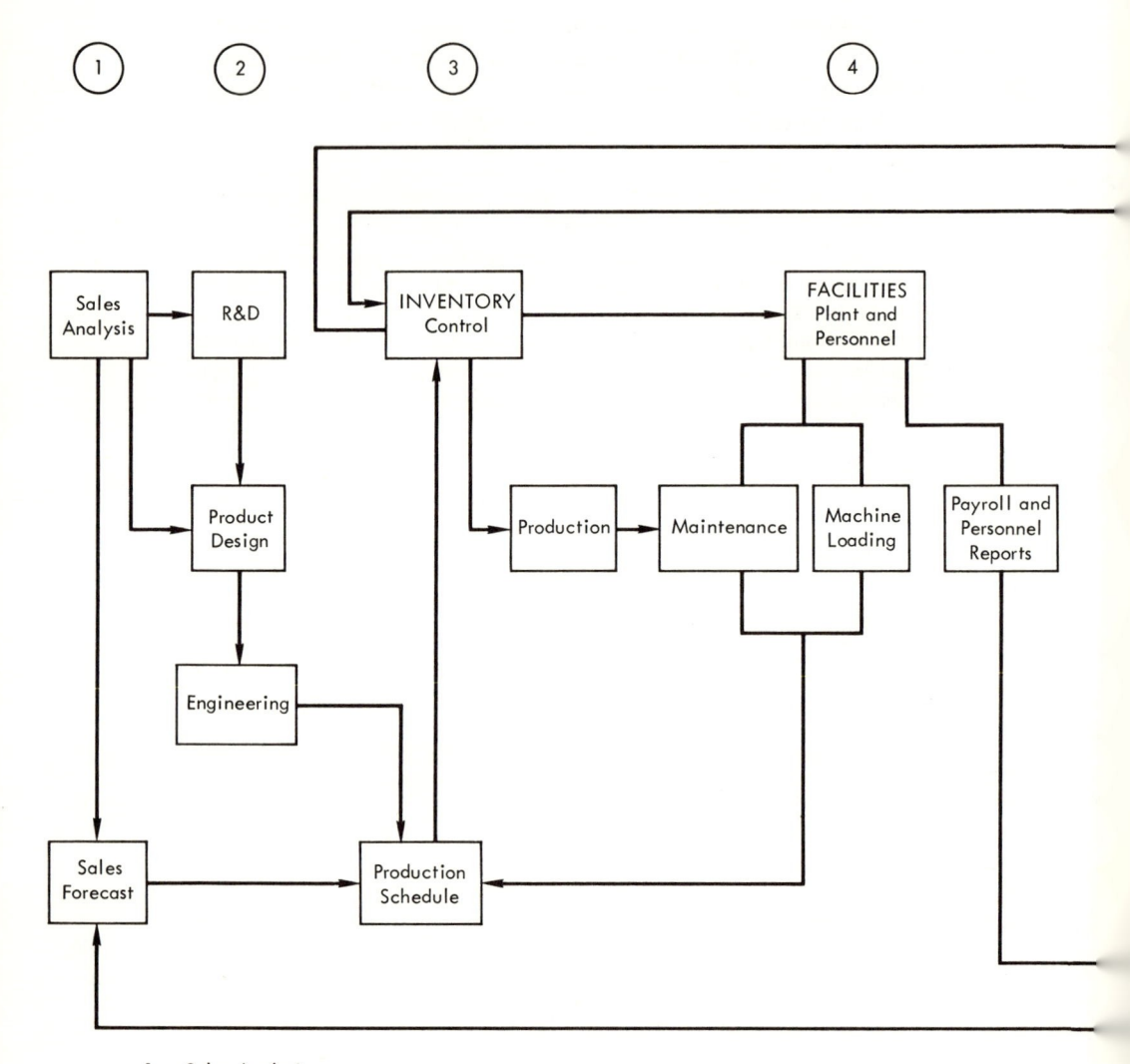

[Flow diagram with boxes: Sales Analysis → R&D; Sales Analysis → Product Design; Sales Analysis → Sales Forecast; R&D → Product Design → Engineering → Production Schedule; INVENTORY Control → Production → Maintenance; FACILITIES Plant and Personnel → Maintenance, Machine Loading, Payroll and Personnel Reports; Machine Loading → Production Schedule; Sales Forecast → Production Schedule; Production Schedule → INVENTORY Control; INVENTORY Control → FACILITIES; Payroll and Personnel Reports → Sales Forecast]

1   Sales Analysis
2   Engineering
3   Inventory Control and Production Scheduling
4   Production/Operations Facilities

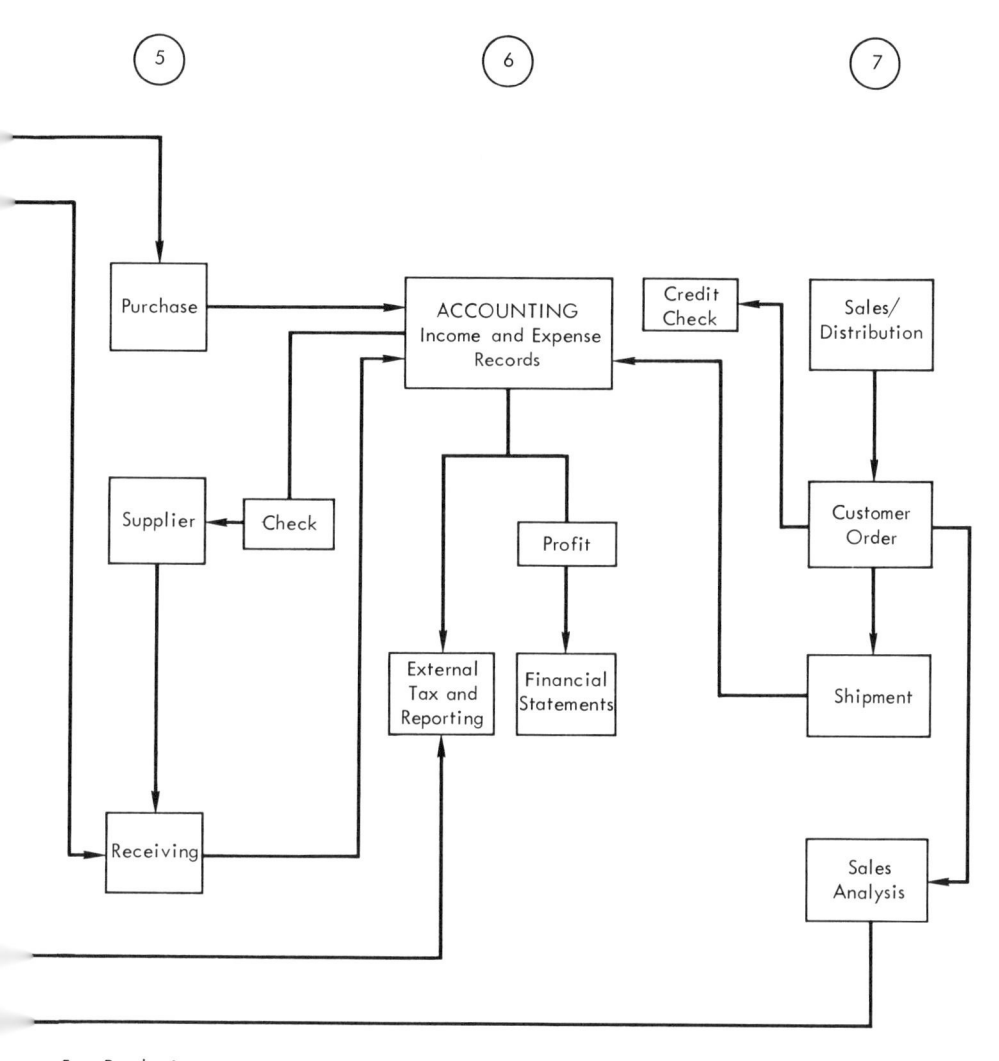

5   Purchasing
6   Financial
7   Sales and Distribution

Figure 5–11 Integration of Subsystems Through the Information Flow in the Production/Operations System

181

In most organizations, the system is concerned primarily with the five basic subsystems of the personnel function: recruiting, placement, training, compensation, and maintenance.

It is probably not unfair to say that many personnel managers are proving to be myopic in their conventional specialization and concern with personnel records for their own sake. Manpower management, as opposed to the traditional view of the personnel function, should be considered a total system that interacts with the other major systems of the organization —marketing, production, finance, and the external environment. Indeed, the primary purpose of the manpower management program is to service these major systems. Forecasting and planning the manpower needs of the organization, maintaining an adequate and satisfactory work force, and controlling the personnel policies and programs of the company are the major responsibilities of manpower management. Plant security is often an auxiliary function.

In order to achieve the foregoing, a *manpower system* is necessary. Like any system, it consists of a number of inputs and outputs, and a number of related subsystems, processes, and activities, all operating through the medium of information. Such a system is shown in Figure 5–12. Note that the output from the manpower subsystems goes to personnel staff specialists as well as to line operating managers. Many personnel managers mistakenly conceive of their information systems as a tool of the personnel function alone rather than as the real reason for a manpower system— organizational effectiveness. A systems-oriented approach to manpower management interrelates and integrates the functions of the personnel man-

Information Input	Manpower Systems	Outputs
Company Objectives Operating Plans Job Related Info Personnel Plans Personnel Policies Other Planning Premises	1 RECRUITMENT, SELECTION, AND HIRING 2 PLACEMENT 3 TRAINING AND DEVELOPMENT 4 PAY AND COMPENSATION 5 HEALTH, SAFETY, AND SECURITY 6 MAINTENANCE	TO OPERATING MANAGERS (Improve personnel performance) TO ORGANIZATION PERSONNEL (Personnel satisfaction) ORGANIZATION GOALS (Related to manpower) PERSONNEL MANAGEMENT (Reports, records, etc., related to manpower)

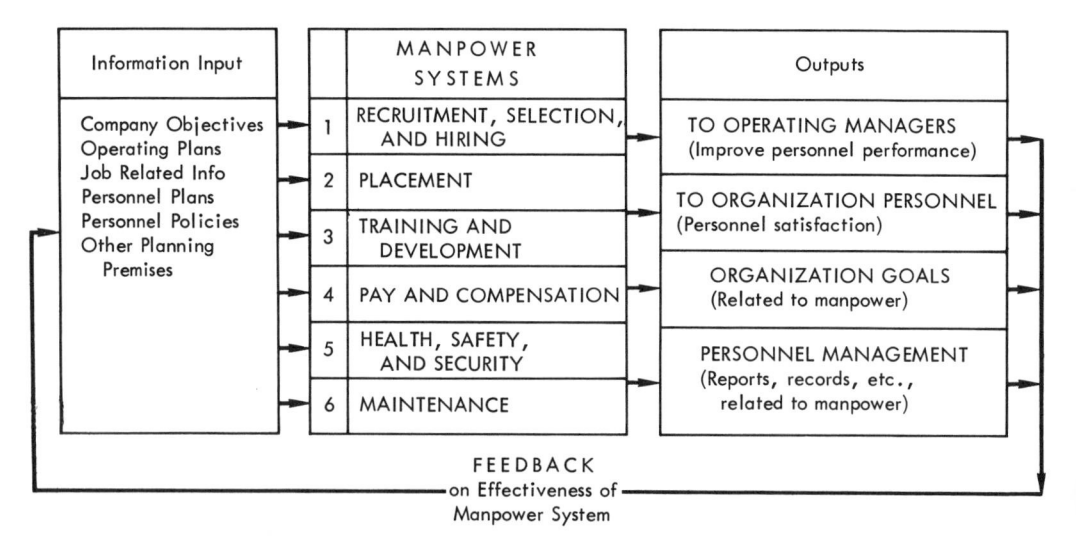

FEEDBACK on Effectiveness of Manpower System

Figure 5–12 Manpower Information Systems

ager with the duties of the operating personnel, who benefit most from a manpower information system.

Briefly, the six major subsystems of the manpower management system, designed to accomplish these objectives, are:

1. *Recruitment.* Properly managed, the recruitment system forecasts personnel needs and skills and recruits the personnel at the proper time to meet organizational needs. A properly designed information system will furnish information concerning (a) skills required for company programs and processes, and (b) inventory of skills available in the organization. Manning tables, job specifications, and other personnel data are also useful in this subsystem.

2. *Placement.* This system is perhaps the most vital of all personnel functions because it matches available personnel with requirements, and hence the effective use of manpower as a resource takes place within this system. A properly designed placement information system takes account of the latest behavioral tools and techniques to ensure that the capabilities of people are identified and placed with properly organized work requirements.

3. *Training and development.* As technological changes and demands for new skills accelerate, many companies find that they must necessarily develop much of their talent requirements from internal sources. In addition, a large part of the work force must constantly be updated in new techniques and developments. This task is the function of the training and development system. Basic information requirements include a continuing skills inventory of company personnel matched against a forecast of current and estimated needs for improved skills.

4. *Compensation.* The pay and other values (fringe benefits, for example) for the satisfaction of individual wants and needs and for compliance with government, union, and other requirements is the basic function of the compensation system. Information included in or required by this system is largely that associated with the traditional payroll and other financial records.

5. *Maintenance.* This system, largely for the benefit of operating managers, should be designed to ensure that personnel policies and procedures are achieved. It may extend to the operation of systems to control work standards, those required to measure performance against financial plans or other programs, and the many subsidiary records normally associated with the collection, maintenance, and dissemination of personnel data.

6. *Health, safety, and plant security.* As the name implies, this system is concerned with the health of personnel and the safety of job practices and related operations. Plant security includes actions necessary to prevent theft, damage, or compromise of classified information.

Other Information Systems

In addition to the major systems described, many organizations have a variety of less important information requirements for which the design of an information system is desirable. Some are manual, some computer based, and some may be combinations of manual and computer. Among the most common are:

1. *Purchasing*. In this rapidly growing area of application, some purchasing uses are: automatic preparation of quote requests, updating order records, handling routine follow-ups, processing requisitions, and checking history files as a means of vendor selection.[20] More advanced applications include order writing, vendor rating, computation of EOQ, and preparation of accounts payable checks.

2. *PERT*. Program Evaluation and Review Technique, PERT, has become a widely used information device for controlling the time, cost, and work in a project or program. Modifications of the basic technique include PERT/TIME, PERT/COST, PERT/CPM (Critical Path Method) and PERT/LOB (Line of Balance).

3. *Research and Development*. This is a vital area for industrial companies but of less importance for financial and service organizations. This information system may include some method for exchanging information on the results of research findings, or in a more sophisticated system, provision can be made for the examination, storage, and retrieval of research information.

4. *Simulation*. Although, strictly speaking, simulation is not an information system, it may be classified as such because it is computer based and it depends upon access to the company's data bank. It is a method for simulating decisions and hence is a vital tool of planning.

5. *Strategic Planning*. This system deals with projections of the future and for the most part uses information developed for other purposes. It is one of the few information systems that utilize the entire range of information developed in the company, both external and internal.

AUTOMATION, COMPUTERS, AND MANAGEMENT

In 1947, the Ford Motor Company announced the organization of an "automation" department in its manufacturing engineering division. The world has not been the same since.

The convenient term *automation* was applied to what has been called "Detroit-type" mechanization, the linkage of successive machines by automatic work transfer and positioning devices. Since that time, however, the new word *automation* has been used to fit a variety and multitude of purposes and phobias.

Information Automation

There is little doubt but that the "automation–cybernation" age has consequences unlike any other development in history for the handling of data and for communication. Consider, for example, its impact on the telephone industry in the United States. It has been estimated that if the communication load of today were to be handled with the equipment and methods of the early 1930's, it would require that every female in the entire nation between the ages of 16 and 60 become a telephone operator. As another example, it is estimated that if the present proliferation of products in the automobile industry were to be produced without the assistance of computers, the entire industry work force would be required to handle the paper work involved.

Because we are concerned here with management information systems, it is advisable to view the possible impact of automation of information in terms of its place in the national economy and in the company. It is estimated that up to 90 percent of the work involved in any white-collar job involves the seeking and obtaining of information. This applies in accounting, marketing, finance, production, and engineering operations as well as in management processes. If we think of 90 percent of man-hours and salaries going into information processing, we can see why management seeks improvements in the concepts and design of information systems and why the automation of this information becomes important. One authority estimates that more than ten million individuals in the United States are directly concerned with the production and processing of information and that at least 50 percent of the cost of running the American economy is information cost.[21] The growing trend toward information systems and information automation is also reflected in costs allocated to the function of information processing. John Diebold estimates that the market for equipment alone has grown from $1.5 billion per year in 1961 to over $7 billion in 1970 despite tremendous advances in the productivity and capacity of this equipment.[22]

Automation and Decision Making

Earlier we examined the potential breakthrough provided by the concept of "automatizing" or *programming* decisions so that they can be made automatically by *decision rule*. This concept cannot be overemphasized. The potential for automating decisions is illustrated conceptually in Figure 5-13.

In the figure are shown four types of decisions: programmed (automatic), semiautomatic, judgment, and unexplored. These types are not distinct but shade into each other along a continuum. The programmed decisions of Type I are automatic in the sense that procedures or rules have been established for them. A major objective of management information systems is to move the boundaries of this type of decision to the right. With the help and participation of managers, the systems approach combined with management science can devise decision rules and thereby delegate to computers the decision-making power that was once the prerogative of management.

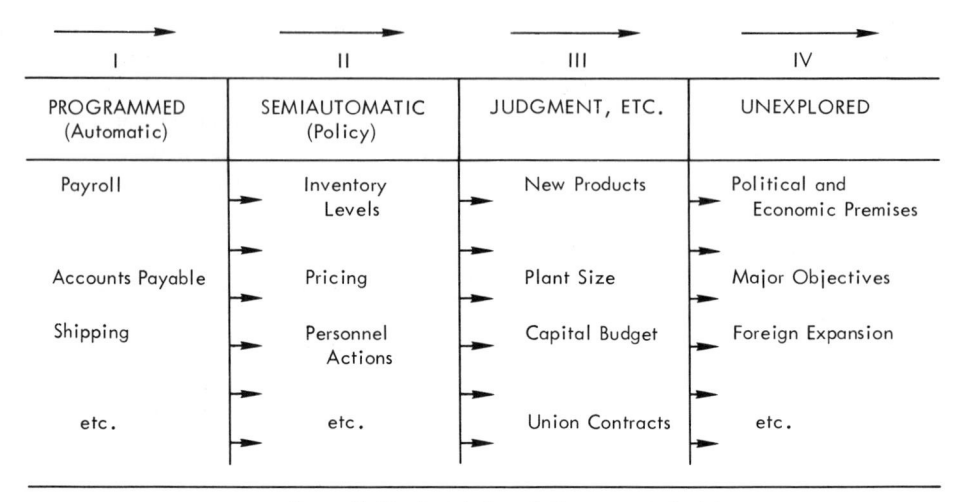

I	II	III	IV
PROGRAMMED (Automatic)	SEMIAUTOMATIC (Policy)	JUDGMENT, ETC.	UNEXPLORED
Payroll	Inventory Levels	New Products	Political and Economic Premises
Accounts Payable	Pricing	Plant Size	Major Objectives
Shipping	Personnel Actions	Capital Budget	Foreign Expansion
etc.	etc.	Union Contracts	etc.

Figure 5–13 Boundaries of Management Decisions

Type II decisions are those that are frequently guided by policy, and some latitude is provided in the boundaries of the decision. Illustrative of these are such decisions as particular inventory levels under an inventory policy and specific pricing decisions under a pricing policy. Frequently these policies are rather general and do not provide for the "optimum" decision in terms of time, cost, or effectiveness. For example, an inventory policy stated in terms of months' supply might be improved by "programming" or "automating" inventory decisions in terms of economic order quantities, thus lending a more "optimum" solution or decision. We see then, in this illustration, how the boundaries of Type I decisions can be moved to the right to include some decisions now covered by incomplete policies.

Given the state-of-the-art in management decision makng today, Type III and Type IV decisions remain largely in the realm of experience, intuition, and judgment. These types of decisions offer the greatest prospect for improvement through management information systems. As the boundaries of each category of decision making are moved to the right and as more and more decisions lend themselves to programmed rules, the manager will have more time and opportunity to concern himself with the more difficult and demanding decisions of Types III and IV and to expand his managerial horizons through the use of information systems.

SUMMARY

Information is absolutely essential to the survival of an organization. As organizations grow in size and complexity, their increased need for communications demands an information system for planning and controlling.

In an information system, inputs of information (both data and planning information) are processed according to plan into an output that provides information for decisions regarding planning and control. If the output exceeds control limits, this fact provides information for direct changes in the processor or for changing allocation of resource inputs.

As an organization simply cannot survive without that critical element of information, neither can the functions of management be performed unless a flow of information is provided to decision makers. The planning process depends upon the availability of planning premises—external and internal information needed to evaluate alternative courses of action. The systems approach to organizing takes into account the integrative nature of information flows as well as the structuring of the organization around decision centers. The function of control is also dependent upon the flow of information for measuring performance against standard and for correcting deviations.

The basic information systems of most companies include the financial, the production/operations, the marketing, and the personnel systems. Although different companies have reached various stages of sophistication in applications within these categories, much remains to be done. The task is to upgrade many of these systems from the historical analytical variety to the type of specific application that will provide better decisions and information for the management process.

The implications of information automation are greatest for the programming of decisions, a basic and extraordinarily important concept for the design of information systems. Future design will focus on advancing the frontiers of programmed decisions so that managers may devote their time to the design of the more advanced systems for implementing company strategies, policies, and supporting plans.

DISCUSSION QUESTIONS AND PROBLEMS

1. It is said that an *information* system will avail you nothing unless it is backed up by a *management* system. Explain.

2. List the steps in the planning process and show how information becomes essential for performing these steps. What kinds of information do we need for planning?

3. Using a university as an example, list the major types of information that could be classified as environmental, competitive, and internal. Do the same for a bank. How do they differ? How are they alike?

4. In a small manufacturing company, Mr. Black is the president, Mr. Johnson is the vice-president of manufacturing, Mr. Symour is the production planning and control supervisor, and Mr. Galt is the supervisor of shipping and receiving. Show this organization structure and indicate what kinds of information would be utilized by all levels and individuals listed. How might the organizational structure be designed around the information flow?

5. How might the planning information in Question 4 also be used as the basis for production control?

6. Design the basic elements of a financial plan (budget) for a manufacturer or a firm of your choice, and show how these elements can be used for (a) a planning system, (b) an operating system, and (c) a control system.

7. Which of the major information systems and subsystems of Table 5–1 would be applicable to a hospital? A retail store?

8. What information systems would you recommend for the Midwest Stationery Company (Question 9 of Chapter 2)? What information would be contained in each of these subsystems? What would be the source of such information? What would be the output of each system?

9. The California Aviation Company has signed a contract with the U.S. Navy for the overhaul and repair of Navy aircraft. Over the years the Navy has "programmed" its support requirements for overhaul and repair and has determined for each aircraft (a) major components to be overhauled, (b) parts required, and (c) labor hours by skill for each component. Contract requirements call for a "cost plus" reinmbursement basis, furnishing of parts by the Navy, and three months' notice prior to the entry of any aircraft for overhaul and repair.

Questions:

(1) Construct a model of a manpower system along the lines of Figure 5–12, indicating information inputs, major manpower subsystems, and information outputs.

(2) From what other subsystems in the company would the manpower system receive an input?

(3) To what other subsystems in the company would the manpower system outputs provide an input? For what purpose would the other subsystems utilize the output from the manpower system?
(4) What kind of system might be established to insure that the actual labor hours within the plant agreed with the standards set by the Navy?
(5) Name at least two subsystems of the company's MIS that might be automated. Describe how this might be accomplished.

REFERENCES

1. George A. Steiner, *Top Management Planning* (Toronto: Collier-Macmillan Canada, Ltd., 1969), p. 475.
2. Ross Parasteh, "Prevent Blunders in Supply and Distribution," *Harvard Business Review*, March–April 1969.
3. Norbert Wiener, *Cybernetics* (New York: John Wiley & Sons, Inc., 1948), p. 187.
4. V. A. Graicunas, "Relationship in Organization," *Bulletin of the International Management Institute* (Geneva: International Labour Office, 1933), in L. Gulick and L. Urwick, eds., *Papers on the Science of Administration* (New York: Institute of Public Administration, 1937), pp. 181–87.
5. Gerald A. Feltham, "The Value of Information," *Accounting Review*, October 1968, p. 684.
6. "From Data to Dollars," *Dun's Review*, June 1969, p. 34.
7. *Ibid.*
8. Jay Galbraith, *Academy of Management Proceedings*, December 1968.
9. For a comprehensive discussion of the problem of people and systems, see Richard Johnson *et al.*, *The Theory and Management of Systems* (New York: McGraw-Hill Book Company, 1967), pp. 365–400.
10. Steiner, *Top Management Planning*, p. 515.
11. Robert W. Holmes, "Information Systems Review for Senior Management," *Financial Executive*, April 1969, p. 56.
12. For a recommended outline of knowledge required by the manager in the field of information systems see Joel E. Ross, "Data Processing Training for Managers: Objectives and Curriculum Content," *Computers and Automation*, September 1968, pp. 16–20.
13. A suggested approach to training technicians in the body of knowledge required for the design of MIS is contained in Joel E. Ross, "Systems Analyst Training: Objectives and Content," *Journal of Systems Management*, February 1969, pp. 7–9.
14. For research results on the way top management obtains relevant information about the environment, see Francis J. Aguilar, *Scanning the Business Environment* (New York: The Macmillan Company, 1967).
15. For a comprehensive coverage of financial systems, see James Bower and William R. Welke, *Financial Information System* (New York: Houghton Mifflin Company, 1968).
16. John Dearden and F. Warren McFarlan, *Management Information Systems* (Homewood, Ill.: Richard D. Irwin, Inc., 1966), pp. 10–11.
17. A comprehensive review of applications in the marketing area is found in Samuel V. Smith, Richard H. Brien, and James E. Stafford, *Readings in Marketing Information Systems* (NewYork: Houghton Mifflin Company, 1968), and in Richard D. Buzzell, Donald F. Cox, and Rex V. Brown, *Marketing Research and Information Systems* (New York: McGraw-Hill Book Company, 1969).

18. In a survey of 122 marketing vice-presidents, their top four choices for utilizing their company's computers were: forecasting sales, customer services, predicting market for new products and services, and sales analysis and control. See "Reading the Crystal Ball," *Nation's Business*, February 1969, p. 16.
19. Buzzell *et al.*, *Marketing Research and Information Systems*, p. 4.
20. *Purchasing Magazine*, June 12, 1969, p. 71.
21. Adrian McDonough, *Information Economics and Management Systems* (New York: McGraw-Hill Book Company, 1963), p. 5.
22. John Diebold, "What's Ahead in Information Technology," *Harvard Business Review*, September–October 1965, p. 76.

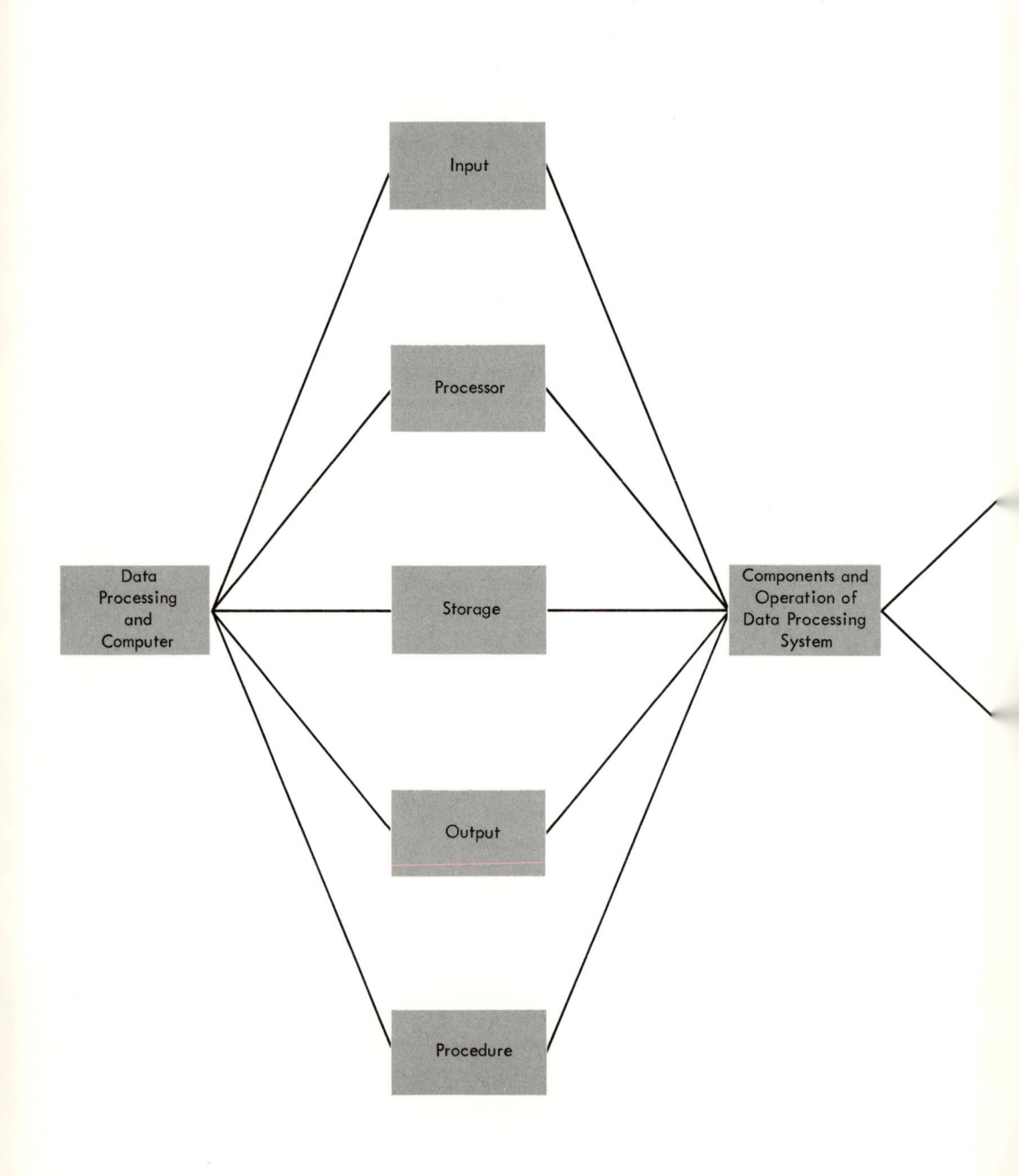

```
                    ┌─────────┐
                    │  Input  │
                    └─────────┘

                    ┌──────────┐
                    │ Processor│
                    └──────────┘
┌────────────┐                              ┌──────────────┐
│    Data    │      ┌─────────┐             │ Components and│
│ Processing │──────│ Storage │─────────────│ Operation of │
│    and     │      └─────────┘             │Data Processing│
│  Computer  │                              │   System     │
└────────────┘                              └──────────────┘
                    ┌─────────┐
                    │ Output  │
                    └─────────┘

                    ┌──────────┐
                    │ Procedure│
                    └──────────┘
```

6
what the manager should know about the computer

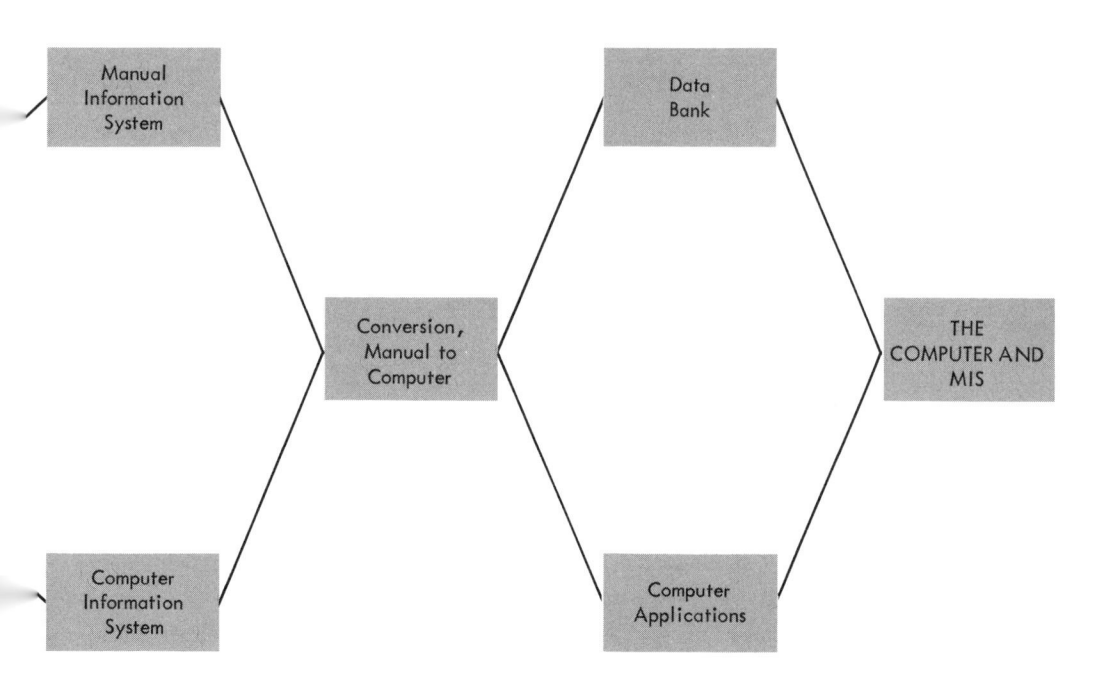

- Manual Information System
- Computer Information System
- Conversion, Manual to Computer
- Data Bank
- Computer Applications
- THE COMPUTER AND MIS

6

Judging from the business press, the "brave new world" of management information systems is upon us. There is hardly a magazine today that doesn't print articles on computers, information systems, data banks, and similar related subjects. However, despite the proliferation of books and articles and the abundance of seminars and courses in this area, few efforts have successfully blended the separate concepts of management, information, decision making, and computer hardware. This synthesis is one of the major purposes of this book.

Another basic task of this book is to develop the concepts, principles, and techniques necessary to design better applications for computer-based management information systems. The enormously increased complexity of large-scale organizations makes the adequate design and utilization of these systems critical for the remainder of this decade. Indeed, the seventies will come to be known as the period of progress from problem solving through "seat-of-the-pants" management methods to the era in which problems are identified, observed, measured, and solved through the systems approach to management.

When we review the factors contributing to complexity in organizations and the advances in management that permit the application of the systems approach, it becomes clear that vital changes lie ahead for the manager. First, we know that the future will bring changes and that the changes will occur at an accelerated rate. Second, these changes will require more information—more knowledge about our product, our customer, and about alternative ways to improve our effectiveness. And third, the requirement for more information will necessitate new methods and new procedures for gathering, retrieving, and evaluating this information for making vital decisions.

It is not the purpose of this chapter to provide either a technical discussion or an in-depth treatment of the hardware or the operation of a computer. We believe that such an exposure is not essential for the manager–user. Just as the driver of an automobile can operate the vehicle without a sophisticated engineering knowledge of its engine, the manager can be quite closely involved in MIS design without a technical background in computer operation.

However, some familiarity with the computer and its role in the processing of information is desirable. The objective of this chapter is to explain the elements and operation of the computer sufficiently so that the manager–user can participate in systems design. In order to do this, he should be able to understand and evaluate the potential and performance of the computer in the accomplishment of his operational effectiveness. A secondary purpose is to help close the understanding and appreciation "gap" between managers and computer professionals. The approach will be by analogy, making the transition from the commonplace and easily understood manual system to the more complex computer application.

DATA PROCESSING AND THE COMPUTER

Not since the invention of writing, about 3000 B.C., has there been an advance with the impact of the computer for both the processing and the storing of information. Consider that in less than fifteen minutes a low-cost computer ($3000 per month rental) can update an inventory file of 25,000 items with 5000 different types of transactions and then print out the status of items that are over or under a predetermined limit. In the next decade the storage capacity of computers will be unlimited for most practical applications. It is estimated that holographic technology will provide the means for storing incredible amounts of information in condensed form —e.g., the entire Manhattan telephone directory on one 8-by-10-inch film card—and for erasing and replacing any single bit of information without disturbing others.[1]

As previously suggested, there are several prerequisites for a modern, effective computer-based management information system. The *first* of these is a *management* system—the organizational arrangements, the structure and procedures for adequate planning and control, and the many other manifestations of good organization and administration. Indeed, such a system is a prerequisite for progress in any endeavor. *Second,* there must exist data and information—information about the company's goals, resources, environment, policies, operations, plans, and performance against plans. These types of information represent knowledge about the company's plans and its managerial and operational processes. *Third,* in order to process these data, it is necessary to have appropriate equipment that will: (a) provide the capability for economic, rapid access to large-scale storage of retrievable data, (b) process this data economically and at high speed, and (c) enter information into the system and retrieve and display it. These three activities are now often performed by special electronic communication devices and by today's computer and related hardware.

A final prerequisite to an effective computer-based management information system is *information management,* an organization for designing, maintaining, and managing the required systems and procedures.

We shall be concerned in subsequent chapters with information management and systems design. In this chapter we want to examine first how information is stored, processed, and retrieved by means of the electronic computer and related devices. The objective is to understand how the computer operates as the fundamental information processor and the essential element of a management information system.

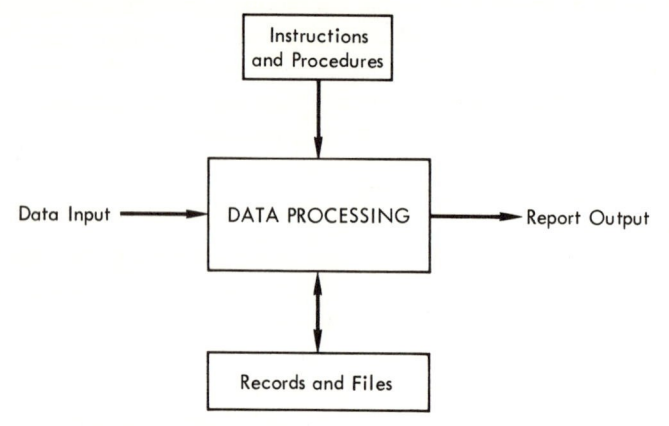

Figure 6–1 Basic Components of an Information System

Components and Operation of a Data Processing System

An information system is composed of five basic components, as shown in Figure 6–1. In a manual system, human beings perform the five basic functions; in a computer-based system, the functions are performed by equipment. In either type of system the basic functions are: (1) entering data into the system; (2) processing the data (rearranging input data and processing files); (3) maintaining files and records; (4) developing procedures that tell what data are needed and when, where they are obtained, and how they are used, as well as providing instruction routines for the processor to follow; and (5) preparing report output.

Man's knowledge and store of information is what can be acquired and stored in his memory or some peripheral source. The information must then be retrieved and manipulated in order to be useful. To augment his memory, man uses a variety of devices, including books, forms, and records. We are concerned here with the two major sources of storage and manipulation for information systems: records and the computer.

If it were not for records, the size and reliability of data storage would be restricted to what people could remember. Records were the earliest device for assisting in the data-processing task. Consisting first of pictures and marks, writing later relied on alphabets and numerals.* The "alphabet" for processing business data consists of ten numerals, twenty-six letters, and twenty-five special characters. This "alphabet" is represented by punched holes in cards (Figure 6–2) or paper tape and by positive and negative charges in magnetizable material. This electronic representation is

---

*To appreciate the value of writing as a memory device, try to multiply two three-digit numbers without the aid of pencil and paper.

necessary in order to provide a scheme that is efficient for processing purposes.

Both manual and computer-based information systems have the elements and attributes of systems in general and can be described in terms of these elements: input, output, and processor. Our examination of computer systems in this chapter will proceed by analogy to make the transition from the easily understood manual system to a slightly more complex computer-based system. The transition and analogy will accomplish two purposes. First, we will be able to see how a computer-based data-processing system can become a vital adjunct to management planning and control. Second, by examining the system through its components (input, output, processor), we will be better able to understand how these components of an information system provide the framework for MIS design.

OPERATION OF A MANUAL INFORMATION SYSTEM

The human being is the earliest and still the most prevalent form of data processor. Despite the fantastic growth of computer applications, manual information systems still outnumber them in quantity of systems and information handled.

People receive input data by seeing or hearing them. These data are then stored in the brain, which also acts as a control and logic unit. The outputs from this type of information processing are oral or written reports and in some cases a variety of physical actions. The human mind, acting as a control and logic unit, can perform many operations on data: adding, subtracting, multiplying, and dividing; storing results; repeating the operations on different sets of data; comparing two items; outputting results in a pre-

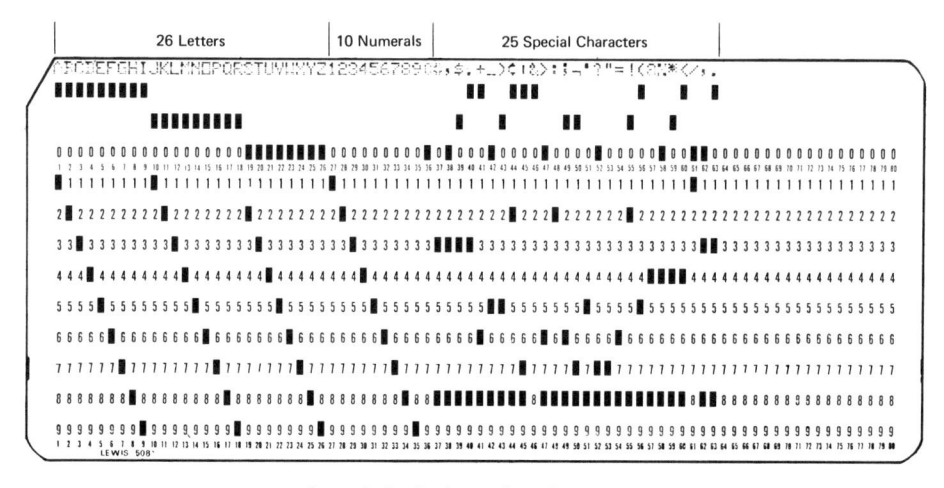

Figure 6–2 Business Data Input

arranged manner and revising the processing operations as a result of changed instructions.

Despite his ability to perform the foregoing processing tasks, the human remains an unreliable processor. The human mind is slow in performing the arithmetical computations required and is rather erratic in applying rules of logic. Fatigue and boredom are among human frailties that cause from 1 to 10 percent of human error in computation and clerical tasks. On the other hand, where judgment is required, the human mind is indispensable. Judgment is needed to make decisions in data-processing systems because of the difficulty of planning to handle all eventualities. In summary, human beings alone are inefficient data processors, but they become a vital element of all data-processing systems because of the need for decisions and judgment.

All the many information systems in the typical company (e.g., payroll, accounts receivable, billing, inventory, production scheduling, shipping) are fundamentally similar in that they possess the basic components of any system: input, processor, and output. Examining a typical manual system will make the understanding of such a system easier and facilitate the transition to a computer-based system. Figure 6–3 shows an inventory clerk operating a manual inventory accounting system. The fundamental elements of data processing, *manual or computer,* may be described in terms of this illustration.

Note that the components of this manual inventory accounting system are the same as those of an information system, illustrated in Figure 6–1.

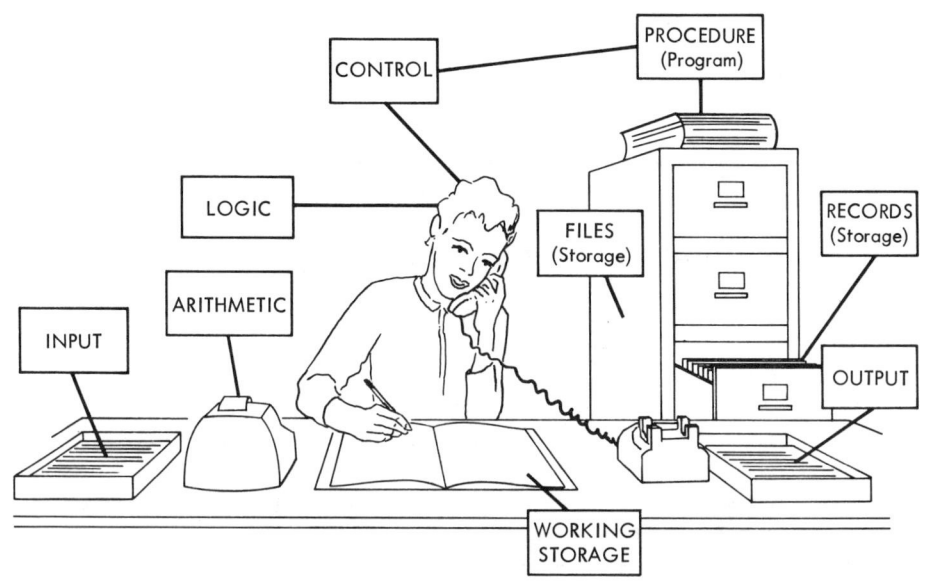

Figure 6–3 Elements of Data Processing (Inventory System)

They are also the same components we will use to describe a computer-based information system:

1. Input
2. Processor
    arithmetic
    control
    logic
3. Storage
    internal
        memory
        working storage
    external
        records and files
4. Procedure or program for instructing the processor
5. Output

Generally speaking, there are two types of inventory control systems, whether manual or computer. The first is the elementary inventory accounting system, which merely adds receipts and subtracts issues from inventory in order to produce an up-to-date inventory of all items. The second, and more sophisticated type of system, computes demand based on prior sales or issues and calculates economic order quantities and reorder points. This application will be discussed in Chapter 7, *Computer-Based Systems for Decision Making*. In this chapter we will utilize the first type of inventory accounting system to illustrate both the manual information system and the conversion from manual to computer based. Refer to Figure 6–3 for the following discussion of manual system components.

Input

We see that the *input device* for the manual inventory-processing system is the in-basket of the inventory clerk. This device receives the *input data* to the system, which may be in various forms and media and is related to information surrounding inventory receipts and issues. Inventory records are updated with receipts on the one hand and reduced with orders for the item on the other. Receipts and issues may be recorded in writing by a storekeeper, stamped on an invoice by a mechanical device, or punched into a card. The resulting cards, invoices, receipt documents, issue papers, shipping documents, and a variety of other *input* information affecting the inventory system are entered into the in-basket for processing and ultimate preparation of output. *Output* can take the form of (a) updated inventory records, (b) an inventory status report, or (c) other reports and documents related to inventory. Note that the input component will accept a variety of information formats.

Processor

From the standpoint of manipulating or processing the data, the *processor* of the manual system is the most important component. It is made up of a control element (contained in the inventory clerk's brain), which keeps the proper relationship among the components of input, processor, storage, and output. An additional element of the *processor* is the calculator or the *arithmetic* element, which performs the four mathematical functions of add, subtract, multiply, and divide. The logic element of the processor, also in the clerk's brain, compares two quantities to see if one is equal to, greater than, or less than the other. It is surprising to most people to discover that these five operations (add, subtract, multiply, divide, compare) comprise the entire processing ability of the computer. However, this ability is a fantastic one, as we shall see.

The three elements of the *processor* component in the manual inventory accounting system can be summarized and illustrated:

Element	*Processing Task*
Control	Decides sequence and extent of processing among data contained in input, storage, and output
Arithmetic	Multiplies units issued by unit price and deducts from on-hand balance
Logic	Compares on-hand balance with minimum inventory level and prepares status report

Storage

The third element depicted in Figure 6–3 is the *storage*. There are two parts to the storage: the *internal* (internal to the processor) and the *external*. The internal storage in this manual system is the working storage represented by the pencil and whatever temporary record the processor (clerk) is working on. This internal storage is sometimes called *memory* because it is stored in and is immediately available to the processor (clerk).

External storage is represented by the individual *records* for an item of inventory. When these individual records are combined they make up a *file*. Prior to performing any processing or calculation upon external storage, the processor (clerk) would have to retrieve the applicable records from the appropriate file. The classification, structuring, and organization of this external storage is very important to the design and operation of any information system, manual or computer-based. In the illustration of inventory accounting, the inventory records may be organized by customer, class, project, or a variety of ways. As a general rule, the costs of classification vary inversely with the costs of using and retrieving the information.

Program/Procedure

Another essential element of this manual system is the *procedure,* which instructs the processor (clerk) on how calculations are to be performed or information processed. This is analogous to the *program* of the computer. The procedures manual may, for example, instruct the processor to "(a) multiply unit cost by units issued, (b) deduct units issued from balance on hand, (c) deduct gross value of issue from dollar value of inventory." The clerk would then perform this processing on the input information, update the inventory balance (external storage), and prepare the required *output* report to go in the out-basket. Preparation of the *output* is the final step of the information-processing system.

Output

The reason we design and operate systems is to achieve some *output*. In the case of the inventory accounting system, the outputs are two: (a) an updated inventory master-file record, and (b) an inventory status report. In the manual system of Figure 6–3, these outputs would be updated files and an inventory status report placed in the out-basket.

A schematic diagram of the foregoing manual information system is depicted in Figure 6–4.

COMPONENTS OF A COMPUTER SYSTEM

Although many managers are awed and sometimes confused by the computer, its operation is essentially no more complex than that of the manual system just described. Indeed, if we make the transition from manual to computer-based system by drawing an analogy between them, there should be no difficulty in understanding the functions and operation of the computer.

We saw in Figure 6–3 the elements of data processing as done manually by a clerk. The field of computers is called *electronic data processing,* and the computer is nothing more than an electronic data processor, with its components the same as those of the manual system described. However, it accepts data in the form of alphanumeric (alphabetic and numerical) characters, as demonstrated in Figure 6–2. If we wish to convert our manual inventory system to computer, the input data would be the same for both systems; only its input *form* would be different. The computer *processes* these data. For example, it adds items received and deducts items issued to update the inventory record, but it does all of this *electronically*. The alphabetic and numerical characters, normally in the form of punched cards or paper tape, are sensed and are represented in electronic form within the computer. The subsequent arithmetic or processing operations are accom-

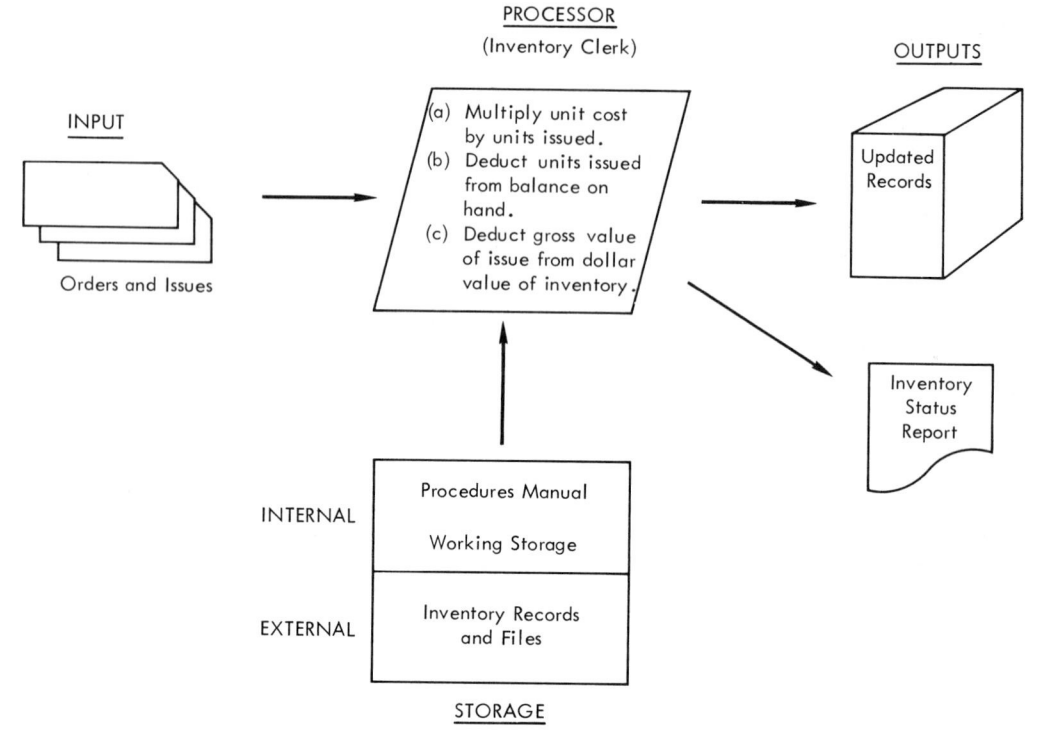

202 Computer-Based Management Information Systems

Figure 6–4 Manual Inventory Accounting System

plished electronically; hence the computer can be described as an *electronic data processor*.

The manual inventory control system previously discussed, when converted to computer application, might appear schematically as in Figure 6–5, which illustrates the basic components of the computer system. Figure 6–6 (page 204) shows the actual hardware components of modern, third-generation computer systems. A discussion of the components follows.

Input

The function of entering data into the computer system is performed by an input device. Unlike the manual system with its human processor, the input to the computer must be in machine-acceptable form. Normally this input takes the form of punched cards, paper tape, magnetic tape, paper documents, and direct input from keyboards. Typical computer input/output devices are shown in Figure 6–7 (pages 206–7).

The input devices read or sense these coded data and make them available in a form acceptable to the computer. Whatever device is used, the data must generally be coded in a form compatible with the characters of

Figure 6–2. In the case of our illustration of the inventory accounting system of Figure 6–5, the input would most likely be in the form of transaction punched cards that contain data representing various kinds of receipts and issues.

The Central Processor

The central processor is the most significant component of the computer. As in the case of our inventory control clerk in the manual system, it consists of a *control* section, which coordinates the system components, and the *arithmetic/logic* unit, which performs the same functions (add, subtract, multiply, divide, compare, shift, move, store) as the clerk–calcu-

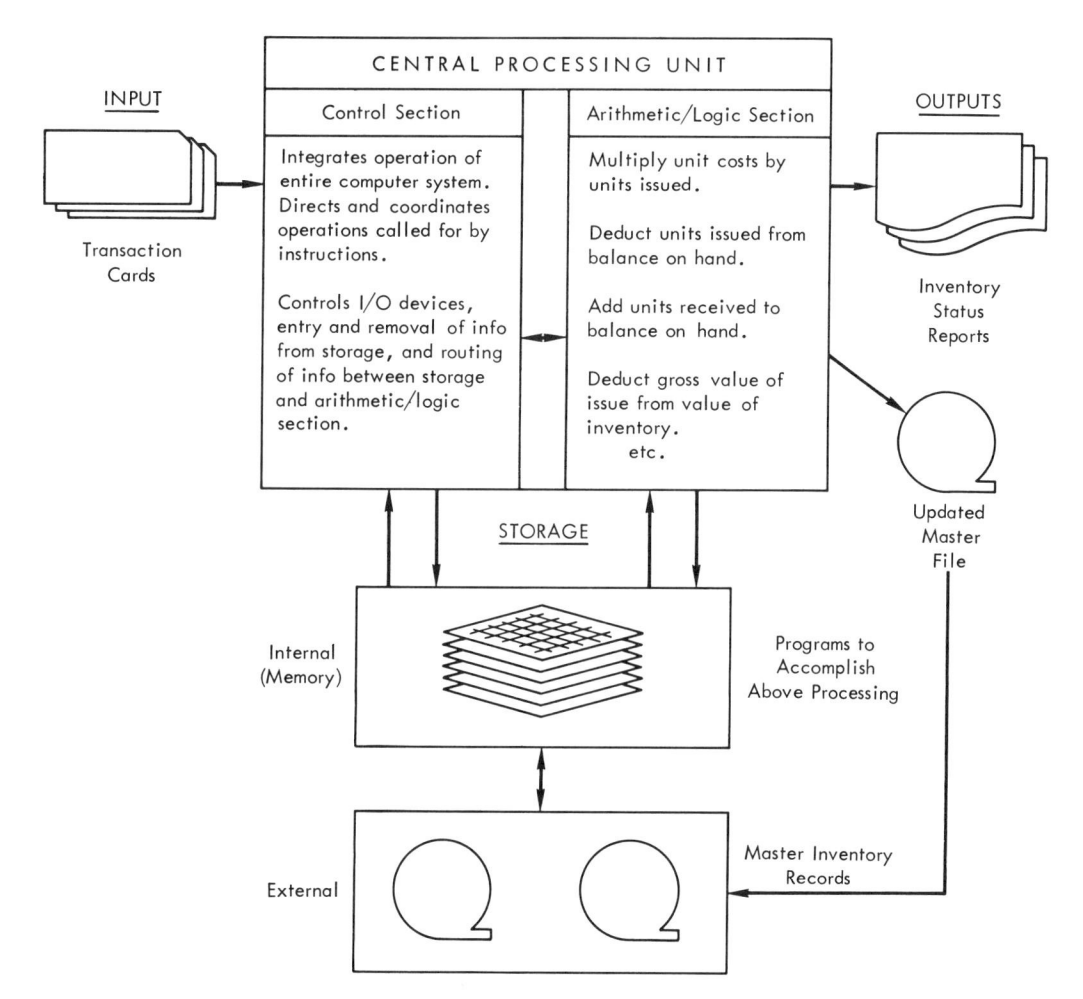

Figure 6–5 Computer-Based Inventory Accounting System

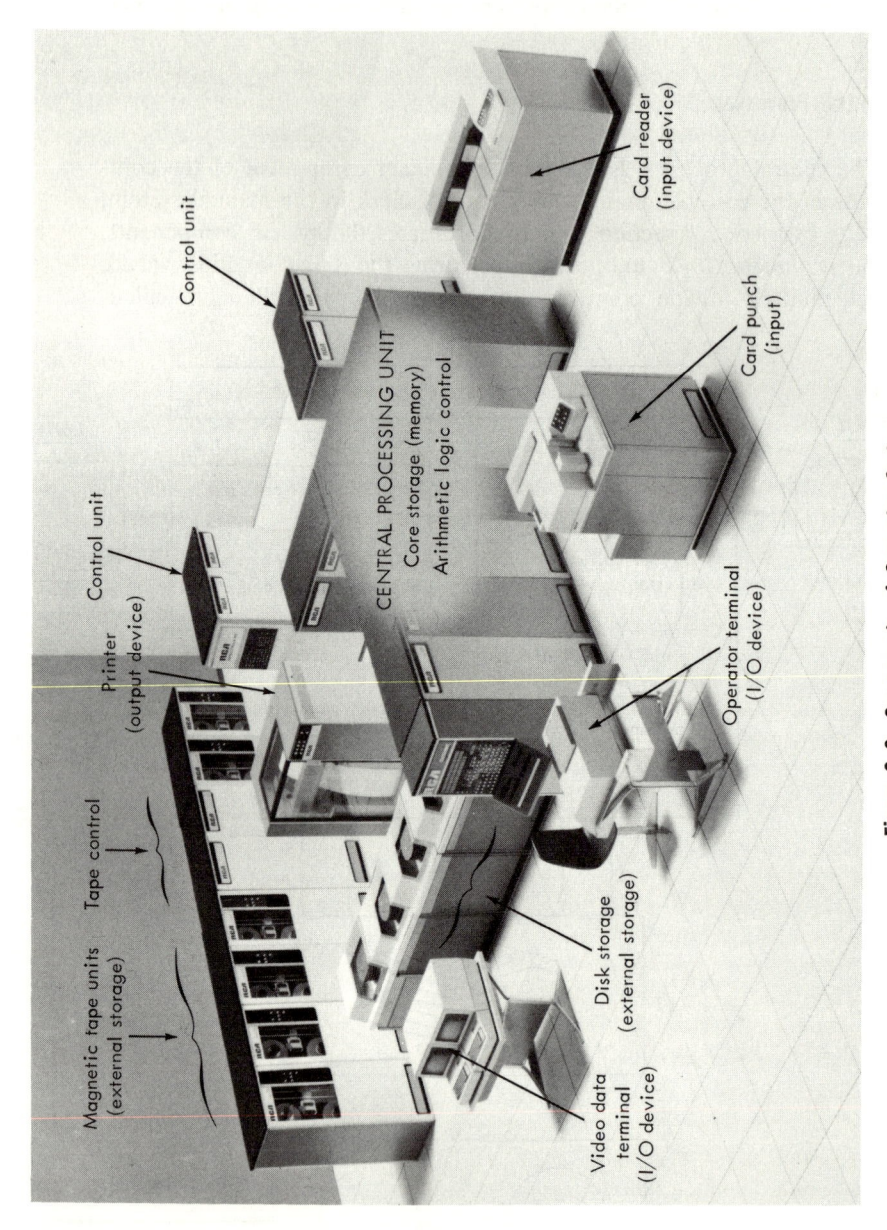

Figure 6-6 Components of Computer System
SOURCE Courtesy of RCA Information Systems

lator combination of the manual system. However, the CPU (central processing unit) of the computer accomplishes these tasks at fantastically increased speed and accuracy. This meager processing logic, accompanied by the five simple functions, accounts for the almost infinite variety of tasks the computer can perform. Figure 6–6 illustrates a central processing unit and console.

The control section of the CPU directs and coordinates all operations called for by the instructions (programs) to the system. It controls the input/output units and the arithmetic/logic unit, transferring data to and from storage, and routing information between storage and the arithmetic/logic unit. It is by means of the control section that automatic, integrated operation of the entire computer system is achieved.

The arithmetic/logic section performs the arithmetic and logic operations. The former portion calculates, shifts numbers, sets the algebraic sign of results, rounds, compares, and performs the other tasks of calculation. The logic section carries out the decision-making operations to change the sequence of instruction execution, and it is capable of testing various conditions encountered during processing.

Storage

Storage is somewhat like a huge electronic filing cabinet, completely indexed and accessible instantly to the computer. All data must be placed in storage before being processed by the computer. Storage consists of *internal,* which is a part of the processing component, and *external.*

Note the similarity between manual and computer systems. Internal storage, frequently referred to as *memory,* is the characteristic that permits the computer to store, in electronic form, data from input devices as well as long series of instructions called *programs* that tell the machine what to do. These programs are similar to the procedures manual of the manual system. It is this memory facility that distinguishes the computer from devices such as calculators and bookkeeping machines, which, although they have input, output, and processing capabilities, cannot store programs internally within the processing unit. The program enables the computer to perform complex and lengthy calculations in order to process specific input data.

In order to understand how programs of instructions permit the computer to process data, we must examine the concept of *computer memory* to see how information and instructions can be stored within the computer. The information can be (1) instructions (programs) to direct the processing unit, (2) data (input, in-process, or output), and (3) reference data associated with processing (tables, code charts, constant factors, etc.). Because the computer memory is the storehouse of this information, it is important to understand how it is represented in memory.

Figure 6–7 Input/Output Devices
SOURCE   Courtesy IBM Corporation and RCA Information Systems

IBM 1403 Printer

IBM 2540 Card Read Punch

IBM 1009 Data Transmission Unit

RCA CRT

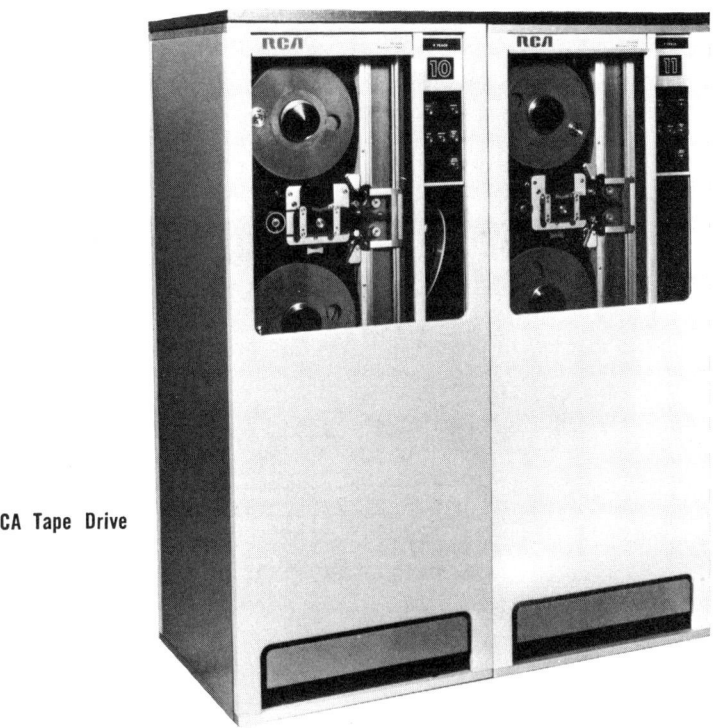

RCA Tape Drive

Memory is comprised of planes of magnetic cores, as shown in Figure 6–8. A magnetic core is a doughnut-shaped ring of ferromagnetic material the size of a matchhead, capable of retaining either of two possible polarities—either 0 or 1—and this representation is therefore called *binary*. A current passed in one direction through the wires magnetizes the core; a current sent in the other direction reverses the core's magnetic state. One state represents a 1, the other a zero.

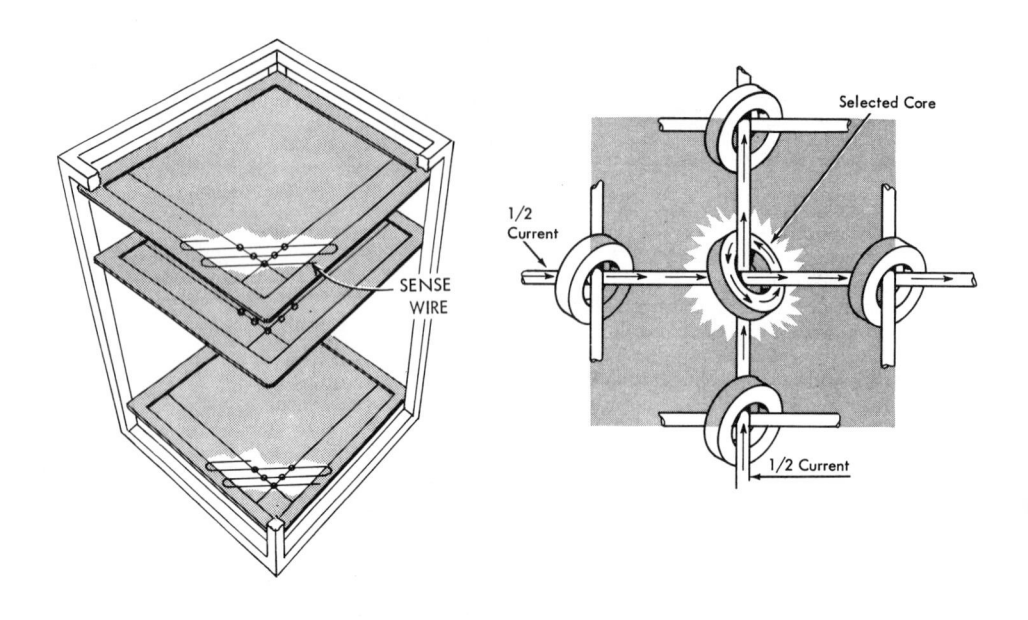

Figure 6–8 Magnetic Cores
SOURCE   Courtesy IBM Corporation

Because each magnetic core holds only one bit and can represent only two states, more than one core is needed to represent a number. Cores are arranged in planes (Figure 6–8) that may have 32, 64, or some other number of cores in each direction for a total of 1024 or 4096 cores. Modular construction of storage planes permits additional storage requirements to be met by "plugging in" additional units.

Unlike the decimal number system, where each position in a number represents a power of 10, the binary system of numbering represents each position by a power of 2. Moreover, in the binary numbering system we can use only 1's and 0's (which represent the polarities of our magnetic cores). Hence the binary number 1001 is $1 \times 2^3 + 0 \times 2^2 + 0 \times 2^1 + 1 \times 2^0 = 9$. This is the manner in which numbers and characters are represented in the magnetic core of the *computer memory*. Binary numbers from 0 to 9 can be represented by the table:

Binary	*Decimal*
0000	0
0001	1
0010	2
0011	3
0100	4
0101	5
0110	6
0111	7
1000	8
1001	9

Computer memory is made up of fixed units comprising a certain number of magnetic cores. We want to be able to represent in memory ten decimal digits, twenty-six alphabetic characters, and twenty-five special symbols (comma, dollar sign, etc.). (See Figure 6–2.) Binary schemes for representing these data vary, but all utilize a prearranged assignment of bits and groups of bits. This system of representation is important because of the need to arrange core storage and locate it by address.

The storage of computer memory is divided into locations, each with an assigned address. Each location holds a specific unit of data, which may be a character, a digit, an entire record, or a word. When a data item is desired, it is obtained from its known location in addressable storage units that are organized to provide data when wanted. There are several schemes for using the processor to assist the programmer in keeping track of the storage locations. These schemes provide *data-names,* such as "update inventory" or "calculate net pay" to automatically refer to sections in the program designed to perform these calculations. Notice the similarity between these programs and the procedures manual of the manual inventory system described previously.

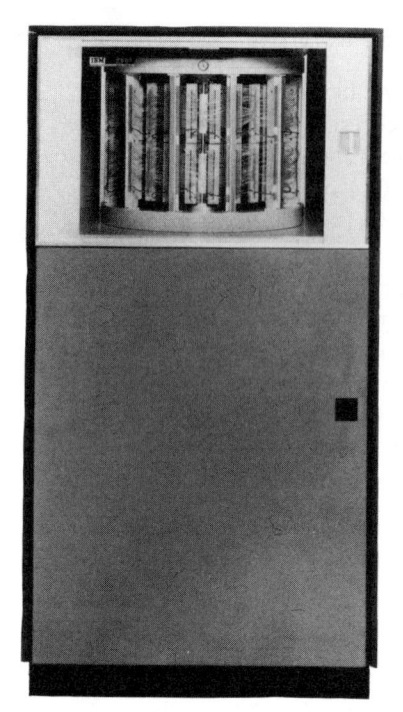

IBM 2303 Drum Storage

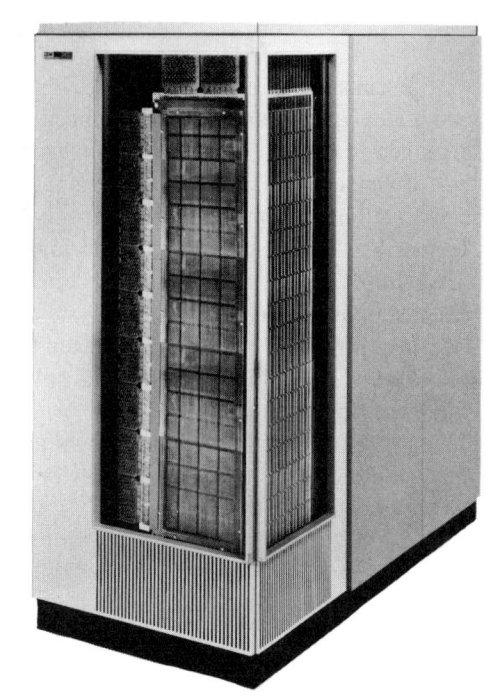

IBM 2361 Core Storage

IBM 2311 Disk Storage Drive

IBM 2321 Data Cell Drive Model 1

Figure 6–9 Storage Devices

SOURCE   Courtesy IBM Corporation

External storage (consisting of records and files, reference data, and other programs) is of two types:

1. *Direct access.* Disc, magnetic drum, and data cell devices providing random-order mass data storage that can be accessed randomly, without having to read from the beginning of the file to find the desired data. Figure 6–9 shows some of these devices that stand apart from the processing unit.
2. *Sequential.* Magnetic tape that is sequentially ordered and that must be read from the beginning in order to read or write a desired record.*

Output

Output devices produce the final results of the data processing. They *record* information from the computer on a variety of media, such as cards, paper tape, and magnetic tape. They *print* information on paper. Additionally, output devices may generate signals for transmission over teleprocessing networks, produce graphic displays, microfilm images, and take a variety of special forms. For the most part, the basic business-type applications take the output form of a paper printout. As indicated in Figure 6–5, the output from the inventory accounting system would be: (1) a printout containing an inventory status report, and (2) an updated inventory master file. Figure 6–7 shows some typical output devices that are linked directly to the computer system.

Summary

We have chosen the illustration of the inventory control system to make the transition by analogy from a manual to a computer-based system.

There is nothing very complex about the computer components, a greater understanding of which can be obtained by comparing the components of the manual and computer systems as in Table 6–1. Both have the basic components: input, processor, storage (internal and external), programs or procedures for processing data, and outputs. A major consideration of the computer system is the structure of data storage in computer memory so that this information can be accessed.

---

*Magnetic tape storage can be compared to a home tape recorder, since the tape media of each are physically almost alike. If we wish to play song number 5 of the tape, we must play through songs 1, 2, 3, and 4 to reach it. So it is with tape storage for the computer. Conversely, random-order storage can be compared to the phonograph. Information is recorded on grooves in a disc, and if we wish to play song number 5, we can place the needle in the proper groove immediately. So it is with disc storage for the computer.

Table 6-1
Comparison of Manual and Computer-Based Inventory Accounting System

Component	Manual System	Computer System
INPUT	Various manual transaction documents	Punched cards
PROCESSOR	Inventory control clerk with calculating machine and human logic	Central processing unit
STORAGE		
Internal	Working storage of inventory clerk	Memory of central processing unit, which contains magnetic core
External	Manual inventory records and files	Master inventory file maintained on magnetic tape
PROCEDURE	Processing instructions contained in procedures manual	Program for processing data contained in memory of internal storage
OUTPUT	Manually prepared status report and updated master file	Automatic preparation of status report and updating of master file

CONVERSION OF MANUAL TO COMPUTER-BASED SYSTEMS[2]

To increase our understanding of computer-based management information systems, we continue our transition from manual to computer system by describing the steps involved in making a conversion or changeover from the inventory accounting system of Figure 6-4, assuming as we do so that a feasibility study has been made and that the system conversion is economical and feasible. The steps involved in the conversion are illustrated in Figure 6-10 and are listed below.

1. System description
2. Input documents
3. Output documents
4. File design
5. The program flowchart
6. Computer assembly
7. Computer program
8. Program operation

System Description

The system description is in narrative form and is usually prepared after preliminary investigation and definition of the problem. The description is essentially a statement of the major inputs, outputs, processing opera-

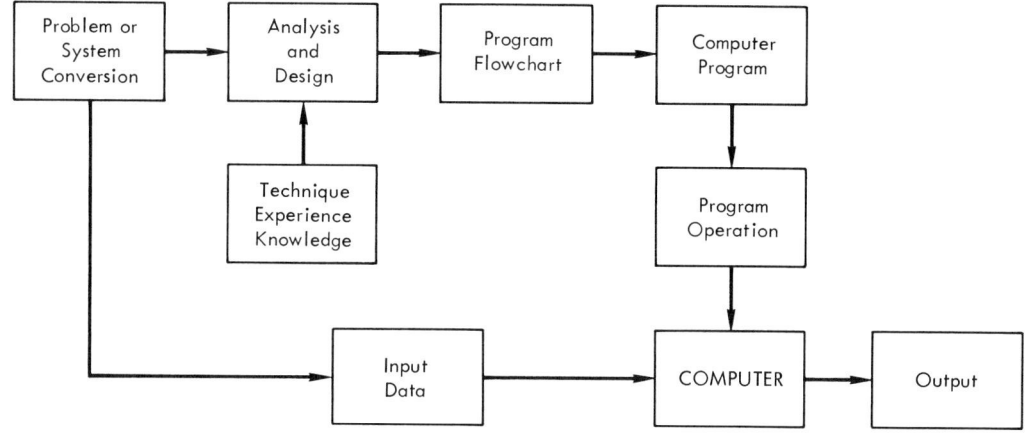

Figure 6-10 Conversion of Problems to Machine Operation

tions, and files needed. The purpose is to show the logical flow of information and the logical operations necessary to carry out the particular design alternative chosen. After the narrative description of the system is prepared, it is almost always depicted in flowchart form.

The *narrative* form of our inventory accounting system could take the following level of narration:

> The activity is concerned with an inventory control accounting system for finished goods inventory. Transactions (receipts and issues) are read from punched cards, the relevant magnetic-tape master record is found and updated, and the new inventory status report is printed.

The *flowchart* puts in symbolic form what has been described in narrative form. It facilitates a quick analysis of the job being performed and provides a general symbolic overview of the entire operation. The flowchart for the narrative description of our inventory accounting system appears as Figure 6-11.

Input Documents

After the system description is completed, it is necessary to specify how the information will be put into a form that is acceptable to the computer. Volume of information, frequency, accuracy and verification requirements, and the handling of the information are considerations in the selection of input format. Sometimes inputs have to be accepted in the form in which they are received from the outside. In this case, the task of conversion is merely one of preparing input to machine-usable form.

The exact layout of input documents is necessary because the computer program is an exact and precise sequence of steps that operates only when

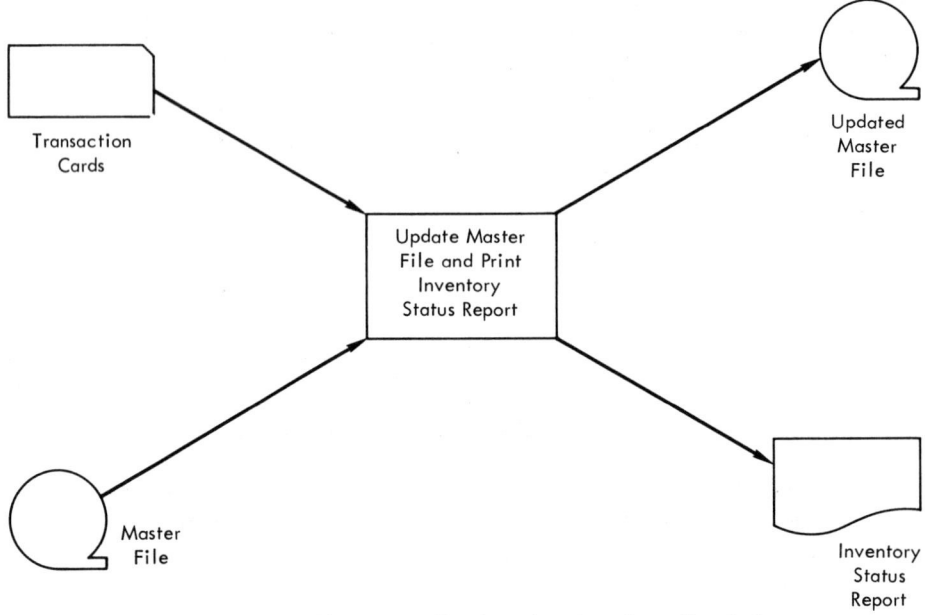

Figure 6–11 Systems Flowchart, Inventory Accounting System

data is located in prescribed positions. In our example, the input format is determined to be punched cards. The holes in these cards are interpreted by the input device of the card reader, converted into computer-readable form, and stored in computer memory for processing.

The card input layout for our inventory accounting example is shown in Figure 6–12. The item number of inventory is represented by an eight-digit numeric field. A separate card is prepared for each transaction, with the quantity involved in the transaction represented by an eight-digit field and the nature of the transaction indicated by the last field on the card,

Figure 6–12 Layout for Input Transaction Card

which has an eight-digit code (this could be transaction by price, territory, customer, etc.).

Examination of the input document reveals that it provides all the relevant information contained in the system description. The typical *item description* normally associated with inventory is not contained in the input document because it is already filed in storage.

Output Documents

Outputs are subject to much the same considerations as input documents, but the output format should be treated with additional care because it represents the purpose or objective of the entire operation. It is the output document with which management is almost exclusively concerned, and because of its critical nature, care should be taken in its design.

The output layout in our example is shown in Figure 6–13. Although the computer is capable of printing much more complex reports than our example, we show the minimum information required to meet the specifications of our system description and output requirements.

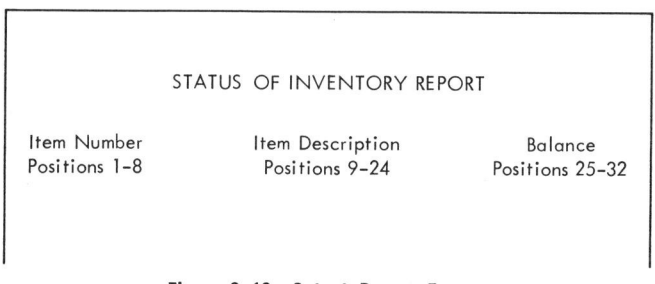

```
                STATUS OF INVENTORY REPORT

    Item Number          Item Description          Balance
    Positions 1-8        Positions 9-24            Positions 25-32
```

Figure 6–13 Output Report Format

File Design

The logic required to control the flow of data through the system is a part of systems design, and the flow is in turn dependent upon the design of data files. These two steps are closely associated and should be considered in conjunction with considerations of type of equipment, storage capacity, input and output media, and format.

The character-by-character contents of every record are specified by the file record layouts. Since magnetic tape files are already specified for our example, we are concerned with the tape input layout. This is shown in Figure 6–14.

The item number is an eight-digit field, the same as that on the punched card of the input document. The item description consists of two eight-digit fields making up sixteen alphabetic characters. This description is an integral

Frames	1.......8	9.......24	25.......32	
	Item Number	Item Description	Item Balance	End of Record Gap

Figure 6-14 Layout of Magnetic Tape Records

part of the inventory file maintained on tape; there is no reason to include it on the input punched card representing individual transactions. The file design of the magnetic tape is completed by the eight-digit item balance field. For the sake of simplicity we have not included several other elements of file design, such as price, unit costs, weight, minimum and maximum inventory limits, and so on.

The Program Flowchart

The program flowchart is the programmer's logic of the detailed, step-by-step representation of how the computer program will accomplish the job. It is the "blueprint" of a program and is used to marshal and organize the facts for examination on paper; to outline problems, logic, and solutions; and to deal with the whole problem in systematic steps. The flowchart of our conversion from manual to computer inventory accounting might appear as shown in Figure 6–15.

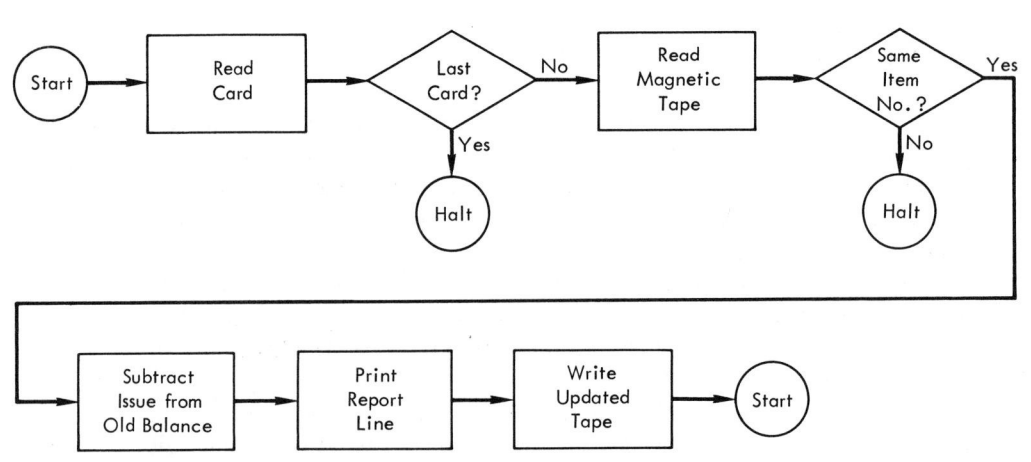

Figure 6–15 The Program Flowchart

The flowchart symbols for both programming and system flowcharting are shown in Figure 6–16. By comparing these symbols with the decisions and actions depicted in our flowchart for the inventory accounting system, we can see how the computer will perform the logic of the application. After the program writes out a new, updated master record on tape (Figure 6–14), it loops back to read another card, and so on, until all cards (transactions) are processed.

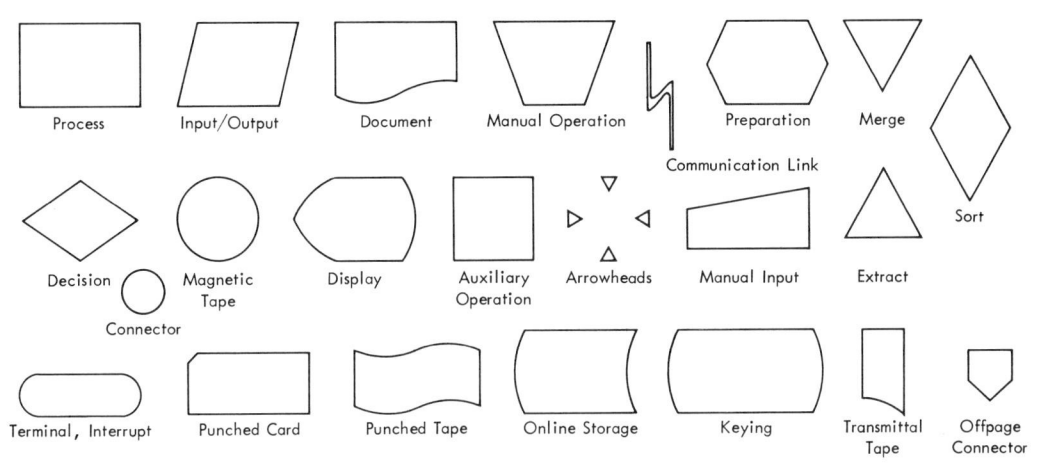

Figure 6–16 Program and System Flowchart Symbols

Computer Assembly

Computer processing units can operate only from instructions expressed in machine-readable form: binary numbers. For example, the instruction to add regular pay to overtime pay giving total pay would look like this:

$$10 \quad 100 \quad 101 \quad 200$$

The 10 indicates the ADD instruction, the 100 and 101 are addresses of storage locations for the numbers representing regular and overtime pay, and 200 is the location for the sum, total pay.

Obviously, it is too tedious for a programmer to instruct the computer in binary form, so assembly programs are written that allow the program to be expressed in alphanumeric notation and "assembled" into binary notation for storage in the computer. Computer instructions are stored in the same way as data.

Computer Program

After data is transcribed to an input medium, and before the program is assembled into binary notation for computer use, the procedural steps that are to take place within the computer system must be defined precisely in terms of operations that the system can perform. Stated another way, the flowchart of Figure 6–15 must be written as an instruction that can be "run through" the assembly and converted into machine-readable format.

A series of instructions pertaining to an entire procedure is called a program. The program is stored internally and the processor has access to the instructions as required.

The details of computer programming are complex, specific, and beyond the scope of this brief investigation. We are concerned only with the general nature of how the processor is instructed to perform its operation on the input data in order to produce the output data in the desired format. For this purpose we can refer to the programming description provided by a leading computer manufacturer:

INSTRUCTIONS

The computer is directed to perform each of its operations by an instruction—a unit of specific information located in main storage. This information is interpreted by the central processing unit as an operation to be performed.

If data are involved, the instruction directs the computer to the data. If some device is to be controlled—a magnetic tape unit, for example, the instruction specifies the device and the required operations.

Instructions may change the condition of an indicator; they may shift data from one location in storage to another; they may cause a tape unit to rewind; or they may change the contents of a counter. Some instructions arbitrarily, or as a result of some machine or data indication, can specify the storage location of the next instruction. In this way, it is possible to alter the sequence in which any instruction or block of instructions is followed.

An instruction usually consists of at least two parts:
1. An operation part that designates read, write, add, subtract, compare, move data, and so on.
2. An operand that designates the address of the information or device that is needed for the specified operation.

Operation	*Operand*
Select	Tape Unit 200
Read	One record into storage positions 1000–1050
Clear and add	Quantity in storage location 1004 in accumulator
Subtract	Quantity in storage location 1005 from contents of accumulator
Store	Result in storage location 1051
Branch	To instruction in storage location 5004

During an instruction cycle, an instruction is selected from storage and analyzed by the central processing unit. The operation part indicates the operation to be performed. This information is coded to have a special meaning for the computer. For example, in a System/360, the letter A is interpreted as "add," the letter C as "compare," SIO as "start input/output," and TR as "translate." Other computers use different coding and numbers of characters or positions to define an operation.

The operand further defines or augments the function of the operation. For example, to perform arithmetic, the storage location of one of the factors involved is indicated. For input or output devices, the unit to be used is specified. For reading or writing, the area of storage for input or output records is indicated or fixed by machine design.

Because all instructions use the same storage media as data, they must be represented in the same form of coding.

In general, no particular areas of storage are reserved for the instructions only. In most instances, they are grouped together and placed, in ascending sequential locations, in the normal order in which they are to be executed by the computer. However, the order of execution may be varied by special instruction, by recognition of a predetermined condition of data or devices within the system, by unpredictable interruptions from outside the system (teleprocessing input), by hardware conditions that require servicing from a special set of programs, or by other programs that require unusual priority.[3]

Program Operation

After the program has been written and run through the assembly process, it is placed in memory in binary or "machine-readable" form and is ready to process the input cards, update the master file tape, and print the required report. The computer will execute the instructions of the program in sequence until the program comes to a halt.

Summary

We have gone through the complete cycle of converting a manual inventory accounting system to a computer-based system. Included were the eight steps in making the conversion, the steps that described the operation of the components of the computer system.

The reader should now have a very good idea of how information needs are translated into the language and operation of the computer. However, we have taken the simplest form of inventory accounting system to illustrate this conversion. Few, if any, applications are as simple and straightforward as the one we have demonstrated by way of illustration. The reader may wish to take the more complicated inventory control system of Figure 6–17 and speculate on the steps involved in bringing this system through the conversion process just described.

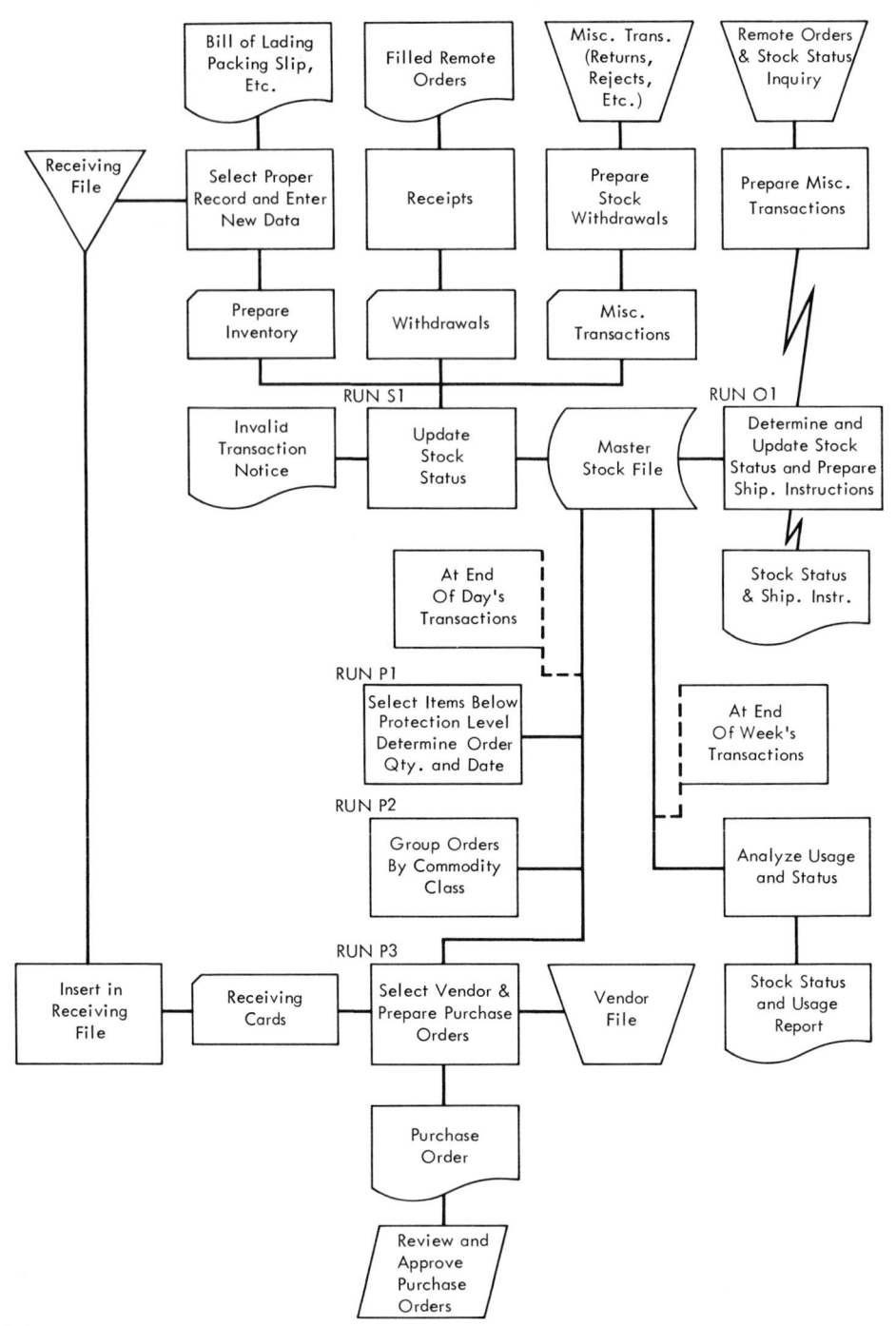

A typical system-flowchart description of an inventory-control application, this chart uses specific symbols for certain processing functions and input/output. The application involves a multiple-warehouse system: items are stocked in a central warehouse for distribution to remote warehouses; all customer orders are received by remotely-located warehouses and transmitted by teletype (communication-link symbol) to the central data-processing installation. The system provides four major groups of operations:

(1) updating stock status [run S1], based on actual transactions; (2) response to inquiries [run O1] from auxiliary warehouses and central warehouse; (3) reorder analysis [runs P1, P2, P3], including purchase-order preparation; (4) weekly analysis reports [run S2] to show slow-moving items, major changes in usage rates, behind-schedule deliveries, economic lot sizes, etc.

Figure 6–17 Flowchart for an Inventory Control System

SOURCE   Courtesy IBM Corporation

THE DATA-BANK CONCEPT

The point has been made repeatedly that the most basic element of a management information system, and indeed the element vital to the management process, is knowledge—information about the goals and objectives of the organization, its policies, resources, operations, and environment. An individual's personal knowledge is only what can be acquired and stored in his memory and then retrieved and manipulated as necessary, and although many managers insist on operating with only the information stored in personal memory, it is essential nowadays to augment this capacity with other storage media. Books, magazines, forms, records, and a variety of other media assist us in storing information until it is needed. However, in today's complex managerial environment it is becoming more and more necessary that the organization turn to the computer for storing, processing, and retrieving information. In developing an information system to serve the diverse needs of today's organization, knowledge and information relative to the organization's management and operations can be stored in the memory of the computer. This knowledge can be described and labeled as a data bank. Conceptually, Figure 6–18 shows the transfer of information from human memory and other media to the memory of a computer. To under-

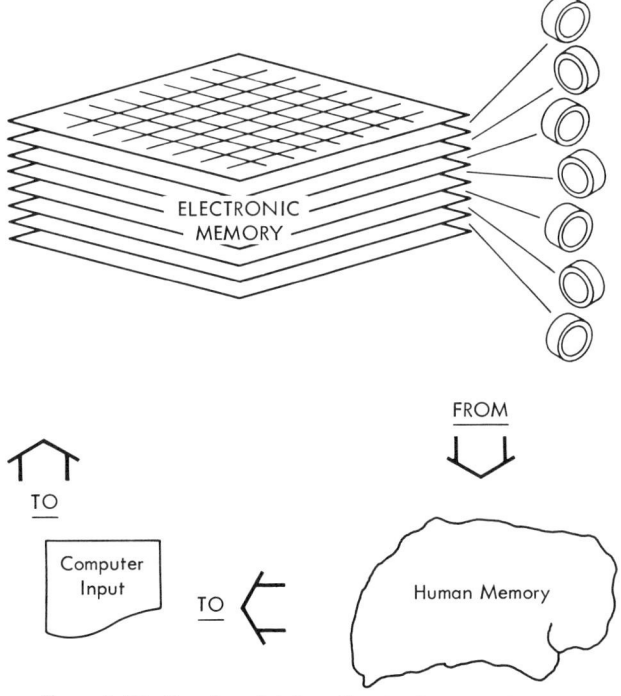

Figure 6–18 Transfer of Information to Computer Memory

stand and appreciate the concept of central storage and the acquisition of information from a data bank, it is helpful to review an elementary sample of storage under a manual system.

Information Storage—Manual System

Today's complex organizations are burdened with a combination of problems, not the least of which is information handling. The ratio of clerical workers to production workers continues to rise, and there appears to be no end in sight to the increasing volume of clerical operations performed in modern companies today. Yet despite the increase in clerical workers and clerical operations, one out of four production workers in manufacturing is handling paperwork, and the percentage is much higher in nonmanufacturing industries.

Managers embroiled in paperwork have no time for planning and evaluation, and their working hours become more crisis-oriented when most of their time is spent searching for information with which to handle crises that arise in addition to the normal work flow. Add this cost of underutilization of management manpower to the rising cost and complexity of information handling, and the conclusion emerges that the gathering and dissemination of information is usually the company's most difficult problem. Information is voluminous, scattered, and often difficult to obtain.

Generally, dissemination of information falls within one or more of five categories: (1) replies to inquiries, (2) standard routine reports, (3) exception reports, (4) shop or operational paper, and (5) special reports. Costs and complexities of maintaining manual information systems for these types of reports usually result from two factors: duplication of conventional record files in two or more departments, and problems associated with *integration* of decentralized planning and operating departments.

The natural inclination of people to hoard duplicate information relating to their jobs, plus the tendency of departments to overlook some of the costs associated with information, results in duplication of record files in many departments. This is not to say that in a manual information system some duplication is not necessary; indeed, it is. Figure 6–19 illustrates how an information *input* of a single transaction (customer purchase order) results in action within a number of other files, each separately maintained. Record files affected are: first, the customer file (for credit checking, preparation of shipping instructions, preparation of an invoice, etc.); second, the accounts receivable records; third, inventory adjustment; and fourth, updating of production scheduling and other production statistics. Depending upon the nature of the company and the organization of its information system, several additional files may be affected by this one transaction.

The integration of planning, operating, and controlling between departments through the medium of information is a problem of even greater im-

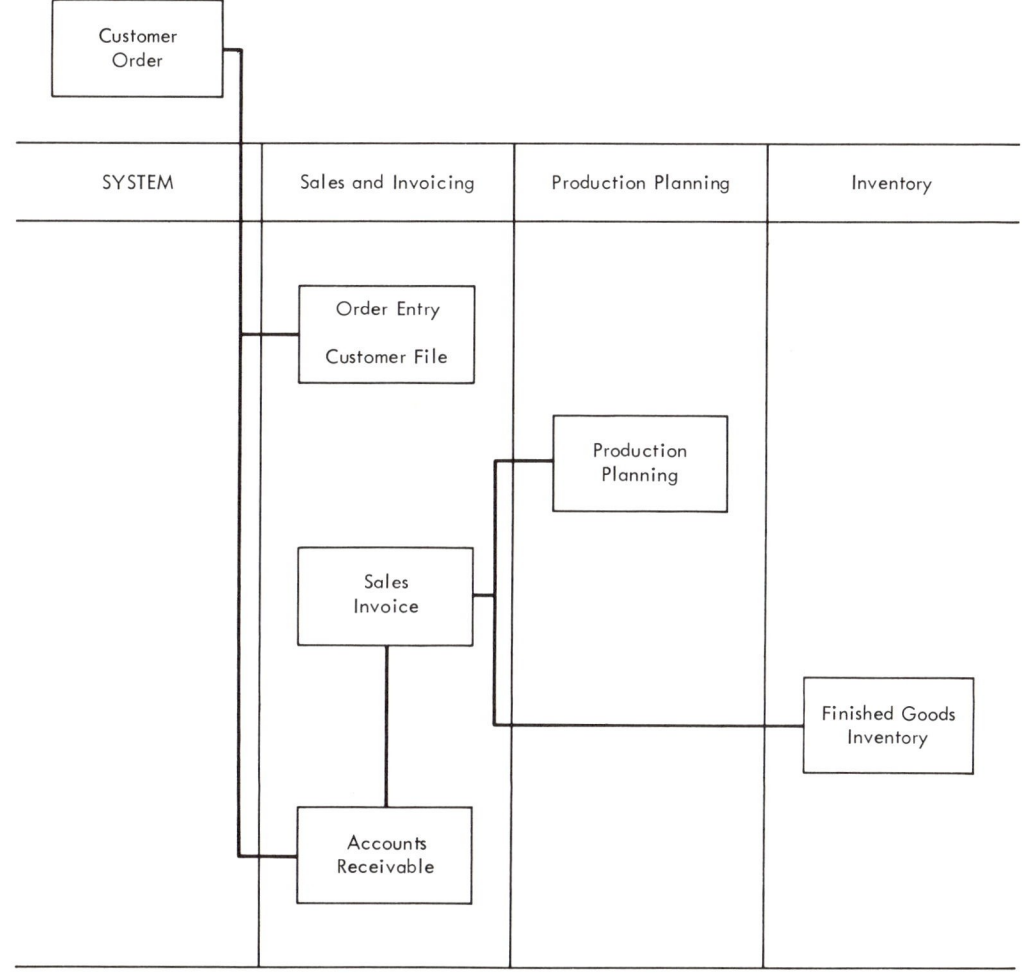

what the manager should know about the computer 223

Figure 6–19 Record Files in Manufacturing Company—Manual System

portance. Departments tend to recognize only some of the costs and information important to them and frequently fail to recognize the interaction of their operations with other departments in the company. The sales department is well aware of customer service and the need for substantial inventories of finished goods, yet is unaware of the planning and resources involved in maintaining optimum inventory levels. The production department is concerned with utilization of employment, overhead, and facilities, yet it is not fully aware of how these actions influence the marketing effort. Finance, on the other hand, watches over excessive inventory and carrying costs, fearful of cash drains and their effect on profits. It is essential that the efforts of these decentralized departments be integrated.

| Owner & Sons — Purchase Order ||||
Quantity	Stock Number	Unit Cost	Total
120	74B 34916-z	3.60	432.00

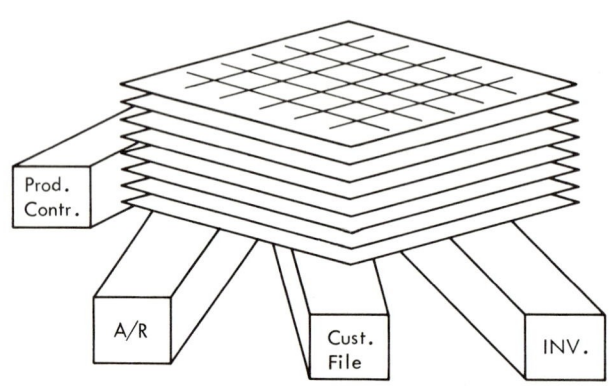

Figure 6–20 Integration of Separate Record Files Into One Data Bank

How can today's manager possibly digest all the pertinent detail in a dynamic company? How can he maintain his information files at a minimum and at the same time ensure that the many departments within the company are integrated into a total system? The answer in both cases appears to lie in the proper design and implementation of a management information system. Yet this is difficult if not impossible with a manual information system. Experience has shown that if today's company wishes to improve its operations, it can do so with (1) a central information system, and (2) a framework to facilitate mechanization. These two attributes are part of the data-bank concept.

Information Storage and Retrieval—Data Bank

The corporate or organization data bank can overcome the two primary objections to the manual system mentioned. The accumulation of information in an information center where "one set of books" is maintained avoids the maintenance of separate record files and also tends to *integrate* the separate functions and departments of the company.

The data bank, or the *central data base,* as it is sometimes called, is constructed to store and retrieve the information used in common by the various subsystems of the company. Using modern information-processing technology, a high-speed, random access, mass storage device is used to store large volumes of data concerning the various aspects of the firm and its environment. All relevant information about the company's operation is contained in one readily accessible file, arranged so that duplication and

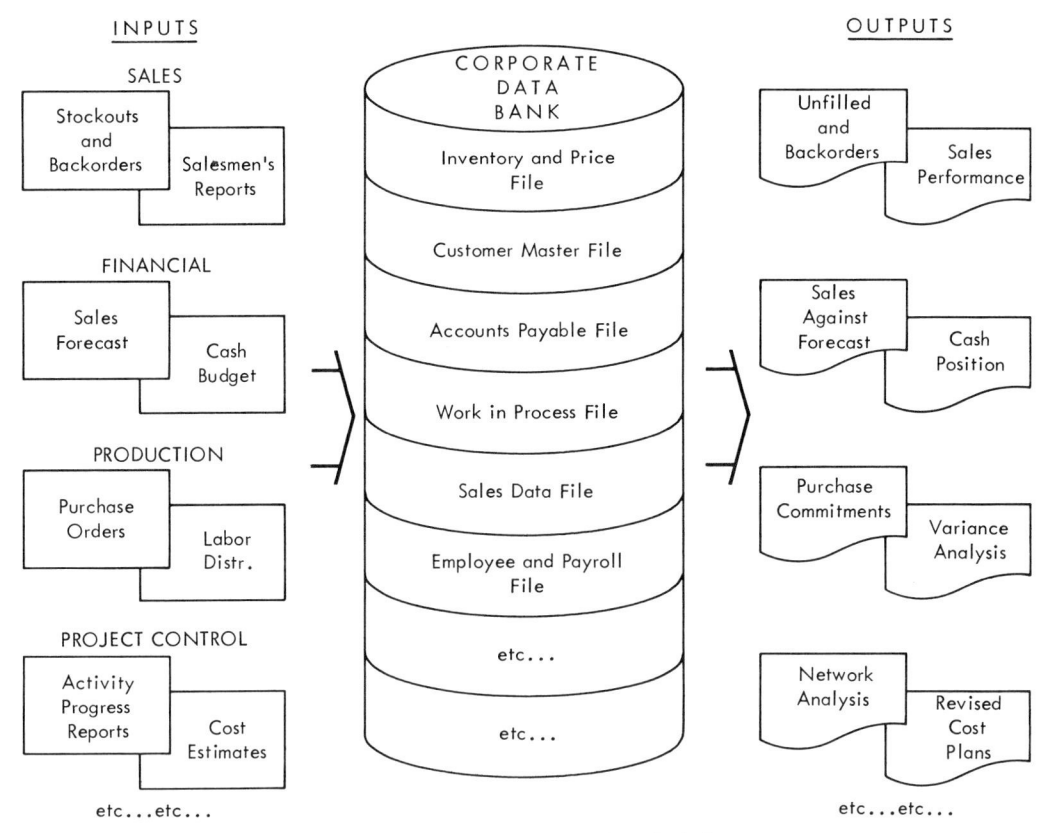

Figure 6–21 Selected Inputs and Outputs from Typical Manufacturing Company's Data Bank

redundancy are avoided. Moreover, because only one set of records is necessary, it will be easier to maintain their accuracy.

Taking the example of the customer purchase order used to demonstrate our manual system, Figure 6–20 shows how the four separate files maintained in four departments can now be combined into one central data bank. Data is captured once, validated, and placed in the appropriate location in the data base.

Figure 6–21 is a more comprehensive illustration of the data-bank concept and illustrates how more, but by no means all, of a typical manufacturing company's information files can be integrated into the central data base. In the usual case, the data base is organized around the major information subsystems required to run the business: (1) general accounting files, (2) inventory file, (3) customer and sales file, (4) vendor file, and (5) personnel file.

It is essential that the data-base system satisfy the requirements of the user, otherwise he will continue to maintain his own system and thereby defeat the purpose of the central data base. The key element in this concept is that each subsystem utilize the same data base in the satisfaction of its information needs. This will yield an additional significant advantage—the integration of departments and functions. Each organizational entity, integrated into a whole through its access and interface with the total information resources of the company, gains a greater understanding and appreciation of how its actions and plans affect others throughout the organization. This integration is demonstrated conceptually in Figure 6–22.

A major side benefit of a central data base is the simultaneous review of company structure, information needs, and management that naturally accompanies the comprehensive review required. The development of the data may act as a catalyst in highlighting such problems as communication, organization, planning, and control.

Potential problems surrounding data-base construction are generally those connected with interdepartmental coordination and agreement. These might include: (1) the possibility of invalid input of information by a unit wishing to maintain *information security;* (2) the "multiplier effect" of erroneously entered data, which has an immediate influence on other depart-

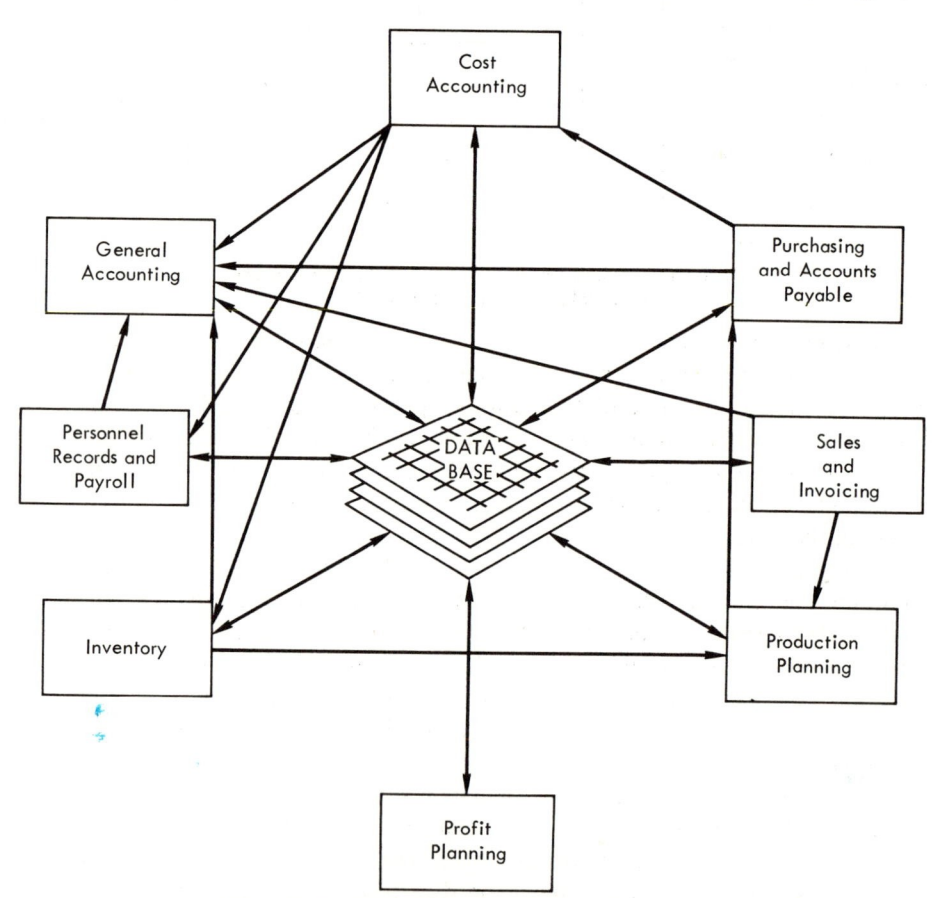

Figure 6–22 Integration of Functions and Departments Through the Integrated Data Base

ments utilizing the data; (3) the *time dimension* of input data, which requires that user departments agree on the time during which a transaction should be reflected by data input; and (4) the interdepartment agreement required concerning the degree of detail to be included in data elements of the data base. Unless some common ground for agreement and solution of these problems is found, organizational units tend to maintain their own system for their peculiar needs. This, of course, defeats the purpose of the central data base.

TYPES OF COMPUTER-BASED APPLICATIONS

An insight into the design of management information systems can be gained by considering three types or classifications of application. We are not concerned with the many classifications by function or process (e.g., payroll, purchasing, inventory control), but with those where batch (cyclical) processing is used—applications that utilize the on-line or real-time capability of modern equipment, and applications designed primarily for making or aiding decisions.

The state-of-the-art in these applications and the effectiveness of each in providing management assistance for planning, operating, and controlling are important factors to consider when designing or modifying a management information system. The characteristics of the three types of application can be compared:

Type of Application	*Degree of Implementation*	*Greatest Use*	*Orientation*	*Integration of Data Base*	*Decision Making*
BATCH	Greatest	Integration of subsystems	Historical and accounting	Integrated	Limited
REAL-TIME	Few	Control	Remote	Moderate	"Pre-set" decision rules
DECISION-MAKING	Very limited	Planning	Decision assistance	Limited	Poor

Batch Processing Applications

Batch processing is the classical method of processing data and is far and away the most frequently used MIS application. It entails the cyclical processing of input information in "batches." The time it takes to process the data and receive an output is known as "turnaround" time.

The batch processing of checking accounts in commercial banks is a good illustration of this type of application. The turnaround time, or the minimum unit of time in processing checks, is one business day, since a depositor's account is considered satisfactory if it has a positive balance at the close of the business day. Thus, checks received from all sources are proved and sorted for processing against customers' accounts. The checks are "paid" by posting to accounts after they are sorted to the accounts on which they are drawn. Any checks that cause an overdraft by reason of insufficient funds may be charged back to the source from which received.

Most applications in the batch processing category involve the automation of routine functions, deal primarily with the data of the accounting system, and are oriented to record keeping and historical information. Most, but by no means all, of these systems are used for (1) payroll, (2) accounts payable, (3) customer billing, (4) general ledger, and (5) accounts receivable.

Because most of the cost of maintaining information in a company is for the batch processing type of application, these systems offer perhaps the greatest potential for reduction of *information-handling costs*. Because of the relatively larger amount of experience with these applications, considerable advances have been made in such large-volume, self-contained applications as payrolls, inventory control, accounts payable, and customer billing.

Some of the more advanced work on improving batch processing applications involves the integration of such separate but related applications as the integration of inventory control and purchasing. Additionally, considerable advance has been made in the data-base concept of these applications whereby multiple applications are obtained from single-source, single-file integrated data bases.

One consideration to keep in mind when developing batch processing applications is the subsequent difficulty involved in integrating a data base from a variety of batch processing systems that were independently developed.

Real-Time Applications

Compared with batch processing, the real-time applications are very few, but they are highly publicized because of their exciting nature and their great potential for the future. These applications feature the computer's exciting capability for direct and instant access in which a dialogue is carried on between computer and user.

Most current real-time applications are little more than on-line versions of previous systems, and most are primarily one-application-oriented, with little integration between subsystems. Characteristically, this type of application features remote terminal access with data transmission through telephone lines or some other means. Illustrative of real-time applications are those systems for airline reservations, room reservations, work-progress control in plants, inventory-status ordering and reporting of geographically dispersed distributors, and credit-status interrogation for a variety of users.

Real-time operation can be defined as "paralleling data processing with a physical process in such a fashion that the results of the data processing are immediately useful to the physical operation."[4] This definition causes some difficulty because of the varying elapsed times required to *complete a transaction* and the varying time required for data processing to be *immediately useful*. To illustrate, we can say that real time in the case of an airline reservation system involves the processing of an answer while the customer is on the phone. On the other hand we have systems that scan and match workers' identification badges and job tickets on a real-time basis but wait days or weeks to process paychecks.

Generally speaking, real-time systems have these three characteristics: (1) data will be maintained "on-line," (2) data will be updated as events occur, and (3) the computer can be interrogated from remote terminals or other devices. There is some doubt whether managers really need this capability in more than a small fraction of their daily information needs.[5] As a practical matter, more systems with real-time capability utilize both the batch processing and real-time modes for their operations. Such a system is illustrated in Figure 6-23, a conceptual design of the U.S. Bureau of Employment Security management information system that is planned to be installed nationwide in the middle 1970's. Note the organization of the central data bank and the capability of the system to service many remote users by terminal. Users can "interrogate" the system as desired.

Decision Applications

Although spectacular breakthroughs have been made in computer applications for command and control decisions, similar uses for management problems are few and quite limited. Nothing approaching decision systems such as the SAGE (Semi-Automatic Ground Environment) air defense system or the one that guides Apollo's flight to the moon have yet been designed for business use.

Computer applications that make and execute low-level, routine decisions are relatively frequent. Examples are inventory reordering and certain types of production scheduling. However, for higher-order top-management decisions, available applications involve much interaction of the decision maker with the computer. This type of man–machine interface may be called *computer-assisted decision making*.

The primary reason for lack of progress in higher-level decision making by management information systems is the difficulty of defining decision rules for business problems. Although management science techniques have been successfully applied to discrete parts of business activity, their application to higher-management decision processes is still an item for further research. Indeed, applications at higher levels are the forthcoming frontier of computer applications.

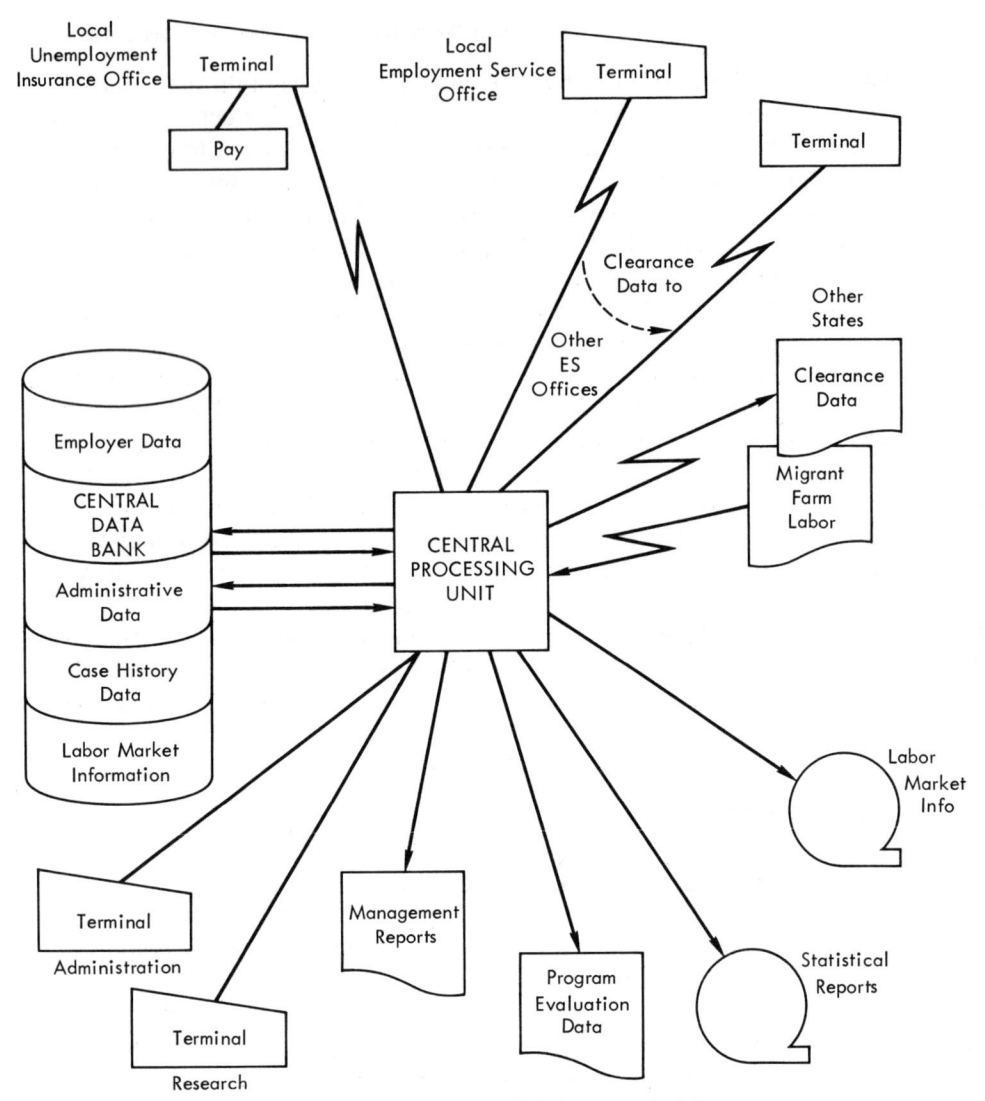

Figure 6–23 U.S. Bureau of Employment Security Management Information System Conceptual Design

With regard to *computer-assisted decision making,* several surveys indicate that the effectiveness of current and near-term applications in assisting management is, at best, below average. However, the majority of firms plan to devote a major share of computer effort to computer-assisted decision making for management in the future.

One of the most rapidly growing applications for computer-assisted decision making is the simulation or model. The corporate model enables management to: (1) reduce the time required to react to change, (2) evaluate alternative courses of action with a full knowledge of all pertinent factors, and (3) make longer-range plans by taking longer looks into the fu-

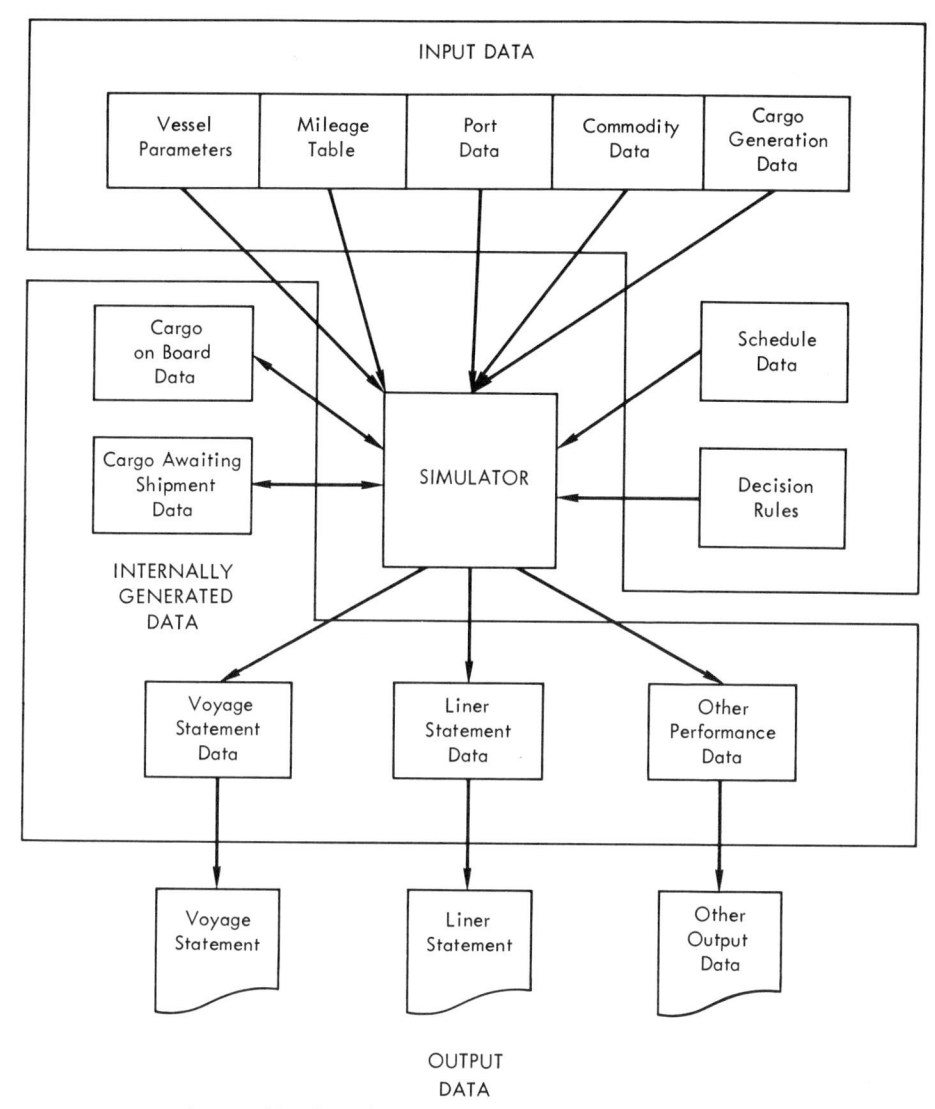

Figure 6–24 Simulation Model—Moore-McCormack Lines, Inc.

ture.[6] By posing "what if . . ." questions to the model, the decision maker can explore different alternatives and weigh the consequences of each. In other words, he can simulate the effects of many decisions without having to wait for the results of the decisions in "real life."

Figure 6–24 demonstrates a simulation utilized very effectively by Moore-McCormack Lines, Incorporated, for scheduling and routing cargo vessels.[7] Two alternative means of varying inputs will illustrate the model. Assuming that some parameters are fixed (i.e., current fleet, freight rates, commodity volumes, origin and destination patterns, operating costs), the following inputs can be varied to determine their effect upon operations:

schedule patterns, vessel assignments, and decision rules. On the other hand, the decision maker can assume that modes of operation are fixed, and he can then vary the following inputs to determine their effects: freight rates, annual volumes, operations costs, and origin and destination patterns. Under each of the foregoing assumptions and variations of fixed parameters and inputs, one valuable output from the model is a financial statement indicating the performance of each individual vessel based on the assumptions put into the model.

SUMMARY

In this chapter we have made the transition by analogy from a manual information system to one that is computer based. With the example of the inventory accounting system, it was shown that the components of both systems are the same: input, processor, storage, output, and procedure. In the manual system, the operations are performed manually or with minimum mechanical assistance, but the computer system processes data electronically; hence we call it an electronic data processor.

In first establishing a computer information system or modifying a manual one for computer use, the programmer and designer go through the steps of system description, design of input document, output documents, file design, flowcharting the program, writing the computer program, and making the program operational.

The concept of a central data base has several advantages over the notion of individual departmental files. The data bank is constructed to store and retrieve information used in common by various subsystems of the company. This centralization avoids the duplication costs involved in maintaining separate record files, but more important, an integrated data base tends to integrate the functions and subsystems of the organization.

Of the three types of applications (batch processing, real time, and decision), batch processing is far and away the most numerous and advanced in degree of implementation. Operational real-time systems are few in number but of great potential for advancing the boundaries of managerial decision making and control. Applications for top-management decision making are pratically nonexistent, although systems designed for computer-assisted decision making are growing in number and degree of sophistication. Modeling appears to offer the greatest potential for decision assistance in the future.

what the manager should know about the computer 233

DISCUSSION QUESTIONS AND PROBLEMS

1. The components of a data-processing system are listed below along with those of a manual information system and of a computer system. Match column A with B and C.

A Data-Processing System	B Manual Information System (Shipping)		C Computer System	
(a) Input	_B_	Shipping Clerk	_B_	Central Processor
(b) Processor	_C_	Records and Files	_D_	Program
(c) Storage	_D_	Procedures Manual	_E_	Printer
(d) Instructions	_A_	Customer's Invoice	_C_	Magnetic Tape
(e) Output	_E_	Shipping Document	_A_	Punched Card

2. Compare the arithmetic, control, and logic functions of the human to those functions and components of the computer.

3. What is the difference between internal and external storage of the computer? What is the function of the internal storage? Where are the programs stored?

4. Take a relatively simple manual application with which you are familiar (payroll, order processing, inventory update) and describe the various steps in converting this system to computer application.

5. Draw a program flowchart for the application chosen in Question 4.

6. To what extent should the manager–user be familiar with the details of system conversion? With programming the computer? With systems analysis? With systems design? With the work of the programmer and analyst?

7. What are the advantages of having a company-wide data bank? What typical items are contained in a data bank and how are they structured? Show how different functions (e.g., cost accounting, sales, inventory) can be integrated with a data bank.

8. Differentiate between batch processing and real-time applications. In what type of application would each be utilized?

9. Name and illustrate what is meant by decision application.

10. The Heritage Furniture Corporation of High Point, N.C., is a full-line furniture manufacturer and enjoys a quality and service reputation unsurpassed in the industry. Furniture manufacturing is partly a production-flow type of process and partly a job-shop process, owing to the large number of special orders received. Manufacturing areas and shops include cutting, assembly, upholstery, finishing, painting, warehouse, and shipping.

The company's management, to improve the manufacturing process, had designed a tentative information system called Manufacturing Information Control System (MICS), the objectives of which were to: (a) improve scheduling and expediting, (b) improve control over work in process, and (c) improve the information concerning raw materials inventory and the location of raw materials throughout the manufacturing process. Conceptually, the MICS would be implemented thus:

a. Develop a market forecast monthly.
b. Explode this forecast into raw materials and labor requirements.
c. Merge current raw materials inventory with any design changes to yield raw material requirements, labor requirements, and production requirements.
d. Achieve production control by attaching travelers (lists of all operations required to complete an item) to each item. After each operation, an attached punched card would be forwarded to the computer center in order to keep financial and production control information complete and up to date.

Questions:

(1) Describe a manual system for production control.
(2) Is the computer system better? If so, how, in terms of cost, accuracy, and time to gather data?
(3) What would be the inputs and outputs of the system?
(4) What dangers might lie ahead in the implementation of this system?
(5) How could the system be revised for real-time application? For decision application?

REFERENCES

1. "New Products of Tomorrow," *Fortune*, May 15, 1969, p. 219.
2. This material is freely adapted from Jerome Kanter, *The Computer and the Executive* (Englewood Cliffs, N.J.: Prentice-Hall, Inc., 1968), pp. 13–25.
3. *Introduction to IBM Data Processing Systems* (White Plains, N.Y.: IBM Technical Publications Department, 1967).
4. Robert V. Head, *Real-Time Business Systems* (New York: Holt, Rinehart & Winston, Inc., 1964), p. 3.
5. John Dearden, "Myth of Real-Time Management Information," *Harvard Business Review*, May–June 1966, pp. 123–32.
6. George W. Gershefski, "Building a Corporate Financial Model," *Harvard Business Review*, July–August 1969, p. 61.
7. Described more fully in Lawrence I. Lipperman, *Advanced Business Systems* (New York: American Management Association, 1968), pp. 51–57.

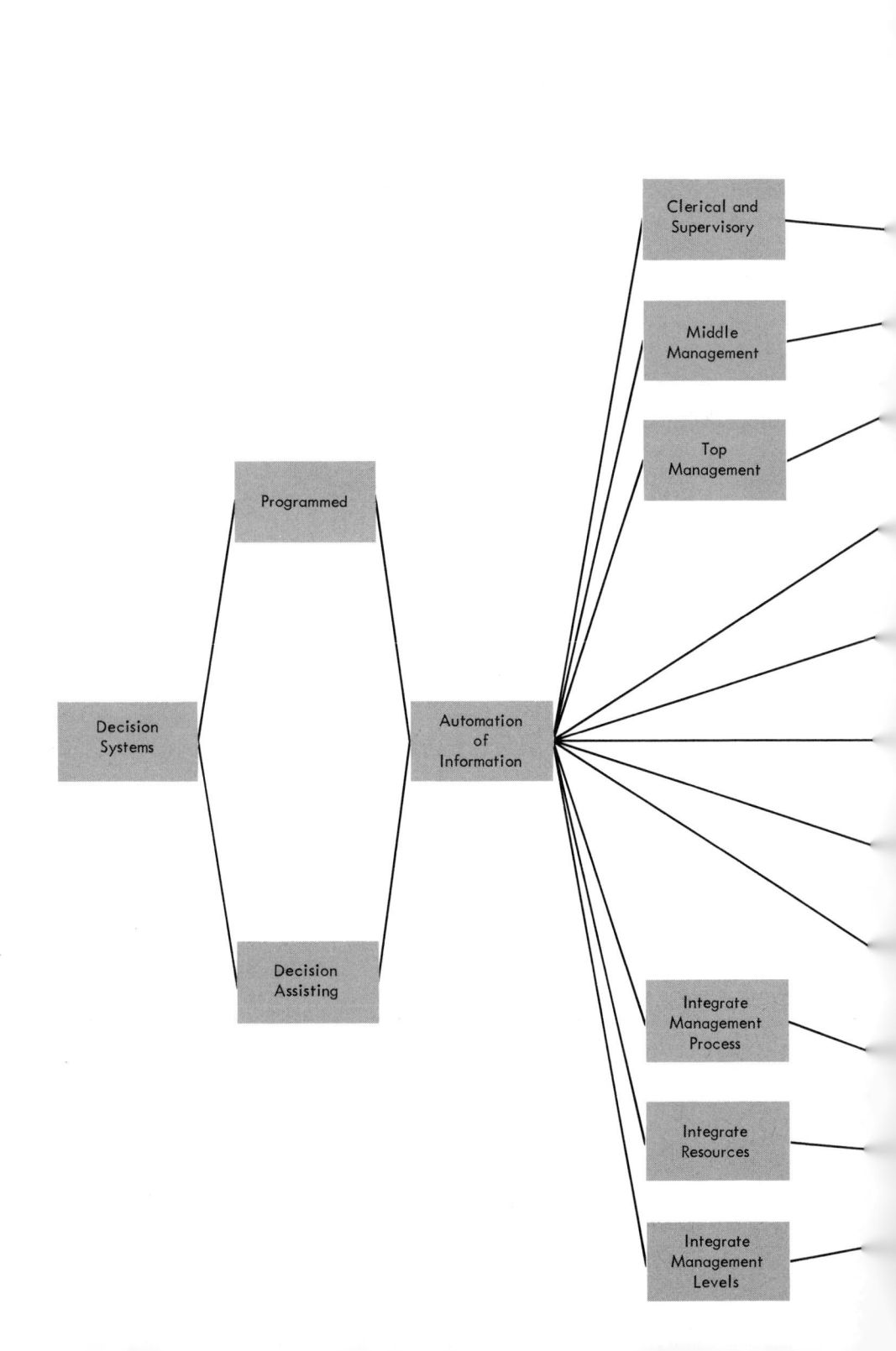

```
Decision Systems
├── Programmed
└── Decision Assisting
        │
        └── Automation of Information
                ├── Clerical and Supervisory
                ├── Middle Management
                ├── Top Management
                ├── Integrate Management Process
                ├── Integrate Resources
                └── Integrate Management Levels
```

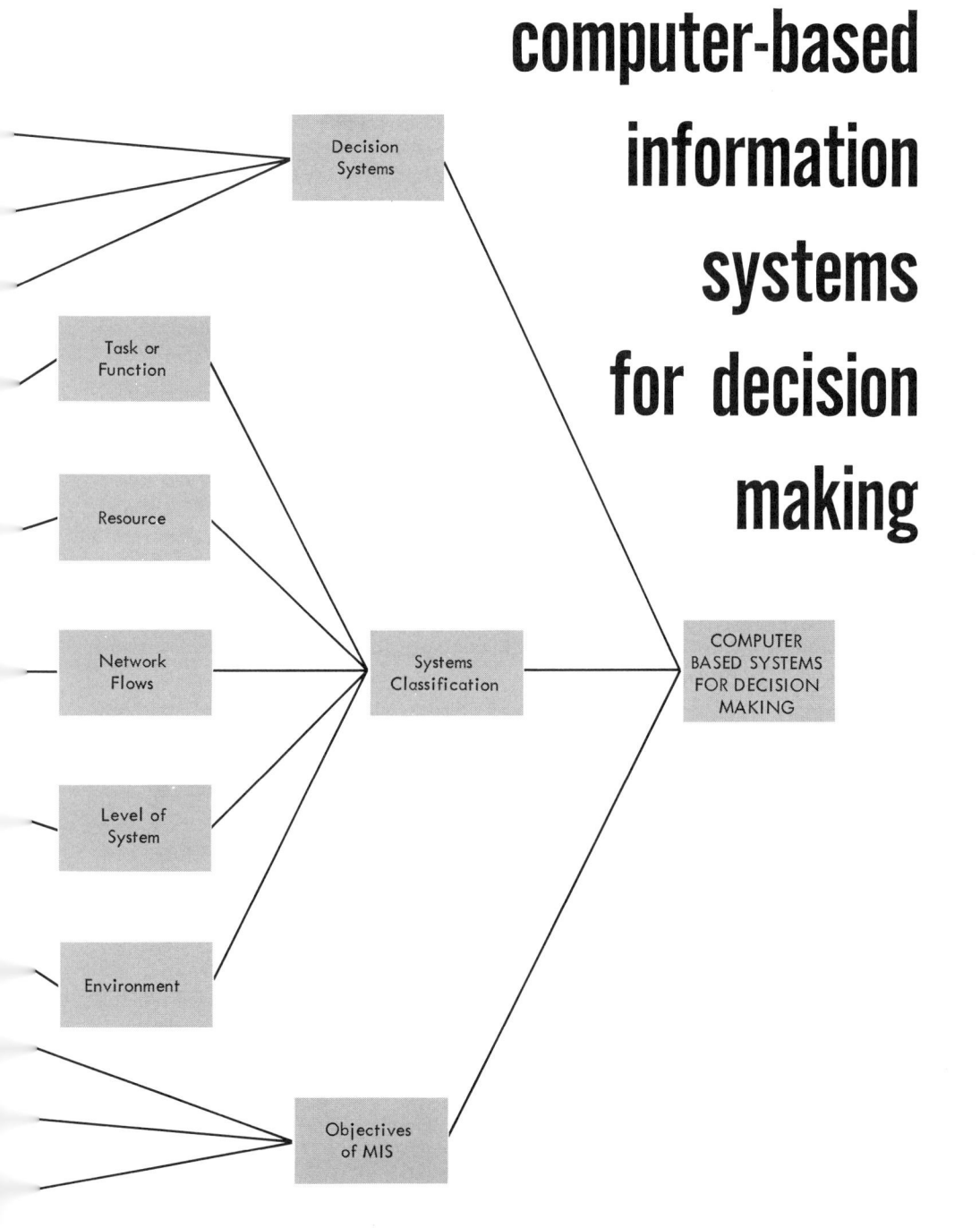

7
computer-based information systems for decision making

- Decision Systems
- Task or Function
- Resource
- Network Flows
- Level of System
- Environment
- Systems Classification
- Objectives of MIS

COMPUTER BASED SYSTEMS FOR DECISION MAKING

7

Consider that in 1970:

1. The revenue from communication of data from one business machine to another in different cities exceeds the revenue from voice transmission over comparable long-distance lines.
2. In ten years the speed of computers has increased by a factor of 1,000:1, costs for computation have gone down by a factor of 100:1, and computer memory capacity has gone up 1,000:1.
3. Approximately 65,000 computer systems are now installed in the United States, representing an investment of about $25 billion.
4. The annual shipment of computers and related equipment in the United States will shortly reach $9 to $10 billion and represent about 12 percent of total new plant and equipment investment.

To state the obvious, computers have arrived on the United States business scene and management will never be the same again. The systems approach to management is facilitated by and indeed is attributable to the digital computer. Perhaps for the first time in history a science of management is possible. Much of the recent history of other sciences can be written in terms of the tools of the computer. Just as the telescope gave science a tool for viewing the distant, and the microscope a tool for examining the minute, the computer gives us a tool for grappling with the complex.

Herbert Simon views the computer as the fourth great breakthrough in history to aid man in his thinking process and decision-making ability.[1] The first was the invention of writing, which aided man's memory in performing mental tasks. The remaining two events prior to the computer were the emergence of the Arabic number system with its zero and positional notation, and the invention of analytic geometry and calculus, which permitted the solution of complex problems in scientific theory. Now the electronic digital computer combines the advantages and attributes of all these breakthroughs and makes them available for decision making and for management of organizations.

As we will see, decision rules, management science, and computers are by definition (p. 359) subsets of information systems design. The task of this chapter is to coalesce or otherwise integrate the topics thus far discussed and to set the stage for MIS planning and design considerations to follow. Hence, we must demonstrate the relationship between the computer on the one hand and its use for decision-making applications on the other. We will be concerned with: (1) how the computer "makes" programmed decisions, provided we program it with appropriate decision rules, and (2) how the computer can provide decision-assisting information for complex decisions that do not lend themselves to automation. These considerations are of primary importance for the manager if he is to utilize the computer and management information systems in improving his decisions and his operations. We will also examine the integrative nature of decision systems and some typical classifications.

AUTOMATION OF INFORMATION

Although everyone is aware of the enormous increases in productivity obtained through mechanization and automation of the physical production process, few managers view the production of information as analogous to that of physical goods. Yet the production of information is at least as important as the production of physical commodities. The now-expanding discipline of management information systems regards information as a resource equal in importance to the traditional ones of men, money, materials, and machines.

Although the potential for progress in the automation of the information production process is great—some 50 percent of the costs of running our economy are information costs[2]—improvements and innovations in the information production process are far less than in the production and manufacture of physical goods. No other field offers such concentrated room for improvement as do informational analysis and the design of information systems for decision making. Formal approaches have begun to appear only recently. It is time for the methods analyst and the industrial engineer to leave the shop floor and enter the office, where the new era of "information technology" is accelerating.

A variety of schemes (function, user, purpose, level, etc.)[3] are available for classifying management information systems. However, we are concerned here with how these are designed to assist the decision maker. It is helpful to identify two types of systems or applications: (1) the automated or programmed system, and (2) the decision information system. This classification does not really identify two distinct types but a whole continuum, from the unprogrammed type of system that merely furnishes information at one extreme to the completely programmed system at the other end.

The Programmed Decision System

The programmed information system is theoretically the ultimate in design and application because discretion is removed from the human decision maker and turned over to the information-decision system. In the "never-never land" of total systems, the complete automation of decisions will have been accomplished and the organization will remain in dynamic equilibrium by means of self-correction obtained by cybernetic feedback.[4]

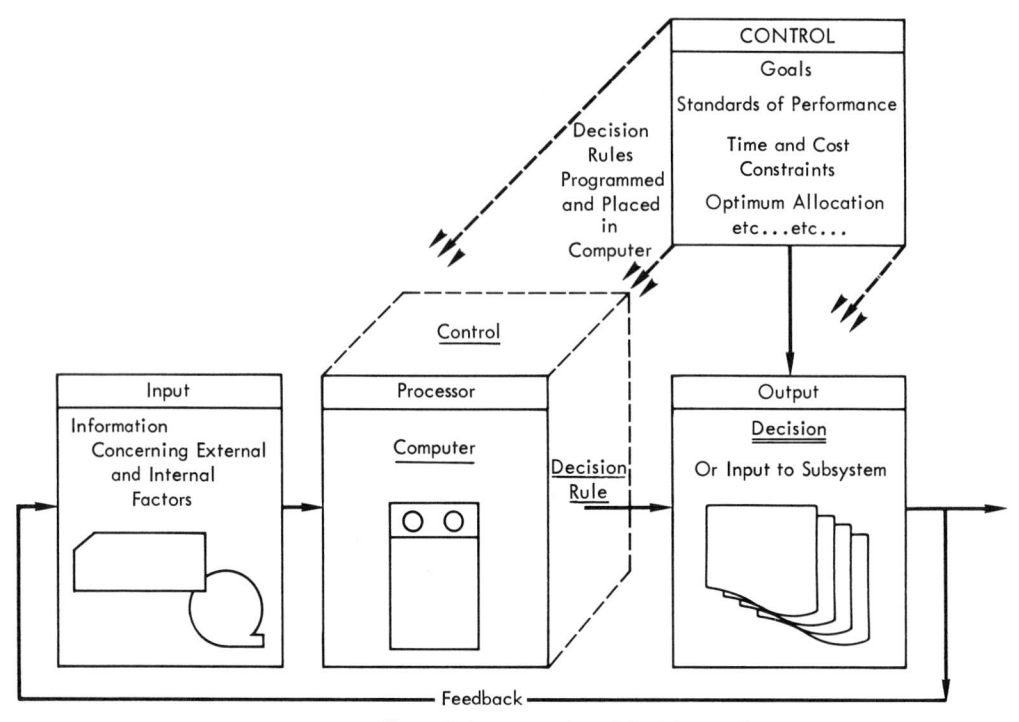

**Figure 7–1 Automation of Decision Making—
The Programmed Decision System**

Figure 7–1 illustrates schematically the notion of programmed information systems. The objective is to design the information production process in such a way that the computer automatically "makes" the decisions. This is accomplished in three steps:

1. Analyze the problem by means of the *management science* approach and design a *decision rule* that solves all applications.
2. Program the *decision rule* for the computer.
3. Design the input and output of the computer information system to provide for automatic decisions by the computer.

Note that under the decision-rule concept of programmed decision systems (Figure 7–1), *the control component of the information system now becomes a part of the processor (the computer), and the human judgment in control and decision making formerly required is now accomplished automatically by computations performed in the computer.*

This concept is essential for an understanding of how programmed decision systems are designed for computer-based information systems. A word of caution, however: in actual practice the complete removal of human intervention for management applications is unlikely, owing to the need to *periodically review the decision rule.* So in the sense that the decision rule is subject to change, for whatever reason, the system is not 100 percent programmed.

Figure 7–2 illustrates some programmed decision systems in manufacturing, planning, and control. From this illustration it can be seen that the systems that are totally programmed are, for the most part, somewhat primitive, consisting primarily of applications that automate the paperwork involved in clerical operations and output decisions formerly supervisory in nature and made by humans. Routine decisions such as accounts receivable, payroll, inventory quantity determination, order placement, customer billing, shipping schedules, and a host of others formerly covered by standard operating procedure for manual processing lend themselves admirably to absorption in a programmed decision system.

Figure 7–3 illustrates a much more sophisticated distribution logistics model (sometimes called distribution management, physical distribution control, or rhochrematics) that, in its more advanced stage, treats the entire

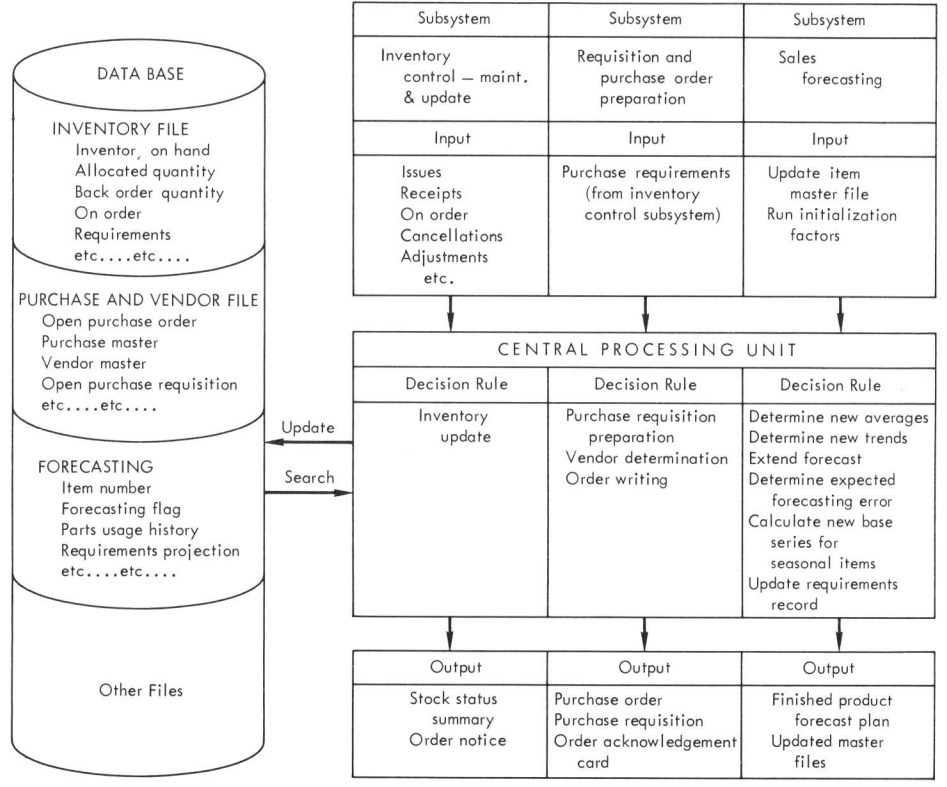

Figure 7–2 Examples of Programmed Decisions in Manufacturing Subsystems

INPUTS

Sales forecast (by territory and product)

Inventory costs and limits

Customer service standards

Procurement leadtimes, costs, etc.

Manufacturing leadtimes, costs, etc.

Transportation leadtimes, costs, etc.

Warehousing leadtimes, costs, etc.

Company Data Base

Central Processing Unit

Decision Rule

DISTRIBUTION LOGISTICS MODEL

OUTPUTS

Management Reports

Program Evaluation Data

Statistical Reports

Research

OTHER MANAGEMENT REPORTS

Procurement & Vendor Schedule

Raw Matl. Warehousing Schedule

Production Schedule

Shipping Schedule

Finished Goods Whse. Schedule

etc.

DISTRIBUTION DECISIONS

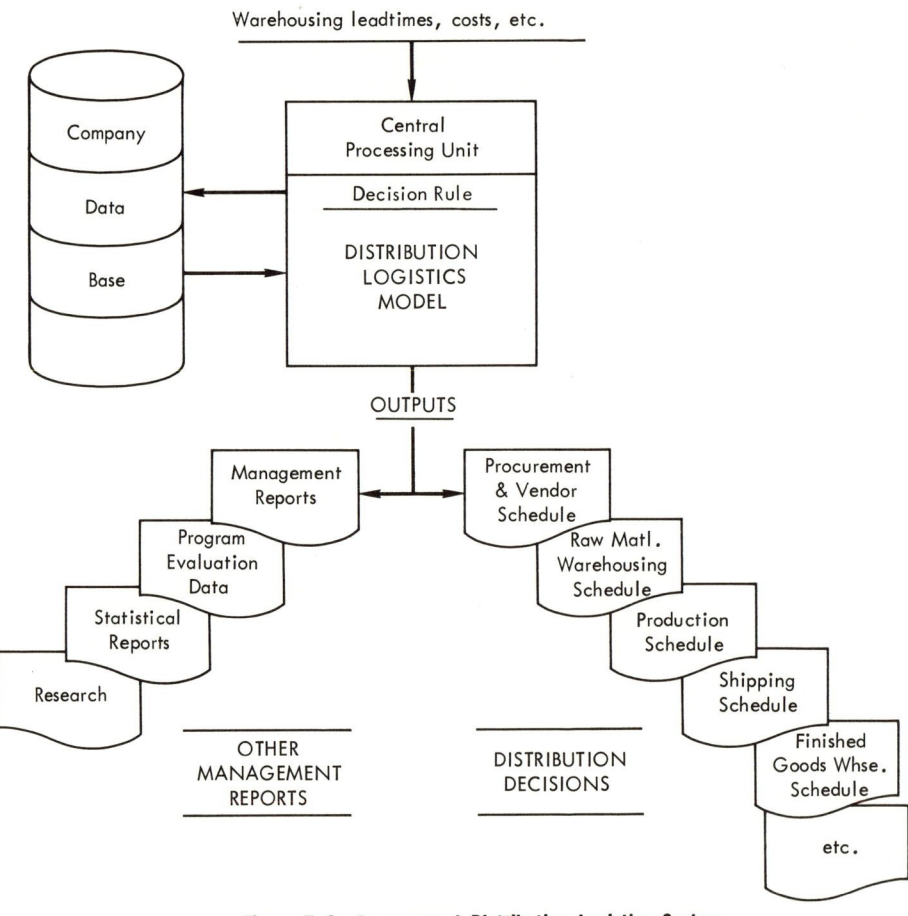

Figure 7–3 Programmed Distribution Logistics System

logistics of a business, from sales forecast through purchase and processing of material and inventory to shipping of finished goods. The objectives of this system include the optimization of total costs and at the same time the meeting of established constraints such as capital cost and customer satisfaction.

From the model illustrated in Figure 7-3 it can be seen not only that the system is exceedingly complex but also that it can be a fine instrument of planning and control. The system is shown as a group of subsystems that are integrated, interrelated, and connected in a total system of distribution. It goes without saying that such a system requires constant review of the variables involved, to insure that the inputs as well as the decision rules have been and remain correct. In this sense it is not truly a fully programmed system.

In practice, the totally programmed decision system is rare, except for the clerical operations involved in routine paperwork. Expansion of applications in the programmed area is unquestionably one of the most fruitful fields for research and also offers the greatest payoff in the future for designing better information systems.[5] Moreover, *and this is important,* the present lack of totally programmed systems for middle- and top-management use does not invalidate the approach. On the contrary, the management science techniques involved in the design of decision rules are fundamental and necessary for improving the *decision information systems* that promise to revolutionize management in the very near future.

Decision-Assisting Information Systems

At one end of the programmed/automated continuum lie clerical functions, so widespread and so familiar that little need be said about them. At the other end are those few totally programmed systems designed for management use. Between these two extremes we have the *decision-assisting information systems,* whose outputs contain decision-making information for use by a human decision maker. This area unquestionably contains the potential applications of greatest importance. Here are some examples of existing systems:
   1. A franchise operator of a major beverage company can "play" his major decisions regarding production, routing, advertising, etc., and choose his best alternatives prior to commitment of funds.
   2. Executives of a large utility gather in the "command control center" to model their decision on a time-sharing terminal.
   3. A major airline uses the company information system for decisions regarding (a) flight scheduling, (b) market forecasting, (c) aircraft design, (d) aircraft acquisition, (e) optimum fleet configurations, etc.
   4. An executive comments, "The greatest advantage of this type of system is the fact that the data can be obtained and mistakes made without the need to commit expensive manpower and equipment."

5. In a retail chain with thousands of stores, the computer checks the stores' stock level against merchandise sold; when merchandise is needed, it transmits purchase orders along with necessary shipping instructions.
6. A manufacturer of micro switches, with a product line of 12,000 items, 38 branch offices, and 312 distributors, reports the following results from installation of a management information system: (a) on-schedule deliveries up from 58 percent to 97 percent, (b) sales/inventory ratio up from 4:3 to 6:2, (c) production cost variances down from 23 percent to 1 percent.

The type of system that we have chosen to call the *decision-assisting information system* is characterized by the fact that it concentrates on the information required by the manager as decision maker. This information may be furnished independently (as in output reports) or in an interactive sense where there is a man–machine relationship in a problem-solving network.

This man–machine, or manager–decision, system is similar to our programmed system in the sense that decision rules are usually required to provide the output in a manner required by the decision maker. In recent years considerable attention has been given to the subject of management science techniques, both in the design of decision rules and in the application of the information output for subsequent decisions. Table 7–1 identifies some techniques available to assist the manager–user, as well as the systems designer, in making decisions and in designing decision rules. These techniques are representative and should not be considered the last word. Moreover, there is some "crossing over" between basic and advanced, as well as between uses. Chapter 11 will expand on similar approaches and on the utilization of management science in systems design.

Table 7–1

Basic and Advanced Techniques for Decision Making

Basic	*Advanced*
Economic and Financial Analysis	Maximum–Minimum Value Problems
Breakeven analysis	(E.g., inventory control, warehousing)
Capital budgeting analysis	Monte Carlo models
Ratio analysis	Decision trees
Marginal analysis	Queuing models
Incremental analysis	
Forecasting	Optimization Problems
Regression analysis	(Resource allocation and sequencing)
Input/output matrixes	Linear programming
Exponential smoothing	Dynamic programming
Probability distributions	Transportation methods
	Assignment methods
Project planning and control	Cost/Benefit Analysis
PERT/CPM	Systems simulation
PERT/Cost	

The manner in which information can be automated and programmed for use in a *decision-assisting information system* is shown in Figure 7–4. Notice that in this illustration the characteristics and outputs of this vital type of system are shown:

1. Some outputs are decisions; the computer has "made" a decision in accordance with a *programmed decision rule.* (The shipment routing order)
2. Some outputs are secondary information in the form of reports to be used by a subsequent human decision maker. (Variance analysis)
3. The methods of Table 7–1 have been utilized in both types of systems for the design of decision rules.
4. There are provisions for man–machine-type interactions in the sense that the manager/decision maker can *"model"* his decisions prior to commitment.
5. *Optimum* solutions are provided by management science decision rules.

Other illustrations of decision-assisting information systems are shown in the following discussion of middle- and top-management use of the computer.

DECISION SYSTEMS AND LEVELS OF MANAGEMENT

If the computer and management information systems are to realize the potential claimed for them, it is clear that they must accomplish two essential tasks: (1) expand the frontier of applications, both in numbers and complexity, for which automated techniques are workable; and (2) improve and increase the applications and their usefulness in more areas of management concern and in higher levels of managerial decision making.

Figure 7–5 demonstrates how the boundaries of management's *programmed* decisions are constantly moving to the right in order to assimilate and program increasingly complex problems. However, the progress in moving those boundaries to the right has been slow. Computers and information systems thus far have been concerned largely, indeed almost overwhelmingly, with clerical applications. Computer-based management information systems properly designed for decision making can be the breakthrough that will program more and more of the managerial decisions that now take so much time and effort.

In order to examine the current state-of-the-art in decision systems and explore how they can be improved in the future, we should examine a classification of applications by level of management. Once again, the categories chosen are along a continuum and shade into each other. However, to overcome in part this arbitrary choice of categories, illustrations will be functional to demonstrate better the potential of information systems.

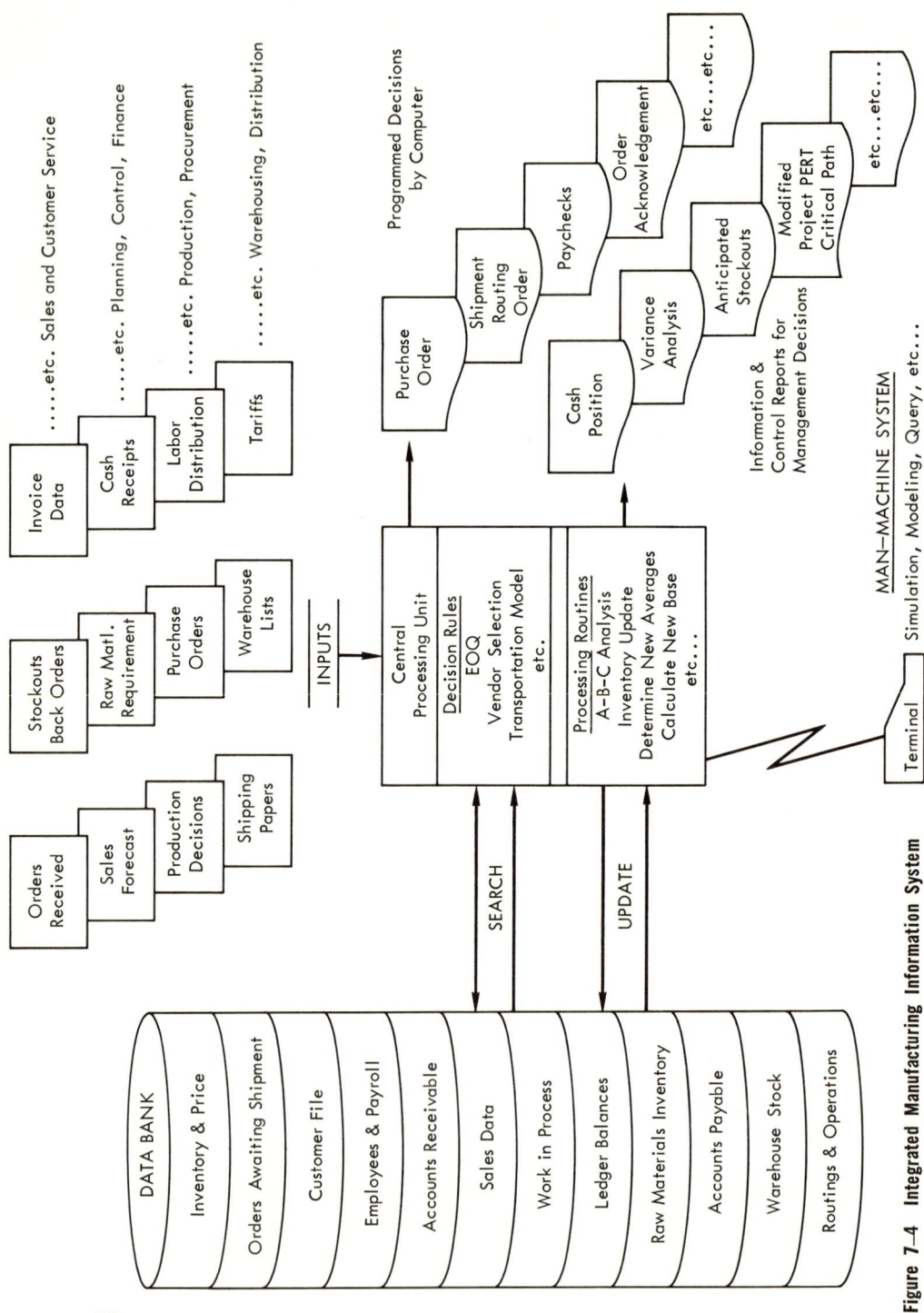

Figure 7–4 Integrated Manufacturing Information System

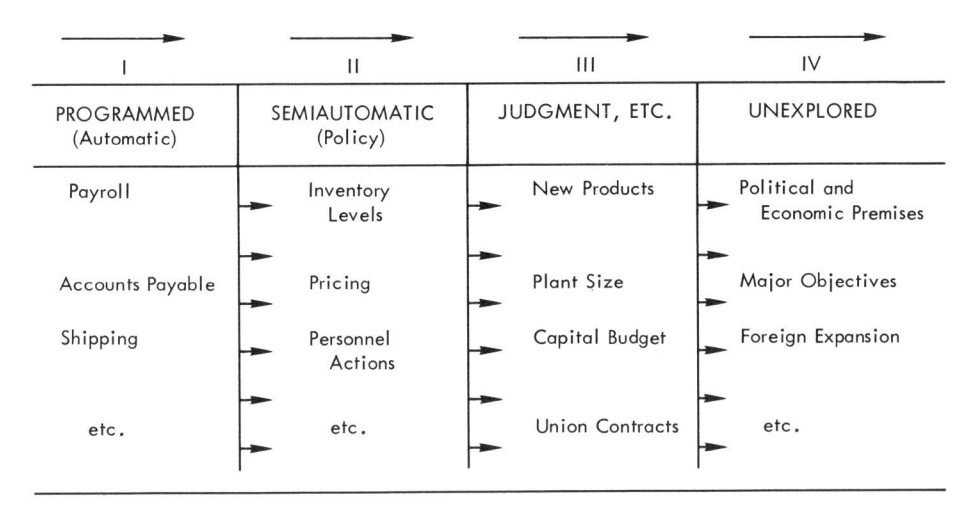

I	II	III	IV
PROGRAMMED (Automatic)	SEMIAUTOMATIC (Policy)	JUDGMENT, ETC.	UNEXPLORED
Payroll	Inventory Levels	New Products	Political and Economic Premises
Accounts Payable	Pricing	Plant Size	Major Objectives
Shipping	Personnel Actions	Capital Budget	Foreign Expansion
etc.	etc.	Union Contracts	etc.

Figure 7–5 Boundaries of Management Decisions

Clerical and Supervisory Level

Although in a strict sense the clerical and supervisory types of application are not oriented to decision making, it is worthwhile to review some of them and see how they may be improved.

Despite the thousands of computer-based installations in the United States, the overwhelming share of applications are concerned with standard tasks of accounting and financial record keeping. Until now, computers have been doing largely what clerks had done before, but doing it electronically. The value of the computer, when it was measured at all, was calculated by a method that compared its cost against the cost displacement of clerical and machine resources such as clerks and tabulating equipment. Naturally, with this view of cost in mind, management turned to the automation of clerical paperwork as the first and frequently the only application.

Most of these clerical applications are not advanced or sophisticated; they are functionally similar to the punch-card tabulating (unit record) equipment that the larger electronic data processing systems replaced. The great majority of smaller firms are just beginning to consider the use of EDP. Even in the country's largest firms the EDP applications are largely clerical. One survey of computer applications in the 500 largest United States corporations showed the frequency of applications in the following order:[6]

1. Inventory control
2. Payroll
3. Cost studies and reports
4. Production planning
5. Raw materials ordering
6. Parts ordering

248   Computer-Based Management Information Systems

The intention here is not to downgrade the use of the computer for clerical applications. On the contrary, the clerical area offers applications with immediate payoff in cost reduction as well as improved accuracy of information. Moreover, much of the information furnished as output from clerical systems has decision-making applications at the supervisory level and elsewhere. The illustrations of Figure 7–6 give a further insight into how sophisticated clerical information systems can integrate the functions of a manufacturing company and provide outputs for decision making at supervisory and middle-management levels. Figure 7–6 also illustrates the "total systems" concept—at least as far as this concept can be adopted in a manufacturing company with the information shown. This illustration shows each subsystem segregated into the primary input of the system, the primary output of the system, and the data flow between systems (pages 250–51).

For the purpose of *decision making* and improvement of operations, what is needed is an approach to the design of an information system and its contribution that measures these not by cost displacement of clerical expenses but by *how well the system improves the operation of the organization*. Figure 7–7 shows some of the applications and ways in which this might be done. Notice particularly the transition from clerical operations to decision applications, which demonstrates how the operations of the company are improved (e.g., customer relations, personnel stability, etc.).

In summary, it is time for the manager to advance from the already firmly established clerical base of applications to the additional use of these applications for making decisions on how operations of the organization can be improved. We should assume as given the benefits of paperwork automation and clerical cost displacement and build from there. Figures 7–6 and 7–7 summarize how this may be accomplished.

Middle-Management Level

From the uncertain premise that top management's primary job is planning, and that middle (or staff) management's job is operating, the clear implication is that the management information system should yield information for improved operating decisions. Also involved are intangible benefits such as improved customer service, vendor relations, planning skills, and the like. In taking into account both the operational and intangible benefits, we find one thread common to both: each is derived from information supplied by the system to various users—managers, customers, salesmen, and others. So in designing and in assessing the use of the system, we start with the questions: "What positive value is derived from having the information in the hands of the user? What can it do for improvement of operations?"

In a landmark article of more than ten years ago, Leavitt and Whisler predicted that as a result of EDP and related technology the practice and structure of management would change enormously. It was suggested that "the horizontal slice of the current organization chart that we call middle management will break in two, with the larger portion shrinking and shrinking and sinking into a more highly programmed state and the smaller portion proliferating and rising to a level where more creative thinking is needed."[7] Other prognosticators of the computer scene have generally identified three developments of EDP that will vitally affect middle management: (1) the flattening of the organization structure because the computer is taking the place of some middle-management positions, (2) the recentralization of control owing to the economies connected with centralized decision making and management of certain functions (e.g., purchasing, accounting, production planning), and (3) the prediction of Leavitt and Whisler that the computer would routinize many of the traditional functions of middle management. All these developments, it was predicted, would result essentially from the phenomenon of moving the boundaries of management decision making to the right, as visualized in Figure 7–5.

Although the changes predicted have not occurred to the extent expected, there is no doubt but that the movement is in the direction forecast. These changes are, after all, dependent upon how rapidly the new developments in management technology are adopted. One of these developments is the knowledge of how to use computers to solve operating problems. As we pointed out in the discussion of clerical and supervisory applications, the overwhelming majority of applications have been in the clerical area, and organizations in general have been slow to adopt the more sophisticated applications for operating decisions. Another development related to the computer is the use of management science techniques to design decision-making information systems. Once again, we can conclude that great progress has not been shown on the part of managers in adopting the available techniques in this area.

But despite the general slowness of organizations to adopt the available computer and related technology, developments thus far seem to bear out the predictions outlined. In many organizations where computer-based systems and applications have utilized new technology, we find a flatter organization structure because of the reduction and consolidation of functions after the computer takes over many of them. Moreover, as organizations are more closely *integrated*, closer cooperation, and in some cases consolidation of responsibilities, has resulted. It appears also that the prediction of centralization of decision making is being borne out in the organizations that adopt the new technology. One outstanding example of this is the centralization in one computer of all airline reservation decisions. Other firms and industries are moving to centralize financial planning, purchasing, production planning, accounting, and a host of other functions that have historically been the concern of middle management.

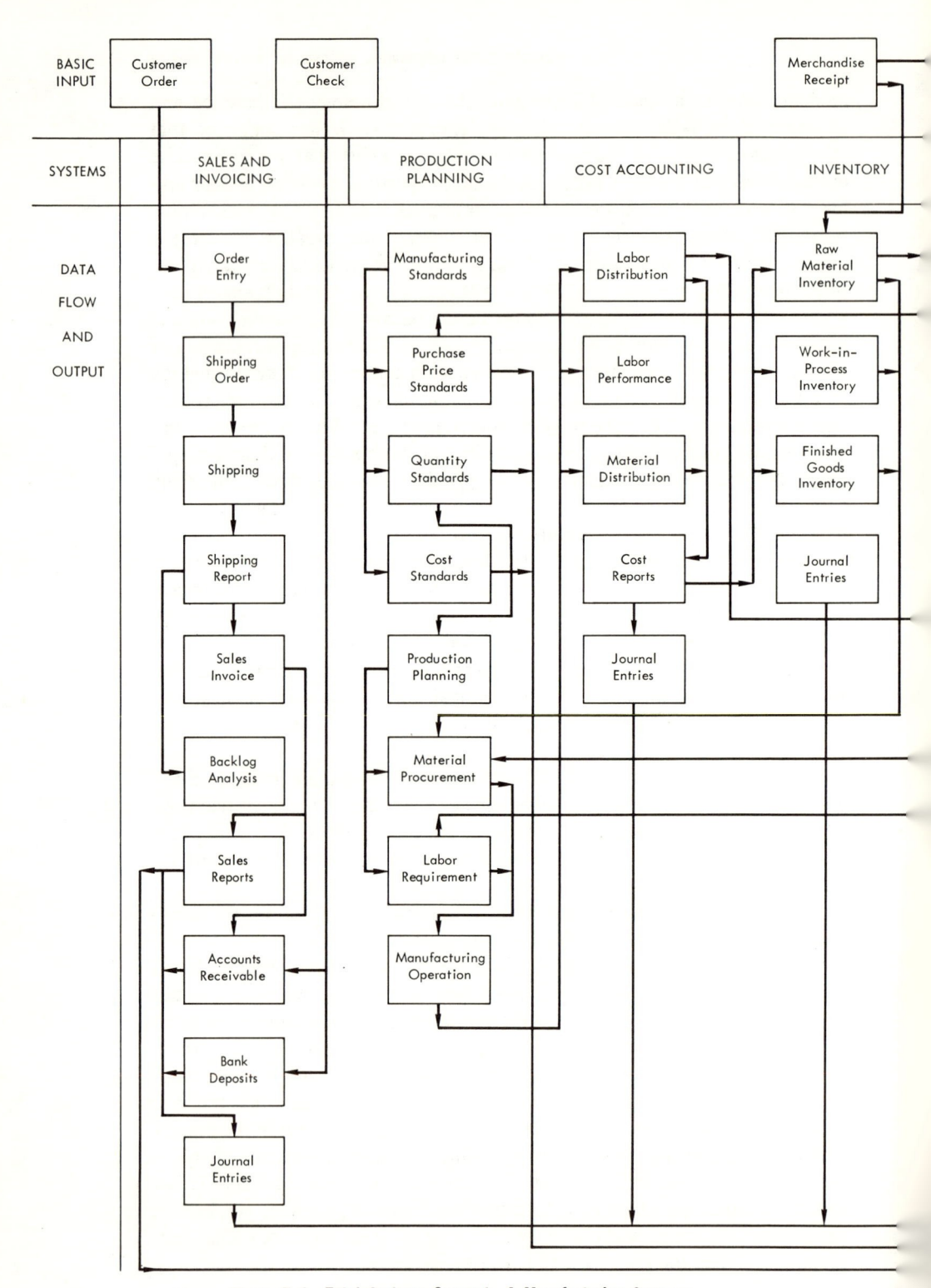

Figure 7-6 Total Systems Concept—A Manufacturing Company

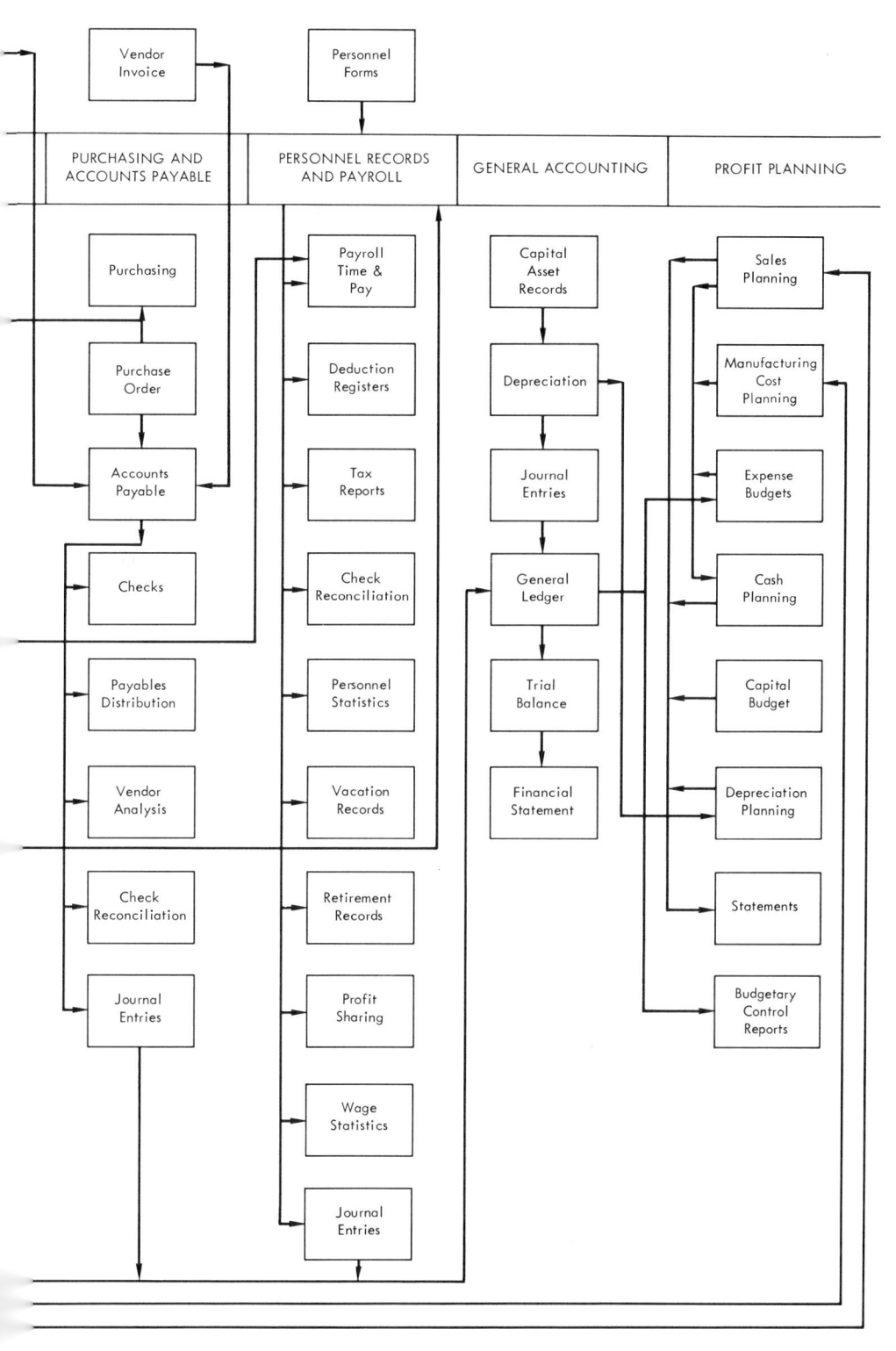

SOURCE   C. C. Wendler, *Total Systems* (Cleveland: Systems and Procedures Association, 1966), p. 33

ADMINISTRATION AND CONTROL			DECISION MAKING AND OPERATIONAL	
Application	Objective		Application	Objective
Ledger Accounting	Clerical Displacement and Control	→	Accounting	Cash Control Budget Control
Marketing Order Entry Billing	" "	→	Personnel Skills Inventory	Personnel Stability
Personnel Payroll	" "	→	Purchasing Replenishment Orders	Vendor/Buyer Relationship
Production Output Reporting	" "	→	Production	Cost Control
		→	Inventory	Optimize Inventory
Inventory Inventory Level	" "	→	Marketing	Customer Relations
		→	Distribution	Optimize Costs Customer Relations

Figure 7–7 Advances in Clerical and Supervisory EDP Applications

  A corollary to the organizational changes just described is the prediction that many of the jobs of middle management would be routinized. As to whether this has happened or is likely to, the answer must be *yes* and *no!* *Yes* in the sense that much of the middle manager's job of *computation*—evaluating information, weighing alternatives, making choices—can be and has been alleviated by the computer. On the other hand, these computational aspects of the manager's job are the very ones that have been routinized in the past and for which the computer can supply the greatest relief. In regard to the broader aspects of the manager's job—communications and leadership—it appears that the computer's advantage lies in computation, and relief from this task will permit the manager to perform better the broader, more human aspects of his job.

  In summary, the available evidence and a priori assumptions concerning advancing computer technology lead to the conclusion that significant and perhaps profound changes may occur in the way middle managers perform the *decision-making* part of their job. What has been a human system of interaction will now become a man–machine system, with the manager carrying on a discourse with the computer. Moreover, many of his routine computational tasks will be taken over entirely by the computer. The trend and direction of this process is demonstrated in Figure 7–8. The ranks of today's middle-management group (in firms that are not yet on the frontier

SUBSYSTEM	NEW INPUT DATA	OBJECTIVE
Marketing	Demographic data Consumer trends	Optimum marketing budget Determination of marketing mix
Purchasing Vendor selection	Catalog information	Vendor performance
Finance Cash management	Money market conditions	Return on portfolios
Personnel Labor negotiations	Control data	Improved negotiating position
Distribution Route optimization	Rate information	Improved shipping schedules
Production Dynamic scheduling	Other subsystems	Optimum use of plant
Forecasting	Economic data	Improved realism in forecasting

TOTAL ENVIRONMENT PLANNING

↑ ↑ ↑ ↑ ↑

REDUCED RANKS OF MIDDLE MANAGEMENT

TODAY'S MIDDLE MANAGERS

Clerical and Supervisory Systems (Figure 7-7)

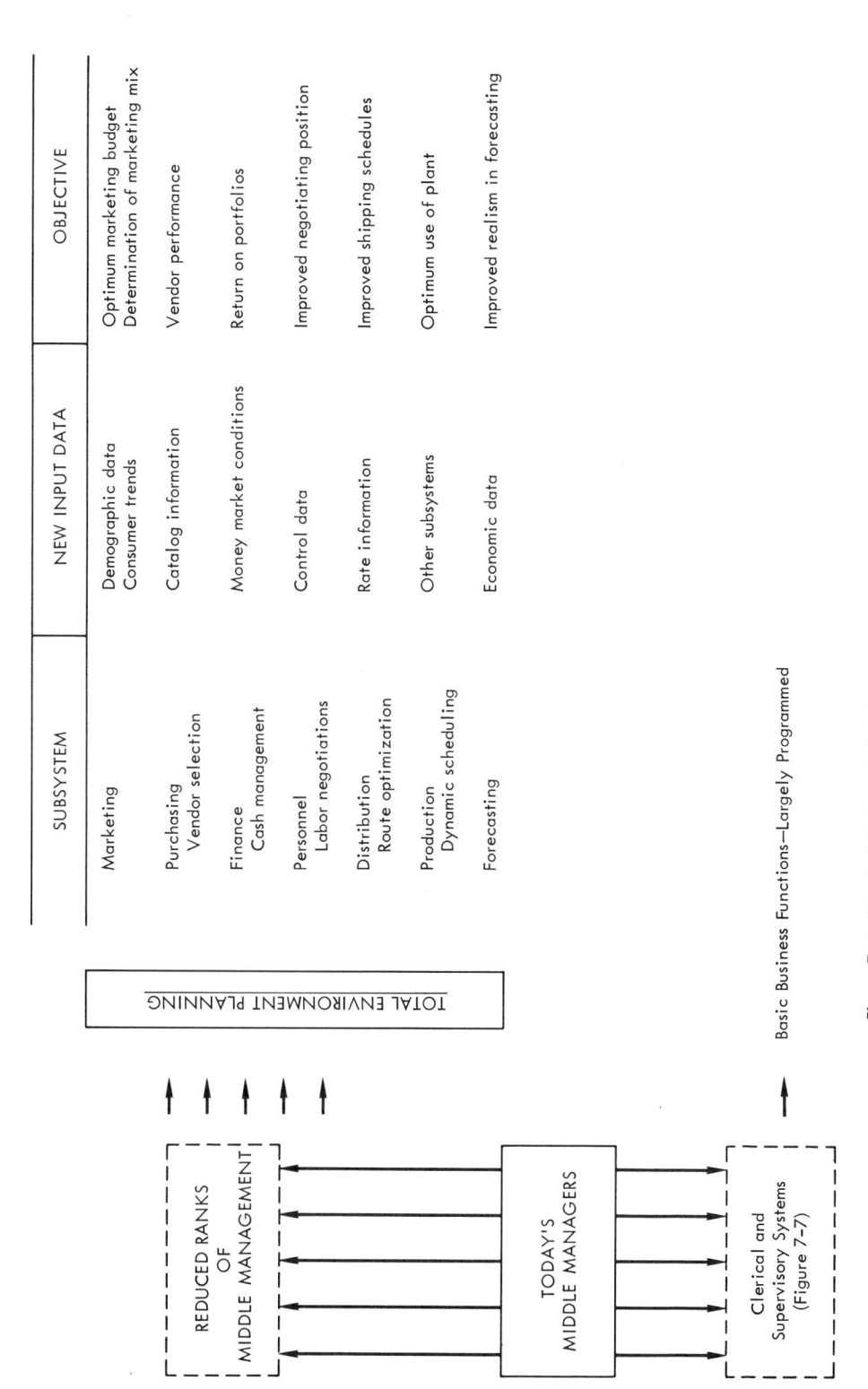

→ Basic Business Functions—Largely Programmed

Figure 7-8 Trend of Tasks and Decision Making in Middle Management

of information systems) will no doubt continue to separate. Those who see and avail themselves of the new systems approach to management will rise to a more creative and demanding level, where computer-based systems are designed and utilized for strategic and tactical planning based on the total environment of the firm's information resource. This exciting and creative level of management will be accomplished in a man–machine atmosphere.

What are now considered to be the basic functions of business and the province of middle management will be more and more subject to decision rules, to routinization, and to management by a lower level of supervision. At both levels, however, the challenges will be greater—the challenge to design better man–machine systems and the challenge to perform the human factors of the job that are not seriously affected by the computer.

Top-Management Level

There has been something less than widespread enthusiasm for the contributions of computers, management science, and decision information systems to the job of top management. Professor Jay Forrester of M.I.T. concludes that "... management science has not penetrated the inner circle of top management."[8] John Diebold is pessimistic, with the view: "... we have not come close to realizing the computer's true potential."[9] This lack of application to top management's problems is frequently blamed on the "communication gap" between managers and technicians. There is little doubt that such a gap exists and that it is attributable to both groups. The general lack of top-management involvement in EDP operations is well established. The Diebold Research Program's recent survey of more than 2,500 executives of 140 companies concluded that *technicians,* not management, are setting goals for computers, and it attributed failure to realize the true potential of EDP applications to management's lack of involvement.[10] The federal government reached a similar conclusion about federal executives and termed the situation "critical."[11] On the other side of the coin, the computer "technocrat" and the "management scientist" are apparently more involved in techniques for their own sake than for application to top management problems.[12] How might some of these problems be overcome in order to get greater benefits for top management?

Although the line between top and middle management is not clear, and in some cases it is indistinguishable, we can generally classify the duties of top management as these:

1. *Management control*—Control over people to whom the manager has delegated responsibility, exercised through a system for evaluating performance against a previously adopted plan, objective, or standard. The

management information system can assist in this task in two essential ways. First, the management science techniques of modeling, simulation, or otherwise calculating the effects of various alternatives can improve the effectiveness of the plan. Second, performance reporting of some type, with variances explained, can greatly assist top management in reviewing performance and discovering means for correcting deficiencies.

2. *Personnel planning*—Organizational planning and actions concerning key personnel. Properly designed, an information system can be of use in this top-management task. For example, certain types of data on personnel analysis are useful; skills forecasting is possible to enable matching with available and projected needs; and basic information required in labor negotiations can be retrieved when necessary.

3. *Coordination*—The harmonizing of organizational efforts and sub-elements, particularly those that cut across organizational lines. This function is similar to top-management control in the sense that a spotlighting of problem areas is desired. An information system can assist in this process by providing early warning signals and advance information concerning deviation from plan.

4. *Operating control*—Direct involvement in operational decisions and day-to-day operations of a nature so important as to suggest the involvement of top management. Where executives become involved in operational situations, the same kind of information required by others is required by them. If operations happen to be in production or similar areas that lend themselves to quantification and close control, the problem is simplified.

5. *Strategic planning*—This function is clearly the most important and the most closely associated with top executives. Setting long-range goals, determining strategies to achieve objectives, and other broad-gauged considerations are the most important of these tasks but the least adaptable to assistance by computer-based information system. This is due partly to the nature of the decision and the general lack of enthusiasm and interest on the part of managers to utilize the tools of the computer.

The major information needs for all the functions listed can be partially or wholly supplied by a properly designed management information system. Given the level of sophistication in most companies, design efforts should probably begin with the elements of Figure 7–8 as the near-term goal. For those firms that have reached that level of sophistication (and there are very few), further design effort might be directed toward a system that will facilitate top management's most difficult job of *strategic planning* in these areas:

1. *Product planning*—based upon demographic data and information concerning consumer trends and competitors.
2. *Labor planning*—including the forecasting of personnel skills and

negotiating considerations based on operational plans of the company and the external environment.

3. *Resource planning and innovation*—optimum selection, utilization, and innovation in materials, productive capacity, inventory, and distribution. Optimum in the sense of lowest cost, best vendor and carrier performance, and most customer satisfaction.

The challenge in systems design is unquestionably greatest in the area of top-management use. However, *with top-management participation* (a must), the frontiers of decision-making assistance and capability can be improved, just as clerical and operating uses have been improved.

INTEGRATION: THE OBJECTIVE OF COMPUTER-BASED SYSTEMS FOR DECISION MAKING

Perhaps the most vital characteristic of a computer-based, decision-making information system is that of *integration,* a characteristic fundamental to the systems approach. This involves the relation of the parts or functions (subsystems) of an organization to each other and to the whole. Instead of concentrating on traditional clerical subsystems or devoting efforts to achieving "islands of mechanization," the design effort should take into account the necessity to integrate sales, manufacturing, finance, personnel, and the other elements going to make up the organization. Equally important is the necessity to integrate the functions of management, the resources of the organization, and management levels. This must be accomplished with some plan for integrating the separate information subsystems—the first step in any overall plan.

Integration of Information Systems

The question arises as to whether the structure of management information systems should be designed according to a "total systems" concept or some other "integrated data processing" (IDP) scheme. There is a wide variety of opinion on whether these concepts are valid. To illustrate, Dearden concludes:

> Present concepts for organizing the systems and data-processing activities have fallen far short of providing a real solution. In fact, the favorite current approach—total systems—is leading us in precisely the wrong direction.[13]

A contrasting viewpoint is held by the U.S. Navy:

> A total "systems design" concept guiding each improvement in information systems is most desirable. An original, objective, detached, comprehensive approach is the essence of this concept. The end product or net final mission requirements of a whole activity should

be the starting point. Thenceforth, with minimum regard for prevailing organization, methods, and equipment, the ideal system should be outlined. The end objective is the optimal informational product by an optimal combination of personnel and equipment, each doing that which is ideally and properly human and mechanical, respectively, in order best to carry out the organizational mission.[14]

Despite the debate surrounding the usefulness of the "total systems" concept, it is still a good one provided it is viewed as the need to fit each new application into an overall *framework* or master plan for an eventual total information system. Without such a framework, expensive redesign efforts are almost certain to occur. The investment in time, expense, and effort should be made at the outset or early in the development stage to develop a sound, long-range system plan that will facilitate the smooth transition and fitting in of subsequent applications.

Integration of the Functions of Management

The ideal management information system should provide for the integration of the functions of management at and between the various levels as well as laterally throughout the organization by providing for:

1. *Planning*—Integration of related information created in the various prime steps of the management cycle; i.e., plans and programs (requirements, forecasts, allowances, allocations, budgets, projects, etc.). This implies the proper design of content as well as of data flow to insure that everyone involved is aware of planning information. An illustration of this might be the plan for distribution expense, which provides planning information vertically throughout the sales organization as well as laterally to finance and operations, whose own plans may be affected by it.

2. *Direction*—The use of information systems design to communicate, coordinate, and give direction to plans at various levels. There is no reason why the information system (structure and outputs) could not be the vehicle through which plans are implemented and controlled. For example, a PERT/CPM schedule, once adopted as a plan, may be the communication device thereafter that can achieve coordination of all organizational elements.

3. *Operations*—Integration of information concerning plans, direction, and necessary data and facts concerning the transformation process of taking inputs (personnel, money, materials, equipment, etc.) and processing them into outputs. Figure 7–4 illustrates this approach to the design of the manufacturing information system. Unless some integrative approach is taken toward the separate operational elements (manufacturing, engineering, shipping, distribution, finances, etc.), these functional units will tend to focus on their own objectives at the expense of the firm's.

4. *Control*—Integration of information concerning progress of plans, programs, and operations can be corrected to achieve desired output. To the extent feasible, automatic control should be built into the information system, not for automatic correction of output (although this is the theoretical ideal) but for automatic exception reporting for management planning and control. Inventory decision rules are common examples of this type of control.

5. *Organization*—Integration of the organization by utilizing its structure to design and implement the information system, notwithstanding the fact that modern integrated information systems frequently transcend conventional organization structures. Conceptually, this linking of subsystems with and through the organization can be shown:

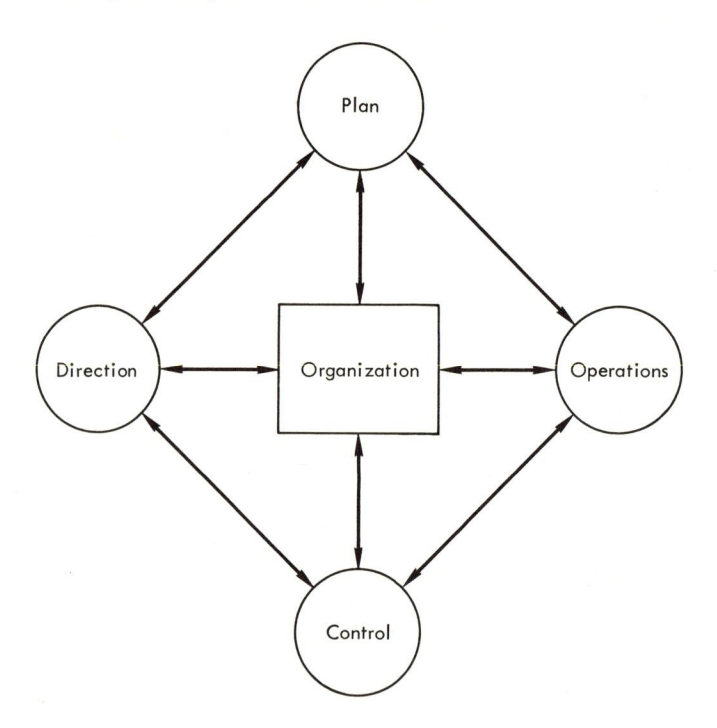

Owing to the complexity of modern organizations, the various levels of management within them, and the decentralization of operations, staff people or departments that develop plans are frequently not the ones who subsequently make them operational or control them. It is therefore necessary that everyone speak the same language. In other words, management information systems must be developed under a plan that recognizes this complexity and provides for integration through the media of information systems. A corollary objective is the integration of computer languages, data classification, and degree of detail for both the planning and performance data.

Integration of Resources

For purposes of systems design, *integration* can be defined as the design of subsystems in such a way that data are processed in a continuous stream until the use of such data has been completed in the total system. Now, since *operational* (as opposed to information) subsystems can be described in terms of their information needs, it follows that integration of resources contained in operational systems can be improved by proper design of the information system. Indeed, it has been made abundantly clear that information is the nervous system, the bloodstream, the physiology that gives direction to the operations that make the transformation process possible. Therefore, in advancing our objective of integration through information we are at the same time allocating scarce resources in a more economical way.

A useful concept to keep in mind is that of the modular elements of information having commonality across different uses of structures. If the lowest-level information elements (as defined by the designer) are called "modules," then integrative operational systems can be constructed from a collection of "modules." Indeed, this notion is the basic approach to the design of integrated systems. It is illustrated in Figure 7–9, which depicts unique as well as common modules. In this illustration the common modules

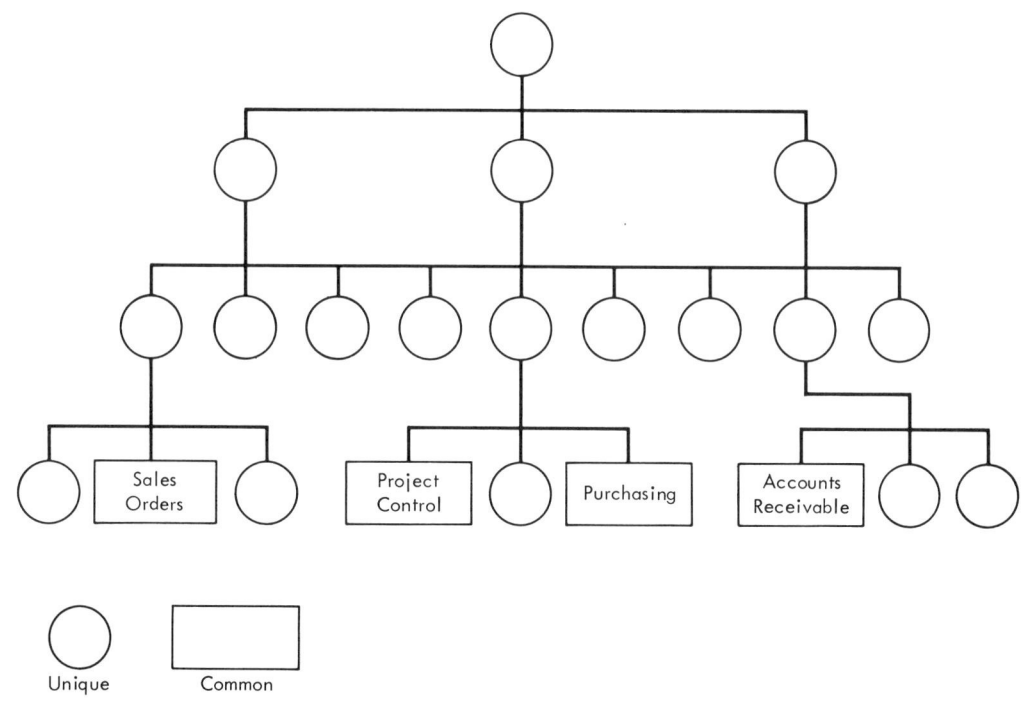

Figure 7–9 Integration of Organization Through Information

are sales orders, project control, purchasing, and accounts receivable. For some purposes two or more of these modules may be combined to provide a modular operational information system.

Horizontal integration of resources may be achieved by systems that interrelate and interlock the lateral functions of the organization (i.e., product development, marketing, operations, finance, personnel, etc.) and keep the managers of these functions apprised of information concerning interfaces and their impact on other functions. This integration is not, and cannot be, achieved by the "islands of mechanization" or "automate now, integrate later" approaches to systems design because development under that approach often proceeds without regard to the interlocking nature of subsystems.

Consider, for example, the rather common situation in which the outputs from an otherwise sophisticated production planning and control or project control system are not utilized or even received by personnel, despite the fact that these systems are designed to forecast the types and amounts of skills required for a project or production plan. Or consider the personnel system that maintains an up-to-date skills bank but does not provide output for the training system.

Integrated design takes account of subsystem interfaces. The manner in which subsystems design can be utilized to integrate functions horizontally and levels vertically is shown in Figure 7–10.

Vertical integration is achieved mainly through the characteristic of hierarchical systems whereby higher-order systems are dependent on lower-order subsystems for input. Lower-order systems are, in turn, dependent on more elementary or still lower order subsystems for input. Orlicky[15] conceives of three levels of vertical subsystems, which are shown in Figure 7–11 and listed in one of two ways:

Location	*Duties*
1. Management	1. Management
2. Office	2. Planning and control
3. Factory and field	3. Execution

The structure of these vertical systems can be shown by system structure level, by area covered, and by organizational level:

System Structure Level	*Areas Covered*	*Organizational Level*
Bottom	Execution of physical processes Control of processes Control of field operations	Factory and Field
Middle	Planning and management controls (Product development, marketing, manufacturing, finance and administration, etc.)	Office or Staff
Top	Overall planning and control Management of superstructure	Top management

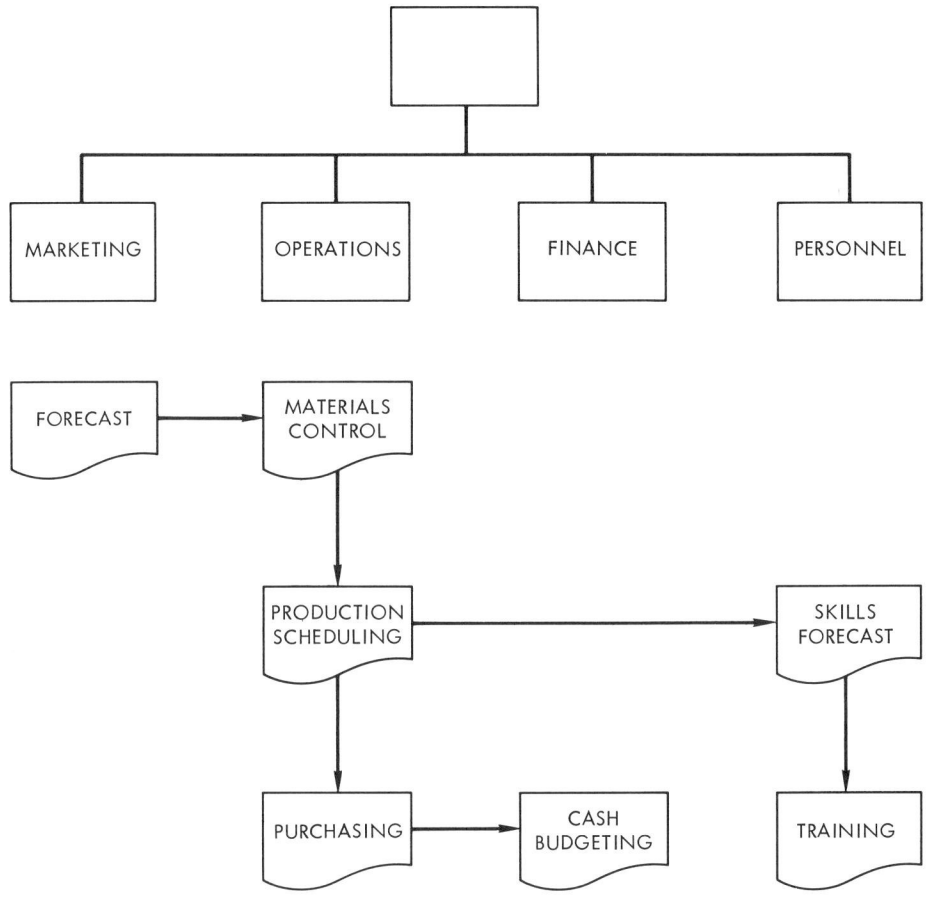

Figure 7–10 Horizontal and Vertical Integration
of Functions and Resources

It becomes evident that information systems are a vital tool for integration and economical operation of these vertical systems. The longer or deeper down in successively lower levels that planning and programming for all elements can be integrated, the higher the probability that the systems "mix" will be in optimal balance. Equally evident is the improved nature of planning and control information when all the pertinent interdependent elements and subsystems are correlated vertically.

Integration of Management Levels

If, as we have demonstrated, the integration of functions, programs, and resources is desirable in systems planning, then it follows naturally that the integration of the levels of management is also to be sought. A rather arbitrary but nevertheless traditional view of the levels of management and the tasks can be shown:

```
                        ┌─────────────┐
                        │ Management  │
                        │ Information │
                        │   Systems   │
                        └─────────────┘
```

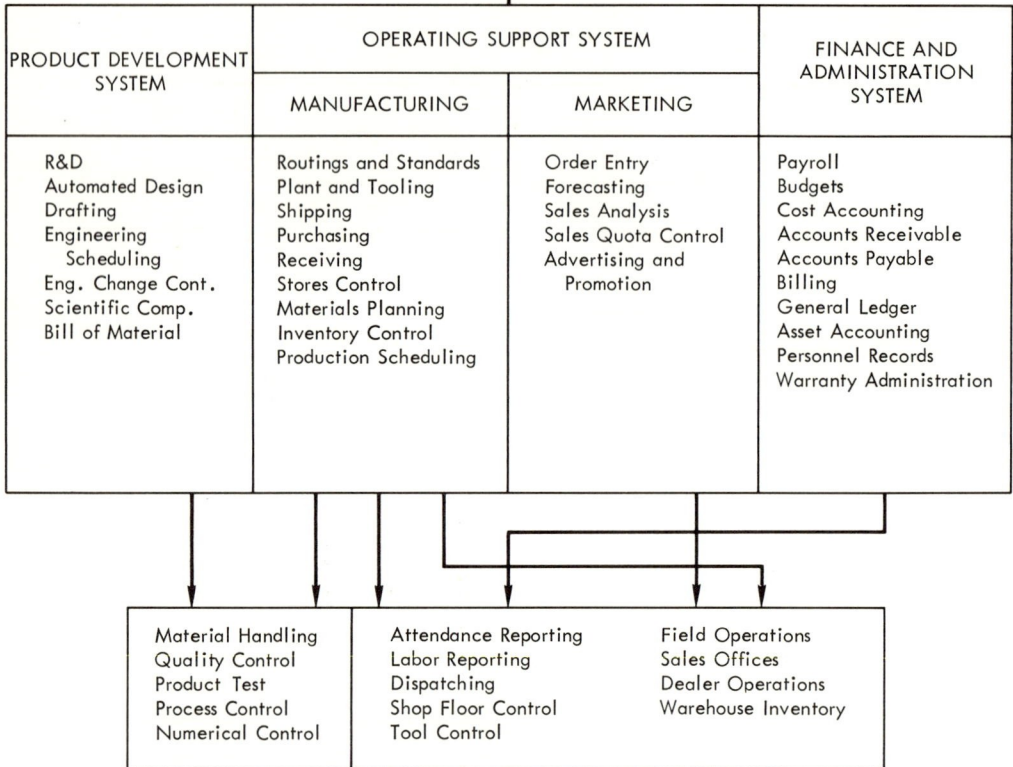

PRODUCT DEVELOPMENT SYSTEM	OPERATING SUPPORT SYSTEM		FINANCE AND ADMINISTRATION SYSTEM
	MANUFACTURING	MARKETING	

R&D
Automated Design
Drafting
Engineering
   Scheduling
Eng. Change Cont.
Scientific Comp.
Bill of Material
	Routings and Standards
	Plant and Tooling
	Shipping
	Purchasing
	Receiving
	Stores Control
	Materials Planning
	Inventory Control
	Production Scheduling
		Order Entry
		Forecasting
		Sales Analysis
		Sales Quota Control
		Advertising and
		   Promotion
			Payroll
			Budgets
			Cost Accounting
			Accounts Receivable
			Accounts Payable
			Billing
			General Ledger
			Asset Accounting
			Personnel Records
			Warranty Administration

Material Handling Quality Control Product Test Process Control Numerical Control	Attendance Reporting Labor Reporting Dispatching Shop Floor Control Tool Control	Field Operations Sales Offices Dealer Operations Warehouse Inventory	

Figure 7–11 Structure of Management Information Systems
SOURCE J. Orlicky, *The Successful Computer System*, © 1969 by McGraw-Hill Book Company. Used by permission of McGraw-Hill Book Company.

Management Level	Task	Decision Making	Type of Information Used
Top	Management	Setting of objectives and selection of courses of action from among alternatives	Decision information
Staff	Operational planning and scheduling	Identification, analysis, and evaluation of alternatives	Operating and some historical information
Functional	Line supervision at lower and middle organizational levels	Control of operations	Historical and some operating information

Despite the definition of top management's job as decision making, research indicates that computer information systems have had little or no effect on the way this task is performed.[16] Even at middle-management levels, the effect of computer-based systems has been very slight to moderate.[17] The general lack of use at these levels for decision making leaves use by only the lower levels of management and supervision. These latter groups depend largely on historical information and clerical applications. Such a situation cannot continue to exist if, like resources, management levels are to be integrated both horizontally and vertically.

The answer to better integration of management levels appears to lie in improved systems planning and design. Despite some lack of appreciation and a frequently defensive attitude on the part of a large segment of management, better systems design effort should be aimed at developing a greater understanding of the factors influencing management decisions. Also helpful would be better education of all levels of management concerning the capability of computer-based information systems to assist in areas of decision analysis.

A large part of the systems design effort can be devoted to upgrading historical information to the operational or decision-making category, or at the very least, to designing future systems with decision making and management in mind. *Integrated* systems are the objective, and the integration of management levels will be advanced by designing information systems around a data base that provides for a minimum of input, a multiple or joint use of the same data at all levels, and a maximum access for anyone with a need to interrogate any part or all of it. There should be no duplication, excess, or inadequacy of informational content flowing between organizational elements, horizontal or vertical.

CLASSIFICATION OF SYSTEMS

We have frequently referred to the prevailing tendency to build systems around some existing classification such as the charts of accounts or simply to automate existing reports. Such one-for-one changeover in systems design results in nothing more than attempted automation of existing files. As one designer stated it, this approach is "the perpetuation of inefficiencies at an accelerated rate." If integration is the primary goal of systems design, it is clear that we must start with some kind of scheme of systems classifications. A classification is designed to organize the facts and information concerning the activities of an organization by the grouping of similar characteristics, traits, and relationships. The major purpose of such classification is the retrieval of the information by persons desiring it for a particular decision or purpose, although these persons and these decisions may vary. An equally important reason for classification is to reach a balance between the costs of classification on the one hand and the costs of retrieval on the other. As the costs of classification go up, the costs of using it go down, and vice versa.

Information systems have been classified by McDonough and Garrett:

1. *Management operating systems* are used to produce working papers, such as purchase invoices, job orders, or paychecks.
2. *Management reporting systems* are used to aid management in the making of decisions.[18]

Some writers prefer to use the classifications of *major* and *minor* systems. For example, Steiner[19] uses the following:

MAJOR INFORMATION SYSTEMS
    Accounting
    Material flows
    Periodic planning information
    Special reports
    The grapevine
    Scanning

MINOR INFORMATION SYSTEMS
    Competitive information
    Research and development
    Sales forecasting
    Special systems

These two classifications are interesting and useful for some purposes but of little use in the development of an overall plan for systems development to structure our plan during the design phase.

For the purposes of systems development and design, and in order to meet our planning objectives, we might use a combination of the following classifications of information needed to manage an organization:

1. *Task*—The job, the function (selling, manufacturing, financing, etc.) represents the *purpose* for which the information is reported.
2. *Resource*—The objects or events reported upon are the resources (personnel, equipment, money, etc.) that are being used or acquired.
3. *Networks*—Flows of information and resources representing a model of the organization; the focus of planning and control.
4. *Level*—Three levels representing the hierarchy of planning and control in the organization: strategic planning, management control, and operational control.
5. *Environment*—The environment in which the firm operates, including information needed to set goals and objectives, information concerning other external environment (suppliers, government, etc.), and other external planning premises.

The job of the systems planner is to devise the master classification scheme that best fits his particular organization, keeping in mind the need to design a *master plan* that will serve for integration of various additional applications over the near and long term. In most cases a combination of the approaches cited will be sufficient, but *some grand scheme* is necessary if the planning objectives previously detailed are to be achieved.

The task of selecting the proper classification framework can be described conceptually in Figure 7–12. From the "menu" offered, the designer must select the combination that suits the needs of management. The combination is multidimensional:

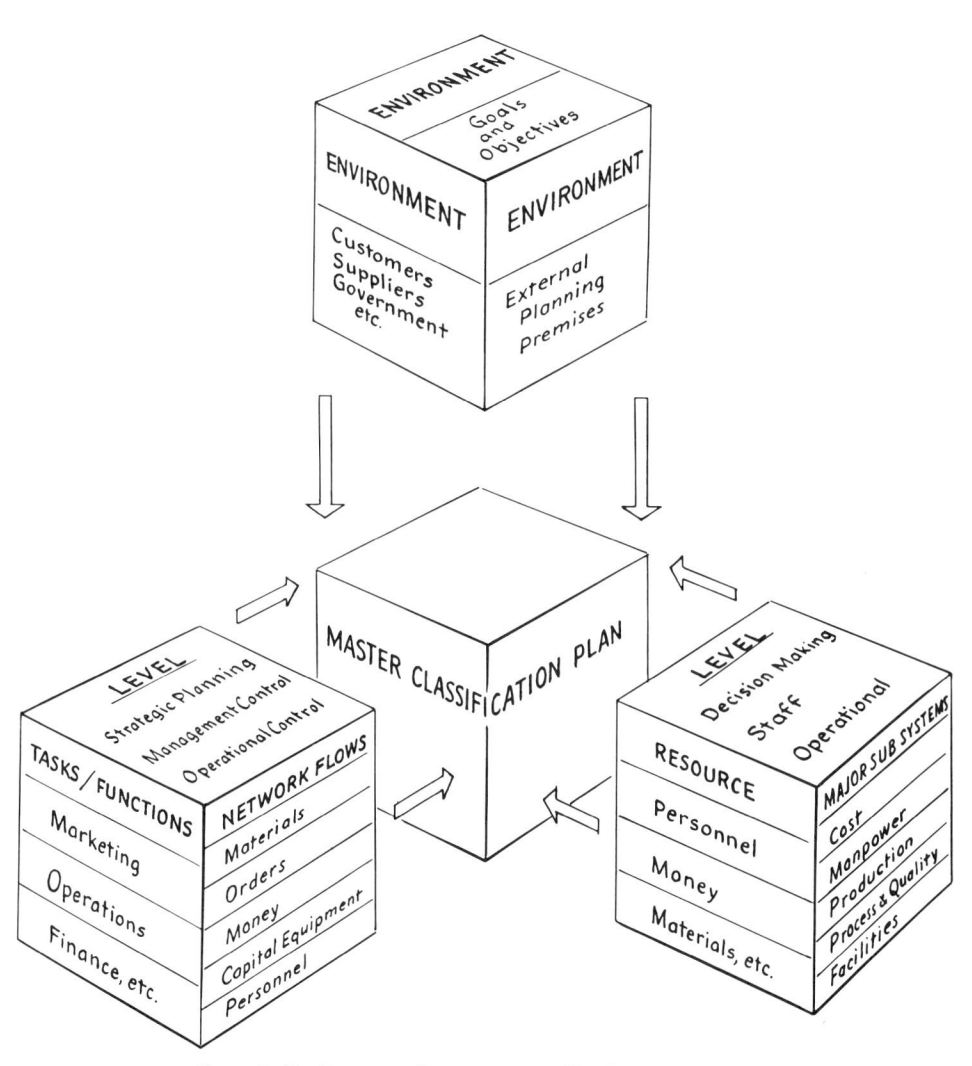

Figure 7–12 Elements of a Master Classification Plan

1. Two hierarchical classifications of systems (function and decision-making)
2. The common tasks/functions among systems
3. Resources to be managed in the transformation process
4. Information and resource flows
5. The environment in which management sets goals and objectives

In addition to these five dimensions, the designer is concerned with additional dimensions of a classification scheme: the common functions and resources among systems in the vertical hierarchy and, finally, informational elements that go to construct integrated subsystems across horizontal boundaries.

Task or Function

The most logical and the most widespread type of categorization in information systems is organized around the job to be done, the task to be performed, and the use to which the information will be put. Classification in this fashion tends to develop for the same reason that most firms choose it for its basic organization: homogeneity of functions performed. This approach produces a natural subgrouping of work as well as of the information required to plan and control this work. Moreover, this approach permits or encourages integration of subsystems, because different functional organizational entities frequently deal with the same resource or with different aspects of the same task. For example, sales orders from the marketing function have an important interface with production control and other subsystems.

Figure 7–10 illustrates some of the major subsystems classified by task or function in a manufacturing organization. Others are shown in Table 7–2, on page 268.

Resource

A second and widely used means of classifying information systems is around the resource (people, projects, equipment, funds, etc.) to be managed. Each resource usually has characteristics peculiar to its description and hence to the information surrounding it. Resources tend to be organized around the functions of the organization: money around treasury department, personnel around personnel department, raw materials around production, and so on. Because of this association there is naturally a great deal of overlap and integration between tasks (functions) and resources.

For each major resource, an information system can be constructed with files that contain information in subcategories; the personnel system contains a subsystem entitled Employee Benefits, which in turn has files on

Insurance, Savings, Retirement, and so on. Major elements of a resource classification system are illustrated below. Note that several of the *task* subsystems are common to two or more *resource* systems. This makes the point once again that subsystems are seldom mutually exclusive; they are usually multidimensional, with dimensions of (a) hierarchy, (b) task, and (c) resource, each of which has two other dimensions of (d) vertical and (e) horizontal boundaries.

TASK/FUNCTION INFORMATION SYSTEM

RESOURCE	Purchasing	Inventory Control	Billing	Scheduling	Job Control	Personnel Administration
LOGISTICS						
Raw material	x	x		x		
Finished goods		x	x	x		
Production facilities		x		x	x	
PHYSICAL ASSETS						
Property and equipment	x	x		x		
FINANCIAL						
Cash and credit	x		x			
MANPOWER						
Payroll					x	x
Benefits						x

Network Flows

Most existing information systems are organized around either resources or what might be called "task-oriented, function-related" categories, but these classification approaches leave something to be desired. Conceptually, they are static and do not adequately take account of the *dynamic* nature of the business firm. Yet we know that business is a dynamic organism composed of systems that process inputs into useful outputs of products or services. This processing or transformation of resources into outputs is made possible through an information system characterized by two attributes: first, *movement* or *flow* through a complex interconnected system, and second, the *integrative* nature of the information used at multiple points throughout the organization. These characteristics are difficult to achieve in an information system organized by resource or task alone. What is needed is an additional dynamic dimension of *flow*. This concept can be applied to either information or physical resources, and these can be classified into *networks*. The idea of flow gives a greater conceptual grasp of the twin notions of upper management's development of plans and lower man-

Table 7–2

Selected List of "Task-Oriented, Function-Related" Subsystems

Product Development	Operations	Finance	Manpower
Engineering	Classification	Accounts receivable	Arbitration
Project control	Cataloguing	Accounts payable	Classifying
Bill of material	Inventory control	Billing	Interviewing
Research and development	Labor scheduling and reporting	Cost accounting	Placing

Styling	Manufacturing
	  Cutting
	  Welding
	  Finishing
	  Etc.
		Cash receipts
		Cash budgets
		Financial planning
		General ledger
		Plant accounting
			Recruiting
			Selection
			Staffing
			Testing
			Services

	Production control	Variance analysis	
	Process control	Taxes	
	Purchasing	Timekeeping	
	Quality control		
	Stores control		

	Scheduling
	  Labor
	  Finished goods
	  Etc.		

	Servicing
	  Maintenance
	  Repair
	  Materials handling
	  Packaging
	  Receiving
	  Shipping
	  Warehousing		

agement's execution and control of these plans. To say it another way, we want to have operational planning and control systems, and these may be achieved through an analysis of the flow process: its inputs, the transformation processes, its outputs, and the *decision points*.

The subjects of the network flows are the inputs to the organization: facilities, materials, manpower, money, orders, and information. To illustrate how an information system can be built around such a flow network, let us take the *materials* flow. Conceptually (and practically), we can depict a system that plans and controls the acquisition of materials; their subsequent transportation to the factory; their allocation, storage, and production transformation within the factory; and their transportation and distribution and final sale to a customer. We can see that an information system built around such an approach would *integrate* a number of activities that have traditionally been organized and managed by function (marketing, purchasing, etc.) or resource (plant, materials, etc.).

The categories or *networks* we shall mention comprise an arbitrary classification around which the systems designer may begin to construct a master classification plan. Regardless of the extent to which this scheme is utilized, it does provide an excellent sketch of the operation as a *dynamic system* whose total objectives can be achieved through the planning, allocation, and control of flows of inputs that are transformed into outputs.

The *materials network* includes the flow and stocks of all materials, whether raw materials, work in process, or finished goods. An information system using this concept would include all decisions from the point at which acquisition decisions are made until final delivery to a customer. Obviously, a number of other subsystems would need to be architecturally integrated with this flow because of interfaces. By taking the systemic network approach to design of this system, planning and control as well as time and cost considerations could be substantially improved over the traditional functionalism associated with management of materials. To illustrate, consider the traditional system in which a sale triggers a change in the production schedule, which triggers a requisition for replenishment, which triggers a change in purchasing, and so on until the entire system has "geared up" to handle this input stimulus. Under a systems or network approach to materials flow, the initial trigger provided by the sale can stimulate responses all the way through the integrated system with much less delay and at less cost than the traditional organization, which is intent upon optimizing subsystem (department) objectives rather than the system (firm) as a whole.

The flows of *orders* comprise another network. These are not physical objects but rather symbolic representations of what will become arrangements of other resources and the allocation of resources to meet the commitment of the order. Viewed in this light, orders become the catalyst that can provide the decision inputs for optimization of transformation resources.

It is important to design a system to track the *money* network because money is the common language of managing and provides a tool for measuring results against plans. Moreover, money is a medium of exchange that reflects the firm's actions with its total environment, outside and inside. Outside, the money flow interfaces with banks, customers, stockholders, government (tax), labor, suppliers, and the community at large. Inside the firm it is a yardstick to measure resource allocation and control. Focusing on the money flows within and without the organization should improve the integration of subsystems at both these levels, as well as the management of the individual functions, resources, or outside entities.

Other network flows consist of the *personnel network,* the *facilities network,* and the *information network*. The first two of these work in much the same fashion as those just discussed in that they improve decision making, shorten the time involved in decision making, and integrate the organization subsystems for greater economies and efficiencies. The *information network* is in a category by itself; it represents the other flows and provides the linkage that causes them to interact in the manner of a *total system*.

Levels of Systems

In Chapter 4 we discussed the impact that the systems approach will have on the function of organizing and the structure of organizations. One major change will probably be the elimination or reduction of the sharp lines of demarcation between existing departments as we know them—purchasing, accounting, sales, manufacturing, engineering. However, one essential feature of organizations will no doubt remain: the managerial hierarchy of planning and control. This hierarchy of management and organizational structure has been described in a number of ways, but almost invariably as having three levels. Some of the ways of structuring this hierarchy have been by layer, task, location, function, and level:

CLASSIFICATION

LAYER	Task	Location	Management Function	Level
FIRST	Strategic planning	Management	Management	Top
SECOND	Management control	Office	Planning and control	Middle
THIRD	Operational control	Factory and field	Execution	Supervisory

Whatever the combination of classifications we choose to describe the organizational hierarchy, different levels and tasks must be recognized and provided for in systems development and design. In Table 7–3 Blumenthal distinguishes among three levels: *strategic planning, management control,* and *operational control*. These levels are further extended to include an information systems perspective on this hierarchy of an organization: inputs, outputs, systems types, and so on. These attributes and levels should be considered in adopting the master classification plan for information usage at different levels and for different purposes.

Environment

The classifications we have discussed thus far (task, resource, information flows, levels) have been concerned for the most part with the interaction of subsystems within the firm and information available inside the organization. However, some of the most vital sources of information are

Table 7-3

LEVEL	ORGANIZATIONAL IDENTITY	ACTIVITIES	CHARACTERISTICS	TEMPO	INPUTS	INFORMATION SYSTEMS	OUTPUTS
Strategic planning	Corporation and division top management	Set objectives Determine resources to be applied	Unpredictable Variable Staff-oriented External perspective	Irregular	Staff studies External situation Reports of internal achievement	Special one-time reports Simulations Inquiries (unrestricted)	Goals Policies Constraints
Management control	Corporation and divisional departments Profit centers	Allocate assigned resources to tasks Make rules Measure performance Exert control	Personal style Organizational change Line-oriented Judgmental Internal perspective	Rhythmic: quarterly monthly weekly	Summaries Exceptions	Many regular reports Format variety Inquiries (restricted) "Data-bank" oriented Abstract	Decisions "Personal" leadership Procedures
Operational control	Supervisors Foremen Clerks	Use resources to carry out tasks in conformance with rules	Stable Logical Predictable Prescribed	Real-time	Internal events Transactions	Formal Fixed procedures Complex Concrete	Actions

SOURCE Sherman C. Blumenthal, *Management Information Systems: A Framework for Planning and Development* (Englewood Cliffs, N.J.: Prentice-Hall, Inc., 1969), p. 29.

external to the firm and concern the external environment in which it operates. Although the satisfaction of the manager's *total* information needs, including those external to the firm, is probably impossible, these needs must nevertheless be taken into account despite the two major difficulties of (1) little control over the environment, and (2) inability to design a system to capture this information. A variety of schemes exist for classification of environmental information needs. In general they follow our breakdown of planning premises. These may include:

- Social
- Legal
- Technological
- Demographic
- Economic
- Political
- Competitive

SUMMARY

The number of installed computer systems is accelerating rapidly, but their use for the automation of information for decision making remains essentially untapped. Two types of systems for decision making are identified: the automated system and the decision information system. The former utilizes management science in the design of decision rules for making decisions that are essentially automated. These are illustrated by the many paperwork and clerical applications in current use, plus such operating applications as production control. The decision information system provides information for the human decision maker in a man–machine interaction. Modeling and simulation provide the greatest potential in this area.

Although the boundaries of computer-assisted decisions have advanced somewhat toward the programming of more complex decisions, the vast majority of applications remain essentially in the clerical areas. As the knowledge of utilizing systems techniques for making operating decisions advances, more and more applications will be made in the middle-management area. The top-management level has remained largely untapped for computer-assisted decisions, and it is here that the greatest potential lies.

The major objective of computer-based systems for decision making is integration of the functions, resources, and management levels of the organization. An important part of the task of achieving this integration is the design of a master plan with a predetermined scheme of classifications of systems.

DISCUSSION QUESTIONS AND PROBLEMS

1. A recent check of several large companies reveals that "general and administrative expense" is less than 10 percent of sales. If this is true, how can it be claimed that 50 percent of the cost of running the American economy is information costs? Would information costs be contained in captions other than "general and administrative"? If so, where?

2. Illustrate several operations now being performed that would be difficult, if not impossible, without the computational power of the computer; without the storage power of the computer.

3. What do we mean by "automation of information"? What is a possible hierarchy of levels of automation? Name one or more applications (e.g., payroll) where automation of information is fairly commonplace. Name several applications (e.g., advertising budget) where automation has hardly begun. Why can't decision rules and hence automation be applied to these areas?

4. What does management science have to do with the design of decision rules? Illustrate.

5. Compare the cybernetic nature of machines with that of organizations. Why can we not achieve automatic feedback and control in the organization in the same way as in the machine? Can we make further advances in programming or automating the decision process in the organization? Show how.

6. Do you think that further advances in MIS will reduce the ranks of middle managers? Lower-level managers? Top management? Justify your answers.

7. Distinguish between decision information, operating information, and historical information. How can these categories of information serve to integrate the levels of management?

8. Choose a commonplace information system (e.g., accounts receivable, raw materials inventory control, sales order analysis) and show how it might interface with other classifications of systems shown in Table 7-2.

9. One of the nation's largest airlines is a pioneer in the use of computers for a limited number of real-time applications. Foremost among these applications is the reservation system, which provides instant information and confirmation of passenger space. By and large, the system has worked out well.

Despite the design of sophisticated systems in the areas of reservations and flight scheduling, the management of the airline is not satisfied with its management applications. A brief survey of executive opinion indicated the following major needs:

Marketing	Operations	Finance	Personnel
S Space forecasting	P Maintenance scheduling	P Cash budget	O Crew training
P Passenger analysis	S Overhaul and repair of engines	P Foreign currency control	D Safety
P Group sales reservation	P Parts requirements and control		
	P Crew scheduling		

Questions:

(1) Which of the foregoing needs, if any, would lend themselves to programmed decision systems (automation)? Which to a decision information system? Which to simulation?

(2) Could company resources and management levels be better integrated through the proper design of MIS to fulfill the above needs? Which ones? How?

(3) How would you classify the needs into an MIS classification scheme?

REFERENCES

1. Herbert A. Simon, *The New Science of Management Decision* (New York: Harper & Row Publishers, 1960), p. 34.

2. Adrian F. McDonough, *Information Economics and Management Systems* (New York: McGraw-Hill Book Company, 1963), p. 11.

3. For example, one classification includes five hierarchies: (1) clerical; (2) information systems—manual and mechanized; (3) decision systems; (4) interactive systems—man–machine and man–man; and (5) programmed systems. G. W. Dickson, "Management Information-Decision Systems," *Business Horizons,* December 1968, p. 19.

4. In cybernetic terms we might call the organization "a homeostatic machine for regulating itself through feedback." Despite the fact that thousands of examples of this kind of control exist for mechanical systems (machines), economic systems (Keynesian theory), biological systems (human brain), etc., it is difficult to think of the company or the organization in these terms; yet the fundamental design idea is the same.

5. Recent research efforts have included the design of decision rules and programmed systems for selection of portfolio investments, selection of optimum vendors, and other activities that lend themselves to mathematical treatment.

6. George Terborgh, *The Automation Hysteria* (New York: W. W. Norton & Co., Inc., 1966), pp. 28–29. Prepared by the Machinery and Allied Products Institute. Several other surveys of EDP applications are included in this work.
7. Harold J. Leavitt and Thomas L. Whisler, "Management in the 1980's," *Harvard Business Review*, November–December 1958, pp. 41–48.
8. Jay W. Forrester, *Industrial Dynamics* (Cambridge: The M.I.T. Press, 1961), p. 3.
9. John Diebold, "ADP—The Still-Sleeping Giant," *Harvard Business Review*, September–October 1964, p. 61.
10. John Diebold, "Bad Decisions on Computer Use," *Harvard Business Review*, January–February 1969, p. 16.
11. U.S. National Bureau of Standards, *Training for Automation and Information Processing in the Federal Service*, October 1966.
12. For example, see discussion of the failure of management science to deal thus far with the "risk-making and risk-taking decisions of the business enterprise" in Peter F. Drucker, "Thinking Ahead: Potentials of Management Science," *Harvard Business Review*, January–February 1959.
13. John Dearden, "How to Organize Information Systems," *Harvard Business Review*, March–April 1965, p. 19.
14. U.S. Department of the Navy, *Automatic Data Processing Program*, SecNavInst. 10462.7B, August 1967 (Washington, D.C.: Department of the Navy), p. H-4.
15. Joseph Orlicky, *The Successful Computer System* (New York: McGraw-Hill Book Company, 1969), pp. 93–94.
16. See page 254.
17. Rodney H. Brady, "Computers in Top-Level Decision Making," *Harvard Business Review*, July–August 1967, p. 97.
18. Adrian M. McDonough and Leonard J. Garrett, *Management Systems: Working Concepts and Practices* (Homewood, Ill.: Richard D. Irwin, Inc., 1965), p. 61.
19. George A. Steiner, *Top Management Planning* (Toronto: Collier-Macmillan Canada, Ltd., 1969), pp. 487–91. John Dearden also classifies systems into major and minor. Major systems are financial, personnel, and logistics. Minor systems include marketing, research and development, strategic planning, and executive observation. Dearden, "How to Organize Information Systems," pp. 23–25.

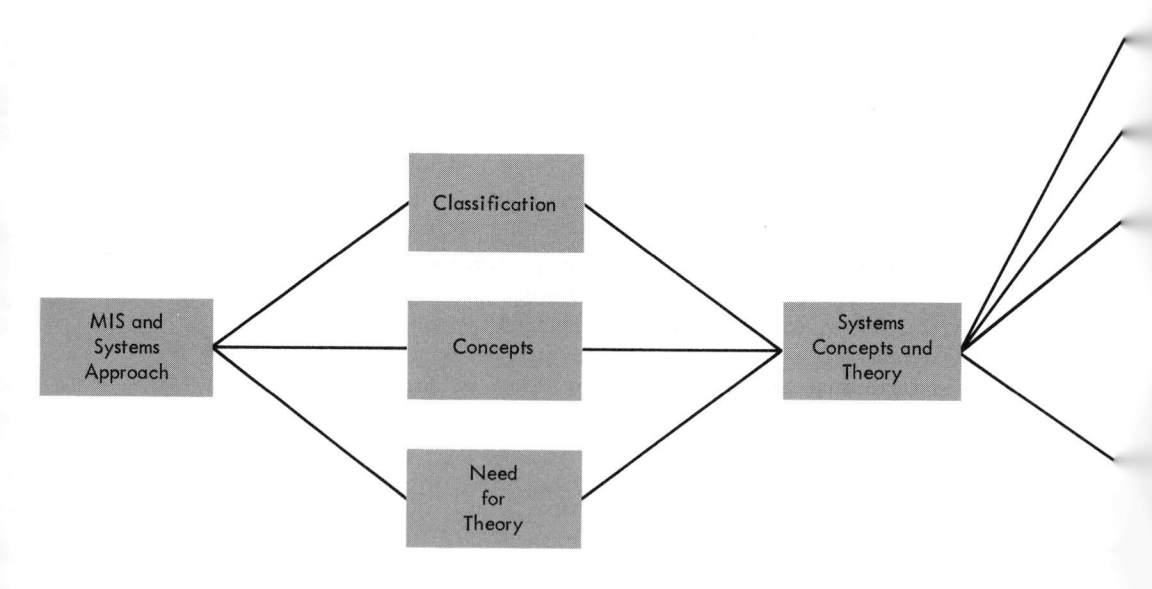

```
MIS and              Classification
Systems  ──────────  Concepts       ──────────  Systems
Approach             Need for Theory            Concepts and Theory
```

8
systems theory and management information systems

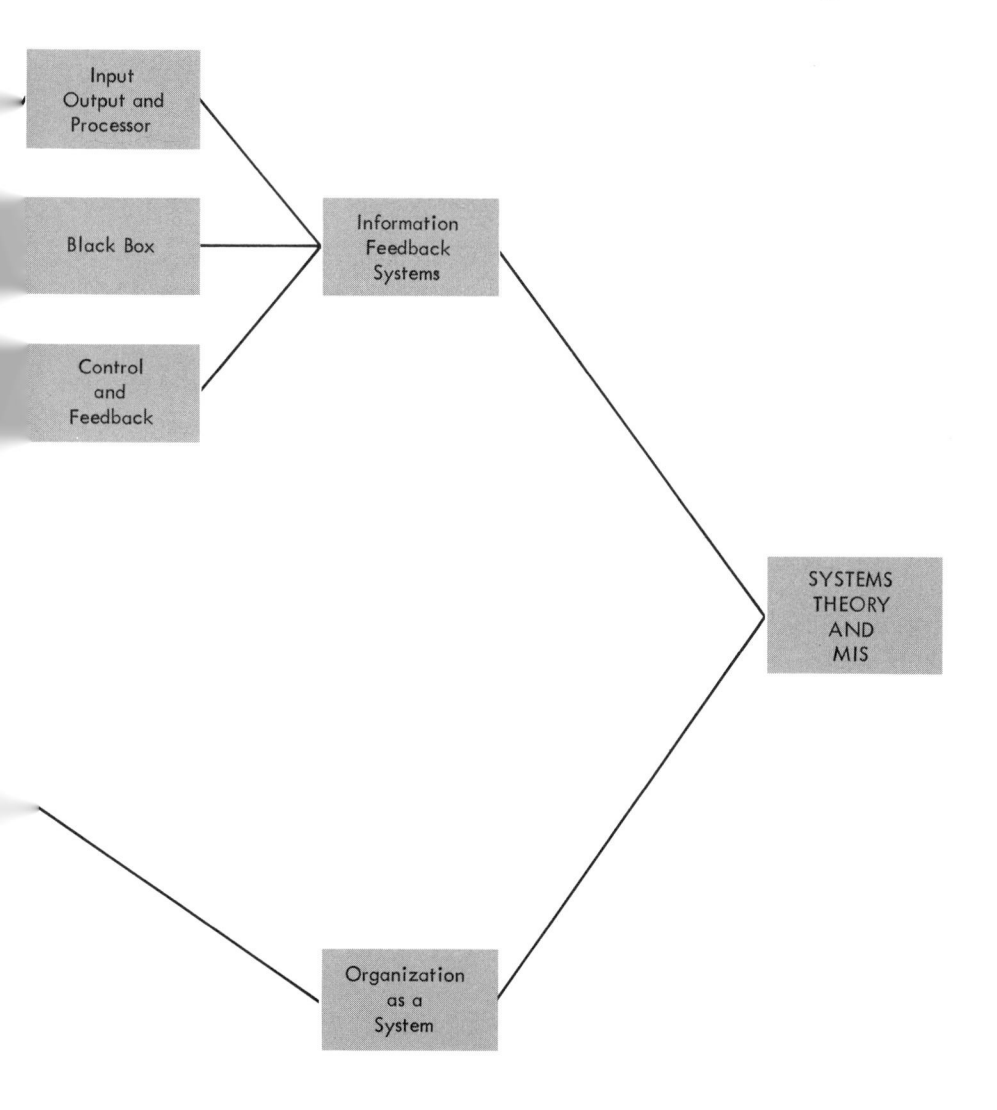

- Input Output and Processor
- Black Box
- Control and Feedback
- Information Feedback Systems
- Organization as a System
- SYSTEMS THEORY AND MIS

8

We are not attempting here to develop a total systems theory but rather to choose the portions of such a theory that are relevant for organization and management and for designing information systems to facilitate these processes. There is serious doubt about whether a general systems theory exists and whether it makes a significant contribution to management theory. Therefore, the manager can hope only for some concepts, principles, and guides that are relevant for decision making in planning, operating, and controlling. This is what the concept of systems can provide.

The systems approach is primarily a way of thinking about the job of managing. It provides a framework for integrating the internal and external environment factors and the diverse operations that affect the success of an organization. It provides for the recognition of subsystems and their functions as well as for the complex network of supersystems within which the manager must operate. In short, the systems concept advances a way of thinking that helps to explain some of the complexity of the manager's environment and also assists him to perceive and explain the nature of complex problems.

Essentially then, the systems approach to management utilizes scientific analysis to provide decision-making information in complex organizations. The fundamental building blocks are these:

Topic	Contribution to Systems Theory and MIS
Systems classifications, concepts, and need	Classifies categories of systems for ease of description and explanation. Defines operation of elements and components of systems. Describes effort at a theory.
Information feedback systems	Describes elements and operation of all systems in order to develop theory and principles for structure and design of management information systems.
Decision making	Process is integral to systems approach since the output of MIS is information for decisions.
Management science	Vital tool for designing programmed decision rules and for problem solving and decision making.
Systems design	Goal is integration of subsystems that provide information for management.
Computer	Necessary device for storing, processing, and retrieving information in MIS.

We have examined the role of the computer in the operation of an MIS. In this chapter we will expand the examination of systems theory to develop the contribution listed. The remainder of the foregoing topics will be developed in subsequent chapters in order to construct a total body of principles for the design and operation of management information systems.

SYSTEMS CLASSIFICATIONS

Systems fall into a number of categories, and confusion may result if we talk about systems behavior and characteristics without identifying and specifying the kind of system we are talking about. The following commonly accepted classifications are the most important ones for a study of business and information systems.

Conceptual and Empirical

It is especially important to distinguish between systems that are conceptual (analytical) and those that are empirical. For example, there will be misunderstanding if a person is talking about an information system as a set of concepts, ideas, or characteristics while his listener is envisioning an operational system of people, equipment, and reports. *Conceptual* systems are concerned with theoretical structures, which may or may not have any counterpart in the real world. Conceptual systems are typified by those of science, such as economic theory, non-Euclidean geometry systems, the general system of relativity, or organization theory. Note that conceptual systems for organizations as composed of ideas are distinct from empirical organization systems made up of people.

Conceptual systems, then, are systems of explanation or classification. They may also appear in practical management affairs in the form of plans, accounting system structures, and classifications of policies and procedures.

Empirical systems are generally concrete operational systems made up of people, materials, machines, energy, and other physical things, although electrical, thermal, chemical, information and other such systems involving intangibles also fall into this category. Empirical systems may of course be derived from or based upon conceptual systems and thus represent the conversion of concepts into practice. In advancing the science of MIS, we deal with conceptual systems such as models, but MIS are themselves, in practice, empirical (real-world) systems.

Natural and Man-Made

Natural systems abound in nature. The entire ecology of life is a natural system, and each organism is a unique natural system of its own. The water system of the world, at least before man affected it, was a natural system. Our own solar system is a natural system.

Man-made systems were formed when men first gathered in groups to live and hunt together. They now appear in infinite variety all about us and extend from the manufacturing system of a company to the system of space exploration. Their objectives likewise vary tremendously. One system may be concerned with national defense; another may be a transportation system. A business organization is a system with many smaller systems included—production, accounting, and so on—as well as others such as communication systems and office layout systems overlaid upon the main economic organization of people.

Social, Man–Machine, and Machine

Systems made up of people may be viewed purely as *social* systems, apart from other systems objectives and processes. Business organizations, government agencies, political parties, social clubs, and technical societies are examples of systems that may be so studied. Admittedly, all of these employ objects and artifacts that form physical systems, yet the most relevant aspects may be considered to be organizational structure and human behavior.

Most empirical (as opposed to conceptual) systems fall into the category of *man–machine* systems. It is difficult to think of a system composed only of men who do not utilize equipment of some kind to achieve their goals. Even philosophers write and record. It is possible to think of some small systems that are purely mechanical, but they are usually a part of larger systems involving people.

Pure *machine* systems would have to obtain their own inputs and maintain themselves. The development of a self-healing machine system would bring these systems closer to simulation of living organsms. Such systems would need to adapt to their environment. Although some electrical power generating systems approach self-sufficiency, self-repairing and completely self-sufficient machine systems are still in the category of science fiction.

Open and Closed

An *open* system is one that interacts with its environment. All systems containing living organisms are obviously open systems because they are affected by what is sensed by the organisms. In a more important sense, organizations are usually systems operating within larger systems and are therefore open systems. For example, a company's marketing organization is a system that is a part of the larger system, the entire company. The company in turn is a system within the larger industry system.

The fact that a company interacts with its environment—a larger system—makes that individual company an open system. The open system may be further identified by its individually small influence on its environment and inadequate feedback of information from the environment. As business managers will readily agree, they must somehow manage their companies in great ignorance about the future impact of environmental conditions. The environmental system with which they can best contend is the particular industry system of which they are a part.

Continuing in this direction, then, we note that the industry is part of the national economic system, which in turn is a system within our society. Our society is a system within the world system; the world system is a part of the solar system; and so on into the unknown.

The question of what constitutes a *closed* system is more difficult. A closed system is one that does not interact with its environment. Whatever environment surounds the closed system does not change, or if it does, a barrier exists between the environment and the system to prevent the system from being affected. Although it is doubtful that closed systems really exist, the concept has important implications. We attempt in research to develop models that are essentially closed systems. When we set up experiments in the laboratory for the study of human behavior, we are attempting to establish a closed system temporarily. The scientist who devises a laboratory system to measure the elasticity of a metal is assuming a closed system such that environmental changes that would affect his results are avoided. Problems in business are sometimes resolved as if a closed system existed in order to simplify the situation enough so that at least a first approximation can be obtained.

Some authors distinguish further between open systems that are simply influenced passively by the environment and those that react and adapt to the environment. These subclasses are designated as *nonadaptive* and *adaptive* systems.

Permanent and Temporary

Relatively few, if any, man-made systems are *permanent*. However, for practical purposes, systems enduring for a time span that is long relative to the operations of humans in the system may be said to be "permanent." Our economic system, which is gradually changing, is essentially permanent for our plans for the future. At another extreme, the policies of a business organization are "permanent" as far as year-to-year operations are concerned. It is true that major policy changes may be made, but these will then last an indefinite and "long" time relative to the daily activities of employees.

Truly *temporary* systems are designed to last a specified period of time and then dissolve. The television system set up to record and transmit the proceedings of a national political convention is only a temporary system. A small group-research project in the laboratory is a temporary system. Some systems that are temporary are not so by design. A company that is formed and quickly goes bankrupt is an example. Temporary systems are important for the accomplishment of specific tasks in business and for research in science.

Stationary and Nonstationary

A *stationary* system is one whose properties and operations either do not vary significantly, or else vary only in repetitive cycles. The automatic factory, the government agency that processes Social Security payments, the supermarket store operation, the high school, and the ferry system are examples of stationary systems.

An advertising organization, a continental defense system, a research and development laboratory, and a human being are examples of *nonstationary* systems.

Let us compare the stationary system—the automatic factory—with the nonstationary continental defense system. In the automatic factory, system quantities may change with time and operating levels may vary within certain limits. However, there is a manufacturing cycle that is repeated with relatively little change. Such a system could be very complex and the cost of failure is high. Failure is not necessarily permanent, though, because the factory could be modified to operate properly. In the case of the continental defense system, the cost is likewise very large. One major difference is that initial failure is apt to rule out the opportunity to revise the system. In nonrepetitive systems, failure in one case does not always lead to successful modification for different cases in the future.

Subsystems and Supersystems

From the preceding discussions, it has become apparent that each system is nested in a larger system. The system in the hierarchy that we are most interested in studying or controlling is usually called "the system." The business firm is viewed as "the system" or the "total system" when focus is on production, distribution of goods, and sources of profit and income. As Stanford L. Optner says, "The total system consists of all the objects, attributes, and relationships necessary to accomplish an objective, given a number of constraints. The term *system* is most frequently employed in the sense of total system. The objective of the total system defines the purpose for which all the system objects, attributes, and relationships have been organized."[1]

Smaller systems within the system are called *subsystems*. This distinction has important implications in practice with regard to optimization and the "systems approach," as we shall see later.

Supersystem is not usually used in antithesis to subsystem; it denotes extremely large and complex systems.

Classification of Organizational Systems and of MIS

It is useful to identify the classifications into which organizational systems and MIS fall. We summarize our conclusions as follows:

Organizational System

1. Conceptual, if we are discussing the theory or organization charts or manuals; empirical if we are discussing the people and their actual relationships and activities.

2. Natural, if we are discussing man as part of the ecology of life on earth; man-made if we discuss any other organization of man.

3. Social. All man-made groupings of people are social systems whose behavior has been subjected to considerable research. Chapter 3 provided some insights into the social system of business organizations.

4. Open. Every social organization is open because it reacts with its unpredictable environment.

5. Permanent, almost, if we consider major political systems and companies that last for centuries. England and Lloyd's of London have existed for centuries. Probably all organizational systems are temporary and doomed to oblivion in the history of Earth.

6. Nonstationary, in general. Organizational systems tend to change to adapt to a changing environment in the long run. In the short run, we may treat some of those listed earlier as stationary for convenience in studying them.

7. Subsystems *and* supersystems. The organizational system varies from the small, supervised group in business or government to the complex, social–political–economic group making up a country like the United States.

Management Information System

1. Conceptual, if we are discussing the models or theory of MIS; empirical, if we are referring to a specific system in action.

2. Man-made. Human information systems are devised by men and are not simply "born."

3. Social *and* man–machine. MIS may be viewed purely from the human aspect, which includes communication/information/decision making. The MIS in its most sophisticated form includes equipment such as electronic computers and is therefore a man–machine system.

4. Open *and* closed. For simple operational and low-level functional management decision making, the MIS may be "decoupled" from its environment to operate on information stored within the system. Most MIS,

284 Computer-Based Management Information Systems

however, are utilized for planning and decision making that require important interactions with the business environment.

5. *Temporary.* MIS are constantly being revised, both formally and informally.

6. *Stationary.* Once designed, the MIS is supposed to handle certain types of problems on a more or less routine basis and supply information to management according to a specified program.

7. *Subsystem and supersystem.* At the present state-of-the-art, MIS are being designed primarily as subsystems of a potential total business MIS. A total, sophisticated MIS for a large corporation or industry would certainly verge on a supersystem, but this is a potentiality rather than a reality.

SOME SYSTEM CONCEPTS

It is the approach of science to ask, "What are the parts?" It is a requirement for design that we ask, "What are systems composed of?" Here we take a conceptual view of systems to answer this question because the answer has already been given: empirical systems are composed of real-life things. Identification of concepts will be important in the development of system theory, in the design of systems, and in the evaluation of systems. System concepts also provide an introduction to models of systems.

In order to make these concepts more understandable, we will show their application to a simple, computer-based marketing information system (MARIS). The concept of this marketing information system is shown in Figure 8–1.

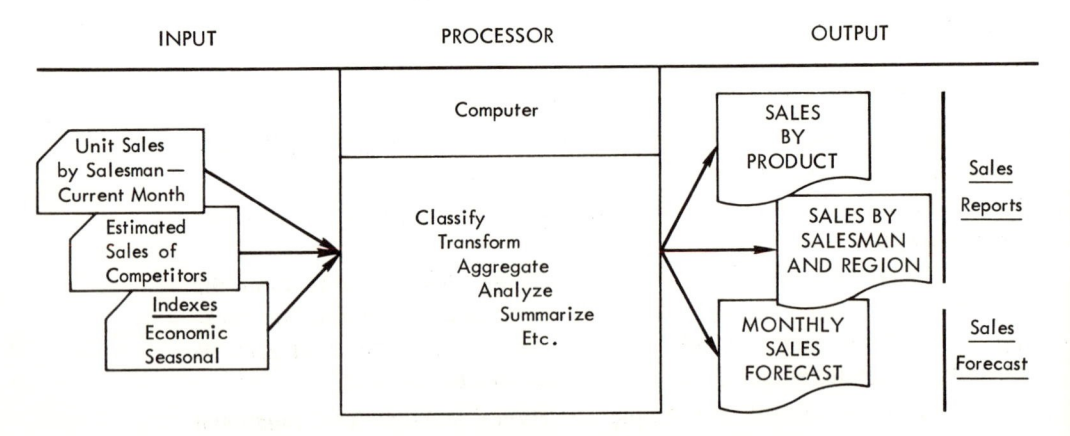

Figure 8–1 Inputs and Outputs of a Marketing Information System (MARIS)

Principal System Quantities or Variables

Every system is a processor, according to the definition given earlier. The principal system quantities or variables are representations of amounts of information, energy, or matter, which appear as inputs or outputs of the system. In our marketing information system, we have as inputs sales in units by each salesman for the past month, sales of competitors (estimated), economic conditions, and seasonal indexes. The outputs are sales by product, salesman, and region, and a forecast for the coming month.

We see first that one of our input variables is sales in units by a particular salesman. This variable might have been expressed in pounds, gallons, other appropriate units, or some other measure such as dollars, but the system designer selected units as the dimension. Similarly, each other input is represented by a name or symbol that has a specified dimension and varies with time.

These input quantities are classified, transformed, aggregated, or analyzed by the computer to yield the desired output variables with values for a particular point in time.

System Parameters

Many quantities that enter into the relationships among the input variables and the output variables are considered constant for a specific period of time or system operational style. In essence, for a fixed set of these values, the system is said to be in a specified "state." These quantities, which determine the state of the system, are called *parameters*. Not entirely jokingly, we might call these parameters "variable constants."

In the MARIS example, it turns out that management scientists who constructed the relationships among the inputs and the outputs included several parameters. One of these is a "fudge" factor to correct the sales forecast in the event that a competitor conducts a special promotion. Normally, this promotion "fudge" factor changes in value from month to month, i.e., it is a constant characterizing the no-promotion state. However, it is turned on to a new value once in a while, when one or more competitors increase their promotional level.

Another parameter in the sales forecasting process is the average age of the salesmen. If the average age changes by more than 15 percent, a change in this parameter is called for, and the selling function has changed its "state."

Components

A system's components are simply the various identifiable parts of the system. If a system is large enough so that it is composed of subsystems, and each subsystem is composed of subsystems, eventually we reach some parts that individually are not subsystems. In other words, in a hierarchy of subsystems, the components exist at the lowest level.

In our MARIS system, there are two subsystems: the sales reporting system and the sales forecasting system. The components of the system are telecommunication devices, people, an electric computer, procedure manuals, and reports. These components, except for some of the people, are shared by both systems.

Attributes of Components

Components, because they are objects or people, possess properties or characteristics. These characteristics affect the operation of the system in speed, accuracy, reliability, capacity, and many other ways. Choices must be made in systems design between the use of humans and the use of machines, and between various kinds of machines, on the basis of attributes and cost.

Humans, for example, have very limited capacity to absorb information per unit of time compared with machines. However, humans are better than machines in analyzing poorly structured problems. It has been said that man is the most effective control component that can be mass-produced by inexperienced labor.

An example of a choice between machines might be the selection of an output device from among a cathode-ray tube, an audio system, a mechanical printer, or a plotting device. In the MARIS, the characteristics of the output component are not high speed, but clarity, economy, and relative permanence. Therefore a printer, auxiliary to the computer, is chosen and the format of the output is a "printed" report, sent to management once a month.

Structure

The structure of a system is the set of relationships among objects and attributes. A description of the way in which the objects and their attributes are connected defines the structure. Levels of relationship may be classified as:

First order—Dysfunctional relationships caused by natural phenomena or conflicting attributes.
Second order—Symbiosis, the necessary relationship between dissimilar organisms, as for example, plant and parasite.
Third order—Synergistic relationships in which attributes of objects reinforce each other to increase or improve system output.

The functional relationships among the people and the equipment form the structure of the MARIS. The organizational hierarchy, the lateral relationships among the people in the system, and the relationship between the computer and the people could be set forth in a block diagram representing the structure of the system.

Dysfunctional relationships among people may be present because of poor system design or personality conflicts among the people. There may be dysfunctional relationships between people and the computer due to humans' inability to perform monotonous, repetitive operations connected with the outputs or inputs of the computer. On the other hand, the computer may fail to operate properly because of rough or careless treatment of punched cards or equipment by humans.

Symbiosis in the MARIS is the necessary relationship between the computer and humans. Each needs the other to accomplish system objectives.

Synergistic effects in the social group making up the system may be achieved by different individuals' supplementing each other so that total output is greater than the simple addition of each individual's work.

Process

The total process of a system is the net result of all ongoing activities in converting inputs to outputs. When management and systems designers have established the data that will be available as inputs to an MIS and the information desired for the output, the systems designers have the major project of designing the conversion process.

The total process is actually made up of many small processes. A parallel between a material-processing system and an MIS may help clarify the meaning of a single process. In a certain factory, a worker receives a square of sheet metal, places it in a punch press, operates the press to produce a formed and perforated piece of metal. This is a single process in the entire production process.

In our marketing information system, the computer flowchart shows the aggregation, by the process of addition, of individual sales reports into total sales. This is a single process among many in the system. The functional relationship between an input and output of a process is called the *transfer function*. This term is commonly used in the design and evaluation of feedback systems.

Boundaries

The concept of boundary of a system makes it possible to focus on a particular system within a hierarchy of systems. The boundary of a system may exist either physically or conceptually. The operational definition of a system in terms of its boundary is:

1. List all components that are to make up the system and circumscribe them. Everything within the circumscribed space is called the system, and everything outside is called the environment.
2. List all flows across the boundary. Flows from the environment into the system are inputs; flows from inside the boundary to outside are called outputs.

We will substitute nested political systems for our marketing information system because the boundaries are easily recognized. Let us start with the city as the smallest system and consider it as part of the county system, which is part of the state system, which in turn is part of the national governmental system.

The boundaries of the city are physical, informational, and legal. The physical boundaries are identified on a map and all physical components of the city system are simply circumscribed on the map. Flows across the physical boundary are inputs from the environment and include flows of people, vehicles, or even animals. Water supply, electrical power, and weather movements are more esoteric examples of inputs. The outputs are of the same type.

The city is an open system that reacts with its environment on the basis of information crossing the boundaries in either direction. The information is usually recorded in newspapers, in the city if it is input or outside of the city if it is output. Television, radio, and word of mouth also provide information flow across the boundaries.

The legal boundaries of the city circumscribe all legal or political actions the city may take. The city is limited to action over its inhabitants, its physical system, and people or companies that operate or pass upon its physical system. However, further restrictions limit the legal actions (or components of the legal system) and reserve them for the state or federal systems.

The city is thus composed of several major systems, each of which has fairly well-defined boundaries. What has been said about the city boundaries may be translated to the county system and then to the state as a system.

Characteristics of Systems

For the solution of a given problem there are good systems and poor ones. The poor systems have characteristics that do not fit the requirements of the problem or of the decision makers. Our marketing information system may be a poor system if its sales forecasts are monthly and manufacturing requires weekly forecasts for planning. It may be a poor system if some salesmen's reports are not included from time to time because of lack of control over reporting.

There are many characteristics of systems that are important for design, production, diagnosis, and evaluation. Man–machine systems have a large spectrum of such characteristics, as shown in Table 8–1.

Table 8–1

Characteristics of Man–Machine Systems

1. Performance of basic and subsidiary functions
2. Accuracy of performance
3. Speed of performance
4. Cost
5. Reliability
6. Environmental adaptability
7. Maintainability
8. Replaceability by successive models
9. Safety and fail-safe features
10. Producibility (feasibility of manufacture)
11. Optimum materials and process for size of manufacturing run
12. Simplification, standardization, and preferred sizes
13. Weight
14. Size and shape
15. Styling and packaging
16. Compatibility with other systems or auxiliary equipment
17. Modular design
18. Ease of operation (human engineering)
19. Balanced design through trade-offs
20. Ease of transporting and installing
21. Legality
22. Social aspects

Table 8–1 is useful because it can serve as a checklist for the designer. Each characteristic must be considered in terms of its degree of importance for the system under scrutiny.

NEED FOR A GENERAL SYSTEMS THEORY

We have noted that there are many types of systems. It is apparent also that for even one type of system, such as MIS, each particular system must be designed on a custom basis. Although we will develop some general *procedures* for systems design in Part IV, we do not yet have a *science of systems*. Such a science has been termed *general systems theory* by researchers in this field.

Admittedly, the present practical value of general systems research to companies is very small, but the student of business will do well to look up from the ground beneath his feet to the horizon from time to time. What is of only theoretical value today may be the essence of practice tomorrow.

The Aims of General Systems Theory

In order to study our world, we have developed scientific approaches and organized total scientific study into subfields or disciplines. The basic structure of these disciplines may be organized as follows:

1. Abstract formal science (mathematics, logic)
2. Empirical science
   a. Natural science
      (1) Physical science (such as geology, physics, chemistry)
      (2) Life science (such as biology, botany)
   b. Behavioral science (behavior of men in societies)
   c. Applied science (such as economics/business, engineering, medicine)

As each of these sciences has developed, a common characteristic of theories has become evident. Theories are structures that tie together the principles and the data; in other words, a theory is a system, and partial theories are subsystems. In the empirical sciences, there appear to be many similarities among systems from different disciplines. For example, the biological organism, as a system, exhibits many of the characteristics of the economic organization, the private corporation. Certain large, engineered electromechanical systems appear to parallel man as a system.

If a structure of parallelisms can be developed so that the essence of systems may be extracted and analyzed, progress in the various disciplines may be greatly expedited and much repetitive research may be eliminated. The procedure is to separate concepts from contents, and then to apply the analysis of the concepts to the contents of the real world.

The aims of general systems theory may be considered these:

1. To identify structural and functional isomorphisms among systems
2. To identify types of systems that appear to recur in various disciplines (horizontal cut across the sciences)
3. To identify types of systems that appear to recur at various sublevels of a discipline
4. To study how systems *are* structured and *do* behave (descriptive) and how systems *should* be structured and *should* behave (normative)

Fundamental Approaches

The development of a general systems theory is still in a primarily speculative stage. At present, the question of what approach to make toward developing a theory has not been answered. Kenneth E. Boulding has proposed two possible approaches: a hierarchical classification by degree of complexity, or the development of models common to many disciplines. The degree of complexity is indicated by definitions of levels as follows:

Level 1. This is the level of frameworks, such as patterns of the universe or arrangements of particles within the atom.

Level 2. This is the level of clockworks or simple moving systems.

Level 3. This is the level of the control or cybernetic system, in which there is a feedback of information to maintain equilibrium.

Level 4. This is the level of an open or self-maintaining system, which is characteristic of life as opposed to non-life.

Level 5. This is the genetic–societal level, or level of plants. Such systems have divisions of cells, each of which performs specialized functions.

Level 6. This is the animal level, characterized by increased mobility and self-awareness. Such systems have specialized information receivers such as eyes and ears, leading to a tremendous increase in information that is absorbed.

Level 7. This is the human level, in which the individual not only knows, but knows that he knows. He is the only one to know that he will eventually die and the only one to be able to pass on knowledge in a cumulative form from generation to generation ("time-binding," as Alfred Korzybsky says).

Level 8. This is the level of social organizations, of which organizations for the development of knowledge and production of goods and services are of particular interest in this book.

Level 9. This is the level of transcendental systems—all those that transcend anything we know about now.[2]

The development of models that appear to recur from one discipline to another might be a more promising approach. Figure 8–2 shows how general systems theory might be structured by this method. Genetic models are those such as human birth process, social organization formation, formation of quantities of an element from radioactive decay, and macroscopic

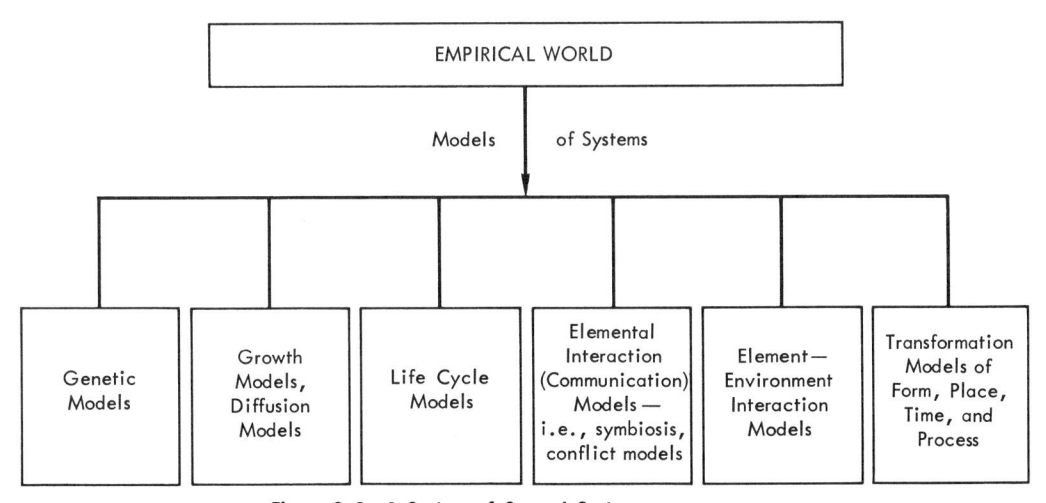

Figure 8–2 A System of General Systems

births of new products in the total economy. Similarly, models of growth and total life-cycle models can be observed in almost all disciplines. The remaining models fulfill all requirements for interaction systems.

INFORMATION FEEDBACK SYSTEMS

An integral part of general systems theory is the notion of automatic feedback control. This is particularly important for the study and design of management information systems because the theory and the practice of cybernation (feedback control) underlie all design and application of computers as well as of information systems that utilize them.

The need for feedback control through information is sometimes illustrated by the example of the automobile driver. We accept as a simple, everyday occurrence the complex system of driver, steering wheel, automobile, street, eye, and steering hand. Yet consider the effects of making very slight changes in the system structure by substituting elements and adding time delays. Let the driver be blindfolded and receive his information input from a front-seat companion. It is unlikely that the system output would be acceptable, given the time delay in information transmission plus the distortion caused by an additional input medium provided by the other person.

Consider the much worse situation in which the driver's information input comes from a companion in the back seat facing the rear, who could see only where the vehicle had been and not where it was going. Yet this kind of situation exists in business all the time. Managers do not have a clear view of the road ahead and must depend upon information gathered from a variety of sources with built-in time delays. Their historical accounting information system usually provides them with information on where they have been, not on the course for the future. Information feedback systems, properly designed, offer a tremendous breakthrough in techniques and in the general approach to decision making that will assist the manager in charting a course for the future.

Systems theory and the notion of information feedback are fundamental to the decision-making process and to the design of supporting information systems. Indeed, an MIS can be defined as a *communication process in which information (input) is recorded, stored and retrieved (processed) for decisions (output) on planning, operating, and controlling.* The concept implied by this definition is shown schematically in Figure 8–3.

The attribute of *information feedback* is essential to an understanding of the self-regulating nature of systems in general and of how this attribute can be applied in a management information system to aid in decision making. The tendency toward self-regulation through information feedback is demonstrated by Table 8–2, which summarizes some characteristics of

```
   ┌─────────┐    ┌──────────┐    ┌─────────┐
   │  INPUT  │    │ PROCESSOR│    │ OUTPUT  │         To
   │         │    │ Recorded │    │         │      Planning,
   │         │    │  Stored  │    │         │      Operating,
──▶│Information│─▶│ Retrieved│─▶ │Decisions│────▶ Controlling
   │         │    │ Processed│    │         │       Systems
   │         │    │   etc.   │    │         │
   └─────────┘    └──────────┘    └─────────┘
        ▲              FEEDBACK        │
        └──────── on Effectiveness ────┘
                    of Decisions
```

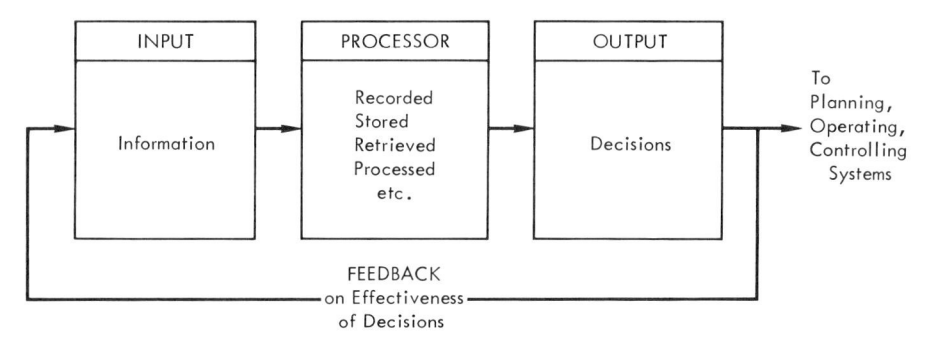

Figure 8–3 Information and Decisions—A System

the major categories of systems. Note that despite the origin or nature of the system and its complexity, all categories have the characteristic of reacting to information feedback, whether internal or external. This characteristic is of the utmost importance in understanding the nature and design of a management information system and appreciating how it serves the processes of communication and decision making within an organization.

The Elements and Operation of a System

We have now formed a workable definition and concept of a system. The remainder of this chapter will advance this concept by examining the elements of a system and how they relate to its operation.

Input, Processor, Output

Regardless of the complexity of a system, the basic elements are functionally and operationally the same. Table 8–3 illustrates some typical systems with the elements of input, processor, and output. An understanding of these elements and their relationships is essential for proper systems design.

Input is the start-up component on which the system operates. Table 8–3 illustrates the variety of inputs to systems. Note that in almost all cases, the input to a system is the output from some other system. The input to an MIS is, of course, data or information. *Output*, the result of an operation and the purpose or objective for which the system was designed, is also demonstrated in Table 8–3. (Note, however, that no standard of performance or yardstick has been placed upon these outputs. Performance standard is integral to another system component to be discussed, the control.) The *processor* is the activity that makes possible the transformation of input into output. Men, machines, functions, operations, organizations, and combinations of these may act as processors and may be analyzed as such in systems design.

Table 8-2

Categories of Systems Classifications

Category	Type	Characteristic	Example
COMPLEXITY[a]	Deterministic	Parts interact predictably	
	Simple	Simple but dynamic	Office layout
	Complex	Complex but describable	Computer hardware
	Exceedingly complex	Complex and indescribable	None
	Probabilistic	No prediction can be made	
	Simple	Simple but dynamic	Quality control
	Complex	Complex but describable	Financial plan
	Exceedingly complex	Complex and indescribable	The company
MAN/MACHINE[b]	Machine-like	Automatic performance	Automatic manufacturing operation
		Information tightness	
		Predictable	
		No human interface	
	Man-dominated	Variable: disturbances	Management information system
		Statistically unstable	
		Nonautomatic	
		Nonautomatically improving	
	Man–machine	Man–machine characteristics	Aircraft and pilot
		Complex, costly, demanding	
		Information feedback for self-improvement	
NATURAL/MAN-MADE	Natural	Complex, static, predictable	Biological system
	Man-made	Complex, dynamic, unpredictable	Economic system
ADAPTIVE/NONADAPTIVE	Adaptive	Reacts to environment	The company
	Nonadaptive	Not affected by environment	Pressurized aircraft
OPEN/CLOSED	Open	Exchanges information with environment	Thermostat
	Closed	Not affected by environment	Traffic light
OPEN LOOP/CLOSED LOOP	Open loop	Does not feed back information for system change	Business firm without MIS
	Closed loop	Automatically feeds back information for system equilibrium	Business firm with MIS

SYSTEM OF SYSTEMS[c] BY LEVEL

Level of frameworks	The static structure—the anatomy of a system	The universe
Level of clockworks	Simple dynamic system with predetermined, necessary motions	Solar system
Level of the thermostat	The cybernetic system moves to maintain an equilibrium through a process of self-regulation	Thermostat
Self-maintaining systems	The open system—moves to and includes living organisms	A cell
Genetic-societal level	Level of cell society, characterized by a division of labor among cells	The plant
Animal systems	Self-awareness and goal-directed behavior. Stimulus response feedback	The brain
Human systems	Level of symbol interpretation and idea communication	Human being
Social systems	Level of human organization—value systems, human emotions, communications, as these affect a system of humans	A nation
Transcendental systems	The ultimates and absolutes and the inescapables and unknowables that exhibit structure and relationships	??

[a] Adapted from Stafford Beer, *Cybernetics and Management* (New York: John Wiley & Sons, Inc., 1959), pp. 12–19.
[b] Described in Stanford L. Optner, *Systems Analysis for Business Management*, 2nd ed. (Englewood Cliffs, N.J.: Prentice-Hall, Inc., 1968), pp. 3–11.
[c] Described in the landmark article by Kenneth E. Boulding, "General Systems Theory—The Skeleton of Science," *Management Science*, April 1956, pp. 197–208.

Table 8–3

Illustrations of Systems Elements

SYSTEM	INPUT	PROCESSOR	OUTPUT
DATA PROCESSING	Raw data	Classify, sort, summarize, calculate	Arranged data
MANUFACTURING	Materials, labor, etc.	Operations	Product
AIR CONDITIONING	Electricity	Motor, compressor, etc.	Cooled air
WEAPON SYSTEM	Instructions	Missile, ground support, equipment, personnel, etc.	Target destruction
COMPUTER-BASED MANAGEMENT INFORMATION SYSTEM	Information	Computer, people, etc.	Decisions
UNIVERSITY	Students	University	Changed students

Input, processor, and output are common to *all* systems and are the terms by which all systems are described. Any system may be defined in terms of these elements and their properties. Moreover, they are set in place in fixed positions, which is important for the systems analyst or designer because he can work forward or backward in identifying the elements and in solving system problems. For example, he may define the output in some specific value or format (e.g., cost of direct labor hours per product per week) and then proceed to deal with the processor (production control system) and input (shop labor control) in order to achieve the desired output. Although many design problems may be examined from left to right (considering input first), we shall see in a later chapter on systems design that a manager should, in general, consider outputs of the system before the other elements.

The Processor as a Black Box

It would be inadvisable to underrate the complexity of the processor. Illustrations in this chapter are very general and at a high level of coarseness; we should not conclude from this that operations within the processor or "black box" are as simple as depicted. Indeed, the "black box" concept of the system processor reflects a fundamental characteristic of information feedback systems, extreme complexity.[3]

This complexity can be illustrated in a simple way by taking the data processing system of Table 8–3. The "black box" or processor of this system describes the four operations: classify, sort, summarize, and calculate. Figure

systems theory and management information systems   297

MAJOR SYSTEM

```
┌─────────────────┐     ┌──────────────────┐     ┌─────────────────┐
│     INPUT       │     │    PROCESSOR     │     │     OUTPUT      │
│                 │ ──► │ Classify, Sort,  │ ──► │                 │
│ Data To Be      │     │ Summarize,       │     │ Arranged Data   │
│ Arranged        │     │ Calculate        │     │                 │
└─────────────────┘     └──────────────────┘     └─────────────────┘
```

Subsystems

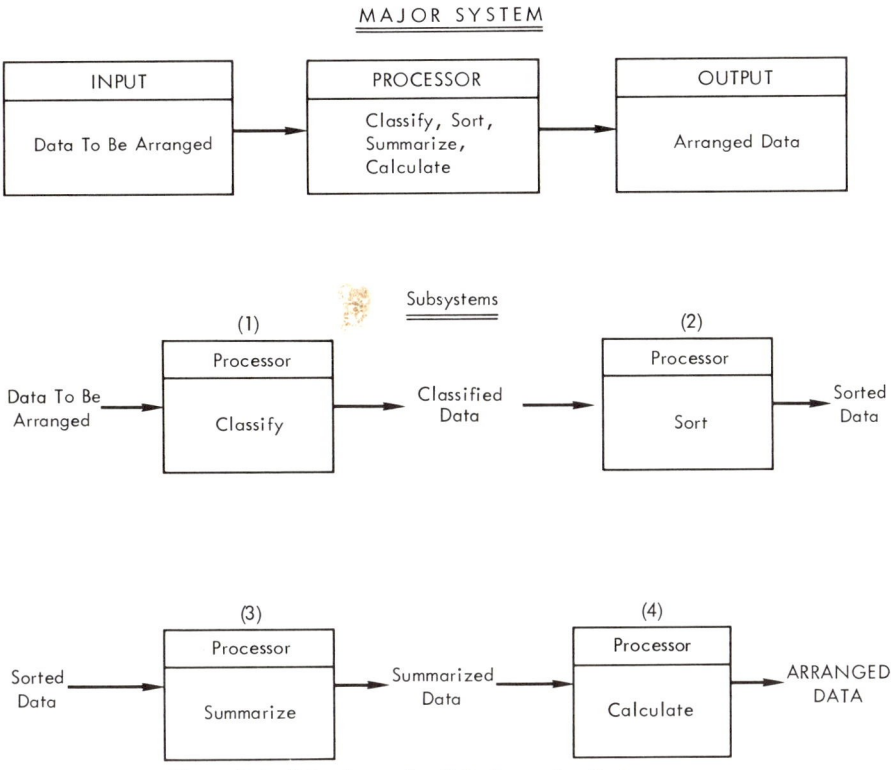

```
                  (1) Processor                    (2) Processor
Data To Be    ──► ┌──────────┐ ─ Classified ─ ──► ┌──────────┐ ─ Sorted
Arranged          │ Classify │   Data               │   Sort   │   Data
                  └──────────┘                      └──────────┘

                  (3) Processor                    (4) Processor
Sorted        ──► ┌──────────┐ ─ Summarized ─ ──► ┌──────────┐ ─ ARRANGED
Data              │ Summarize│   Data               │ Calculate│   DATA
                  └──────────┘                      └──────────┘
```

Figure 8–4   Subsystems of a Data Processing System

8–4 illustrates how, if we wish to think of the details of our system, it might be redesigned and shown as four separate subsystems. So it is with most system processors that at first glance appear to be simpler than they are in reality.*

Another reason for complexity in the processor is the difficulty of defining the constraints or boundaries. Where, for example, does the manpower management system start and stop? Does it include the subsystems of training, recruiting, placement, safety, discipline, payroll, labor relations, and scheduling? No doubt top management's view of the system differs from that of a personnel department supervisor, whose definition of the system

---

*Consider the shop floor as a processor or "black box," with inputs of material and outputs of product. The shop houses ten processes and it is possible to schedule incoming material to these processes in any order and to sell the product at any stage. This planning problem has about ten million alternatives, and if we assume one minute per alternative, it will take us about nineteen years working day and night to find the best plan. Yet, with the tools of the computer and linear programming, the best solution can be determined in less than one minute.

may include only personnel records. Neither of these views is incorrect; they merely indicate the alternative ways of defining the processor. One of the first tasks of the system designer is to define the boundaries of the system. This places limits on the subsystems to be studied and has the advantages of (1) emphasizing the need for integrating subsystems, (2) concentrating effort in the most profitable areas, and (3) reducing the problem to manageable size.

Control and Feedback

We have previously explained that a system can be defined in terms of the elements and properties of input, processor, and output, and in a strict sense this is so. However, systems are dynamic and changes inevitably occur. Moreover, in a dynamic system it is necessary to review, periodically or continuously, the state of the output in order to make necessary alterations because of changes in the environment or for other reasons. In the system of the business organization we need to determine whether the product output is profitable and acceptable to the customer; otherwise the system will ultimately come to a standstill. In the air-conditioning system it is necessary to determine whether the output of cooled air oscillates within the range that we, the users, have determined; if it does not, this system will stop operating. The system elements that permit the system to remain in equilibrium are *control* and *feedback*.

A management information system is in all respects an information feedback system that can be defined as a *system measuring changes in output that leads to a decision resulting in action that affects the output.* Information feedback control is a fundamental characteristic of all systems and is essential to the design of a management information system. To illustrate:

1. A thermostat receives information on the temperature and starts the air-conditioning system; this lowers the temperature and the system stops.
2. The output of the direct-labor control system is standard labor hours. The information system measures performance and reports deficiencies; this activates a training system that brings performance up to standard.
3. The sales manager receives information that sales are down because competitive prices are lower; he lowers the price of his firm's product, which raises the sales level to normal.

We speak of control and feedback together because they occur together; by definition, the purpose of feedback is control. *Control is defined as the system function that compares output to a predetermined standard. Feedback is the function that provides information on the deviation between output and control standard and delivers this information as input into the*

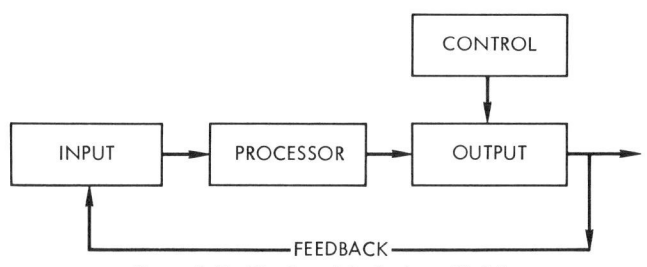

Figure 8-5 The Complete Systems Module

process from which the output was derived. The place of feedback and control may be illustrated as in Figure 8-5.*

The nature of these two all-important components becomes clear if we recall the steps in the control process: (1) setting standards of performance, (2) measuring performance against the standard, (3) correcting deviations. Because we are considering an information control system, the control element is concerned with comparing output against a predetermined standard. This standard is fundamental to the systems of *management, information,* and *control.* The concept is illustrated in Figure 8-6 for the generalized business system. The *feedback* element is the arrangement for collecting information on the comparison of output to control standard and for delivering this information (measuring performance) as input to the system so that deviations from expected output can be corrected through the management process.

THE BUSINESS ORGANIZATION AS A SYSTEM

It is important to understand how the elements of an organization function as a system because, like any other system, the organization operates through the medium of information. It is also necessary to understand that because the functions of management are served by an information system, these functions should be considered in the design process. These concepts can be better understood by relating them to the organization as a system, as is done in Figure 8-7.

---

*In all systems we are striving to achieve a state of self-regulation. The state of self-regulation through automatic feedback is demonstrated by the classic case of the Watt governor of almost 200 years ago. The engine has a valve that controls its power and hence its speed. The *control* (desired speed) is set on this valve. As the engine turns at increasing speed, with it turn weighted arms, also at an increasing speed. The arms are mounted on pivots so that they are free to rise by centrifugal force as they revolve. The arms operate a valve that admits fuel to the engine so that the valve is closed in proportion as the arms rise and the speed grows. Hence we have a self-regulating automatic feedback control system. The more the machine tends to exceed a given speed (output), the less it is supplied with the energy to do so. Conversely, if it fails to reach the desired speed (the output as set on the control), the governor will regulate the power upward until it does. The input to the machine is adjusted by the output itself, and both settle down to a state of equilibrium.

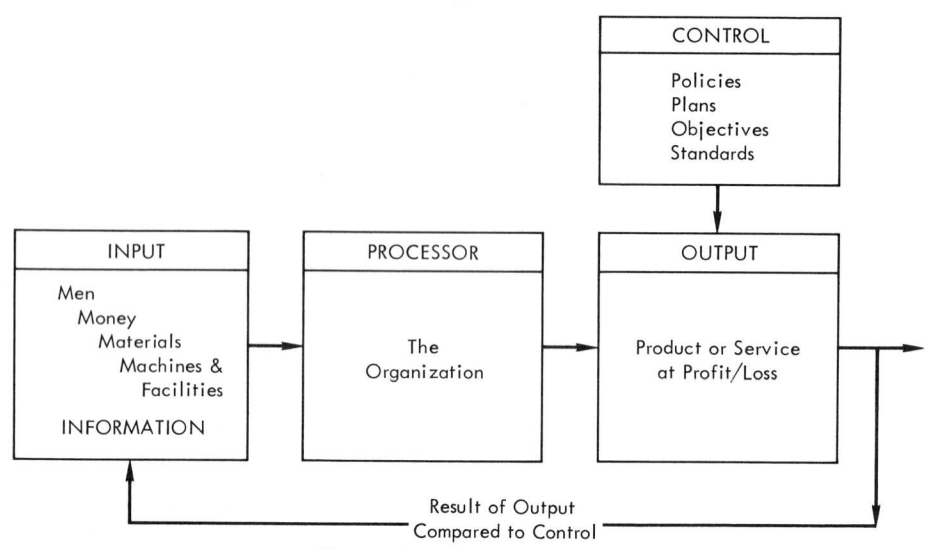

```
                                    ┌─────────────────┐
                                    │     CONTROL     │
                                    ├─────────────────┤
                                    │  Policies       │
                                    │  Plans          │
                                    │  Objectives     │
                                    │  Standards      │
                                    └────────┬────────┘
                                             │
                                             ▼
┌─────────────────┐   ┌─────────────────┐   ┌─────────────────┐
│      INPUT      │   │    PROCESSOR    │   │     OUTPUT      │
├─────────────────┤   ├─────────────────┤   ├─────────────────┤
│      Men        │   │                 │   │                 │
│     Money       │──▶│      The        │──▶│ Product or Service │──▶
│   Materials     │   │  Organization   │   │  at Profit/Loss │
│   Machines &    │   │                 │   │                 │
│   Facilities    │   │                 │   │                 │
│  INFORMATION    │   │                 │   │                 │
└────────▲────────┘   └─────────────────┘   └────────┬────────┘
         │                                           │
         │              Result of Output             │
         └──────────── Compared to Control ──────────┘
```

Figure 8–6 The General Business System

The organization must be viewed as a system. Because the outputs of the system establish the purpose for which the system exists, we examine the outputs of the business organization, and we find that the output is the objective for which the company exists. These objectives are multiple, but for the manufacturing firm they must necessarily include the manufacture and sale of a product at a profit. Later we will examine the subsystems and outputs of the subsystems that contribute to this objective. Note that, as in the management process, if no objective is established the organization has no stated reason for existing, and therefore no system can be described or designed.

Inputs to the organization include the four classic items of men, money, materials, and machinery, plus the vital fifth input of information. Again, as we begin to analyze the subsystems of the organization, the inputs will break down into subclassifications (e.g., direct labor, indirect labor, and so on).

What controls operate on the output of the organization? There are considerations outside the firm, such as custom, competitive environment, and government regulation, that imply *external control*. These must be considered limitations on the operation of the system, and information measures must be designed to measure output against them. However, for most purposes the *internal controls* are more important, certainly more frequent in systems design. Each subsystem has one or more measures of control and, as in the *central process,* these consist of *standards of performance* or some other measure of whether the output is within the limits previously established in the control process. Listed here are four examples of subsystem outputs and *control measures* (standards of performance) that operate on them:

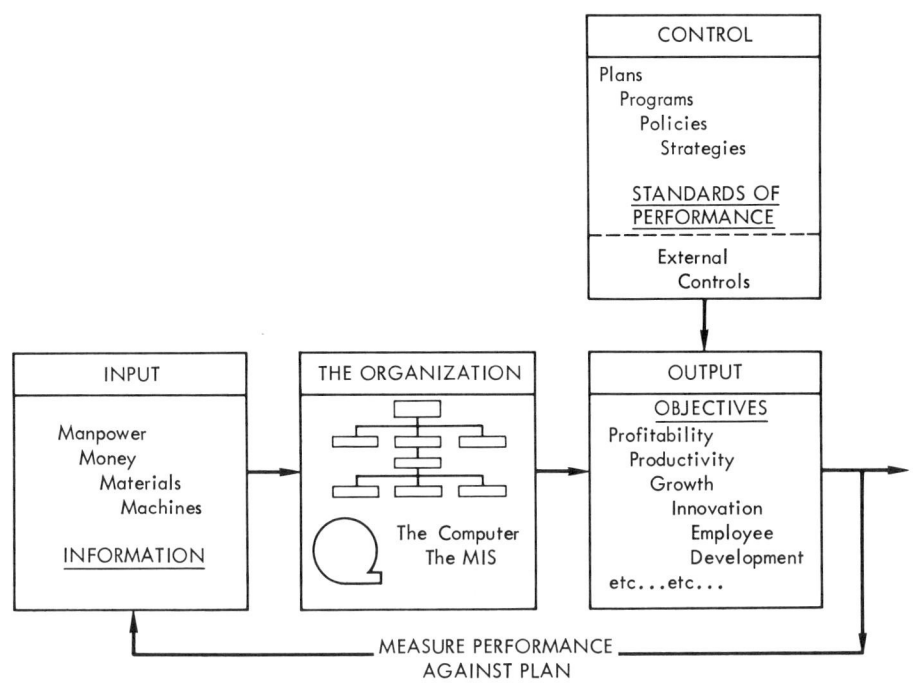

```
                                    CONTROL
                                    Plans
                                      Programs
                                        Policies
                                          Strategies

                                    STANDARDS OF
                                    PERFORMANCE
                                    ─────────────
                                    External
                                    Controls
                                         │
                                         ▼
   INPUT          THE ORGANIZATION        OUTPUT
                                         OBJECTIVES
   Manpower                              Profitability
   Money                                 Productivity
   Materials                             Growth
   Machines                              Innovation
                   The Computer          Employee
   INFORMATION     The MIS               Development
                                         etc...etc...

         ▲────────── MEASURE PERFORMANCE ──────────
                    AGAINST PLAN
```

Figure 8–7 The Organization as a System

Subsystem	Output	Control
Sales	Sales orders	Quota
Industrial relations	Employee morale	Turnover
Quality control	Quality product	Rejections
Accounts receivable	Collections	Bad debts

The final element of *feedback* is essential for system operation and for self-regulation or correction of deviations. If sales quotas are not met, if labor turnover is high, if bad debts exceed expectations, this information must be fed back into the system as input so that corrections can be made.* In the ultimate (and perhaps theoretical) management information system, the feedback provides information for system self-correction.

One of the best ways to conceptualize the total business organization as a system is to view its major components as parts of an overall financial plan. Figure 8–8 illustrates the major subsystems of such a plan for a manufacturing company. The total output of the organization is measured in terms of return on investment or a similar financial standard. The total objective can be, and is, broken down into major subsystems, some of which are demonstrated in Table 8–4. Notice that these subsystems can be, and are, controlled by information systems that utilize the outputs and controls listed in Table 8–4.

---
*See Chapter 4 for a discussion of what action the manager takes if output is not within the limits set by the control process.

Table 8–4
Outputs and Controls of Selected Subsystems of the Financial Plan

System and Subsystems	Output	Control
FINANCIAL PLAN	PROFITABLE OPERATIONS	RETURN ON INVESTMENT/ PROFIT ON SALES/ PROFITABILITY OBJECTIVE
Purchasing	Raw materials cost within control limits	Standard purchase price
Raw materials inventory	Meet production schedule	Optimize inventory costs
Cash budget	Cash to meet operations	Cost of capital
Programs	Program completion	Time and cost limitations
Distribution expense	Sell and deliver product	Cost objectives and limits
Direct labor	Manufactured product	Direct labor hours
Promotion	Promote qualified persons	Promotion policy
Training	Meet skill demands	Time, cost, quantity standards
etc. . . .	etc. . . .	etc. . . .

SUMMARY

The purpose of this chapter is to define more precisely, intensionally, extensionally, and contextually the meaning of "system." In so doing, we have developed various systems classifications, system terms, and system characteristics fundamental to the modeling, design, operation, and evaluation of systems.

We have also enlarged the focus of our view of systems to include the idea of a science of general systems. General systems theory offers the hope that knowledge about diverse systems may be unified and system design made more objective.

The notion of automatic control through information feedback is essential to understanding systems theory and to applying it to management. Control measures changes in output, which in turn leads to decisions resulting in actions that affect the output. This idea is basic to the structure and design of the organization as a system and to the utilization of information as the central catalyst for integrating the many subsystems of the organization.

The components of any system include input, processor, output, control, and feedback. All systems can be explained in these terms, and the interaction between subsystems can be examined as an operation of these components. The management information system (MIS) is the common system that permits the other four resource systems to function as a whole.

```
                    ┌─────────────────────────────────────┐
                    │        A PLAN OF OPERATIONS         │
                    │ Management's Goals and Objectives   │
                    │            for the Year             │
                    └─────────────────────────────────────┘
                                formalized in
                                      │
                         ┌────────────────────────┐
                         │ THE ANNUAL PROFIT PLAN │
                         └────────────────────────┘
                           wherein management specifies
                                      │
                       ┌──────────────────────────────┐
                       │ THE OVERALL INCOME OBJECTIVE │
                       └──────────────────────────────┘
                                detailed in
```

| Sales Budget (in Quantities and Dollars by District, Product, and Time Period) | | Other Income Budget
Interest Income
Royalty Income
Others |

                                     less
                   ┌───────────────────────────────────────┐
                   │ THE OVERALL COST AND EXPENSE OBJECTIVE │
                   └───────────────────────────────────────┘
                                detailed in

| Production Budget (Units to Be Produced) | Distribution Expense Budget by District and Time Period | Administrative Expense Budget by Department and Time Period | Other Expense Budget
Interest Expense
Others |

                          involves

| Purchases Budget Cost of Materials Used |

| Direct Labor Budget |

| Factory Overhead Budget |

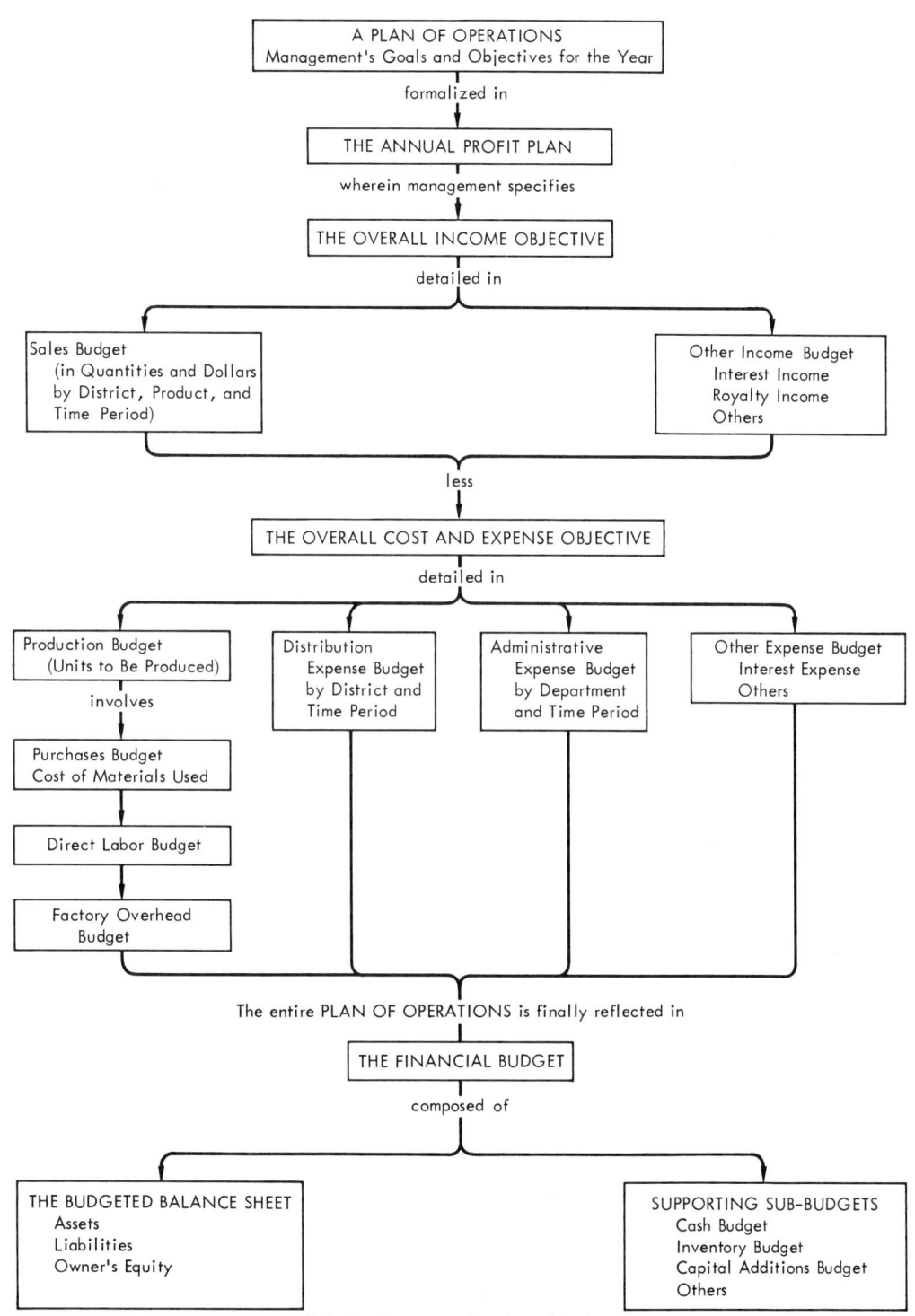

The entire PLAN OF OPERATIONS is finally reflected in

                        ┌──────────────────────┐
                        │ THE FINANCIAL BUDGET │
                        └──────────────────────┘
                                composed of

| THE BUDGETED BALANCE SHEET
Assets
Liabilities
Owner's Equity | SUPPORTING SUB-BUDGETS
Cash Budget
Inventory Budget
Capital Additions Budget
Others |

Figure 8–8 Development of a Financial Plan

SOURCE Glenn A. Welsch, *Budgeting: Profit Planning and Control,* 3rd ed., © 1971. By permission of Prentice-Hall, Inc.

DISCUSSION QUESTIONS AND PROBLEMS

1. What relationship can you identify between the ecological system of the earth and many business firms? Explain by means of an example.

2. Describe a system that is very small in size but very complex in its functioning.

3. Review and criticize the definition of a system given in this chapter, and attempt to develop a better one.

4. Relate a marketing system of business to the definition of a system given in this chapter. (Use the three illustrations in the text as guides.)

5. If you wished to study the function of business as an institution in society using the systems approach, would you proceed "inside out" (business, industry, economy, society) or "outside in" (society, economy, industry, business)?

6. Consider a young lady who is charged with managing a room in which duplicating services of several kinds are supplied. People from various offices throughout the plant go to a counter opening out from the room and place orders. Define all elements of the basic system of which the young lady is a part. Next, list all systems that link with her basic system (consider equipment, materials, costing, etc.).

7. A firm has available about a dozen concepts for proposed new products. It must evaluate, select, develop, and launch the products selected. This new-product planning cuts across all functions of the organization. Show how each characteristic of the systems approach, as discussed in the text, is applicable to the new-product project.

8. We identify two types of business systems: operational and informational. Show by discussion which classifications each of these falls into (conceptual versus empirical, natural versus man-made, etc.) according to the classification explanations given in the text.

9. If you grant that every system is a part of a greater system, discuss the meaning and the advantages and disadvantages of "decoupling" a system.

10. The components of an organizational system may be identified in many ways. What do *you* identify as such components?

11. Consider a one-man real estate office in terms of the discussion on page 264, SOME SYSTEM CONCEPTS. Relate each concept to this one-man business and identify or define all attributes and characteristics listed as applicable to this specific business.

12. In general systems theory we often come across hierarchies of system functions, hierarchies of physical material (from atomic particles to galaxies), biological hierarchies, and so on. Develop a hierarchical system of information starting from the smallest unit and proceeding to the largest.

13. A problem in logic arises when subsets are not "proper subsets." Does this have any significance for systems of systems or general systems theory?

14. A certain company paid its president $250,000 and its vice-president $100,000 and gave them a total of $100,000 in expenses and "considerations." Some stockholders gained control of the company, fired both these executives, and substituted a decision-making computer. The rest of the organization remained unchanged, so that managers of manufacturing, engineering, marketing, finance, and personnel reported to the computer. When a conflict arose between two managers, each presented his prediction of an outcome if his course of action were followed. At first the computer made a decision at random; then, as actual outcomes were supplied to it, the computer "learned" the relative value of each manager's judgment and the probability of a successful manager's obtaining a favorable decision if a conflict situation arose or increased.

Compare the characteristics, attributes, and effectiveness of these two systems. (Consider that some distinguished managers and presidents have stated that they are fortunate if they make correct decisions 50 percent of the time.)

15. A gasoline company is developing a new layout for its gasoline stations. Apply the systems approach to the location, design, and facilities of one as opposed to two restrooms (as determined by the systems approach). Proceed by starting with the objectives. Be sure to identify components, variables, parameters, structure, process, boundaries, and trade-offs involved.

REFERENCES

1. Stanford L. Optner, *Systems Analysis for Business and Industrial Problem Solving* (Englewood Cliffs, N.J.: Prentice-Hall, Inc., 1965).
2. Kenneth E. Boulding, "General Systems Theory—The Skeleton of Science," *Management Science,* April 1956.
3. See Stafford Beer, *Cybernetics and Management* (New York: John Wiley & Sons, Inc., 1964), pp. 52–53. Beer argues that the "black box" concept of the processor is of paramount importance to feedback control systems. Many boxes are *absolutely* black (e.g., the economy or the industrial firm), and most others are so black as to be indescribable. Therefore, the methods we should use to handle exceedingly complex systems are those of input manipulation and output classification, not those of cause-and-effect analysis.

CASE STUDY

AMERICAN SCIENTIFIC PRODUCTS COMPANY, INC. (B)

In the fall of 1970, the American Scientific Products Company engaged a consulting firm in the Boston area to design and install computer-based systems for control of raw materials inventory, accounts receivable, and payroll. About a month after the project was begun, it became evident to the consulting firm that operations in other areas could be improved by the utilization of management information systems. Dr. Robert Dobrynski, president of the company, authorized a preliminary study for the conceptual design of a company-wide MIS. He admonished the consultant, "Now, be careful with my vice-presidents and department heads. When we talk about information for decision making, it leads us to responsibilities and the identification of important decision makers. Some of these people might be offended." Some of the areas investigated by the consultant are briefly described below. Major elements and subsystems are shown in Figure 1.

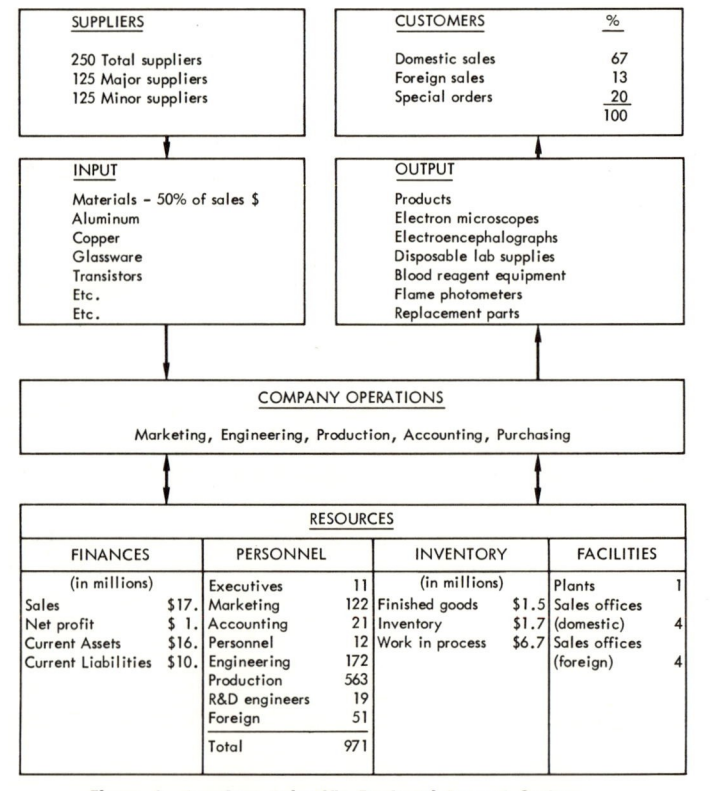

SUPPLIERS		CUSTOMERS	%
250 Total suppliers		Domestic sales	67
125 Major suppliers		Foreign sales	13
125 Minor suppliers		Special orders	20
			100

INPUT	OUTPUT
Materials – 50% of sales $	Products
Aluminum	Electron microscopes
Copper	Electroencephalographs
Glassware	Disposable lab supplies
Transistors	Blood reagent equipment
Etc.	Flame photometers
Etc.	Replacement parts

COMPANY OPERATIONS
Marketing, Engineering, Production, Accounting, Purchasing

RESOURCES

FINANCES		PERSONNEL		INVENTORY		FACILITIES	
(in millions)		Executives	11	(in millions)		Plants	1
Sales	$17.	Marketing	122	Finished goods	$1.5	Sales offices	
Net profit	$ 1.	Accounting	21	Inventory	$1.7	(domestic)	4
Current Assets	$16.	Personnel	12	Work in process	$6.7	Sales offices	
Current Liabilities	$10.	Engineering	172			(foreign)	4
		Production	563				
		R&D engineers	19				
		Foreign	51				
		Total	971				

Figure 1 American Scientific Products' Present System

Marketing and Distribution

Since its founding, the company had maintained a policy of building superior products. Stringent quality controls were maintained, and this aspect was widely advertised in trade and professional journals. Although a substantial advertising budget (3 percent of sales) was utilized, the effectiveness of this advertising was open to question.

The company's standard line of products was being marketed through its worldwide sales force of 173 salesmen, all of them salaried. Sales of replacement parts, a growing source of revenue, were normally handled by a telephone call or on a mail-out basis as the customer needed the part. This portion of total sales was beginning to increase as the age and number of units in use increased. The company generally viewed this source of sales as a convenience to customers rather than as a primary profit item.

Another growing segment of sales was that of custom-designed units, manufactured to meet the particular needs and specifications of research institutions and other customers needing one-of-a-kind products. A.S.P. had not generally been able to ascertain production costs on items of this nature and as a result did not devote active sales effort to their marketing. Distribution of such units was handled by the sales engineer from the production plant at Stoughton or the distribution center at Boston.

It was believed by some A.S.P. managers that custom-designed units could represent a significant portion of total revenue, but the absence of accurate production cost information made this a difficult fact to prove.

Production

Except for custom-designed units, almost all the company's products were manufactured for inventory. The procedure of manufacturing for inventory was the subject of constant debate between marketing and manufacturing personnel. Because of the high cost of the items and the inability to forecast sales accurately, the manufacturing group hesitated to produce for a finished-goods inventory that might never sell; but the sales force wanted the full line of products on hand for immediate delivery to customers.

Inventory was categorized as follows:

1. Shop stores—Parts that had been purchased for production of standard products
2. Work-in-process inventory—Material and labor already expended against preplanned and project stock
3. Finished-goods inventory—Completed standard products ready for sale or in fulfillment of customer orders

NOTE: General and administrative expenses were recorded and applied to inventory production costs.

Costs of producing standard products were recorded on a material-cost card and a payroll report. Each of these forms was prepared daily, i.e., materials drawn from stock and the transaction were recorded by the stock clerk on a material-cost card. Labor hours were recorded on the payroll report by the accounting department as the time cards were collected each day.

When a particular unit or lot of units was completed, the total costs were computed and then compared with historical cost data that had been collected in the past for the production of the same units.

Production problems and production cost data problems arose when custom-designed units entered into the production process. The manufacture of custom-designed units, specially produced rather than produced for inventory, caused production and assembly difficulties because their utilization of engineering, supervisory, and production personnel talents interrupted the producing-for-inventory process. Not only did these custom-designed and -manufactured products require the services of various personnel normally involved in the standard production process, but they also caused an interruption of the use of production-line equipment, machinery, and materials. Quite often the costs of producing the custom units were in part unrecorded or charged against products manufactured for inventory. Basically, cost data was to be recorded in the same manner as standard inventory products, but due to the uncertainty and inaccuracy of machine time, personnel hours, and material allocation, it was difficult to determine the accuracy of the production costs of special or custom units under the current system.

Materials and Supplies

Material purchases accounted for approximately 50 percent of A.S.P.'s sales dollar. A.S.P. currently controlled the input of materials and supplies by a procedure based on estimated annual parts costs. There was a normal six-week time lag for material purchased. The company had about 250 suppliers, half of which could be considered major suppliers. In accordance with sound purchasing practices, A.S.P. aspired to have multiple supply sources, but because of the exotic nature of some of the materials, this was not always possible.

The purchasing function generally worked in this way: a requisition for materials or supplies was sent to the purchasing agent, who originated the purchase order or purchase authorization. A number of different purchasing agents handled different classes of supplies and materials. Almost all items handled through inventory control (Incoming Materials Department) had an A.S.P. job number, or a standard part number if the device was a production line piece of equipment. When part numbers were not assigned or were missing, as was often the case, it was difficult to determine to which project the item belonged. (This was especially true or common on custom-designed units.)

Financial

Profit planning existed in the company, but it was a major source of frustration for Dr. Dobrynski. Sales forecasts were made annually and updated monthly. Generally, these forecasts were met. However, it was in the area of cost control that need for improvement was most evident. When costs exceeded plan, as they often did, it was practically impossible to trace the variance to specific products or departments.

III

Information, Decision Making, and Management Science

The necessary ingredient for management decision making and action is information. It is not data, masses of microscopic bits delivered in macroscopic batches, that underlie effectiveness in problem solving and decision making.

Better decisions can be made when the quality, frequency, reliability, and format of information are available to the manager at his moment of need.

A careful study of the nature of data, the storage, processing, and retrieval of data, the characteristics of information and communication, and the solving of decision problems is essential to the understanding of management information systems. The symbiotic roles of management science and computers in relieving managers from making many decisions (or improving on managerial decisions) has led to the debated question, "Can machines think?" Regardless of the conclusion, sophisticated, computerized management-science models are increasingly becoming a part of management information systems.

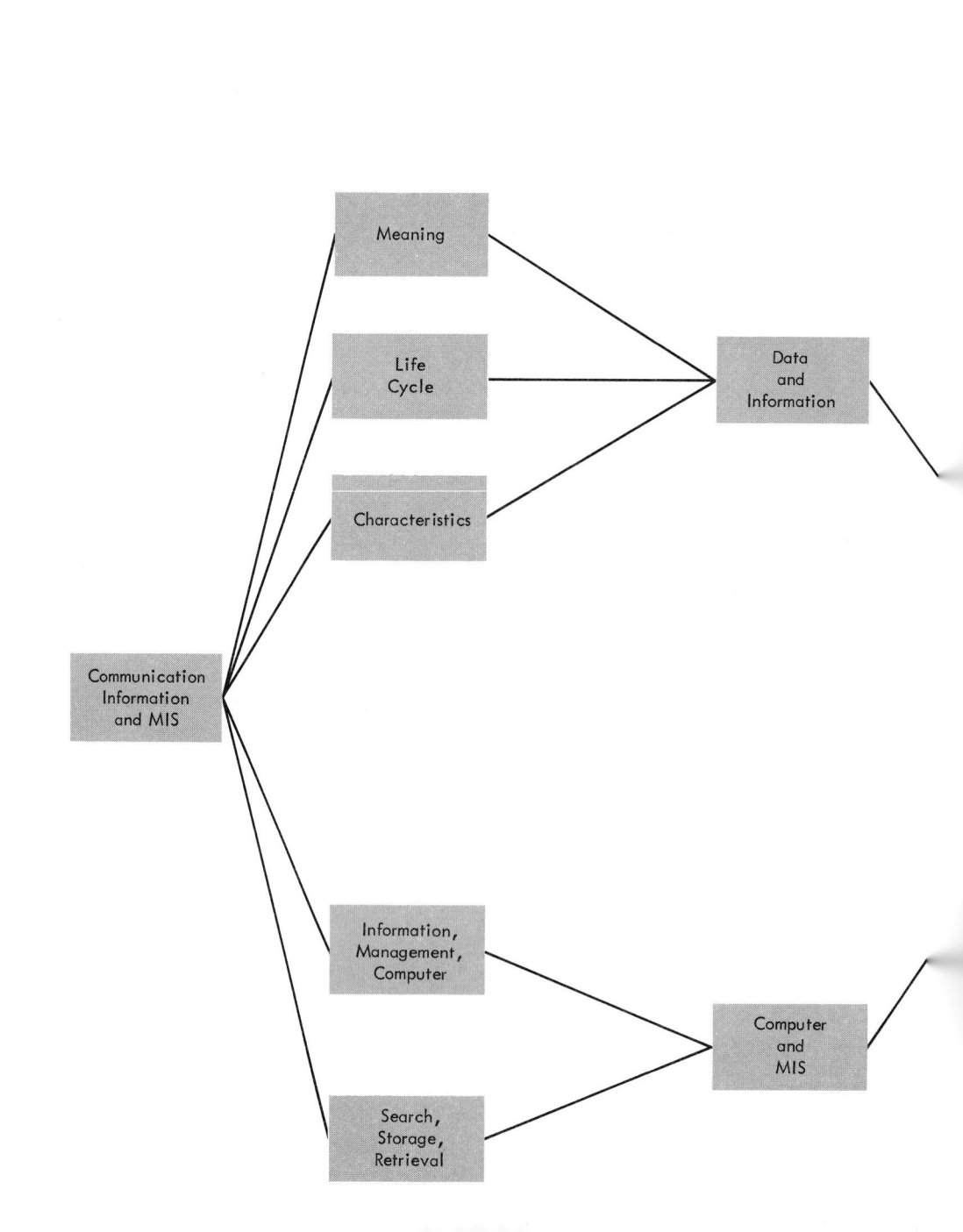

```
                          Meaning

                          Life
                          Cycle         ─────►  Data
                                                and
                                                Information
                          Characteristics

Communication
Information
and MIS

                          Information,
                          Management,
                          Computer
                                        ─────►  Computer
                                                and
                          Search,               MIS
                          Storage,
                          Retrieval
```

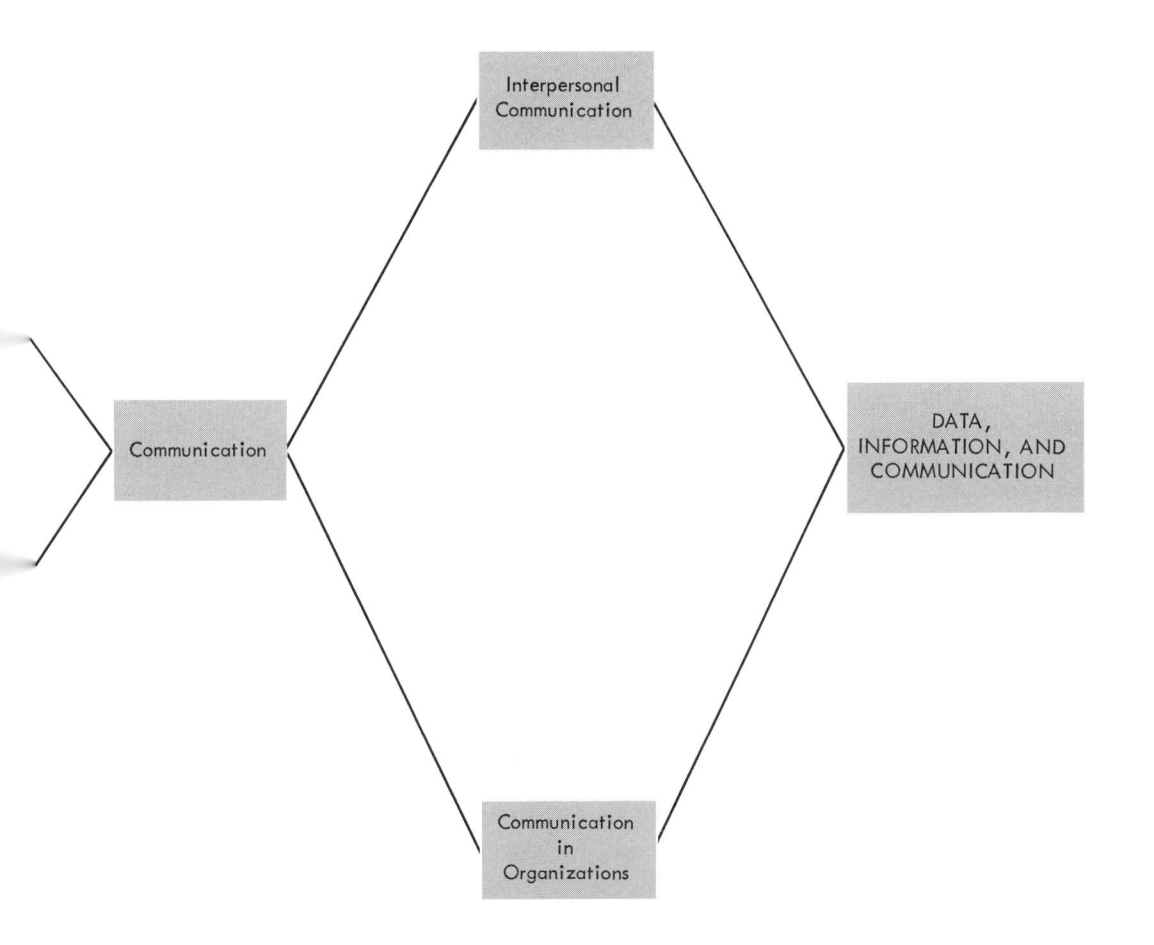

9
data, information, and communication

Interpersonal Communication

Communication

DATA, INFORMATION, AND COMMUNICATION

Communication in Organizations

9

Organized and goal-directed activity by two or more people or devices would not be possible without communication. Our definition of a "system" requires a set of elements that "interact" or are related by communication among them. So we may say that communication is the enabling process of a system, and especially of MIS. Although communciation may take several different forms—depending upon whether we are studying systems of people, man–machine systems, or machine systems—it is essential to all of them.

Therefore, in order to design effective systems, we need to know the nature of the role of communications, the structure and characteristics of the systems when viewed as communication systems, the nature of information and data, and the operations performed on information and data.

In management information systems, in particular, the focus is on the information aspects. It is important to study the economics of information in terms of management's needs and goals. Problems of getting the right information in the right form to the right man at the right time need to be identified before MIS can be developed. Without information communicated from sources outside himself, the individual manager would find meaningful planning, direction, and control impossible.

MEANING OF INFORMATION AND DATA

In organizational (human) systems, the elements are the individual people in the system. If these individuals are to act in concerted fashion, they must communicate, or transmit and receive signs. A sign is a preparatory stimulus that predisposes a person to act in a certain way based on his past experience. There are two kinds of signs, according to Charles Morris.[1] One is a signal that originates from an experience-act. Thus, observation of an overflowing warehouse is a signal to a manager that there is an oversupply of finished goods. The other is a symbol that the individual produces as a synonymous substitute for another sign. A symbol is illustrated by a high production report or low sales report characteristic of oversupply of goods. The report is a substitute for the sign presented by actual observation.

How are signs related to information? Signs that stimulate or affect behavior (or response, in the case of machines), either immediately or after the passage of time, constitute information. Information may have the form of language signs, behavior signs, phenomenological signs (such as smoke coming out of a computer console), or other forms of signals and symbols. Where systems include human beings, it is, of course, important to know what kinds of signs affect their behavior, in what way, and to what degree.

Very often, as managers have discovered, their actions communicate to subordinates completely different messages than do their words. Subordinates are also aware of the impact of various signs. In particular, they have learned the signs and messages most suitable for communicating bad news to superiors. In systems designs, both formal and informal means for communication among workers must be planned for.

Because *information affects* the *behavior* of men or machines, a useful distinction may be made between data and information. Data may be considered signs, usually recorded observations, that are not *currently* affecting behavior. However, data may *become* information if behavior becomes affected. For example, the data base for computer systems consists of masses of such signs that are not affecting behavior. Until the data are actually viewed, and properly organized for a manager so that he reacts to them, they are not information. The manager also has many facts stored in his mind. These are data until he calls upon them in connection with some activity he is pursuing or some decision he is required to make. The data are transformed to information when the manager is conscious of meaning associated with them. It should be noted that if a stack of reports is delivered to the manager and he throws up his hands in disgust, the *data in the reports* have not become information, but rather *the fact that piles of reports must be read* is information. (An interpretation of an observation.) It is the latter that constitutes information because it affects behavior. To put it in decision-making terms, it may be said that information is *data in use,* or, "Information is the net value obtained from the process of matching the elements of a present problem with appropriate elements of data."[2] This concept is important to remember in the design of MIS because data must be delivered to decision makers as information to be acted upon. The problem with most so-called information systems is that they are treated as *data* systems rather than *information* systems.

THE DATA LIFE CYCLE

Data within an MIS have their own life cycle. Three aspects of this life cycle are particularly important in the development, design, and operation of systems. First, we need to know how data are *generated,* i.e., how they are born. Secondly, we need to know what *manipulation* or processing of data is carried out. Finally, we need to know *how* certain types of information processing are carried out, particularly the *transmission of data* (and *communication of information*) and storing/retrieving of data. The reproduction of data may occur at various points in the life cycle, and therefore it is not shown on the life-cycle diagram of Figure 9–1.

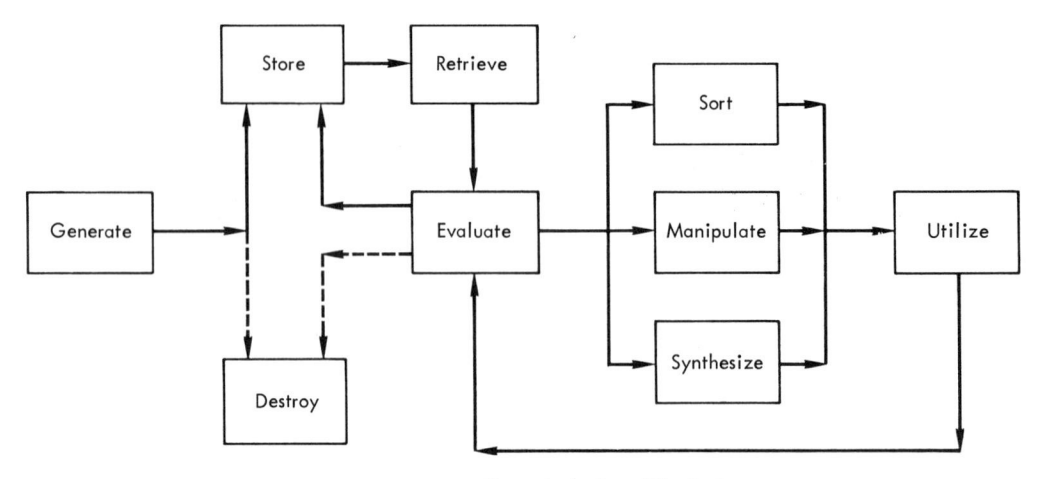

316 Information, Decision Making, and Management Science

Figure 9-1 Data Life Cycle

The generation of data, indicated by the first block in the figure, may occur externally or internally to man. External events may be observed by either man or equipment. As soon as data are created, or as part of the process of creation, they are stored at least briefly. Further processing after the generation consists of:

1. *Storage.* The birth of data or information is the result of some phenomenon in the environment or in the the company that is observed and recorded. Experiments or simulations represent the planned generation of data. At any rate, data must be stored in man's mind, in a document, or in a "mechanical" device of some form before they may be operated upon or utilized.

2. *Conversion* to a different form of storage or presentation. Data are usually converted from storage in the mind or the primary recording instrument to some more convenient form, such as documents, reports, or computer inputs.

3. *Transportation.* Data are constantly being transported from source to storage to processing to user to storage.

4. *Reproduction.* Data as stored are often not in a convenient form for interpreting. Storage on tape, on cards, or in files often must be reproduced in different form. Further, many more copies may be required than exist in storage.

5. *Classification.* Data are often accumulated at random and must be sorted to be useful. Even data that have been sorted and classified may be needed in a differently ordered form. In marketing, sales data may be stored on the basis of salesman, and then sorting on the basis of product and customer may be needed.

6. *Synthesis*. Aggregation of many pieces of data to structure a meaningful whole or complete report is often required. Individual salesmen's reports, the collection of all factory costs, or marketing intelligence data on a particular competitor are illustrations.

7. *Manipulation*. Quantitative data must often be operated upon, by adding, subtracting, and so on, to change their form or to develop their meaning through formulas or equations. Statistical methods for estimating sales potential or for sales forecasting and computation of financial ratios are examples.

8. *Utilization*. When data are finally put in a usable form and the time is right, they are retrieved as information for decision making.

9. *Evaluation*. The value of data depends upon their accuracy, reliability, and time reference as well as on the needs of potential users. There is also an economic aspect of cost of storage versus value of the data and of other data that could be stored. Therefore, data files should be continually monitored to eliminate useless and low-priority data.

10. *Destruction*. Data records may be stored again or destroyed following their evaluation or use. Destruction of data records may be on a purely routine basis following one-time use or may occur in review of old records. Destruction is, of course, the end of the life cycle.

Probably the major practical problem involved in the data life cycle is that of storage and retrieval. The rapidly growing field of management information systems is based on determining what to store, what to retrieve, and how to retrieve information (the data that have significance to managerial tasks) at the right time. Although the development, design, and operation of an MIS must take account of all these processing steps, storage and retrieval require special attention.

CHARACTERISTICS OF INFORMATION

The design of MIS requires consideration of some important characteristics of information. Characteristics for man–machine and machine systems differ somewhat, and are as follows:

For Men and Machines

1. *Purpose*. Information must have a purpose at the time it is transmitted to a person or machine, otherwise it is simply data or noise. Information communicated to people has a wide diversity of purposes because of the variety of activities of people in organizations and systems. The basic purposes of information are to inform, evaluate, persuade, or organize other information. Creating new concepts, identifying problems, solving problems, decision making, planning, initiating, controlling, and searching are just

some of the purposes to which information is directed for human activity in business organizations. The purpose of supplying information (not data) to machines is to provide instructions or to provide information for stored instructions to act upon.

2. *Mode and format.* The modes for communicating information to humans are sensory (through sight, hearing, taste, touch, and smell), but mainly visual and aural in business organizations. Machines are capable of receiving information in a wide variety of modes that include the equivalent of human sensory perceptions and also extend to electrical, chemical, and other means. Sound-activated recorders, gamma-ray quality control devices, electrostatic moisture monitors in paper manufacture, and numerical control machine tools suggests some of the machine modes of receiving information. Voice communication between man and machine is at the frontier of current research.

The format is also a common characteristic of information for man or machine. Humans receive most of their information in the formats of verbal material or documents. The cathode-ray tube (CRT) is being increasingly used as a format. Machines receive information in the format of energy patterns, tapes, cards, or even written form.

3. *Redundancy/efficiency.* Redundancy is, roughly, the excess of information carried per unit of data. Redundancy is a safeguard against errors in the communication process. One of the simplest and most common examples of redundancy is in correspondence or contracts that spell out a number (three) and follow it by the numerical character in parentheses (3). The redundancy concept is very important in systems design. Where the cost of error, misinterpretation of instructions, or failure of a portion of a system is critical, considerable redundancy may be built into the system. It may appear in the form of parallel design, whereby two parts of the system perform the same operation and the results are reconciled before the next step. Redundancy occurs in every organization by supervisory checkups on workers.

The efficiency of the data language is the complement of the redundancy:

$$\text{Efficiency} = 1 - \text{Redundancy}$$

Obviously, in any man–machine system, high efficiency, without offsetting errors, favors high speed of operation and economy. Higher-order computer languages, for example, pack in much more information per unit of data than do the detailed programming languages. The English language is not very efficient, as we can see by taking a sentence, crossing out many words such as articles, crossing out letters in the long words, and then observing how the sentence may still be easily interpreted. Numerical calculations indicate that English has a redundancy of about 75 percent.[3]

4. *Rate.* The rate of transmission/reception of information may be represented by the time required to understand a particular situation, such as a major foul-up in the factory. Quantitatively, the rate for humans may be measured by the number of numeric characters transmitted per minute (such as sales reports from a district office), or by the number of short messages (ideas) per unit of time. For machines, the rate may be based on the number of bits of information per character (sign) per unit of time, a definition derived from mathematical information theory as originally developed by Claude Shannon.

Generally, in MIS, the human component is easily overloaded at low rates of transmission. High transmission rates are of interest in telecommunications and in real-time systems such as a nation-wide airlines reservation system.

5. *Frequency.* The frequency with which information is transmitted or received affects its value. Financial reports prepared weekly may show so little change that they have small value, whereas monthly reports may indicate changes big enough to show problems or trends. Further, information that appears too frequently tends to act as interference, noise, or distraction and to overload the receiver.

The frequency with which information is transmitted must, of course, be related to an operational need. Information on capital expenditure plans may require only annual transmission to management. At operating levels, information may need to be transmitted with a frequency corresponding to actual events (real time). At the top-management level, real-time frequency transmission is less pressing because top-management decisions are strategic in nature and require deliberation.

6. *Deterministic or probabilistic.* Information may be known with certainty, as is usually the case with historical information. Information concerning the future must always have an element of doubt, yet often it is considered deterministic in the sense that a single value is assumed to exist. The computation of inventory, of return on investment, of next month's sales, or of the P&L statement is often performed to yield a single value, the deterministic solution of a problem.

If information is probabilistic, a range or set of possible outcomes and their association probabilities is given. In simulating the operation of a firm, the model may be so constructed (with Monte Carlo techniques) that return on investment appears stochastically as:

ROI	*Probability*
5%	.1
10%	.4
15%	.3
20%	.2

A major consideration in the design of MIS is the utilization of probabilistic as well as deterministic information for decision making. As we will show in Chapter 11, both deterministic and probabilistic techniques of management science are concerned with the development of decision aids.

7. *Cost.* Cost is a limiting factor in obtaining information. A small, nonscientific sample for determining market potential costs far less, generally, than a probability-sample survey or test-marketing a new product. Even internal information from company records may be extremely costly because of the necessity to gather, store, process, and retrieve it. Both the systems designer and manager must constantly evaluate or trade off the value of the information against its cost.

8. *Value.* What is the value of a specific piece of information? This may be too complex and expensive a question to answer in a going business. Management may have to evaluate by judgment the possible gain from the information or the possible loss from its absence. Because many pieces of information are employed in making a decision, the difficulty of evaluating any one of them is evident. However, the systems designer may be in a better position to evaluate the total value of a certain subsystem. For many programmed decisions, the "expected value" of perfect information may be computed and the cost of uncertainty determined. In conclusion, it may be said that the measurement of the value (both qualitative and quantitative) of information is a fertile area for designer ingenuity. The value is highly dependent on other characteristics, such as mode, rate, frequency, deterministic/stochastic features, reliability, and validity. The concept of value of information in MIS will be touched on again in Chapter 13.[4]

9. *Reliability.* Reliability may be expressed as the degree of confidence the decision maker places in the information. In a statistical sense, the reliability of an estimate is the percentage of times the estimate will lie between two limits that represent the precision of the systems. Such a statement might be expressed: "I am 95 percent confident that the average income of households in this city falls between $7100 and $7800."

It is more expensive to obtain more reliable information. Hence reliability offers another characteristic of information that may be traded off with value and cost of the information.

10. *Validity.* The validity of information is a measure of the degree to which the information represents what it purports to represent. Suppose we develop an index that we say represents the efficiency (output/input) of a system. We may then find out that the index is also influenced somewhat by cost and some external economic factor. The fact that the index actually measures (and is influenced by) factors other than what we want to measure lowers its validity.

Primarily for Machines

11. *Steady state or dynamic.* Characteristics of information especially related to machines are derived from the difference in types of "sensing" by

machines and in the response purposes of machines. Although machines may sense information in many ways, electrical, mechanical, and optical are by far the most common. Electrical inputs from card or tape sources, variations in power, switching circuits, and mechanical keys and levers are examples of methods for providing information inputs. A characteristic of such information is that it may be steady state or dynamic. Information that does not vary with time is called steady state. A numerical control machine may receive information from a tape that tells it to cut ⅛ inch off a unit for one unit in process after another. This is a steady-state situation.

Now consider a real-time warehouse and factory inventory system. Information on the number of units in each warehouse, forecasts of demand, and factory production rate is supplied to a computer for determination of future production rate and shipments to warehouse. Both inputs to and outputs from the computer vary with time and so represent information with dynamic characteristics.

12. *Linear or nonlinear.* When information inputs are linear functions of some variable, the information is linear, as opposed to nonlinear. Much information that management utilizes is linear, mainly because it is easy to comprehend and no better information is available. Some examples of *nonlinear* information are: (a) double-declining-balance method of depreciation, (b) forecast of sales as increasing at the *rate* of 5 percent per year, and (c) compound interest value of money in evaluating capital budget items on a discounted cash-flow basis. Although the ratio method of forecasting, a linear method of relating accounts for the present and the future year, is still popular, analysis of more complex models made possible by the computer has introduced more nonlinear information into the business world.

13. *Continuous or discrete.* The information may represent a continuous variable and hence be a continuous input, or it may be discrete in form. Most information is discrete. That is, managers receive reports on sales, production, personnel problems, crises in the plant, or financial data at separated periods of time. Real-time information systems supply information continuously as a function of time (a continuous variable), but managers do not make decisions by monitoring such information, obviously. Continuous, real-time information is utilized for managerial decision making when it appears in batches. Continuous information is also suited for input to machines requiring such information for uninterrupted operation.

INFORMATION, MANAGEMENT, AND THE COMPUTER

The first step in developing a science is usually developing a taxonomy of ideas, as we have just done for information characteristics. For an applied science, we next seek some guiding principles and theory for using the results that we deduce from the taxonomy. As a first principle, we might state that only information—the data that have relevance to a manager's problems—should be referred to him. Today, most managers are overwhelmed with irrelevant data and spend much time doing their own screening. The practical problem posed for the MIS is to distinguish between what is relevant and what is irrelevant to each manager. The manager who understands and believes in the "management by exception" concept is apt to work most closely with systems designers. In our taxonomy of information characteristics, we would deduce from these problems the fact that purpose, mode, and format are considerations in the information field.

The computer has been a blessing and a curse with respect to purpose, mode, and format of information. It has been used to produce drearily detailed stacks of data with little purpose. Yet, properly used, it has made analyses for project control, simulated complicated problems in business, and made possible many timely financial reports. As the computer becomes recognized as a tool or component in MIS rather than being mistaken for an MIS, it will reach its potential for revolutionizing the management process.

The thoughtful manager of the future will not spend his time gathering all types of data at random and will not intersperse planning and decision-making activities with such random search. He will concern himself with determining the kinds of problems he must solve, the areas of knowledge he must stay abreast of, and the kind of sampling of the environment he must conduct in order to sense impending changes. Even today, managers should be aware of the characteristics of information so that they may participate in MIS development by establishing trade-offs among characteristics of information obtained. In most cases, cost is the common factor that links these trade-offs.

The actual search, storage, and retrieval of data that will be converted to information for management pose some difficult problems. An introduction to this subject follows.

INFORMATION SEARCH, STORAGE, AND RETRIEVAL

In organizational systems and man–machine systems, decision-making elements are not usually supplied automatically and gratuitously with data; the data must be selectively retrieved or obtained from any or all of three sources:

1. The environment
2. The storage system developed for the operating system
3. Actualized situations (laboratory or similarly controlled operation)

Methods of obtaining information from each of these sources for the operation of a system may be extremely difficult.

The problem of searching for information in the *environment* is difficult because often we do not know what will represent information and what will be irrelevant data. Even when we do know generally what we are looking for, the source and form may be completely unsuspected, F. J. Aguilar defines four modes of scanning the environment:

1. *Undirected observation.* The searcher has no specific object in mind except to scan for items that may be useful to him now or in the future. The manager accomplishes this by reading newspapers and trade journals, listening to shop talk at social gatherings, attending industry meetings, and generally staying alert to word of anything that may bear upon his company.

2. *Conditioned viewing.* The observer directs his attention to a more or less clearly identified area without making an active search. If a signal of some kind appears, he is ready to evaluate it. The manager is apt to follow closely the activities of his company's competitors or read the financial news for significant changes.

3. *Informal search.* This is active, directed, but relatively unstructured search for specific information. Often an investigation into the possible market for potential new products follows this informal type of search. Recruiting of personnel or a search for new product ideas are other examples.

4. *Formal search.* This is a systematic method following a preestablished plan to obtain specific information or information relating to a specific problem. Carefully developed, scientifically planned sample survey designs, some types of industrial intelligence search, or the recruiting of a new president for the company typify this search pattern.[5]

The *storage system* within the company contains data obtained from the environment and data obtained from internal operations of the company. The modern term for a carefully designed aggregation of data in an MIS is *data base.* Storage systems designed especially for the operating systems of a company may range from simple card files to complex, computerized storage and retrieval systems. One advantage of installing an internal information storage and retrieval system is that it forces management to formulate rules for including data, the first step in the selection of relevant data. Also, if we put the data into the system as it becomes available we should presumably be able to get it out more easily than by searching the environment at some later time when we need it. This may or may not be the case in practice, however. One of the major problems of internal storage/retrieval systems is classifying, indexing, and coding incoming material so that queries may retrieve *all* relevant data and *only* relevant data.

When large amounts of data are to be put in storage for later retrieval, the data must be classified in some way so that particular items can be withdrawn. Classification consists of arranging subject matter into batches on the basis of *differences* and *similarities.* Classification is commonly by hierarchy or by attribute. For example, a hierarchical arrangement of marketing data would be:

    Marketing
      Selling
        Sales expense
          Telephone expense
            John Smith's telephone expense

Attributes offer the opportunity for narrowing down classes without developing highly detailed hierarchies. Thus, "John Smith, telephone expense, eastern region" would be sufficient to identify the information concerning the telephone expense of John Smith of the eastern region as the intersection of three classes.

When classes have been developed, indexes must be used to describe their contents. For example, the index at the back of a book provides words or descriptors that represent certain paragraph contents in the book. Word indexes, key-in-word-in-context indexes, and controlled indexes are other examples.[6]

Hierarchical classification is omitted in the key-word or uniterm index method. Suppose we wish to store a document that deals with test marketing of TV sets by a competitor. We assign the three key "words" or uniterms: (1) test market, (2) TV, and (3) competitor. There will be many documents with some of these terms assigned as well as other terms. If we consider the terms as representing three classes of information, we may represent the situation by a "set" diagram, Figure 9–2. With the aid of the computer and the application of logic statements, the search for information may be greatly refined. The statement for the data in Figure 9–2 simply asks for the intersection:

TV and Test Market *and* Competitor

1. Each circle represents a class of documents.

2. Dark area represents documents that belong to all three classes.

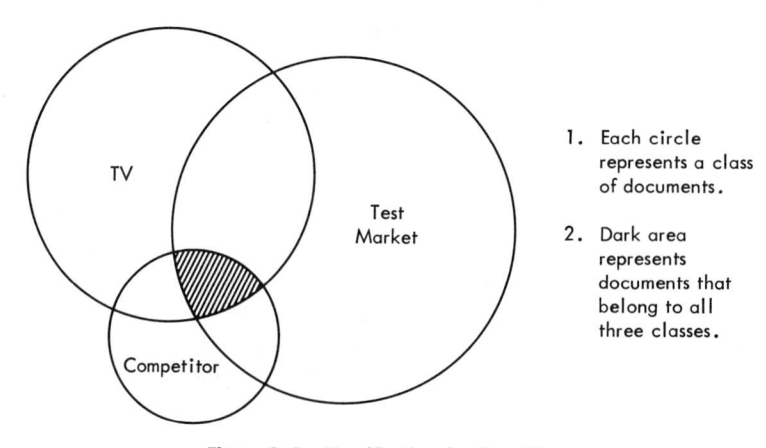

Figure 9–2 Classification for Searching

More refined statements might read as:

A and B and C and not D
(A or B) and (C or D)
Not A and not B and C

Finally, statements or index terms are usually coded to save space and time. Codes are shorthand representations of words or statements. Thus the Dewey Decimal System uses codes as representations of content descriptors. In a hierarchical system, a letter might designate a major area of information, and numbers might be used for subclasses. Decimals are sometimes employed to aid in establishing subclass level. Three examples of "alphanumeric" code terms are:

M 9232
A 1.200.28
HB/128/5

Company policy manuals and many business systems attempt to provide memory aids in their codes: for example, ADM stands for administrative, LEG for legal, and PER for personnel in some systems. This makes coding and decoding easier. A. M. McDonough has developed a comprehensive four-character alphanumeric code for business. The general category of management problems and new products is coded as M230. For the area of management problems and market needs, the code term is M232.[7] It is important to note that the more refined the index and the code classification, the more expensive the storage of data. However, the more refined the index and classification system, the lower the cost of retrieval, because relevant data may be pinpointed better. Costs for classifying information and for writing retrieval specifications rise rapidly with complexity in either. It is therefore important for the system designer to develop an optimum storage and retrieval system by trade-off between indexing and retrieval requirements. The system itself is expensive to design and usually even more expensive to revise if it fails to meet future needs.

Although the mechanics of storage and retrieval of data represent some of the most complex aspects of MIS, there are other aspects of importance. An overview of the total problem is summarized here:

1. *Identification of the users and their needs.* The user of information is certainly the principal figure in the MIS. The success of any system depends on how effectively and efficiently it serves the user's needs.

2. *Selection of data* for storage and retrieval. The user's needs must be well defined and the relative importance of these needs must be established. Only the user can do this, and therefore the specification of type of data to be stored and to be made available is the responsibility of the user. In other words, *the manager must actively take part in the design of the MIS.*

3. *Maintaining "interest profiles"* of users. The MIS must include a means for recording current and changing needs of users. As new data flow into the company or are generated, the MIS must compare the data with the requirements of the user profiles so that timely information is automatically sent to the managers.

4. *Method of classifying and indexing.* As we have said, service and economics are critical to classifying and indexing in MIS design. Further, it is not only today's needs that must be considered. The system should be able to encompass changing and increasing demands upon it so that it will not have to be redesigned and reconstructed repeatedly, a very costly undertaking.

5. *Procedures for retrieval.* Procedures need to be established for the manager, the information specialist, and the computer operation group to function in the search process. The information specialist is an interpreter who links the manager and the computer by his knowledge of the information classification and coding system.

6. *Type or types of storage.* Although the computer cards and tapes are usually considered to be the main storage unit, data are stored in other places and forms in an MIS. Reference and document libraries, file cabinets, reports (including computer printouts), microfilm, microfiche, aperture cards, engineering drawing files, and manual card-sort systems are examples of types of storage that may all be present. The selection of such types of storage is often based upon tradition rather than on economics, modern technology, and MIS considerations.

7. *Dissemination of information.* Although managers may call for information as they need it, there are many formats for presenting it to them. Verbal, visual, and hard copy are the most common means of dissemination. Another aspect of dissemination is related to the "interest profile." Procedures must be established so that relevant information that the managers may not even know is existent or available may be disseminated in a timely and useful form.

8. *Updating of storage files.* Unless a completely mechanical procedure can be employed, removing obsolete material from storage files as new data are added is a major problem. Managers simply do not have time to review complete files periodically. Most companies either continue adding data to a file until it collapses or they remove data from an accessible file like a computer system to some remote storage space where it is practically inaccessible on an economic basis. Again, this illustrates the need for professional information specialists in the design of these systems.

In the final analysis, the information storage and retrieval system must be measured by its efficiency and effectiveness. Figure 9–3 indicates an approach to evaluating the effectiveness of the system.

Needed and
High Importance

+

— (Successes)

(Misses)

Not Received ← → Received by Manager

— (Noise)

+

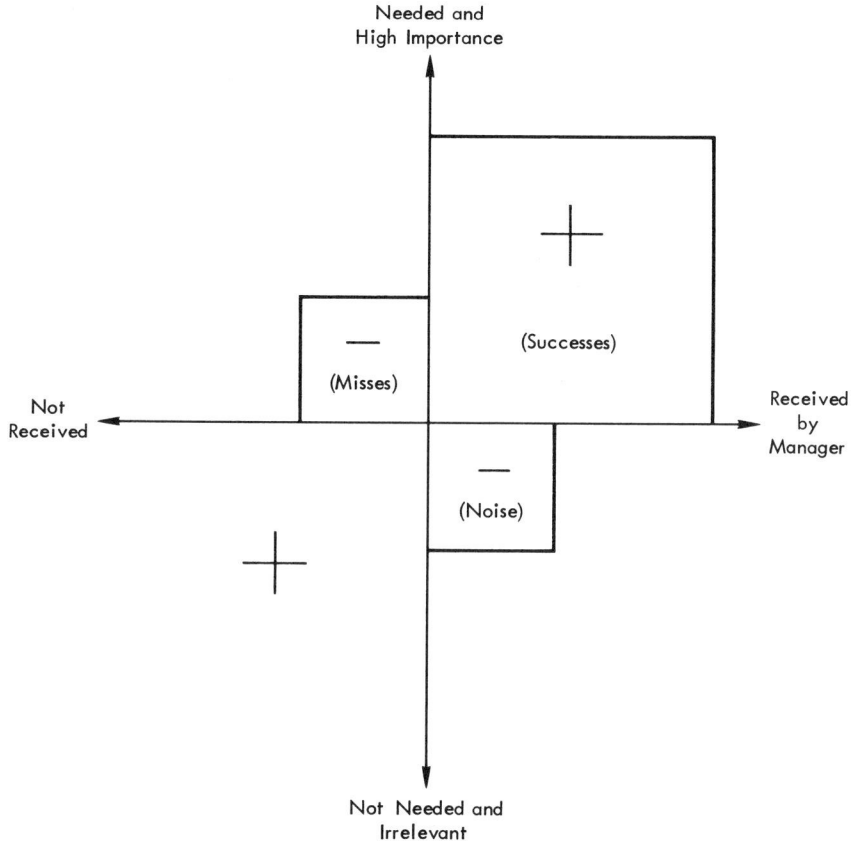

Not Needed and
Irrelevant

Figure 9–3 Measure of the Information Storage and Retrieval System

COMMUNICATION

Communication means the transfer of *information* as distinguished from the transfer of data. The term *message* is usually used to represent an amount of information intended as a specific stimulus. It is unfortunate that the mathematical approach to data transmission measurement and analysis was called "information theory," because of the confusion it creates. The mathematical theory of data transmission deals with the efficiency of the transmission system only, not with the meaning of what is transmitted. In mathematical data transmission theory, the "message" is the output of a source of transmission and is a *sample* of data drawn from the population of all data. A "character" is the unit of a message, as for example, a letter, word, or phrase. The population of data is any set of characters (distinct symbols) denoted as the alphabet for the system.

A. D. Hall raises the major questions that we like answered in the analysis of communications in a system and points out the very narrow limitations of mathematical information theory for MIS design:

> Suppose that in trying to understand how some system behaves, a systems engineer stands astride a path carrying messages from one place in the system to another. Among the many questions he might raise about the messages are:
> a. How much information is flowing?
> b. How many different kinds of messages are there?
> c. What is the meaning of each message to the recipient?
> d. How valuable are the messages?
> e. How frequently does each kind of message pass by, and is the passage of one kind correlated to the passage of another kind?
>
> The answers to these questions might be quite relevant to the design of some new system. However, information theory is not even concerned with *c* and *d*. It is concerned with questions *a*, *b*, and *e*, but the measure of information the theory provides is very special—much narrower than that required for the engineering of practical systems.[8]

Despite the narrowness of application, the principal concepts developed in mathematical data transmission theory as listed below *suggest a structure* for some aspects of MIS:

1. Definition of a unit of "information"
2. Noiseless systems
   a. Discrete sources
      (1) Average "information" transmitted
      (2) Channel capacity
      (3) Redundancy of "message" symbols
   b. Continuous sources
      (1) Average information transmitted
      (2) Channel capacity
3. Noisy systems (Same subtopics as for 2.)

From this list, and from a broader perspective, communications theory as related to systems design in general comprises the following major areas:

Concept generation. For any system, there must be a generation of concepts or information, either within or without the system. Such information provides the system goals and is the basis of communication among system components. (See Figure 9–4a.)

Source or transmitter. Once a concept has been generated for some purpose, it must be transmitted from some source. The transmitter and the generator may be the same element in the system (a person) or the concept (information) may arise from some phenomenon outside the system and be transmitted by some mechanical device. Figures 9–4(a) and 9–4(b) show the separate functions. The messages must be put into a form that can flow from source to destination as indicated by the encoder.

data, information, and communication

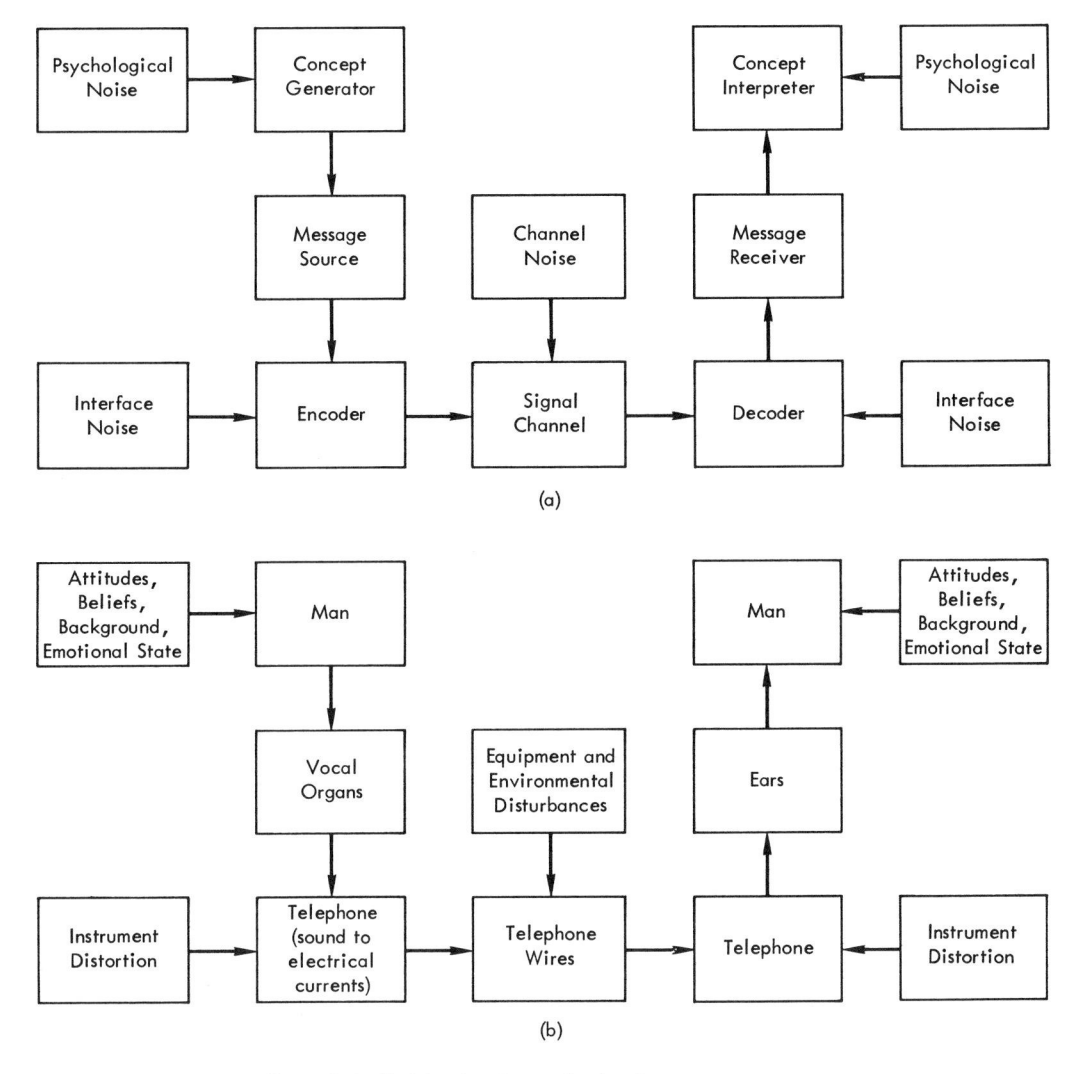

Figure 9–4 Models of a Communication System

Channels. The channels provide the means for the flow of energy that carries the information.

Noise. There are no 100 percent noise-free systems in real life. Unwanted data or signals always appear in systems, owing to human or mechanical performance. The task for systems designers is to minimize noise and prevent its reception from being accepted as true information.

Transmission efficiency. Efficiency in communication, the ratio of useful output to input, may be affected by the performance of all elements in the communication system. Inefficiencies in energy conversion, inefficiency of semantic properties of language, and poor filters against mechanical or psychological noise in the system may reduce transmission efficiency. How many MIS designers evaluate and consider such system efficiency?

Receiver. Because communication is the linking of two components of a system, there must be a receiving component as well as a transmitting component.

Interpretation. Information that represents reality in its entirety cannot be transmitted. There are always gaps, so that interpretation is needed to make the whole and develop the meaning and significance.

Man–machine interfaces. The study and the design of modern systems require the study of man–machine relationships and the improvement of interface operations.

A model of the basic communication system between two elements such as man–man, man–machine, machine–man, or machine–machine is shown in Figure 9–4(a). Figure 9–4(b) shows a specific example of the model.

In summary, the question could be asked: Is the mathematical theory of data transmission useful in the analysis and design of MIS? The answer is that the theory does provide concepts of value to MIS designers. Specifically, the concepts of unit of information, message, noise, channels, efficiency/redundancy, and message frequency may draw upon developments in the mathematical theory.

Interpersonal Communication

Communication among people may be in the form of one-to-many, one-to-several, or one-to-one, or the complements of many-to-one and several-to-one. In organizations, the hierarchical discipline generally rules out the many-to-one case (such as mobs or pressure groups). Even when many people are present, communication is usually conducted between two people or among a few people at a time within the context of an organization.

The study of interpersonal communication is complex and involves such factors as:

1. Psychological, social, and cultural characteristics of the people in the organization
2. The nature of language and problems of semantics
3. The social and the formal structures of the organization
4. Modes of communication, such as:
   a. Speaking
   b. Writing
   c. Other visual transmission
   d. Behavior

Some authorities believe that most of the problems in society (and in organizations) exist because of our inability to communicate with each other. Each of us perceives the world around him uniquely and for this reason has a difficult time seeing exactly how someone else feels in critical situations. Barriers inherent in interpersonal communication are primarily:

1. *Perceptual.* A person perceives (senses and interprets) events about him in terms of his own unique psychological, social, and cultural background. Thus no two people perceive things exactly the same. When in communicating they refer to the same event, an event each has reconstructed differently, obstacles to communication arise.

2. *Psychological.* The same words or events mean different things to different people, depending upon their needs and thinking processes. An elderly lady limps slowly down the street. To the two confidence swindlers, she appears to be an easy mark. To the social worker, she is a symbol of the need for greater care of the elderly. To the passing physician, she is a reminder that there is as yet no cure for arthritis.

3. *Social.* Social barriers arise because people in organizations are conditioned by the roles imposed upon them by their social backgrounds. Some aspects of this have been discussed in Chapter 3. Vocabulary, idioms, social group restraints on behavior, and different social needs underlying communication tend to thwart interchange of ideas.

4. *Cultural.* We need only observe the interchanges between unions and management to show how cultural values separate people into two worlds. The cultural barrier is often so great that the disinterested observer wonders if the two groups are talking about the same problems.

5. *Semantic.* Semantic problems arise most frequently in the interpretation of written documents, where two-way exchange between parties is impossible. The implication for the systems designer and the manager is that written procedures and policies require special attention and probably periodic interpretation by verbal means.

6. *Media* (of transmission). Each medium of communication has weaknesses—the sloppy phrases and poor organization of verbalizing and the limitations of space in writing are obvious ones.

7. *Physical.* Channels of communication between people—such as physical, electrical/electronic, audio, or other—may distort messages or introduce "noise."

A survey of numerous writers in the field of communications leads to the list of barriers in Table 9–1. Some of these overlap several of the classes just cited, so that no attempt has been made to categorize the barriers. Examination of them suggests means for improving interpersonal communications.

Table 9-1
Barriers to Communication

1. Distorted perception of events outside the individual.
2. Misinterpretation of signs coming to an individual from the outside environment.
3. Heightened emotions, misunderstandings, friction, laziness.
4. Resistance to change. Many people tend to resist new ideas because of the mental or physical effort involved in learning. Therefore they tend to ignore or misunderstand ideas that are in conflict with long-held views. This makes the communication of new ideas difficult.
5. Failure to "listen." This occurs when the receiver does not give his full attention and effort to understanding the sender. People are able to think faster than a speaker can express himself, so that there is a tendency for the mind to wander.
6. Uncritical assumption by the listener that he understands what the sender is saying.
7. Failure of the sender to recognize the situational context and frame of reference of the receiver.
8. Cultural differences, which affect language, viewpoints, and values of the sender and the receiver.
9. Lack of feedback between the individuals who are attempting to communicate with each other.
10. Confusing facts with inferences, "sentiments," and value judgments.
11. Failure to appraise motives. What is the speaker trying to accomplish? His words may not uncover his true objective or what he really means.
12. Failure to assemble the facts before passing judgment.
13. Extrapolation or overgeneralization. This covers such a situation as grasping for the first ideas communicated and immediately jumping to conclusions of great generality. Guilt by association would also come under this heading.
14. Rigid application of two-valued logic, the assumption that everything is either black or white. A categorizing of people, events, or ideas into dichotomies. (A thing is either *A* or *not-A*.)
15. Overcommunication. Too much information may be transmitted to a listener at one time, so that he cannot absorb it in an organized fashion. As a result, the entire communication may be a failure.
16. Confusion of abstract symbols (words) with concrete events.
17. Limitations of language and symbols.
18. Gobbledygook, the ostentatious use of technical terms and over-verbalization.
19. Lack of organization of the ideas being communicated.
20. Conflict between verbal communication and behavior signs. The receiver may interpret the sender's actions and behavior at either the receiver's conscious level or the subliminal level.
21. Inappropriate channel of communication.
22. Blocking or intermittent operation of the channel of communication.
23. Extraneous signals or "noise" associated with the communication channel.

24. Distance between the sender and receiver, or length of channel of communication.
25. Time between the sending of a message and its reception.
26. Structure of the social organization.
27. Social barriers.
28. Status barriers.
29. Number of individuals involved in the communication process (size of the social group).

The systems designer must take these barriers to communication into account. For instance, training programs for people who will man the system reduce misunderstandings that might arise if only procedural manuals are provided. People selected to run a system might be chosen because of similar backgrounds and compatibility. Where communication failures in operating a system seem possible on occasion, owing to some of the barriers listed, the designer might arrange for redundancy or special controls in particular parts of the system.

Communication Network in Organizations

Organizations are systems for goal achievement. Goals are achieved by solving problems and performing operations. Decisions for operations must be based on the information in the problem solution. Decisions must be communicated to other decision makers (managers) or to operators (individual contributors or "doers"). Both decision makers and operators receive and give information as part of communication networks. These networks are of two types, which bear an important relationship to informal and formal organization (see Chapters 2 and 3):

1. Informal systems developed by interaction among individuals
2. Formal systems established through the process of organizing

Informal systems may consist of "grapevine" patterns as shown in Figure 9–5, or they may fall into task-solving patterns as in Figure 9–6. Formal patterns are generally hierarchical in nature.

In the design of an MIS, the fundamental problem is to develop a structure and pattern of communication consisting of:

1. Decision centers
2. Action points
3. Channels of communication
4. Information flow

which produce optimum performance directed toward system goal achievement.[9]

In a business firm, from a systems viewpoint there are management control points at various parts of the system. These management control points are the decision centers of the system. The identification of a decision

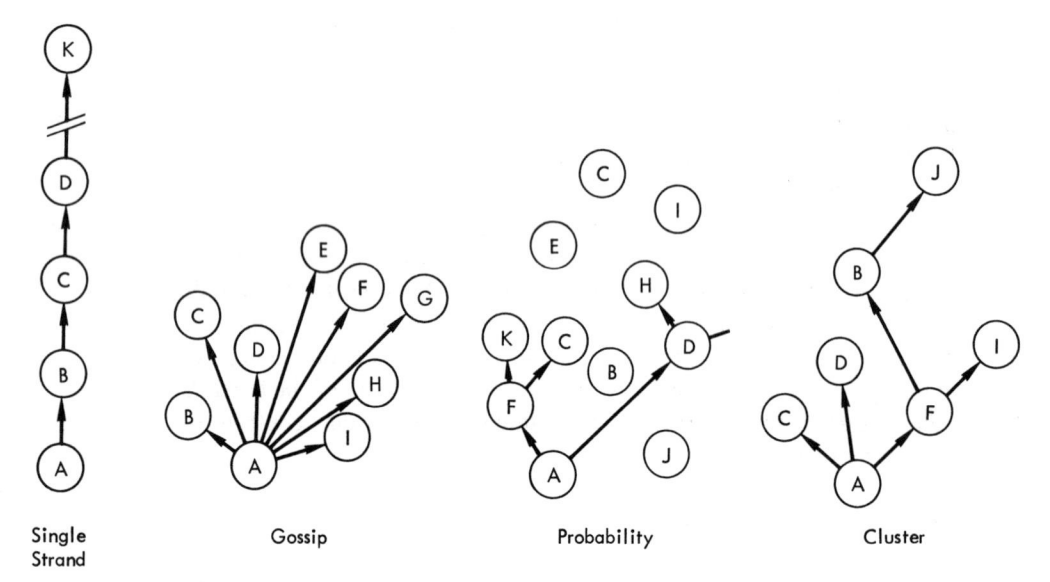

Figure 9-5 Grapevine Patterns

SOURCE Keith Davis, "Management Communication and the Grapevine," *Harvard Business Review*, September–October 1953

center is not always easy. Some questions that help the systems designer reconcile organizational reality with system concepts in establishing decision centers are:

1. What decisions need to be made?
2. What information is required and available for making the decision?
3. What individuals have the knowledge, judgment, and formal authority to make a particular decision?
4. Is the decision best made by an individual or by a group?

Because managers make managerial decisions to control subsystems, these decisions must be communicated to the processors (see Chapter 4), that is, to people at action points in the system. It has now become apparent that a breakdown in communication between decision centers and action points may cause an entire subsystem to fail, and failure of a subsystem is likely to lead to a breakdown in the entire business system.

The distinction between decision centers and action points has a parallel in the distinction between information systems and operational systems. Decision centers belong to the former and action points to the latter. The information system is, of course, an overlay of the operational system and is designed to provide direction and control. S. C. Blumenthal classifies the information systems as shown here.[10] The corresponding operational systems are readily apparent.

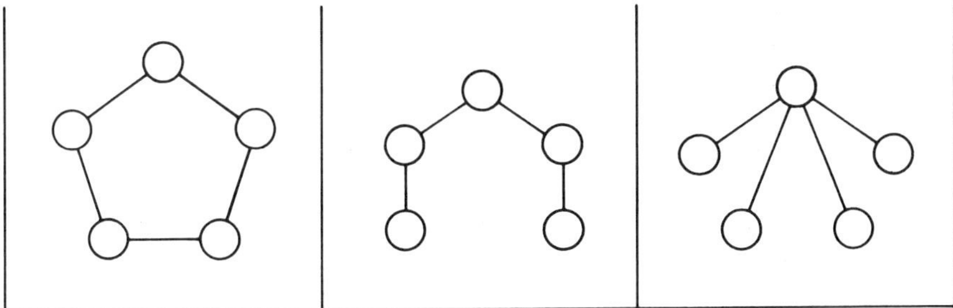

Speed	Slow	Fast	Fast
Accuracy	Poor	Good	Good
Organization	No stable form	Slowly emerging but stable	Almost immediate and stable
Emergence of a leader	None	Marked	Very pronounced
Morale	Very good	Poor	Very poor

Figure 9–6 Task-Solving Patterns
SOURCE Adapted *from Alex Bavelas and Dermot Barrett,* "An Experimental Approach to Organizational Behavior," in *Studies in Personnel and Industrial Psychology,* Edwin Fleishman, ed. (Homewood, Ill.: The Dorsey Press, Inc., 1961), p. 406

Physical Operational Control Information Systems
    Logistics
        Raw materials
        Production
        Saleable product
    Physical assets
        Facilities and equipment
        Capital projects
Administrative Operational Control Information Systems
    Financial
        Accounting
        Treasury
    Manpower
        Payroll
        Benefits
        Personnel administration

The pattern of communication is a function of the number, kinds, and quality of the channels of communication as well as of the amount and frequency of information flow through the channels. In most companies there are *required* channels and flows and *permitted* channels and flows. The information systems designer must structure the required channels and flows so that breakdowns cannot occur either because of time-consuming reporting or because of inadequate reporting for ultimate control. The *permitted* channels and flows are useful and necessary, but they do not guarantee the control that the required information flows do.

The distinction between the engineering design of hardware systems and the design of operational and information systems is derived from the complexity of human organizations. Machines perform in fairly predictable ways and there are a relatively limited number of relationships among components in the engineered system. Communication networks in human organizations involve all manner of behavioral characteristics of people and an infinite variety of constantly changing relationships. The MIS designer must be aware of the underlying principles of organizational behavior and communications theory if he is to design realistic, workable systems.

SUMMARY

Because information and communication link the elements of a system together and, in fact, are necessary for the existence of systems, a study of their nature and functions is vital for the system designer. Definitional problems, which arise immediately, are significant because behavior-instigating implications versus processing implications for data are important in developing information systems. The processes that apply to data are also important in terms of system diagnosis and design. One of the most important sets of processes is the storage/retrieval set.

The transfer of information—that is, *communication*—is the most vital aspect of MIS. There are numerous approaches to the study of communications. Although mathematical analysis of data transmission has been highly developed, the interpersonal side of communication is probably far more operationally significant to the systems designer.

All these topics have been treated very lightly in comparison with the extensive research and literature available. Our goal is to indicate the route for a more rigorous study of information communication in order to develop improved systems.

DISCUSSION QUESTIONS AND PROBLEMS

1. The general manager of a plant holds weekly staff meetings with the managers who report to him. The managers, in turn, hold meetings with their subordinates the following day. The general manager has often wondered why his messages appear to be misunderstood from time to time at the lower levels of the company, and why misleading or fragmentary information is sometimes given to him by his managers. Discuss various explanations.

2. Give an example of the life cycle for some particular data, such as test market data or a production report.

3. Develop a simple expression (either verbal or mathematical) to show how the cost of redundancy of information in a report to management should be balanced with the cost of a misunderstanding.

4. An on-line printer located at the desk of a production control clerk prints out production reports at the rate of 200 lines per minute. The EDP manager states that such a slow machine is obsolete and recommends a new 800-line-per-minute printer. What factors should be considered before such a purchase is made?

5. Marketing research develops an indicator that predicts the success of a certain product if it is introduced. The present value of the profit over the life cycle of the product is estimated to be $2 million. There is, of course, a risk that profits in the latter years of the life cycle will not materialize. The indicator of success is believed to be only about 60 percent reliable. Interpret the usefulness of this probabilistic information for management.

6. What is meant by "random access" to a file?

7. Compare methods of updating computer files (such as personnel or payroll) and physical files kept in a filing cabinet.

8. Draw a block diagram showing the flow of all sources of information and noise that a functional worker, such as a clerk, engineer, production line worker, or salesman, receives during a working day.

9. Arrange a visit to a local department store or manufacturing plant and, with the help of an executive, identify the operational systems and the information systems in a classification similar to (but not necessarily identical with) the classification given in this chapter.

10. A large textile manufacturer operates about 45 mills turning out unfinished gray goods, semifinished textiles, and finished fabrics. These are sold through eight regional sales offices to apparel makers, home furnishers, and industrial users. Presently, inventory reports are two weeks late, but executives would like to know on Monday the inventory position on the previous Friday. There is lack of coordination between mills, which results in duplicate setups. Payroll procedures are not consistent among plants.

The new business-school-educated president is wondering whether plants and offices should be tied together or connected to a central information center. He would also like to see improved sales forecasting and financial planning.

11. The controller of a television network stated, "The order of a sales entry in the sales department leads to a whole series of dependent business events." The network had sales offices all over the United States. Orders could be placed, for example, for commercial positions between the hours of 1 and 3 P.M. for 52 weeks starting at a given date. The problem appeared to be one of taking orders immediately without risk of duplication. Still, the controller did not want to invest in a system, and its corresponding equipment, that was too specialized. What about sales forecasting, payroll, sales analysis, and discounts?

12. A railroad executive lamented his company's lack of control over its inventory of rolling stock. Like other railroad companies, it owned numerous types of cars, rented cars from other companies on a per diem basis, and also rented its own cars and telephoned reports of their locations. The railroad executive felt that there must be some system to provide management with instant information on idle cars and their locations, cars rented by other railroads, cars the company is renting from other roads, the age and physical status of its stock of cars, and the cars in the shops for repair. Also, if the executive could obtain estimates of carload requirements by customers of his company for six months in advance, he could reduce movement of empty cars.

13. A wholesaler with a large warehouse in Miami sells electronic parts, vacuum tubes, and TV tubes to 41 retailers in southern Florida. Once every three days, he sends a truck on a circuit up to West Palm Beach, over to St. Petersburg and Tampa, and back to Miami. At periodic intervals, trucks bringing his supplies from the manufacturers could make stops at West Palm Beach and Fort Lauderdale to drop off shipments ordered by his customers. He wondered if he could develop a system to minimize inventories in both his warehouse and his customers' stores as well as to reduce the number of trips his truck was making. Could he perhaps use a larger or smaller truck more economically? If he could only forecast shipments for his 1200 different products 30 days in advance!

REFERENCES

1. See Charles Morris, *Signs, Language and Behavior* (New York: George Braziller, Inc., 1955), pp. 24–25.
2. Adrian M. McDonough, *Information Economics and Management Systems* (New York: McGraw-Hill Book Company, 1963), p. 76.
3. From *A Methodology for Systems Engineering*, by Arthur D. Hall, copyright © 1962 by Litton Educational Publishing, Inc., by permission of Van Nostrand Reinhold Company.
4. For a good discussion of this subject, see Rudolph E. Hirsch, "The Value of Information," *The Journal of Accountancy*, June 1968.
5. See Francis Joseph Aguilar, *Scanning the Business Environment* (New York: The Macmillan Company, 1967).
6. See Allen Kent, *Textbook on Mechanized Information Retrieval* (New York: John Wiley & Sons, Inc., 1962), pp. 156–58, for an explanation of these indexes.
7. McDonough, *Information Economics,* Appendix 2.
8. Hall, *A Methodology for Systems Engineering,* pp. 384–85.
9. An interesting view on communication patterns is given in M. D. Mesarovic, J. L. Sanders, and C. F. Sprague, "An Axiomatic Approach to Organizations from a General Systems Viewpoint" in W. W. Cooper, H. J. Leavitt, and M. W. Shelly II, eds., *New Perspectives in Organization Research* (New York: John Wiley & Sons, Inc., 1964), pp. 493–512.
10. Sherman C. Blumenthal, *Management Information Systems: A Framework for Planning and Development* (Englewood Cliffs, N.J.: Prentice-Hall, 1969), p. 52.

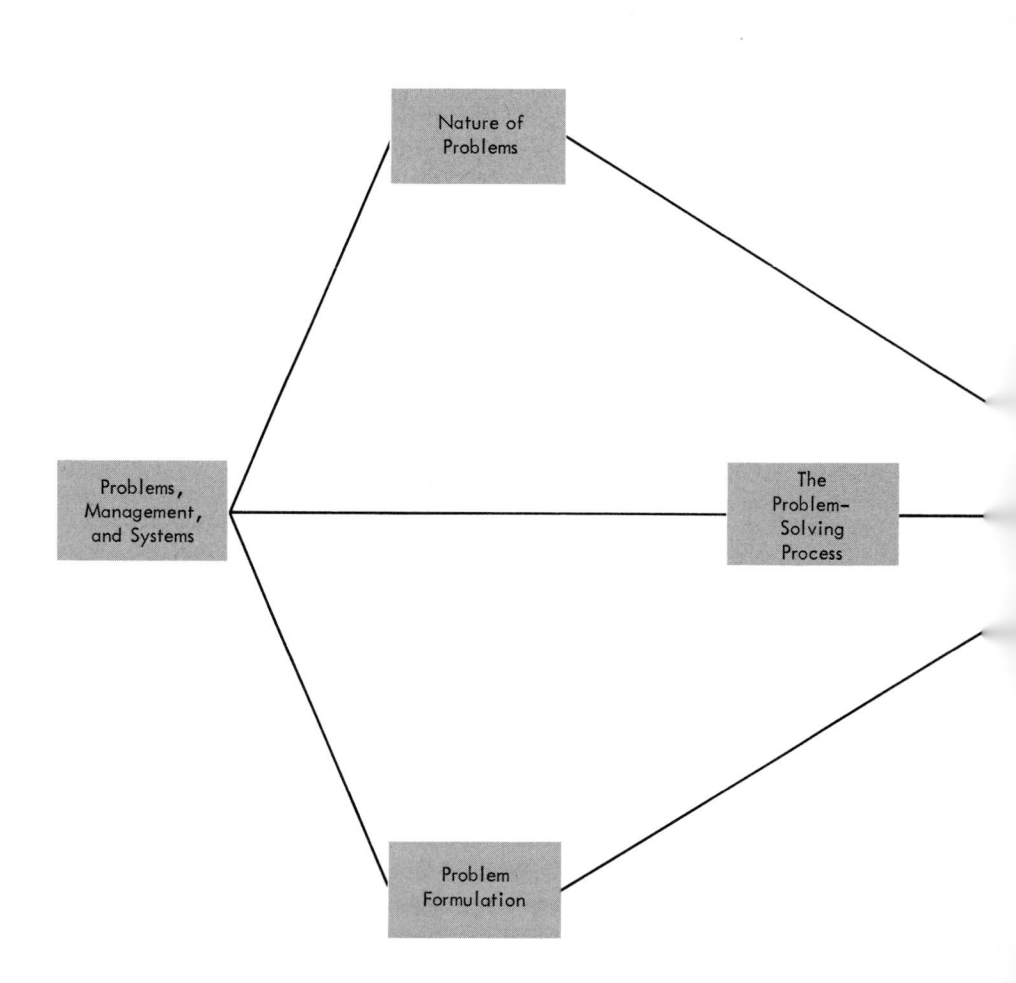

```
                    Nature of
                    Problems


Problems,                                The
Management,                              Problem-
and Systems                              Solving
                                         Process


                    Problem
                    Formulation
```

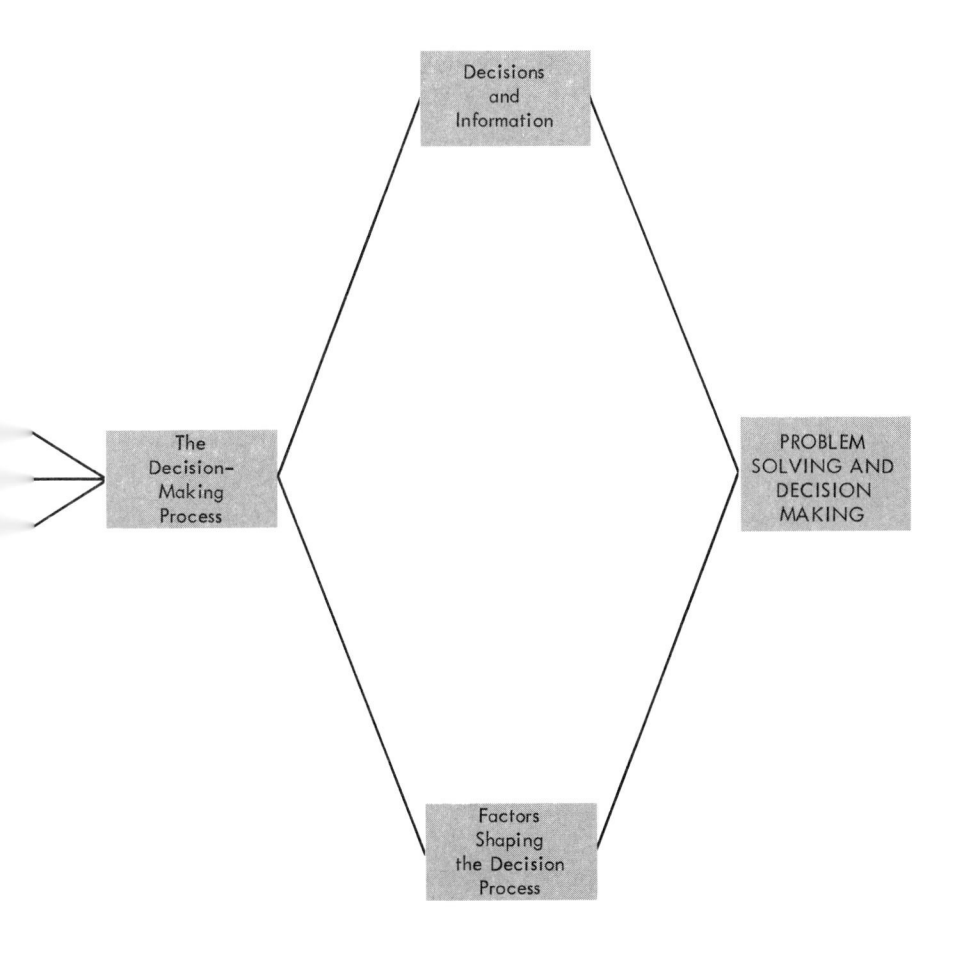

10
problem solving
and decision making

- Decisions and Information
- The Decision-Making Process
- Factors Shaping the Decision Process
- PROBLEM SOLVING AND DECISION MAKING

10

What is problem solving? Decision making? Are they related, different, or the same? What do they have to do with systems, management, and organization? We will try to answer these questions first, and then concentrate on the elements and processes of problem solving and of decision making. Although we will not be able to give a recipe for carrying out these processes, we hope to give their constituents and their flavor.

We will maintain in this book a distinction between problem solving and decision making. Problem solving, in its essential form, is the *seeking of answers to a question*. Decision making is the *cutting off* of further consideration of the problem, the elimination of all alternatives but one; it is a commitment to action. The solving of applied problems usually involves a means—end chain of subproblems. For each subproblem, alternatives are developed and a decision is made to follow a course of action, which requires the solution of another subproblem. Thus, decisions are made at a number of points in the sequential problem-solving process, for example:

1. Decisions as to goals. These involve both values and empirical considerations.
2. Decisions as to subgoals and means in means–ends chains of action.
3. Decisions as to ranges of input values.
4. Decisions as to the selection from among alternate means–ends chains.
5. Decisions regarding basic assumptions.
6. Decisions regarding available data. Should they be accepted or rejected, or should a search for further data be carried out?
7. Decisions on final action to implement the selected solution to the problem.

It is the initial selection of goals and of the general strategy to be followed in solving means–ends chains that is usually referred to as executive decision making.

It is only fair to point out that some scholars view decision making as the dominant process and problem solving as only a means for developing alternatives. Whereas we have used a broad meaning for problem solving and a narrow meaning for decision making, these scholars assume the converse. Our justification is that with our outlook we can relate the narrow view of decision making to computers. That is, computers may make logical decisions on the basis of programmed instructions, criteria, and inputs; however, computers generally do not solve problems by developing alternative solutions for human decision making. Therefore, the narrow view of decision making ties into computer processing, while the narrow view of problem solving does not.

PROBLEMS, MANAGEMENT, AND SYSTEMS

Problems in the form of dissatisfactions abound in human society. As a result, man has created institutions that are devoted to solving certain classes of problems. One such institution is the business firm, whose functions are to solve the problems of providing services and of upgrading materials into products. Other problem-solving institutions are the municipal, state, or federal governments with varied functions of providing services and well-being. The military establishment, nonprofit philanthropic foundations, hospitals, and penal institutions are other examples. The common characteristic of these institutions is the organization of human beings into goal-seeking systems. In business organizations, the key people are the managers. Their primary responsibilities are to direct the solution of problems. Figure 10-1 relates the functions of managers to the inherent problem-solving, decision-making characteristics of business as a system.

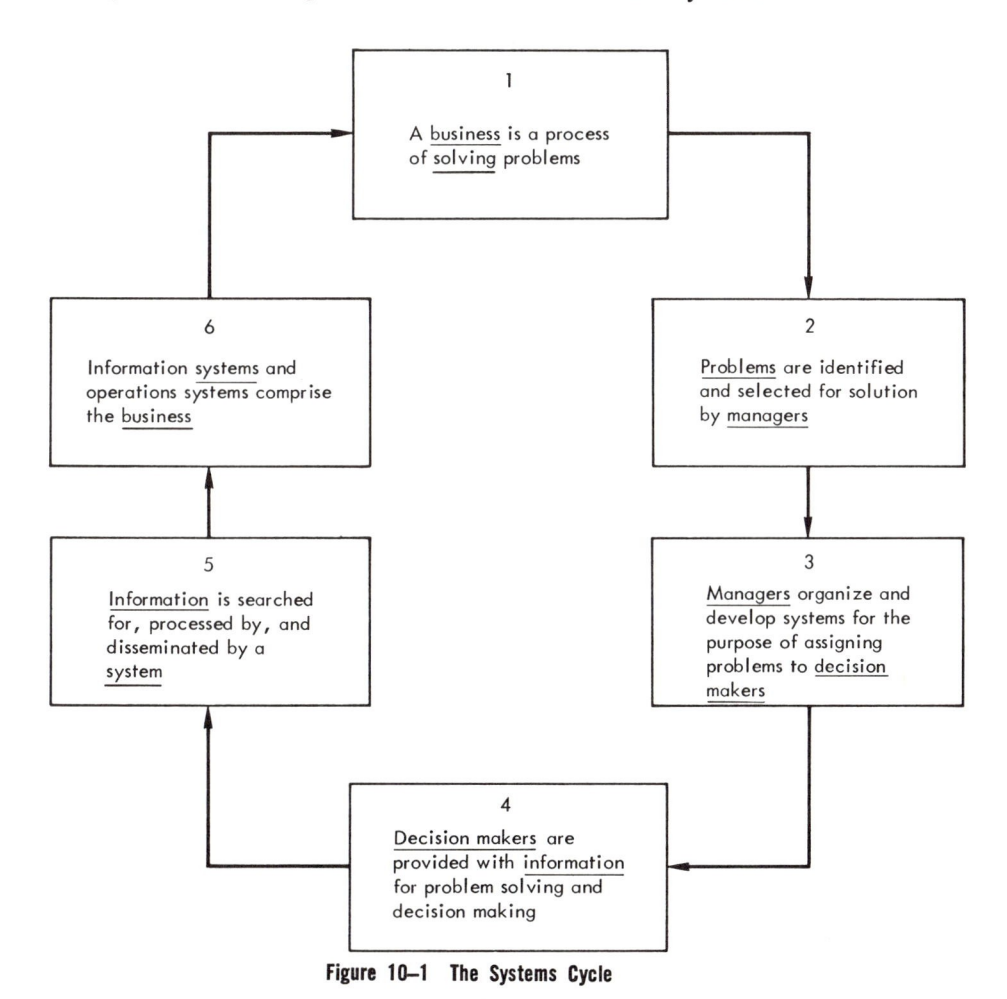

Figure 10-1 The Systems Cycle

1. A business is a process of solving problems
2. Problems are identified and selected for solution by managers
3. Managers organize and develop systems for the purpose of assigning problems to decision makers
4. Decision makers are provided with information for problem solving and decision making
5. Information is searched for, processed by, and disseminated by a system
6. Information systems and operations systems comprise the business

From Figure 10–1 we note first that a business comprises information and operating systems. These systems solve planning, implementation, and control problems directed toward achieving the goals of the business. That is, the purpose of a business (and hence of systems) is to solve problems (Block 1). The basic problems to be solved—such as establishing company goals, developing strategies for achieving them, and managing operations—are identified by managers. Obviously not every problem can be solved, because companies have limited resources, and therefore managers must establish priorities and select problems to be solved (Block 2).

Managers must then organize human effort into synergistic systems, which conduct further problem solving at the operational levels by people who will eventually terminate the problem-solving process by making decisions (Block 3). In order to solve problems and make decisions, however, such decision makers must be provided with information (Block 4). This information is provided by a portion of the MIS (Block 5). The MIS and the operations systems (concerned with implementation activities) together compose the business (Block 6) and hence function as problem solvers (Block 1), starting the recycling. The start of the cycle requires some knowledge of the nature of problems.

THE NATURE OF PROBLEMS

Although managers spend much of their time in solving problems, one of their most important and often overlooked responsibilities is recognizing that a problem exists or impends. Too often managers remain unaware of problems until a crisis is reached or affairs have gone beyond the point of no return. Perhaps they have been misled by the naive idea that a problem exists only when something "bites" them. The manager must look further and discover what will "bite" him if he does not start solving problems in advance. With this in mind, we can say that major symptoms of present or impending problems are:

1. Performance is *presently* not meeting present objectives.
2. It is *anticipated* that at some future time performance will not continue to achieve present objectives.
3. Objectives of the present *are going to be changed* and *present* operating procedures will not result in the achievement of the new, future objectives.

A problem is, therefore, a felt need, a deviation between *that which is* (or is anticipated) and *that which is desired,* or between *that which is known* and that which is *desired to be known.* It is an indeterminate situation in which doubt or uncertainty is felt, and a stimulus presses for a solution.

In business, or other innovative institutions, major problems appear in a four-stage cluster of problems. These broad problem types are:

1. The *problem of searching* for and identifying the primary problem to be solved. Consider, as an example, a company that produces fertilizers and chemicals. Symptoms of declining sales, declining prices, and stiff competition indicate fundamental problems are present. What are these problems? Is one of them an overproduction of phosphates? Have technical innovations made entry into the industry so easy that the industry is overcrowded? Have substitute chemical fertilizers been found? Is the company's marketing program at fault? Has world demand declined?

2. The problem of *diagnosing the situation to determine the primary problem* (or problems) in the presence of many symptoms of problems. For the fertilizer company, the diagnosis showed that the industry was overcrowded, production too high, and prices unrealistically low for the current world demand.

3. The *primary problem itself*. Solution of the primary problem requires the development of alternative courses of action and selection of the best course. One alternative might be to increase demand by arranging financing for countries that urgently need fertilizer but lack the foreign exchange to pay for it. The fertilizer company adopted another strategy, however: it diversified into other chemicals; it eliminated uneconomical and geographically undesirable facilities; and finally, it introduced greater efficiency into its remaining operations.

4. *Secondary problems* connected with the first three classes of problems. They may be problems of method or of a subsidiary nature. One of the problems arising from falling sales and profits might be an attempted take-over by another company. Another might be a shortage of working capital at some time.

The primary and secondary problems cited are *decision problems,* because the objective of finding feasible solutions is to select and implement one. In the case of the fertilizer company, we note that for the decision problems, there was a decision maker who had a problem, an outcome or goal of reversing the sales and profit trends, several alternative courses of action that might achieve the goal, uncertainty as to which course to follow, and a set of environmental conditions and constraints of time and resources. Criteria for a solution are also usually defined, although none were given in our case. Such a set of elements is usually present in all business decision problems.

FORMULATION OF THE PROBLEM

Although the formulation for definition of the problem is often considered a part of solving the problem, we will separate the two in order to develop greater precision. It has been said that a problem well define is a problem half-solved. So that we don't swallow old generalizations without suspicion, we might recall from algebra Fermat's last theorem, a well-defined problem that has resisted solution for several centuries. It is true in complex business situations, however, that verbalization, discussion, and reflection can do much to refine a problem, leading to its formulation and thereby ultimately contributing to its solution. It is also true that some problems are never solved because they are not formulated correctly. The right answer to the wrong problem may be more damaging than no solution at all.

Well-structured problems may be formulated quite precisely by means of mathematical models. The formulation, again, must be valid if the model describes the true problem. Formulation in this case requires that all variables, parameters, and constants be defined. (See Chapter 11, Management Science and Systems Modeling.) Complex problem situations in which the problems themselves are not readily identifiable nor describable are called ill-structured problems. Here, formulation plays a much larger part in the development of a solution.

In each of these two extreme cases, formulation requires a statement of the elements of the problem, the present state and the desired state, the constraints involved in solving the problem, and the criteria the solution must meet. The elements are the factors that are relevant to describing the various states and the relationships among the factors. Consider the fertilizer company again. We might list the elements of the problem, the states, constraints, and criteria as:

Elements
1. Company resources
2. Competition
3. Chemical makeup of fertilizer
4. Pricing activities in the market
5. Current demand and potential demand for fertilizer
6. Availability and cost of raw materials
7. Efficiency of production
8. Efficiency and effectiveness of the marketing program
   Etc.

Present State
1. Company has faced declining sales of 10 percent per year for three years
2. Profits have dropped 5 percent per year in the last two years
3. Production is conducted in widely scattered plants
4. Eight new companies have gone into production in the past two years
   Etc.

Desired State
1. A major role in the industry
2. Higher prices
3. Steadily increasing sales and profits
   Etc.

Constraints
1. No capital expansion funds available for one year
2. Diversification to be accomplished internally rather than through acquisition

3. New research authorizations not to exceed $100,000
   Etc.

Criteria for the solution
1. As a major factor, obtain at least 25 percent of the market
2. Price per unit of fertilizer to be at least $2.25
3. Sales to increase each year at a rate of at least 3 percent
4. Profits to increase each year at a rate of at least 5 percent
   Etc.

In practice, formulation of the problem facing the fertilizer company would be a lengthy one, partly verbalized and partly quantified. The greater the degree to which actual numbers may be attached to items describing the states, constraints, and criteria, the clearer the problem formulation.

There are four common, basic approaches for developing a good formulation of a problem:

1. Start with the general, vague statements characteristically employed to describe complex and amorphous situations. "The problem appears to be a marketing problem, somehow related to our production scheduling, our distribution system, and something that our competitors are either doing better or convincing the customers that they are. Of course, it may lie in our product. At any rate, sales have become more variable from month to month."

Ask questions about the meanings of statements, particularly about goals to be achieved. Redefine the problem over and over until it is clearly described by elements, present and desired states, constraints, and criteria for solution.

2. Start with the usual broad statement, then reformulate the problem very specifically as a narrow one, expand again to a broad problem, and thus oscillate in scope and specificity until we have zeroed in on the problem. Let us examine the hypothetical case of a company that has decided it will diversify, and its problem is, "Into what?" Analysis of its resources and of market opportunities suggests that the problem should be "How do we get into the food distribution business?" This is too broad a problem statement, since there are thousands of kinds of food businesses. The problem is reformulated, "How do we get into the franchised snack business?" This is too narrow for a company of our size, and we enlarge the scope of the problem. "Our problem is the determination of whether to become a franchiser or an operator of a chain of snack-type food outlets or of low-variety restaurants." Of course, the complete formulation of the problem should follow the pattern we have previously described.

3. Start with a problem symptom and define a very narrow, specific problem, then expand by steps to include all aspects of the total problem. A production manager notices that he is exceeding standard costs consistently on a certain type of product. He enlarges the scope of the problem as one of production control. This is expanded to include the training of operators

and quality control personnel as well. This problem is expanded further to a consideration of priority of orders and to improved recruiting, selection, and assignment procedures.

4. Start with objectives to be achieved, rather than with the symptoms of the problem. Redefine objectives until they are clearly expressed and quantified as much as possible. Then specify other parts of the problem that are related to the achieving of these objectives. With this method, the relevance of problem elements, current state of the situation, constraints, and criteria for the solution may be determined as each factor is analyzed.

In the fertilizer company, the goals may be set as part of long-range plans. Possible goals in terms of marketing objectives might be established for classes of products—agricultural, industrial, and consumer. Specific quantitative goals might then be developed for the agricultural line by first breaking it down into feed ingredients and pesticides, to meet identified needs for plant nutrition, plant health, animal health, and flavor enhancement. Similar development of industrial and consumer product lines could be established. Company resources, market position, future environmental conditions, and constraints would then be developed in terms of these goals.

This fourth method of problem formulation is used to develop plans that may solve anticipated problems by advance problem solving. Figure 10–2 shows the complete structure for the development of plans. We start by assuming that columns 1 and 2 are given and develop the 4th column, which lists goals, and the 5th column, criteria, to complete the formulation of the problem. The remaining 3rd column is concerned with solving the total problem.

Since problem formulation is crucial in systems design, many resources are usually devoted to it before the detailed design and implementation of systems. The further along the systems work has progressed, the more costly is the lack of a good definition of the problem. Management systems have probably been established that solve a nonrelevant problem because the real problem was not formulated initially.

THE PROBLEM-SOLVING PROCESS

Once a problem has been formulated, we proceed to solve it. We have all come across a wide range of problems that we found difficult to solve. Further, methods of solution seem to diverge widely. Contrast the solving of a plane geometry problem with the solving of some complex personal or business problem. In the first case, any approach that achieves the objective is satisfactory. In the second case, we may have to *decide* among several courses of action, none completely satisfactory, to reach only a partial solution.

The PLAN	WHY?	Take what ACTION with what RESOURCES?	To ACCOMPLISH what? when?	What CONDITIONS must be met?
STRATEGIC	Corporate Purposes	Corporate Strategy	Corporate Goals	Forecasts Policy Decision Guidelines
CORPORATE DEVELOPMENT				Forecasts Policy Schedules & Budgets
Divestment	Purposes	Projects	Goals	Goal Feasibility Criteria for Decision
Diversification				Forecasts Criteria for Decision
Acquisition and Merger				Availability of Candidates Criteria for Decision

Jurisdiction of Corporate Management

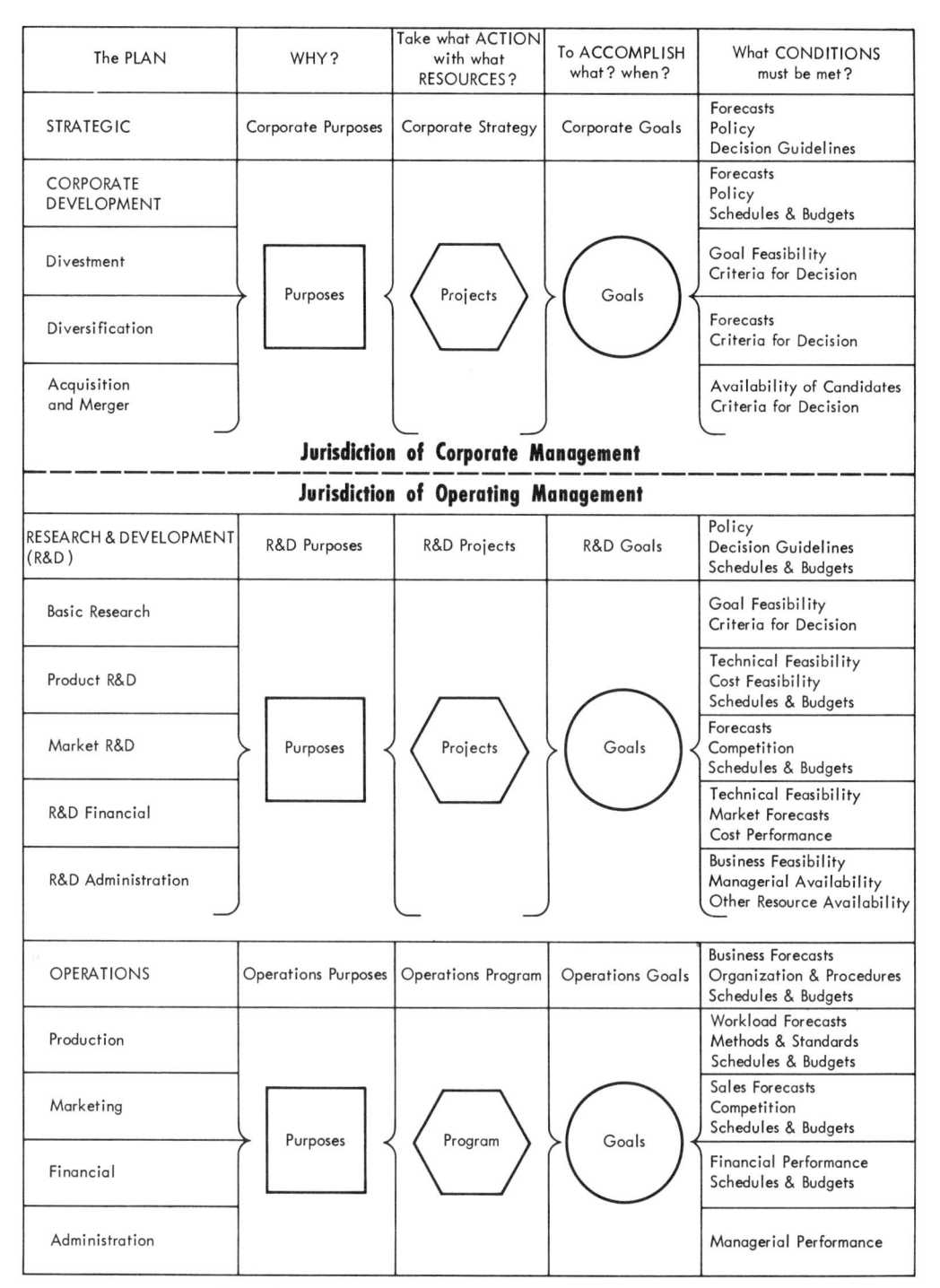

Jurisdiction of Operating Management

RESEARCH & DEVELOPMENT (R&D)	R&D Purposes	R&D Projects	R&D Goals	Policy Decision Guidelines Schedules & Budgets
Basic Research				Goal Feasibility Criteria for Decision
Product R&D	Purposes	Projects	Goals	Technical Feasibility Cost Feasibility Schedules & Budgets
Market R&D				Forecasts Competition Schedules & Budgets
R&D Financial				Technical Feasibility Market Forecasts Cost Performance
R&D Administration				Business Feasibility Managerial Availability Other Resource Availability
OPERATIONS	Operations Purposes	Operations Program	Operations Goals	Business Forecasts Organization & Procedures Schedules & Budgets
Production				Workload Forecasts Methods & Standards Schedules & Budgets
Marketing	Purposes	Program	Goals	Sales Forecasts Competition Schedules & Budgets
Financial				Financial Performance Schedules & Budgets
Administration				Managerial Performance

Figure 10–2 The Essential Elements of Each Plan

SOURCE Based on a table in Stanford Research Institute Report #162 (1963)

A Pragmatic Approach

The pragmatic approach to problem solving in business firms, which has proved effective throughout the years, is clarified by means of the model in Figure 10–3. The general approach is "handling" the problem to avoid the intellectual process of creating an original solution except as a last resort. This is because it is simply more economical to either bypass the problem, find someone who has solved similar problems (an expert), or find a published solution.

Let us follow through some of the principal steps in Figure 10–3. Obviously, if the problem is overlooked, it is not solved. This is not necessarily bad, since only a limited number of problems may be solved with the resources available. If it is a critical problem and is overlooked, of course disaster may result. MIS should be designed to provide information so that critical problems will be identified.

If the problem is obviously unsolvable, we try to avoid it. In a sense, this *is* a solution. We run around a barrier if we can't get over it. If we use cyclamates in our diet drink and the government orders us to stop production, the problem of maintaining production is unsolvable. We do not determine that we can get the government to change its mind, nor do we intend to bootleg the product. We avoid the problem by concocting a new beverage or substitute.

Block C indicates that a solution may be useless, i.e., too late, too costly, or perhaps illegal. Again we try to avoid the problem itself.

When we cannot avoid a problem that appears to have some sort of useful solution (Block D), we proceed to Block E, gather information. Information is gathered by asking other people—experts and operational people—consulting the literature, or passing the problem itself on to people who have the expertise (Block H). If the problem is completely novel, or no one else is available to work on it, or we ourselves are the experts, we attempt to solve it ourselves (Block K). From here on, if the problem is unsolvable we avoid it; if it is solvable, we use the solution and try to generalize it for future problems of a similar nature.

A Procedure for Solving Ill-structured Problems

Block K of Figure 10–3, Do It Yourself, leaves a lot to the imagination. We will try to fill out this block with a discussion of a method of solving ill-structured problems. The solution of well-structured problems is placed appropriately in Chapter 11.

Ill-structured problems in business are both common and difficult to attack. They are called ill-structured because the objectives to be achieved are not defined, the symptoms may lead to various formulations of what may be different control problems, the current situation is muddled and

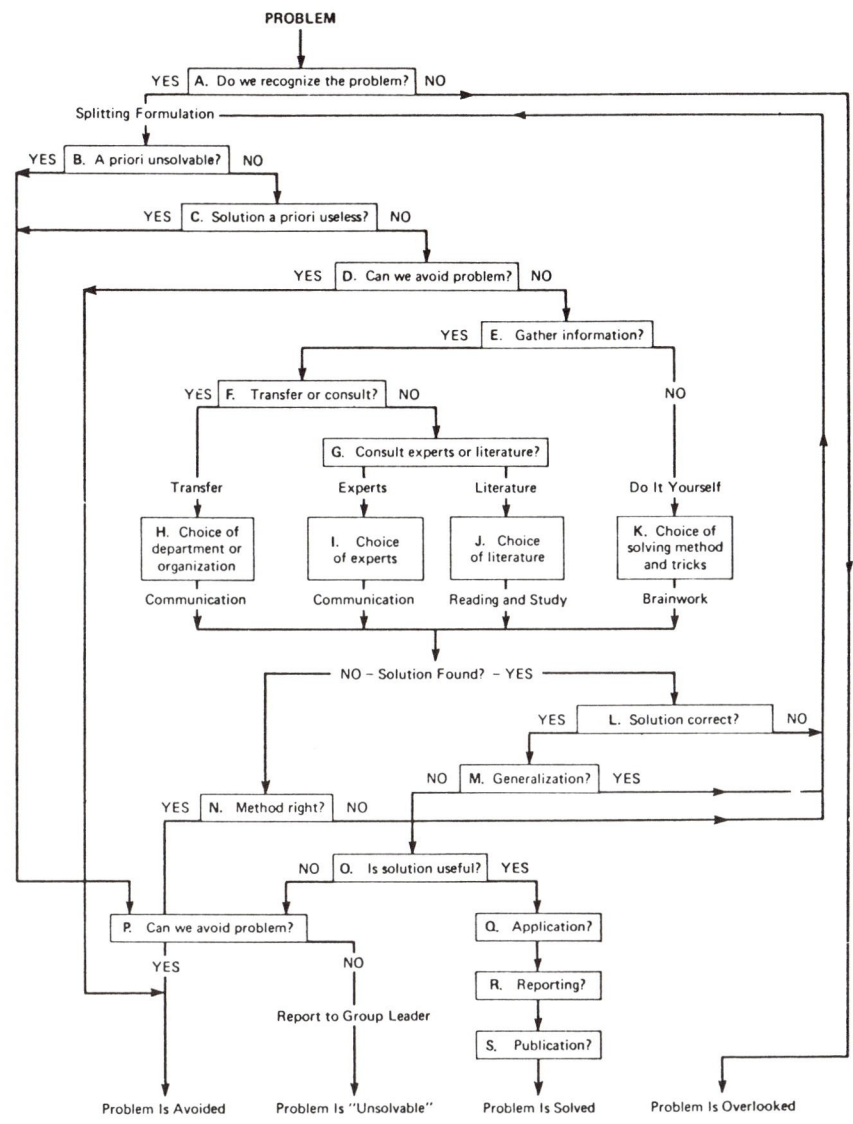

Figure 10–3 Problem-Solving Decisions in an Organization
SOURCE Dr. Ir. A. H. Boerdijk, "Step-by-Step Guide to Problem-Solving Decisions," reprinted from *Product Engineering*. Copyright 1963 by McGraw-Hill, Inc.

difficult to describe, and procedures for solving the problem are not self-evident.

In order to attack such problems, we must first study and analyze the system in which the problems exist. Next, we step outside the system to ask, "What are management's problems in making this system work?" And then we formulate the research whose outcome will provide the solutions to management's problems. This problem formulation we call Phase I. Phase

II is the attempt at solution. It requires searches for data, relationships, and alternative solutions. Let us detail these phases:

Phase I, The Formulation Process
A. Analyze the functions of the system, its components, its operation, and the information system that controls it. This step clarifies the structure in which the problem is imbedded.
  1. Identify and trace each channel of communication that links components (humans, machines, facilities) in the system.
  2. Identify each transformation of data in the system.
  3. Identify each operation performed in the system.
  4. Locate control (decision) points in the system. Generally, a control point is associated with either a manager or a checkpoint that controls on a routine basis (such as an individual operator or a machine).
  5. Drop from consideration each operation or transaction that has no effect on the objectives of the system.
  6. Group together the operations performed between every pair of control points.
  7. Prepare a flowchart showing:
      a. Control points and kind of decisions made at each control point.
      b. Information that flows between every connected pair of control points.
      c. Materials, if any, that flow between every connected pair of control points.
      d. Times required for flow of information and flow of materials in (b) and (c).
B. Formulate management's problems.
  1. Identify decision makers and the decision-making procedure.
  2. Determine the decision makers' relevant objectives.
  3. Identify other participants and the channels of their influence on a solution.
  4. Determine objectives of the other participants.
  5. Determine alternative courses of action available to decision makers.
  6. Determine counteractions available to other participants.
  7. Establish criteria for evaluation of solutions.
C. Formulate the research problems that are most likely to lead to a solution of management's problems.
  1. Edit and condense the relevant objectives.
  2. Edit and condense the relevant courses of action.
  3. Define the measure of effectiveness to be used.
      a. Define the measure of efficiency to be used relative to each objective.
      b. Weigh objectives (if qualitative) or units of objectives (if quantitative).
      c. Define the criterion of best decision as some function of the sum of the weighted efficiencies (e.g., maximum expected return, minimum expected loss).[1]

Phase II, The Search Process
The search process consists of uncovering data and transformations that bring the problem solver closer to his final goal. If the final goal is un-

problem solving and decision making 353

defined in the problem formulation, the search involves also the development of trial goals along with alternative chains of means–ends.

The construction of all possible alternative paths that link the present state of affairs with the desired state of affairs is usually impossible. Even if many alternatives could be constructed, evaluating all of them to find the best is too difficult. Therefore, general, heuristic rules, either objectively framed or so complex that they are internalized in his mind, guide the problem solver in a sequential series of steps or among major strategies. The following steps can only crudely represent this search process.

A. Gather data that seem relevant to the specific research problem to be solved. Find conditions imposed on the problem. Look for trends in data.
B. Classify the data. Draw charts, diagrams, and tables if they will help to organize the data. Look for conflicting data.
C. Devise a plan of attack.
   1. Hypothesize complete broad solutions to be detailed subsequently.
   2. Devise an incremental approach whereby a small part of the problem is solved first, the remainder is studied, and another small part is solved. This way we arrive at a solution by a step-by-step or means–end approach.
   3. Design research to answer specific questions that, when answered, will make a set of solutions evident to the decision maker.
D. Carry out the plan of attack by employing reflective processes and systematic questioning.
   1. Find relationships among the variables of the problem.
   2. Draw upon experience and creative reflection to develop hypotheses (trial solutions) to be tested.
   3. Search for analogies, differences, inversions, substitutions, and similar past problems that may produce hypotheses for solutions.
   4. Start with the desired state of affairs and work backward to determine what is required to achieve the goals.
   5. Develop tests, if possible, to check out parts of the tentative solution or the entire solution. At this stage, models or simulation may be helpful.
   6. Evaluate test results and iterate the first five steps to the extent that modification is indicated.
   7. Evaluate the alternative solutions in terms of criteria established in the formulation of the management problem.

Organizational and Individual Problem Solving

Observation of problem solving in large institutions such as business corporations reveals that there is a spectrum of problem situations and problem solving. At one end of the spectrum is the individual who solves a problem completely independently and implements the solution. At the other end is the solving of the organizational problem of viability, to which everyone contributes on a continuous basis. It is very probable that the janitor solves more problems independently than does the president of a large corporation. The president deals with problems of such breadth that he must seek guidance, counsel, and evaluation at every step of the problem-solving process. Although he may make some lonely major decisions, the development of alternatives that offer him a decision situation is a shared process.

Organizational problem solving is affected by conflicting values and interests of organizational members. Conflict and compromise are mixed with rationality. A comparison of individual and organizational problem-solving activities in greatly abbreviated form is shown in Table 10–1.

Table 10–1

Problem Solving: Individuals and Groups

	Individuals	Groups
Goal setting	A. Task demands	A. Task demands
	B. Personality	B. Group vs. individual conflicts
	C. Establish operational hypothesis	C. Establish operational plan to problem
Search	A. Invoke basic strategy	A. Development—seek discussions
	B. Recall and manipulate information	B. Summarizing—seek discussions
	C. Consider information in light of the hypothesis	C. Consider supporting and opposing discussions
Hypothesis testing (proposed solution)	A. Suggest solution as "correct"	A. Agree to solutions as "correct"
	B. If no solution, use feedback to develop another hypothesis	B. If not, try different planning of problem on feedback basis
	C. Repeat, if necessary	C. Repeat, if necessary
	D. If (A) is correct, problem solved	D. If (A) is correct, problem solved

SOURCE: Marcus Alexis and Charles Z. Wilson, *Organizational Decision Making* (Englewood Cliffs, N.J.: Prentice-Hall, Inc., 1967), p. 75.

The institutionalization of problem solving is becoming more firmly established by the development of management systems and management information systems. For the Type I problem-solving process (see Figure 7–5), computerized systems are rapidly taking over. For the more ill-structured problems, man–machine systems are being developed in which information and the computer are featured. The core topic of this book is the development and implementation of such computerized management information and problem-solving systems.

DECISION MAKING AND MIS

"You don't know how you do it; you just do it."

"I don't think businessmen know how they make decisions. I know *I* don't."

"It's like asking a pro baseball player to define the swing that has always come natural to him."

These candid remarks about their inability to analyze the process of decision making are typical of those of some of America's most successful corporate chief executives, as reported by *Fortune* magazine. The business executive is by profession a decision maker; yet the *process* of how he arrives at a decision is not well understood.

Despite the fact that decision making can be treated as a central aspect of managing, the literature and teaching surrounding decision making have generally focused on the *moment* of decision rather than on the whole lengthy, complex process of defining and exploring the many alternatives in a decision that precedes the final act of deciding. For the systems analyst and for the manager who participates in or utilizes the management information system to assist in the decision-making *process,* the steps in problem solving and systems design are extremely important. Peter Drucker's comment that "over the next 20 years the emphasis in management will be on the understanding of decision making" reflects a growing need to formalize the process as a fundamental and necessary part of management and of information systems design. And because information is the essential ingredient of management and decision making, the aspect of the organization described by the information flow process is a growing concern. The ultimate purpose of the MIS is to make decisions at all levels of operations based upon the information flow.

Although decision making and problem solving are very closely related, they are not identical. Decisions are intertwined with problem solving, because in the process of solving problems, decisions must be made regarding data to be used, assumptions, constraints, and boundaries for the problem. In addition, decisions must be made with respect to procedural methods to be used, intermediate sequential goals to be sought, criteria for evaluation of alternatives, and termination of the search process at all phases of the problem-solving process.

A decision is the termination of questioning; a problem is the beginning of questioning. A decision is a commitment to action; problem solving is a search for the answer to a question. Decision making implements the resolution of a problem. For the management information systems designer, these distinctions are extremely important. The MIS designer must start with determining *what problems are to be solved* so that he can then determine what decisions must be made, when they must be made, and who (or what) is to make them.

356 Information, Decision Making, and Management Science

Within the MIS, who is it that makes decisions? Obviously the managers make the major decisions that guide the operations and strategy of the firm. But there are others within the information system who continually make decisions on lesser problems. Do managers act as individuals to make decisions? Much confusion arises because of the implied assumption that they do. Even the most authoritarian manager today cannot continue for long to make decisions without regard to organizational influences. The more significant the problem under consideration, the more diffused the decision process is likely to be. Management consultations, committees, plans developed through the contributions of many people, and covert sabotage of unacceptable decisions all influence top-level decision making. The more trivial or routine the problem, the more likely it is that only one individual makes a decision, and vice versa.

Programmed and Nonprogrammed Decisions

It is very important to distinguish between two types of decisions representing the extremities of the range of decisions: *programmed* and *nonprogrammed decisions*. These labels are derived from the jargon of the computer field, where a program is defined as a plan for the automatic solution of a problem. Programs are simply a string of instructions to accomplish an assignment. Since few problems lend themselves totally to automatic solutions, we have few totally programmed decisions. We do have many cases of problem solving that combine varying mixtures of combined programmed and nonprogrammed problem solving. The concept of programmed decisions is important because *the ultimate* (and unachievable) *goal of information systems is to provide purely programmed decisions*. Because this is not possible, wee seek to provide the optimum type of information to the human decision maker, who then makes nonprogrammable decisions.

Decisions lend themselves to programming techniques if they are repetitive and routine and if a procedure can be worked out for handling them so that each is neither an *ad hoc* decision nor one to be treated as a new situation each time it arises. Numerous examples of programmed decisions are available in almost any organization, the most familiar being the computation of pay in accordance with a union agreement, contract, company policy, or regulation. Hence the *program* or *decision rule* is contained in the agreement, contract, policy, or regulation. Other examples are pricing orders, credit checks, payment of accounts receivable, and the dozens of decisions made daily in accordance with company policy (decision rule).

Decisions are nonprogrammed to the extent that they are unstructured, new, of high consequence, elusive, or complex, or involve major commitments. Advertising budgets, new-product decisions, acquisition and merger considerations, board-member selection, and similar problems illustrate the nonprogrammed type of decision that cannot be automated.

problem solving and decision making

Can we not say that the hypothetically ideal situation in an organization would be to have all decisions programmed? Without a decision rule to cover a situation, the manager must fall back upon the general problem-solving methodology, which depends so much on human judgment. The cost of solving the organization's problems in this manner is usually high, and solutions may sometimes be unsatisfactory. One of the goals then of MIS design is to devise decision rules for the problems that lend themselves to solution by decision rule and the programmed approach.

The major reason for distinguishing between these two types of decisions is to arrive at some classification of decision-making methods in order to improve decision making. This is done in Figure 10–4, which classifies two types of decisions, programmed and nonprogrammed, and two general approaches, old and new, to the techniques involved.

TYPE OF DECISION	METHODS OF DECISION MAKING	
	OLD	NEW
PROGRAMMED Repetitive and Routine	Habit Standard Operating Procedure Organization Structure Policy etc...	Management Information Systems (Includes Management Science Techniques and the Computer)
NONPROGRAMMED One-shot. Ill-structured	Judgment, Intuition, Insight, Experience Training and Learning	Decision Theory ? ?

Figure 10–4 Methods of Decision Making

Making Nonprogrammed Decisions

It is apparent that we do not have a complete theory of decision making. Equally clear is the lack of understanding among practicing executives and academicians on just how decisions are made in organizations. When asked to explain the decision-making process in business organizations, we usually say that executives exercise "judgment" and that this judgment is largely a function of experience, intuition, and insight.

Managers seem to make better decisions when exposed to training in an orderly thinking process. For example, military officers attend war colleges to learn the military problem-solving and planning steps: (1) determination of the mission; (2) description of the situation and courses of action; (3) analysis of opposing courses of action; (4) comparison of own courses of action; and (5) the decision. The Harvard Graduate School of Business exposes the would-be executive to hundreds of case situations, presumably with the expectation that by solving many problems, the student will become proficient at the process. Over the years, the manager has been

358 Information, Decision Making, and Management Science

urged to learn, practice, and acquire the habit of making decisions based on the problem-solving process: (1) define the problem; (2) identify the alternatives; (3) choose the best alternative. This process, defined by Dewey decades ago, is largely intact today and is still good advice for solving the unstructured, nonprogrammed problem.

There is some evidence that problem solving can be learned. At least we recognize and reward those who have had some success at it. Selection processes for managerial advancement are largely devoted to identifying past success at decision making and attempting to predict future success. We also tacitly admit that experience improves problem solving by our practice of exposing managers to increasingly varied and difficult decision-making situations as they advance in a career.

Despite the abundance of research and literature on the topic, we still do not completely understand the decision-making process nor have we devised new or different methods that have significantly improved the process. It appears, in short, that the new and emerging "decision theory," which may provide a breakthrough in the understanding of the process and in improving actual decision making, is still emerging. The answer appears to lie partly in a process whereby more and more decisions can be programmed because of better-structured approaches available for programmed decision making—*management information systems*.

Making Programmed Decisions

By far the greatest number of business decisions are repetitive and routine. One survey found that about 90 percent of management decisions are routine ones. If this is true, then there is an overriding need to automate or *program* these decisions so that the executive can get on about his true task, the design and plans for improved organizations and operations. If the manager's job is primarily that of decision making, he should get away from short-term tactics and routine, place these types of decisions in the programmed category, and have them made by one or more techniques of programmed decisions. To draw an analogy, there is no reason why we should not standardize information for mass production of programmed decisions in much the same way we standardize materials for production of products.

Some of the traditional ways of making programmed decisions are shown in Figure 10–5. The most general and most pervasive way is by force of habit. We go to the office, make decisions regarding the disposition of the in-basket correspondence, and take dozens of actions daily that are "programmed" through force of habit. These habits and skills are valuable to the organization; one of the major costs in personnel turnover is involved in having new people acquire the habits of the organization and the job.

problem solving and decision making 359

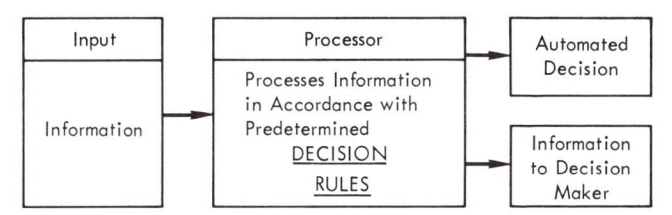

Figure 10–5 Making Programmed Decisions with a Management Information System

Following habit, the most prevalent technique for programming decisions is with the company procedure—written, oral, or understood. Standard operating procedures provide a means for indoctrinating and training new personnel and for guiding experienced personnel in the performance of specific tasks. The procedure has the additional advantage of forcing a certain amount of detailed planning, because it cannot be adequately designed, reviewed, or implemented without careful thought. In a strict sense, policy cannot be classified as a programming technique; by definition it provides only a general guide to action. However, the decision-making process in the organization is vastly improved by the establishment and communication of clearly understood policies.

MIS as a Technique for Making Programmed Decisions

Future prospects for programming the decisions of the organization through the proper design of an MIS are enormous. If we include the *computer* and *management science* as integral parts or tools of computer-based information systems, the prospects for a revolution in programmed decision making are very real. Just as the manufacturing process is becoming more and more automated, so is the automation of programmed decisions increasing to support this production and other information needs throughout the organization.

How will this revolution come about? What is there about management information systems that will program so many of our routine decisions? The answer lies in three basic considerations surrounding the design of an MIS:

1. The problem to be solved, the decision process to be programmed, or the process for which information is desired. The essential element in programming a decision is the *decision rule* (e.g., reorder if inventory declines below x level).
2. Management science. We define this broadly to include operations research, associated mathematical tools, and the scientific approach to problem solving. Management science, thus defined, gives us the methods and techniques to design the *decision rules*.
3. The computer. This is a fantastic device for processing information and "making" programmed decisions in accordance with predetermined decision rules.

360 Information, Decision Making, and Management Science

Schematically, the management information system will operate as shown in Figure 10–5. The importance of this concept of making programmed decisions by management information system cannot be overestimated. It is at the heart of good systems design.

THE DECISION PROCESS

The detailed decision process is a function of information and behavioral and environmental factors that shape the process. An exhaustive presentation of the processes of decision making would require separate treatment for decisions made by (1) an individual, (2) a small group, and (3) large, complex organizations. A description of the process of decision making in a large organization might astound the young, inexperienced student, because of the large number of people who may be involved. Let us consider a company that wishes to buy jet engines for an advanced airplane it is developing. It must choose among a number of proposals put forth by outside companies. The decision to select a certain proposal may depend upon engineering approval, legal approval, accounting evaluation, manufacturing evaluation, top management approval, and even governmental approval, if it is a defense contract. Conceivably, more than 100 people could contribute to and influence the decision.

In this chapter we cover primarily the general aspects of decision making, which describe the process for the individual. Group interaction, bargaining, compromise, conflict, and other forms of negotiation are beyond the scope of this book, except as covered in Chapter 3 and 7.

Decision Making and Information

We have previously defined an MIS as a processor of information (input) to yield decisions (output). The quality, quantity, rate of flow, and timing of information supplied by the MIS to the decision makers are critical to effective operation of the company. The function of the system must be to seek out, evaluate, select, and manipulate information and disseminate it to decision makers within the organization.

The *quality* of information was discussed in Chapter 9. With regard to the *quantity* of information supplied to decision makers, the inexperienced person may believe that the more information disseminated, the better the decision that results. But there are several points that contradict this view. Decisions in practical affairs face deadlines, and the cost of additional information to be supplied in a short time rises rapidly. Also, the quantity of information that humans can handle per unit of time is limited; although humans may be able to detect and transmit to the brain millions of bits per second of sensory information, they can handle only a small fraction of them in the form of concepts or signs.[2] Therefore, it is possible to overload the decision maker with too much information and consequently obtain poorer decisions than with little information.

The systems designer must be concerned with the *timing* of information as well as the *rate*. If the information is transmitted too soon, the decision maker may forget it. Also, information that is sent too early may become obsolete, so that the decision maker either employs out-of-date information or is interrupted again for a new transmission. On the other hand, information that is transmitted at a time beyond the decision deadline is useless. There is a natural tendency for people in an organization to fear sending incomplete or inaccurate information to decision makers; so high is the aversion to such risk that suppliers of information often take time to check and recheck. There must instead be a mutual understanding between the information collector and the decision maker on the degree of risk of faulty information. Unverified information received on time is better than volumes of perfect information received too late to be used.

Very often, better information may be obtained within a given time span if we are willing to pay the price. The cost of additional information in terms of dollars, time, and risk/size of outcome of the decision should be estimated before purchasing it. We must remember one of the basic rules of information management: information is the measure of the value (worth) of a message to a decision maker in a specific situation.

The reception of information is affected to a great degree by the perception or "filtering" process of the receiver and the format of the presentation. The systems designer and the manager–user must therefore consider carefully the format of information presentation to reduce distortion. For example, visual media such as charts may be effective in communicating to marketing executives, whereas tables and schedules may be more meaningful to accounting and financial personnel. Flowcharts and raw computer output may be most appropriate for computer and management scientists in the organization, while verbal communication may be most effective among operative workers and their first-line supervisors.

Factors That Shape the Decision Process

Managers often say, "Get me the facts and then I'll make the decision." This implies that once the facts are available, they will be able to make well-reasoned, objective decisions. In reality, decisions by managers are influenced by a wide variety of factors, most of which they are not even aware of. These may be classified as:

1. Rational factors
2. Psychological characteristics of the decision maker
3. Social influences
4. Cultural influences

These factors provide constraints in the design of **MIS**.

Rational Factors

Rational factors are those that the manager consciously employs to arrive at a decision—such as cost, time, management principles, and forecasts. To him, they are *measurable* things.

Systems designers tend to focus on the rational aspects of decision making, with the result that the system cannot be implemented. Rational choice implies complete information, the establishment of objective goals, the development of objective standards and measures, the availability of all feasible alternatives, and the means for selecting the optimum alternatives. In practice, of course, we have only incomplete information for complex problems. Though objective standards and measures in the form of dollars, share of the market, turnover rate, or number of units per month are often available, there are usually many other criteria that cannot be measured. Goodwill, employee morale, air pollution, quality of management, or company image are examples of factors that may affect decisions and are difficult to define, let alone measure.

Humans engaged in solving complex problems are able to consider only a limited number of alternatives within the restraints imposed by time. They search among the limited number to find one or a few that appear to meet at least minimum requirements. Considerable effort may then be expended in selecting from among these few. Generally, it may be said that if an optimum solution may be found in a real-world situation, the problem may be solved by a machine or computer, because it is of such limited scope that logic, objective criteria, and measurement are sufficient to reach a decision.

Psychological Factors

Rational factors represent common methods and criteria for decision making, but psychological factors are not interpersonal. Psychological factors are what the individual brings to the decision process; they involve his personality, capabilities, experience, perceptions, his values and aspirations, and his perceived role. There is, of course, considerable overlap among psychological, social, and cultural influences, since it is a rare individual who stands apart from his society and culture in terms of his behavior processes.

Attempts to develop a theory of decision making based on psychological factors have been based largely on the "utility" curve of the individual. The utility function represents the values, aspirations, and risk aversion of the individual, perhaps to the greatest degree. The development of utility functions depends upon stated preferences of the individual and certain assumptions regarding the ordering of preferences. Unfortunately, either humans cannot discriminate well enough or they change their minds, so that ordering rules run into difficulty.[3]

A general description of psychological criteria for decision making is given by Herbert Simon. The decision maker does not try to maximize his satisfactions but settles for satisfactory solutions that "suffice." Finding solutions that both satisfy and suffice is therefore called "satisficing" by Simon. This means that the manager searches for the optimal alternative but discontinues his search and evaluation when a reasonable choice is found.[4]

What is satisfactory depends on the decision maker's level of aspiration, and according to numerous studies, the aspiration level depends on past experience. If the decision maker has achieved his goals in the recent past, his level of aspiration will rise. If he has not fully achieved past goals, he lowers his level of aspiration.

Social Factors

Decisions in an organization must be made with due regard to acceptance by members of the organization, otherwise implementation will suffer. The decision maker must therefore consider not only his own values, but the values and goals of the individuals affected. Thus, "participative" decision making is often employed to reach a decision that will be accepted by the group, or in the case of manager–subordinate situations, by the subordinate.[5]

Decisions involving great or sudden change in organizational structure are usually avoided by experienced managers unless it is obvious that everyone in the organization benefits immediately. Instead, decisions are limited to incremental changes over a period of time so as to reduce resistance to what is really a major decision. The use of committees often helps to diffuse responsibility for decisions among organizational members so that acceptance is achieved more readily.

Cultural Factors

Cultural factors are learned behavior patterns. For business organizations in the United States, three cultural influences predominate. These are the culture of the particular firm, the culture of the geographical region where the firm is located, and the culture of the American people.

Let us give an example of a cultural influence from each of these classes. The learned behavior in an R&D-oriented firm is one of innovation, aggressive change, and search for new ideas, whereas in the United States shipbuilding industry, there is resistance to technological changes and a desire to retain old ways. Regional cultural differences are most evident to those who have worked in the frenetic, competitive pace of New York City and then in firms in the South where activity is more moderate.

National cultural differences are great. In the United States, the workday differs from that of many countries; some countries have a long siesta period and the workday ends later. In the United States, there is a greater opportunity for young men to exercise a voice in corporate affairs, whereas in many countries, firms are dominated by single families and elderly leaders. In United States firms, continuing education is a strong cultural characteristic rarely found in other countries. Many other differences could be listed that distinguish the culture of United States firms from those in other particular countries.

Besides the more obvious cultural differences in firms in different countries, there are some that most of us are not aware of. These are internalized and rarely verbalized differences in values and thought processes. For example, we behave as if youth were the most valuable attribute of people, whereas in some countries the elders are held in high esteem. We believe that Americans have the best management, the most advanced technology, and the greatest "know-how," and this unspoken assumption is often reflected in our dealings with businessmen from other countries and in our decisions. We believe our system of ethics is superior to that of others, and yet we often engage in business practices abroad that we would not condone in the United States. Our decisions are influenced by the reasoning processes we have learned in our schools. Without realizing it, our approach to problem solving and decision making is quite different from that of people in other cultures.

Management and the Decision Process

We would like now to tie information and decision factors into management from a systems view. Figure 10–6 does this by picturing management

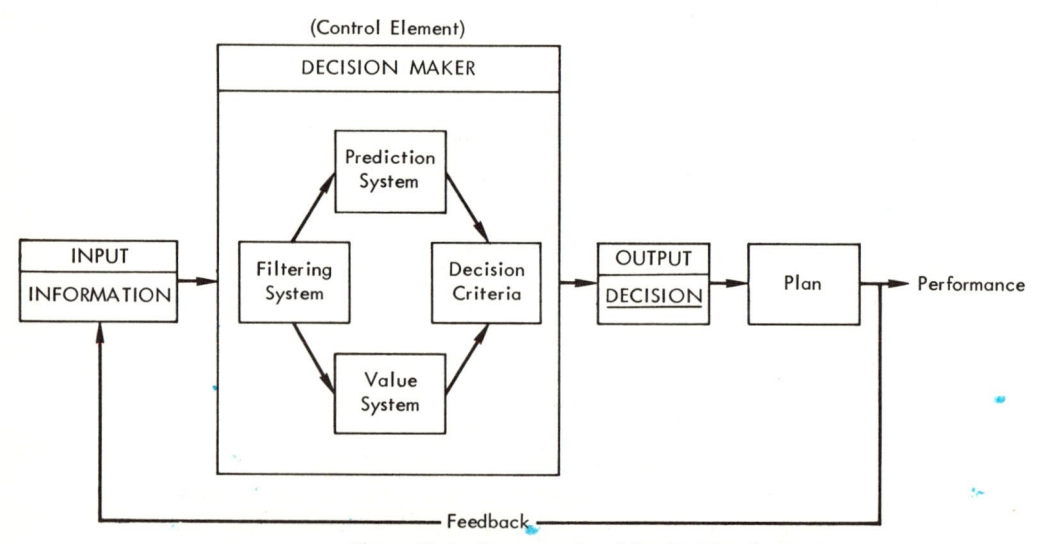

Figure 10–6 Management and the Decision System

and the management system as an information processor for planning and controlling to achieve objectives. Management is represented as the decision maker in this figure.

ANATOMY OF CHOOSING

To a great extent, the process of actually making the choice is hidden in a "black box," the Decision Maker block in Figure 10-6. Whereas psychologists attempt to explore the psychological process, management scientists attempt to develop normative methods. The systems designer must, to a great extent, use as a basis the more objective, rational approaches to decision making in MIS design. We start, then, by describing the rational decision process.

First, we note that information about the real world is the starting point, as shown in Figure 10-6. So either the MIS system must supply information or the manager must search for and recall it. The information is then filtered by the manager to select what he believes is most useful to him in the solution of his problem. This filtering is the selection of the key variables to be used in a model of the problem.

The model of the problem provides the predictive system. The decision maker can vary the inputs to the model so that the model can predict the alternative outcomes. Decision criteria must be established to provide objective evaluation of the alternative input-outputs. Let us now examine the process of choice in a more specific and rigorous fashion.

The elements of the process are:

1. Objectives of the decision maker
2. Decision criteria and decision rules
3. Possible states of nature (A state of nature is simply the real-world situation. Often our focus is on a single key variable whose value is said to represent a "state" or condition.)
4. Outcomes of research, each of which predicts the likelihood of various states of nature occurring
5. Alternative actions that may be taken

The relationships among these elements are indicated approximately by Figure 10-7. We note that at the top of the diagram we must formulate objectives, establish criteria that our choice must satisfy, and establish decision rules for making the choice once we have the information that predicts alternative outcomes. Outcomes of research, such as market research, indicate the probable states of nature. The reliability of such indicators depends upon a combination of the future we assume and random events in the world in which we operate. Outcomes are sometimes called premises, which state, "If we do this, then that will happen," or, "If this event in the environment occurs, then such-and-such a condition of the environment will

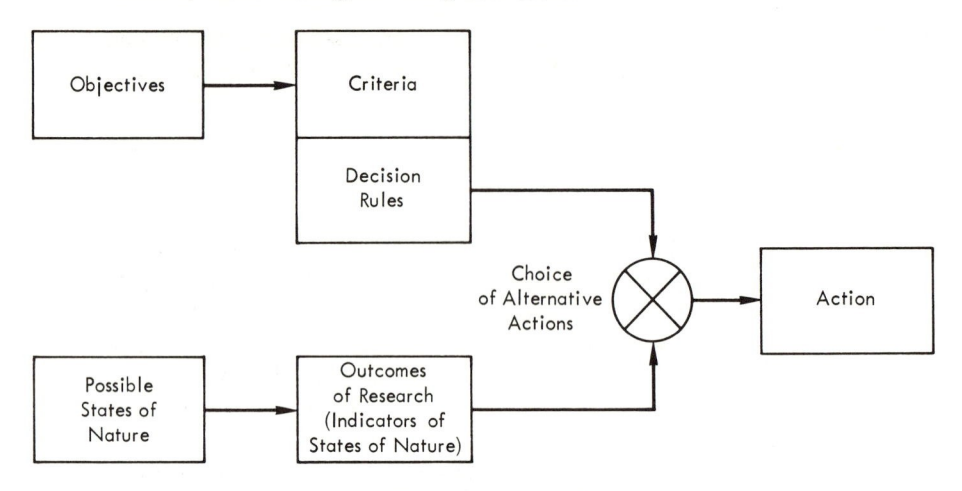

Figure 10-7 Anatomy of the Decision Process

result." Outcomes of research constitute the information that, when processed through the decision rules and criteria, leads to a choice.

A simplified concrete application of the decision-making model of Figure 10-7 is as follows. Suppose that the objective of a company is to introduce a new product, and several products are then developed. Only one may be brought out in the current year because of limited company resources. The company establishes certain criteria for inclusion in its decision rule. These might be the requirements that profit exceed 20 percent of sales, that return on investment before taxes exceed 30 percent, that present excess manufacturing capacity be utilized, and that the product fit into the current channels of distribution.

Possible states of nature might consist of a large sales potential, a medium sales potential, or little sales potential. Market research provides indications of the market potential for each product. The reliability of such indicators depends, of course, on the extent (and hence costs) of the research.

Alternative actions consist of marketing alternative products on a local and expanding basis, a regional basis, or an immediate national basis. The entire process derived from Figure 10-7 is shown in Figure 10-8.

Simplifying the Choice Process for Complex Decision Problems

The complexity of our environment is such that the abstractions of management science models remove too much of reality. The decision maker must find some way of selecting important elements and evaluating them to reach a decision. Some of the ways in which complexity is handled are suggested by William T. Morris:[6]

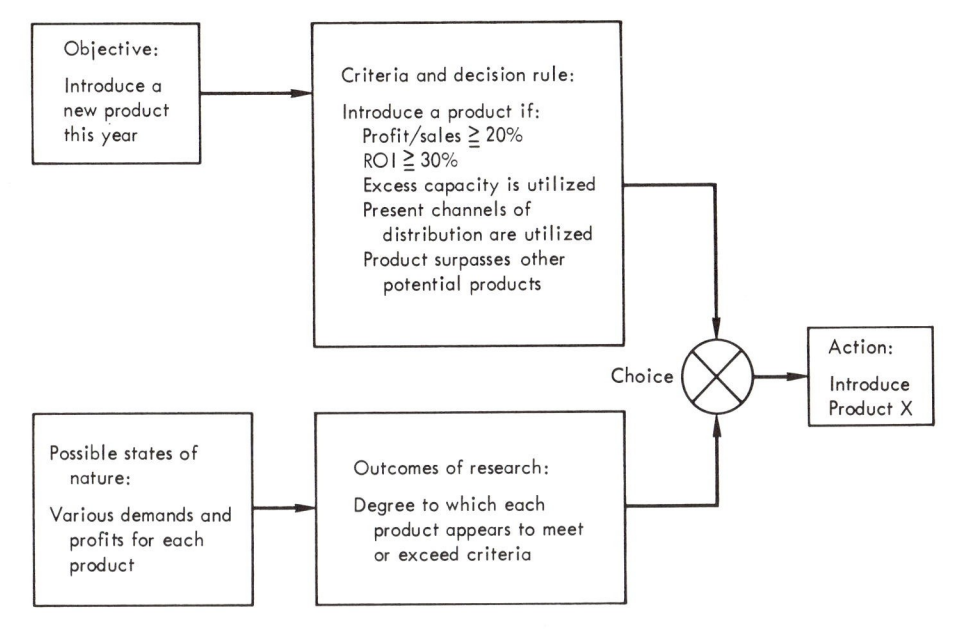

Figure 10–8 Example of a Decision

1. Rules of thumb based on past experience are employed to narrow the search for alternatives. Examples: Three-year payback for capital investment. Hire only experienced salesmen. Keep thirty days of inventory on hand. Allow an annual increase in payroll of only 6 percent.

Often these rules are poor guides to choice, and their only merit is that they lead to a choice in a short time.

2. Categorization of guidelines provides general guidance and rules. Company operating and policy guides, standard operating instructions, procedure manuals, and administrative memos and circulars circumscribe behavior to limit choice to a great degree.

3. Suppression of intangible values such as employee morale, customer goodwill, ethical considerations, public welfare, and industry relationships simplifies the choice process greatly. The focus is on economic units, profits, costs, number of employees, and efficiency.

4. Adoption of a short-range view is common. It is much easier to make a choice if the ramifications of the art beyond today, next week, next year, or the next five years are not taken into consideration.

5. Suppression of risk or a rough estimation of the total risk has sufficed in the past. Deterministic estimates of sales, costs, and new-product profits are still common. Management science and the computer have steadily introduced more and more subjective risk estimates into the choice process in recent years.

6. Quasi resolution of conflict has simplified organizational decision making. Goals of different departments are treated as independent constraints. Problems are broken into parts and treated separately. Different goals and aspirations of individuals are treated at different times in order to reduce conflict. Compromises and "satisficing" are employed to find mutually agreeable decisions.

7. An indifference approach is taken to making small decisions. Where two choices are apparent and the import of the action is obviously not significant, a snap judgment is made to eliminate the time-consuming effort of evaluating all the tangible and intangible aspects of each choice.

8. "Muddling through" is a common approach to complex situations in which the organizational decision makers face a very complex problem with greatly significant consequences attached to the total series of acts required to resolve the problem. They make an initial decision on a first act and observe the consequences. Sequential decisions are made on a similar trial-and-error basis so that considerable maneuverability is maintained at all times. This approach is precisely the opposite of making a clear-cut decision on long-range objectives and plans.

SUMMARY

Problem solving is finding the answer to a question. Business organizations must develop information systems to supply the information that managers require to solve complex, ill-structured problems. Alternative solutions to a problem should be developed, so that managers may make a decision based on knowledge of the implications of various courses of action.

The symptom of a problem is observed when performance is not meeting, or will not in the future meet, present or future plans. The resultant problem cluster may then be identified as (1) the problem of searching, (2) the problem of diagnosing, (3) the primary problem, and (4) secondary problems. The formulation of these problems is critical because improper definition may prevent the real problems from being solved.

An approach to "handling" problems in a practical way has been given, as well as an amplification of the problem-solving process employing a systems approach. The relationship of problem solutions to management decision making and the place of technical decisions in the problem-solving process has been discussed.

Parallel to the concept of the extremes of ill-structured and well-structured problems are the important concepts of nonprogrammed and programmed decisions. Although the MIS assists managers in solving problems and making nonprogrammed decisions, the MIS also makes programmed decisions for repetitive problems. This is accomplished by application of the computer to logic systems. Chapter 11 discusses the role of management science in developing logic systems and decision rules.

In nonprogrammed decision making, the MIS, the computer, and management science play a supportive role. High-level decisions tend to be the result of many contributions. Rational, psychological, social, and cultural factors all influence the ultimate choice among alternatives.

In the final analysis, the entire problem-solving decision process depends upon the flow and processing of information in a system. This system, the MIS, is the nervous and cognitive system of the organization.

DISCUSSION QUESTIONS AND PROBLEMS

1. Select a company from *Fortune* magazine's top 500. By studying its annual reports, speeches of its officers (usually available from its public relations department), and actions as reported in the newspapers and trade journals, write a description of the goals and objectives of the company. Compare what it says with what it does.

2. Select a small local firm whose owner or manager will grant you an interview. Ask him what goods he has in mind for his company for this year and for five years ahead. Ask him what he considers to be his major problems. Do you believe he has problems that he does not recognize?

3. Identify a problem of your own or of some company with which you are very familiar. List the elements of the problem. Describe the present state of the situation, and the desired state. List the constraints. Develop criteria for solutions. Suggest several possible solutions.

4. The text indicates that executives do not know how they make decisions. Suppose that a decision is made by considering a known number of factors. Can you hypothesize how marginal changes in the values of these factors change the decision? (A simple example is a purchase of a needed item in which price is the sole factor.) Do you believe it is possible to structure all decision problems? Why, or why not?

5. Outspoken executives have admitted that they are lucky if they make correct decisions 50 percent of the time. Would structuring a decision problem to provide an analytical decision, or even flipping a coin, be a more economical substitute for paying over $200,000 a year for the decision making of top executives? Discuss.

6. List the problems you have faced over the past week. Next select the ones that are somewhat repetitive. Develop a programming logic for solving several of these problems.

7. Look up in a textbook on management science the method of developing a utility curve by means of the "standard gamble." Develop your utility curve for money.

8. Develop the elements of the decision problem for a homeowner who is considering replacing his old refrigerator.

9. Joe and Bill Turnip have developed the Turnip Nursery in Florida into a $500,000 annual business. The business has boomed, along with the rapid population growth of the state. About 30 percent of revenue comes from sales of plants, 20 percent from lawn maintenance. Bill, Jr., has been attending a business school in upper New York State and working summers at the nursery. As he has grown familiar with the business, he has been asking questions of the partners about the future of the firm—questions such as: "What are your plans for the company for five years from now?"

"What are the objectives of the company, in terms of growth, services supplied, geographic area to be served, and ROI?" "You are growing at a rate of 15 percent a year; how will you be able to operate from this limited, hemmed-in site three years from now?" "Why don't we have inventory records of shrubs?" "Why don't we forecast sales?" Since the nursery has always operated very profitably from the beginning, the partners have responded somewhat grumpily to such persistent questioning, but they are beginning to wonder if they do have problems without realizing it.

10. The Delmar Box Company, located in Albany, New York, was formed by Mr. Ronald Harrison for the manufacture of industrial pallets. Although he had had no formal business education, Mr. Harrison was a very shrewd and enterprising individual. By aggressive selling and heavy investment in the most modern equipment, he built a highly profitable business. He knew the cost of manufacturing each pallet within a fraction of a cent and he usually bid on the basis of this knowledge. Eventually a problem appeared that endangered his business. Some large-farm operators in the surrounding areas put their unutilized farm labor to work in the long winters making pallets; bidding was below cost because of the farmers' lack of cost accounting methods. They would remain in the market for a few years before they discovered this and left it, but there were always a few new entries. In addition, Delmar Box had grown enough to catch the eye of the unions. If all box companies became unionized, this would present no problem, but small companies generally escaped and were able to pay minimum wages. Mr. Harrison was seriously reevaluating his business objectives because he knew something had to be done fairly quickly.

11. The Galactic R&D Company's business depended upon developing new products, getting them into production, and then either selling the product and plant or forming a separate subsidiary. Its major problem, according to its president, Mr. Rolly Joss, was selecting products for development and commercialization. No formal procedures for pre- or post-evaluation of projects existed.

12. "An airline is a very closely coupled operation with a lot of time dependencies," Robert B. Parsons, vice-president of computer science for Eastern Airlines, has been quoted as saying. Airlines operations need to keep track of customer reservations on an on-line basis, maintain flight surveillance, control maintenance and spare parts inventories, plan flights, and bill credit card companies. The continual development of more efficient systems to accomplish this, with an eye to the basic objectives of the business, requires more and more careful formulation of total system objectives.

13. The Wood Products Company grows timber and sells 15 classes of lumber, from soft to hard woods and from rough construction types to interior plywood. The new manager of business systems, Keith Millslot, a recent M.B.A. graduate, is attempting to take a systems approach to the business. He notes that most trees require planting 15 years in advance of cutting. He has been attempting, unsuccessfully so far, to get top management

to formulate corporate objectives so that he can consider future markets, future products, land to be acquired, and location of processing plants. Mr. Millslot has finally obtained the president's permission to explain, at a meeting of top management, the long-range systems problems and the need for company objectives. As he sits at his desk pondering what his approach should be at the meeting, his assistant hands him an article from *Business Week,* August 23, 1969. The article mentions that the executive vice-president at Boise Cascade is experimenting with a computerized model of the Timber and Woods Products Division with almost 8,000 equations.

REFERENCES

1. See C. West Churchman, Russell L. Ackoff, and E. Leonard Arnoff, *Introduction to Operations Research* (New York: John Wiley & Sons, Inc., 1957), p. 132.
2. See George A. Miller, "The Magical Number Seven, Plus or Minus Two: Some Limits on Our Capacity for Processing Information," *Psychological Review,* March 1956, pp. 81–97; and Alfred Kuhn, *The Study of Society, A Unified Approach* (Homewood, Ill.: Richard D. Irwin, Inc., 1963), pp. 178–79.
3. For a further discussion of applied decision making, see Arthur D. Hall, *A Methodology for Systems Engineering* (Princeton, N.J.: D. Van Nostrand Co., Inc., 1962).
4. Herbert Simon, *Administrative Behavior,* 2nd ed. (New York: The Macmillan Company, 1958), p. xxiv.
5. For a discussion of this topic, see Aaron Lowin, "Participative Decision-Making: A Model, Literature Critique, and Prescriptions for Research," *Organizational Behavior and Human Performance,* February 1968.
6. William T. Morris, *Management Science, A Bayesian Approach* (Englewood Cliffs, N.J.: Prentice-Hall, Inc., 1968), p. 15.

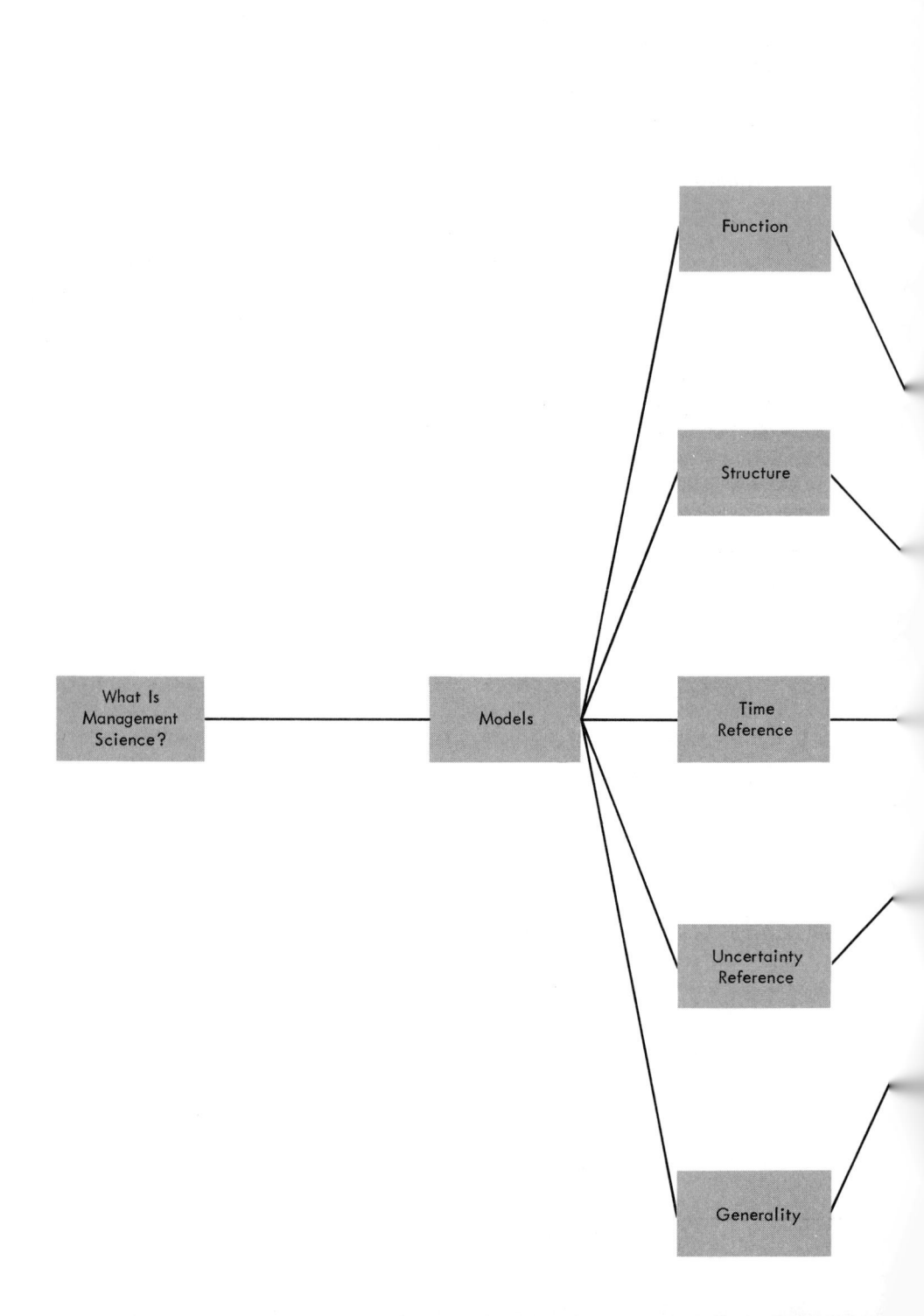

```
What Is Management Science? ── Models ──┬── Function
                                         ├── Structure
                                         ├── Time Reference
                                         ├── Uncertainty Reference
                                         └── Generality
```

11
management science and systems modeling

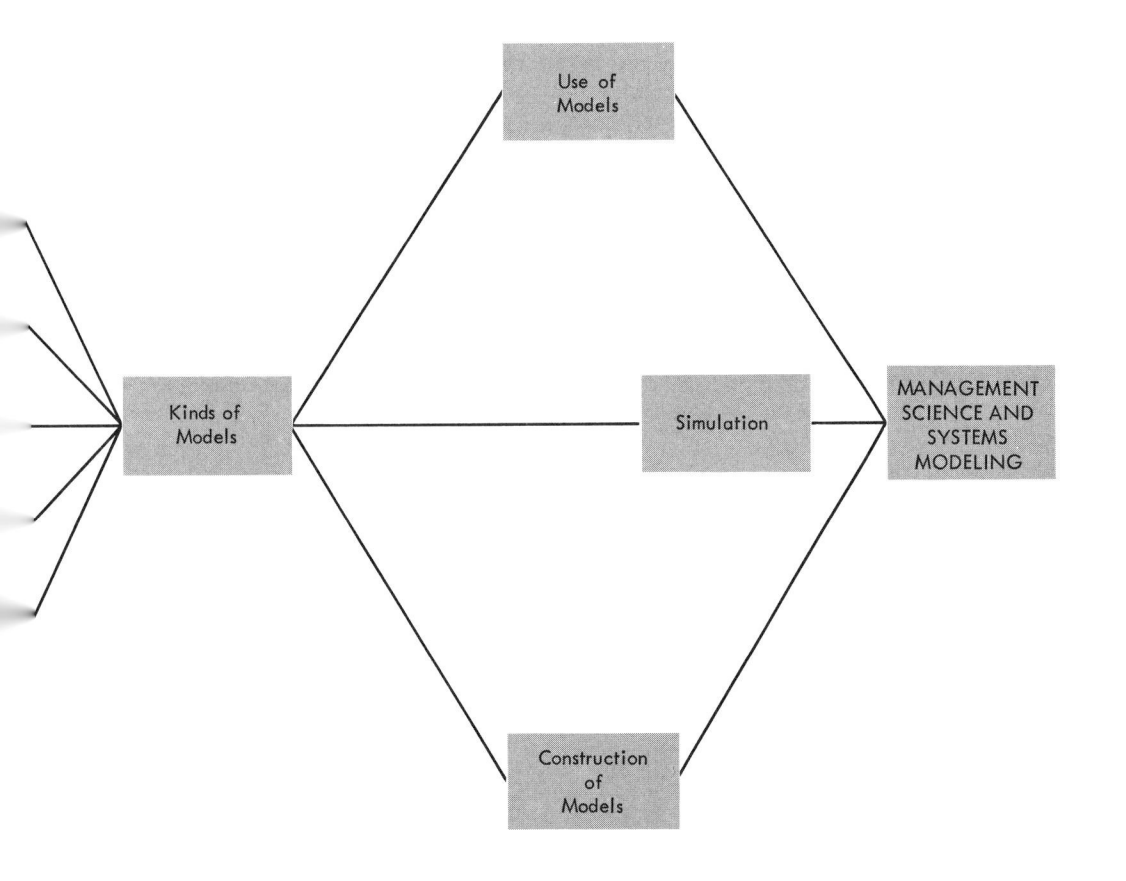

11

"The techniques involved—computer-based information systems, the mathematical wizardry known as operations research, decision analysis, and theories of group behavior—all have been around for years. Now they're coming out of the specialized departments and staff deep-freezers to create systems that look at the business as a whole."[1]

"Operations research," "management science," "modeling," or just "science"—all represent pretty much the same process. That process, which we shall call management science, is a sophisticated aid to practical decision making, directed toward the solution of broad business problems by means of specialized techniques. The application of management science to MIS represents a tremendous advance over the disorganized collection of information and management by experience based on "feel." Management science requires the manager to define his problems and assumptions carefully, usually in terms that may be quantified and measured, so that he may achieve better problem definition. When it is applied to the design of organizational and operating systems for problem solving, management science utilizes a considerable volume of man's knowledge of many related sciences. Therefore, problem-solving systems may be designed that are more effective and more efficient for the organization as a whole.

The techniques of management science are also incorporated *in* the system. Basically, these techniques, employed in conjunction with modern computers, provide "programmed" decision making for the solution of many subproblems in the system. Optimum solutions to such subproblems may be obtained in minutes. This contrasts with rule-of-thumb, intuitive, and approximate solutions that decision makers were forced to rely on in the past. Without the computational power of the computer, management science techniques usually could not be applied within the time span of realistic operational requirements. Thus the computer and management science combine to free humans from repetitive decision making, so that they may concentrate on more complex, novel, and ill-constructed problems as well as on "nonprogrammed" decision making.

The dysfunctional aspects of the increased application of management science are twofold. The first is the failure of the systems designer to recognize that his models of systems and problems will always be abstractions of the real world. Qualitative factors and human judgments must find a place in all higher-level decisions. Mathematically derived solutions must be checked against intuition and variances must be accounted for. Failure to do this may result in absurd and costly decisions. The second drawback to the introduction of management science techniques is organizational resistance to change. This resistance is further complicated when the management scientist fails to communicate with manager–users in terms that the manager understands.

We have brought out in general terms the role that management science plays in designing decision rules for programmed decisions and in helping managers make nonprogrammed decisions in the man–machine mode. It is now necessary to explore in more detail the nature of management science and its applications to MIS design.

WHAT IS MANAGEMENT SCIENCE?

Management science is simply a scientific approach to the solution of operational problems. It is concerned with providing management with *decision aids* or *decision rules* derived from:

1. A total-system orientation
2. Scientific methods of investigation
3. Models of reality, generally based on quantitative measurements and techniques

In previous chapters, Chapter 8 in particular, we have presented the systems approach. The systematic approach to problem solving, covered in Chapter 10, parallels the generally accepted steps of management science (operations research). These steps consist of:

Problem Solving	*Management Science*
1. Observation	1. Search for problems
2. Statement of a problem	2. Statement of a problem
3. Collection of data	3. Collection of data
4. Development of hypotheses for solution of the problem	4. Development and testing of a model representing the problem solution
5. Evaluation of the alternative hypotheses	5. Manipulation of the model to determine the outcomes of various input conditions

Subsequent to the problem-solving process of developing feasible alternatives is the decision process, in which the parallelism continues:

Decision Making and Action	*Management Science*
1. Selection of best alternative	1. Selection of the best course of action
2. Implementation of best alternative	2. Implementation of the solution
3. Review of results	3. Control of the model by maintaining a check on its validity as time goes by

We now look at the third characteristic of management science—modeling. Since the time when cave men drew symbols and pictures on the walls of caves, man has utilized "models" to represent aspects of his environment. It is only recently that scientists in many disciplines have discovered that the term *model* applies to what they have been doing all along. It now appears that most scientific conversations start with a mention of a model. The field of MIS is no exception; models are a necessity for both study and design of MIS. Since models are so important, we need to know what they are, what their characteristics are, and how they help us.

WHAT ARE MODELS?

We can solve both simple and complex problems of the practical world if we concentrate on some *portion* or some *key features* instead of on every detail of real life. This approximation or *abstraction* of reality, which we may construct in various forms, is called a *model*. Models do not, and cannot, represent every aspect of reality because of the innumerable and changing characteristics of the real world to be represented. If we wished to study the flow of material through a factory, we might construct a scaled diagram on paper showing the factory floor, position of equipment, tools, and men. It would not be necessary to give such details as the color of the machines, the heights of the men, or the temperature of the building. In other words, models deal with the relevant variables, and often only the relevant variables that have a major impact on the decision situation.

Many forms of models exist, and the particular form selected depends upon the purpose. Generally, models may be used to define or describe something such as an MIS; to assist with analysis of a system; to specify relationships and processes; or to present a situation in symbolic terms that may be manipulated to derive predictions. This last purpose, to provide a prediction system that can be manipulated to aid a decision maker, is perhaps the most important attribute of models.

Models provide two very important benefits that are closely related but distinct. The first is economy in representation and inquiry. It is cheaper, for instance, to represent a factory layout or an MIS visually in a diagram than to construct either one. It is also cheaper to try out modifications of such systems by rearrangements on paper. Second, models permit us to analyze and experiment with complex situations to a degree that would be impossible by constructing the actual system and its environment. For example, the experimental firing of an Apollo lunar vehicle may cost tens of millions of dollars and require months of preparation. If the lunar flight puters permits the simulation of many flights under various conditions. By and the systems are simulated by a model, the application of large com-

simulation, information may be obtained in a few minutes that could not be obtained in generations of time or with billions of dollars of expenditure if the life-size system were used for experimentation.

KINDS OF MODELS

Models may be divided into four different classes. The characteristics of a particular model may then be represented by a term from each class. Thus a manager might ask a management scientist in his marketing organization to construct a model for the selling and logistics system of a new shoe-cleaning product. The management scientist might then ask, "Shall we make that a symbolic, dynamic, probabilistic, and general model, or should we try to keep costs under $10,000 and construct an iconic, static, deterministic, and specialized model?" When put as a single question, this may seem facetious; in practice the answer to this question must be evolved in the discussion.

It is apparent that a few terms must be defined to describe classes of models, simply for economy of expression. It is also desirable to know what options exist when we are about to embark upon the construction of models. Models may be classified in five ways:

Class I—Function

Type	Characteristics	Examples
1. Descriptive	Descriptive models simply provide a "picture" of a situation and do not predict or recommend.	(a) Organization chart (b) Plant layout diagram (c) Block diagram representing the structure of each chapter of this book
2. Predictive	Predictive models indicate that "if *this* occurs, then *that* will follow." They relate dependent and independent variables and permit trying out "what if" questions.	(a) $BE = \dfrac{F}{1 - v}$, which says that if fixed costs (F) are given, and variable costs as a fraction of sales (v) are known, then breakeven sales (BE) are predicted (deterministically) (b) $S(t) = aS(t - 1) + (1 - a)S(t - 2)$, which says that predicted sales for period t depend on sales for the previous two periods
3. Normative	Normative models are those that provide the "best" answer to a problem. They provide recommended courses of action.	(a) Advertising budget model (b) Economic lot size model (c) Marketing mix model

Class II—Structure

Type	Characteristics	Examples
1. Iconic	Iconic models retain some of the physical characteristics of the things they represent.	(a) Scaled 3-dimensional mock-up of a factory layout (b) Blueprints of a warehouse (c) Scale model of next year's automobile
2. Analog	Analog models are those for which there is a substitution of components or processes to provide a parallel with what is being modelled.	An analog computer in which components and circuits parallel marketing institutions and facilities and processes so that by varying electrical inputs, the electrical outputs provide an analog simulation of the marketing system outputs
3. Symbolic	Symbolic models use symbols to describe the real world.	(a) $R = a[ln(A)] + b$, which says in symbols that sales response (R) equals a constant times the natural log of advertising expenditure (A), plus another constant (b) $TC = PC + CC + IC$, which says in symbols that total inventory cost (TC) equals purchase cost (PC) plus carrying cost (CC) plus item cost (IC)

Class III—Time Reference

Type	Characteristics	Examples
1. Static	Static models do not account for changes over time.	(a) Organization chart (b) $E = P_1 S_1 + P_2 S_2$, which states that the expected profit (E) equals the probability (P_1) of the occurrence of payoff (S_1) multiplied by the value of the payoff (S_1), plus the probability (P_2) of payoff (S_2) multiplied by the value of (S_2)
2. Dynamic	Dynamic models have time as an independent variable.	$dS/dt = rA(t)(m - S)/M - \lambda s$, which gives the change in sales rate as a function of a response constant r, advertising rate as a function of time $A(t)$, sales saturation (M), sales rate (S), and sales decay constant (λ)

Class IV—Uncertainty Reference

Type	Characteristics	Examples
1. Deterministic	For a specific set of input values, there is a uniquely determined output that represents the solution of a model under conditions of *certainty*.	Profit = Revenue minus costs
2. Probabilistic	Probabilistic models involve probability distributions for inputs or processes and provide a range of values of at least one output variable with a probability associated with each value. These model assist with decisions made under conditions of *risk*.	(a) Actuarial tables that give the probability of death as a function of age. (b) Return on investment is simulated by using a probability distribution for each of the various costs and revenues with values selected by the Monte Carlo (random) technique. ROI appears in graph form as return in dollars vs. probability of the various dollar returns.
3. Game	Game theory models attempt to develop optimum solutions in the face of complete ignorance or *uncertainty*. Games against nature and games of competition are subclassifications.	Two gasoline stations are adjacent to each other. One owner wonders: "Shall I raise or lower my price? If I raise mine, my competitor may raise or lower his. If I lower mine, he may raise or lower his. I know the gain or loss in any situation, but once each of us sets the price, we must keep it for the week. We can't collude."

Class V—Generality

Type	Characteristics	Examples
1. General	General models for business are models that have applications in several functional areas of business.	(a) Linear programming algorithm for all functional areas (b) Waiting line model. Applications appear in production, marketing, and personnel.
2. Specialized	Specialized models are those that have application to a unique problem only.	(a) Sales response as a function of advertising may be based on a unique set of equations. (b) The probabilistic bidding model has a single application to one functional area.

Model	Objective	Nomenclature for Relevant Variables	Pictorial Representation	Mathematical Representation of the System
Inventory Model	Find Economic Order Quantity by trade-off of carrying costs and ordering costs so as to minimize the system cost.	Q = size of order K = carrying costs S = ordering costs D = estimated annual demand TC = total system cost	(sawtooth inventory diagram with Reorder Level; Cost vs Q, Order Size showing Total Cost and K curves)	$TC = (Q/2) \cdot K + (D/Q) \cdot S$
Progress Model	Find time, cost, or price per unit after declines due to experience gained.	K = cost of first unit N = N-th unit produced ϕ = fraction of initial cost required to produce a unit after any doubling of production C_N = cost to produce N-th unit	(Cost per Unit $ vs Number of Units Produced curve)	$C_n = KN^{(\log \phi / \log 2)}$
Waiting-Line Model	Find the average length of a waiting line, the average waiting time, or the optimum number of service facilities.	Poisson arrival rate with exponentially distributed service times for a single service facility. λ = average number of arrivals/period μ = average number of service completions/period C_w = cost per period for a person or unit waiting C_f = service facility cost for one unit TC = total system cost	(Population → Waiting Line → Service Facility; Probability vs Length of Line; Average Length of Line curve approaching 1.0)	Average number of units in system $= \lambda/(\mu-\lambda)$ Average time a unit waits in the system $= 1/(\mu-\lambda)$ Service rate for minimum cost, min $= \lambda + \sqrt{\lambda C_w / C_f}$

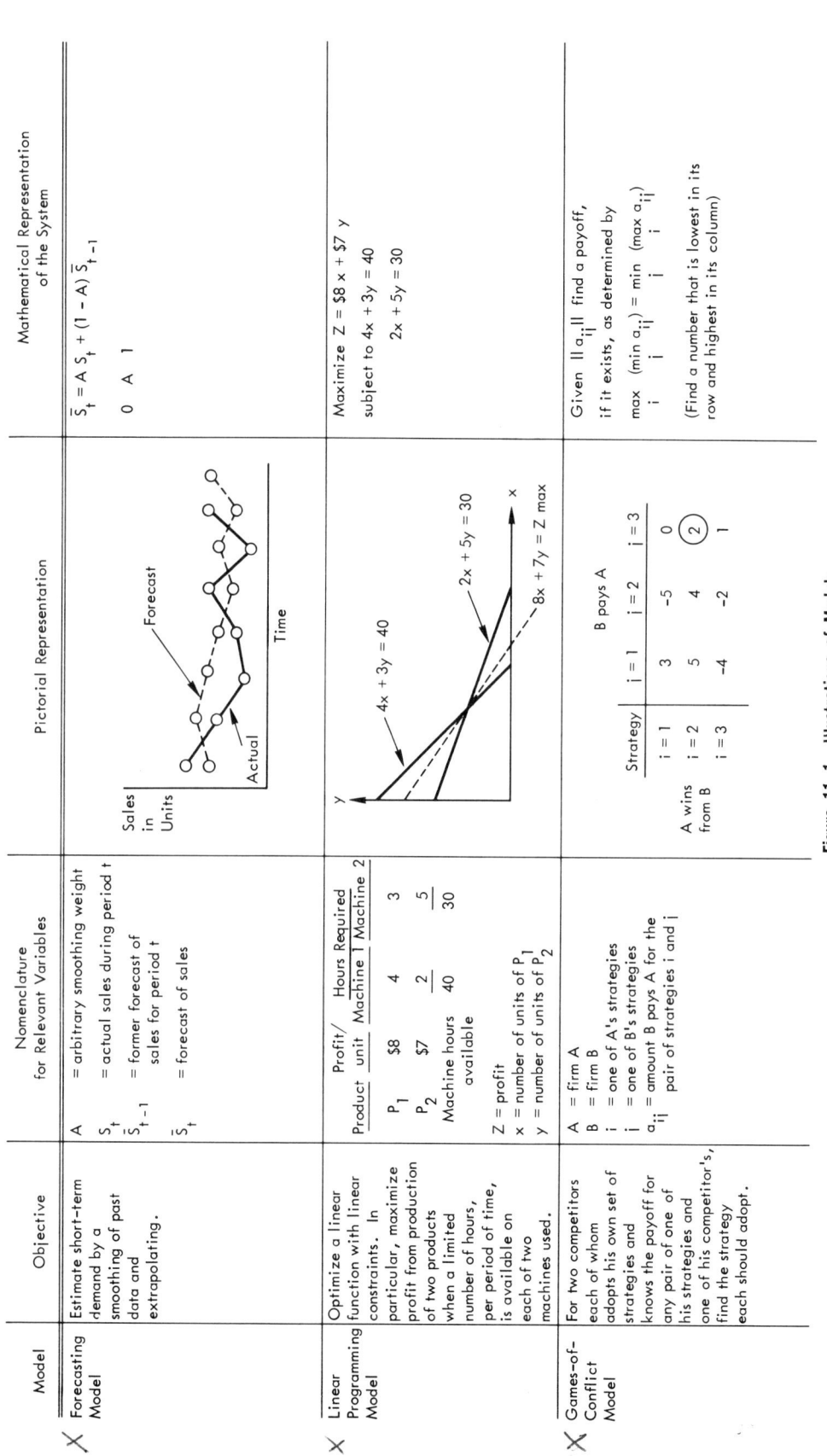

Model	Objective	Nomenclature for Relevant Variables	Pictorial Representation	Mathematical Representation of the System
Forecasting Model	Estimate short-term demand by a smoothing of past data and extrapolating.	A = arbitrary smoothing weight S_t = actual sales during period t $\bar{S}_{t-1}$ = former forecast of sales for period t $\bar{S}_t$ = forecast of sales	Sales in Units plotted vs Time, showing Actual and Forecast curves	$\bar{S}_t = A\, S_t + (1 - A)\, \bar{S}_{t-1}$ $0 \leq A \leq 1$
Linear Programming Model	Optimize a linear function with linear constraints. In particular, maximize profit from production of two products when a limited number of hours, per period of time, is available on each of two machines used.	Profit/unit and Hours Required: Product | Profit/unit | Machine 1 | Machine 2 P_1 | \$8 | 4 | 3 P_2 | \$7 | 2 | 5 Machine hours available | | 40 | 30 Z = profit x = number of units of P_1 y = number of units of P_2	Graph showing constraints $4x + 3y = 40$, $2x + 5y = 30$, and objective $8x + 7y = Z_{max}$	Maximize $Z = \$8 x + \$7 y$ subject to $4x + 3y = 40$ $2x + 5y = 30$
Games-of-Conflict Model	For two competitors each of whom adopts his own set of strategies and knows the payoff for any pair of one of his strategies and one of his competitor's, find the strategy each should adopt.	A = firm A B = firm B i = one of A's strategies j = one of B's strategies a_{ij} = amount B pays A for the pair of strategies i and j	A wins from B: Strategy | $j=1$ | $j=2$ | $j=3$ $i=1$ | 3 | -5 | 0 $i=2$ | 5 | 4 | (2) $i=3$ | -4 | -2 | 1	Given $\|\|a_{ij}\|\|$ find a payoff, if it exists, as determined by $\max_i (\min_j a_{ij}) = \min_j (\max_i a_{ij})$ (Find a number that is lowest in its row and highest in its column)

Figure 11–1 Illustrations of Models

Model	Objective	Nomenclature for Relevant Variables	Pictorial Representation	Mathematical Representation of the System
Markov Process Model	Find the share of the market held by each company if the probabilities of brand switching by the customers can be estimated.	S_{11} = share of market for brand 1 in period 1 S_{12} = share of market for brand 2 in period 1 S_{21}, S_{22}, similarly P_{11} = probability that a customer who bought brand 1 in period 1 will buy brand 1 in the next period P_{12} = probability of switch from brand 1 to brand 2 P_{21}, P_{22}, similarly	(Two-state diagram with states 1 and 2, transitions P_{11}, P_{12}, P_{21}, P_{22})	$\begin{pmatrix} S_{12} \\ S_{22} \end{pmatrix} = \begin{pmatrix} P_{11} & P_{12} \\ P_{21} & P_{22} \end{pmatrix} \begin{pmatrix} S_{11} \\ S_{21} \end{pmatrix}$
Expected-Value Model	Determine the course of action that will yield the greatest expected gain.	☐ Decision point ◯ Random event in the world p_i = probability that a particular event occurs a_i = gain or loss resulting from outcome of random event EV = expected value of a course of action	(Decision tree: Alternative 1 with $p_1=.2$, $a_1=-\$20$ and $p_2=.8$, $a_2=\$100$; Alternative 2 with $p_3=.6$, $a_3=\$50$ and $p_4=.4$, $a=\$60$)	EV (alternative 1) = $P_1 a_1 + P_2 a_2 = .2(-20) + .8(100)$ EV (alternative 2) = $P_3 a_3 + P_4 a_4 = .6(50) + .4(60)$

Model	Objective	Nomenclature for Relevant Variables	Pictorial Representation	Mathematical Representation of the System
Network Planning Models— Critical Path Method (CPM) or Program Evaluation Review Technique (PERT)	Schedule a project and control it by maintaining surveillance on time and costs. Find critical (longest) time path in the planning network and slack times for events outside the critical path.	○ Event → Activities 1 - 2 Mold frame — 4 hours 1 - 3 Cut axle — 2 hours 2 - 3 Machine the frame — 6 hours 3 - 4 Insert axle — 1 hour 2 - 4 Get motor from warehouse — 8 hours 4 - 5 Install motor — 2 hours t = time of activity between event i and event j, when it exists	(network diagram with nodes 1,2,3,4,5 and edges 4,2,8,6,2,1,2; critical path indicated)	Find the maximum $\sum_{i,j} t_{ij}$ subject to the given order and time constraints of the activities
Flow Graph Model*	Interrelate variables in a complex situation and derive a mathematical expression for dependent variables.	The nodes are: X_s = customer funded research and grants, X_i = new capital investment, X_p = return to the investors. Then the parameters of the system are: $R(s)$ = fraction of sales spent for research, $R'(s)$ = fraction of capital used in research, $I(s)$ = income from research, $I'(s)$ = fraction of net profit returned to investors, $S(s)$ = return on manufactured products, $P(s)$ = fraction of capital in products, inventories, etc., T = tax rate.	(flow graph diagram with nodes X_s, X_i, X_p and edges labeled $R(s)$, $I(s)$, $S(s)$, $P(s)$, $R'(s)$, $I'(s)$, -1, $-T$)	The mathematical relationship for the investor income may be written directly as: $$x_p = \frac{X_i I'(s)[1-T]/[R'(s)I(s)+P(s)S(s)-P(s)]+X_s I'(s)I(s)[1-T]}{E}$$ where $E = 1 - R(s)I(s) - [1-T]/[1-I'(s)]\,[R'(s)-P(s)+P(s)S(s)]$ $- P(s)[s)R(s)/[1-T][1-I'(s)]$

Figure 11-1 Illustrations of Models (continued)

*Flowgraph model is reprinted from Gary Whitehouse, "Model Systems on Paper with Flowgraph Analysis," *Industrial Engineering*, June 1969.

The foregoing classification provides a structure for the understanding of models; specific descriptions of elementary forms of general models will shed more light on their use in business applications. In Figure 11-1, therefore, we show the objectives of some selected models, usually in a specific application. It is necessary to introduce definitions of terms in Figure 11-1 so that a pictorial description of the situation and the mathematical representation may be made meaningful, to some degree at least. We admit that only an impression of the nature of models is given by the figure; only through the detailed derivation of a model can the student gain a complete insight.

What does all of the preceding mean to the student of MIS? First, information systems should solve as many problems as possible on a routine basis. The computer and the application of models make possible much routine problem solving to relieve management. Second, the solutions from models may supply valuable information to aid managers in solving problems. Managers must evaluate the amount of aid that a particular type of model can supply, as well as the associated cost. A probabilistic dynamic prediction model may be very helpful, but it may cost $100,000 to develop and utilize for a year. On the other hand, a deterministic model may be reasonably helpful and cost only $10,000 to develop and process on the computer for a year. In some instances, development of a complex model of a firm's operations may be necessary for survival because of modeling being carried out by competitors. Modeling has become an extremely potent tool in the hands of those who know how to use it in MIS.

USE OF MODELS FOR ANALYSIS OF SYSTEMS CHARACTERISTICS

There are a number of questions that we would like to ask about a system, regardless of whether it is an inventory, financial, operating, or information system. These questions relate to the efficiency of the system, the "state" of the system, the amount of feedback, the stability of the system, its speed of response to changes in input, and the effect of transient inputs to the systems. The answers to these questions assist us in evaluating current systems or in evaluating alternatives for a system being designed.

Certain types of iconic models combined with their mathematical counterparts are particularly helpful in making such analyses. Some of these appear in Figure 11-1 and will be apparent from the descriptions. There is a large body of knowledge dealing with the manipulation of these models by mathematical means, which is beyond the scope of this book. From the management viewpoint, it is enough to know that such models exist. Here we present an introduction to some of them.

Block Diagram and "Black Box" Concept

A block diagram usually consists of a network of blocks linked by lines with arrowheads. The blocks are labeled to indicate the processing performed. The lines indicate the order of processing as well as inputs and outputs as labeled. Such a format is consistent with the pictorial and mathematical development of engineered control systems (servomechanism theory). A conceptual model of this type, modeling in gross terms an entire business operation, is shown in Figure 11–2. Only the information processing is indicated in this figure.

The inverse or dual model uses blocks to designate information and the network of lines to designate processing. Some authors use mixed versions of the basic block diagram and its dual form in order to present concepts, but mixed diagrams may render quantitative analysis more difficult.

In order to present an overview of modeling with block diagrams and parallel quantitative methods, we will first expand on the nature of block diagrams and then indicate briefly the nature of the quantitative, analytical, parallel analysis. The reader is directed to texts on servomechanisms for an in-depth treatment.

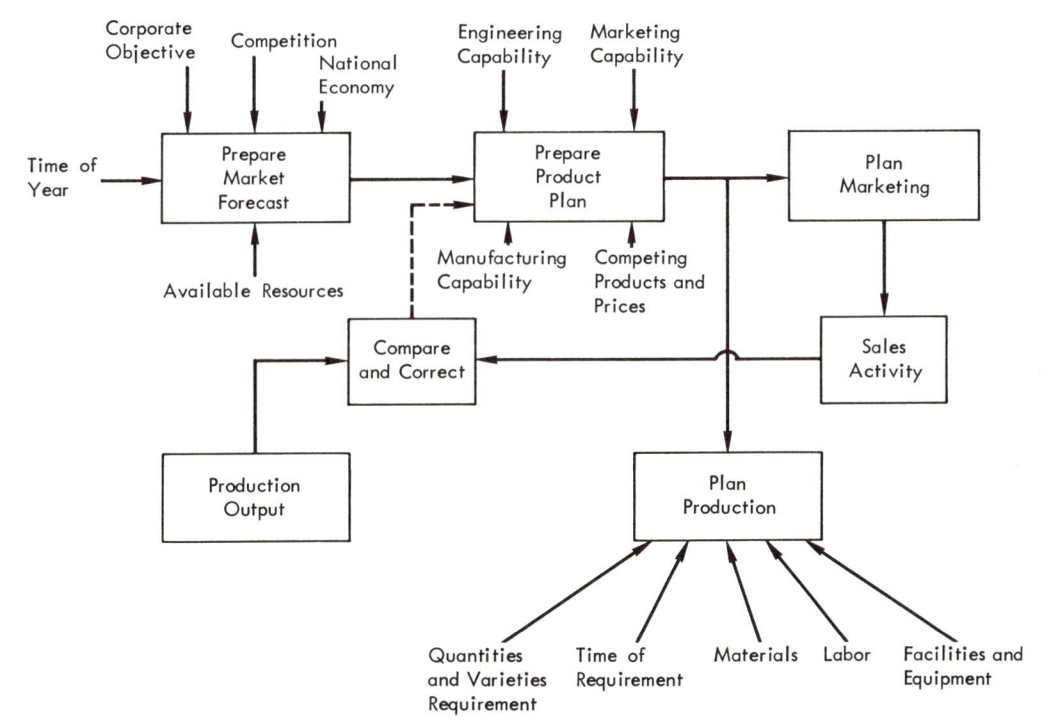

Figure 11–2 Gross Model of a Business Information Processing System

Basic Module

Regardless of the complexity of the block diagram model, the basic modules are the same. Each module consists of one or more inputs, a processor that acts upon the inputs, and one or more outputs. In information systems, both inputs and outputs are either raw data or information, depending on the purpose of the input or output. Chapter 9 gives a detailed distinction between "data" and "information" based on nonutilization or utilization in a decision or control process.

The *input* is the start-up source in an information system block or operational system block. Figure 11–3 shows both operational (physical) and informational inputs. In Figure 11–2 one or more inputs may also be identified for each block. The *processor* is the activity that transforms input into a new form called *output*. Man, machines, decision procedures, organizations, or even environmental phenomena may act as processors. If we refer again to the basic module of Figure 11–3, we see that the activity of selling performed by a salesman results in a physical movement of a product. It also results in a conversion of information about ownership and location of the product from input to output.

If the activity in a processor is well defined so that we describe in detail how the input is converted to the output, we have a good model. Unfortunately, a number of activities must usually be grouped together in a single processor because they are so numerous, complexly interrelated, or not determinable. Such a processor block is usually referred to as a "black box," because we cannot see what goes on inside the block (in a conceptual sense). We try to observe in an empirical situation what happens

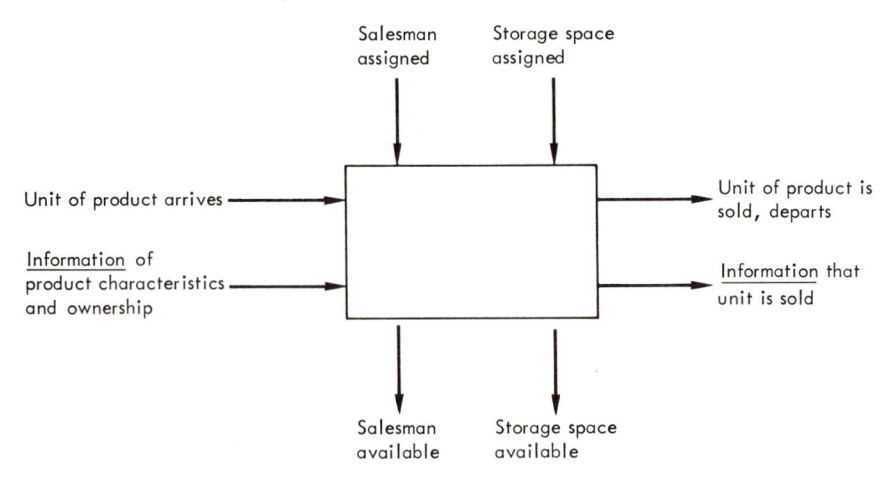

Figure 11–3 Basic Module for Operation and Information Processing, Showing Both Physical Inputs and Outputs and Information Inputs and Outputs

management science and systems modeling 389

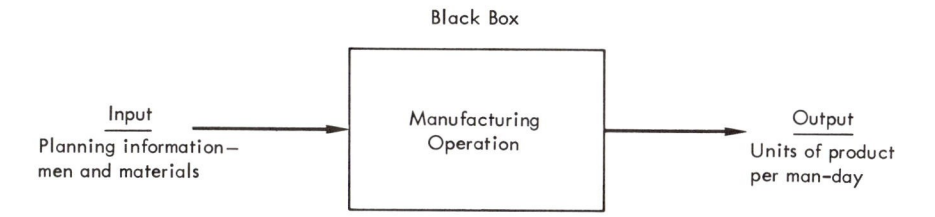

```
                        Black Box
                   ┌──────────────────┐
  Input            │                  │        Output
Planning information ──▶│  Manufacturing │──▶   Units of product
men and materials  │   Operation       │        per man-day
                   │                  │
                   └──────────────────┘
```

Transfer function = manufacturing progress function

Figure 11–4 Black Box Model

to inputs when the "black box" activity takes effect. We hope that we may develop from such data a predictive model for the basic module in which the processor activity can be described by means of a mathematical *transfer function*. Figure 11–4 shows a black box representation of the complete manufacturing operation for a single run of a new complex product. If we consider the input of man-days, the number of units of output per day will tend to increase. This relationship or transfer function assumes one form of the several well-known manufacturing progress functions or "learning curves."

When an input (I) and output (O) are expressed *in the same units*, then the transfer function is simply the ratio of the output to the input, called the *gain* or efficiency:

$$O/I = G \text{ and hence } O = (G)(I)$$

Suppose we represent the entire operation of a company by a block and consider the output (O) as the revenue in dollars and the input (I) as the costs in dollars. We might observe from historical data that if L units of labor and C units of capital are employed, the number of units produced is:

$$O/I = L^{1/2} \, C^{1/2}$$

If we use constants a, b, and c to convert amounts of resources and units of production to dollar values, then the transfer function would be:

$$\frac{O}{I} = \frac{cL^{1/2}C^{1/2}}{aL + bC}$$

How do we know what operation is performed on the input? In man-made systems, we design the system by specifying what transformation of the input is to be made. We do this also when we construct the model of the system, but this does not mean that the system will actually work that way when it is finally designed and put into operation. It becomes necessary to measure or observe how the input is being affected in order to verify our design.

If we are called upon to analyze a system that has been in operation for some time, again we must observe how the input is being changed by the process. We hope that there is a stable enough relationship between input and output so that we can develop a prediction (transfer) function. The black box representing the system process must not vary with time, or, if it does, it must vary in a way that is possible for us to determine.

The fundamental block is just the starting point for specification or analysis of systems. Inputs or outputs may be broken down into their components and analyzed. Blocks in series or in parallel may be combined by mathematical methods for determination of O/I.[2] When there is feedback, the determination of the effect of the transfer function is further complicated.

Feedback and Control

Business systems are dynamic because changes with time in such systems are inevitable. For a dynamic system, it is necessary to review either periodically or continuously the nature of the output in order to adjust the system for changes in its own operation or changes in the environment. In a business system we need to observe whether the output of products is profitable and acceptable to the customer; otherwise the system will come to a standstill. In Chapter 8 we introduced the concept of *feedback* in *control* of dynamic systems.

By means of models and associated quantitative methods derived from servomechanism theory, we may often quantify and analyze portions of business systems. The previous models of basic system modules, Figures 11–3 and 11–4, have represented *open-loop* systems in which there is no control to insure that output does not vary greatly from the desired value. A common and simple way of controlling a system for a constant or static level of operation is to compare the output with a fixed standard and then feed back this information. Let us consider the example, described previously in Chapter 8, of the thermostatic control system in the home. The thermostat is set at a fixed level (I). When the temperature of the room (O) deviates from (I), the difference activates the heating device to bring the temperature back to the thermostat setting. The black box model for such a system is shown in Figure 11–5. The transfer function (G) converts the input of temperature information into a revised room temperature by means of the black box activities of the heating system.

The output of the system is given by:

$$O = G \times (I - O)$$

If we solve for O, we obtain

management science and systems modeling

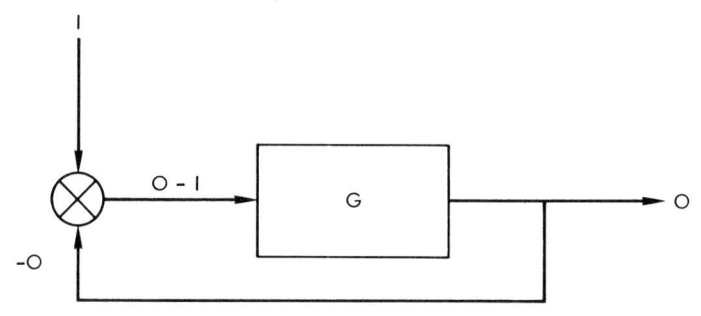

Figure 11–5 Control by Direct Comparison with a Standard

$$O = I \times \frac{G}{1 + G}$$

and hence the transfer function for the system is

$$O/I = \frac{G}{1 + G}$$

In many systems, the input is continually changing and output must adapt accordingly. For example, a company may make monthly forecasts of sales and feed this input to the manufacturing system. The output of the factory at any given time must be transmitted back to the production planners so that they can compare the output rate with the input demand and adjust production accordingly. Figure 11–6 illustrates the application of negative feedback to control fluctuations in output, which are not related to the current input. The concept of "negative feedback" is most easily grasped by considering the automatic gain control of a radio receiver. When the volume of output sound starts to rise, a portion of the output signal is fed back to the input stages of the radio in the form of a signal, which opposes the input signal and hence reduces it.

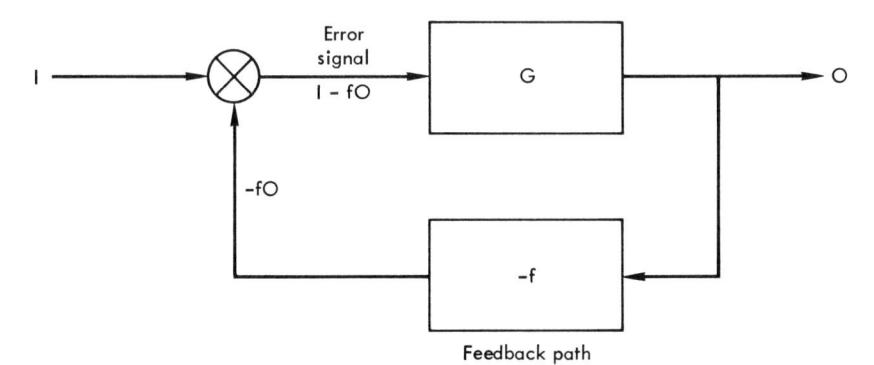

Figure 11–6 Basic Feedback System

The output is given by

$$O = G \times (I - fO)$$

The transfer function for the entire system is

$$O/I = \frac{G}{1 + fG}$$

The effectiveness of feedback may be illustrated by a simplified production or conversion system. In Figure 11-7 the input is number of units of material brought into the workplace, the conversion function is assumed to be a constant, $G = 50$, the output is number of units produced, and the feedback signal is $f = 0.1$. Then,

$$O/I = \frac{G}{1 + fG} = \frac{50}{1 + .1(50)} = 8.33$$

Now suppose the efficiency of the labor force drops by half due to illness and absentees. Then,

$$O/I = \frac{25}{1 + .1(25)} = 7.14$$

A 50 percent drop in the conversion function without feedback would result in a 50 percent drop in the output/input (efficiency) term. With the feedback, the change is only 14 percent. Note also that if there are no time delays, changes in the input of materials produce a corresponding change in output of units produced as long as G and f are constant.

The preceding discussion has assumed no lag in feedback. When a time delay is present, the amount of feedback and the form of input are critical to the stability of the system. If too much negative feedback is applied, the system will tend to overcorrect itself, and "hunting" or oscillation of output will result. If the feedback is too small, wide swings may result because the system corrects itself too slowly. Analysis of linear feedback systems is found in books on servomechanisms and control systems.[3]

State-Descriptive Models of Systems

Most phenomena in the world change continuously with time, but many situations represent discrete changes. Some illustrations of both types of change are:

management science and systems modeling   393

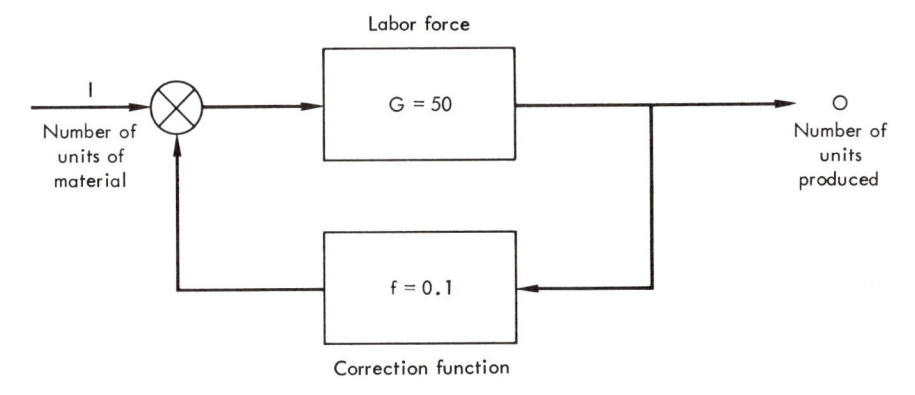

Figure 11-7 Simple Application of Feedback Concept

Events that change *continuously* with time	Events that represent *discrete* changes with time
1. Age of individual employees	1. Number of owners of Fords; of Chevrolets; of Plymouths
2. Experience of a manager	2. Number of units in inventory
3. Obsolescence of a product	3. Number of machines in the shop
4. Utilization of electrical power	4. Number of employees
5. System operation time of an MIS	5. Waiting line or no waiting line at a store's checkout register
6. Hours of computer time employed by an MIS	6. Market position ranking of three firms in an industry

There are several very useful modeling approaches to representing the important problems in which elements fall into discrete "states" or classes. Even continuous-time variables may be classified into intervals, each interval designated as a "state," and a state description of all variables treated as a discrete case. Since we often wish to hold some quantities *constant with time to represent a particular state*, we call these quantities *parameters* of the model. A simple but common model involves the evaluation of the present value V of a future stream of n annual revenues R_k for the value of money, r. The rate of return (r) is the parameter that describes possible states of the business system:

$$V = \sum_{k=1}^{n} R_k/(1 + r)^k$$

A "state" is thus a particular system condition. In the case just cited, a particular system condition might be $r = 6$ percent. A state of a system may vary with time in some known manner, or the state of a system may be under the control of management. For example, in an inventory system, management might wish to avoid the stockout state and therefore design a system with a buffer stock, making such a state extremely unlikely.

Some commonly employed models of system states and transitions from state to state are Markov models, matrix models, and tree diagrams. An example of each appears in Figure 11–1. Since business operating systems and information systems are constantly undergoing state changes, preferably under the partial control of management, modeling systems by state-descriptive methods is very useful. Obviously, the systems designer must have a thorough knowledge of management science to perform such modeling. Managers do not require such depth of knowledge but should be aware of the existence of these techniques. The following sections are designed to provide this brief introduction.

Markov-Process State-Descriptions

A special case, the Markov process in simple pictorial form, will illustrate the application of state-descriptive models. Consider two lily pads floating on the water. A frog sits on one of them and contemplates leaping. The state of this system is described by the frog on the lily pad, and thus two states exist (Figure 11–8). The transfer functions are probabilities. Thus, p_{12} is the probability that if the frog is on pad 1, he will leap from pad 1 to pad 2. Also p_{22} is the probability that if the frog is on pad 2, he will be on pad 2 at the next time interval. If there are n states, there are n transfer functions (probabilities) for each state to represent the probabilities for changing from a given state to any of the n states in the next time period. (This includes the no-change transition case.)

An example of a two-state system is an inventory system. It has two states: goods in inventory and stockout. If the period of time is one week, the probabilities of state changes relative to the current state are the transfer functions.

A more complex system is the organization of a company or institution. In state 1, let us say, there are a number of individuals, each with a special

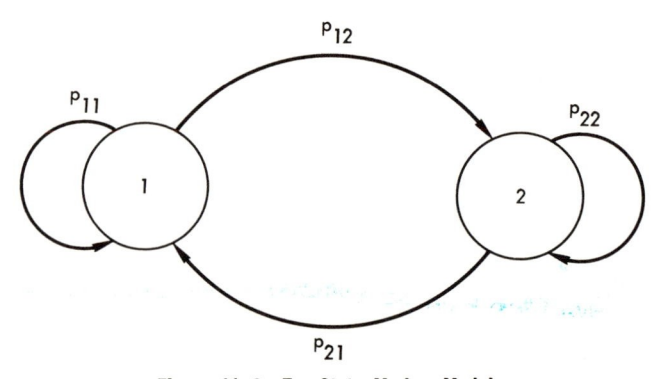

Figure 11–8 Two-State Markov Model

Probabilities of changing from
one state to another at a later period of time

To state (market position)

		1	2	3
From state (market position)	1	.70	.10	.20
	2	.40	.50	.10
	3	.10	.10	.80

(a)

Probabilities of changing states
To specified values

		Assets	Liabilities	Net Worth
From specified values	Assets	P_{11}	0	0
	Liabilities	0	P_{22}	0
	Net Worth	0	0	P_{33}

(b)

Figure 11-9 Matrix State-Description Models

skill. In the next time period, the list of skills present has probably changed, owing to loss or gain of personnel or substitution of people by leaves and additions. The transfer functions are the transition probabilities, as before.

Matrix State-Descriptions

Matrices may also be used to describe systems that change from one state to another. For example, if there are three competing firms in an industry, a state of a firm may be identified as its rank in the market. The matrix shows the probabilities of changes of state from one time period to another (Figure 11-9a).

396 Information, Decision Making, and Management Science

Another matrix representation of systems states and state transitions is that for the balance sheet of a firm (Figure 11–9b). There are, of course, an infinite number of possible states, but a few conceivable cases could be listed. A matrix may then be prepared for this limited number of states so that the sum of the p_{1j}'s equals unity, and similarly with the p_{2j}'s and p_{3j}'s.

Tree Diagrams

Tree-diagram models are useful for showing sequential changes of states for a very limited number of states and transitions combined. They have the added advantage that decisions can be worked into them. Figure 11–10a shows an elementary model and Figure 11–10b a stochastic and decision model. The probabilities of transition from any given state to possible next states are shown on the branches.

SIMULATION

Another powerful application of modeling is the numerical simulation of a system process. A simulation is carried out by specifying a set of starting conditions and a set of rules for the system action. Numerical values are then calculated for the change in the system due to a random input of the exogenous variables. The new state of the system becomes the starting point for another "pass." Simulation is a very valuable technique because (1) it provides for testing of explicit models, those that can be stated in a complete "formula" fashion; and (2) it makes possible the solution of implicit or "chain" types of models whose analytic solution may not even be possible. Figure 11–11 shows pictorially the latter case. The model is composed of parts, each depending on the results of the previous part.

We will attempt to present an explanation of a simulation of an inventory system without lengthy development of many details. The purpose is to give the reader the flavor of the technique rather than a treatise on how to do it.

The following "facts" are given:

1. The objective is to study an inventory system to determine probability distributions for the size of the inventory and for the size of shortages (stockouts), to aid management in evaluating inventory policies.

2. The procurement level is 4 units. This is a parameter, since it is held constant for this simulation, but it could be changed for another simulation of the system. It is also under the control of management. Thus, when inventory drops to 4 units, an order is placed.

3. The size of the order placed each time, the procurement quantity, is 12 units. This is also a parameter under the control of management.

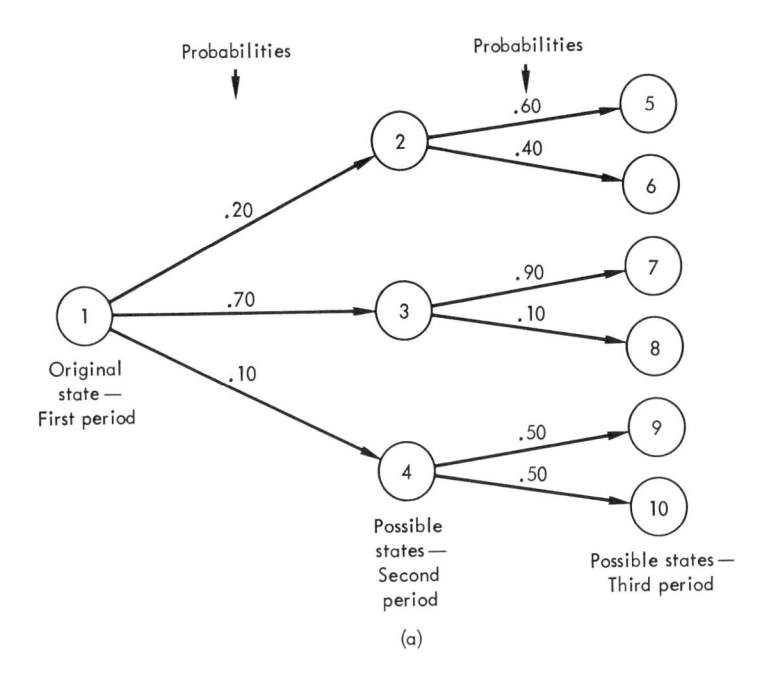

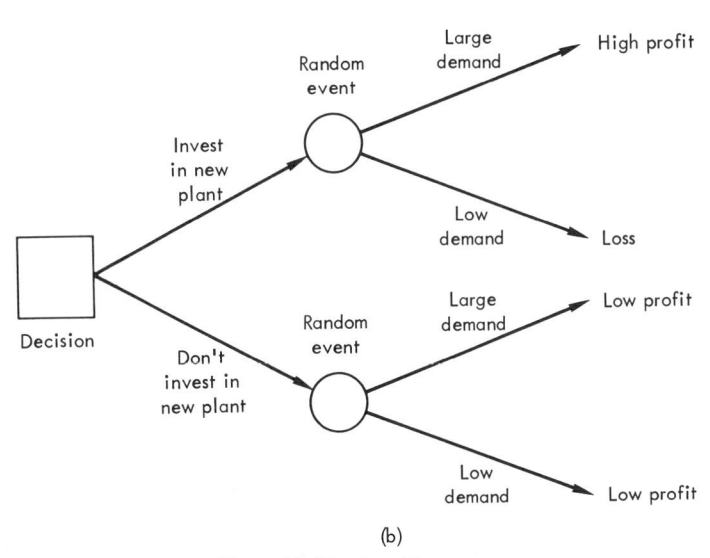

Figure 11–10 Tree Diagrams

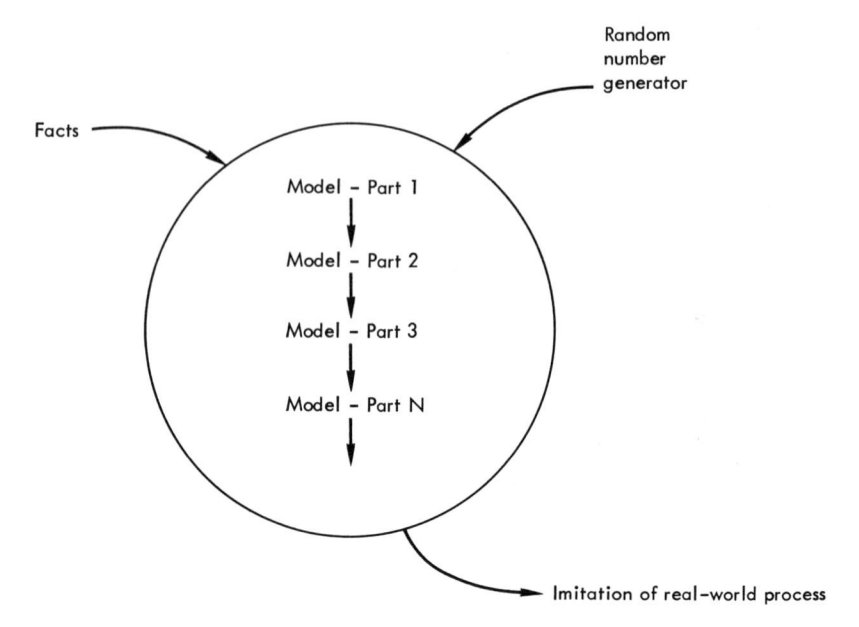

Figure 11-11 Simulation

4. There are two exogenous input variables, variables not under the control of management. These are demand and lead time. The demand is simply the number of units to be withdrawn from inventory in a time period, and this obviously fluctuates.

The lead time is the number of periods of time from placing an order to receiving the goods that replenish the inventory. This also obviously fluctuates.

5. A cumulative probability function or graph links probability values to demand values. This may be constructed from historical data or from a theoretical basis.

A cumulative probability function or graph links probability values to lead time values. This may be constructed similarly to that for demand.

6. A cycle consists of the number of periods from placing an order to the placing of the next order and is determined therefore by the time it takes the inventory level to drop to 4 units.

7. Assume that the initial stock is 4 units.

Now we set up a table, Figure 11–12, to represent the system. Since initial stock is 4 units, we must place an order for 12 more units, according to management policy given under "Facts" 2 and 3 above. In order to find the lead time, we utilize a table of random numbers to give us a number from 0 to 100 and convert it to a probability index by dividing by 100. Suppose the number drawn were 72; this becomes a probability of .72. Corresponding to this probability, we obtain from the graph mentioned in "Fact"

5 a value of the lead time as 4. This is entered in Column (D) of Figure 11–12.

We now obtain a value of demand by the same process, and this value turns out to be zero. We enter this in Column (E). Since no units were demanded in this period and no units arrived, final stock remains at 4, the number of units on hand for the period is 4, and there is no shortage.

The simulation is continued in this manner until Period 4, when 12 units arrive at the end of the period. Figure 11–12 shows the computations into a portion of the third cycle. In practice, *several hundred cycles* would be carried out. The necessity for an electronic computer in such work is apparent. The results in Columns (G) and (H) permit management to determine average inventories, average stockouts, and costs associated with each. Probability distributions for inventory size and shortage amounts may also be obtained.

This simulation is of only a small subsystem; many companies are developing models and simulating entire product ventures. Du Pont has developed a model for its Corfam® product. General Electric has been simulating the development of venture models at the department (business profit center) level. The Boise Cascade Corporation is experimenting with a computerized model of the Timber and Wood Products Division, which has almost 8000 equations and 15,000 variables.[4] The Sun Oil Company has developed a complex, computerized, corporate financial model that uses simulation to improve budgeting, operational control, and planning.[5]

(A) Cycle	(B) Period	(C) Initial Stock	(D) Lead Time	(E) Demand	(F) Final Stock	(G) Units On Hand	(H) Units Short
1	1	4	4	0	4	4	0
	2	4		2	2	2	0
	3	2		1	1	1	0
	4	1		0	13	1	0
	5	13		5	8	13	0
	6	8		2	6	8	0
	7	6		3	3	6	0
2	1	3	2	0	3	3	0
	2	3		4	0	3	1
3	1	0	5	1	10	0	1
	2	10		2	8	10	0
	3	8		2	6	8	0 Etc.

Figure 11–12 Inventory System Simulation

CONSTRUCTION OF MODELS

The construction of models often depends upon recognizing a problem and then finding a matching technique for its solution. The danger in this method is that the analyst may find himself looking for problems to match his techniques instead of vice versa. A general procedure for constructing a model, especially in complex situations, is as follows:

1. Identify and formulate the manager's decision in writing.
2. Identify the constants, parameters, and variables involved. Define them verbally and then introduce symbols to represent each one.
3. Select the variables that appear to be most influential so that the model may be kept as simple as possible. Distinguish between those that are controllable by the manager and those that are not.
4. State verbal relationships among the variables, based upon known principles, specially gathered data, intuition, and reflection. Make assumptions or predictions concerning the behavior of the noncontrollable variables.
5. Construct the model by combining all relationships into a system of symbolic relationships.
6. Perform symbolic manipulations (such as solving systems of equations, differentiating, or making statistical analyses).
7. Derive solutions from the model.
8. Test the model by making predictions from it and checking against real-world data.
9. Revise the model as necessary.[6]

Let us amplify some aspects of this procedure with the aid of the model pictured in Figure 11–13. We begin with the goals of the manager. The manager is faced with a decision problem in achieving a particular set of goals. His decision problem involves the selection of one alternative from among many possible alternatives that are available because of his control over certain variables of his situation. He seeks an alternative that will maximize some benefit, minimize some cost, or optimize some conflicting conditions.

The alternatives in the problem are depicted as A, B, C, and so on, in Figure 11–13, and the problem is to choose the one that will best achieve the goal. The business may choose, for example, the number of salesmen to hire, the amount to be spent on advertising or research, the reorder inventory level, or the products in the product line. The *independent* variables in the system consist of the factors that are internal to the firm, and therefore controllable, and the factors that are *external* to the firm and generally *noncontrollable*. (A company may exert significant influence on external variables through a trade association, political lobbying, market position, or economic leadership.) The decision maker may control *resources* of the firm or *activities*—for example, the mix of manpower and capital, pricing, main-

management science and systems modeling 401

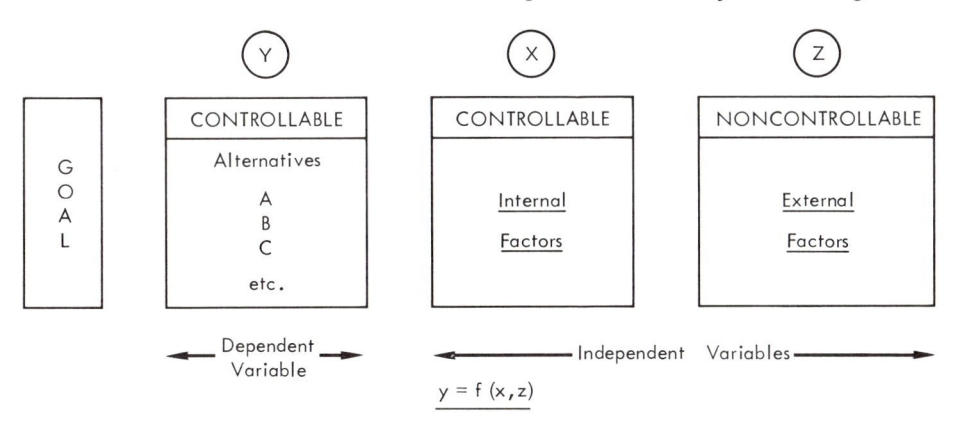

Figure 11-13 A General Model of the Management Science Solution to Decision Problems

Diagram: GOAL | CONTROLLABLE (Y): Alternatives A, B, C, etc. | CONTROLLABLE (X): Internal Factors | NONCONTROLLABLE (Z): External Factors. Dependent Variable ← Y; Independent Variables → X, Z. $y = f(x, z)$

tenance policy, or product strategy. With regard to most *external* factors, such as the vagaries and intransigence of nature and society, the whims of politicians, and the activities of his competitors, the decision maker can exercise little or no influence.

The decision maker must identify the factors, internal or external, that will have a bearing on the dependent variable he seeks to optimize. In practice, the mathematical model should be kept as simple as possible by selecting the factors that have a significant effect on the goal to be achieved and dropping those that add only small refinements. The relationships should be verbalized in complex situations as the first step in structuring relationships. A decision maker who believes that his inventory costs are high might structure his problem in this fashion:

"I'm tying up a lot of money in inventory. In fact, we carry so much inventory that we're running out of warehouse space. Carrying cost is a controllable variable that I could reduce by improving efficiency in warehousing, but I think we're doing well there; I'll consider the cost of storage per unit per year as fixed at $5. What I should do is to lower the amount of inventory I carry at any one time by ordering in small quantities. (The order size is a controllable variable.)

"If I order smaller quantities I'll have less average inventory, but I'll have to place more orders, at $10 for the paperwork on each order. Also, if I can stand short periods of stockout to build up back orders, my average inventory will be lower, but there is a penalty cost in loss of goodwill, probably $5 for each unit per period of time. The length of time of stockout will depend on order size and lead time from ordering to receiving goods (both controllable and independent variables)."

The management scientist would then draw a representation of the model and introduce symbols to identify the variables in Figure 11-14 as:

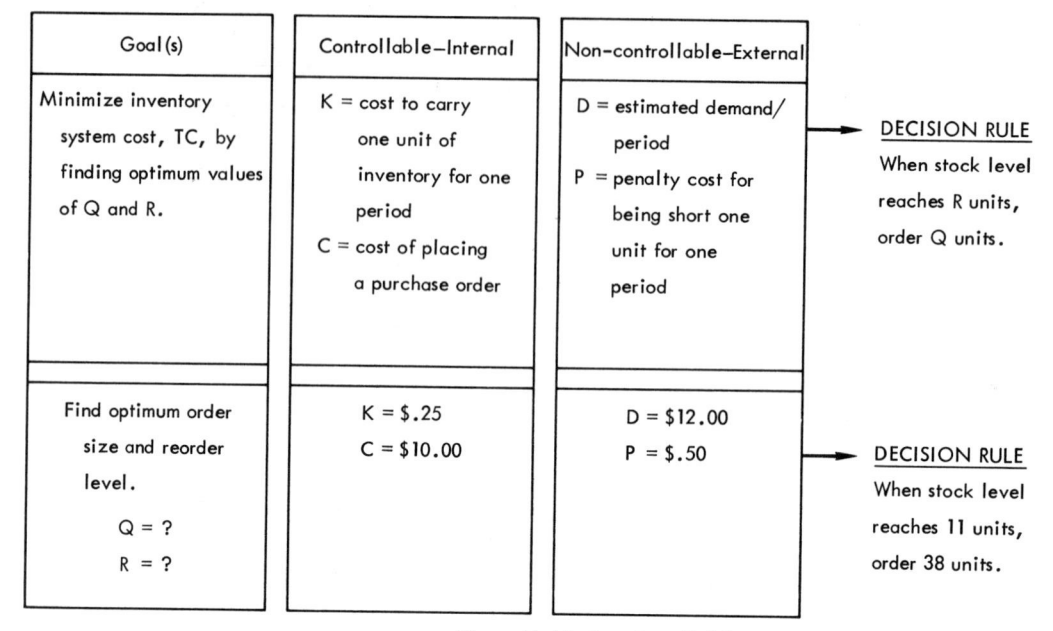

402 Information, Decision Making, and Management Science

Goal(s)	Controllable–Internal	Non-controllable–External	
Minimize inventory system cost, TC, by finding optimum values of Q and R.	K = cost to carry one unit of inventory for one period C = cost of placing a purchase order	D = estimated demand/period P = penalty cost for being short one unit for one period	**DECISION RULE** When stock level reaches R units, order Q units.
Find optimum order size and reorder level. Q = ? R = ?	K = $.25 C = $10.00	D = $12.00 P = $.50	**DECISION RULE** When stock level reaches 11 units, order 38 units.

Figure 11–14 Inventory Model

L = lead time = 2 periods
Q = order quantity (independent variable)
C = cost of placing a purchase order = $10
K = carrying cost per unit of product per period = $.25
P = shortage penalty cost per unit per period = $.50
D = demand in units per period = 12
R = reorder level (independent variable) related to Q and S
S = maximum shortage to be allowed (independent variable)

The system cost is first stated in words to express the relationship among the variables, and then in symbols:

total system cost/period = carrying cost/period + purchase cost/period + shortage cost/period

In symbols,

$$\text{total system cost/period} = \frac{K(Q+S)^2}{2A} + \frac{CD}{Q} + \frac{PS^2}{2Q}$$

The model is then manipulated (by setting the derivatives of total system cost with respect to Q and S equal to zero and solving for Q and S) to yield:

For minimum cost,

$$Q = \sqrt{2CD(1/K + 1/P)} = \text{(about) 38 units}$$
$$R = DL - KQ/(K + P) = \text{(about) 11 units}$$

Figure 11–14 illustrates this situation in which a *decision rule* is determined, a decision rule that can be programmed on a computer so that the computer can "make" the reorder decision. We must keep in mind two very important considerations in using the quantitative techniques related to this model. First, the external factors are not controlled by the decision maker, and hence the *values assigned to these variables must be estimated*, predicted, or forecast by him. For example, the demand per period in Figure 11–14 must be estimated. A second important consideration involves the assignment of values and relationships among the controllable (internal) factors, particularly cost, price, and volume relationships. In many cases, the conventional accounting system does not yield this kind of decision information properly, and care should be taken to determine real (not necessarily accounting) costs. In Figure 11–14, the cost of holding in inventory one unit of product for one period of time is an example. Finally, the restrictions that limit the value of internal factors must be stated for values that exceed the capacity of our warehouse.

SUMMARY

In the early history of technology, new inventions were developed by constructing a device and then tinkering with it until it worked. As science advanced, it became possible to work out on paper in advance the design of a new device. Actual construction of impractical and costly devices could be avoided and more nearly optimum devices designed by application of scientific knowledge.

In the complex world of business, we have seen managers blunder and firms fail because of deficient understanding of the operation of businesses. "Trial" was often followed by "error," and errors often proved to be disastrous. The development of modeling signals the beginning of science in business. Experimentation on models is a tremendous advance over betting the company on every real-world experiment.

We have defined the purpose and nature of models in this chapter. The classifications of models by function, structure, time reference, uncertainty reference, and generality have afforded insights into their nature. We have provided in Figure 11–1 simplified presentations of some models, including their goals, schematic representations, and mathematical representations.

Models are used not only for decision problems, but for analysis and evaluation of complete systems. System efficiency, system response, and system simplification may be studied by means of system modeling. Many valuable techniques for the study of business operational and information systems may be drawn from the literature on servomechanisms and engineered control systems.

Finally, we have attempted to provide guidelines for the construction of models. Because of the limited scope of the coverage of management science in this book, we gave only a general approach and a single example. The construction of models requires a highly specialized business generalist/mathematical specialist to produce the final result. Managers can perform a most important part of modeling by verbalizing the problem, constraints, and qualitative relationships. From the point of view of MIS, the most significant aspect of modeling is its use to provide programmed decision-making and information aids to management decision makers.

DISCUSSION QUESTIONS AND PROBLEMS

1. Describe briefly how management science might be applied in a specific company for the following problems:
   a. Systems evaluation
   b. Detailed system design
   c. Information flow design
   d. Economics of design
   e. Implementation of a system

2. A bank has a drive-in teller system. Long lines form on Fridays, when people cash paychecks. On other days, the lines are rarely longer than five cars, even when there are only one or two tellers. Develop possible variables and objectives. Then develop a verbalized model.

3. There are many alternative sales forecasting objectives and hence many sales forecasting models. What are such objectives and what models are suitable in each case? (This will require reference to books on sales forecasting methods.)

4. Why is it difficult to model consumer behavior? Organizational behavior? Long-range plans?

5. Select a model of a system from either *Management Science, Journal of Marketing Research,* or *Operations Research,* and discuss the utility of the model in the actual business world.

6. An example of each type of model is given in the text for the classification system of models; name a different example of a model for each class.

7. What are the advantages of the concept of a "module" in the construction of systems?

8. Are all business models concerned with "optimizing" some variable?

9. Give an example of a business problem that lends itself to simulation, both because of complexity and because of the economics of obtaining a solution.

10. A "materials" division of a company anticipates, on the basis of executive judgment, that a major expansion will be required over the next 15 years. A management scientist in the marketing department believes that more than intuition should be applied to the whole question. Little study has been made of the growth rate of sales. Further, the company has the choice of overbuilding initially by constructing a plant with one large efficient vat or of constructing a plant with a small vat and adding more small vats in the future. The vats, in which the chemicals are mixed, represent the major cost of the capital expansion. If the large vat is decided upon, only a fraction of its output would be used for many years. The management scientist wishes to formulate the problem and a verbalized model to stimulate management into taking a more analytical look at the system.

11. Du Pont modeled its Corfam® (material for shoes) for analysis on a computer. The variables considered (aggregated in some cases) were: consumers' attitudes, advertising, merchandising, retailer, shoe manufacturer, costs of leather versus Corfam®, cutting yields, key leather prices, shoe market segments, profit incentive to shoe manufacturer, Corfam® shoe sales, market penetration, Du Pont's sales and administrative expense, capital investment, and return on capital. Using these variables, and others if desired, draw a block diagram that represents a model of the venture.

12. A small firm with annual sales of $5 million per year produces a line of specialized and varied medical items, such as electronic heart pacers, ultrasonic machines for orthopedics, and operating room instrumentation. Although many suggestions for needed products are called to its attention by the medical profession, not all will be commercial successes. Mr. Lee, manager of an industrial management group, wondered how the company could evaluate its products. He requested ideas from one of his former professors, who suggested that characteristic development stages of the products be specified so that products could receive a complete "systems" evaluation at key development points. At these "screening" points, the technological, marketing, and economic factors could be considered. The professor also suggested that the "life cycle" of each product be forecast so that time and risk for return could be taken into account. Develop a detailed systems approach and verbal descriptions of models (or quantitative models) to help Mr. Lee solve the problem.

13. Mr. M. Doll, a department manager in a large department store, has decided that he has "had it" working for someone else and decides to set up a men's clothing store of his own. He has good contacts in the clothing industry, good taste in clothes, and plenty of business experience. He has found a good location in an uptown business district. A friend, who is an engineer, suggests that he model the business venture with a particular view to "sensitivity analysis." In other words, he could determine, with the help of a model, the effect of changes in the quality level of clothes, size of store, variety of items, merchandising expenditures, and traffic count on sales and profits. Mr. Doll admitted he had no knowledge of management science techniques and asked his friend to help him work out such a model.

REFERENCES

1. "The 'New Management' Finally Takes Over," *Business Week,* August 23, 1969, p. 58.
2. See Arthur D. Hall, *A Methodology for Systems Engineering* (Princeton, N.J.: D. Van Nostrand Co., Inc., 1962).
3. See, for example, Y. H. Ku, *Analysis and Control of Linear Systems* (Scranton, Pa.: International Textbook Co., 1962).
4. "The 'New Management' Takes Over," p. 58.
5. George W. Gershefski, "Building a Corporate Financial Model," *Harvard Business Review,* July–August 1969. For further discussion of systems modeling, see A. F. Moravec, "Using Simulation to Design a Management Information System," *Management Services,* May–June 1966; and Albert N. Schrieber, ed., *Corporate Simulation Models* (Seattle: Graduate School of Business Administration, University of Washington, 1970).
6. See also William T. Morris, "On the Art of Modeling," *Management Science,* August 1967.

CASE STUDY

An Information Problem*

To: J. Berkman, Manager, Systems Planning

From: J. Manley, Executive Vice-President

Re: Repairs

Our policies and systems for handling goods returned for repair and orders for repair parts should be reviewed. Our customers and our operating personnel are dissatisfied.

With respect to customers, my attention has been directed to numerous complaints, in the following areas in particular:

1. Delays occasioned by correspondence.
2. Requests for payment of nominal amounts before repairs are undertaken by us. In some instances, I understand, customers were industrial firms having established accounts with us. Further, payment requests have been made in instances where items are still under warranty.
3. Where items have been repaired within the last year and are returned a second time, customers believe a new warranty period was established at the date of the first repair and that no further charges should be made. The two repairs may or may not be related. Admittedly, our policies are vague in this area.

With respect to our internal deficiencies, I am aware of the following problems:

1. Customer service requires two men and four clerks to match receiving reports, customer correspondence, and repair cost estimates from the Repair Department, and then to carry on the necessary correspondence with customers.
2. As I understand it, over eight different forms are involved in our handlings, some with five copies. This does not include individually dictated letters to customers. Included are receiving reports, item identification tags, cost estimate forms, work orders and material requisitions. There may be others.
3. The Repair Department claims they are not informed of the exact nature of customer complaints and must therefore conduct a text search to ascertain malfunctions.
4. As I understand it, warranty cards are not now being used. Repairs are being made based on serial numbers of items. This causes diffi-

---

*Prepared by William J. Waldman, Florida Atlantic University.

culties because of item layover in our warehouse, distributors' warehouses, and retailers' shelves. Thus, a customer may be entitled to service under warranty but we refuse him, basing our decision on elapsed time from date of manufacture.

5. Engineering and Product Development inform me there is no formal means of channeling data to them on the nature and causes of malfunctions.
6. The Sales Department believes analysis of warranty cards returned could provide the basis for sales forecasting by product, distributor area, etc. Since much of our distribution is from our warehouse—to distributors, to dealers and, finally, to consumers—demand can actually be strong at consumer levels and we might not know of it for weeks or months.

   Sales also has some ideas about using the warranty names and addresses for direct mail promotions to support national advertising.

These observations are not meant to be exhaustive but rather to indicate some of the areas that need to be explored.

I shall appreciate your comments.

(Author's suggestion: As a point of departure, read Warren W. Menke, "Determination of Warranty Reserves," *Management Science*, June 1969; or "Call Out the Reserves—Warranty, That Is," *Management Services*, January–February 1970.)

CASE STUDY

The Development of a Management Information System for Field Office Managers of the Northwestern Insurance Company*

The Northwestern Insurance Company currently has fifty full-line field offices located throughout the United States, each consisting of a number of service units that perform processing and administrative services for producers (agents) in the geographical area served by the field office. Although the exact composition varies from location to location, most field offices have separate service units for processing transactions relating to life and accident insurance, fire and marine insurance (e.g., homeowner and business coverage of losses from fire, theft, rain, and windstorm), other casualty insurance (including workmen's compensation, public liability, burglary, plate glass, multiperil commercial, and auto fleet coverage), automobile insurance, and fidelity and surety insurance. In addition to the primary service units, each field office normally has an accounting unit.

Administrative and Policy-Related Processing Operations

The primary service units provide processing services to the agent in the field. Each service unit processes four basic types of transactions: new policy applications, policy changes, policy renewals, and claim registrations. Transactions in the field offices arise from correspondence received from the home office, from the producer-agent, and, in some cases, directly from the policyholder.

All incoming mail is transferred in bulk to a record desk. A clerk sorts the mail by unit (e.g., fire, other casualty, automobile). The incoming documents are matched with any existing file records pertaining to each transaction. Although the principal policy records are maintained in the home office, the field offices also keep extensive manual records, some of which duplicate the home office files. Once transaction documents have been matched with appropriate file records, the resulting package is forwarded to the proper service unit for further processing. At the conclusion of processing, existing documents are refiled or otherwise disposed of. New documents created provide the basis for extending or changing coverage to new and old policyholders.

---

*Northwestern Insurance Company is a fictitious name. This case study is based on the operations of a large multiline insurance company, with a few minor modifications. It is adapted from "The Development of a Management Information System for Field Office Managers of the Northwestern Insurance Co.," a paper presented by William C. House at the 1969 TIMS meeting in Atlanta, Georgia. By permission of the author.

The accounting unit is not directly involved in the major flows of paperwork through the field office, and so it does not ordinarily have direct contact with producers in the field. However, it does perform some important processing functions, including the collection of premiums, reporting of premiums received to the home office, and payroll and expense accounting for the field office.

Management Information Requirements for the Field Office Manager

The performance of each field office manager is judged by how well he meets certain basic objectives in the areas of service, personnel, and expenses. These objectives are largely determined by the home office administrators who are responsible for supervising field office operations. Examples of objectives for each performance area are:

SERVICE

Volume of unfinished business (e.g., no more than 2 days work left undone at the end of the week)

Quantity of work done (e.g., number of transactions processed per day)

Quality of work done (e.g., no more than 5% errors)

PERSONNEL

Available hours for each service unit (i.e., number of man-hours available to perform work)

Earned hours for each service unit (i.e., standard processing times for each type of transaction, multiplied by number of transactions processed)

Number of employees hired

Turnover rate—by office, by service unit, by salary grade, by position code

EXPENSE

Actual costs : Provisional budget costs

Actual costs : Budget costs (adjusted for volume changes)

Cost per hour (by field office)

The field office manager needs information relating to service, personnel, and expense performance within ten days after the end of the (usually monthly) reporting period, so that he can determine if any service unit is failing to meet one or more of the basic objectives and can take corrective action before serious deterioration occurs. To determine the basic causes and sources of inadequate performance often requires quickly accessible and detailed information on the performance of particular service units and of specific individuals within these units. In addition, all basic performance information should be provided to the field office manager in one package at one time, instead of in several reports issued at different time intervals, as is now the case.

In the service area, timely information is needed on the rate at which work is coming into the unit and the speed with which it is being processed. If a unit is falling behind in its work, the field office manager needs to take corrective action quickly, to avoid a serious bottleneck. For such purposes, a two-week reporting period would be much better than a monthly one, and weekly reports on the volume of unfinished business by unit would be even more valuable.

In order to utilize data concerning service levels and work backlogs most effectively, the manager needs to know the size of the work load facing him and the number of people he has to handle it. If he is facing a peak volume period and his office is understaffed, he may have to consider the use of overtime, of contract services, of transferring some work to another office, or of hiring and training additional employees. In making such decisions, the manager needs to know probable service requirements by line of business, since some lines are more difficult to handle than others or require specialized training to handle, and by type of transaction (e.g., new business, policy changes, renewals, and claims), since some types of transactions require more employee processing time than others. Therefore, a forecast of service requirements sixty to ninety days in advance would be extremely helpful in determining staffing and training requirements.

To project future requirements, the manager needs past data on the number of new policies, number of endorsements (changes), number of renewals, and number of claims for each service unit for comparable periods. If a relationship could be established between new policies issued and the probable number of changes, claims, and renewals that could be expected in each period per 100 or 1000 policies issued, a complete work-load forecast could be developed simply by predicting the amount of new business. The estimated number of new policies, changes, renewals, claims, and premium payments developed from past experience and considered judgment about the future could be exploded into volume requirements for service to be performed by the various service units.

These volume requirements could then serve as the basis for establishing the size and composition of the work force needed to meet expected volumes, in terms of hours and experience required. Work-load requirements in hours would indicate the amount of work required for each service unit for each type of work (e.g., rating, typing, duplicating), and such information could then be used to decide the best way of meeting work-load requirements (e.g., increasing or decreasing the existing work force, using overtime, employing contract services, shifting some of the work load to other offices, or finding ways to improve present unit productivity).

To decide how to meet these estimated work-load requirements most efficiently and economically, the field office manager needs an up-to-date picture of the status of his current work force. In particular, he needs to know the amount of lost time he is experiencing, because of absences owing to illness and other causes, and the personnel losses of each service unit because of turnover. A realistic forecast of the lost time each service unit is likely to experience during the next three months would help him determine the probable number of available hours he can expect to obtain from his existing work force. By matching available hours with required hours forecast, the manager could determine in advance if he is overstaffed or understaffed in terms of work-load requirements for the coming quarter.

If an increase in service is forecast and the manager is understaffed to meet such an increase, he has a number of alternatives open to him. If he is willing to pay the training costs entailed and can afford to wait until the end of a normal training period, he can increase the existing work force. For temporary work-load peaks, the use of overtime or contract services may be considered. The manager may find it economical to transfer some of the peak load to other field offices that have idle time, at a cost per hour less than other feasible alternatives. In some cases, improving the productivity of the existing work force may be the best solution. Fewer people may be able to do the work required if they are placed in the right positions and are paid large enough salaries. In order to choose wisely from among these alternatives, the manager must be provided with the cost per hour involved in each alternative.

In essence, the manager must decide whether he can perform the projected work load with the staff available at a reasonable cost. If he cannot get the work out with the available staff, he must consider other alternatives. In most cases he will select the least costly alternative, but not at an unreasonable sacrifice in terms of service provided. Some balance must be maintained, since it is possible to meet service objectives satisfactorily at an unreasonable cost, or to provide inadequate service at satisfactory costs. In the dynamic situation faced by the office manager, he must make continual and rapid adjustments to keep the entire office operating at a satisfactory level. Timely and complete information about all aspects of service, personnel, and expense performance is essential if he is to make sound and effective decisions.

Service Reporting

Each field office has the objective of providing twenty-four-hour service on new business and claim registrations and forty-eight-hour service on policy changes. Objectives for renewal service are more flexible, since renewal processing can be accelerated or delayed in many cases without ill effects.

Service reports are prepared manually for each week of a month and are transmitted by mail to the home office once a month. Each field office reports the current status of 55 different processing activities on its service reports. Thus, 2750 transactions (i.e., 55×50) must be processed monthly for all field offices. These reports, normally received by the home office within seven to ten days after the end of the reporting period, are used to evaluate the service status of each field office, and the transaction counts in the reports are also used as basic inputs for expense reporting.

At present, field office managers do not, in many cases, receive information on deteriorating service quickly enough to prevent work-load bottlenecks. Although the manager is informed of the amount of unfinished business in the various service units, he is given no idea of the volume or composition of the service requirements he should anticipate for the next quarter, or the cost of maintaining or changing desired service levels.

Personnel Reporting

Each field office maintains basic personnel files on clerical employees. However, the home office also maintains personnel files, and each field office is responsible for advising the home office of changes in the clerical work force, so that company-wide statistical information can be compiled and payroll information maintained for the preparation of tax withholding information.

Three basic input documents—the personnel employment authorization, the personnel change slip, and the absence report—are used to collect data on personnel changes. Owing to a lag in the forwarding and posting of change slips, the home office personnel file is normally at least ten days out of date.

Transactions affecting the personnel file occur at irregular intervals, but are substantial in number over the entire working year. On an annual basis, the total volume of typical personnel transactions might be estimated as follows:

Transaction Type	Number of Transactions
Salary changes	18,000
Absences	38,000
Personnel time off	1,000
Name changes	2,000
Annual updating	16,000
	75,000

Assuming 300 working days in a year, there would be an average of 250 (i.e., 75,000/300) personnel updating transactions per day for all field offices. And assuming six service units per field office, there would be 300 transactions (6 $\times$ 50) each time the number of available hours is calculated for all service units in the company.

The time lag in updating personnel files makes it difficult to produce personnel information such as turnover statistics, average salaries, etc., in time to be of the greatest potential value to users. High turnover rates and high costs of recruiting and training clerical personnel make it imperative that managers select the best-qualified people with the greatest potential for long tenure; but the present reporting system does not provide information as to what age, education, and experience groups are producing the best results and in which areas recruiting efforts should be concentrated. Also lacking is sound, factual information on the causes of turnover in a particular service unit (e.g., salary inequities, specific job-related dissatisfaction, unit morale problems), which the manager could use to select, train, and motivate individuals so as to achieve higher levels of unit efficiency.

Expense Reporting

Expense performance in the field offices is measured through the use of a provisional (planned) and earned budget system that includes both fixed and variable budget items. Fixed-cost items include stenographic services, telephone operations, mail handling, etc., and variable-cost items include such activities as the screening, rating, coding, typing, duplicating, and disassembly of various types of insurance policies. "Earned hours" are calculated by multiplying the number of transactions processed by the budgeted time rates in the provisional budget. For all field offices, a maximum of 2750 transactions would be involved for each reporting period.

In preparing the provisional budget, the field office manager estimates the volume of each type of activity, the time rate required to process each activity, and employee salaries (including increase programs) for the coming year. The number of hours needed by each office to handle the expected work load is obtained by multiplying the time rate by the number of items to be processed for each activity and then summing the expected activity times. The dollar costs of providing the necessary clerical hours, and the estimated cost per hour for each service unit and for the total office, can then be developed. The completed provisional budget shows planned hours and planned costs for each service unit in the field office.

Comparisons between actual expense performance and budgeted expense levels are presented in monthly and quarterly performance reports. Available hours and earned hours for each service unit and for the total office are shown in the monthly report on a current-month and year-to-date basis. Available hours are the man-hours actually worked by each unit (i.e., gross hours minus vacation time, time lost to illness, and other miscellaneous causes). Earned hours are calculated as previously described.

The monthly expense reports come out approximately twenty days after the close of the month being reported. Quarterly expense reports are not available until approximately forty-five days after the end of the reporting period. As a result, many supervisors are currently figuring productivity ratios by hand from work counts. By the time reports arrive from the home office, the unit supervisors already know the results. Although this practice gives the supervisor information more quickly than would otherwise be possible, it is time-consuming, costly, and cumbersome. Also, the lag between the receipt of information on service status and corresponding information about expense performance means that the office manager does not have a complete picture of service-unit status at a given instant of time and cannot make completely informed decisions about work-load scheduling, hiring new employees, using overtime, employing contract services, etc., at the time when such decisions must be made.

Monthly and quarterly expense reports are needed by field office managers much sooner after the end of the reporting period so they can make better-informed decisions about alternative ways of providing clerical service. Under the present reporting system, information is frequently received too late to be of real value in controlling expense levels, and the manager cannot determine from the information he receives what actions he should take in order to correct present performance. The system does not relate expenses to expected volumes and does not indicate to the manager how he should plan to achieve best results. Finally, there is no way at present of coordinating expense performance with service results, nor does the manager know the economic resources he must use in order to improve service, personnel, and expense performance.

Design of an Information System to Meet Management Information Requirements

At the present time, policyholder records and many other administrative records are maintained in the home office, although some duplicate records are kept by the field offices. Most of the inputs for creating new records and updating those existing in the home office come from the field offices. A large amount of performance data is forwarded to the home office through the use of mail and telegraph services. In addition, two-way data and voice communication channels rapidly transmit data collected for policy record creation and policy updating to the home office data center for batch processing at appropriate times, and inquiries from the field offices about the status of an individual policy are answered promptly on a real-time basis by means of the same network.

The home office maintains four basic but separate files pertinent to performance reporting: policyholder, service, personnel, and expense files. Each file requires a separate processing run. Consideration is being given to consolidation of service, personnel, and expense data into one centralized file. Input devices used to transmit messages to the central computer center (i.e., paper-tape punches connected to telephone lines) could be utilized to input office service, personnel, and expense performance data. A second alternative being considered is the use of two regional processing centers, one in the eastern and the other in the western United States, to divide the total data-processing load.

Another important issue is the frequency of reporting. At the present time, the bulk of reporting is done on a monthly basis, with an average time lag of twenty to thirty days from the end of the reporting period to the receipt of desired management reports by field office managers. This time lag is caused by delays in forwarding data to the home office; in processing data, owing to the occurrence of transaction volume peaks at the end of each month; and in consolidating data items that are obtained from several different processing runs on different computer systems into a single performance report.

More frequent reporting, on a bimonthly, weekly, or even daily basis, is feasible but will probably require integration of existing files, a greater degree of compatibility between existing computers, and expansion of the on-line processing capability now largely restricted to certain classes of policyholder records. For example, if transactions for the service, personnel, and expense areas were processed for all fifty field offices on a daily basis, the estimated number of transactions to be processed would be as follows:

Service	2750
Personnel updating	250
Personnel available hours	300
Expense	2750

Assuming 300 working days in a year, 1,815,000 transactions (i.e., 6050 × 300) would be handled annually by the consolidated system. On a monthly basis (corresponding to the present reporting period), 72,600 transactions (i.e., 6050 × 12) are processed. Thus, daily updating would necessitate about a thirty-fold increase in the number of transactions processed.

The field offices are now processing approximately 20,000,000 policy-related transactions per year. The number is expected to increase at a rate of at least 5 percent annually as new policyholders are added and the coverage of existing policyholders is increased to meet changing needs. Office performance transactions can also be expected to increase at approximately the same rate as new employees are added, as the scope of performance reporting is increased, and as new field offices are created to handle the ever-expanding increase in volume of business.

Expansion of business volume will also increase the number of data calculations that must be performed by existing data-processing equipment. Consideration is being given to development of simulation models in conjunction with existing computers, which would allow field office managers to develop their own forecasts and to test alternative methods of meeting service requirements before making decisions.

IV

Planning, Design, and Implementation of MIS

The overview of management and MIS has been presented and the conceptual groundwork has now been laid for the development of the MIS in practice. Part IV delineates a blueprint for the planning/programming, the design, and the implementation of the MIS. Whereas most literature attempts to give characteristics of well-designed systems, the active, how-to-do-it, step-by-step method is adopted here. Managers must be concerned with action, and the managerial action of MIS development is presented.

The complexities of design and implementation can be ordered only by the planning/programming process. There are numerous variations to the basic design and implementation given in this Part. Once the logic of design is understood, management and designer creativity opens the way to new advances in MIS that yield competitive advantages.

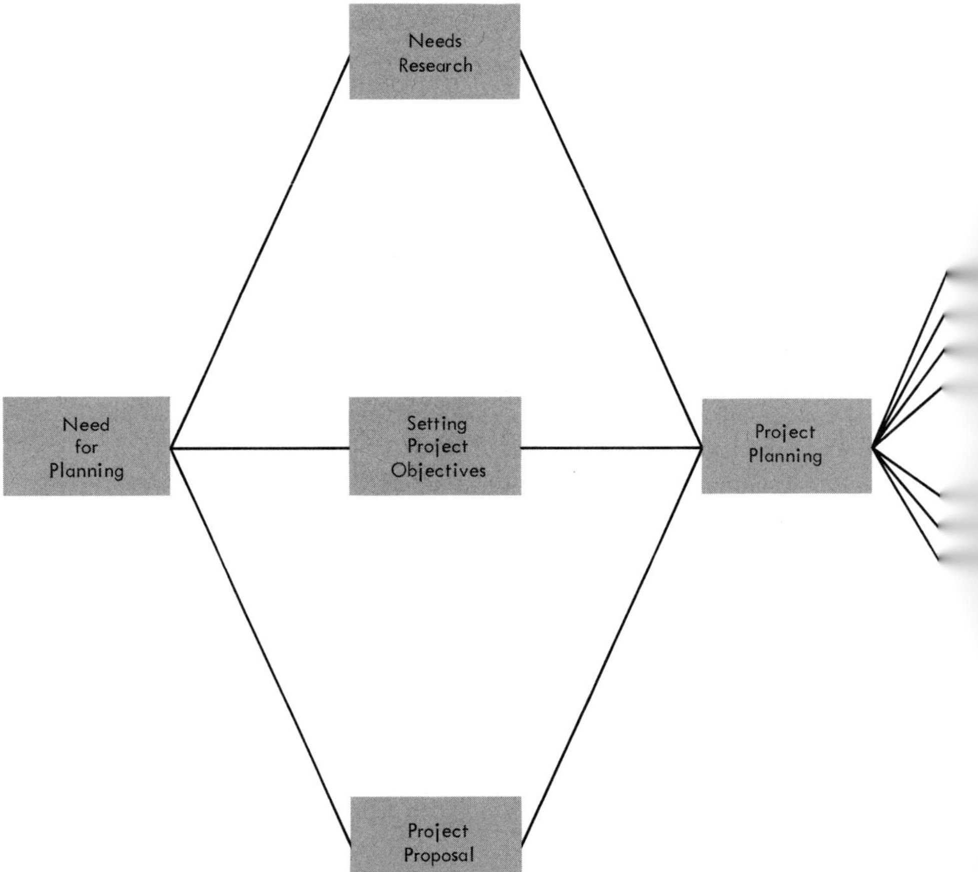
Needs Research
Need for Planning
Setting Project Objectives
Project Planning
Project Proposal

12

planning and programming management information systems

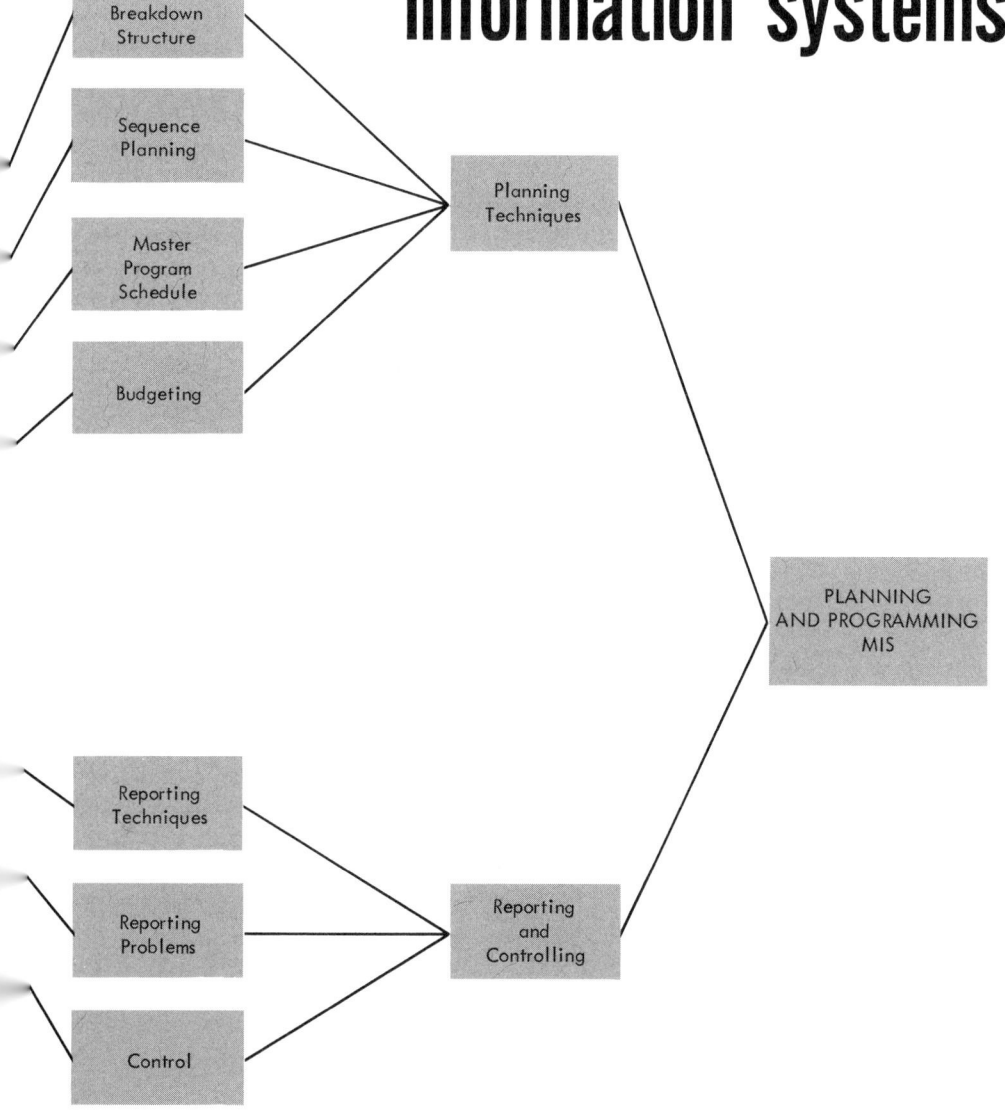

12

It is evident that the improving capability and capacity of modern computers are outracing the ability of the average company to utilize them properly. Several research studies and surveys reveal that the *utilization* of third-generation equipment and techniques falls far short of the computer's potential for processing the information needed for up-to-date management information systems.[1] For the most part, the third-generation equipment is being used on systems with second-generation design, and few companies are without at least some programs essentially intact from their "tab shop" days. With regard to assisting in the top-level decision-making function, managers of firms utilizing computers report that the decision-making process at corporate or division level is not being directly affected by the computer to a significant degree.[2] In a survey of the literature, the National Association of Accountants reports that "descriptions of 'what we have done' shade into 'what we are now doing,' which, of course, immediately lead to 'what we plan to do' next week, month, or next year."[3] It is fair to say that one major reason for the underutilization of computers and the failure to fully utilize the potential of information systems is lack of *managerial* involvement in planning for systems development and design activities.

In this book we have divided the MIS development work into four phases:

1. *Planning and programming.* This phase, covered in the previous chapter, is concerned with the planning, organizing, and control of effort devoted to MIS development.

2. *Gross design.* Sometimes referred to as feasibility study or conceptual design, gross design is the development of alternative MIS's in preliminary form for evaluation and selection of the most promising. It is comparable to the rough sketches that engineers and architects make. Sufficient investigation is made to determine which designs are "feasible"—can be produced to operate.[4]

3. *Detailed design.* Once the critical decision—the selection of the gross design—has been made, the detailed design work is conducted to develop the operational and information systems in detail. The steps in this process are covered in Chapter 14.

4. *Implementation.* The output of design work is a set of specifications; implementation is the conversion of these specifications to a working system.

To a great extent, these phases overlap. Thus, in some cases planning and programming cannot be properly completed until the gross design has been completed. Detailed design and implementation frequently overlap because the design may require testing of partial systems or installations.

The boundaries of the systems planning topic, as we will treat it here, are somewhat more limited than in the usual technical sense. It is viewed as the necessary first step in systems development, and for the purposes of this chapter we will restrict the discussion surrounding this topic to considerations of primary concern to the manager. After tracing the need for and objectives of systems planning, we shall examine in some depth the nature of project planning as it applies to MIS.

THE NEED FOR SYSTEMS PLANNING

Judging from the literature and from observations of real-life applications, little more than lip service has been paid to the widely promoted concept of a "total" single system or to the goal of a highly integrated set of subsystems. Instead, we have seen the development of "islands of mechanization" following unrelated starts in quick-payoff areas such as payroll and some clerical accounting functions. This patchwork approach has resulted in the development of unrelated and sometimes incompatible subsystems.

This patchwork or piecemeal approach to systems development, which has no unifying framework and is without a master plan, has several disadvantages. One of these stems from the unrelated nature of the subsystems developed. Frequently autonomous departments and divisions have developed individualistic systems without regard to the interface of such systems elsewhere in the organization. The result has been an inability to communicate between systems and the incompatibility of subsystems of a like nature throughout the company.

A fairly common example of failure to relate subsystems is the way personnel information is structured. Several departments (sales, production, accounting, personnel) may maintain employee files that overlap with other similar files but do not provide for interface between them. In one instance, critical engineering and labor skills shortages developed in several geographically separated divisions of a multidivision company. But despite the fact that these skills were available elsewhere in the company, no identification could be made because of the lack of a common personnel-skills information system.

A second and serious disadvantage is the cost involved, cost in time, resources, and money. The longer a master plan is put off, the more costly will be the inevitable need to overhaul, unify, and standardize the approach to integrated systems design. Many companies have invested in the automation of clerical records and subsequently discovered that a complete overhaul of the system is necessary when it becomes integrated with a larger effort. A popular one-for-one conversion in the past has been the materials inventory "tab" system, which frequently requires complete rework when a production planning and control system is implemented.

The questions arise, first, Why has the piecemeal approach been allowed to develop? And second, What should and can be done to improve the design situation so that an improved, integrated approach can be taken?

The answer to the first question is complex but the major reason probably is that managers have generally failed to realize in the early stages of systems development the scope of the computer and information systems, the investment it would represent, and the impact it would have on the operations of the business.[5] Belatedly, many firms have realized the need for integration through the implementation of a master plan, and they are now undertaking massive efforts to correct the situation. The signs are favorable. Evidence seems to indicate that future systems development will be characterized by four improving trends:

1. A much greater share of systems effort will be devoted to the planning and control of operations rather than, as previously, to the clerical and routine paperwork of finance and administration.[6] Operations, marketing, product or process development, and personnel management are among the areas expected to have increasingly sophisticated applications.

2. An increasing percentage of expenditures for new plant and equipment and an increasing percentage of sales will be spent on data-processing equipment and activities.[7] This trend reflects primarily the growing recognition on the part of management that information systems are a vital resource. Moreover, increasing expenditures will be made on managerial applications, the surface of which has barely been scratched.

3. An increasing fraction of computer and related expenditures will be devoted to design and "software" as opposed to mainframe and hardware. This changing "mix" of systems expenditures reflects the relatively unsophisticated state-of-the-art in systems design in most companies and the recognition that greater efforts under a master plan are needed.

4. The tendency toward the integration of subsystems will accelerate. Integration not only is economical but yields much more effective information for management planning, operating, and control. More and more companies realize this and are moving in that direction.

The answer to the second question, regarding the means to achieve an integrated approach to systems development, lies clearly in the adoption of a master plan. Working to a long-range blueprint is desirable: it is proven, and it is practical. Indeed, the same reasons that can be advanced for business planning in general can apply to the argument for systems planning.

These four special reasons for systems planning are:

1. *To offset uncertainty*
2. *To improve economy of operations*
3. *To focus on objectives*
4. *To provide a device for control of operations*

Aside from the uncertainty of business operations and the resulting need for better forecasting information, the special need for a systems plan is evident because of advancing computer technology and its widespread effect on business operations. Both software (programming languages, systems design, etc.) and hardware (computers, related devices, data transmission equipment, etc.) have become so complex that the job of selection and utilization is much more difficult. As a result, the majority of organizations have fallen far short of their potential to use computers for processing the information necessary to manage the company effectively. A master plan may not remove the uncertainty, but it will almost surely place the firm in a better position to deal with the unknowns and to take advantage of developments as they occur.

Planning the overall approach to an integrated systems timetable is also *economical*. The prevailing pattern of design effort in most companies reflects the short-term approach of automating those clerical operations that offer an immediate payoff in terms of reduction of paperwork and staff. Customer billing, payroll, accounts payable, and inventory records (not inventory control) are favorite targets for automation of clerical tasks. However, experience has shown that in the long run this approach is likely to be more costly than proceeding under a predetermined plan. Once one job or function has been automated, the need for the design and automation of contiguous functions frequently becomes obvious. Take, for example, the well-designed production-planning system whose inputs come from a manual sales order and forecasting system, and whose outputs are largely ignored by purchasing and personnel. It becomes obvious that money can be saved and performance improved by an effective linking together of these neighboring functions through a good plan for integrated systems design. However, if adjacent or interacting systems are not considered under a plan, costly rework will almost surely result.

Economies surrounding organizational changes, personnel considerations, and equipment purchase or rental may also be realized by working to a predetermined grand scheme rather than permitting systems applications to "grow like Topsy."

A good plan for systems development also serves to *focus on company and systems objectives.* Conversely, firms without explicit organizational objectives and explicit plans for achieving them, that make expedient responses to environmental factors rather than shape their own environment, are unlikely to have definite systems objectives and a plan for their attainment. Indeed, if we review the fundamental process of planning, we discover that planning cannot proceed in any area of endeavor until adequate objectives have first been set. It follows that development of a master systems plan forces examination and definition of objectives.

The question arises: What are the objectives of an information systems plan? Although we will discuss this in detail later in this chapter, it is appropriate at this time to point out that if systems objectives are to be supported, those in charge of systems development will have to ask the following questions: What will be the nature of the firm in the future, and what information will be needed to assist in the satisfaction of the needs arising from management of the company in the future changing environment? What will be our products . . . our customers . . . our competition . . . our distribution channels? What kind of sales forces will be needed . . . what facilities . . . etc.? Only after these questions are specified can the designer begin to determine the objectives of the systems plan and the specifics of information needs and sources.

Systems development, implementation, and operations are among the most difficult of activities within the company to control. The fourth major advantage of the development of systems effort under a predetermined plan is that the plan provides a means for subsequent *control*. Plans and objectives also provide the means for measuring progress. If systems development activities and events are organized on a project basis with specific objectives (e.g., optimize cost of raw materials inventory) to be achieved within a certain time period and at a predetermined cost, then these goals can be used as yardsticks to measure subsequent accomplishments.[8]

Yet despite the fact that the real reason for the development of management information systems is their use to improve the management of organizations, the planning and control of systems development efforts are frequently left to chance. Perhaps those responsible for this effort should take their own advice: "What you need is a system!"

OBJECTIVES OF MANAGEMENT INFORMATION SYSTEMS PLANNING

We have previously described the nature of planning by saying that "Planning involves the development and selection from among alternatives of the necessary course of action to achieve an objective." This definition is but one of many, but planning is invariably defined in terms of those actions necessary to achieve an *objective*. The objective is therefore the essential prerequisite to planning, and planning can be useful and commence only when objectives are properly selected. Improper selection of or failure to define objectives results only in frustration and failure of the entire planning process.

Although the previous discussion relates to general business planning, there is no reason to believe that it does not apply to the more limited context of information systems planning as well. Indeed, the argument advanced here is that systems planning cannot proceed to a master plan or any other constructive scheme unless the objectives of the information systems plan are detailed and well understood.

We are referring not to specific *objectives* (e.g., explosion of bill of materials, requiring that stock orders be billed and shipped within twelve hours after receipt) of subsystems but to the overall *systems planning objectives*—in other words, to the characteristics of the information systems that should be developed for both the near-term and long-range effort. Included herein are objectives having to do first with the systems-planning effort and second with how this effort will improve the allocation of resources and hence the profitability of the organization. An excellent framework of objectives for the systems-planning function has been developed by Blumenthal:

> The systems-planning function must therefore encompass the review of proposed systems in terms of planning criteria designed to minimize the number of systems, to broaden their scope, and to place them in the proper sequence for development. All these requirements can be expressed by the following list of systems-planning objectives:
> 1. To avoid overlapping development of major systems elements which are widely applicable across organizational lines, when there is no compelling technical or functional reason for difference.
> 2. To help ensure a uniform basis for determining sequence of development in terms of payoff potential, natural precedence, and probability of success.
> 3. To minimize the cost of integrating related systems with each other.
> 4. To reduce the total number of small, isolated systems to be developed, maintained, and operated.
> 5. To provide adaptability of systems to business change and growth without periodic major overhaul.
> 6. To provide a foundation for coordinated development of consistent, comprehensive, corporate-wide and interorganizational information systems.
> 7. To provide guidelines for and direction to continuing systems-development studies and projects.[9]

With any organizational resource it is necessary to achieve some sort of economic balance. This balance with regard to information systems applies in two ways: first, an optimal use of resources allocated to information systems; and second, an optimal balance between MIS resources and the resources allocated to other uses in the company. In other words, the organizational objective is to allocate the correct amount of resources to information systems development and design and to get the best systems possible out of the resources allocated to information systems. Here we see the economic principle of marginal utility at work. If no allocation were made to the gathering and dissemination of information, the company would probably go out of business. On the other hand, if all or a substantial amount of company resources went into information systems, there would be no product and the same result would occur.

The practical problem, however, is rarely the allocation of resources to information systems vis-à-vis other uses, but rather where to apply the limited personnel, equipment, and dollars available for the systems effort. The obvious answer appears to be payoff, i.e., the application in which the highest benefits can be obtained for the systems effort. This choice is easier said than made, however, and practical considerations of estimating benefits must be faced.

The benefits of any one or group of applications is not always self-evident. Many companies have tended to take the easy way out by automating the routine bookkeeping and clerical functions because these appear to be the "obvious" areas and because personnel replacement costs can be estimated. This approach is rarely the correct one, however. There are a few organizations (perhaps the Social Security Administration or Internal Revenue Service) whose clerical displacement savings outweigh the savings to be realized in the improvement of planning and control applications. Although the benefits in these managerial areas are intangible and difficult to measure, it is in these types of applications that system development effort has the most impact on costs and on company operations.

Orlicky identifies three areas that consistently yield the greatest benefits in industry:

1. Planning and control of finished goods in the distribution network
2. Planning and control of the use of materials, machines, and labor in manufacturing operations
3. Planning and control of the material procurement function.[10]

He also makes the point that precedence relationships of functions being automated should be followed. Precedence relationship is given by the time sequence in which related functions take place. For example, if materials planning is chosen to be automated, then forecasting or inventory control should be next because these functions are immediately adjacent to materials planning. The approach assures the most orderly growth with a minimum of costly system rework.

In short, the manager or systems designer should focus on an overall plan and the applications that provide the greatest payoff in terms of improved planning and control. In almost every case this approach is more economical than concentrating on areas that offer a quick short-term payoff in terms of clerical savings.

PROJECT PLANNING AND MIS

If MIS designers know how to design systems to assist management with planning and control, they should put this knowledge to work in conducting their own projects. Prior to the entire MIS design project or to any major step, the project manager should develop an overall plan, a detailed program for implementing the plan, and a method for controlling the progress, cost, and time variables of the project. The planning–controlling project cycle is indicated by Figure 12–1. This chapter covers the method and techniques of project management and how these are used for planning and programming MIS.

How do projects arise, and what distinguishes a project? The flow of work in much of a business is a continuous process whose changes are gradual over time. However, there are major dislocations from time to time, caused by needs for major innovations. The introduction of a new management information system is such an innovation.

A number of tasks related in a complex fashion to achieve a one-time objective, such as design of an MIS, is called a *project*. Projects differ from processes because they are discrete—they have a beginning and an end, as opposed to company functional operations such as marketing, manufacturing, or accounting. Projects are complex because they require a wide variety of skills. Moreover, they cut across traditional organizational lines, and involve a substantial number of interrelated activities. And because each project is a one-time effort, unusual problems arise that call for nontraditional solutions. In addition, projects usually require the development of new techniques and advances in the state-of-the-art while the project is in progress.

Projects are carried out under the leadership of project managers. Because of the complexities and high costs of completing projects, these managers must provide coordination and leadership of an unusual order. Good functional managers may fail miserably as project managers. In particular, when a project manager operates from a staff position, as MIS project managers usually do, the difficulties are greatly compounded.

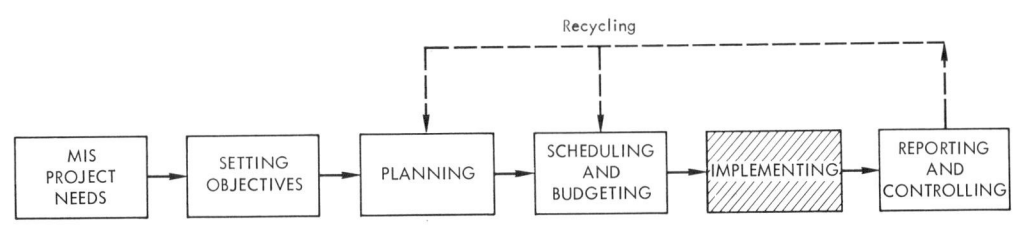

Figure 12–1 The Planning–Controlling Cycle for Project Management

The basic foundations for successful project management are good planning and control systems within the project management cycle. This chapter focuses on the techniques for project management as related to the development, design, and implementation of MIS.

NEEDS RESEARCH

The first stage in the MIS project-management cycle is the search for MIS *needs*. If needs of managers are not identified, many thousands of dollars may be lost by developing systems that serve little purpose. Management then finds it necessary to return to the starting point again and again until needs are properly defined. The identification of needs, in terms of MIS, consists of:

1. The search for planning and operating problems
2. The search for areas of recurring difficult decisions or erroneous decisions
3. The search for company opportunities that depend upon expanded information systems
4. Delineation of problems and opportunities (No. 3) so that priorities may be ranked
5. Selection of projects whose payoff in terms of cost and limitations of resources is justified

Let us amplify some of these concepts. Each company should have an MIS manager or a counterpart whose job is to search continuously for major company problems and opportunities. He must, of course, rely heavily on personal contacts with line managers and top managers as sources. His job is primarily that of gathering together problems, stimulating managers to think about opportunities, and generally getting managers to look beyond their daily jobs, both outside and inside the company. From problems and opportunities thus identified, MIS needs can be recognized in a general way. MIS projects may then be identified by summary descriptions and crude cost estimates, after which they must be evaluated on three basic criteria:

1. How valuable is the solution to the problem or the opportunity (for expansion, market penetration, acquisition program, new production system, reorganization, etc.) to the company?
2. How valuable is the MIS project to the problem solution or the opportunity achievement? What is the net payoff?
3. What is the technology required?

It is evident from these criteria that before any project is undertaken, it should be carefully assessed by asking such questions as:

1. What are management's purposes? In what direction is it guiding

the company in terms of products, services, market position, and return on investment? In other words, what is the corporate shape intended to be?

2. What possible MIS projects will aid management in planning, controlling, problem solving, and decision making? Is a "total system" feasible, or are the projects so large that only a few may be undertaken at a time?

3. Is the scope of each project defined? Unless descriptions of the project, its contribution, and its required utilization of resources are spelled out, the projects cannot be evaluated and ranked.

4. What are the major assumptions underlying each project? These assumptions relate to the environment, to management's needs, to available resources within the company, to desired goals of managers, and to time.

5. What are the short-term and long-term objectives of the MIS project? Too often MIS systems are proposed and designed to solve today's problems with no consideration for changes in organization, environment, and operations in the next five years.

6. What specific criteria should be used to evaluate and rank projects? The aggressive viewpoint of, "What will the system do to advance the company in the long run?" should be used. Criteria are often based erroneously on cost and savings.

7. Is the project technically sound? That is, is it practical in terms of the state-of-the-art of management science, computer science, organizational behavior, and other relevant factors?

8. Are there deadlines or simply desired times for completion of the project?

The needs-research stage is sometimes called the preliminary analysis, or the preproposal stage.

SETTING PROJECT OBJECTIVES

As opposed to the definition of overall MIS planning objectives discussed earlier, in the planning–programming–control cycle objectives must be in more detailed form for each potential project. Needs research indicates the general nature and scope of MIS projects that are required, but once a project is selected, its purposes must be developed to fulfill the needs. An objective is an end result that is to be accomplished by the execution of the plan.

Objectives of information systems may vary widely in scope and direction. Objectives might be:

1. Unify the financial and accounting system of a multidivision company or conglomerate.
2. Develop an environmental scanning system to keep corporate manage-

ment alerted to new market opportunities and competitive strategic moves.
3. Develop a production and inventory control system that interfaces with the current purchasing and marketing information systems.
4. Develop an on-line information system for company-wide materials and finished goods in terms of in-transport and warehouse location.
5. Develop an engineering management information system for control of technical work, costs, and schedules.
6. Develop an MIS for manpower inventory and long-range needs.
7. Update the current MIS for marketing to bring to bear new forecasting techniques and to adapt the system to the new computer being installed.
8. Revise the present financial reporting system to supply more decision-oriented information and to provide it on a weekly basis instead of a quarterly basis.

Besides such major objectives as suggested, each MIS project will have a number of supporting or secondary objectives. It is not enough, as in the first example, to simply specify unification of financial and accounting information. Objectives must be set regarding the nature of reports for each level of the organization, who gets what reports, how frequently reports are to be issued. Secondary objectives might be enlarging and automating the data master file, relating sales information to production planning, or obtaining measurements of morale through classification of reasons for absenteeism and quits. A complete list of objectives at the lowest level in the hierarchy of objectives is established subsequently during the planning of specific tasks. The topic of systems and project objectives will be expanded in Chapters 13 and 14.

PROJECT PROPOSAL

Two alternative sequences of action are possible for developing project proposals and obtaining management approval. As various projects are identified by needs and objectives, a preliminary definition of the scope of the project work, scheduling, costs, and benefits may be prepared as a *project proposal*. The projects are then evaluated by management and selections made on the basis of criteria discussed previously. Subsequent to this, detailed plans are prepared and reviewed once again by management.

In the second alternative, an MIS project is singled out. Then the complete and detailed planning, scheduling, and budgeting for the implementation is worked out. At this point a detailed project proposal is presented to management for acceptance or rejection. Because of the cost of preparing such proposals for all known projects, only those likely to be approved are developed in this much detail. Management thus does not have an opportunity to evaluate a broad range of proposals.

The format for the MIS project proposal consists of an introduction, a management summary, a system description, and an estimate of the cost and schedule. The detail given in each section depends upon whether a brief proposal is prepared for a large number of projects (alternative 1) or whether a single project is selected on a judgmental informal basis and a proposal developed for management's approval (alternative 2). The nature of the information contained in a proposal is outlined in Table 12–1.[11]

Table 12–1

MIS Project Proposal Outline

1. Introduction
   a. A brief, clear statement of the problem or technical requirement.
   b. Purposes of the proposed MIS.
   c. Conservative estimate of the performance of the proposed system, its limitations, its life, and its cost.
   d. Premises and assumptions upon which the MIS is to be developed. These give organizational limitations, special requirements imposed by managers, vendors, or customers, environmental restrictions, or other ground rules.
2. What Is Offered
   a. Description of present method of operation and its weaknesses and problems.
   b. Information requirements, present and future. General description of proposed data base.
   c. Hardware, present and future, available within the company.
   d. Alternative approaches to the information–decision–operational systems. A brief summary of each approach is given and the advantages and disadvantages of each are discussed to show why the proposed system is being offered.
   e. A somewhat more detailed description of the proposed MIS is given. The general plan of action, the budget estimate, and the schedule are provided.
   f. Management action required for adoption of the proposal and for planning and implementing the MIS are stated.
3. Method of Approach
   An outline of the plan of attack on the gross design, detailed design, and implementation. This demonstrates that the project manager has a practical approach for planning and executing the project.
   a. Method of data gathering and analysis.
   b. Personnel assignments.
   c. Programming techniques to be used for the project.
   d. Project reports and review. A description of the type and frequency of reports to keep management abreast of progress on the MIS project.
4. Conclusion
   This is not usually required. If an MIS project looks especially good from a highly technical viewpoint, the conclusion may summarize the strong points to give additional emphasis.
5. Appendixes
   Organization charts, schedules, flowcharts, quantitative analyses, and other detailed substantiating data of a technical or detailed nature that will aid management or technical staff personnel in evaluating the proposal.

PLANNING TECHNIQUES

For very small projects, commonsense techniques for planning and documenting the plans for the MIS project are sufficient. We will discuss here the more elaborate techniques for planning for larger projects. Most of these techniques and tools have been borrowed from engineering project-management theory and practice, where they originated.

The planning techniques rest on some fundamental management premises. The first is that all work can be planned and controlled. The second is that the greater the difficulty in planning the work, the greater the need for such planning. Techniques exist for a rational approach to planning the design and implementation of large systems. The third premise is that the assignment of project management to a project manager with wide responsibilities is an important factor in increasing the probability of success of a project. The project manager must control all funds required for the project. However, the project manager may direct the activities of a program without having direct line-command over all persons involved in the program. He achieves this by means of a clearly defined work breakdown structure for the project.

Work Breakdown Structure

A fundamental concept in project management is the work breakdown structure, which starts with the total end result desired and terminates with the individual detailed tasks. The project breakdown structure is a natural *decomposition* of the project end result. It is created in a level-by-level breakdown from:

1. System to subsystem
2. Subsystem to task
3. Task to subtask
4. Subtask to work package

The manner in which the project is broken down into tasks is illustrated in Table 12-2.

The work breakdown structure, referred to as WBS, starts with a word description of the entire project and is then decomposed by word descriptions for each element of each subdivision. The organizational structure should have no influence on the development of the WBS. The primary question to be answered is, What is to be accomplished? Next, an acceptable way of classifying the work must be found. The classification should be such that natural systems and components are identified and milestone tasks for accomplishing their design are related. Neither gaps nor overlaps must be allowed, yet the structure should interlock all tasks and work packages.

Table 12-2
Standard Task List of the Work Breakdown Structure for Project Control

I. Study Phase
    Task 1   Study organization goals and problems.
        Subtask   1.1   Interview managers and study internal documents.
        Subtask   1.2   Survey operating problems.
        Subtask   1.3   Study informational problems.
    Task 2   Study company resources and opportunities.
        Subtask   2.1   Evaluate company resources.
        Subtask   2.2   Study needs of the market and environmental trends.
        Subtask   2.3   Evaluate competitive position.
    Task 3   Study computer capabilities—equipment and manpower skills.
    Task 4   Prepare proposal for MIS design study.

II. Gross Design Phase
    Task 1   Identify required subsystems.
        Subtask   1.1   Study work flow and natural boundaries of skill groupings and information needs.
        Subtask   1.2   Develop alternative lists of subsystems.
        Subtask   1.3   Develop conceptual total-system alternatives based upon the lists of subsystems.
        Subtask   1.4   Develop scope of work to be undertaken based on need of the company and estimated resources to be allocated to the MIS.
        Subtask   1.5   Prepare a reference design showing key aspects of the system, organizational changes, and computer equipment and software required.

III. Detailed Design Phase
    Task 1   Disseminate to the organization the nature of the prospective project.
    Task 2   Identify dominant and principal trade-off criteria for the MIS.
    Task 3   Redefine the subsystems in greater detail.
        Subtask   3.1   Flowchart the operating systems.
        Subtask   3.2   Interview managers and key operating personnel.
        Subtask   3.3   Flowchart the information flows.
    Task 4   Determine the degree of automation possible for each activity or transaction.
    Task 5   Design the data base or master file.
        Subtask   5.1   Determine routine decisions and the nature of nonroutine decisions.
        Subtask   5.2   Determine internal and external data required.
        Subtask   5.3   Determine optimum data to be stored in terms of cost, time, cross-functional needs, and storage capacity.
    Task 6   Model the system quantitatively.
    Task 7   Develop computer support.
        Subtask   7.1   Develop computer hardware requirements.
        Subtask   7.2   Develop software requirements.
    Task 8   Establish input and output formats.
        Subtask   8.1   Develop input formats (design forms).
        Subtask   8.2   Develop output formats for decision makers.
    Task 9   Test the system.
        Subtask   9.1   Test the system by using the model previously developed.
        Subtask   9.2   Test the system by simulation, using extreme value inputs.
    Task 10   Propose the formal organization structure to operate the system.
    Task 11   Document the detailed design.

IV. Implementation Phase
    Task 1   Plan the implementation sequence.

Subtask	1.1	Identify implementation tasks.
Subtask	1.2	Establish interrelationships among tasks and subtasks.
Subtask	1.3	Establish the performance/cost/time program.
Task 2		Organize for implementation.
Task 3		Develop procedures for the installation process.
Task 4		Train operating personnel.
Task 5		Obtain hardware.
Task 6		Develop the software.
Task 7		Obtain forms specified in detailed design or develop forms as necessary.
Task 8		Obtain data and construct the master files.
Task 9		Test the system by parts.
Task 10		Test the complete system.
Task 11		Cut over to the new MIS.
Task 12		Debug the system.
Task 13		Document the operational MIS.
Task 14		Evaluate the system in operation.

The smallest element in the WBS, usually appearing at the lowest level, is the work package, a paragraph description of the work that is to be done to achieve an intermediate goal. Requirements of time, resources, and cost are listed, including definite dates for starting and completing the work—a short duration compared to that of the total project. The breakdown of the project into work packages, each assigned to a single responsible manager, provides the means for control of the entire project. A typical list of items of information contained in a work package form is given in Table 12-3.

Table 12-3

Work Package Information Checklist

1. Project identification, title, and number
2. Title and number of work package
3. Responsible organization and manager
4. Interface events and dates
5. Start and end date for work package
6. Dollar and labor estimates, projections of dollars and labor on a weekly or monthly basis, and a schedule of actual application of resources maintained as current
7. Contract or funding source identification
8. Account charge number
9. Work order or shop order, to be opened when authorization is obtained to expend a specified amount of money under a particular account number

Sequence Planning

The relationships among tasks must be set forth by a chronological ordering, starting with the terminal task of the project and working backward. As each task is set down, it is necessary to determine what immediately preceding tasks must first be completed. When a network of events has been established, estimates of the time required to complete each event, based upon the work package information, may be entered.

There are a number of time paths through a network that run from the starting event to the terminal event. The longest is called the *Critical Path*. On the basis of management decisions, resources may be added or redeployed to change the length of time of a current Critical Path to yield a new one, thus gaining time by a trade-off involving increased costs. The final network is sometimes called the *Master Project Network Plan*.

Master Program Schedule

The Master Program Schedule (MPS) is a management document giving the *calendar dates* for milestones (major tasks and critical-path minor tasks), thus providing the control points for management review. The MPS may be in the form of a Gantt chart for small MIS projects or in machine (computer) printout for large projects whose networks have been programmed for computer analysis and reporting. In the latter case, the MPS is derived from the network schedule by establishing a calendar date for the starting event.

Budgeting

The establishment of cost and resource targets for a planned series of periods in advance is project budgeting. Although cost constraints may be applied in a top-down fashion during planning, such constraints must be reconciled with a *bottom-up* approach through the work breakdown structure. Reconciliation is accomplished by either (1) allocating more funds or (2) narrowing and reducing the scope of the work and redefining the objectives of the project.

Cost and resource targets must be established for a work package by:

1. Performing organization
2. Funding organization
3. Elements of cost: labor, materials, and facilities

Only direct costs are included in the project budget, because they are the only costs over which the project manager has control.

Cushioning should not be added to the resource costs because meaningful measures of control depend upon realistic goals. However, since experience has shown that project cost overruns are far more common than underruns, a contingency fund should be budgeted to cover unanticipated problems. The project manager's use of the contingency fund is also a measure of his performance.

REPORTING AND CONTROLLING

Control of the project means control of performance/cost/time (P/C/T). These elements, P/C/T, must be reported in a way that ties them all together, otherwise the report is meaningless. Consider, for instance, a project in which performance and costs are on target. It is possible for such a project to be behind and in trouble from the time standpoint. On the other hand, a project may show an overrun of costs as of a particular date, yet if the work performance is ahead of schedule, this is good news instead of bad news.

Reporting Techniques

The reporting system for a project is its own MIS. Some methods of project reporting are:

1. Integrated P/C/T charts as shown in Figure 12–2.
2. Financial schedules and variance reports.
3. Time-scaled network plans and computerized reports based on them.
4. Problem analysis and trend charts.
5. Progress reports.
6. Project control room and computerized graphic systems.[12]
7. Design review meetings and "reference designs." A common "reference design" must provide a formal description of system specifications and goals at any particular time. All designers work on the basis of assumptions about parts of the system other than theirs. If they are not working on the same assumptions, chaos results. The reference design may change with time, and the design review meeting of all key personnel is a good time to make formal changes.

Reporting Problems

Control is difficult if the only reports are written narratives requiring interpretation by management. At the other extreme, reams of computer data reports are equally poor. Managers prefer graphic displays, which reduce large amounts of complex information into easily understood pictorial form. Comparisons and trends of major variables are also effective in communicating. Graphic display must be designed to guard against too gross a level of reporting, however, or else growing problems may be obscured.

Other problems in reporting are the use of complex grammatical structure; high "fog index" of writing; excessive and unexplained abbreviations, codes, and symbols; and too much technical jargon. Projects may fail if the project manager and his technical specialists do not make clear to management what is happening and how the money is being spent.

PERFORMANCE/COST/TIME
PLANNING AND CONTROLLING

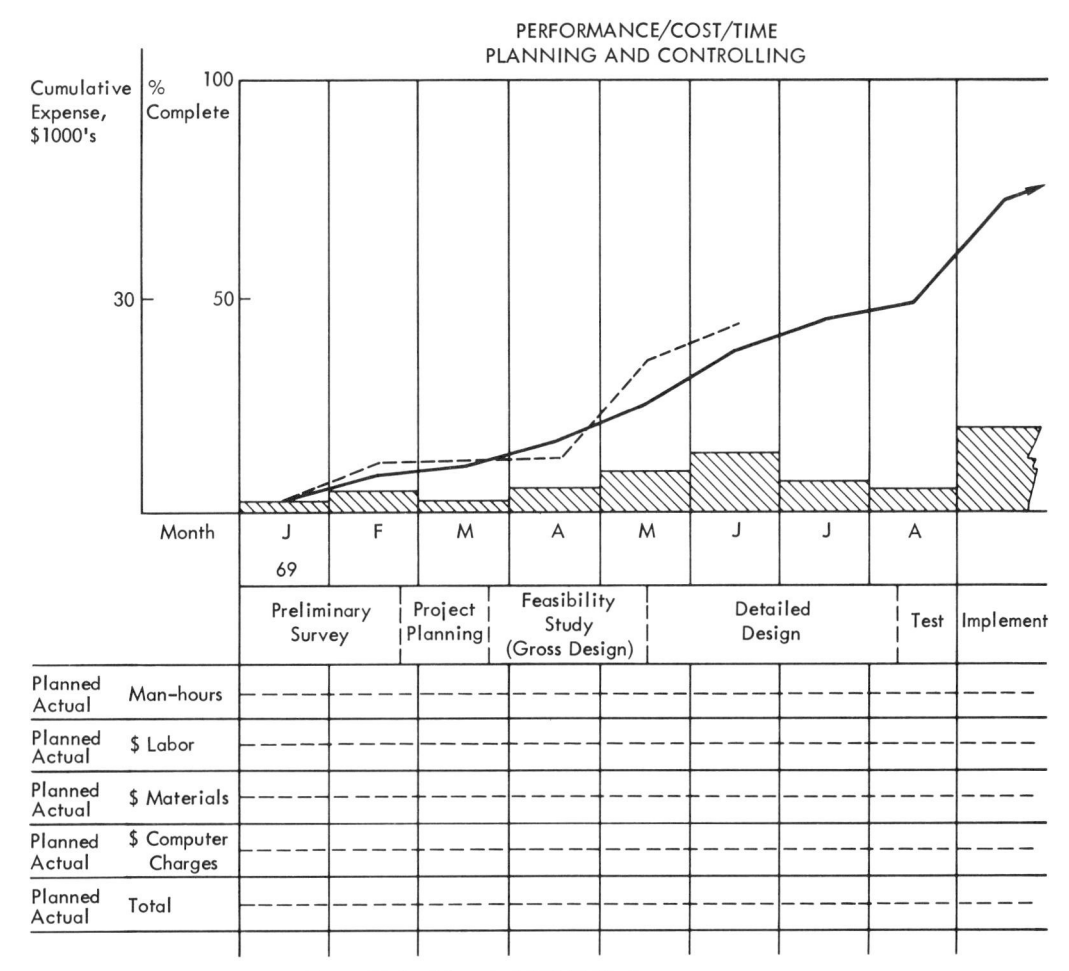

Figure 12-2 Integrated P/C/T Chart

Control Through "Completed Action"

A manager in a chain of command cannot divest himself of accountability for a task that is delegated to him. Responsibility for a work package may be delegated to the lowest level in the organizational hierarchy, but each manager up the line is evaluated on the basis of completed action on the work package. The worker who has responsibility for a work package should be supplied with adequate reports of P/C/T. As variances are reported to the responsible performer, the burden is on him to take corrective action. His ultimate responsibility is "completed action," the presentation of a completed job to his manager. Only in emergencies and cases of wide variances from planned action should the managers at various levels in the organization step in to reclaim delegated responsibility. The control in a well-run project is essentially self-control, based upon a good reporting system.

SUMMARY

The design and implementation of an MIS cannot be carried out on an unplanned trial-and-error basis. The complex assemblage of tasks involved and the cost of the design and implementation are such as to constitute a major project. Project management is conducted with special management techniques of its own, techniques related to establishment of project needs and objectives and to planning, scheduling, budgeting, reporting, and controlling.

The outstanding characteristics of these techniques are the breakdown structure, the network approach to defining task relationships, and the integration of performance/cost/time for planning and control. The detailed techniques for implementing these major-project management techniques have provided powerful aids to management. We have summarized the project-planning and control cycle in Figure 12–3.

DISCUSSION QUESTIONS AND PROBLEMS

1. Some people view systems design as a continuous, ongoing activity, others as a project that must be undertaken at the conclusion of the system's life cycle. The latter view is that a completely fresh systems approach can be accomplished only by the project concept. Discuss.

2. List five systems problems that you have noticed in your recent dealings with stores, service firms, or manufacturing plants.

3. If you were or are working for a company, what kinds of systems problems would you look for whose solutions would provide the greatest payoff?

4. Visit a local firm and obtain interviews with several employees in order to develop a list of possible system projects.

5. Prepare a project proposal for an MIS for the marketing activities of a large department store or of an industrial firm in the locality.

6. Consider some major project on which you are currently working (getting through college, for example), and develop a Work Breakdown Structure.

7. Develop an activity network for the project of Question 6.

8. A systems project is planned for a small store. The "start" event is labeled Event 1. The subsequent activities and required times are:

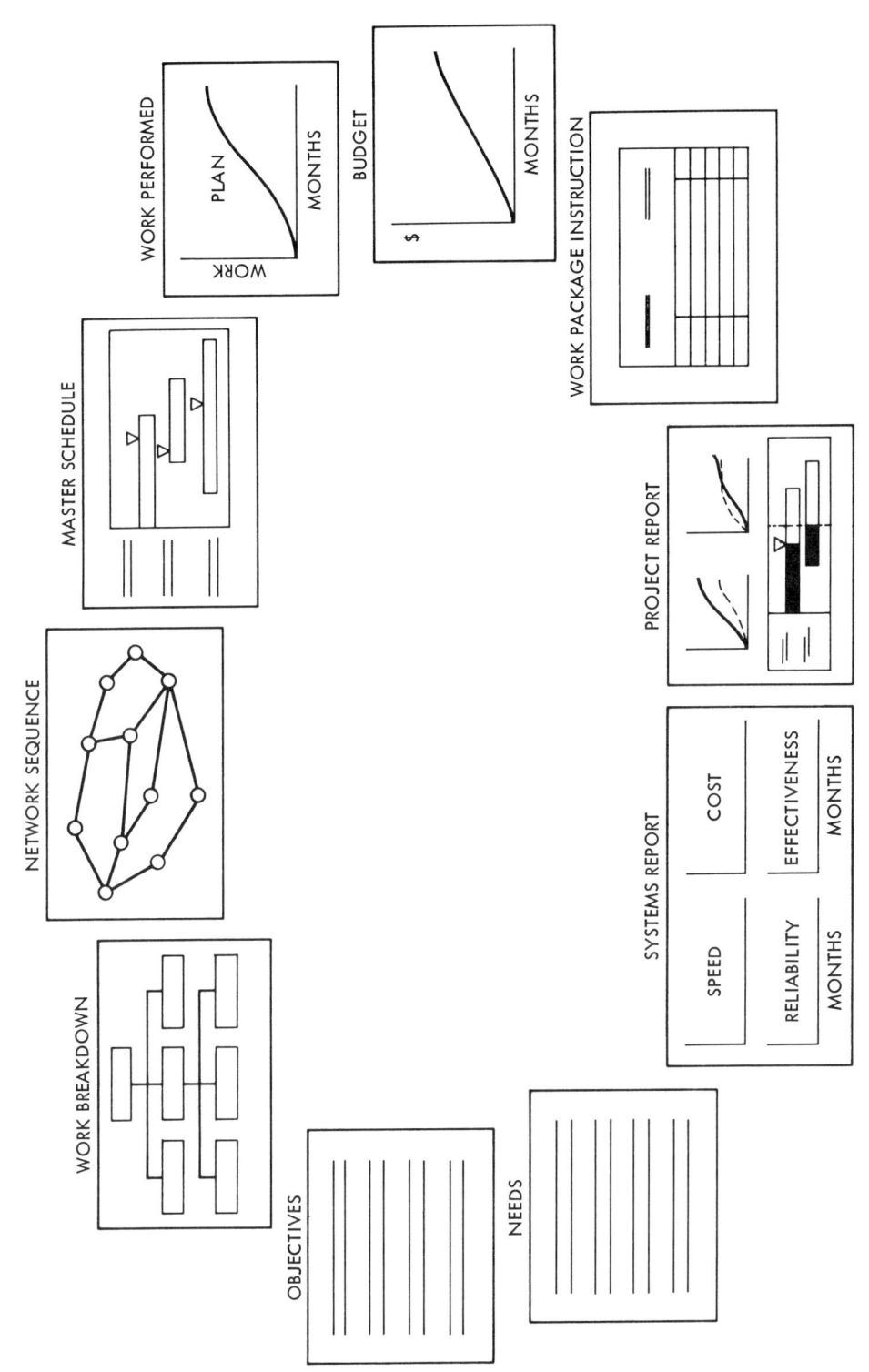

Figure 12-3 Project Planning and Control Cycle

Activity	1–2	Determine information needs	2.6 weeks
	1–3	Analyze store operations	4.0 weeks
	2–3	Define subsystems	1.5 weeks
	2–4	Develop data base	2.1 weeks
	3–4	Identify system constraints	.2 weeks
	4–5	Design the MIS	4.2 weeks

Draw the network diagram, indicate the critical path, find the time for the critical path, and find the slack time for each activity.

9. If you are utilizing a management game in one of your courses, develop a network diagram for the project of developing an MIS to support your play of the game.

10. The South Mall Project is a planned series of buildings that will provide office facilities for more than 10,000 state employees in downtown Albany, New York. Construction started in 1964 and was scheduled to be completed in 1973. A computerized MIS was developed to provide the basis for control of PERT plans for constructions. Fuller Construction Company was selected as the general contractor, or consultant, to coordinate the building of the South Mall. Actual construction work was under the control of prime contractors, who were required to submit all data necessary to enable the construction contractor to prepare network charts. Network charts were to be reviewed once a month. Prime contractors could submit their own schedules and formats without regard to each other, and Fuller was responsible only for summary networks.

As the project progressed, estimates of completion costs doubled and actual expenditures exceeded initial plans at an appalling rate. An evaluation by Mr. Ronald P. Quake concluded that:
 a. The information entering the PERT system was biased.
 b. The interaction between subsystems was not being modeled.
 c. There was no effective feedback mechanism.
 d. The responsibility for constructing a unit was divided among the prime contractors.

Some analysts raised the questions: Was the distinction between the construction project and the MIS project recognized? Should a clear-cut project for the development of the MIS precede project planning for construction? What factors could contribute to cost overruns?

11. An American firm with international operations manufactures and sells a wide variety of electromechanical devices ranging from calculating machines to sewing machines. It owns more than 1,500 stores or outlets for its products and has about 400 approved independent dealers. Heavy competition both at home and abroad has made management very aware of the need for a better MIS directed toward on-line information. An MIS project must now be planned and programmed. The new MIS must tie the following to corporate headquarters:
 a. Retail outlets, to provide sales reports
 b. Regional warehouses and distribution center, to provide inventory, shipping, and receiving information

c. Agencies that handle commercial sales, to provide sales reports and inventory information
d. Factories, to provide demand information to each factory and to receive production, inventory, and shipping reports.

The development of an MIS for such a billion-dollar (sales) company requires considerable planning prior to undertaking of the actual design and implementation. In particular, management wishes to be able to evaluate the progress of the MIS design, when it is initiated, by means of a simple chart relating time, cost, and performance.

REFERENCES

1. For example: Booz, Allen and Hamilton, Inc., "The Computer Comes of Age," *Harvard Business Review*, January–February 1968, p. 83; Rodney H. Brady, "Computers in Top-Level Decision Making," *Harvard Business Review*, July–August 1967, p. 67; The Diebold Group, Inc., "Research Study Conclusions," *Computer Digest*, August 1967, p. 8; and Neil Churchill, *Computer-Based Information Systems for Management: A Survey* (New York: National Association of Accountants, 1969).
2. Brady, "Computers in Top-Level Decision Making," p. 67.
3. Churchill, *Computer-Based Information Systems*, p. 3.
4. Three excellent sources that outline the detailed steps in analysis, design, and implementation are: Sherman C. Blumenthal, *Management Information Systems: A Framework for Planning and Development* (Englewood Cliffs, N.J.: Prentice-Hall, Inc., 1969); Thomas B. Glans et al., *Management Systems* (New York: Holt, Rinehart & Winston, Inc., 1968); and W. Hartman, H. Matthes, and A. Proeme, *Management Information Systems Handbook* (New York: McGraw-Hill Book Company, 1968).
5. Joseph Orlicky, *The Successful Computer System* (New York: McGraw-Hill Book Company, 1969), p. 91.
6. Churchill, pp. 140–43.
7. The Diebold Group, "Research Study Conclusions," p. 8.
8. A comprehensive treatment of how to plan and control systems-development activities is shown in Blumenthal, *Management Information Systems*, pp. 102–65; and Brandon Systems Institute, *Project Control Systems for Data Processing* (New York: Brandon Systems, Inc., 1967).
9. Blumenthal, *Management Information Systems*, p. 13.
10. Orlicky, *The Successful Computer System*, p. 96.
11. See also David I. Cleland and William R. King, *Systems Analysis and Project Management* (New York: McGraw-Hill Book Company, 1968), Appendices; and Hartman, Matthes, and Proeme, *Management Information Systems Handbook*, Chapter 2.2.
12. See, for example, Irwin M. Miller, "Computer Graphics for Decision Making," *Harvard Business Review*, November–December, 1969.

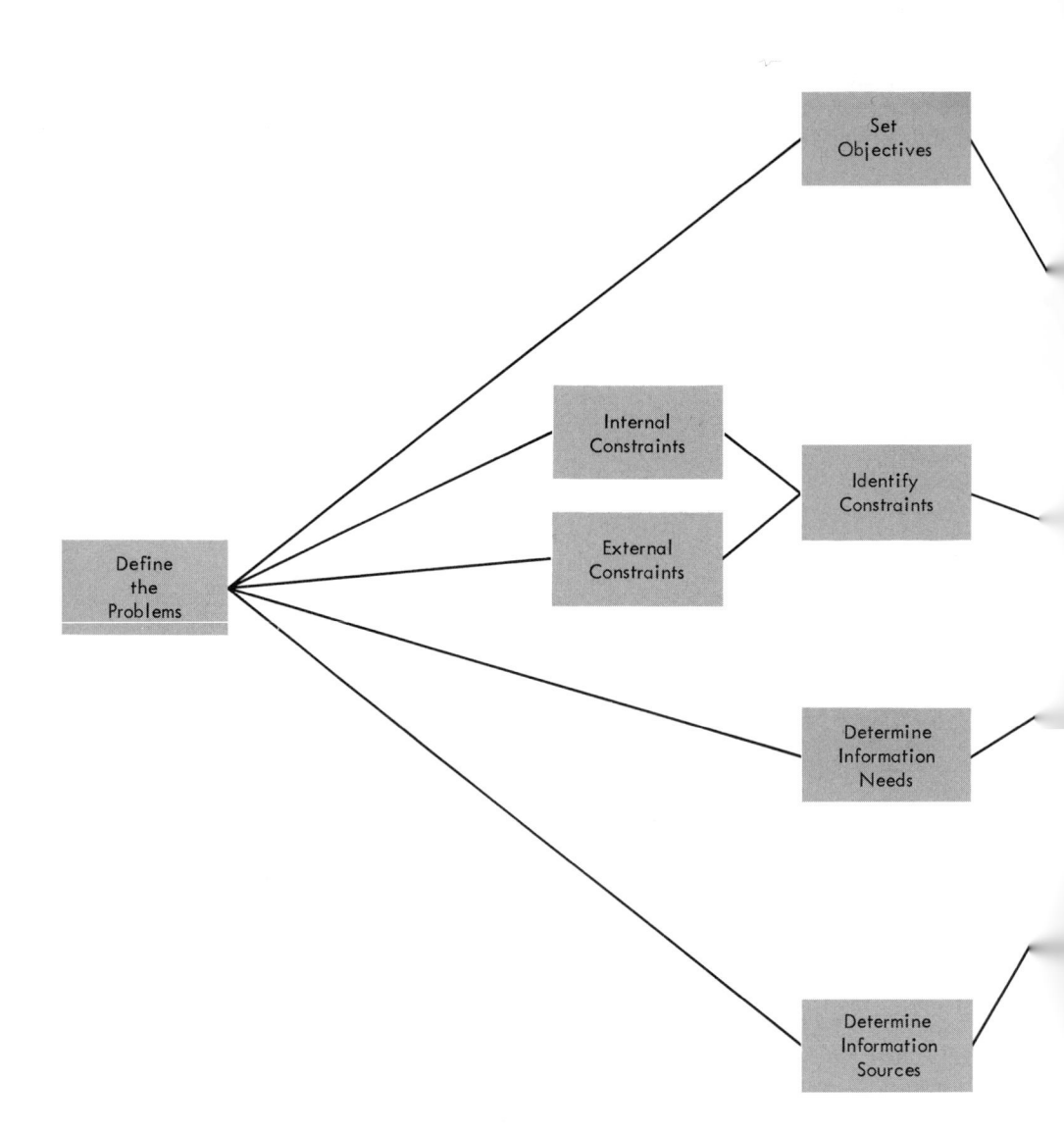

```
Define            Set Objectives
the
Problems          Internal Constraints
                  External Constraints    Identify Constraints

                  Determine Information Needs

                  Determine Information Sources
```

13
MIS design: gross design concepts

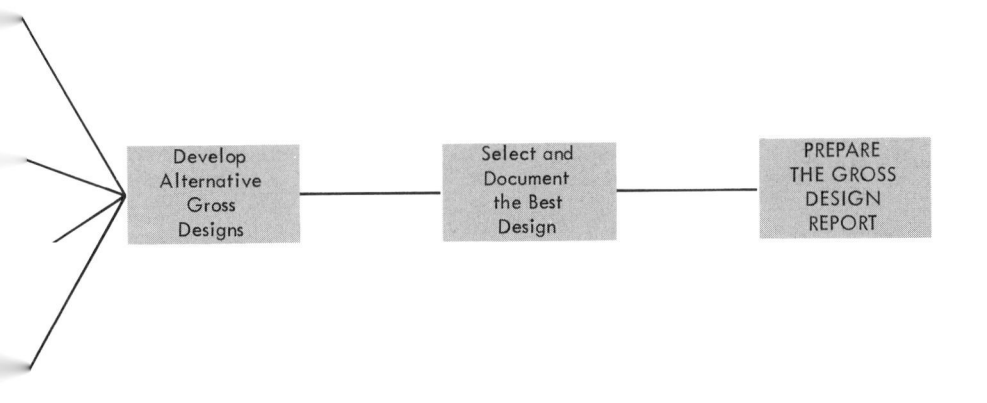

Develop Alternative Gross Designs → Select and Document the Best Design → PREPARE THE GROSS DESIGN REPORT

13

Since the gross design sets the direction for the MIS project, it is vital that managers participate heavily at this stage. The gross design should not be relinquished to technicians.

The gross design involves three fundamental ideas:

1. Consideration of "reference businesses." By this we mean that top management, in its long-range planning, considers alternative directions and growth strategies for the firm. In parallel, the MIS concepts must be based on the direction that the company will most probably follow, which we may call the "reference business" for the designers to work with. The development of alternative feasible MIS designs must be tied closely to management's thinking about the future of the firm. Lower-level technical personnel simply do not have the insight for such planning.

2. Creative aspects of gross design. Gross design is a creative function that involves producing new patterns and arrangements for processing resources and information. For this reason, it requires the broad thinking, experience, and creativity characteristic of employees who have risen in the managerial ranks. What is conceivable, effective, and practical should be management's major contribution to the development of MIS.

3. A look ahead at the potential problems of detailed design and implementation. In essence, the set of alternative concepts of the MIS must be evaluated in terms of feasibility of detailed design and feasibility of implementation.

DEFINE THE PROBLEMS

Problems undoubtedly exist in any dynamic business. What are usually lacking are clear definitions of the problems and a priority system for their solution. Therefore, management must take the first step in MIS design by formulating problems to be solved.

Current problems, however, are not the only concern. MIS design should be related to long-range planning for the company. Long-range plans are dependent on MIS capabilities, and, at the same time, MIS design concepts must be based on the future reference business. A reference business description is the blueprint for the company at some particular time. For MIS gross design, we must look at alternative potential reference businesses for the firm *one year, three years,* and *five years* hence. If we can provide several MIS gross design concepts for each of the several long-range plans, then we should be able to match opportunity and capability for selection of the best combination of business and MIS concepts.

Without giving a complete directory of every item in a long-range plan, we have listed below a few of the key items for management to consider in the development of MIS design concepts:

Sales in units and dollars
Products, sales by product, share of the market
Number of customers and location
Plants—location and size
Warehouses—location and size
Number of employees
Key executives—identification of each
Number of middle executives
Number of vendors and locations
Working capital and cash inventory
Identity of competitors and share of the market of each
Computer capabilities and locations
Communications network within the company
Environmental factors, such as general business conditions, political–legal factors, and social factors

When such information has been gathered, the problems associated with achieving a particular reference business may be exposed. Following problem definition, we must next establish the objectives for systems that will help us solve these problems. Our interest, of course, lies with the MIS in particular.

SET SYSTEM OBJECTIVES

Despite our understanding of the nature of objectives in the operating activities of the company, it is frequently quite difficult to state objectives for systems that cut across all functional areas.

Unlike the *technician*, who frequently turns to topics such as file structure and retrieval techniques and who views the objectives of a subsystem only in terms of its input to a larger system, the *manager* must define system objectives in terms of legitimacy of information demands and not in terms of the satisfaction of demands that are not related to an objective. Systems analysts (and computer salesmen) tend to stress processing efficiency, and staff and functional supervisors commonly believe that their objective is "to complete the required report on time for management use." This view disregards the real objective of the systems design—*management effectiveness*. The value of systems lies in the benefits to their users, not in mere efficiency of transactions. We have witnessed the design of information systems in several government agencies where the system objective was the automation of hundreds of reports, without regard to management of the many tasks related or to functional or resource subsystems represented by the reports (e.g., training, employee relations, safety, recruitment, staffing, etc.). Such focus on the automation of records or the processing of existing data overlooks the true objectives of the operational organizational entity represented by the subsystem.

Yet it is not an easy matter to determine the real objectives of an information system any more than it is easy to determine the objectives of the operational system served by it. A common fallacy in stating objectives is to emphasize the obvious or to state objectives in vague terms; "reduce costs," "improve efficiency," "keep accurate records," "meet the production schedule." When asked for his objectives, a university president may reply, "Provide quality education," and a government bureaucrat may say, "Provide more jobs for the unemployed"; yet in neither case is the objective stated in terms specific enough to provide a measure of performance of the system or to design an information system to help achieve the objective.

Despite its difficulty, being specific is necessary. System objectives must ultimately be stated in terms of the objectives of the department, group, function, or manager to be served or in terms of the functions the information system is to perform. In other words, system objectives should be expressed in terms of what managers can do after their information requirements have been met. Such expression may use descriptive statements, flowcharts, or any other means that will convey to management the objectives that the systems designer must meet in order to develop the system. If possible, the objectives should be stated in quantitative rather than qualitative terms so that alternative system designs as well as system performance can be measured for effectiveness. That is, a statement of objectives should include exactly what it is that the system is supposed to accomplish and the means by which it will subsequently be evaluated. Table 13–1 shows an example of such a statement.

The table contains a statement of objectives for the material control system of one of the nation's major electrical manufacturers. Notice how specific objectives are defined. Listed here are a selected group of functional subsystems and a hypothetical statement of objectives for each. *These examples will be used for illustration throughout the remainder of this chapter.*

Subsystem	Objective
INVENTORY	Optimize inventory costs through the design of decision rules containing optimum reorder points, safety stock levels, and reorder quantities, each capable of continuous and automatic reassessment.
ACCOUNTS PAYABLE	Pay 100 percent of invoices before due date.
PURCHASING	Provide performance information on buyer's price negotiations with suppliers in order that purchase variance can be controlled within set limits.
PRODUCTION CONTROL	Identify cost and quantity variances within one day in order to institute closer control over these variables.
PROJECT CONTROL	Identify performance against plan so that events, costs, and specifications of the project can be met.

Table 13-1

Objectives of Material Control System:
Major Electrical Manufacturer

Subsystem	Objective
ROUTINGS	Capture routing information and time values that can be used by manufacturing for cost of completed work, labor status by contract, effect of changes by rerouting, etc.
STATUS	Establish a system that can be used by manufacturing to determine workload in shop, effect of accepting additional work, overload in various cost centers, status of self-manufactured work in process, etc.
TOOLS	Capture all tool information that can be used by manufacturing to determine tool status *prior* to release of work to shop, and maintain a tool inventory by contract for auditing purposes both by the company and the government on government contracts.
COST CONTROL	Establish an overall system that can be used by manufacturing to very quickly determine labor costs, material costs, tool costs, overruns, etc., by contract.
SCHEDULING	Determine effect of engineering changes, lack of material, tool shortages, etc.
MAKE OR BUY	Make decisions on those items to subcontract, based on cost, load, schedule, etc.
REQUEST FOR PROPOSAL INFORMATION	Establish a system that can be used by manufacturing to produce immediately the necessary information needed for customer requests and requests for proposals.
ELAPSED TIME	Analyze, improve, and prepare an orderly procedure that can be used by manufacturing to report elapsed time, if required by contractual obligation.

In summary, the first steps in systems design attempt to answer the questions: What is the purpose of the system? Why is it needed? What is it expected to do? Who are the users and what are their objectives? These questions relate to the *what* of systems design and the remainder of the steps relate to *how* it is to be achieved.

Finally, the establishment of management information system objectives cannot be divorced from a consideration of organizational objectives, near term and long range. Over the near term, system objectives can usually be framed in terms of management planning and control and decision making: lowering costs, strengthening operating controls, improving data flow, and meeting customer and external requirements. These short-range system objectives must, however, take into account the environment in which a business will be operating five to ten years hence. *Today's* system design must take account of *tomorrow's* environment.

ESTABLISH SYSTEM CONSTRAINTS

The iterative nature of the systems design process is easily understood when we consider the third step in the process—establishing constraints. Sometimes called *problem boundaries* or *restrictions,* constraints enable the designer to stipulate the conditions under which objectives may be attained and to consider the limitations that restrict the design. To state it another way, constraints, which are provided by the manager–user or the designer himself, limit freedom of action in designing a system to achieve the objective. It is clear then that a constant review of objectives is necessary when considering system constraints. Indeed, the two steps of setting objectives and establishing constraints may be considered together as one.

Although constraints may be viewed as a negative limitation on systems design, there is a positive benefit as well. We should not let our desire to design sophisticated systems run away with reality, or make promises that cannot be kept. Identification of the problem or setting the objective may be evident, but the solution is not always easy. Moreover, the designer who thinks his system can run the organization is as mistaken as the manager who believes he can run his organization without a system. Establishing constraints will help insure that the design is realistic.

Constraints may be classified as internal or external to the organization. This concept is shown in Figure 13–1, which forms the basis of the following discussion.

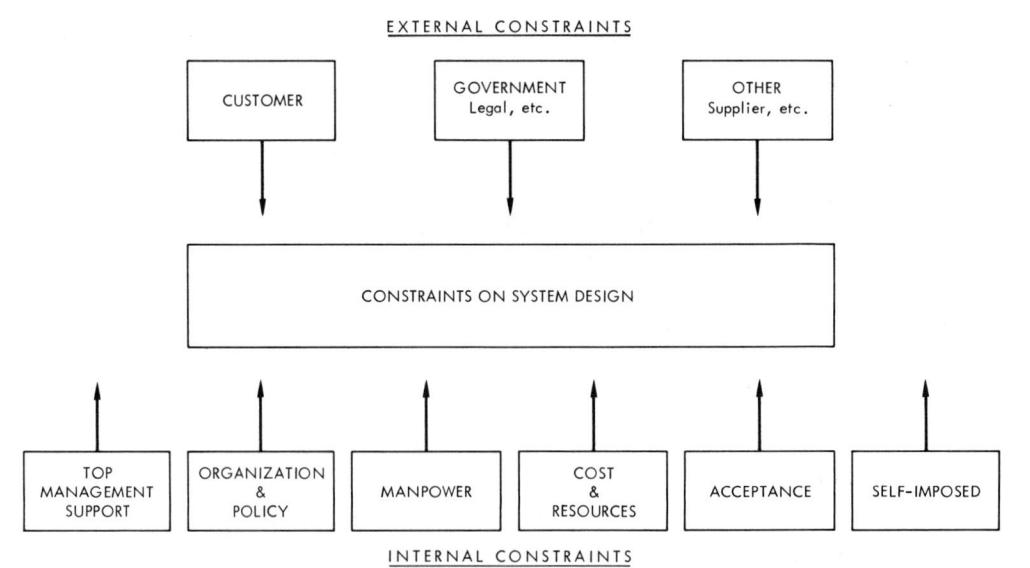

Figure 13–1 Constraints on Management Information Systems Design

Internal Constraints

If *top management support* is not obtained for the systems concept and for the notion that computer-based information systems are vital for management planning and control, the type of design effort discussed in these chapters cannot be implemented. A good environment for information systems must be set, and one essential ingredient is the approval and support of top management. This constraint definitely influences the kind of system the manager–user may design.

Organizational and policy considerations frequently set limits on objectives and modify an intended approach to design of a system. The structure of the organization and the managers occupying various positions influence information flow and use of system outputs. In a decentralized multiplant organization with a wide product line, the design of common systems in cost accounting or production control is obviously less acceptable than in a more centralized organization with fewer products. An additional organizational difficulty is related to the turnover of managers. More than one head of computer operations has stated that his major difficulty is the abandonment or redesign of systems due to the turnover among manager–users. Also, company policies frequently define or limit the approach to systems design. Among these policies are those concerned with product and service, research and development, production, marketing, finance, and personnel. For example, a "promote from within" personnel policy would have an impact on the type of systems design to build a skills inventory. Other important considerations in design are those concerning audits.

Manpower needs and personnel availability are a major limiting factor in both the design and utilization of information systems. Computer and systems skills are among the most critical in the nation; rare indeed is the manager who admits to having sufficient personnel to design, implement, and operate the systems he desires. Additional considerations concern the nature of the work force and the skill-mix of users. Elaborate and sophisticated systems are of little value if they cannot be put to use.

Perhaps the most significant constraint of all is the one concerning *people*. "People problems" is probably the factor most often mentioned where failure to achieve expected results is concerned. Here we have the difficulties associated with the natural human reaction to change, the antagonism, and the lack of interest and support frequently met in systems design and operation. Automation, computer systems, and systems design often call for the realignment of people and facilities, organizational changes, and individual job changes. Therefore, these reactions are to be expected and should be anticipated in designing systems to achieve the objective.

Cost is a major *resource* limitation. The cost to achieve the objective should be compared with the benefits to be derived. You do not want to spend $20,000 to save $10,000. Although a cost–benefit analysis is frequently difficult, some approach to priority setting must be undertaken. Considerations similar to those surrounding cost apply also to the use of other resources. *Computer capacity* and other facilities relating to operation of data-processing systems should be utilized in an optimum way.

Self-imposed restrictions are those placed on the design by the manager or the designer. In designing the system to achieve the objective, he may have to scale down several requirements in order to make the system fit with other outputs, equipment, or constraints. Usually, he will also restrict the amount of time and effort devoted to investigation. For example, he may want to design a pilot or test system around one product, one plant, or one portion of an operation before making it generally applicable elsewhere. Functional requirements also define constraints placed on the system by its users. The data requirements, the data volumes, and the rate of processing are constraints imposed by the immediate users. More remote users impose constraints by the need to integrate with related systems.

External Constraints

Foremost among the considerations surrounding the external environment are those concerning the *customer*. Order entry, billing, and other systems that interface with systems of the customer must be designed with his needs in mind. If certain outputs from the system are not acceptable to the customer, a definite limitation must be faced up to. He may require that bills be submitted in a form that provides input to his system of accounts payable. For example, standard progress-reporting and billing procedures are among the requirements imposed for processing data under many military procurement programs.

A variety of additional external constraints should be considered in addition to the customer. The *government* (federal, state, local) imposes certain restrictions on the processing of data. Among these are the need to maintain the security of certain classes of information (e.g., personnel) in order to comply with law and regulation in the conduct of business (e.g., taxes, reporting), and to meet certain procedures regarding record keeping and reporting to stockholders (e.g., outside audit). *Unions* can and do affect the operation of systems involving members in matters such as compensation, grievances, and working conditions. *Suppliers* are also an important group to be considered when designing information systems because these systems frequently interface with that group.

In summary, it is important to recognize the constraints that have an impact on systems design. Having recognized them and made appropriate allowance in the design function, the manager will then be in a position to complete the remaining steps toward the design of an operating system that will achieve the objective he has previously determined.

The nature of constraints is illustrated here by stating a hypothetical constraint for each of our selected functional subsystems.

Subsystem	Statement of Constraint
INVENTORY	Regardless of reorder points and reorder quantities, the supplier will not accept orders for less than carload lots for raw materials 7 and 12.
ACCOUNTS PAYABLE	The individual who prepares the check for payment of invoices must not be the same individual who approves payment.
PURCHASING	It is not necessary to negotiate purchases in amounts under $500.
PRODUCTION CONTROL	System output for shop control will be identified by department only and not by the individual worker or foreman.
PROJECT CONTROL	We are required to report weekly to the U.S. Department of Defense any slippages in time or cost exceeding 10% of any event in the project control critical path.

DETERMINE INFORMATION NEEDS

Before the installation of the first computer for business purposes in the United States, Ralph Cordiner, then chairman of the board of General Electric, made a prophetic comment on the need for information in systems design:

> It is an immense problem to organize and communicate the information required to operate a large, decentralized organization. This deep communication problem is not solved by providing more volume of data for all concerned, by faster accumulation and transmittal of conventional data, by wider distribution of previously existing data, or by holding more conferences. Indeed, the belief that such measures will meet the . . . [management information] challenge is probably one of the great fallacies in business and managerial thinking. What is required, instead, is a far more penetrating and orderly study of the business in its entirety to discover *what specific information is needed at each particular position in view of the decisions to be made there.*[1] [Italics added.]

A clear statement of information needs is fundamental and necessary to good systems design. Too many companies spend lavish sums on hardware and software to perpetuate existing systems or build sophisticated data banks, without first determining the real information needs of management: information that can increase the perception of managers in critical areas such as problems, alternatives, opportunities, and plans.

Unless managers can provide the specifications for what they want out of an information system, the design effort will produce less than optimum results. If, on the other hand, the manager–user can define his objectives and spell out the items of information that are needed to reach the objective, he is then at least halfway home in systems design. Failure to be specific on these two steps probably accounts for the downfall of more design efforts than any other factor. If systems design begins without such clear-cut statements by the manager, the systems analyst or technician will provide *his* objectives and *his* information needs.

Yet it is not easy for a manager to spell out the specific information requirements of his job, and therein lies a basic frustration in the improvement of systems. In an attempt to get a clear statement of information needs, the analyst frequently meets with an interviewing situation somewhat like this typical exchange:

ANALYST: Could you tell me what the objectives of this cost accounting system are, as you see them?

FINANCIAL MANAGER: Sure . . . to get the reports out faster . . . to do something about keeping the costs in line . . . to keep management informed. . . .

ANALYST: Yes, I understand . . . let me put it another way. What are your responsibilities as you see them?

FINANCIAL MANAGER: Whatta you mean? I'm in charge of the treasury department.

ANALYST: Yes, I know, but we need to get a better statement of your department's objectives, how the cost accounting system can further these objectives, and what information is needed to do this.

FINANCIAL MANAGER: Well, we need the information we've been getting, but we need it faster and with a lot more accurate input from those fellows in operations.

This hypothetical conversation reflects the difficulty of getting managers to be specific about information needs. One approach, sometimes used by consultants, is to get top management to require in writing from subordinate managers a statement containing: (1) a list of four or five major responsibilities for which the manager believes himself to be accountable, and (2) the four or five specific items of information that are required to carry out the responsibilities. These requirements could be framed in terms of duties performed or decisions made; the idea is to get the manager to think of information needs. If this can be done, the information system is well on the way to being designed.

Another approach is avoidance of the direct question: What information do you need? Instead, the designer requests that the user describe what occurs in the decision-making process; then the designer concerns himself with the identification of the questions that are to be resolved in the activity for which the system is being designed. This approach is also a good one for the manager–user, because he is intimately familiar with his operation and presumably with the difficult decision operations in it.

A manager needs information for a variety of reasons concerned with the management process. The type of need that he will have at various times and for various purposes depends largely upon two factors that we shall examine briefly: the personal managerial attributes of the individual manager, and the organizational environment in which decisions are made.

Personal Attributes

Knowledge of information systems. If the manager is aware of what computer-based systems can do, his information requests will probably be more sophisticated and more specific. His knowledge of capabilities and costs places him in a much better position to aid in the design of a good system.

Managerial style. A manager's technical background, his leadership style, and his decision-making ability all affect the kinds and amount of information he requires. Some prefer a great amount of detail; others like to decide with a minimum of detail and prefer personal consultation with subordinates.

Manager's perception of information needs. "You tell me what I need to know" and "Get me all the facts" represent two opposite perceptions of information needs. This dichotomy is due partly to the fact that many managers are ignorant of what information they need. Another dimension of the problem is the widely differing views of managers regarding their obligation to disseminate information to subordinates and to groups outside the firm. The manager who cannot or will not delegate authority is likely to keep information closely held.

Organizational Environment

Nature of the company. Problems in communication and in controlling operations seem to be a function of the company's size and the complexity of its organization. The larger, more complex firms require more formal information systems, and the information needs of these systems become more critical to operations.

Level of management. We outlined in Chapter 10 the three levels of management (i.e., strategic planning, management control, operational control) and the varying needs for information at each. Each level needs different types of information, generally in different form. Top levels need the one-time report, the summary, the single inquiry. The management control level needs the exception report, the summary, and a variety of regular reports for periodic evaluation. The operational control level requires the formal report with fixed procedures, the day-to-day report of transactions, in order to maintain operational control of actions as they occur. Managers at *all* levels have changing information needs, depending on the nature and importance of the particular decision.

Structure of the organization. The more highly structured the organization, the easier it is to determine the information needs. Where authority and responsibility are clearly spelled out, relationships understood, and decision-making areas defined, the information needs of managers can be determined more easily.

Returning to our illustrative subsystems, some information needs might be stated:

Subsystem	Information Needs
INVENTORY	Daily report on items that have fallen below minimum inventory level, in order that expediting action can be taken.
ACCOUNTS PAYABLE	Incoming invoices coded according to "days to due date," since invoices should be paid no sooner than two days prior to due date in order to conserve cash.
PURCHASING	The performance of each individual buyer, indicated by comparing actual purchases with hypothetical purchases at base or standard prices.
PRODUCTION CONTROL	Exception report to identify by shop order and lot number the variances in cost and quantity that are over or under by 5%.
PROJECT CONTROL	Weekly report on progress against plan for the events in critical path. Also need to know where float exists in other events so that resources may be shifted.

DETERMINE INFORMATION SOURCES

The step of determining information needs is hardly completed before it is necessary to consider the information sources. Indeed, these two steps are overlapping and, as we stated before, iterative.

Although some systems require considerable external information, for the most part the natural place to turn for information is inside the firm: books, records, files, statistical and accounting documents, and so on. Thus, most analysis refers to the step of determining information requirements as analyzing the present system.

The extent to which the existing system should be studied in a redesign effort of a new system has long been the subject of debate. One school of thought maintains that detailed analysis of the existing system should be a preliminary step to determining information requirements and that as much information as possible should be gathered and analyzed concerning the in-place system. This approach is justified on four grounds:

1. A minor modification in the existing system may satisfy the information requirements without a major redesign effort.

2. A look at the existing system is required in order to determine the specific areas that need improvement.
3. Since most systems utilize some common sources of input, a study of existing systems is necessary to determine these.
4. A study of existing systems is necessary to determine the data volume and costs associated with new designs.

The second theory of systems design, sometimes called the "fresh approach" or the "logical approach," holds that detailed analysis of the existing system is not necessary because the new system will be substantially changed and should not be predicated on the restraints of the existing one. Moreover, too close an identification with existing systems may compromise objectivity in the construction of logical methods to satisfy the information needs required to meet the systems objectives.

The choice of one or a combination of these approaches by the manager or designer is probably a matter of the state-of-the-art of information systems in the company under study, the objectives and existing information sources of the subsystem being designed, and the preferences of the manager himself. Sooner or later during design, some examination of existing company files as well as of external sources will become necessary, if only to determine the source to satisfy a portion of the new information needs or in order to integrate the subsystem under study with the total system for the organization.

Analysis and Integration

During this step in systems design, the determination of information sources, the form of the new system begins to take shape. We must not only uncover information sources for the particular subsystem under consideration but also take into account how they fit into the overall integrative sources of information and techniques of analysis.

Sources of information may be categorized:

1. *Internal and external records.* Internal records most often take the form of written materials and could include examples of inputs or outputs, file records, memoranda and letters, reports containing information about the existing system, and documentation of existing or planned systems. External data may come from a variety of sources such as trade publications, government statistics, and the like.

2. *Interviewing* managers and operating personnel is a valuable method of identifying possible sources of information and of analyzing the existing system. This form of data gathering can be the most fruitful method of securing information, provided it is conducted properly. Unlike the reading of written records, the gathering of facts from an interview involves human communication problems; these can be largely overcome by proper planning and by gaining the confidence of persons interviewed.

3. *Sampling and estimating* methods may become necessary when the accumulation of data is so large that only a portion of it can be examined. The major advantages of sampling techniques lie in the saving of time and cost, particularly on nonrecurring events where data are not available. One frequently used form of sampling is *work sampling*, which can be used to analyze the actions of people, machines, or events in terms of time. Estimating is an acceptable method of analysis and is a timesaver; however, estimates should be checked to control totals or be verified by interview where possible.

A number of *techniques of analysis* and synthesis have been published and are in widespread use. For our purposes in discovering information sources, two of these are of particular interest—input/output analysis and multidimensional flows. These two techniques permit us to summarize the available sources of information input so that we can avoid duplication by integrating them.

Input/output analysis is demonstrated in Figure 13–2 with the input/output chart, a visual portrayal of information inputs to a system and the information output that results. With a listing of inputs along the left side and outputs across the top, the relationship can be established by the dot at the point of intersection. For example, to produce an output of invoices, the information designated by the dots for company order number, tax data, net price, and shipping papers is required as input.

Figure 13–2 also demonstrates how data can be reduced and subsystems integrated through proper design. The top half, or "before analysis" portion, reveals that several items of output appear also as input, indicating rehandling and reprocessing of the same information to produce an output. The bottom half of the figure illustrates how consolidation and integration can reduce the number of information sources (i.e., input items). Figure 13–3 demonstrates the multiple uses of information sources and how information requirements may be identified and combined in a systems design that can serve more than one user. Files of input can be utilized by various organizational elements and various information subsystems.

Multidimensional flow is an additional technique of organizing information sources or depicting the existing design of a subsystem. A flowchart can be constructed to trace the routing or flow of information from origin to destination and to arrange this flow in a chronological sequence that shows the progression of information through the organization. Although they are not specifically required for identification of information sources, the factors of frequency, volume, time, cost, and physical distance can also be shown on such a chart.

Information Sources—Summary

Now that information sources have been identified with information needs, the next design step is to prepare a list that matches needs and

BEFORE ANALYSIS

OUTPUT DATA

INPUT & SUPPORTING DATA	Invoices	Shipping papers	Shipping labels	Quantity shipped	Back orders	Replenishment orders	Net price	Shipping terms	Shipping register	Stock ledgers	Stock bulletin	Stock report	Billing & cost dist.	Price realization	Tax reports	Royalty reports	Face sheets	Unfilled orders ($)	Orders entered ($)	Statistical analysis
Customer orders																				
Order number		•	•			•														
Quantity ordered				•	•				•									•	•	•
Item ident.		•			•				•									•	•	•
List price							•											•	•	•
Company ord. no.	•	•	•		•			•	•											
Customer reg. record																				
Pricing policy (Dis.)	•						•	•										•	•	
Traffic routing		•						•												
Tax data	•																			
Quantity shipped		•																		•
Net price	•																			•
Invent. cost at stand.										•	•	•								•
Stock replen. proc.					•	•			•											•
Receipts					•	•			•											•
Invoices													•	•	•	•	•		•	•
Shipping papers	•		•					•	•											
Stock ledgers				•	•						•	•	•							•
Price & cost refer.													•	•						
Peg board forms													•	•	•	•				
Royalty ident. codes																•				

AFTER ANALYSIS

OUTPUT DATA

INPUT & SUPPORTING DATA	Invoices	Shipping papers	Shipping labels	Quantity shipped	Back orders	Replenishment orders	Net price	Shipping terms	Shipping register	Stock ledgers	Stock bulletin	Stock report	Billing & cost dist.	Price realization	Tax reports	Royalty reports	Face sheets	Unfilled orders ($)	Orders entered ($)	Statistical analysis
Customer order no.	•	•	•				•													
Cust. ident. no.	•	•	•		•		•	•	•			•						•	•	•
Item ident. no.	•	•		•	•	•	•		•	•	•	•	•	•				•	•	•
Quantity ordered	•	•		•	•	•			•	•		•	•	•	•			•	•	•
Receipts	•	•		•	•	•			•	•	•	•	•	•	•			•	•	•

Figure 13–2   Input/Output Chart (Customer Order Processing)
SOURCE   Victor Lazzaro, ed., *Systems and Procedures,*
2nd ed., © 1968. By permission of Prentice-Hall, Inc.

ACTIVITY	Customer File	Product File	Open Order File	Master Assembly and Parts File	Labor Planning File	Plant Master Schedule	Vendor File	Open Purchase Order File	Accounts Receivable, Credit, and Collection	Accounts Payable	Employee Master Record	Product Development Resource File	General Ledger and Subledger Account File
Pre-Award	X	X		X		X						X	
Order Processing	X	X	X										
Design and Document Product		X	X			X						X	
Buy Materials, Supplies, and Services			X			X	X	X		X			X
Make Product	X		X	X	X	X			X		X		X
Distribute Product and Service It After Installation	X	X											
Plan and Control the Above Activities											X	X	
Report Job Status	X	X	X	X	X	X	X	X	X	X	X	X	X
Report Job Cost	X				X				X	X			X
Report Personnel Statistics											X		X

Figure 13–3   Multiple Uses of Information

SOURCE   Donald F. Heany, *Development of Information Systems,* copyright © 1968, The Ronald Press Company, New York

	Accounting	Production	Purchasing	etc.
Ordering Costs	X			
Carrying Costs	X			
Requirements		X		
Consumption Time		X		
Usage Rate		X		
Lead Time			X	
etc.				

Figure 13–4   Information Needs/Information Sources Matrix

sources. Such a list is evaluated and reevaluated until a final valid list of information sources is generated to match against previously determined information needs. This matching can take the form of a matrix diagram, a valuable device for the integration of subsystems as well as for use in the remainder of the systems design process. Figure 13-4 illustrates how such a matching process might be useful for the economic order quantity subsystem of the inventory management system.

Information sources can be further illustrated by giving examples of our selected subsystems:

Subsystem		Information Sources
INVENTORY	NEED	Items falling below minimum inventory level
	SOURCE	Stock-level determination subsystem compares current balance against minimum inventory level
ACCOUNTS PAYABLE	NEED	Code invoices "days to due date"
	SOURCE	Coded upon entry into accounts-payable subsystem
PURCHASING	NEED	Performance of individual buyers
	SOURCE	Purchasing system compares outgoing purchase prices against predetermined standards
PRODUCTION CONTROL	NEED	Cost variances over or under 5%
	SOURCE	Integration of costing with manufacturing applications: shop control, stores requisitioning, labor distribution, etc.
PROJECT CONTROL	NEED	Progress against plan for events in critical path
	SOURCE	Project control subsystem

DEVELOP ALTERNATIVE GROSS DESIGNS AND SELECT ONE

The development of a *concept* of a system is a creative process that involves synthesizing knowledge into some particular pattern. In our case, the concept of an MIS would consist of the major decision points, patterns of information flow, channels of information, and roles of managers and competitors. The concept must also include the relationship of the MIS to all functional operating systems, both existing and planned. The concept is a sketch of the structure or skeleton of the MIS, guiding and restricting the form of the detailed design. If gross design is the skeleton, then detailed design is the flesh.

Let us present two very simplified examples of alternative gross designs. For the first example, consider a company that wishes to introduce a new compact car. Two teams of engineers are put to work to conceive a design. One concept produced is a sketch showng a three-wheeled vehicle of a specified maximum length, weight, and horsepower, with the engine in the rear. The other team produces a sketch and description of a four-wheeled vehicle with front-engine drive and a specified minimum length, maximum weight, and horsepower limits.

In the second example, a company has twenty warehouses scattered about the United States to provide rapid shipment to customers. Headquarters and production facilities are at a single location. An MIS is needed to regulate production and inventories because of constant crises that have arisen with respect to deliveries. Two teams are asked to develop an MIS. The first team proposes that all orders from customers be sent directly to marketing at company headquarters. Marketing management will then provide demand forecasts to the factory and shipping instructions to the warehouses. A computer at company headquarters will maintain a perpetual inventory of all products in all warehouses. The second team proposes an MIS whereby orders are transmitted by the customers directly to the nearest warehouse. Each warehouse maintains its own inventory records; each forecasts its demand for the month ahead and transmits it to the factory.

It is obvious that each alternative concept of a system has advantages and disadvantages. Sometimes one concept will dominate all others by every major criterion. More often, a cursory evaluation will indicate that several concepts are not feasible or have little to recommend them. When there are several good contenders, careful evaluation of each is required. The bases for evaluation that appear to be most practical are:

1. Compare anticipated performance of the gross design with the objectives of the system as previously developed.
2. Prepare a rough or preliminary cost/effectiveness analysis of the system. This forces some *quantified* comparisons among systems.
3. Examine the flowcharts and identify strong and weak points of each gross design. Examine the quality of the data bases and information to be made available. Study the number of operations, dispersion and duplication of files, and potential breakdown points.
4. Expand the gross designs in more detail if none of these provides a preferred design.

DOCUMENT THE SYSTEM CONCEPT

At this point, sufficient information has been accumulated to begin a more detailed description of the system concept. This description includes essentially a flowchart or other documentation of the flow of information through the system, the inputs and outputs, and a narrative description of the operations.

Here we are describing the *manager's* participation in the system design and not the detailed specifications and documentation included in subsequent expansion by the designer. The manager's involvement in the design process is analogous to the homeowner's participation in the architect's planning, where the basic design and many of the details are shaped by the wishes and needs of the person buying the house. So it is with a computer-based information system. The manager should be involved to the extent that the system provides information for his needs; the designer is concerned with the nature of the materials and equipment as well as with technical processing considerations. Details to be worked out later by the designer will include explicit instructions as to *what data* are to be captured and *when*, the *files* that are to be used, the details of how *processing* is to be done, what *outputs* will be generated by the system, and how the outputs and files are to be *distributed*.

The scope of management design effort in documenting the system concept can be appreciated by recalling the previous discussion of a "black box" concept of a system. The system elements include inputs, outputs, master files, and rules for processing the data through the "black box." The processor element remains essentially "black" to the manager–user except for the decision rules that he has designed. The rules (programs) for processing the data include: (1) processing of input data against the file data and producing an output, (2) processing input data for file update, (3) processing input data into outputs without reference to the file, and (4) producing an output from the file without having processed an input.

Generally speaking, the system concept is not too concerned with the interior of the "black box" or the file construction. It is concerned very much with a definition of the job to be done, without specifying the detailed methods of implementation. To say it another way, the concept defines the problem without much regard to the solution of processing the information through the "black box." These processing details and some input/output specifications may be left for the implementation stage.

Major topics for managerial concern are discussed next. Once again, the design process is iterative.

General System Flow

The general system flowchart is a common method of indicating the general structure of a computer-based information system. Shown in such a chart is the description of the data-processing logic in general terms. The system flow also reflects the design efforts that have gone on before this step: setting objectives, establishing constraints, and determining information needs and sources.

The system flow, as illustrated by a flowchart, is quite general in nature and indicates only the main components of the system. At this stage in the design, the chart does not indicate what processing occurs at particular steps in the flow or what specific data, equipment, or people are involved. However, the chart is extremely important because it provides the foundation upon which a great many detailed specifications will follow.

Notice some important characteristics of the gross design flowchart:

1. System *objectives* are achieved and reflected in the flow diagram (e.g., optimize inventory costs through the design of decision rules containing optimum reorder points, safety stock levels, and reorder quantities).
2. Information needs and information sources are designed into the system.
3. Decision rules and decision points are shown.
4. Inputs and outputs are designated.
5. Most important—*subsystems are integrated.*

System Inputs

From the user's point of view, the inputs were structured when information sources were determined. However, there remains the task of design of input format. Since inputs frequently have to be accepted in the form in which they are received from outside the firm (e.g., sales orders, shipping documents, receiving papers, personnel information, etc.), input design becomes a matter of converting these to machine-usable form. Where inputs are from other subsystems within the firm, the problem becomes one of integrating these systems through common data elements and other means.

More detailed input data specification includes the sources of data—i.e., where they come from, what form they are in, and who is responsible for their production. Some inputs may be machine-readable and some may have to be converted. Because *forms* are so often used in collecting inputs and for other aids in operating a system, they are indispensable in modern business, and forms design is a primary concern of the systems designer.

Although the manager is not concerned in detail with these input specifications, he should be aware that the designer must specify the source of each input, its frequency, volume, and timing, plus its disposition after processing is completed. Since input must be checked for validity and volume, the editing procedures for accomplishing this are also required. Another important consideration is the specification of how inputs are to be converted into machine-readable form. These and other details of input design are usually contained on forms designed for that purpose.

System Outputs

From the technical standpoint, output-data definition includes the specification of destination—i.e., where they go, what form they take, and who is responsible for receiving them. Included in these specifications are the distribution of output (who gets what, how many copies, and by what means), the frequency with which output will be called for and its timing, and the form the output will take (tape, hard copy, data terminal, etc.).

Questions that the designer will ask in the process of developing output specifications include:

1. What form are the output reports to take? Can it be off-line?
2. Should the information be detailed or summarized?
3. What can I do with the output data that will be reused?
4. What kind of output form will be required? How many copies?
5. Are reports generated on demand? By exception? On schedule?

Despite the need to answer these details of output specification, the manager is concerned primarily with getting his information needs as previously determined in some type of output format. In other words, the consideration is how to *present the information to the eye or the ear of the manager*, and the answer lies in the content and form design of the output document. The form design is a direct function of information needs and should be constructed to fill those needs in a timely fashion. Care should be taken not to ask for *too much* information *too frequently*. "Management by exception" and "information by summary" should be the guiding principles.

Three illustrative subsystems that we have been using for design in this chapter are inventory management, production control, and purchasing. Figure 13–5 shows examples of outputs that might be designed to provide managerial information needs determined earlier in the design process for these subsystems.

Other Documentation

Other frequently used means of describing or documenting the system concept are the activity sheet and the system narrative. Figure 13–6 is a system description for our illustrative inventory management system and is designed to provide information on volumes, time relationships, and specific functions or requirements.

The system narrative is another way to document and describe a system. The justification for such an approach is based on the caution of the systems designer: "If you haven't written it out, you haven't thought it out." The following excerpt from our inventory management system narrative indicates the kind and level of system description that should be available at the end of detailing the system concept.

> *Inventory Management of Raw Materials*
>
> This system is concerned with inventory control of raw materials for manufacturing. There are four plants, each with its own computer and each utilizing the same inventory control system. Raw materials move from receiving to storekeeping and thence to manufacturing as required by the production planning and control system. There are three major groups of operations within the system: *stock level subsystem,* based on transactions; *reorder*

DAILY RAW MATERIALS EXPEDITE REPORT

Item Number	Description	Unit	EOQ	ROP	Bal	On Order	Del.	Received	Action
zz	Gasket Material	yd	900	400	327	900	6/6		Expedite with vendor
f73	Spring	doz	60	10	12	60	7/3	42	Check receipt

SHOP VARIANCE REPORT

No.	Lot	Description	Unit	Run	Start	Due Compl.	Shop	Variance ± 5%
3B2	R44	Alum. Tube	each	2	6/13	6/19	Weld	Cost variance + 7.2%
zzx4	R44	Alum. Tube	each	3	6/13	6/26	Bend	Time over 7 days

BUYER NEGOTIATIONS VARIANCE REPORT

Material	Unit	Part No.	Vendor	Standard Cost	Actual Cost	Variance
Steel Pl.	Lb.	274345X	Bay Metals	.32	.35	.03 9.4% +
Dr. Shaft	ea.	B33-165	Zimmer	9.55	8.72	.83 8.7% **

Figure 13–5 Selected Outputs for Three Subsystems: Inventory Management, Production Control, Purchasing

ACTIVITY:	Inventory Control			
		Key	Name	Volume
Stock Level Subsystem			Inputs	
Freq: As received		1600	Receipts	100/day
Inputs: 1600, 1610, 1620		1610	Issues	1000/day
		1620	Misc. Transact.	100/day
Reorder Point Subsystem			Outputs	
Freq: Daily				
Inputs: 3610, 3640		2600	Stock Status	400/day
		2610	Purchase Orders	25/day
Reporting		2620	Expedite Report	1000 lines/day
		2630	Exceptions	200 items/day
Daily		2640	Stock Status	5000 lines/week
Inputs: 3610				
			Files	
		3600	EOQ & ROP File	5000 records
		3610	Master Stock	5000 records
		3620	Receiving File	5000 records
		3630	Vendor File	100 records

Note: Purchase orders for commodity class 7Q4 must be in carload lots.

Figure 13–6 System Description—Activity Sheet for Inventory Control Subsystem (Materials Control)

point subsystem, including purchase order preparation; and *economic order quantity subsystem.*

Stock Level

1. As material arrives at receiving, the receiving report is marked to show quantity and quality acceptance. The receiving report is then matched against the receiving order file (prepunched card) and actual quantity received, date received, and quality acceptance are key-punched. The receiving order card is then transmitted to the computer center for updating the inventory file.
2. As the storekeeper issues items from stores, a prepunched card is . . . etc . . . etc. . . .

Once the gross design concept has been documented, the responsible manager or task force leader should prepare a report for the top managers who must authorize further development of the system.

PREPARE THE GROSS DESIGN REPORT

The gross design report is, in a sense, a proposal for the expenditure of funds and for organizational changes. Because it is directed to management, it should have a concise summary of the problems that necessitate the system, the objectives, the general nature of the system, reasons why the concept was selected over others, and the time and resources required to design and implement the system. Along with this summary, possibly in a separate volume or volumes, the documentation should be provided. In essence, the proposal shows performance specifications of the system. Performance specifications describe the functions that must be performed by the system and the means by which each function is measured.

SUMMARY

The gross design represents the conceptual structure of the MIS. It specifies the performance requirements for those who will develop the detailed design. Because it sets the broad outlines of the MIS, the managers who will make use of the MIS must have a large role in the development and evaluation of alternative concepts.

Management must identify basic business problems and objectives of the MIS. System constraints may be of an environmental, basic business, or technical nature. Management is responsible primarily for specifying the first two. The needs of management for information are a function of the problems to be solved and of individual managerial style. Thus, only the managers can factor these into the gross design. Sources of information, on the other hand, are often best determined by the technical specialists.

The gross design is ultimately described by formal documents such as flowcharts, input/output matrices, data-bank requirements, hardware and software requirements, organizational changes, and time and cost refinements of the project program proposed.

DISCUSSION QUESTIONS AND PROBLEMS

1. Distinguish between *performance* specifications and *design* specifications by reference to engineering literature.

2. Develop a form that could be used to guide the designer in presenting a gross design of an MIS to management.

3. Why is the term *feasibility design* often used to designate gross or conceptual design? Which of the three terms do you think is most appropriate? Why?

4. Should detailed design work ever overlap the development of the gross design? Why, or why not?

5. Develop in detail a possible "scenario" between the systems designer and a manager of marketing at the stage of development of alternative concepts for a marketing management information system.

6. Develop a list of criteria for comparing alternative gross designs.

7. When the engineering department in a certain large company wishes to order materials or components for the development of a prototype model, it sends a materials request form to the purchasing department. The purchasing department selects one of several vendors that can most closely meet the specs, and prepares a purchase order. The purchase order must be signed by engineering management and, depending upon the amount, by the finance department, or even the general manager.

The vendor encloses a packing slip with delivery of the items, and the company's receiving department sends a receiving report to both engineering and accounting. The vendor also sends a separate invoice to the accounting department to bill the company. The company checks the invoice, the packing slip, the receiving report, and the purchase order. If they all agree, the bill is paid; otherwise an investigation is initiated. Problems arise when partial shipments are made.

The new senior systems designer is appalled at such a cumbersome system and has told management he can devise at least three superior gross designs.

8. Cooper Textile Mills has its home plant in Wycombe, Pa.; a second manufacturing plant in Puerto Rico; a dyeing plant in New Jersey; a manufacturing plant in France; and its primary sales office in New York. Cooper Mills' major product is power nets, the basic material in women's foundation garments. It is one of the most difficult materials to produce on a continuously high-quality basis. According to President Gilbert Cooper (in *Textile World*), "We need the raw materials on hand to be able to react to a sudden switch-over in customer style preference—from nylon to rayon, for example. At the same time, some of our raw materials are so expensive—up to $6 a pound—that tying up capital in a glut of stock could ruin us financially." Without knowledge of market trends, panic pricing may result in heavy

losses. Trends in style could be noted early, if prompt reports of sales could be obtained and analyzed.

Could several good gross designs for a management information system be developed?

9. According to Walter E. Trabbold, controller of the Bank of Delaware, "We have defined it [development of management information systems] in terms of six subsystems."

These are:
a. Development of a central (customer-information) file
b. Computerization of all operations: demand deposits, savings, commercial loans, mortgage loans, investments, and clubs
c. Integrated accounting subsystem to meet reporting requirements of management, stockholders, and regulatory agencies; this includes general ledger, cost, budgeting, and statistical information
d. A reporting subsystem in two parts: standard reports and exception reports
e. An on-line inquiry subsystem to provide management with current operating and marketing information
f. A sophisticated model of the entire business system

For a bank considering installation of a total management information system, draw a block diagram of the gross design to represent the subsystems listed and their relationships.

10. A real estate firm employs five clerical people and twenty salesmen. It has on-line access to multiple listings of real property in the large city in which it operates. Nevertheless, the president feels that a really sophisticated MIS could improve profits greatly. He plans to sketch several alternative systems based upon the conceptual framework opposite, which he came across in an article (J. H. McRainey, "Data—The Crucial Element," *Automation,* August 1961).

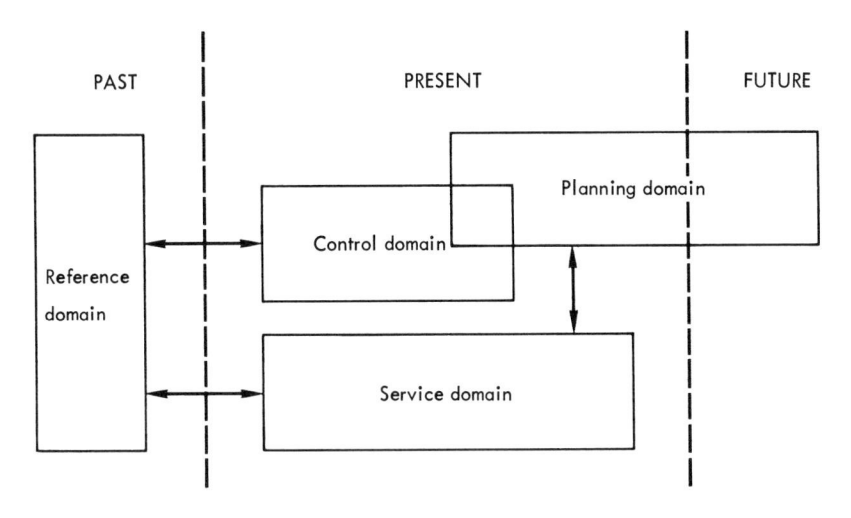

```
              |                       |
     PAST     |       PRESENT         |    FUTURE
              |                       |
              |         ┌─────────────┼──────────┐
              |         │   Planning domain      │
        ┌─────┼───┬─────┼─────┐       │          │
        │     │   │ Control domain    │          │
  ┌─────┤  ◄──┼──►│     │     └───────┼──────────┘
  │     │     |   │     │    ▲        │
  │Reference│ |   └─────┼────┼┘       │
  │ domain  │ |         │    │        │
  │     │◄──┼─┼────►┌───┼────▼────────┼──┐
  │     │   | │     │ Service domain  │  │
  │     │   | │     │   │             │  │
  └─────┘   | └─────┴───┴─────────────┘  │
              |                       |
```

REFERENCES

1. Ralph J. Cordiner, *New Frontiers for Professional Managers* (New York: McGraw-Hill Book Company, 1956), p. 102. Used by permission of the McGraw-Hill Book Company.

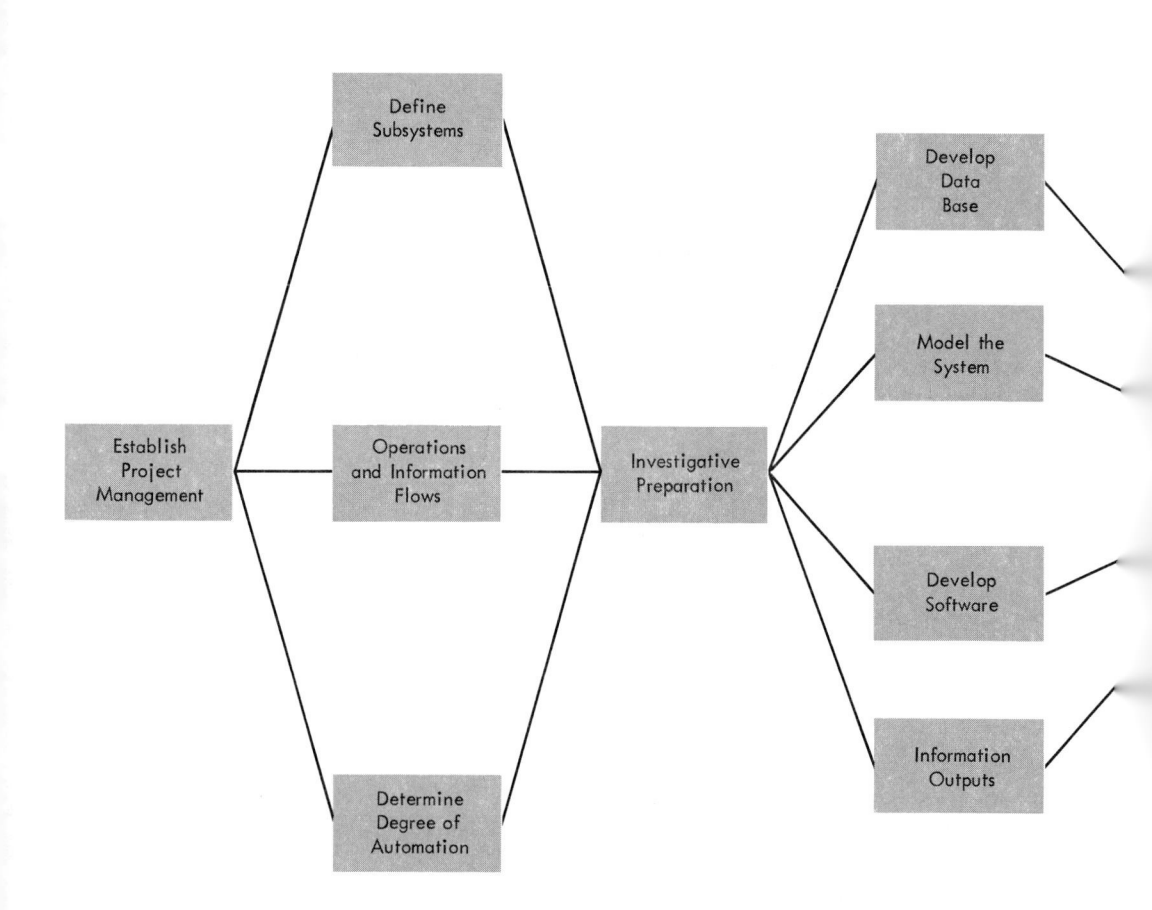

```
                    Define
                  Subsystems

                                              Develop
                                               Data
                                               Base

                                              Model the
                                               System

Establish      Operations          Investigative
 Project       and Information     Preparation
Management         Flows
                                              Develop
                                              Software

                                              Information
                                               Outputs

                  Determine
                  Degree of
                  Automation
```

14
detailed systems design

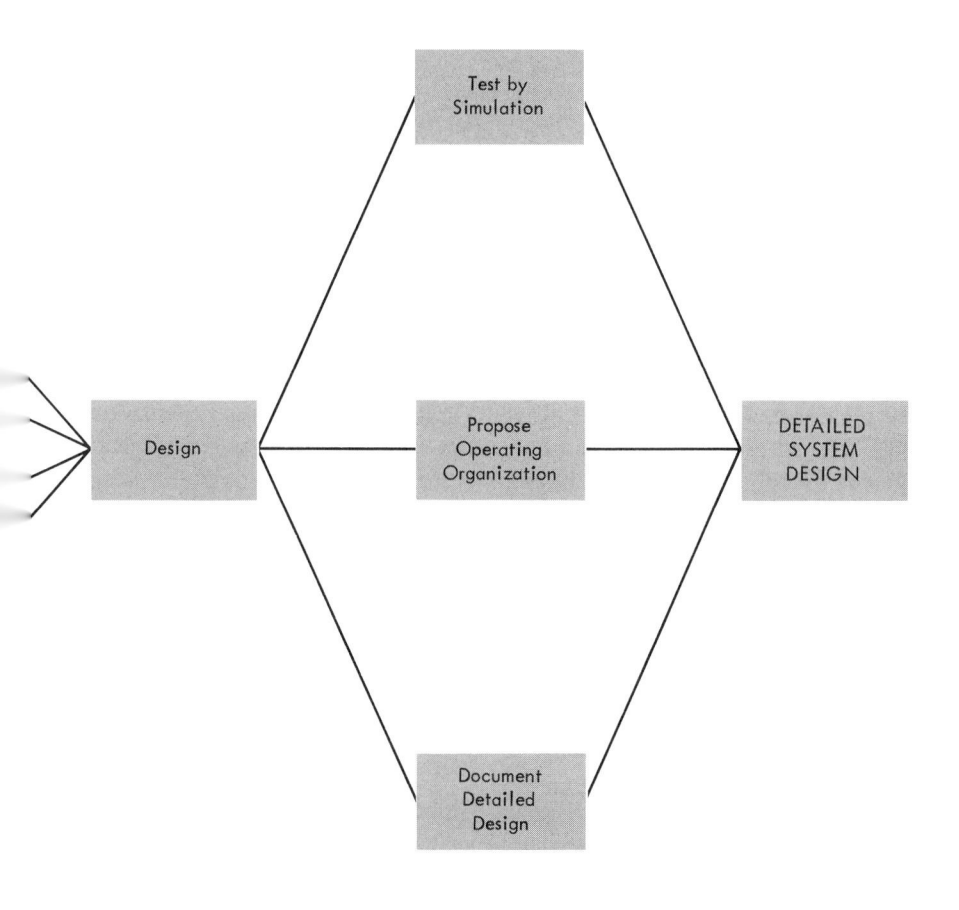

Design → Test by Simulation, Propose Operating Organization, Document Detailed Design → DETAILED SYSTEM DESIGN

14

Once the scope and general configuration of the MIS have been established, the detailed design of the system may be started. A step-by-step explanation of a how-to-do-it procedure for detailed system design applicable to all systems is impractical, for the following reasons:

1. There is a wide variety of approaches to system design in terms of organizing for it, conducting it, and defining its output.

2. A basic question rarely treated by writers deals with the state-of-the-art and to what extent it should be incorporated into systems design. In other words, should we describe management information systems design as it *could be* if the latest state-of-the-art knowledge were utilized, or should we describe it in terms of what will become feasible within five years?

3. Systems design is a complex of concurrent activities, whereas the nature of our description can proceed along only one line at a time.

4. It is difficult to describe a process of rational design that must be tested in an organization from time to time to determine the likelihood of its being accepted by the members of the organization. That is, the design of a management information system is both a rational and a social process.

5. If it is to represent the design of information systems in general, the explanation may be at such a level of generality that it gives no clues to the multitude of detailed steps involved. On the other hand, the explanation of a detailed procedure can describe only one among thousands and gives no clue to the general nature of design. Attempting to find a middle course sacrifices the advantage of one extreme without gaining much from the other.

6. An explanation of detailed systems-design procedure must be interrupted frequently by descriptive essays on some aspect with which the designer deals.

Within the limitations on clarity and objectives imposed by these considerations, we will attempt to present the nature of systems design at the "edge of the art." The edge of the art is broad, with part in the present and part in the near future. A general approach will provide the framework, but frequent resort to detailed procedures and descriptions will bring substance to the framework.

INFORM THE ORGANIZATION OF THE PURPOSE AND NATURE OF THE SYSTEMS DESIGN EFFORT

The first step in systems design is not a technical one. It is concerned with gaining support for the work that follows. Systems designers must have the support of most members of the organization in order to obtain information for the design of the system and to obtain acceptance of the final system. At a minimum, members of the organization should be informed of the objectives and nature of the study. It is preferable, if possible, to draw many members into the study, at least in some small way. Furthermore, it is desirable to reassure the employees, if possible, that changes will benefit them or that they will not suffer financially from the implementation of the system. Even so, the natural human resistance to change requires that sufficient information on general progress be disseminated to gradually accustom the employees to their future roles.

The contrary approach, that employees should not be disturbed during the system design, can be quite hazardous. When people are not informed, they seize upon bits of information, construct concepts that may be completely erroneous, and in consequence often take up detrimental activities. The final system, when announced, may be met with shock, resentment, and both open and covert resistance.

AIM OF DETAILED DESIGN

The detailed design of an MIS is closely related to the design of operating systems. Sometimes, it is true, the operating system must be accepted without change and a new MIS appended to it. However, it is preferable to design both systems together, and as we discuss the detailed design of the MIS, this parallel effort will be apparent, even though our principal focus is on the MIS.

By drawing upon the analogy of engineering design, we can clarify the meaning of detailed design. The direct goal of engineering design is to furnish the engineering description of a tested and producible product. Engineering design consists of specifications in the form of drawings and specification reports for systems as a whole and for all components in the system. Further, justification documents in the form of reports of mathematical analysis and test results are part of the detailed design. Enough detail must be given so that engineering design documents and manufacturing drawings are sufficient for the shop to construct the product. The production of operating and maintenance instructions is also considered part of the design output.

The analogy of detailed design of MIS readily follows. The aim of the detailed design is to furnish a description of a system that achieves the goals of the gross system-design requirements. This description consists of drawings, flowcharts, equipment and personnel specifications, procedures, support tasks, specification of information files, and organization and operating manuals required to run the system. Also part of the design is the documentation of analysis and testing, which justifies the design. The design must be sufficiently detailed that operating management and personnel may implement the system. Whereas gross design gives the overall *performance* specifications for the MIS, the detailed design yields the *construction* and *operating* specifications.

PROJECT MANAGEMENT OF MIS DETAILED DESIGN

Any effort that qualifies as a system design has the dimensions of a project. The first step in the detailed design is therefore a planning and organizing step. For small projects, all phases may be planned for, as described in Chapter 12, *before* the gross (feasibility) design is undertaken. Often, in larger projects, not enough is known about the prospective system in advance of the gross design to plan for the detailed design project. Further, if the gross design indicates that a new system design is not appropriate at this time, any project planning for the detailed design in advance would be wasted.

Once the project manager and key project personnel have been designated, the steps in project management fall into two classes: *planning* and *control*. The amount of effort expended in each step is obviously a function of the size of the MIS project and the cost of developing the detailed design of the project. The key steps in planning and control of detailed design, as based upon Chapter 12, are recapitulated here.

Project Planning

1. Establish the project objectives. This involves a review, subdivision, and refinement of the performance objectives established by the gross design.
2. Define the project tasks. This identifies a hierarchical structure of tasks to be performed in the design of the MIS and may be documented by work package instructions for large projects.
3. Plan the logical development of sequential and concurrent tasks and task activities. This usually requires a network diagram of events and activities.
4. Schedule the work as required by management—established end date and activity-network constraints. Essentially, the work and schedule are tied together by completion of the PERT diagram.
5. Estimate labor, equipment, and other costs for the project.

6. Establish a budget for the project by allocating funds to each task and expenditures month by month over the life of the project.
7. Plan the staffing of the project organization over its life.

Project Control

1. Determine whether project objectives are being met as the project progresses.
2. Maintain control over the schedule by changing workloads and emphasis as required by delays in critical activities.
3. Evaluate expenditure of funds in terms of both work accomplished and time. Revise the budget as required to reflect changes in work definition.
4. Evaluate manpower utilization and individual work progress, and make adjustments as required.
5. Evaluate time, cost, and work performance in terms of schedules, budgets, and technical plans to identify interaction problems.

IDENTIFY DOMINANT AND PRINCIPAL TRADE-OFF PERFORMANCE CRITERIA FOR THE SYSTEM

Dominant criteria for a system are those that make an activity so important that it overrides all other activities. For example, a dominant criterion might be that the system operate so that there is never a stockout. This overrides the criterion of minimizing inventory cost. Such a criterion might hold for a company selling human blood, life-preserving drugs, or electric power. It might even hold for a company selling a consumer product where loss of a customer is permanent and all competitors have a no-stockout policy.

Examples of other dominant criteria might be one-day customer service, zero-defect product, specified price range for products, maintenance of multiple sources of supply for all materials and components purchased, or conformity of all research and engineering to long-range corporate plans. It is obvious that identification of the dominant criteria is necessary before subsequent design steps can proceed.

Trade-off criteria are those in which the criterion for performance of an activity may be reduced to increase performance of another activity. For example, the criterion of low manufacturing costs might be balanced against that of long-range public image of the firm achieved by reduction in environmental pollution. Again, the criterion of producing styles or models for many segments of the market might be balanced against that of maintaining low manufacturing and service costs.

The reason for identifying dominant and trade-off criteria is that as the detailed design is developed, decision centers (managers or computers) must be identified to achieve such criteria or make trade-offs. The MIS must

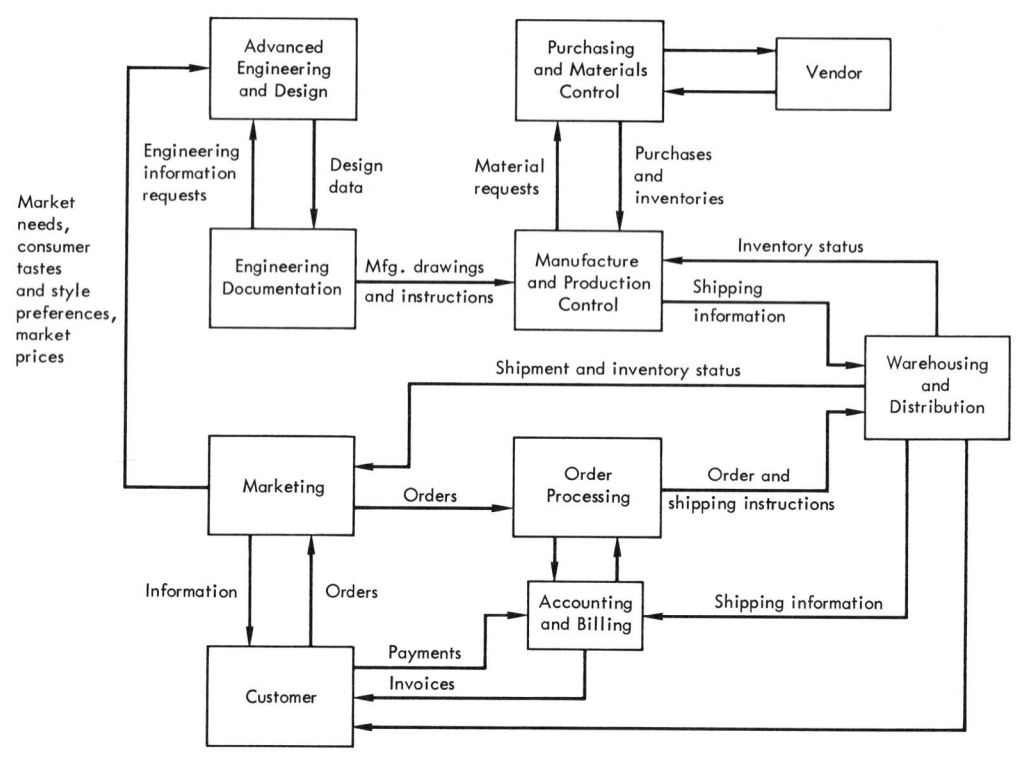

Figure 14-1 Gross System Concept for a Business System

be designed to provide the information for the decisions, or at lower and programmed levels, to make the trade-offs.

DEFINE THE SUBSYSTEMS

We start the process of defining the subsystems with two principal blocks of information: (1) the gross design concept, and (2) the dominant and trade-off performance criteria. Although the gross design requires some assumptions concerning the subsystems, it is necessary now to review these subsystems and to redefine them if it seems appropriate. Based upon the gross design, investigation of the detailed activities of each major activity block must be undertaken. Consider, for example, the gross design representation of a business system given in Figure 14-1. (It should be emphasized that this is a greatly simplified representation of the gross design. A gross design should be fully defined, as described in Chapter 13.) Each large block (or system) must be broken down to determine all activities required and the necessary information inputs and outputs of each activity. Careful analyses of such activities is critical in detailed design. Figure 14-2 shows a typical form, which helps to develop descriptions of each activity.

ACTIVITY (TRANSACTION)		NETWORK DIAGRAM ACTIVITY NUMBER
PURPOSE AND DESCRIPTION		
INPUTS	MEDIA	
OUTPUTS	MEDIA	
SEQUENCE OF ELEMENTS OF ACTIVITY	PERFORMER	DECISION RULE

Figure 14–2 Activity Design Form

480 Planning, Design, and Implementation of MIS

```
                    Equipment      Men
                    assigned       assigned
                         │           │
                         ▼           ▼
B, batch or      ┌─────────────────────┐
lot arriving ───▶│                     │────▶ Batch leaving
                 │      Quality        │
                 │   Control Activity  │────▶ Defective parts
I, inspection    │                     │
instructions ───▶│                     │────▶ Information results
                 └─────────────────────┘
                         │           │
                         ▼           ▼
                    Equipment      Men available
                    available      (Original
                    (Original      available
                    equipment less manpower less
                    equipment      men assigned)
                    assigned)
```

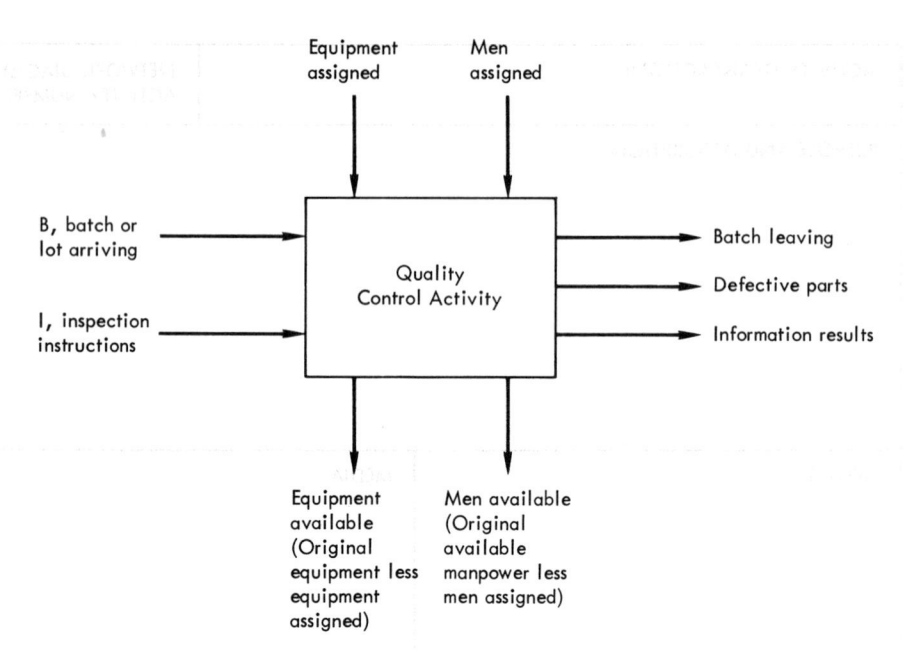

Figure 14–3 Model of Activity Operation and Information

The quality control activity, one of many in the manufacturing subsystem, might be analyzed as shown in Figure 14–3. The activity processor is made up of equipment and men assigned. One form of information output is the revised figure for resources available after commitment to the activity. The operating input is a batch or "lot" of parts, and the output consists of reduced-size batches of a statistically specified quality plus defectives that have been separated out. The information results give the average quality of batches, the number of rejects, and the number of batches inspected per unit of time. The kind of information output captured must be based upon decisions to be made for planning and control. At this stage, only speculations on needed information for an activity may be made.

The information system must be based upon the operating system. Once this operating system is outlined by the selection of the gross concept, certain basic relationships among major activities become more or less fixed. However, there is still considerable freedom in establishing the detailed activities and their relationships. The detailed activities, once defined, may be related in network form, as shown in Figure 14–4.

The degree of breakdown of the major activities, of course, determines the size and complexity of the network. If the activities are broken down too finely, the design will never be completed. If a major activity is broken down too coarsely, vital material, information, and decision needs will not be factored into the design. Furthermore, optional rearrangement or re-detailed systems design   481

grouping of activities will not be examined. If we could conceive of a hierarchy of activities such as:

System
  Subsystem
    Functional component
      Task
        Subtask
          Operation element

then we would probably want to develop our *activity network* at the "functional component" level. Once activity networks have been developed to include each major activity of the gross design, the subsystems are then redefined. A subsystem may consist simply of the activities corresponding to a major block activity of the gross design, or some detailed activity blocks may be transferred from one group to another to make up the network of the subsystem. Any changes such as this will require a redefining of the major activity block in terms of its performance requirements. Quite often, however, a major block activity must be considered as comprising several subsystems. Grouping of activities into a subsystem may be based upon various considerations, such as (1) common functions, (2) common techniques or procedures, (3) logical flow relationships, or (4) common inputs or outputs.

The revised subsystems can be identified on the network diagrams by drawing a loop around the aggregate of activities to be included in a particular subsystem. At this point, all connecting lines for activities that cross over the loop represent either inputs or outputs to the subsystems, as dis-

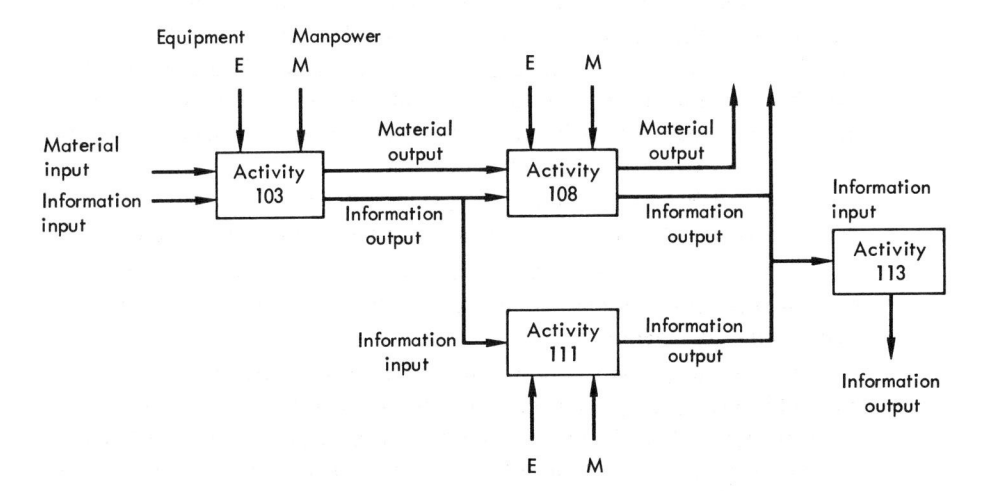

Figure 14-4   Interrelating Activities

cussed in Chapter 8. The loop itself is a boundary of the subsystem and an interface between two or more subsystems. Because organizational authority and responsibility structures are often divided by subsystem boundaries, problems of interfacing subsystems require careful attention; that is, inputs and outputs between interfacing systems must be matched.

The approach that we have given here for identifying subsystems is analogous to one method of development of a new company's organization structure by analysis followed by synthesis. This consists of identifying activities and tasks, grouping tasks into positions, and then grouping positions into components on some rational basis. An alternative approach that is quicker but not so thorough is simply to divide the major activities of the gross design into the subsystems apparently required to fulfill the major activities. Such a procedure may lead to incompletely defined subsystems, mismatches between subsystems, and missing activities.

Information for Defining Subsystems

The objective of the design search is to find a set of subsystems that satisfies the performance requirements specified by the gross design. In order to do this, we must search for information that helps us select and define the subsystems. Such information consists of:

1. Dominant and trade-off criteria for the operating and the MIS systems as a whole. Dominant criteria—such as the decision to utilize only current manufacturing area available, to use company salesmen rather than manufacturer's representatives, to utilize current computing facilities, or to install time-sharing terminals for executive use—impose some clear limitations on alternatives for the designer. Where dominant criteria are absent, trade-offs that permit different emphasis on different functional activities must be identified, so that subsystems can be defined realistically. Analysis may indicate, for instance, that the logistics activities should be separated from both manufacturing and marketing management for greatest effectiveness and efficiency. This will require the study and development of a logistics system closely coupled to the other two systems.

2. Available resources the company will commit. Systems must be designed, obviously, in terms of what is available to implement them.

3. Required activities for achievement of systems operations and performance specifications. Each activity and its relationship to other activities must be identified.

4. Necessary control positions in the system. Every system has a hierarchical structure of control points, usually corresponding to the organizational responsibility structure. However, organizational responsibility for control of variances is often not well defined. The MIS designer must get control positions clarified in order to develop information flows.

5. Management decision points for system planning and control. At the upper levels of the organization, important decisions must be made regarding system operation and variances from major company goals. These top management positions and their information requirements must be identified.

6. Information required for programmed decision making. Complete information requirements for decisions capable of being processed by decision tables and models with the aid of the computer must be uncovered.

7. Specific output requirements of all systems. This includes a detailed list of purposes to be served by the information output. The specific content of each report or communication and the method of utilization should be determined. The frequency of reports, their formats (written, visual, audio, etc.), distribution, and filing must be established. This information assists with the development of activity descriptions just discussed. Such information may be recorded on the activity form shown in Figure 14–2.

Obtaining Information

The designer utilizes four principal sources for the development of the MIS. These are:

1. Task force meetings
2. Personal interviews
3. Internal and external source documents
4. Personal observation of operations and communications, when feasible

Task Force Meetings

For the design of large systems, the use of task forces for the development of information and ideas is usually advantageous. The task force for a single major activity block should consist of both managers and key specialists. The designer should chair the task force meetings. His function is to draw out ideas and information, synthesize ideas, including his own, and present in diagrams and documents the synthesis for evaluation and modification. The task force meetings serve to bring out information gaps, operating needs, and controversial points. In repeated meetings, the design of a subsystem is hammered out.

Interviews

Instead of, or supplemental to, task force meetings, the designer should conduct interviews with key managers at top and intermediate levels, with key specialists, and with a sampling of operating employees. Although it appears obvious, it cannot be emphasized enough thàt the designer *must use tact in interviews*. Whether he is interviewing the top manager or the lowest-level employee, his role is that of *a searcher* for knowledge, *not a lecturer* on systems.

In interviews with managers, the designer should seek information on

1. Objectives of the firm or organizational component
2. Major policies in force or needed to accomplish these objectives
3. The categories of information the managers desire
4. Speed of access to the various categories of information desired by managers
5. Intervals of time desired between receipt of various types of information
6. Format desired for information presented
7. Style of decision making of the managers
8. Resources that will be committed for the implementation and operation of the system
9. Degree of manager involvement in classes of decisions: individual decision making, participative decision making, or partially routine (programmed) decision making
10. Organizational relationships that would facilitate system operation and management decision making

Systems designers should not expect too much from managers in the way of defining information needs. Rather, they should work with managers to identify objectives and develop plans. The identification of necessary information will follow from this.

Internal and External Source Documents

The use of internal source documents primarily provides the systems designer with a point of departure. From a practical viewpoint, it is likely that many traditional operations and reports must be retained simply to provide some continuity of operations; and this is appropriate, since the current methods are usually the result of continued minor improvements. Modification or regrouping of activities or data batches is still feasible for the systems designer, however. The number of internal source documents may be great, depending upon the company, so that no complete listing is given here. Organization and policy guides, procedures manuals, master budgets and account structure, and the many functional reports of engineering, manufacturing, marketing, purchasing, and employee and public relations should be examined according to their relevancy to the system being designed. Sometimes, reports such as records of customers' complaints or of service calls may provide the key to system design needs.

External source documents provide economic, marketing, industry, and financial information related to the firm that may be of assistance. A review of the company by a securities analyst in a financial journal may provide very valuable insights.

Direct Observation

The designer should not isolate himself in his office to sketch out designs; he should make on-the-spot surveys of operations in action. It would be foolish, for example, to develop a systems design in which foremen in the factory provide hourly personal reports to a planning/control center if the factory were a half-mile in length or if the planning/control group were in a building some distance away. Similar absurd situations could be conjectured for sales reports or physical distribution reports. On-site inspection will reveal the physical and environmental restraints that may have to be accepted in a new system. Conversely, however, such inspection may also lead to a major revision of the physical facilities to suit the system design.

The designer should record, as he goes along, the relevant (and probably much irrelevant) data he is gathering. In the case of large documents, he would, of course, merely make notes of points vital to his investigation. At the end of certain phases, he should try to organize the data so that future information may be related to that already gathered. Finally, at some point, he sketches alternative designs for the operating subsystems.

SKETCH THE DETAILED OPERATING SUBSYSTEMS AND INFORMATION FLOWS

The development of the detailed design is first carried out for the subsystem, functional, and task levels of detail. It is very similar to detailed engineering design, which requires trial and error, shifting operations to find good arrangements, and performing calculations to check out the system. The equivalents of engineering sketches in MIS design are the flowcharts. Figure 14–5 shows the graphic symbols and their meanings as used by designers. There are three types of systems flowcharts:

1. *Task-oriented charts.* These are block diagrams showing the relationships among the various tasks or activities. (See Figure 14–6). Subsequently, the detailed elemental steps required to complete an activity are analyzed and described step by step on an operation analysis form (sometimes called a flow-process chart).

2. *Forms-oriented charts.* These charts identify the forms used in communicating or reporting and trace the flow of all copies through the organization. In some cases, the chronological movement may receive emphasis.

3. *Program flowcharts* (block diagrams). Prepared by the people who give instructions to the computer, the program flowchart is a fundamental tool of programming, designed to show the logical sequence of steps to be carried out by the computer. It structures the logic that the coding of the programs will follow. Program flowcharts will be of interest at a later stage in the design, but we include them here for completeness.

486   Planning, Design, and Implementation of MIS

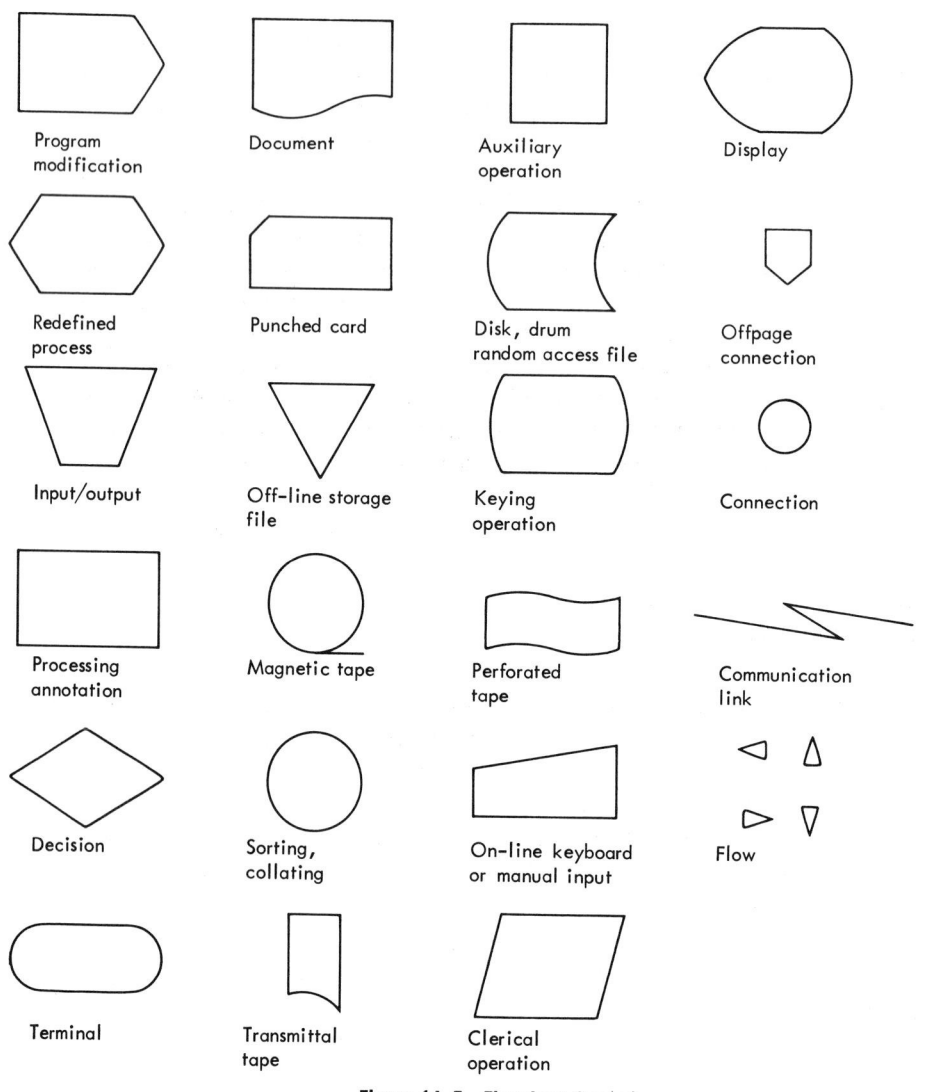

Program modification	Document	Auxiliary operation	Display
Redefined process	Punched card	Disk, drum random access file	Offpage connection
Input/output	Off-line storage file	Keying operation	Connection
Processing annotation	Magnetic tape	Perforated tape	Communication link
Decision	Sorting, collating	On-line keyboard or manual input	Flow
Terminal	Transmittal tape	Clerical operation	

Figure 14–5   Flowchart Symbols

The flowcharts are *not* the complete detailed design. They show primarily flows and relationships. Inputs and outputs are shown only in gross form. The quantitative relations among elements in the systems must be expressed in terms of mathematical models. Where this is not possible, detailed verbal descriptions must be used to actually develop the detailed operating design. The flowcharts are important, however, in developing the information necessary for managerial decisions with respect to the design for model constructions, and for programmed decision making in system operation.

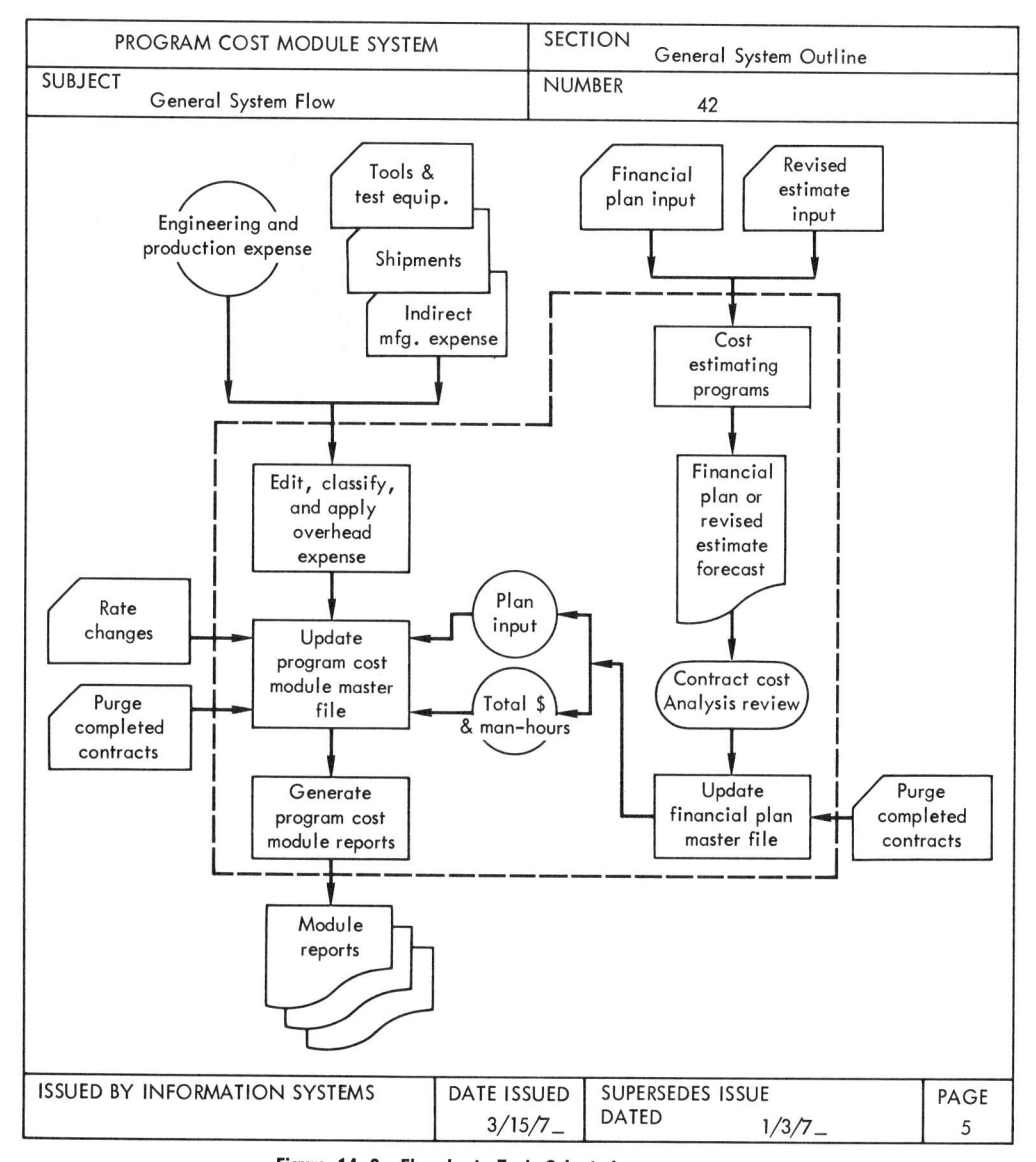

PROGRAM COST MODULE SYSTEM	SECTION General System Outline
SUBJECT General System Flow	NUMBER 42

[Flowchart with the following elements:
- Engineering and production expense
- Tools & test equip.
- Shipments
- Indirect mfg. expense
- Financial plan input
- Revised estimate input
- Cost estimating programs
- Edit, classify, and apply overhead expense
- Financial plan or revised estimate forecast
- Rate changes
- Plan input
- Update program cost module master file
- Total $ & man-hours
- Contract cost Analysis review
- Purge completed contracts
- Generate program cost module reports
- Update financial plan master file
- Purge completed contracts
- Module reports]

| ISSUED BY INFORMATION SYSTEMS | DATE ISSUED 3/15/7_ | SUPERSEDES ISSUE DATED 1/3/7_ | PAGE 5 |

Figure 14–6 Flowchart: Task Oriented

DETERMINE THE DEGREE OF AUTOMATION OF EACH OPERATION

Each operation in the flowchart should next be examined to establish the level of automation possible. Levels of automation may be classified as shown in Table 14–1. By listing each operation along the horizontal axis of a chart and levels of automation along the vertical axis, an "automation profile" may be plotted.

Table 14-1
Levels of Automation

	Function Performed by Machine	Characteristics
L 1	None	All work performed by humans, manual aids are used.
L 2	Supplies action, energy	Mechanical or electrical energy is supplied for the basic process action.
L 3	Supplies all action, energy	Energy is supplied for all control, auxiliary, and basic functions.
L 4	Stores the control instructions	Machine follows the established, step-by-step, stored instructions.
L 5	Controls intermediate and auxiliary actions	Feedback in minor loops assists in control.
L 6	Controls output by main-loop feedback	Closed-loop feedback produces controlled output by iterative process.
L 7	Modifies or creates control instructions	Machine determines what to do and requires no human control.

SOURCE Delmar W. Karger and Robert G. Murdick, *Managing Engineering and Research,* 2d ed. (New York: The Industrial Press, 1969), p. 325.

Widely contrasting levels of automation in a system may be suspect and should be examined. It is not at all incorrect, however, to choose an "all manual" (low-level automation) system. Low-level automation may be preferred when:

1. Problems are not well structured
2. The decision criteria cannot be well defined
3. The rules for making decisions must be constantly modified or changed
4. There are gaps in the data entering the system
5. The data entering the system are ambiguous, inconsistent, or somewhat unreliable
6. The processing steps are simple and few in number
7. The cost of human labor is low relative to the cost of the equipment
8. Storage of data is negligible

DEVELOP THE DATA BASE

The data base is the data that must be obtained (sometimes called "captured") and usually stored for later retrieval for managerial decision making. It also consists of data that will be utilized in programmed decision making and real-time control. As discussed in Chapters 9 and 10, the data base is derived from the needs of management for information to guide the total business system. We start with the study of management's problems and information needs, develop flowcharts of systems that meet management's requirements, and then detail the data requirements of the systems.

detailed systems design   489

A systematic approach to the development of the data base is as follows:

1. Identify all points on the flowcharts that require data inputs. Generally these are inputs to activities or transactions as well as decision tables or modeling operations.

2. Prepare a data or file worksheet for each data element, giving:
   a. Source of data
   b. Length and form
   c. Current and potential frequency of updating
   d. Retention schedule for the data
   e. End use of the data

3. Group all data worksheets by system and check for omissions.

4. Group all data worksheets by activity and by organizational component and note duplications. A matrix approach to this analysis along the general lines indicated by Figure 14–7 is very helpful.

5. Eliminate duplicated data requirements to develop an integrated data base for which cross-functional use of the master file is employed. See Figure 14–7.

6. Evaluate the items in the master file for frequency of need and value of the data to the system versus cost of obtaining the data. Judgment must now be used to prune the file for possible revision of the system design if the cost of file construction and file maintenance exceeds the estimated value of the system or the available resources.

MODEL THE SYSTEM QUANTITATIVELY

We next proceed with the quantification of as much of the system as possible. We attempt to determine quantitative ranges for inputs and outputs, quantitative relationships for the transfer functions, and time and reliability responses for operations in the system. Decision models are developed in both mathematical-equation form and decision-table form. The purpose of modeling at this stage is to define the system more precisely and to improve it. An example of the modeling of two closely related subsystems, demand forecast and purchasing, is the TRIM (test rules for inventory management) model. Figure 14–8 shows the model and makes it evident that every input and output can be expressed in quantitative terms.

Besides the mathematical modeling of systems discussed in Chapter 9, logic tables may be developed for decision models. Such "decision tables" may include both quantitative and qualitative bases for decision making. Decision tables are valuable for both design and documentation of systems. Decision structure tables are in the form of:

IF these conditions exist . . .
THEN perform these actions . . .

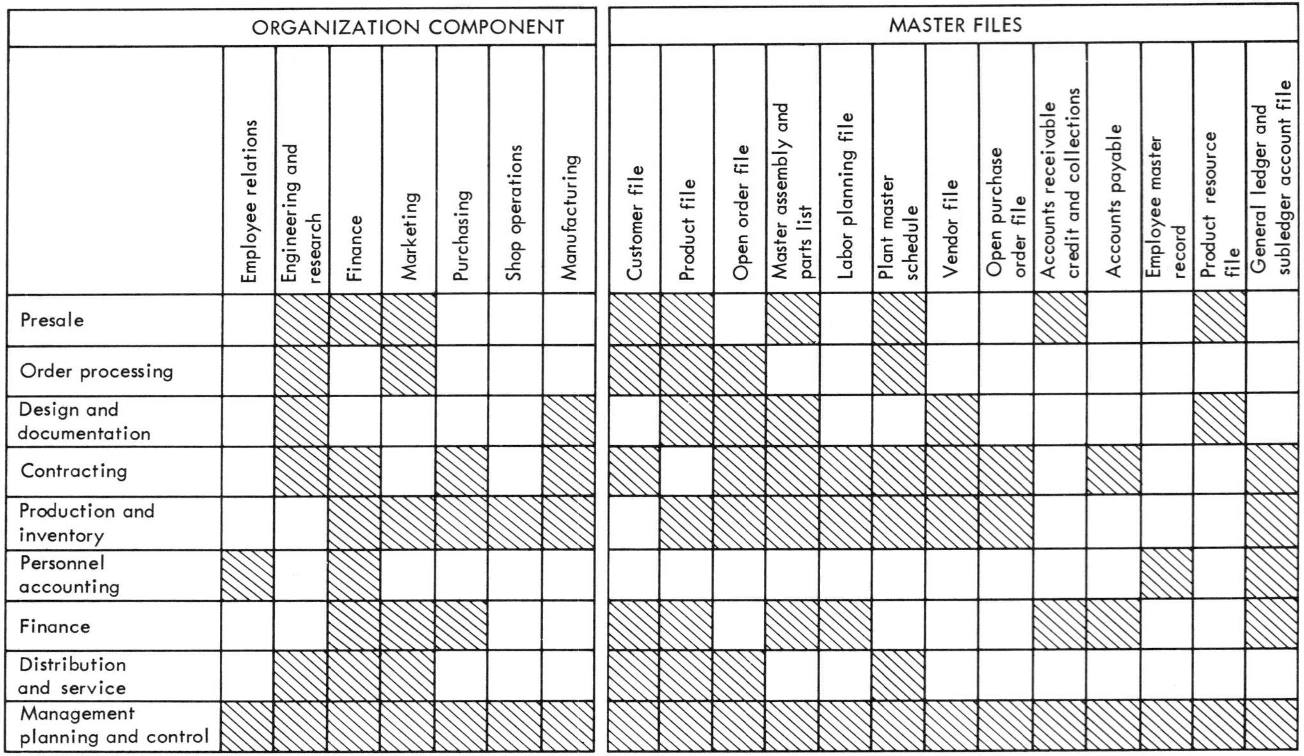

Operation of MIS across organizational components

Integrated MIS involves cross-functional use of master files

Figure 14–7 Development of the Master File

SOURCE Based on a figure by John Ryan, Manager of Internal Automation, General Electric Co., in *Automation,* May 1964. Reproduced with permission of The Penton Publishing Co., Cleveland, Ohio.

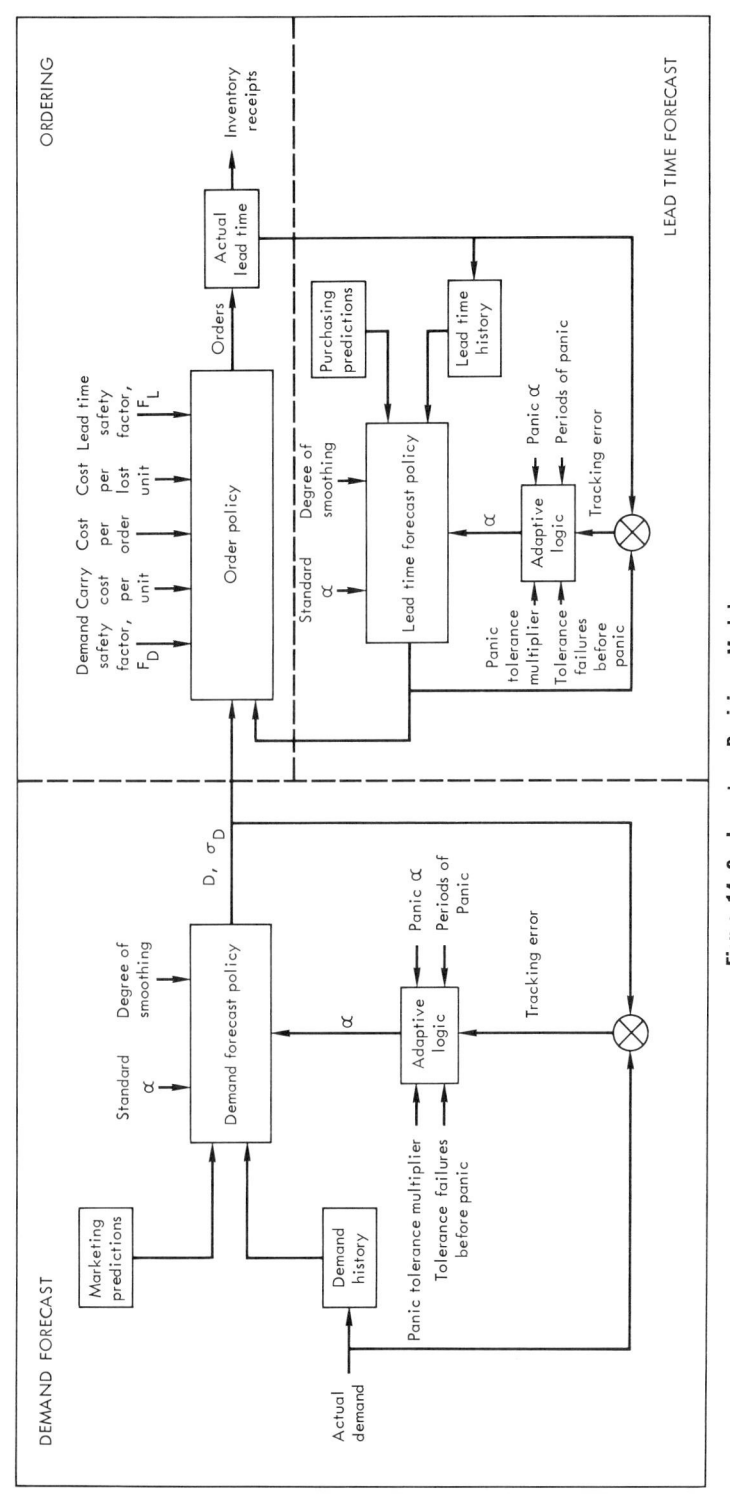

Figure 14–8 Inventory Decisions Model

SOURCE H. Chestnut, T. F. Kavanagh, and J. E. Mulligan, "Applying Control to Inventory Management," *Control Engineering*, September 1962, p. 100.

492 Planning, Design, and Implementation of MIS

The "If" listings form the *condition stub*. The "Then" listings make up the *action stub*. Figure 14–9 shows a simplified decision table for purposes of explanation. The first column, under "Decision Rules," is read as follows:

IF the car is driven less than 10,000 miles/year and
if the age of the youngest driver is over 25 and
if no drivers have major physical defects and
if no driver has had more than one accident in the past 3 years and
if no driver has had a speeding conviction and
if the major use for the car is pleasure driving,
   THEN the policy limit is $100,000/$300,000
and the policy rate is $1.12/$1000
and our policy identification type is A.

DEVELOP THE SOFTWARE

We are concerned in this book primarily with the managerial and decision-making aspects of MIS. Although software programming development in the technical sense is not a primary concern of management, management does have the responsibility of insuring that the software is an economical and effective part of the MIS. Software development, particularly good programming, is generally an expensive activity that cannot be slighted.

The coordination of the systems design group and the computer organization should start at the time of the gross design. Trained programmers

Auto Insurance Policy Coverage	Decision Rules			
Miles driven per year	< 10,000	< 10,000	< 15,000	< 15,000
Age of youngest driver	> 25	> 25	< 25	< 25
Physical defects of driver (one eye, one arm)	None	None	None	None
Accidents in last 3 years	≤ 1	≤ 1	≤ 2	≤ 2
Speeding convictions	None	None	None	None
Major use	pleasure	business	pleasure	business
Policy limit, $1,000's	100/300	100/200	50/100	25/50
Policy rate per $1,000	1.12	1.50	1.74	2.50
Type of policy	A	D	F	H

Figure 14–9 Decision Table for Insurance Decisions

should be on hand at the start of the detailed design work and at least nine months prior to installation. There are some principal steps in software development for systems over which management, through the systems designers, should maintain surveillance. These steps, carried out by the computer organization, are:

1. Develop standards and procedures for programming. Standardized charting symbols, techniques, and records should be maintained.

2. Study the gross system specifications and work with the system designers in the development of the detailed design. The computer programmers should be a part of the design team by contributing their expertise as needed.

3. Develop the data-processing logic and prepare the programming flowcharts. When the programming charts are completed, they should be reviewed by the systems design group.

4. Code the instructions given by the flowcharts. This is the writing of detailed instructions to the computer. Good coding should balance gains from economical use of machine storage capacity with possible speed of machine operation. Another important goal for the coding process is to build error control into the machine instructions.

5. Test the program. The aim is to find, diagnose, and correct errors by running sample problems and checkout programs on the computer. Actually, this "debugging" often continues into the implementation phase, where it is a much more expensive process.

6. Document the programming, coding, and testing. This is an extremely important step. Too often rough sketches, preliminary programs and codes, and test results are not updated to the "final" or most recent status. Not only should documentation be maintained completely up to date, but the contents should be easily interpreted by anyone skilled in the field. It is management's responsibility to insure that this proper documentation takes place.

ESTABLISH THE INFORMATION OUTPUT FORMATS FOR MANAGEMENT

Too little attention is paid to the format and timing of information communicated to managers to assist their decision making. Too often managers are swamped with raw computer printouts, neatly bound to impress them. They are routinely fed reports that occupy their time in the search for problems when operations are progressing smoothly. Finally, when a crisis does occur, a day or more is required to collect the relevant information.

Management reports should be of two kinds: brief summaries of the total system for which the manager is responsible and relevant information on specific problems he has selected to work on. Problems may be brought to his attention in three principal ways. His superiors may detect a future or current problem arising from factors other than his own system. The manager himself may identify problems from summary reports or needs of the future. Subordinates may bring problems to him as part of their functioning in his system.

A system of reports should be established, not to isolate the manager from routine detail but to provide him with increasing detail at each level of operation as he needs it to solve problems and make decisions.

Standard typed reports and well-planned computer-output summary reports will probably be the basic formats for communication of information to managers for some time yet. Video communications and cathode-ray-type presentation of information offer speed and flexibility. Where group decision making on major problems is fairly frequent, some leasing firms use a "decision room" (war room) with wall-mounted charts and means for quickly projecting on a screen large displays of information.

The growing computer sophistication of today's managers is increasing the use of time-sharing terminals as a means of getting information to managers. High-level managers of a number of companies now have these terminals in their offices at work, at home, or at both. They are able to utilize models to ask the "What if I do this . . .?" type of question and receive the information within seconds or minutes.

In general, the format should be established to *save the manager's time*. A wide variety of new communications and display equipment is being developed, and the systems designer should remain abreast of these developments.

TEST THE SYSTEM BY SIMULATION

For very small systems, the best test may be conversion to on-line operations. In very large systems, simulation of the entire system may be too complex and costly. However, for many systems and for subsystems and functional components of large systems, testing by simulation should be carried out. The alternative, conversion to the new system and debugging and redesigning during changeover, should be held to a minimum. It is costly and damaging to the morale of the people responsible for implementing the system. Simulation has a further advantage in permitting evaluation of the system against the criteria of the gross-design performance specifications.

The procedure for a simulation test of the whole system is as follows:

1. By random methods, select values of exogenous data from within the anticipated ranges of each variable. Let us illustrate with the input to

our business of the variable we identify as share of market held by our principal competitor. The range for this is 20 to 35 percent. By the Monte Carlo technique, described in Chapter 11, we choose a random number and find the corresponding value of our competitor's market share is 23 percent. We do the same for other exogenous inputs, such as economic indexes, interest rates, cost of raw materials, size of new markets, and labor costs. Nonquantitative inputs may be handled just as easily by listing alternatives and selecting one by random-number means.

2. Trace the effect of the exogenous inputs through the system. Where the activity processors are automatic, as in the case for computerized systems or decision tables, the process is straightforward. Where humans are involved, errors and time lags of a random nature may be introduced, or, as a first approximation, the humans may be considered to perform routine operations with machine-like efficiency.

There will be numerous points in the system at which human decisions, and more important, managerial decisions, will be required. If the system is to be properly tested, it is necessary to have an appropriate manager make the decision based on the information available from the system at that stage of the simulation. Inadequate information, lack of understanding of the situation by the manager, and inability of the system to control errors in judgment may be uncovered by this realistic type of simulation.

3. Examine outputs of various subsystems. Have cost variables been kept under control? Have outputs been restricted to specified ranges? Will the subsystems be able to respond rapidly enough to inputs so that the entire system will respond in time to maintain itself in its environment? Are all operations being performed according to specifications or are crisis decisions being made constantly to keep them in line?

4. Repeat steps 1 through 3 several times. It is not feasible to test the whole system in the way that some operations are checked out. That is, a Monte Carlo simulation of a stochastic inventory system may require several thousand simulation cycles, but the process is mechanistic enough so that they can be carried out on a computer.

PROPOSE AN ORGANIZATION TO OPERATE THE SYSTEM

The development of a new organization structure when the company executives and organization are in place is fraught with practical obstacles. Managers would consider it an imposition if the MIS group were to suggest regroupings, particularly if an individual manager's position may be abolished. The MIS group should work with incumbent and top managers to *suggest* organizational changes that will correspond to requirements of the new system. The group should not attempt to press or sell a reorganization. Major changes in organization are the prerogatives of top management.

Organization for systems management requires an outlook different from that of organization for functional component management. Subsystem managers should recognize that their main objective is that the subsystem should function in a way that is best for the whole system. Subsystem management requires a knowledge of the dynamics of systems and of the need for trade-offs to optimize system performance. The manager must be able to interface his subsystem operations effectively with coupled subsystems.

The hierarchy of management should follow the hierarchy of systems and subsystems, rather than of technical disciplines. Assignment to activities by technical discipline should be primarily at the lower level, except for some overlay service systems like financial planning and control.

DOCUMENT THE DETAILED DESIGN

The end product of the detailed design project is production of the documents that specify the system, its operation, and its design justification. Documentation consists of:

1. A summary flowchart.
2. Detailed flowcharts.
3. Operations activity sheets showing inputs, outputs, and transfer functions.
4. Specification of the data base or master file.
5. Computer hardware requirements.
6. Software (programs).
7. Personnel requirements by type of skill or discipline.
8. Final (updated) performance specifications.
9. Cost of installation and implementation of the system.
10. Cost of operating the system per unit of time.
11. Program for modification or termination of the system.
12. An executive digest of the MIS design. This is a report that top management can read rapidly in order to get the essence of the system, its potential for the company, its cost, and its general configuration. We point out that a high-level MIS official at General Electric remarked, "If the MIS can be justified on the basis of cost savings, it isn't an MIS." The executive digest should be directed toward showing how the system will aid managers' decision making by gains in information or in time.

Some documentation should be on standardized forms. Input–output–activity diagrams or listings are an example. Obviously, standard symbols should be used on flowcharts and guidelines should be established for flowchart format. Some documentation is unique to a project, such as the data base, and the format and classification of items should be determined by the needs of the particular user. Other documentation should simply follow good reporting style.

SUMMARY

Detailed design of the MIS system commences after the conceptual framework of the gross design has been formulated. Detailed design begins with the performance specifications given by the gross design and ends with a set of specifications for the construction of the MIS. Unless the operating system is to remain unchanged, the design of the MIS must be developed in conjunction with the design of the operating system.

A unique recipe for detailed design cannot be given, because design work is a creative, problem-solving activity. Blind alleys, iterative cycling processes, and new techniques are developed during the design process itself. We have tried here to describe major phases and activities of the design process. These design activities utilize all the concepts and tools developed in Part III of this book. Part III could provide only an indication of these techniques, and this chapter can supply only an indication of their application. The prospective MIS professional must develop in-depth skill in the problem-solving, decision-making, and management science areas by further study. He must develop his skill in systems design through actual experience. A textbook can only point the direction.

DISCUSSION QUESTIONS AND PROBLEMS

1. What characteristics of organizational behavior discussed in Chapter 3 indicate the desirability of keeping employees informed about a systems study before and after it has been started?

2. How are dominant criteria for systems design related to policies of the company?

3. Obtain interviews with executives at a local business firm or manufacturing plant and develop dominant and trade-off criteria that you think would be used in some selected MIS for the firm.

4. Refer to books on engineering design and management to note how specifications for a product are formulated (documented). Compare with the format or presentation of detailed systems design specifications as commonly given.

5. Define the subsystems for a marketing system. (See Donald F. Cox and Robert E. Good, "How to Build a Marketing Information System," *Harvard Business Review,* May–June 1967.)

6. What data and information would be relevant for an MIS that predicts sales of a branded consumer product sold in retail outlets? (See Samuel G. Barton, "A Marketing Model for Short-Term Prediction of Consumer Sales," *Journal of Marketing,* July 1965.)

7. Develop a decision table for an automobile rental firm for accepting or rejecting applicants.

8. In the R&D project type of organization, the performance specifications for a financial reporting system are:
   a. Summary report of expenditures by task and by direct labor and materials for each task is to go to the project manager.
   b. Report of expenditures for each section's own task and subtasks, broken down by direct labor, materials, and organizational unit within the section, is to go to the section manager.
   c. Report of charges for work performed for other sections is to go to each section manager.
   d. Report of direct labor and materials, broken down for task and subtask and for all "shop orders" making up each subtask, is to go to all "fund owners," i.e., engineers and managers responsible for a shop-order job, subtask, or task.
   e. All the reports listed are to be distributed within five working days after the close of each month.
   f. Cumulative year-to-date expenditures are to be included.
      (Note: One of the problems is gathering materials expenditures and determining assignment of personnel (labor) to different

shop orders. Also, travel expense and training programs are considered direct labor charges to keep the overhead rate low.) Develop a detailed design for the system, except for the computer programming. Make assumptions or estimates for missing data.

9. The Electronic Component Division manufactures plugboards for such varied items as television sets, communication equipment, and digital computers. It has undergone extremely rapid growth in the last five years and now employs more than 2500 employees.*

Information Requirements for the Plant

Each of the electronic components used in the manufacture of a plugboard, such as transistors, resistors, diodes, capacitors, and so on, requires a basic amount of information that must be kept as up-to-date as possible. Typical information required for each is the following:

a. Design engineering data—expected life, electronic characteristics, size, reliability if applicable, etc.
b. Process engineering data—description of the material needed to manufacture a given product so that, given the number of finished units that must be manufactured, these units can be "exploded" into their component requirements.
c. Purchasing data—list of approved vendors for the part, rating for each vendor based on quality control and delivery-time feedback, price-break information, maximum capacity of each vendor, status of all open orders for the part, including balance of material to be received, requests for additional material for the part from production, planning, and control.
d. Financial data—standard purchase price to cost the value of the product to be built, variances from standard, such as labor and raw materials price variances; accounts payable information.
e. Finished goods inventory—total quantity of finished plugboard, by type, that can be applied to the production schedule in order to determine the balance to be manufactured.
f. Production forecasting—information about the projected need for each plugboard for the next year, broken down by monthly periods.

Each of the information needs described corresponds to a function under the plant manager (see Figure 14–10 for a plant organization chart). The manager of each function has been instrumental in developing his own information subsystem to obtain the information he needs for his job. As soon as the plant started its operations, isolated systems were developed to supply management with some of the information needed—for example, a system for purchasing/receiving functions and one for the bill of materials

---

*The authors gratefully acknowledge the collaboration of Mr. Edgardo J. Marill in the preparation of this problem.

```
                              Plant Manager
    ┌──────────┬──────────────┬──────┴──────┬──────────────┬──────────┐
  Finance   Manufacturing  Engineering   Production     Purchasing  Personnel
    │                                     Planning
MIS Manager                               & Control
```

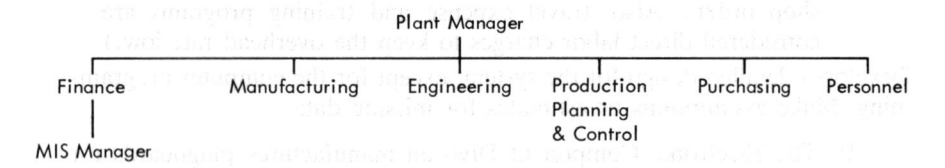

Figure 14–10 Plant Organization Chart

used by process engineering and production planning. These isolated systems were manual at first, and, with the support of a modest pool of programmers under a data-processing department, evolved into separate, unrelated, computerized systems of varied degrees of sophistication.

As these isolated systems become more complex, the advantages of having them work as one master system became overwhelmingly apparent. A lot of processing was being duplicated by calculating the same intermediate results in different systems for use in related control functions. Forecasting information could be fed directly into the purchasing system, the financial system, and the production system. Financial data, such as variances from standard material cost, could be used by purchasing in developing price history information and purchasing performance. The history of finished goods inventory could influence the forecasting system.

Integrated MIS Systems Design

The intial three-month study by the company's MIS group resulted in several very important recommendations to top management. The main points of the report were as follows:

   a. Due to the lack of uniform design practices in the design of most of the present support systems, it is not feasible to modify them for merger into an integrated information system. The subsystems were not designed for the complex controls envisioned in the integrated system.

   b. Any modification of the present support systems would be extremely undesirable, because there is so little documentation available for these systems, and that little is poorly written. The personnel who originally developed the major portion of the present support systems are no longer working for the company, a result of job swapping in an industry that is in desperate need of qualified analysts.

   c. Further, present data files are poorly structured and do not lend themselves to expansion. There are numerous discrepancies among the present systems owing to lack of enforcement of programming standards. The same data items are formated differently in different systems. For example, stores balances use nine significant digits in the stock transaction system, yet ten are used in the gross-to-net requirement analysis system. The use of a one-digit year in some purchasing transactions makes them unacceptable to most other systems.

   d. A random-access data base must be developed as soon as possible, to merge all the information now scattered among many tape files. This data base will be the hub around which all the system data requirements revolve.

e. A functional gross block design is proposed in this report (see Figure 14–11). In it, the basic relationship of the various proposed subsystems is described. The design is flexible and lends itself to future expansion and diversification programs that the plant may undertake.

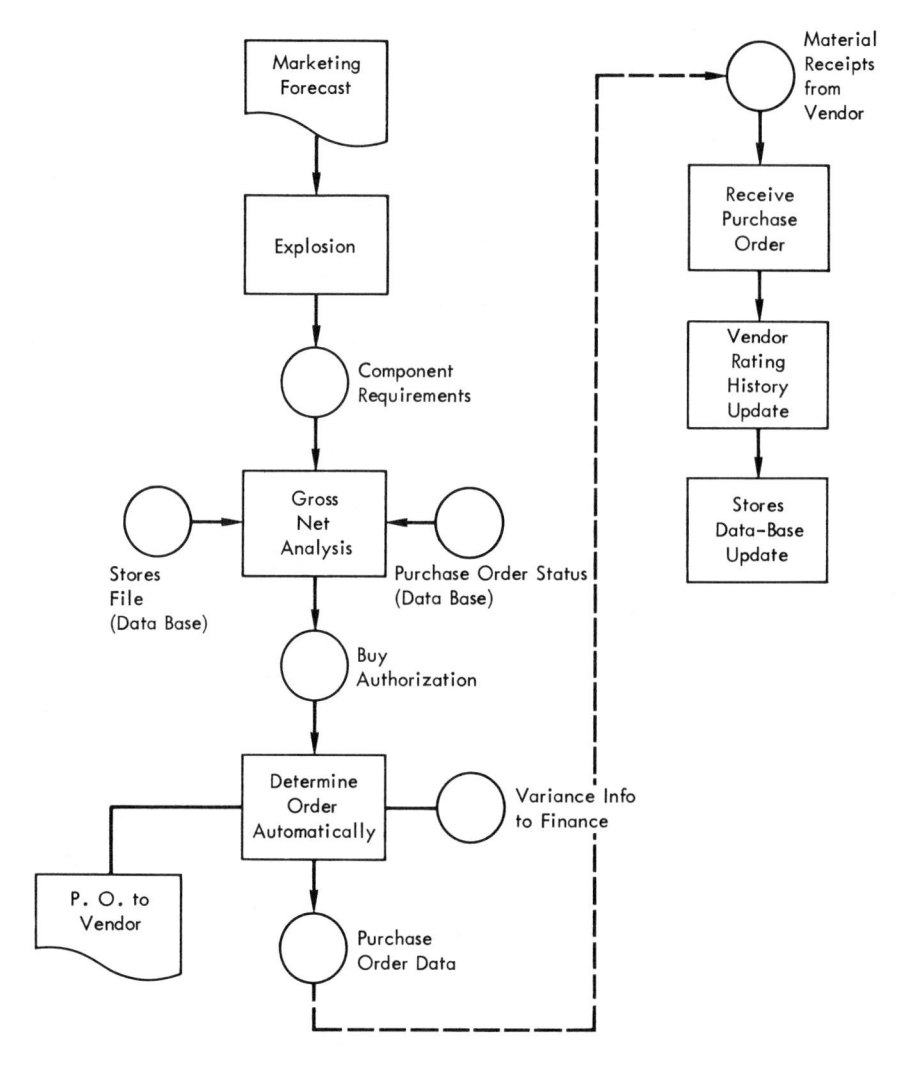

Figure 14–11 Proposed Integrated System

Applied Electronics, Inc.
Electronic Component Division

CARD AND/OR TAPE LAYOUTS

Date ______

Job No. ______ Program Title Data Base Update

File Id. SysData File Name Master Data Base Design

BLOCKING FACTOR ______ RECORD COUNT ______

Input [X] Output [ ]
Card [ ]
Mag. Tape [ ]
Paper Tape [ ]
Disk [X]

Part Number	Part Description	Planner	NPA % Material	Commodity Code	Inventory Account Number	ABC Class	EOQ Quantity	MIN Quantity
1–16	17–31	32–34	35–39	40–52	53–63	64–67	68–74	75–80

MAX Quantity	Lead Time	Material Handling	Standard Cost	Average Usage	Buyer Code	Unit of Measure	Loc	Quantity in Stock	Loc	Quantity in Order	Quantity on Requisition	Variability Coefficient	Source Code
81–86	87–90	91–96	97–102	103–110	111–114	115–119	120–124	125–130	131–134	135–141	142–148	149–156	157–160

Approved Vendor #1				Approved Vendor #2				Approved Vendor #3				Approved Vendor #4		
Vendor #1 Code	Lead Time	Price Break	Julian Date	Vendor #2 Code	Lead Time	Price Break	Julian Date	Vendor #3 Code	Lead Time	Price Break	Julian Date	Vendor #4 Code	Lead Time	Price Break
161–166	167–170	171–176	177–182	183–189	190–193	194–199	200–204	205–210	211–214	215–219	220–225	226–231	232–235	236–240

	Approved Vendor #5				
Julian Date	Vendor #5 Code	Lead Time	Price Break	Julian Date	
241–247	248–253	254–257	258–262	263–269	270–319

MIS-207 Sept. 1968

Figure 14–12 Data-Base Detailed Design

f. A proposed format for the data-base input is given in Figure 14–12.

Urgency

Management has asked the MIS group to proceed with the detailed design and make a presentation within two months.

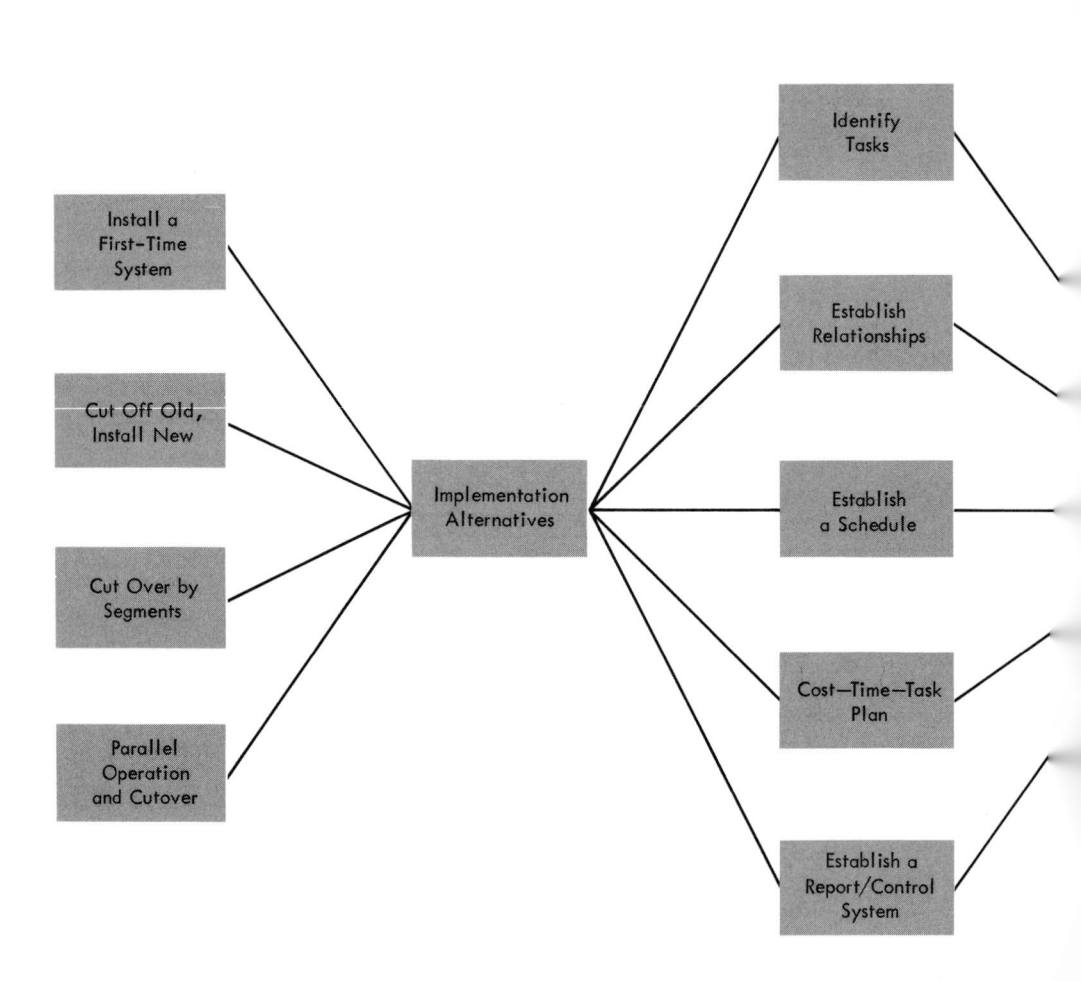

```
                                          Identify
                                           Tasks

  Install a
  First-Time
   System                                 Establish
                                         Relationships

  Cut Off Old,
  Install New        Implementation       Establish
                      Alternatives        a Schedule

  Cut Over by
   Segments
                                         Cost—Time—Task
                                              Plan
  Parallel
  Operation
  and Cutover                             Establish a
                                         Report/Control
                                             System
```

15
implementation of the new MIS

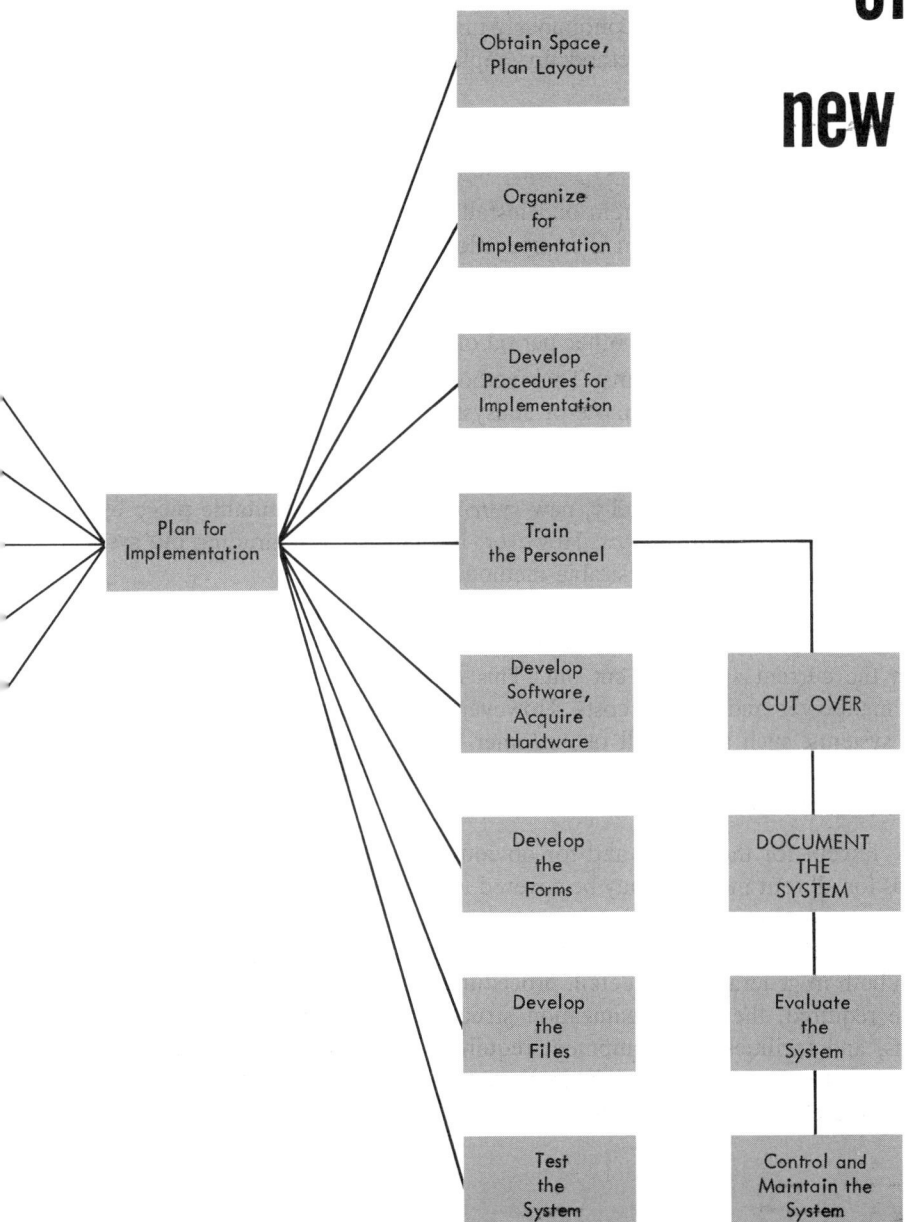

15

Although the design of a management information system may seem to management to be an expensive project, the cost of getting the MIS on line satisfactorily may often be comparable to that of its design. The cumulative expenditures for the design and installation of an MIS follow the pattern sketched in Figure 15–1. The implementation has been accomplished when the outputs of the MIS are continuously utilized by decision makers.

There are four basic methods for implementing the MIS once work has been completed. These are:

1. Install a system in a new operation or organization, one just being formed.

2. Cut off the old system and install the new. This produces a time gap during which no system is in operation. It is practical only for small companies or small systems where installation requires one or two days. An exception to this would be the installation of a larger system during a plant's vacation shutdown or some other period of inactivity.

3. Cut over by segments. This method is also referred to as "phasing in" the new system. Small parts or subsystems are substituted for the old. If this method is possible, some careful questions should be asked about the design of the new system. Is it really just an automation of isolated groups of clerical activities? Generally, new *systems* are not substitutable piece by piece for previous *nonsystems*. However, in the case of upgrading old systems, this may be a very desirable method.

4. Operate in parallel and cut over. The new system is installed and operated in parallel with the current system until it has been checked out; then the current system is cut out. This method is expensive because of the manpower and related costs. However, it is required in certain essential systems, such as payroll or customer billing. Its big advantage is that the system is fairly well debugged when it becomes the essential information system of the company.

Except for the timing and for obvious variations, the implementation steps for all four methods may be covered together. We now proceed to give step-by-step procedures for implementation, support, test, and control of the specified MIS. We assume that the specification provides the system description both in general and in detail, procedures for operation, forms and data base required, the new organization structure including position descriptions, and facilities and equipment required. The step-by-step procedures are given for major phases of the implementation that are usually conducted in a parallel or network time-format.

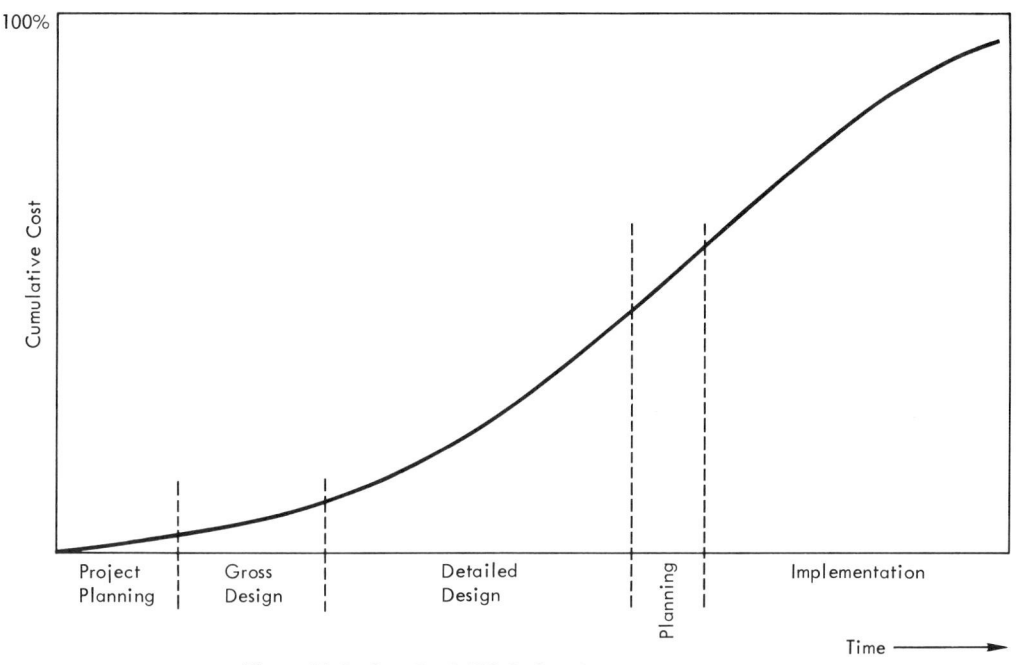

Figure 15-1 Growth of MIS Project Costs

It should be pointed out that occasionally design and implementation are carried on simultaneously. Such a process provides operational testing of the design on a continuous basis, but it limits consideration of major design alternatives. It is a trial-and-error process. Completion of conceptual and analytical design in advance of equipment installation offers many advantages besides cost.

PLAN THE IMPLEMENTATION

The three main phases in implementation take place in series: these are the initial installation, the test of the system as a whole, and the evaluation, maintenance, and control of the system. On the other hand, many implementation activities should be undertaken in parallel in order to reduce implementation time. For example, acquisition of data for the data base and forms design for collection and dissemination of information may be carried out in parallel. Training of personnel and preparation of software may be in parallel with each other and with other implementation activities.

It is apparent, then, that the first step in the implementation procedure is to *plan the implementation*. Although some analysts include the planning of the implementation with the design of the system, we believe it is operationally significant to include it in the implementation stage, for several reasons. First, the planning and the action to implement the plan should be bound closely together. Planning is the first step of management, not the last. Further, the MIS design and the urgent need for the system at the time the design is completed will weigh heavily on the plan for implementation. And finally, the planning process is a function of line management, at least as far as key decisions or alternative plans are concerned. The systems analyst may prepare plans to assist managers, but *managers must have the last say.* At the same time, managers require the services of the systems analyst to detail plans. The managers prefer to make decisions based upon the most recent information: the MIS specifications, the proposed plans of the systems analyst, and the current operating situation.

The planning for the project of implementation should follow the procedures for project programming described in Chapter 12. Once the conversion method has been described, the specific steps are as we shall delineate here.

Identify the Implementation Tasks

The major implementation tasks, or milestones, usually consist of:

1. Organizing the personnel for implementation
2. Acquiring and laying out facilities and offices
3. Developing procedures for installation and testing
4. Developing the training program for operating personnel
5. Completing the system's software
6. Acquiring required hardware
7. Designing forms
8. Generating files
9. Completing cutover to a new system
10. Obtaining acceptance
11. Testing of the entire system
12. Providing system maintenance (debugging and improving)

The plans should list all subtasks for each of these major tasks so that individuals in the organization may be assigned specific responsibilities.

Establish Relationships Among Tasks

For small projects, the order of performance may simply be described in text form. However, even in small projects, a Gantt chart or network diagram makes visualization of the plan and schedule much clearer. In large projects, many concurrent and sequential activities are interrelated, so that a network diagram must be employed in any good plan. Figure 15-2 shows a Gantt chart and Figure 15-3 shows a network diagram (condensed) for illustrating task relationships.

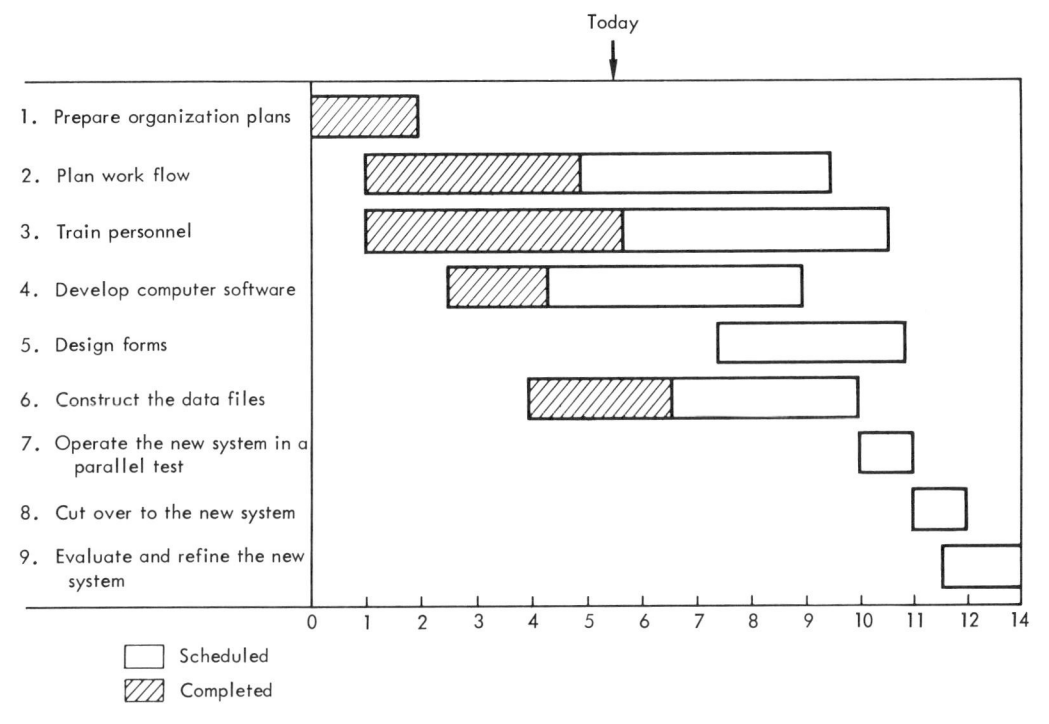

Figure 15–2 Gantt Chart for MIS Implementation

Establish a Schedule

A first estimate of the schedule is prepared by having the system designers estimate the times between the events in the program network. The critical path (longest time through the network) can then be calculated. The end date is thus established once the starting date is specified. Figures 15–2 and 15–3 indicate how times are shown for the implementation activities.

The actual desired end date is then usually specified by management on the basis of this information. Obviously, management may apply pressure or provide additional manpower to shorten the network times.

In a somewhat simplified representation (although possibly true to life), the decision scenario might run like this:

> [The top manager involved and the managers who report to him, the MIS design manager and an analyst, and the computer center manager and a programmer attend a conference.]
> TOP MANAGER (to his managers): Well, you fellows have worked on this MIS to get rid of the problems of lack of information and obsolete methods. Now's the time to see what you have really got. Bill [MIS design manager] has given us his plan for getting this

510 Planning, Design, and Implementation of MIS

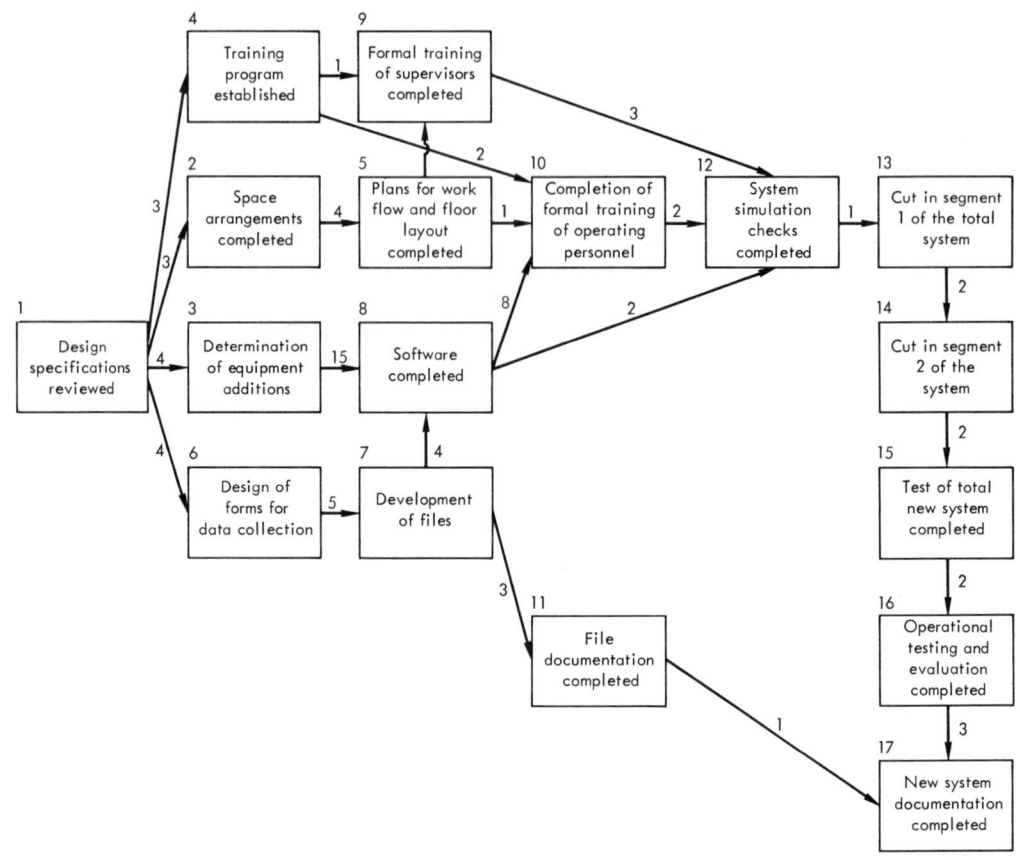

Figure 15-3 Network Diagram for MIS Implementation

MIS into action. I see from his plan that this will take seven months. That's a pretty long time. It seems to me that about three months of good, concentrated effort should swing it.

[Bill has already estimated that it could be done in three months if nothing at all went wrong. His previous consultations with the computer center manager, Ken, have led to his present estimate. They have learned from past experience that the safe course is to double the estimated time required. They have also agreed privately to add on another month for the purpose of the meeting.]

BILL: Ken and I have gone over this very carefully, and we think that the very best time we could make with full pressure applied by your managers would be six months.

[The top manager plays this game every day and interprets this correctly as double the ideal time, but recognizes it as a schedule that could be met in practical circumstances. He also knows that most schedules tend to slip, so he continues.]

TOP MANAGER (to his managers): You guys are the ones that are going to have to live with this and spend time working on it. How about it, should this be cut back?

ONE OF THE MANAGERS: If we cut some corners and shoot for completing the data base at a later time, I think we could make it in four months.

TOP MANAGER: Let's do it this way so that Bill has no complaints. We'll schedule complete installation in five months and really bear down. We *need* this system. If we get a little behind in our work over this period, we can more than make it up as soon as the system's in—OK? Let's start in immediately along the lines of Bill's plan. Bill, you revise the details of the schedule as you think necessary and get new copies of the plan out tomorrow. If there are no objections, that's all, then.

[Heads nod in agreement and murmurs are heard that "this is a great system but we're really going to have to sweat to get it in." The meeting ends.]

Prepare a Cost Schedule Tied to Tasks and Time

The cost for completing each milestone, and possibly each task required to complete a milestone, should be established as part of the plan, then the rate of expenditures should be budgeted. The techniques for this phase of planning were covered in Chapter 12.

Establish a Reporting and Control System

Reporting and control of the work in progress may be obtained by weekly meetings of the key people involved or by brief written progress reports. The financial personnel must make certain that report formats allow them to show cost and technical progress relationships as well as cost–time relationships. When large numbers of people are both conducting regular operations and introducing new equipment, arrangements, and operations, some confusion is inevitable. The object of the control system is to minimize this confusion and the associated delays and costs.

ACQUIRE FLOOR SPACE AND PLAN SPACE LAYOUTS

The installation of a new system to replace a current one may require a major revision of facilities as well as completely new office, computer room, and production layouts. The MIS project manager must prepare rough layouts and estimates of particular floor areas he feels will be needed. He should then prepare cost estimates and submit a proposal for management's approval.

Facilities and space planning should begin as soon as approval of gross space allocations has been obtained. The urgency for such planning is twofold. First, there may be a long lead time if new partitions, electrical work, air-conditioning, or even new buildings are required. Second, the detailed work flow depends upon the physical arrangements of the buildings. The training of operations personnel will be more successful if it is based on exact physical relationships among the people and the equipment.

Space planning must take into account the space occupied by people, the space occupied by equipment, and the movement of people and equipment in the work process. Related to these are the number and kinds of exits; storage areas; location of utilities, outlets, and controls; environmental requirements for the equipment; safety factors; and working conditions for the personnel. A large investment in good working conditions will repay its cost many times. It is a short-sighted and costly policy to scrimp on facilities and human environment when a major renovation is required to install a new system.

ORGANIZE FOR IMPLEMENTATION

Once the implementation tasks have been defined in the planning phase, management usually assigns a project manager to guide the implementation. A manager of management information systems may assume this responsibility by virtue of his permanent assignment. In smaller companies, someone from the finance/accounting department, or even the computer center manager, may be placed in charge. A project manager, who is responsible for the entire MIS development and implementation, as described in Chapter 12, usually works best.

The role of line managers must be made clear. Since the purpose of the MIS is to increase the amount and quality of their contributions, the system is really *their* system. Top management must take explicit steps to make the middle managers aware of this and of the necessity for their involvement in implementation. Essentially, the systems specialists are there to *assist* management with the implementation; they are assigned to the project as needed for this purpose.

Besides assigning responsibilities to line managers, systems specialists, and computer programmers, top management should make sure that line functional personnel have active parts in the implementation. These are the people who will operate the system and they also must feel that it is *their* system.

Proper organization by assignment of specific leadership and task responsibility diffused widely throughout the whole organization can prevent the moans and wails so often heard after a new MIS is installed and fails. As discussed in Chapter 3, mature people respond to work assignments that call forth their full talents. They resist the control that is implied when they are simply handed a system installed by specialists and told exactly how to operate it. But when they have a hand in shaping and constructing the system they must operate, employees react favorably. Without such acceptance, management finds that new systems fail because of inertia, apathy, resistance to change, and employee feelings of insecurity.

DEVELOP PROCEDURES FOR IMPLEMENTATION

The project leader has available the network plan for proceeding with the implementation. He must now call upon key people in the project to prepare more detailed procedures for system installation. For example, suppose that the detailed design specification calls for the manufacturing manager to receive a report on raw materials stored on the factory floor at the end of each day. The source of data is the foreman, who will fill out forms and send them to a production planner for compilation. The systems analyst must develop the procedure for delivering instructions and forms to foremen, for coordinating and integrating this very small portion of the MIS with other parts of the manufacturing system, and for working out problems with the people involved.

As another example, suppose some files must be converted from filing cabinets to magnetic tape or to some kind of random-access storage. The systems analyst must develop the procedures for making this conversion without upsetting current use of the files.

Procedures for evaluating and selecting hardware must be spelled out. Procedures for buying or constructing software should be established. Procedures for phasing in parts of the MIS or for operating the MIS in parallel must be developed. Obviously there are *many* procedures that must be delineated in advance if the entire implementation is to be saved from chaos.

A major part of implementing the MIS is the testing of each segment of the total system as it is installed. So far, the only testing that has been done is a simulation of the system during the detailed design stage. The testing of segments of the MIS during installation requires application of line personnel to actual files, software, and hardware for either current operations or specially designed test problems. This is equivalent to the physical laboratory testing of parts of an engineered product after the theoretical evaluation (testing) and before construction of the parts.

It is necessary to develop the testing procedures on the basis of the design and test specifications. The procedures should prescribe:

1. Which segments of the system will be tested
2. When such tests are to be performed
3. Test problems to be run
4. Who will perform the tests
5. How the tests will be run
6. Who will evaluate test results and approve the system segment or recommend modification

We might review at this time the sequence of test development and conduct up to the point before system acceptance. The steps are listed under the appropriate steps of system development.

1. Detailed design stage:

Prepare a test description for each test. The test description is a concise statement of the ultimate objective of the test and the systems, components, and facilities involved in its accomplishment.

2. Detailed design stage *or* implementation stage:

Prepare a test specification for each test. The test specification is derived from the test description. It is a completely detailed statement giving information on conditions under which the test is to be run, duration of the test, method and procedure to be followed, data to be taken and frequency, and analysis to be performed on the data.

3. Implementation stage:

Prepare a test operating procedure for each test. A completely detailed procedure for the accomplishment of the test specification includes organization of personnel for conduct of the test; provision of necessary test forms and data sheets; statement of conditions to exist at the start of the test; a list of all equipment, software, and file data required for the test; and step-by-step procedure for all the people participating in the test.

4. Implementation stage:

Prepare an acceptance test program. This requires a test description, test specification, and test operating procedure for the entire MIS, to check out the system before it is accepted by operating personnel for sole continuous use.

TRAIN THE OPERATING PERSONNEL

A program should be developed to impress upon management and support personnel the nature and goals of the MIS and to train operating personnel in their new duties. In the case of management, many of whom participate in the development of the system, two short seminars are usually adequate. If the first meeting is held at a time when the detailed design is well along, some valuable proposals may be offered that can then be incorporated in the design. Another meeting near the end of the implementation stage may review the benefits of the system and the roles of the executives.

Particular attention should be paid to the training of first-line supervisors. They must have a thorough understanding of what the new MIS is like and what it is supposed to do. Since, in essence, they oversee the operation of the system, they must learn how it will operate. They are faced with many changes in their work and they must obtain acceptance of changes by their subordinates. Supervisors will therefore have an intense interest in the answers to:

1. What new skills must we and our people learn?
2. How many people do we gain or lose?

3. What changes in procedures do we make?
4. What are the new forms? Are there more or fewer?
5. What jobs will be upgraded or downgraded?
6. How will our performance be measured?

Certain professional support personnel—such as computer center personnel, marketing researchers, production planners, and accounting personnel who provide input to the MIS or are concerned with processing data and information—should also attend one or several orientation meetings. Since these people will be working with only a small part of the MIS, the seminars should be designed to provide them with an understanding of the complete system. This will furnish direction for their own jobs and give them a perspective that may reduce the likelihood of blunders.

Finally, longer and more formal training programs should be established for people who perform the daily operational tasks of the MIS. These are the clerks, the computer operators, the input and output machine operators, file maintenance personnel, and possibly printing production and graphic arts personnel.

In most medium and large companies, a training specialist arranges such programs. He schedules classes, arranges for facilities, and assists the technical people (in this case, the systems analysts) in developing course content and notes for distribution. In small companies, the MIS manager will probably have to develop the training program himself.

DEVELOP THE SOFTWARE; ACQUIRE THE HARDWARE

A comprehensive discussion of the preparation of computer programs and the evaluation and acquisition of computer and peripheral equipment does not fall within the objective of this text. We are concerned rather with identifying the managerial considerations of MIS design. The *management of automation of logic, communication, and display* is important as a *basis for systems design* and as a *factor in systems implementation*. In Chapter 14, we mentioned the principal steps in software development that must be carried out. To a great extent, however, the detailed design of the MIS has provided some criteria for the hardware and software, if it has not in fact specified it. One complicating factor in systems installation is that a new computer is often required along with the new MIS.

Systems designers and programmers provide the flow diagrams and the block diagrams during the detailed design stage. Some modification may be required, however, as the implementation stage progresses. In the implementation stage, coders convert block diagrams into sequences of statements or instructions for the processing (computer) equipment. The development of software is described by the block diagram of Figure 15–4.

516 Planning, Design, and Implementation of MIS

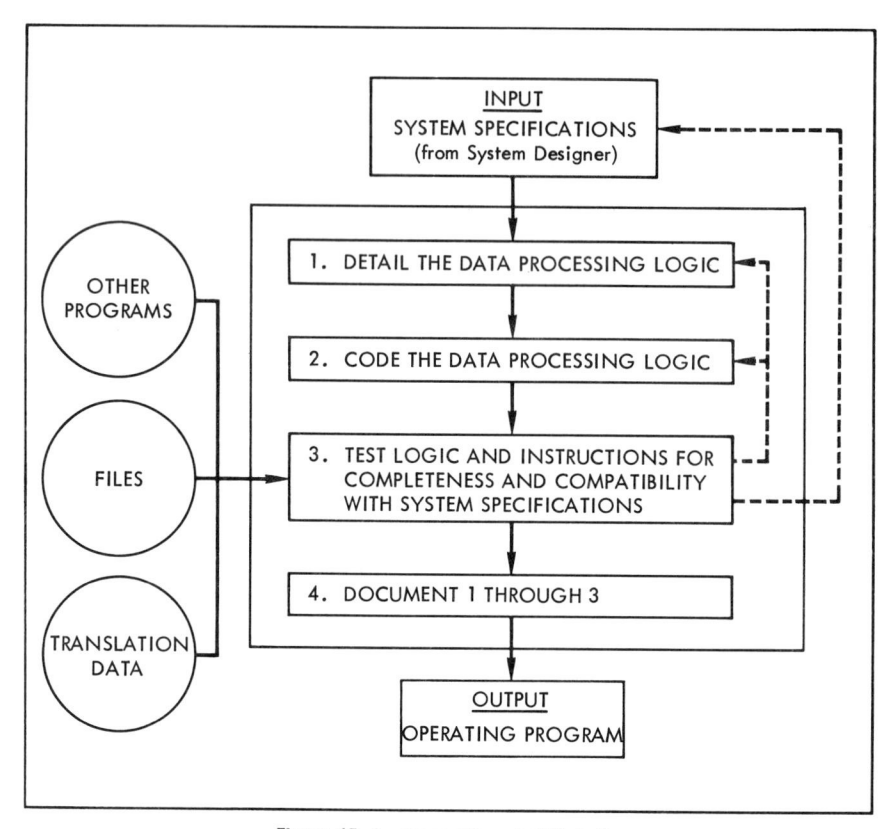

Figure 15-4 Preparation of MIS Software
SOURCE Donald F. Heany, *An Introduction to Information Systems,* General Electric Company, 1966, p. 10

The development of software and the acquisition of new equipment are usually the limiting items in getting an MIS implemented. When possible, these tasks should be started during the design stage. There is, of course, some risk of loss in starting early, but it must be balanced against the considerable delay involved in the sequential approach to design and implementation of the MIS.

DEVELOP FORMS FOR DATA COLLECTION AND INFORMATION DISSEMINATION

A vast amount of detailed data, both external and internal to the company, must be collected for input to the MIS. If control over marketing is to be exercised or sales forecasting carried out, then somewhere, every day, a salesman must sit in a room and fill out a form summarizing the day's activities. Obviously, the form insures that the right information is supplied in a manner that simplifies processing for computer storage. We might ask, What about a truly modern firm in which the salesman may plug in his time-sharing terminal and transmit his information directly to a computer thousands of miles away? Even in this case, the salesman must have a form (or format) for his guidance.

Forms are required not just for input and output but also for transmitting data at intermediate stages. In a personnel system, input to the computer may consist of all known applicants for all known jobs within a company. The computer may provide sorted output to match jobs and applicants. The personnel recruiting specialist may then have to add a statement of his activities—*on a form*, which is attached to the computer output. The entire package is then forwarded to the manager of personnel.

Output forms of the MIS must be prepared at the implementation stage, when they can be both designed and tested. Further, the problems of printing and inventory size and location must be resolved. Management science may provide some guidance to the ordering and inventory solutions.

The output forms are what the managers see, and so these forms should be designed so that key information and variances are easily discernible. A periodic report form should be a summary form that is keyed to a hierarchy of increasingly detailed forms. Managers may then pursue specific questions easily by calling for the underlying details.

DEVELOP THE FILES

The specifications for the files have been developed in the detailed design stage. In the implementation stage, the actual data must be obtained and recorded for the initial testing and operation of the system. This requires a checklist of data, format of data, storage form and format, and remarks to indicate when the data have been stored. The implementation also requires the development of a procedure for updating each piece of the data and for updating entire sections of the file as required. This collection of data used in routine operations is often called the *master file*.

When data are obtained from the environment—as are economic, competitive, and financial data, or vendor sources—a procedure for obtaining the data may be developed along with the initial acquisition. Responsibility for file maintenance for each file item should also be assigned. For internal data, the generating source or the compiling source (such as marketing) is usually assigned responsibility for file items. The structure of such information is more generalized than that of the master file. This file is often called the *data base*, although in practice the master-file and database elements are usually stored together.

In the detailed design phase, each item of data for the files is specified and the retrieval methods (indexes) are developed. In the implementation stage, forms must be designed so that the data may be analyzed by the programmers and coders for storage in the computer. Thus, the file name, maximum number of characters required to record each data element, frequency of access, volume of operations on the element, retention characteristics, and updating frequency are examples of relevant information required to translate a specification into a file element. A sample form, not to be taken as ideal or generalized, for recording a file element is shown in Figure 15-5. Although separate forms are often used for recording data before they are stored, Figure 15-5 includes a space for initial values.

The development of files or data bases belongs in the conceptual realm of information systems designers and storage and retrieval experts. The translation of specifications for files into computer programs is a function of computer specialists. For our purposes, only an insight into the relation of these specialists' problems to management decision systems is needed.

TEST THE SYSTEM

As each part of the total system is installed, tests should be performed in accordance with the test specifications and procedures described in Chapter 14. Tests of the installation stage consist of component tests, subsystem tests, and total system acceptance tests. Components may consist of:

1. Equipment, old or new
2. New forms
3. New software programs
4. New data-collection methods
5. New work procedures
6. New reporting formats

Components may be tested relatively independently of the system to which they belong. Tests for accuracy, range of inputs, frequency of inputs, usual operating conditions, "human factor" characteristics, and reliability are all of concern. We do not require vast amounts of input data for this, but rather representative elements of data and limiting or unusual data. During component testing, employees are further familiarized with the system before the organization switches over to complete dependence on it. Difficulties occurring during component tests may lead to design changes that will bring large benefits when systems tests and operations are carried out.

One point difficult to cover in a general discussion of testing, but a very important and *practical* one, is: How are the new pieces of equipment, new forms, new procedures, and so on, being tested in an organization where daily operations must be maintained? This is particularly relevant where substitution of components cannot be made, but the entire new system must

```
                    DATA ELEMENT DESCRIPTION


    File Name _____

    File Number _____          Date _____

    Data Element _____

    Field Element _____   Group Label _____

    Form _____   Source _____

    Maximum Length (Characters/Item Group) _____

    Storage Medium _____

    Retention Characteristics      _____
    _____

    Update Procedure        _____
    _____
    _____

    Initial Value  _____

    Units          _____
```

Figure 15–5 File Form

be installed, operated in parallel, and then cut in on a given day. It is a test of the ingenuity of the MIS project manager in preventing utter chaos. One possible approach is to plan for new equipment to be in different locations from old equipment and available areas. Sometimes it is possible to have operating personnel, using a few files and tables fitted into the room, handle both old procedures and testing of the new components from their regular work stations. In other cases, adjacent available office space may be utilized for testing, and the physical substitution of the new for the old system may take place in overtime on the night before cutover. The fact that partitions may have to be removed may permit temporary, crowded, side-by-side arrangements until the acceptance testing is complete.

As more components are installed, subsystems may be tested. There is a considerable difference between the testing of a component and the testing of a system. System tests require verification of multiple inputs, complex logic systems, interaction of humans and widely varied equipment, interfacing of systems, and timing aspects of the many parts. If, for example, the programming for the computer fails to work in the system test, costly delays may take place. Often, minor difficulties cropping up require redesign of forms, procedures, work flow, or organizational changes. The training program itself is being tested, since, if the supervisors and operators lose confidence in the system at this point, they may resist further implementation of the new system in subtle ways.

Although complete parallel testing before a target day cutover is perhaps the most difficult to implement, it is sometimes necessary. Consider a bank that must collect and process millions of dollars in checks before shipment to various points in the country for collection. A delay of a day, or even of several hours, can be very expensive in terms of interest foregone. Order processing, payroll operations, project management control, retail operations management, and airline reservation service are other examples in which a break in system operation is extremely undesirable.

CUT OVER

Cutover is the point at which the new component replaces the old component or the new system replaces the old system. This usually involves a good deal of last-minute physical transfer of files, rearrangement of office furniture, and movement of work stations and people. Old forms, old files, and old equipment are suddenly retired.

Despite component and system testing, there are still likely to be "bugs" in the system. One of the chief causes of problems is inadequate training of operating personnel. These people are suddenly thrown into a new situation with new equipment, procedures, and co-workers. If the training has been superficial, mass confusion may result. Having extra supervisory help, with the systems designers on hand, is one way of preventing first-day cutover panic. Design analysts should also be present to iron out "bugs" of all kinds that may arise.

The systems designer may observe the cutover and the smoothing out of system operations over a few weeks with some gratification. If he is naive, he will depart believing that his system is installed. The more experienced designer will make a few informal return calls later on; he knows that often employees go through the motions of adopting the new system while maintaining secret files in their desks and performing old procedures in parallel with the new. This resistance to change, belief that the old methods were best, or lack of confidence in the new system must be detected and overcome. The systems designer may detect such activities, and he should report them to the supervisor for corrective action. The supervisor should recognize that improper handling of such cases may make it more difficult to ferret out future instances.

The debugging process associated with the cutover to the new system may extend for several months. Programs may require improvement, forms may need to be changed for more efficient operation, or employees may desire transfer to different jobs within the system. In particular, the operational testing of the system over a period of several months exposes it to a volume and variability of data and conditions that could not be practically achieved in preacceptance testing. Production records such as productive time and nonproductive time give indications of future maintenance requirements and idle-time costs.

DOCUMENT THE SYSTEM

"Documentation" of the MIS means preparation of written descriptions of the scope, purpose, information flow components, and operating procedures of the system. Documentation is not a frill; it is a necessity—for trouble-shooting, for replacement of subsystems, for interfacing with other systems, and for training new operating personnel, and also for evaluating and upgrading the system.

If the system is properly documented:

1. A new team of operators could be brought in and could learn to operate the MIS on the basis of the documentation available.

2. Designers not familiar with the organization or MIS could, from the documentation, reconstruct the system.

3. A common reference design is available for managers, designers, and programmers concerned with system maintenance.

4. The information systems analyst will have a valuable data source for developing new MIS, schedules, manpower plans, and costs.

Documenting a Manual Information System

The documentation of a manual information system may consist of the following documents:

1. A system summary of scope, interfaces with other systems, types of outputs and users, assumptions and constraints for design, and name of design project leader
2. Old and new organization charts and comparison of number and kinds of people before and after the new system is installed
3. Flowcharts and layout charts
4. Desk equipment
5. Forms
6. Output reports and formats
7. Manual data-processing procedures
8. Methods for controlling and revising the system—that is, specification of faulty operation and organizational procedures for initiating changes.

Documenting a Computer-Based MIS

Documentation of a computer-based MIS is similar to that of a manual system except that all software development, programs, files, input–output formats, and codes should be documented. Of particular importance is the documentation of the master file and the means for entering, processing, and retrieving data.

EVALUATE THE MIS

After the MIS has been operating smoothly for a short period of time, an evaluation of each step in the design and of the final system performance should be made. There is always the pressure to go on to new jobs, but the feedback principle should apply to the work of the MIS as well as to the product. Thousands of dollars are invested in an MIS, and it is good business to measure the value of the results.

Evaluation should not be delayed beyond the time when the systems analysts have completed most of the debugging. The longer the delay, the more difficult it will be for the designer to remember important details.

The evaluation should be made by the customer as well as by the designers. For each step we have covered in this and the last three chapters, the question should be asked, "If we were to start all over again, knowing what we now know, what would we do differently?" The customer may ask, "How does the system now perform and how would we like it to perform?" In addition, though it is less important than the previous evaluations, the financial specialists should evaluate the project in terms of planned cost versus actual cost of design, implementation, and operation. They should also attempt to identify cost savings and increased profits directly attributable to the MIS.

CONTROL AND MAINTAIN THE SYSTEM

Control and maintenance of the system are the responsibilities of the line managers. Control of the system means the operation of the system as it was designed to operate. Sometimes operators will develop their own private procedures or will short-circuit procedures designed to provide checks. Often well-intentioned people make unauthorized changes to improve the system, changes that are not approved or documented. Managers themselves may not be factoring into decisions information supplied by the system, such as sales forecast or inventory information, and may be relying on intuition. It is up to management at each level in the organization to provide periodic spot checks of the system for control purposes.

Maintenance is closely related to control. There are times when the need for improvements to the system will be discovered. Formal methods for changing and *documenting* changes must be provided. There are times when failure to change the system will cause confusion and error. Changes in the tax rate, in price of the firm's products, or in assumptions about competitors, among many possibilities, must be entered into the system by means of a formal maintenance program.

SUMMARY

The implementation of the MIS is the culmination of the design process. We have pointed out the close pre- and post-implementation relationships between design and implementation. We have discussed three major approaches to implementation from the design-time standpoint. Finally, we have given a step-by-step procedure for implementation. As we pointed out in the chapters on design, such a procedure is only an approximation of the timing, since there may exist a parallel execution of some steps. Thus, it seems logical to document the system after it has been debugged and is in final form. In practice, however, it is necessary to document the system as installation takes place, so that there will be an up-to-date reference design during the design phase. The final documentation should be a complete, formal, accurate version of the MIS as it exists in operation.

We have given the major implementation steps as:

1. Plan the implementation
2. Acquire the floor space and plan space layouts
3. Organize for implementation
4. Develop procedures for implementation
5. Train the operation personnel
6. Develop the software; acquire the hardware
7. Develop the necessary forms for data collection and information dissemination

8. Develop the files
9. Test the system
10. Cut over to put the new system on-line
11. Document the system
12. Evaluate the MIS
13. Control and maintain the system

In conclusion, we point out that many practitioners believe that the design and implementation of an MIS is always an evolutionary process. There are, however, many advantages to a complete redesign of the MIS despite the difficulties of installing a new system while an old one is in operation. The "big-step" approach permits complete rethinking of the entire system and encourages innovative ideas. Indeed, it *is* the systems approach.

DISCUSSION QUESTIONS AND PROBLEMS

1. Specify the principal subsystems and segments of a marketing information system for a company you are familiar with or find described in the literature. Develop a network diagram to show the principal steps in the cutover by segments that would have been required to introduce this system.

2. Prepare an outline of tasks typical of an implementation program for a new MIS.

3. Describe in a "scenario" a possible discussion between a systems designer and a supervisor in their first contact concerning implementation of an MIS. Assume that there has been no training program for the supervisor, that her job is to be completely changed, that she will be using totally new equipment, and that she must transfer two of her five girls to another department in the company.

4. Prepare a test specification for testing a portion of an MIS of your own choosing.

5. Revise the competitive activity report form on page 526 so that it will be easier for both the salesman and the computer personnel to use.

6. Arrange for an interview with an MIS manager at a local plant. List all the problems he encountered when he implemented his current MIS; prepare a summary report on these problems, with suggestions as to how they might have been avoided.

7. Prepare a detailed list of documents that record the newly-implemented MIS in a department store, and state their general contents.

8. Bill Maxwell is manager of business systems development in a large, decentralized corporation with a diversified product line. The executive vice-president one day said to him, "Bill, we would like to find out if our management information system for the whole company is really helping management cope with significant problem areas. We are not interested in procedural audits or efficiency of computer operations in this connection, but rather in decisions relating to project priorities. We want to know whether systems projects are related to long-range plans that have measurable, consistent objectives."

Bill replied, "We have been preparing just such a post-implementation study this past month, sir. Here is an outline of the key action items we are examining."

9. At present, the Snocan Company, which manufactures 25 products, has 103 sales offices throughout the United States with an average of ten salesmen per office. Every week, the sales reports in each office are tabulated by a clerk on a rotary calculating machine. The reports divide sales according to salesman, product, and customer. The reports are mailed to headquarters where they are combined by clerks using calculating machines. The results are then typed and given to marketing research and to management. While top management is studying the reports, marketing research analyzes them and forecasts sales for the next six months. Unfortunately, by the time management receives the reports, they are from three to six weeks old.

A new system has been devised in which daily sales by salesman, product, and customer are sent over a data-communication line from each office to headquarters. (See, for example, "Getting Mail by Phone," *Business Week,* September 28, 1968.) A new electronic computer is to be installed to compile and analyze the data and forecast sales. The computer will also handle payroll calculations and replace three clerks in payroll.

The detailed design has been approved by management. The company's system designer is now ready to detail plans for implementation. Nobody in the company has had any experience with computers or computer languages. About 2000 square feet of floor space is available at present for the computer center. The kind of data transmission equipment and the computer have not yet been specified.

To: ☐ _____ DISTRICT
(check ☐ _____ DIVISION
one)

COMPETITIVE ACTIVITY REPORT
(Report Only One Type of Activity on Sheet)

Brand _____
Manufacturer _____
Area in which effective _____
Type of Activity (check all applicable boxes):
  1. ☐ New Brand (complete 5)
  2. ☐ Package or Product Change
  3. ☐ Price Change (complete 5)
      a. ☐ Decline – Effective _____
      b. ☐ Increase – Effective _____ Orders at Old Price through _____ , For Shipment By _____ .
  4. ☐ Promotion – Effective From _____ To _____
      a. ☐ Price Pack – _____ ¢ Off On _____ Unit(s). (complete 5)
      b. ☐ Merchandise Pack – _____ ☐ On Pkg. ☐ Near – Pack
      c. ☐ Mail – In Offer – _____ For _____
              (PREMIUM)   (CONSUMER REQUIREMENT)
      d. ☐ Coupon – _____ ¢ Off On _____ Unit(s), ☐ Mail, ☐ N'Paper, ☐ Mag., ☐ Pkg.
      e. ☐ Allowance (complete 5) –
         Paid On –
           ☐ Purchases For _____   ⎫ Customer
                        (PERIOD OR NUMBER ORDERS) ⎬ ☐ Has
           ☐ Movement For _____   ⎭ Option
                             (PERIOD)
           ☐ Other (explain) – _____
         Performance Required – ☐ Ad, ☐ Display, ☐ Reduced Price, ☐ Other _____
         Contract – ☐ Yes ☐ No
         Payment made by – ☐ Check, ☐ Invoice Deduction, ☐ Optional
         Stocks Protected – ☐ Yes ☐ No
  5. Price Information

Sizes or Flavors	Previous or Regular C/L Cost	Amount Per Case This Activity	C/L Case Cost with This Activity

Additional Details _____

Sources of Information (2 or more) _____

Reported By _____ Unit _____ Section _____

526

CASE STUDY

The Artcraft Company*

The Artcraft Company was formed in 1924 to service sign painters with supplies required by their trade. The company began simply as a jobber; sales were made through a simple 24-page catalog directed to sign painters and to stores dealing in such supplies.

In 1928, Mr. E. C. Parsons, Artcraft's owner, developed a lettering device suitable for use by draftsmen, advertising art studios, sign painters, and others. At first, Artcraft had the parts made on the outside and then assembled and packaged the item. Subsequently, they undertook manufacture of a number of the component parts.

The lettering device filled a particular market need; it was successful on its own and also was responsible for attracting business to the company's general line of supplies. Although the general economy deteriorated following 1928, Artcraft's sales went from $750,000 to $1,800,000 by 1935.

Following World War II, popular interest in painting escalated, and Artcraft's sales increased greatly, particularly with art supply stores. By 1960, their sales were nearly $10 million, of which $6 million was in items they manufactured—paints, brushes, palettes, and related items. The balance was imported or purchased domestically and packaged under Artcraft's name.

In 1962, E. C. Parsons II entered the business after his graduation from business school. From the outset it was clear that he was both alert and aggressive. He concluded rather quickly that the company had been the fortunate victim of circumstances, that it had beeen carried along by the tides of a generally improved economy and the growing popularity of art as a hobby. In line with his belief that the company was far from having reached its potential, he proposed that the product line be increased, by amplifying the art supplies offerings and by extension into engineering and drafting supplies, and that a sales force be added to reinforce the catalog.

In 1964, the elder Parsons died. Young Parsons took over and immediately set the wheels in motion to move the company onto higher ground. He decided it would be too much of a financial strain on the company to both increase manufacturing activity and develop a sales force, and so it was decided to increase the line by jobbing rather than manufacturing additional items and to concentrate on sales force development.

By 1969, company sales had reached $18 million. Company strategy had taken hold. There were now 300 employees, handling 100,000 orders annually from distributors, art supply and drafting supply stores, hardware and paint stores, college book stores, advertising agencies' art departments, and industrial and research firms. In all, Artcraft had 18,000 customers, of whom 500 had annual purchases of $15,000 or more, and a line of

---

*Prepared by William J. Waldman, Florida Atlantic University.

nearly 12,000 items. Further increases in the range of 10 percent per year were expected.

Artcraft's accounting and information systems, which relied on manual and mechanical methods, were under the direction of Ed Simpson, who had been with the company for twenty years. Recently a number of problems had arisen. Although none were of a critical nature, in the aggregate they suggested that with further growth, present methods were likely to prove inadequate. The situation was reflected in comments by various company executives and workers:

George Saunders, sales vice-president: "Our catalog is vital, both for mail orders and to support our salesmen. Considering the thousands of items we carry, a salesman could not function without it. Our problem here is our inability to get a catalog out on time even once a year. Even then it is filled with items that should have been dropped, and new items are often omitted. Under pressure of getting it out, we do not change prices to reflect cost changes. Actually, we should produce two catalogs a year, with supplements quarterly."

Al Beven, production vice-president: "I'm spending too much time putting out fires. Most of our production problems are a matter of deciding between Urgent, Very Urgent and Extra Very Urgent. This business was built on service to the customer. We still think this is the most important thing. Consequently, we make one short run after another just to have something in stock. The high cost of short runs takes a back seat to customer service."

Joe Dean, purchasing agent: "We now have many low-value, low-volume items on which we can't afford to keep unit inventory records. The warehouse is supposed to notify us when items reach reorder quantities. They don't; they either forget or don't care. You know, there is a lot of turnover in help there. In any event, most of my buyers spend half their day on the phone expediting shipment. They should be shopping for prices and new items and helping me with the catalog."

Al Parker, credit manager: "We have a lot of small accounts that I believe should be written off if they do not pay after a couple of reminders. Understand, I'm not sure our collection costs exceed our collections for small accounts, but it is my educated guess they do. Actually, just going through customer-account ledger cards to flag delinquent accounts costs us a fortune. On top of this, half the reminders that go out should never have been sent; during busy seasons it takes three days or more between receiving a collection and getting it onto the customer's records."

Mitch Weber, warehouse supervisor: "We keep feeding the order-editing department lists of items going out of stock and to be taken off back-order status. It doesn't seem to make any difference. Practically every order we get lists out-of-stock items, and this means retyping and refiguring these invoices. Even worse, they are backordering items we have presently in stock. By the time they release the backorders, the items will be out again."

Artcraft's sales are firm; they are making money. In fact, they are having the best year in their history by a considerable margin.

CASE STUDY

QUANTUM ENGINEERING ASSOCIATES, INC.*

Company Background

Quantum Engineering Associates, Inc., was an industrial electronics manufacturer with headquarters in Chicago. Its products were oriented toward information handling; the principal categories were information display equipment, communication terminal equipment, recording equipment, and magnetic recording supplies.

Quantum was founded in 1961 by Joseph A. Beatty, Lawrence H. Cummings, and Phillip W. Hayward, who felt that during the 1960's there would be a market for specialized computer peripheral (input/output) equipment that could be designed and developed by a small company and sold to computer manufacturers for subsequent reshipment as part of computer systems. All three men were engineers with experience in the design of computer systems. They located in suburban Chicago, where they set up their headquarters, a research and development center, and a small manufacturing facility. Phillip Hayward was elected president and chairman of the board of Quantum; Joe Beatty, chief engineer; and Larry Cummings, vice-president of manufacturing and marketing. Their initial products were console typewriters and digital plotters, all of which were well accepted.

In 1964, they realized that communications would be an important part of the forthcoming third generation, and therefore they began to design communications terminals that would interface with these new systems. In 1965, they acquired Consolidated Electric Corporation, a Denver manufacturer of power supplies and electronic measurement equipment. Larry Cummings was put in charge of long-range planning; Robert Adams was brought in from outside the company to become vice-president of production and marketing for products manufactured in Chicago; and Frank Perkins, who was president of Consolidated Electric, became vice-president and general manager for that division. Quantum's philosophy on acquisition was that the sales and earnings growth of the company to be acquired should be greater than 25 percent per year; that there should be a similarity of products; that the existing management of the acquired company should be strong enough to remain and manage it; and that the acquired company should be operated as a separate organization—except for engineering, for which Quantum set up a centralized division upon the acquisition of Consolidated Electric.

In 1967, Quantum acquired Systemagraphics, Inc., of Framingham, Massachusetts, which marketed information display devices, such as large video screens that could be tied via communications to a computer, com-

---

*This case was prepared by Mr. Charles M. Dye under the direction of Dr. R. G. Murdick and Dr. J. E. Ross.

munications terminals that used cathode-ray tubes for visual display, and keyboard-to-tape transcribers.

In late 1969, Midwest Magnetic Company was acquired. Midwest was a Chicago manufacturer of recording equipment, magnetic discs, and magnetic tape for both home recorders and computers.

During 1968 and 1969, Quantum had outstanding increases in sales. However, Phillip Hayward felt that for continued growth in the future, certain organization changes were required. He eliminated the position of general manager at the various divisions and cut the divisions' administrative staffs substantially, transferring some of the people to corporate headquarters in Chicago. Because of similarity of the products, control of production and of marketing was brought into the Chicago headquarters. Frank Perkins was elected executive vice-president of production and moved to Chicago from Denver.

Quantum had management information systems (MIS) in use at each of the four manufacturing locations, as well as at corporate headquarters. Each facility's MIS was designed by its own MIS department, and management at the plants was generally satisfied with the results from the MIS. In the summer of 1970, William K. Doyle was hired to be corporate director of MIS. His first assignment was to take a look at a problem Quantum was having with the manufacturing plants.

The plants had recently started having material shortages. Three of them were falling behind in making deliveries to customers; there appeared to be insufficient material of the right type on hand to support production. In addition, Hayward was concerned as to whether the resources Quantum was using on MIS were achieving effective results in relation to Quantum's volume of business. Generally, electronics manufacturing companies spend up to 2 percent of sales on MIS.

Organization

An organization chart for Quantum Engineering Associates is shown in Exhibit 1.

As treasurer, John Zimmerman was responsible for corporate financing, economic analysis, and acquisition planning. It was expected that in the early 1970's Quantum would assume a more aggressive role in acquisition of information-handling companies, and as Larry Cummings was involved in long-range planning in the technical area, his job was to counsel Engineering, provide guidance to Market Planning, and lend technical assistance to Zimmerman.

Julian Peel was vice-president of public and industrial affairs, a function brought about by Hayward's growing awareness and concern regarding social issues that affect business. He felt that many business concerns were ignoring some of the unpleasant problems in the economy, such as hard-core unemployment, lowering standards of education, pollution, and lack of equal opportunity. Peel's job was to get the company involved in relevant issues where it was possible for Quantum to provide tangible assistance.

President and Chairman of the Board
Phillip W. Hayward

Treasurer – John L. Zimmerman
V.P., Public Affairs – Julian S. Peel
V.P., Long-Range Planning – Lawrence H. Cummings

- **Vice-President, Administration** — Reilly Dobson
  - Controller — William E. Weiskoph
  - Dir., Personnel — Roland C. Finley
  - Director, MIS — William K. Doyle
- **Vice-President and Chief Engineer** — Joseph A. Beatty
- **Executive Vice-President, Production** — Frank Perkins
  - General Manager, Chicago #1 Plant — Philip Rigby-Jones
  - General Manager, Chicago #2 Plant — Harry Fawcett
  - General Manager, Denver Plant — Thomas Anderson
  - General Manager, Framingham Plant — Kurt Krueger
- **Director, Quality Assurance** — Lewis L. Quillen
- **Executive Vice-President, Marketing** — Robert Adams
  - Manager, Field Service — Jefferson Coe
  - Director, Market Planning — James Price
  - Vice-President, Advertising — John Haines
  - Vice-President, Sales — Whitney Archer
  - Manager, Marketing Administration — Philip Koch

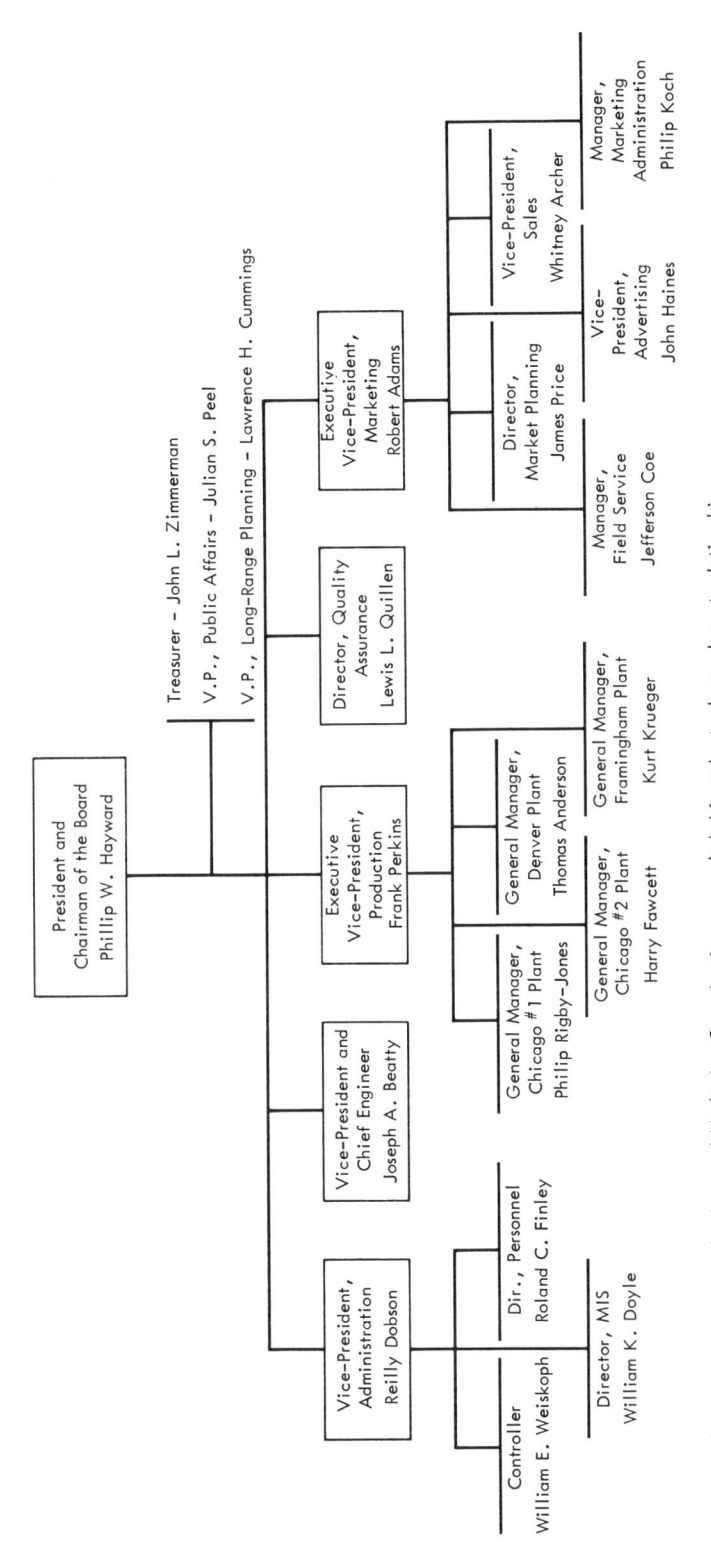

Note: Only Administration, Production, and Marketing Organization are exploded in order to show relevant relationships.

Exhibit 1 Quantum Engineering Associates, Inc., Organization Chart (as of January 1, 1970)

The vice-president for administration, Reilly Dobson, was a CPA and had previously been an MIS manager in a similar-sized company. He was responsible for MIS, treasury operations, operating and capital budgets, general accounting, auditing, and personnel. The personnel function included organization development, salary administration, training, manpower planning, and employment.

Director of MIS was a new position brought about by consolidation of Production and Marketing. Hayward felt that there was no one qualified in the various MIS departments and therefore brought in Bill Doyle from another company. Doyle had had ten years of experience in data processing and had previously been an MIS manager for a smaller manufacturer.

As executive vice-president of production, Frank Perkins was in charge of four plants: Denver, Framingham, Chicago #1, and Chicago #2.

Joe Beatty, vice-president and chief engineer, had a staff of 150 engineers and scientists at the Chicago location. In addition, at each of the manufacturing plants, he had sustaining engineers who provided support to production by handling post-release engineering design problems.

As executive vice-president of marketing, Bob Adams was responsible for advertising, marketing research, market planning, sales, field engineering and service, and marketing administration. The sales department was organized into four regions and twenty-one district offices.

Finally, the director of quality assurance, Lewis L. Quillen, was responsible for the quality of the product in all functional areas. This included design, manufacturing and testing, and field performance auditing.

Financial Condition

The income statement and the balance sheet for 1968 and 1969 are shown in Exhibits 2 and 3 respectively. Plant contributions as budgeted for 1970 are shown in the table below.

($ in thousands)

	CHICAGO #1	CHICAGO #2	FRAMINGHAM	DENVER
Material	11,747	13,449	29,228	23,720
Direct labor	3,654	5,085	9,419	4,466
Overhead	4,891	6,850	10,969	6,139
Cost of goods sold	20,292	25,384	49,616	34,325

Quantum had achieved significant sales growth each year, and this was expected to continue into the 1970's. Because of their technical nature, the products had a high material content compared with other manufacturing costs.

EXHIBIT 2

Quantum Engineering Associates, Inc.
Consolidated Earnings
Years Ending December 31

	1969	1968
	(thousands of dollars)	
Net Sales	131,035	97,348
Costs and Expenses:		
Production, shipping, and delivery costs	92,231	69,090
Research and development expenses	14,485	11,379
Selling and administrative expenses	10,164	7,619
Total expenses	116,880	88,088
Earnings from operations	14,155	9,260
Other income:		
Dividends	455	358
Interest	210	172
Patent licensing	841	514
Gain on sale of assets	703	154
Miscellaneous	417	349
Total other income	2,626	1,547
Earnings before interest charges	16,781	10,807
Long-term debt and miscellaneous interest	595	446
Earnings before taxes	16,186	10,361
Provision for federal and other income taxes	8,473	5,199
Net earnings	7,713	5,162
Dividends paid	0	0

Facilities and Information Systems Utilization

The Chicago corporate headquarters contained offices for all executive officers plus the engineering, administration, marketing, and quality assurance staffs. Although headquarters did not have a computer, it did have a programming staff of ten people and used the computer at the Chicago #1 facility for processing of most headquarters applications. In addition, they used a time-sharing service for solving engineering problems, and for management planning they used a financial model and a market-planning model. There was a teletype network set up for message communication with all plants; however, there was no direct communication link between computers or into computers at any of the plants. Headquarters' 1970 budget for MIS was $316,334.

The Chicago #1 plant, Quantum's original facility, was located on the west side of the city, several miles from corporate headquarters. In 1970 it had 805 direct and 375 indirect labor employees, who were responsible

EXHIBIT 3

Quantum Engineering Associates, Inc.
Consolidated Balance Sheet
Years Ending December 31

	1969	1968
	(thousands of dollars)	
Assets:		
Current assets:		
Cash and short-term securities	7,635	5,698
Receivables (less allowances for losses and discounts)	11,953	7,153
Inventories at lower of cost or market:		
Raw materials and supplies	8,669	6,488
Work in process	13,586	9,107
Finished goods	1,434	934
Prepaid expenses	607	448
Total current assets	43,884	29,828
Investment and deposits	2,529	—
Fixed assets:		
Buildings and equipment, at cost	22,578	13,521
Less: Accumulated depreciation	5,483	3,684
Total fixed assets	17,095	9,837
Deferred charges:		
Repair parts inventories, at cost	168	119
Research and development expense	9,424	9,184
Other deferred items	79	158
Total deferred charges	9,671	9,461
TOTAL ASSETS	73,179	49,126
Liabilities and Shareholders' Equity:		
Current liabilities:		
Short-term loans	8,968	4,283
Accounts payable	9,308	5,311
Salaries and wages payable	2,184	1,471
Federal and other income taxes	1,316	717
Other accrued liabilities	2,450	1,674
Long-term debt due within one year	1,119	889
Total current liabilities	23,345	14,345
Long-term debt	8,269	6,395
Shareholders' equity:		
Common stock:		
Authorized—10,000,000 shares of $1 par value		
Issued—4,109,469 shares (3,314,122 in 1968)	4,109	3,314
Less: Treasury stock—223,358 shares	223	192
(192,477 in 1968)	3,886	3,122
Capital in excess of stated value	19,243	16,541
Retained earnings	16,436	8,723
Total shareholders' equity	39,565	28,386
TOTAL LIABILITIES AND SHAREHOLDERS' EQUITY	73,179	49,126

for manufacturing console typewriters, digital plotters, and communications terminals. Functionally, they handled procurement, inventory control, assembly, and shipping. In addition, accounting services, such as payroll, general accounting, and manufacturing budgets, were performed at this facility. The MIS department, consisting of 20 programming and 32 operations people, had an IBM 1410 System with disc storage, renting for $16,300 a month. At that time, they were considering conversion to a System 360 Model 50 or Spectra 70/45. The 1970 MIS budget here was $975,435.

The Chicago #2 plant, located on the northwest side, had 1120 direct and 448 indirect labor employees, manufacturing recording equipment used primarily by industry, magnetic tape for home recorders and computer tape stations, and magnetic discs for computer disc-storage devices. Their functional responsibility was similar to that of the Chicago #1 plant. The computer facility included an IBM System 360 Model 40. The rental for this system was $22,457 per month, which was part of a $1,037,298 annual MIS budget. There were 26 programmers and 35 computer center personnel at the facility.

The Denver plant was responsible for manufacturing power supplies, industrial recording equipment, and electronic gauges. The direct and indirect employees at this facility were 985 and 397 respectively. The functional responsibilities upon consolidation of the organization were similar to those of the Chicago #1 plant. The computer center included a Univac 1050 and a Univac 1004, computers renting for $14,800. There were 19 programmers at the facility and 21 people in operations, and the 1970 MIS budget was $874,177.

The Framingham plant was the largest in the corporation, employing 2095 direct and 850 indirect personnel. Framingham manufactured communication information displays, large screens, video projection equipment, communications terminals, acoustical couplers, keyboard-to-tape recorders, and optical scanning equipment. Like the other three plants, it was functionally responsible for material procurement, inventory control, and manufacturing accounting. The computer facility was budgeted at $1,314,761 in 1970. They had an RCA Spectra 70/45 system that rented for $25,085 per month. There were 27 programmers on the staff and 48 employees in computer operations.

Information Flow

Quantum Engineering Associates utilized a standard cost system in their manufacturing plants. Although they procured material to a forecast requirement, products were built based on actual orders, and as a result there was little or no finished goods inventory. Upon completion of assembly and final testing, the product was shipped to the customer. Any finished goods inventory was the result of last-minute requests by customers for delay in delivery or of order cancellations.

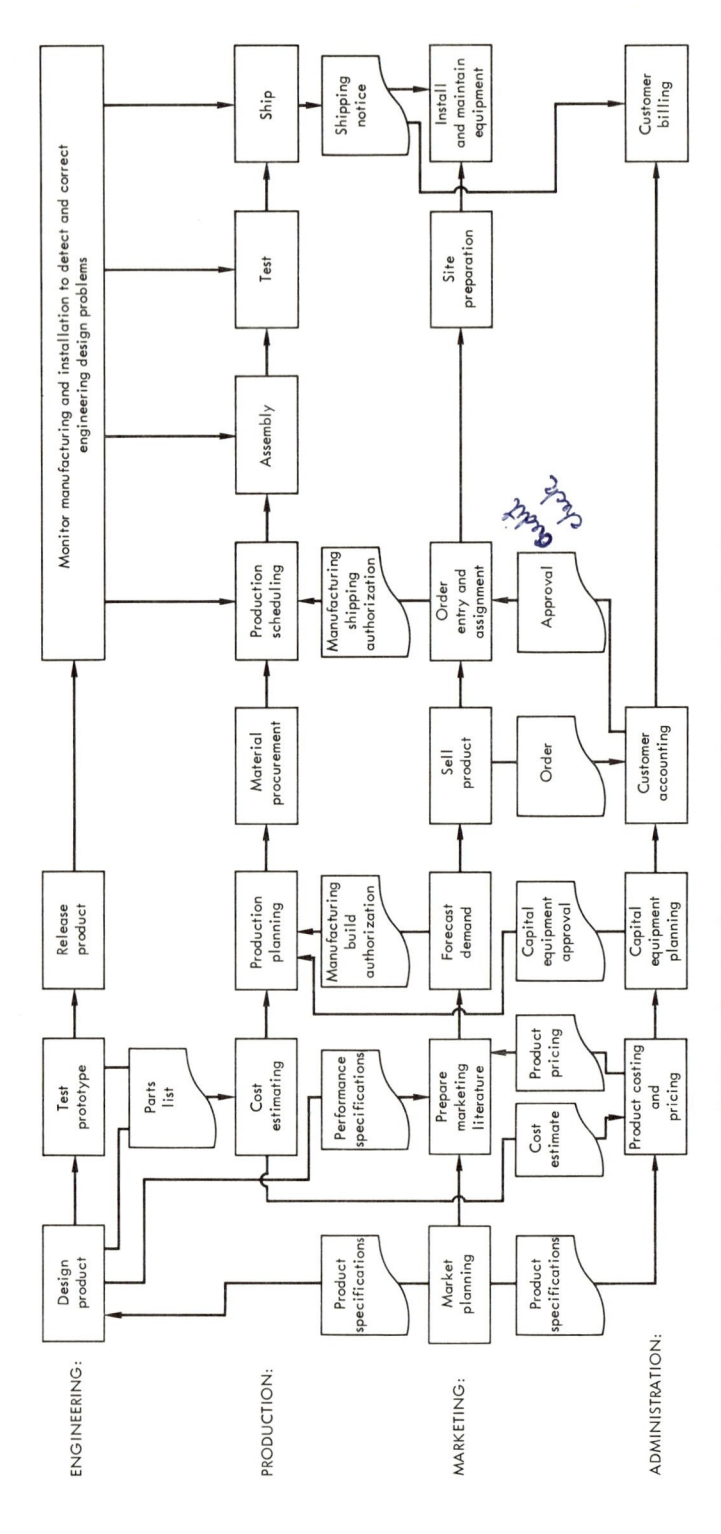

Exhibit 4 Quantum Engineering Associates, Inc., Information Flow

Phillip Hayward, in trying to determine why production had poor delivery performance, told Bill Doyle to look into the existing systems to see if the way information was being handled was incorrect. He told Doyle to stay within the boundaries of information needs rather than worrying about the hardware—that is, to assume that any specific piece of computing equipment was doing an adequate job.

Doyle began his assignment by visiting each plant for an orientation. He found a reasonably mature MIS at each location. The operating managements were familiar with the systems, and most of the using departments had acquired sufficient discipline to use the systems effectively. At the conclusion of the tour, he drew up an information flow depicting the major transactions that occurred in Quantum Engineering Associates. This is shown in Exhibit 4. In addition, he drafted a diagram of location relationships, shown in Exhibit 5.

Engineering

Because of the nature of the products manufactured, there were continual new-product releases. The dynamic nature of the industry and the relatively long lead time between design concept and actual delivery to the customer led to the company's policy of announcing new products anywhere from six to twelve months prior to actual delivery of the first unit. The information flow would begin with recognition by the market planning (or long-range planning) department of a new product opportunity. Market Planning would write a product specification, including price, cost, and

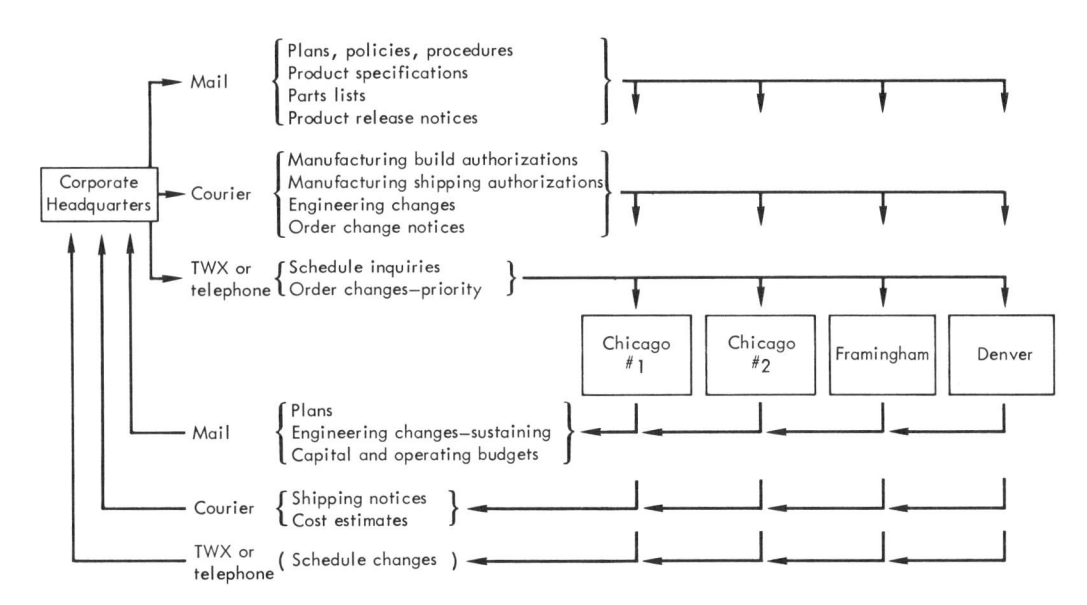

Exhibit 5 Quantum Engineering Associates, Inc., Information Flow to and from Plants

usage constraints, and give these to Engineering. Then Engineering would design the product according to the specifications, boundaries, and design goals.

As soon as the product was committed to design, Engineering released bill-of-material information to Production, meanwhile keeping their own bills of material because of the necessity to delineate additional items such as reference drawings or the parts structure of assemblies purchased from suppliers. Although the early release of material information led to some changes in parts—usually 3 percent—during the assembly or test phase of manufacturing, it permitted Production to order material with long lead time well in advance of actual need. In addition, this early release of material was required by Production to estimate manufacturing costs.

At the completion of design, Engineering tested the prototype and made changes to their bill of material as design problems were corrected. When testing was finished, the product was released to Production. Because of the complexity of the product and the necessity of getting it out of Engineering as soon as possible, newly designed products frequently required a number of engineering changes after release. Therefore, Engineering monitored manufacturing and installation on the pilot production run for newly released products. This pilot run normally consisted of ten units. After the pilot run was completed at the individual plant, Sustaining Engineering became responsible for enhancements to the product or remedial engineering changes, and sent all these changes to Corporate Engineering for final approval and for distribution to the affected functions. The MIS for Engineering included bills of material, project accounting, and design automation. Engineering changes were supplied to the manufacturing plants for inclusion of the material and/or process change in the plant's bills-of-material system.

Production

Production participated in initial planning for new products with Marketing, Engineering, and Administration. They submitted their requirements for new tooling, test equipment, etc., to Administration, and upon approval of top management, Administration authorized acquisition of the capital equipment. Requests for capital funds were usually required twelve months in advance of Production's actual need for the equipment. For new products, Production was authorized to order enough material for the pilot run immediately upon receipt of a parts list from Engineering.

Manufacturing cost estimates prepared for Administration were usually made from sketchy information supplied by Engineering, since a product-pricing decision was required well before completion of the Engineering release of the new product. The complete list of parts would not be available until the final Engineering release.

To procure material for released products not in a pilot-run status required a manufacturing build authorization from Marketing. This authorization was revised monthly; upon receipt of it, all plants reforecast their material requirements by exploding parts requirements from the manufacturing bills of material. Then, based upon the build authorization, the forecast system applied inventories and outstanding purchase orders in order to determine the net procurement requirements. It took an average of one month to get a purchase order placed and two months to receive the material from the vendor, although some material had a procurement lead time of ten months or longer. Production had an agreement with Marketing that schedules would not change significantly within 120 days of shipment. The manufacturing build authorization usually covered a period of twenty-four months.

A manufacturing shipping authorization was provided by Marketing to schedule products to be assembled. This acted as an order on Production to accumulate parts from their raw materials inventory and schedule discrete products to be built. The manufacturing shipping authorization covered a period of 120 days. Weekly order changes, additions, and deletions were sent via a courier to the manufacturing plant. The average assembly and test time for a product was sixty days; upon completion of testing, the product was shipped and a shipping notice sent to Marketing and to Administration.

The manufacturing plants were experiencing severe materials shortages. With the exception of the Chicago #2 plant, they had fallen as much as thirty days behind in shipments during the previous six months. Each plant had a bills-of-material system that had been designed by its own MIS staff. In addition, each plant had its own material forecasting and procurement system, with the exception of the Chicago #1 plant, which had recently scrapped its own system and was using that of Chicago #2.

Production management and operating personnel used a number of different documents in decision making. Information supplied to them from corporate headquarters included the ten-year plan, the yearly operating plan, and corporate policies and procedures. From Marketing they received product specifications, manufacturing build authorizations, manufacturing shipping authorizations, and periodic market analyses. Bills of material for specific products were received from Engineering, in addition to product release notices and engineering changes. Information used within the manufacturing facility included raw material and inventory status, material requirement forecast, outstanding purchase order status, production schedule, work-in-process inventory and production status, and labor efficiency.

Because there was often a shift in the product mix from one manufacturing build authorization or shipping authorization to another, Production in their decision-making process asked the following typical questions:

—What is the extent of the shift in the product mix in the current manufacturing build authorization or manufacturing shipping authorization?
—Is the material on hand and on order sufficient to build the mix?
—Will material on order arrive on time?
—Can material that is needed earlier than planned be rescheduled and brought in from the vendor on time?

—Assuming that there has been an increase in production requirements for the immediate period, can some of the production be shifted out in time without impacting the overall schedule or material requirements of other products?

—Is there excess material at the other plants that could be used to augment any material shortage occurring because of mix change?

—Is the present direct labor force adequate to meet the schedule?

—If it is inadequate, can the schedule be changed to compensate for unavailable labor?

—If the available labor is inadequate, is this temporary, and can the inadequacy be made up by overtime?

—If the inadequacy is permanent, what type of labor mix will be required, and can the acquisition be made in time to meet the schedule?

If, after these questions were answered, there still remained a material or labor shortage, then the marketing schedule would be rejected or renegotiated.

Marketing

After a new product opportunity had been originated by Long-Range Planning, a special research and development group in Engineering, or by Market Planning, Market Planning and Administration used a financial model at a time-sharing service center to forecast resources required and profit potential. Then Market Planning had the tasks of drafting product specifications and making sure that the product was consistent with the corporate ten-year plan. Product specifications were furnished first to Engineering and Administration, forming the basis for Engineering to start conceptual design and for Administration to begin gathering production costs for eventual pricing of the new product. Documentation that helped formulate marketing strategy included product specifications, engineering performance specifications, product pricing, and results from the financial model. Strategic alternatives were run through a market planning model, which provided a final forecast of demand by month over a two-year period. This forecast became the basis for the manufacturing build authorization and in addition was used to determine the amount of sales and promotion effort needed to support the new product during the next twenty-four months. The model was used each month to revise the manufacturing build authorization.

Doyle noted that Engineering, Production, and Marketing often referred to the same product differently. Engineering would include in their bills-of-material system a complete list of all parts, even those included in an assembly purchased from a vendor. Marketing's equipment list referred to model numbers along with identifying features—e.g., 2392 Communication Typewriter with a 60-cycle power supply and blue styling. Engineering assigned unique numbers to the completed units to permit better identification by their engineers; e.g., the 2392 with the above configuration would be given a discrete number different from that of a unit with a 60-cycle power supply but *tan* styling. Production, in their bills of material, used a numbering system similar to that of Engineering; however, they recorded only those parts identifiable to a "buy" level. For example, in the assembly structure shown here, Manufacturing and Engineering would use the same numbers for Assemblies 1, 2, and 3 and Parts 1, 2, and 3; but Production purchased only Assembly 3 and therefore did not carry Assembly 4, Part 4, or Part 5 on their bill of material.

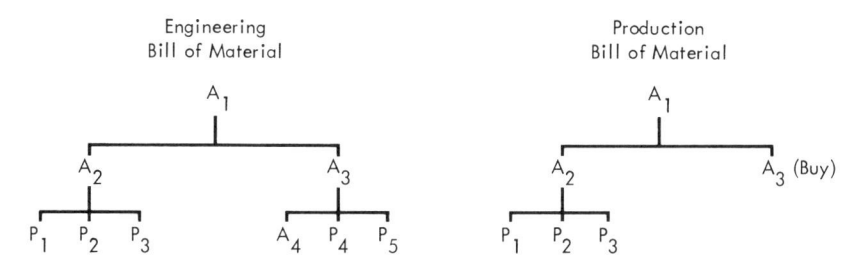

```
       Engineering                         Production
      Bill of Material                    Bill of Material

           A₁                                  A₁
           |                                   |
      ┌────┴────┐                         ┌────┴────┐
      A₂        A₃                        A₂        A₃ (Buy)
      |         |                         |
   ┌──┼──┐   ┌──┼──┐                  ┌──┼──┐
   P₁ P₂ P₃  A₄ P₄ P₅                 P₁ P₂ P₃
```

When a sale was made, the order was sent to Administration for accounting approval and to Marketing Administration for entry. (All revenue for equipment was the result of sales, not of rental. When a customer wished to rent EDP equipment, an arrangement was made with a third-party leasing company.) The lead time from order entry to shipment of equipment was normally six months. Upon approval of credit, Marketing Administration made a schedule assignment. They issued a manufacturing shipping authorization to Production 120 days before the delivery date, and any subsequent change to the order was made on a weekly order-change notice transmitted to the affected plant by either a courier or TWX. Approximately 30 percent of the orders were changed during the 120-day period; common causes included the addition or deletion of special features, change of shipping request date or styling, or upgrading of the order to a larger-size unit. During the period of assembly, Marketing was responsible for preparation of the site to receive the equipment, and later for installation and subsequent maintenance. Information systems that Marketing used included applications such as the financial and market planning models, sales efficiency, field performance and service, and the manufacturing scheduling system that interfaced with each plant's MIS.

Administration

Administration's task was to work with Long-Range Planning and Market Planning on new market opportunities, formulate the prices of new products upon the receipt of cost estimates and production specifications, and handle the review and approval of tooling and capital equipment requests from Production. The management information systems used included application areas such as financial forecasting, fixed asset accounting, budgeting, accounts receivable and billing, and financial statement consolidation.

At the conclusion of the organization survey and the drafting of the information flow, Bill Doyle decided to review the development history of a specific product. The one he selected was the Quantum Communications Terminal, Model 2392, designed to operate via communication lines with a computer. The terminal had a keyboard similar to that of a typewriter and printed information received over a communication network. It could send and receive characters at the rate of forty per second, which gave the product an excellent price–performance ratio.

During the second half of 1967, Market Planning had determined that existing printing terminals on the market were too slow (most sent and received at the rate of ten characters per second) and that a market existed for a faster terminal. They released product specifications to Engineering in January 1968, and the product, priced at $3100, was announced the following September. First deliveries to the field were to start in April 1969.

Engineering began to release preliminary material information to Production during the spring and summer of 1968. Production planned to build a pilot run of ten units for shipment in April, and, in preparation for the product announcement, made an estimate in August that post-pilot production cost would run $2136 per unit. The time segments that Production required were: eight months to order and receive long-lead items (about 10 percent of the parts); four months to order and receive normal material; one month to pull the material from stock and prepare it for production; two months to assemble the products; and finally, one month to test them.

The production version of the terminal consisted of 28 assemblies and 326 unique parts. Bill Doyle found that about 60 percent of these parts were also used on other products.

In August 1968, Marketing gave Production a manufacturing build authorization for post-pilot production as follows:

Ship Month	Number of Units
May 1969	25
June 1969	75
July 1969	90
August 1969 to April 1971	100

Engineering had planned to have testing completed by January 1969, but they began having mechanical design problems with the terminal in November, and testing was not completed until March. During that period, engineering changes on forty-two parts and assemblies were sent to Production, where it was decided to hold up all phases of pilot production except for procurement until they were assured of design stability. It was during the final two weeks of prototype testing that Production felt confident enough to release material for assembly. Because of parts shortages, the pilot products were not shipped until July 1969.

The acceptance of the terminal by computer users was much better than Market Planning had anticipated. In March 1969, Marketing issued a revised manufacturing build authorization:

Ship Month	Number of Units
May 1969*	50
June 1969	90
July 1969	115
August 1969	130
September 1969	140
October 1969 to April 1971	150

*Subsequently moved back to August 1969.

With the information he had assembled, Bill Doyle felt he was in a position to determine whether to revise the existing MIS or to design a new system. His initial concern was to eliminate the existing problems, his long-range task to improve the effectiveness of and value received from MIS.

Information-Handling Industry

In 1970, the anticipated annual growth rate of the industry was over 15 percent. The terminal and communications equipment segment of the EDP market was expected to grow from $1.6 billion in sales in 1970 to $5.5 billion in 1975. Growth during that period for all computer hardware was forecast to be from $8.5 billion in 1970 to $15.5 billion in 1975. The reason for this was the far greater emphasis being placed on communication-oriented systems by users, as well as a proliferation of service bureaus whose revenues were expected to increase from $.3 billion in 1970 to $6.4 billion in 1975.

From 1965 through 1969, leading companies in the information processing field, such as IBM, RCA, Sperry Rand, and General Electric, experienced an average sales growth of 12.6 percent. During that same period, electronics companies had a 13.9 percent increase in sales per year.

V

The Future of MIS

To focus only on the concepts and practices of today is to fail to educate. Some attempt must be made to stimulate the student to speculate about the future, perhaps to dream a little. Without vision, the student is obsolescent by the time he starts to practice the concepts he has learned. Part V presents a synthesis of the ideas of many who peer into the future of management and information systems.

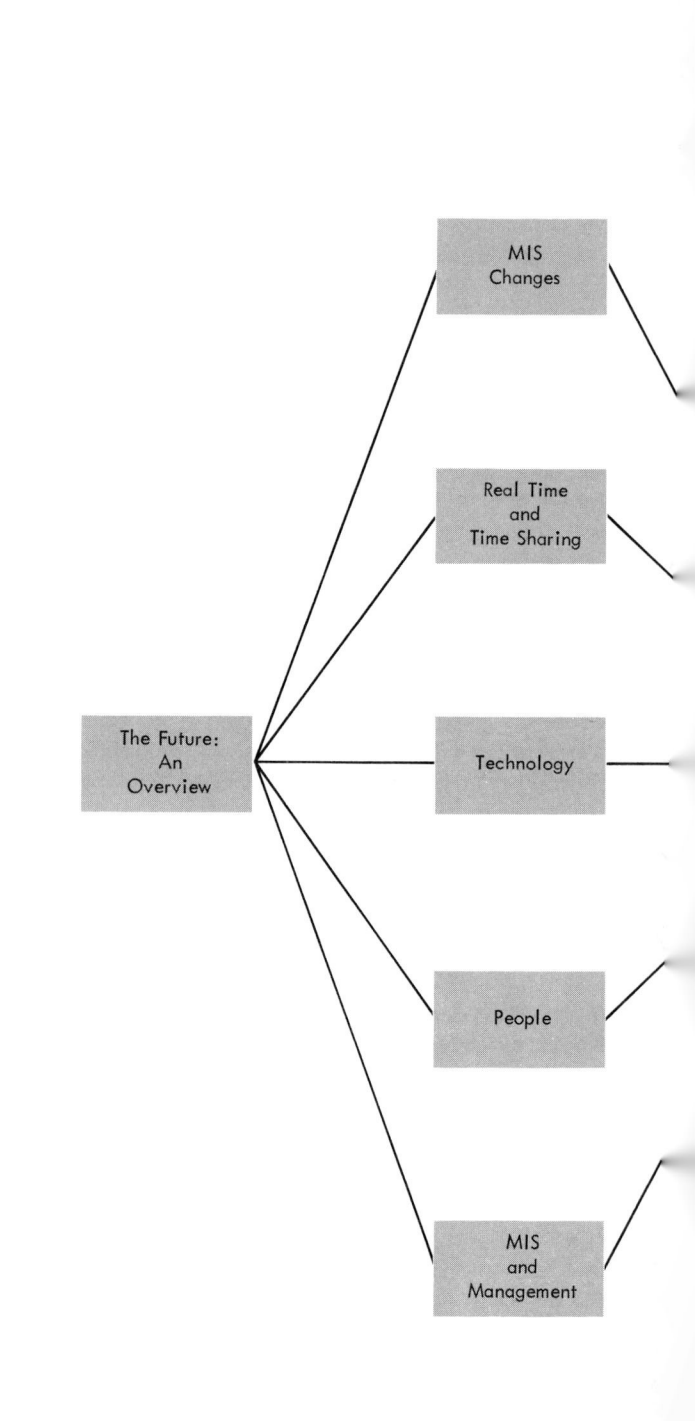

```
                                    MIS
                                   Changes


                                 Real Time
                                    and
                                 Time Sharing


    The Future:
        An                        Technology
     Overview


                                   People


                                    MIS
                                    and
                                 Management
```

16

management information systems: the future

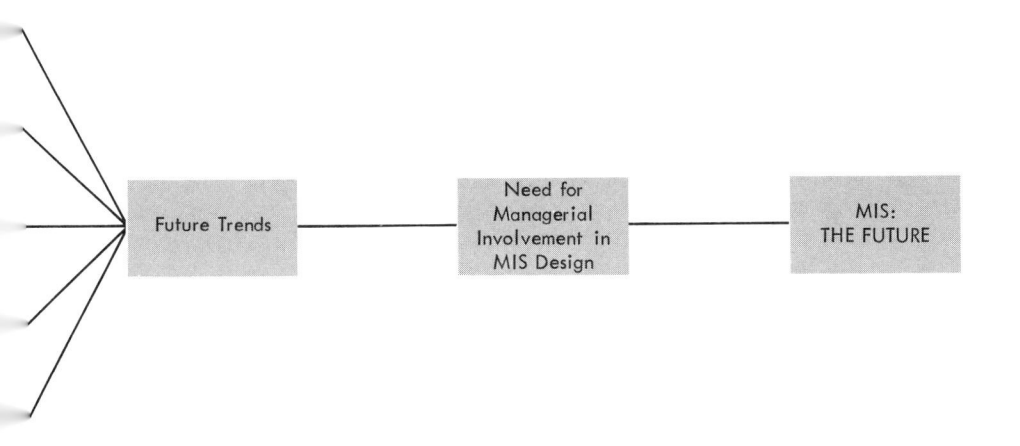

Future Trends → Need for Managerial Involvement in MIS Design → MIS: THE FUTURE

16

No single development since the Industrial Revolution has changed the business scene so much as has the electronic digital computer. In less than two decades, the character of business information systems, and to a lesser extent the character of management, has changed dramatically. The questions arise, What will be the extent of these changes in the future? Is the past merely prologue?

Predictions about the future impact of the computer and the course of developments in management information systems are tenuous at best. Some forecasts have called the trend but were optimistic with regard to the timetable. No less a prognosticator than Professor Herbert Simon predicted in 1960 that ". . . there is every prospect that we will soon have the technological means [through management science and heuristic programming] to automate all management decisions, nonprogrammed as well as programmed."[1]

In what has become a landmark article, Leavitt and Whisler foresaw in 1958 that the new information technology would have these effects:[2]

1. There would be a return to recentralization, as opposed to the then decentralization trend, because of the economies and centralized control encouraged by computers and centralized information systems.
2. The boundary between planning and operations would move upward due to the increasing sophistication of and need for management science techniques and information technology.
3. The line separating top management from middle management would become clearer than ever because of the "routinization" or programming of many of the types of decisions then made by middle management.

Generally speaking, predictions of the computer's impact on management have proved to be somewhat off target in three respects: (1) the progress has not been as rapid as expected, (2) the focus has been on how the computer would affect management rather than on how management would affect the computer, and (3) the joint interaction of the computer and the firm with events outside the firm has largely been overlooked.

The *timetable* for the computer's impact has been slowed because of inadequate staff, lack of managerial involvement, and the economics of adapting to the new technology. Although the fourth generation of equipment is now available, most firms are struggling with second-generation applications and look forward to the day when they can consider the initial steps in designing an integrated system. The bottleneck has not been technology or hardware but "brainware"—the necessary design and programming talent to develop the third-generation software systems and the vital management participation, prerequisites for up-to-date management information systems.

A second factor that has slowed progress in computer applications has been delay in adoption of the attitude that the *manager is going to employ the computer*, not the reverse. The need to take this "management first" approach to the use of the computer was expressed by McDonough: "My assumption is that information systems serve managers in their job responsibilities. The reverse assumption, which is being made too often, is that the managers exist to serve the information system."[3] This elementary and obvious point has frequently been overlooked.

The third reason to modify predictions of the computer's impact has been the newness of the tool, and consequently our tendency to concentrate on it as "gimmickry" to the partial exclusion of other, equally important, factors not necessarily related to the computer. For example, in a broader and more contemporary view of the manager's role, the factors that current forecasts say will have the most impact on management in the next decades have to do with the businessman's role in his environment. A group of 200 leading businessmen and educators has suggested that this role should be concerned with three tasks: solution of the nation's social problems, reevaluation of the profit motive on a longer-term basis, and effective cooperation with government in solving social problems.[4]

Whatever changes face the manager in the future and whatever his needs, it is quite clear that computers and information systems will play an increasingly important role on the business scene. This chapter attempts to give some insight into that role and into some of the developments that can be expected over the near and long term. The predictions made here stem largely from the views held by the majority of other prognosticators and from the assumption that a vacuum cannot exist for long before it is filled. There is a vacuum today in the practice of management; the fundamental tenet of this book is that it can be filled partly through the design of computer-based information systems.

THE FUTURE: AN OVERVIEW

Despite the fact that the average manager, and to a lesser extent the average man on the street, sees evidence of computer activity all around him, the industry can be described as entering the stage of advanced adolescence. When speculating about the future of a child, we can attempt only to read the signs, inject some opinion, and hope for the best in predicting its welfare and growth.

Many economists expect the computer industry to be the single largest employer in the United States by the year 2000.[5] Aside from being large in terms of physical output, the computer and related industries (e.g., information systems) will have an expanding influence on the world we live in and the offices we work in as managers. We live in a time and place where rapid social and technological change is endemic. According to Professor Warren G. Bennis, the managerial competencies needed for effectiveness in such an environment include a knowledge of large, complex systems and "an ability to develop and use all types of information systems, including high-speed electronic computers. The job of the leader will be to collect, organize, and transmit information."[6] Many forward-thinking leaders deem computer-based information systems a prerequisite for survival in the forthcoming decades. As the president of Pillsbury stated, "There is one other condition to success in 1975—that is an information-oriented management system."[7]

Not withstanding its importance in managing the affairs of the business firm, it is in other areas that the computer may have its greatest impact in the years ahead. More important perhaps than business is the area of social applications: education, medicine, transportation, urban planning, and welfare. The potential in education alone is staggering when we consider the enormous contribution the computer can make in educational methodology, which is little different today from what it was hundreds of years ago. Until now the computer industry has been of and for experts. The next decade will see the computer's impact on every man, woman, and child, as computer terminals take their place in the home, the office, or the schoolroom. This "everyman" approach to computer use was expressed by S. F. Keating, president of Honeywell, Inc., in this fashion:

> With the help of computers, he will learn to take a systems approach to his life and its responsibilities. The computer industry has been compared in its effects on mankind to the automobile industry, and the comparison is valid. I do not expect, at least in this century, that every man will have a two-computer garage. But the time will come when he will have, in his home or business, one, two, or more computer terminals available to him and have the knowledge to use them intelligently for the benefit of his career and of his family.[8]

None of these developments will seem unusual to the manager of the 1970's. It will be natural for him to encounter computer output at work in dealing with customers, vendors, government agencies, and others in the company. He will realize also that computer-based systems will become an even more important part of his social and industrial life as time goes by. Rather than being confused by these developments, he will welcome them. He will understand the computer and will become involved in the design of systems affecting his job. Moreover, he will put the computer in its proper perspective with the philosophy, "Render unto the machine the things that are the machine's and unto man the things that are man's . . . the things of the spirit, the personality, and leadership, which no machine can do."

FUTURE TRENDS IN MANAGEMENT INFORMATION SYSTEMS

It is impossible, of course, to forecast the future of computer-based management information systems in toto. However, by reviewing the literature, by listening to the experts, and by observing events, we find several trends emerging that may reflect the course of events in the 1970's and 1980's. We shall discuss these under the headings:

1. The changing nature of management information systems
2. Real time
3. Time sharing
4. Hardware technology
5. The people problem
6. The impact of MIS on the manager

The Changing Nature of MIS

The existing state-of-the-art in management information systems could probably be described as having reached a plateau—a condition in which the automation of historical record keeping and routine clerical applications has come of age and where most companies are at least thinking of advancing to the next plateau of integration and advanced decision-making systems.

Many companies have computer-based systems for (1) payroll, (2) accounts payable, (3) customer billing, (4) accounts receivable, and (5) general ledger. And most of these companies feel that their computer efforts have more than paid for themselves; indeed, many firms are developing new applications under a general framework that increases compatibility and takes into account needs for future integration.[9] The accent, in other words, appears to be shifting from the glamour of clerical automation to managerial applications that make a contribution to profit. As attention moves in this direction, the emphasis will be increasingly on: (1) developing a grand scheme or master plan for systems development, (2) auditing current systems to determine ways to improve them, and (3) increasing objectives and determining information requirements.

The shift of concentration *away from hardware and clerical automation* and *into improved systems design for managerial use* is reflected in company plans for the future. In a year-long study, the consulting firm of Booz, Allen and Hamilton found that among the 33 firms studied, all had future plans for allocating less effort to the finance and accounting area and more to the other functions of the business.[10] The existing 47 percent of systems effort allocated to finance and accounting would be reduced to 31 percent in the future, and the difference would be allocated to production, R&D/engineering, distribution, marketing, and planning and control. Moreover, among the same firms, the current 28 percent of computer applications rated as above average in effectiveness in assisting management was expected to increase to 70 percent after planned system improvements were implemented. Several subsequent studies have indicated similar plans on the part of well-managed companies.

In short, the direction is definitely toward improved systems for management applications. This is not to say that the computer is going to take over management; it suggests rather that the manager should explore for ways to employ the computer to routinize internal operations, so that he can concentrate on his more important problems concerned with planning, people, and the external environment of the firm. *Good management* will have much more effect on the use of the computer than good computer usage will have on management practice.

The Growth of Real Time

Anyone who has observed the process of making a reservation at an airline ticket counter has seen *real-time* information processing in operation. Essentially, in real-time processing the computer (central processor) responds to inquiries and processing requests in so short a time frame that decisions controlling current operations can be made from these responses. Usually, the response is immediate. Additional characteristics of real-time processing include data that is maintained "on-line," data that is updated as events occur, and a computer that can be interrogated from remote stations. Hence, the single greatest advantage of real-time processing is speed.

Despite some debate about whether management planning and control information systems require the speed of real-time processing,[11] use of this mode is certain to accelerate. Part of this increased usage lies in improved technology, primarily *computer-communications* systems. Currently, about 12 percent of the computers installed around the world are communications-oriented. By 1972 this figure should increase to 52 percent, and by 1975 to between 60 and 70 percent.[12] Not all these computers will be business-oriented. Nevertheless, the growing emphasis on computer-communications systems will usher in a new era of real-time business applications.

The developments in real-time processing coupled with the design of common data-base systems will provide the necessary tools to give reasonable responses to management requests from a central data base. The time when the manager, in a paperless, peopleless office with a computer terminal, will make decisions based on his real-time access to a data bank is not likely to be in the 1970's; nevertheless, several management applications will be available. Model building will become much more commonplace as systems designers and managers familiarize themselves with this excellent tool of problem solving. The manager can ask questions of the "what-if" type and thereby explore more alternatives at greater depth. The remote terminal, the data bank, the real-time processing, and the library of easily retrieved programs and mathematical models will provide a business laboratory in which the manager can explore the results of his decisions before making them.

The movement toward real-time applications has already started in many forward-thinking companies, and more will follow soon. A side benefit from this type of processing is managerial involvement. As one corporation president said, "In our firm we find the most effective method of involvement comes from the use of a direct-access console. Togetherness is *time-sharing!*"[13] [Italics added.]

Time Sharing

The state-of-the-art in time sharing has been described as "a conglomerate of third-generation hardware, second-generation software, first-generation terminals, and 'zero' generation in management enlightenment."[14] Despite this pessimistic view, the advancement in communications technology, together with the design of common data-base systems previously mentioned, will undoubtedly make the 1970's the decade of time sharing.

Time-sharing developments will have a marked effect on individual company systems; there is little doubt but that the larger companies with regional or single-plant computers will probably move to a central, large-scale, time-sharing system to do most of the data-processing work for the entire organization. Each plant or region may retain a small-scale computer for local processing tasks and to act as a satellite of the larger, central one.

Although time sharing at its current stage of development offers limited attractiveness (on a real time basis) for the housekeeping variety of applications (payroll, billing, etc.), its use will no doubt grow in the future as communications and other costs come down. The typical small organization will probably use a terminal connected to a commercial time-sharing service bureau. Advantages of time sharing under this type of arrangement include:

1. Real-time response to queries.
2. Access to a library of easily used "canned" programs.
3. Convenience of installing a terminal wherever there is a telephone.
4. Low cost. Because the central computer can handle so many customers (the Scientific Data Systems Sigma 7 provides conversational time sharing for more than 200 users at once), the data-processing costs are reduced substantially over the same processing in a batch mode.

Service Systems

A step beyond the time-sharing method of data processing is the concept of the "dedicated services" system or the "complete" data-processing service bureau, which can provide a wide range of services to eliminate the need for the customer to have his own data-processing staff. The idea is to sell the customer answers instead of machine time.

These service systems will be designed to create support for specific industries, markets, or applications on a regional or national basis, providing a complete range of information services. The data-processing firm that deals in such services to selected industries will be able to provide in one package the advanced equipment, the systems programs, and the human and financial resources that individual users are unable to provide for themselves. It is essentially "one-stop shopping" for the user (lawyer, doctor, association, firm in a particular industry) who subscribes to the service. Because of the proliferation of users and applications in the 1970's, off-the-shelf programs and applications designs may be another service provided by the specialized "complete" data-processing service. Estimates of the market for dedicated services range up to $1 or $2 billion by mid-1970.

Improved Technology

All the foregoing predictions depend upon the development of improved hardware and design capabilities. In a very brief period of time we have witnessed the transition from first- to third-generation computers. Additions per second have shot up from 16,000 in the first generation to a million and a half in the third. As speed and capacity have increased, costs have gone down dramatically, and there is no indication that this trend will reverse itself. The emphasis in the future will therefore be on software and personnel costs because these will place a severe limit on how the fourth-generation equipment will be used.

The need to emphasize the software and people components of future systems cannot be overemphasized. We have been accustomed in the past to think of computers in terms of their computational ability and storage capacity. These surpassed long ago the ability of designers and managers to take full advantage of them in systems design. The "computer revolution" has now become the "information revolution" as our interest turns from hardware considerations to the effect of information systems on the practice of management. Some of the technical developments that will assist or facilitate the design of better management information systems are mentioned briefly here.

1. The current state of *data communications* is probably the major obstacle to overcome in the near future if real-time and time-sharing applications are to reach their potential. Telephone lines are at present the only practical general means of communication. The future growth of this means is indicated by AT&T's projection that 75 percent of its revenue by the middle or late 1970's will be derived from data transmission rather than

voice. Microwave transmission, satellite communications, and laser transmission are other potential methods of communication not available today on an economical basis. Despite the communication barrier, real-time and time-sharing applications will grow dramatically. Remote job input, on-line terminals ranging from Touch-Tone telephones to improved cathode-ray tubes, and computers of small size will bring EDP to the smallest firm. Many more people will be given on-the-job computer interface by removing EDP from the computer room and utilizing these remote input–output devices.

2. The *man–machine interface* will be significantly improved as direct interrogation of the computer is made through improved keyboard or voice input. Output will be received in the form of printed, displayed, or audio media. The real task in developing these systems is managerial, not hardware. The design and structuring of the system will be aided as managers participate in design in a more meaningful way. Modeling and simulation techniques should also be more widely available.

3. *Large data bases* will become much more common as the cost of storage continues to decrease. Cost reductions and expanded use of random access files and memory will permit the substitution of an integrated data base for the multiplicity of independent files now maintained. However, as in all other developments, the boundaries will be limited by human ability. For example, the organization of data bases and the search techniques for retrieval will continue to limit the use to which they can be put.

4. Present *input/output devices* have been the bottleneck to full use of the computer processor. These must and will be improved. Among the developments that will help to narrow the current performance gap between the central processor and its associated I/O equipment are remote data terminals, optical character recognition, voice input, automatic copying equipment, voice output systems, and revolutionary computerized indexing systems. These and other devices still in basic research will enable the user to communicate with the wealth of information to be contained in the large central data banks.

The People Problem

We can surmise what the future trends in information technology will be and conclude that the industry has the technological capability to produce virtually any kind of hardware with capability and capacity far greater than that in use today. However, the unequivocal conclusion emerges that the limitations upon the use of this equipment are set by the availability and competence of people. The manner in which the equipment is used—systems design, programming, software, and supporting services—will be the critical factor in the development of future management information systems. The people affecting these systems can be classified as the technician and the manager–user, although the sharp distinction between these two groups will tend to diminish in the future.

The projection of technician shortages can only be termed dismal. Starting with an estimated shortage of 100,000 in 1970, the number of computer technicians needed, it is estimated, will increase by 40 percent a year while the *supply* increases by about 20 percent.[15] Moreover, to compound the difficulty, the *qualitative* shortage will probably be worse than the *quantitative*. People required to design and implement the increasingly sophisticated management information systems of the future must be much better qualified and trained than the practitioners of today.

Equally important are the state of training and the state of acceptance of the manager–user. The pace at which the foregoing technological developments occur will depend on management's response to these trends. And, as one observer concluded, "This response will be a function of management's understanding of the achievements in information systems, management's disposition to change, and management's commitment to change."[16]

For achieving the potential of the technology, education is the only answer; great emphasis will have to be placed on teaching techniques. There is some evidence that the educational system may even now be gearing up to handle the tremendous need for better-informed people. Colleges and universities are accelerating their offerings of computer-related courses and are engaging in a number of cooperative research activities with industry. College curricula are moving toward the inclusion of information systems, computers, and quantitative methods.[17] Professional associations (e.g., the American Institute of Certified Public Accountants) are recognizing the need for systems education and making provision for it. Several computer-related associations have begun earnest efforts to determine the needs for future computer and systems education and to have curricula implemented.[18] The federal government, with 25 percent of the nation's computer inventory, has taken giant strides to overcome the shortage of both technicians and managers.[19]

MIS: Impact on the Manager and the Management Process

In Chapters 1 through 4 we examined at some length the development of the systems approach and the manner in which it has affected organization theory, the management process, and hence the job of the manager. Can we speculate about the future? Although we cannot predict the future with any degree of certainty, there are two characteristics of the managerial environment of the 1970's and 1980's about which we can be certain: there will be change and increasing complexity, and they will occur at an accelerating rate. What effect will this have on the manager and the management process as we try to handle change with better management information systems?

As the systems concept pervades organizational life, the manager may find that the nature of his job and the way he perceives his role may change greatly. The "systems" nature of this job has been pointed out by Herbert Simon:

> I suppose that managers will be called on, as automation proceeds, for more of what might be described as "systems thinking." They will need, to work effectively, to understand their organizations as large and complex dynamic systems involving various sorts of man–machine and machine–machine interactions. For this reason, persons trained in fields like servo-mechanism engineering or mathematical economics, accustomed to dynamic systems of these kinds, and possessing conceptual tools for understanding them, may have some advantage, at least initially, in operating in the new world. Since no coherent science of complex systems exists today, universities and engineering schools are understandably perplexed as to what kinds of training will prepare their present students for this world.[20]

The manager of the future who "thinks systems" will be of a breed different from that of the contemporary manager, who is technically oriented or a specialist in some functional area such as engineering, sales, accounting, or manufacturing. The new breed of manager will be a generalist who understands the need to bring the diverse elements of the organization together in a *system*. He will be concerned with organizational goals, not with a specialty, a technique, or a subsystem.

This systems approach to managing requires a completely different outlook, a new way of thinking. The *system* (organization) is *integrated* by the common medium of information, which is furnished by a properly designed *management information system*. This view is certainly not the total substance of the systems approach, but it provides the essence of it and the vehicle through which decisions are made and implemented.

The need for information and data in tomorrow's complex environment was expressed recently by James E. Webb, former manager of a complex organization (administrator, National Aeronautics and Space Administration, 1961–68): ". . . [executives] cannot leave it to others to 'keep on top of the data' while they attend to 'more important things.' If they do, they cannot accomplish their jobs."[21]

THE NEED FOR MANAGERIAL INVOLVEMENT IN SYSTEMS DESIGN

Evidence continues to mount that the results obtained from existing computer-based information systems are something less than expected and that lack of *adequate management support* heads the list of causes. The most critical prerequisite to the proper design of information systems is unquestionably the personal involvement of managers at all levels, but there is still a widespread tendency for manager–users to abdicate their responsibilities in systems design to the computer specialist.

Research supports this view. Thurston found that control of information systems work tended to fall into the hands of staff specialists, and that results from these specialists were generally not as satisfactory as those from operating managers.[22] In a study of computer effectiveness in 27 companies, Garrity concluded that the companies utilizing computers effectively were those that involved operating management in the selection and manning of computer projects and in the responsibility for those projects.[23] After a screening of more than 50 companies to determine the state-of-the-art in *marketing* systems, another study revealed that the most striking characteristic of the successful company is its view of the development of the information systems as a responsibility of both top management and operating line management.[24] In a survey of more than 2500 executives in 140 companies, the Diebold Research Program determined that failure to reach the true potential of the computer is due partly to the fact that *technicians*, not management, are setting goals for computers.[25] Even the federal government concluded: "Without question, the single most critical problem in ADP training is the need for understanding and support by top management."[26]

Causes of Systems Difficulties

Judging from research studies, from a review of the literature, and from what can be observed in actual organizations, we can summarize the major causes of systems difficulties. Notice that all of these difficulties could be overcome to some extent by appropriate *management involvement*:

1. *Computer rather than user orientation.* This reflects the "automation of records" or the "one-for-one-changeover" syndrome, which emphasizes the use of the computer for clerical processing applications rather than for managerial decision making. As the computer comes of age, the orientation must change from the record-keeping function to one concerned with operational improvement.

2. *Improper definition of user requirements.* Related to the first difficulty is the need to clearly define systems objectives and information requirements. These are frequently the most difficult steps in design and the ones in which the manager–user must be involved.

3. *Organization of the systems function.* Traditionally, computer organizations were placed under an accounting or financial manager because of the "most use" principle. As companies extend applications from finance

into operations and other widespread areas, the organization should be examined also. The successful company follows the same basic pattern or organization in operation of the systems function as elsewhere in the company—placement of overall responsibility near the top and involvement of operating management in increasing the effectiveness of computer operations.

4. *Overlooking the human side of information systems.* The impact of computer applications elsewhere in the organization is frequently minimized or overlooked. Human fears and natural reluctance to change must be overcome with better communications regarding the nature, the purpose, and the impact of the computer. Gaining acceptance and participation in the systems effort is also a function of top management.

5. *Underestimating complexity and costs.* Unless there is adequate experience upon which to base estimates, the likely tendency in a period of initial experimentation is to underestimate the cost and complexity of systems design and implementation. This initial phase is critical because it frequently sets the mood and the course for the future.

Prerequisites for Useful Management Information Systems

From what we have outlined thus far in this chapter, it appears that the prerequisites to a successful management information systems effort are three. Indeed, this was ably stated in the research study sponsored by the National Association of Accountants:

> In examining the differences between apparently successful and unsuccessful approaches to these more advanced systems, three requirements were isolated:
> a. A good information system or information base upon which to build a data base.
> b. A system staff that understands the management aspects of the problems being studied and an involved management that understands something of the computer and the systems approach—*a management base.*
> c. Sufficient highly placed executive support to help cross organizational boundaries, to restructure activities where needed, and to overcome natural resistance to change—top-level management support.[27]

The data or information systems base requires at least a minimum of computer hardware, software, and experience with applications—that is, a support base from which to build an integrated system—and people who not only appreciate the need for integrated systems and a good data-collection system but who have first-hand knowledge of the operations of the company and its information needs.

The management base is composed of two interacting and overlapping groups: (1) computer people who know something about the process of management, about decision making, about the information needs of management planning and control, and about utilization of the computer to coalesce the design of an information system to facilitate these needs; and (2) management people who understand the operation of a computer and can work with systems technicians in designing a system to provide information for management needs. In other words, the management base will go far toward eliminating the constant gap between manager and technician, a gap that must be closed for good systems design.

The top-level management support base is necessary for three reasons. First, subordinate managers are naturally lethargic about activities that do not have the support or interest of their superiors. To illustrate, consider the findings of the NAA study cited, which found that "the company with the most primitive systems had a management 'completely unconcerned with the computer,' and a company with serious conversion problems had a management that 'used to be interested.'" Second, the resources involved in computer-based information systems are large and are growing larger as a percentage of company sales and capital investment. Such a significant investment in resources requires top-management attention. Finally, if we are to build *integrated* systems that cut across organizational boundaries, upper-level support is necessary if only to achieve the coordination required in an effort that transcends these boundaries.

Managerial Involvement—Conclusion

The almost universal applicability of the computer and the acceleration of increasingly sophisticated applications make inevitable the day when all managers must become involved in computer information systems design. In summary, there appear to be three major reasons. First, the time is rapidly approaching when, for personal reasons, the manager must **bring to the job** at least a minimum familiarity with the topic. Second, from the point of view of the organization, a company's information system will have to become a vital part of its operation, just as marketing, operations, and finance are today. Third, it simply makes good sense for managers to become involved, because much better and more effective information systems will be the result of their involvement. Let us examine each of these reasons more closely.

For personal reasons the manager should keep abreast of new information techniques that increasingly affect his job. In this area the seat-of-the-pants operating manager is a thing of the past. If he plans to be a manager in a computer-using company or one that will eventually obtain a computer, he cannot take the position that he knows nothing about computers or that "the computer won't affect my job." He cannot delegate the job of systems design and use because only he, not the technician, can develop systems objectives and information needs. More and more modern corporations are turning to a new generation of management in order to utilize the third- and fourth-generation equipment and techniques necessary to remain competitive. If today's manager does not join this new generation through interest, education, and involvement, the organization must of necessity turn to others who will.

It is increasingly evident that the company's information system is becoming part and parcel of the total organizational resources that make up the company. Indeed, in many companies the information system is considered to be as important as market strategy, product design, or manufacturing technology in giving the company a competitive edge. The day will probably come when no company will be better than its information system. *For organization reasons,* therefore, the executives who view their job as the economic allocation of resources will become involved in the allocation of systems resources, because these are becoming as important as other major functions in the conduct of the business.

Since effective *systems design* cannot take place in a managerial vacuum, it also makes sense for the manager to become involved. Aside from the reasons outlined previously, the participation of operating management in the design of its own systems will result in better systems design at lesser cost in the long run because design requires a reasonably intimate knowledge of the problems of the particular field. It is as difficult for the accountant to design the production control system as it is for the personnel officer to design the accounting system. On the other hand, it is not difficult to provide the accountant, the personnel officer, and the production control manager with sufficient knowledge of the computer to enable them to participate in the design of systems that will help them in their own operation. Indeed, it is much easier to impart knowledge of the computer to the operating manager than to teach the computer technician the details of an operation in sufficient depth for him to design a system by himself.

In conclusion, it can be said that although most executives pay lip service to computers and systems design and are willing to invest company resources of money and personnel, something more is needed. This something more is *time and effort.* Executives must invest the time and effort to support systems design efforts, upgrade their skills in this vital area of management, and become actively involved in the development and design of management information systems.

The key to the Systems Age is *involvement,* and there is little time to lose.

REFERENCES

1. Herbert Simon, "Will the Corporation Be Managed by Machines?" in Melvin Anshen and George L. Bach, *Management and Corporations: 1985* (New York: McGraw-Hill Book Company, 1960), p. 22.
2. Harold J. Leavitt and Thomas L. Whisler, "Management in the 1980's," *Harvard Business Review*, November–December 1958.
3. Adrian M. McDonough, "Keys to a Management Information System in Your Company," in *The Third Generation Computer* (New York: American Management Association, 1966), p. 27.
4. "Tomorrow's Leaders View the Problems of the Next 25 Years," *Saturday Review*, January 13, 1968, pp. 31–66.
5. Steven Norwood, "Wanted: Human Skills for the Computer," *Electronics Age*, Autumn 1968.
6. Warren G. Bennis, "New Patterns of Leadership for Tomorrow's Organizations," *Technology Review*, April 1968, p. 37.
7. Terrance Hanold, "A President's View of MIS," *Datamation*, November 1968, p. 62.
8. "An Overview of the Information Processing and Computer Community," *Journal of Data Management*, June 1969, p. 32.
9. Neil Churchill, *Computer-Based Information Systems for Management: A Survey* (New York: National Association of Accountants, 1969), p. 139.
10. James W. Taylor and Neal J. Dean, "Managing to Manage the Computer," *Harvard Business Review*, September–October 1966.
11. See, for example, John Dearden, "Myth of Real-Time Management Information," *Harvard Business Review*, May–June 1966.
12. This estimate was made by James Bradburn, executive vice-president of RCA Information Systems, in the *Journal of Data Management*, June 1969, p. 73.
13. Hanold, "A President's View of MIS," p. 62.
14. Lee Pryor, "Time Sharing at This Point in Time," *Journal of Data Management*, May 1969, p. 30.
15. An estimate made by Dick Brandon, president of Applied Systems, Inc. See "An Overview of the Information Processing and Computer Community," *Journal of Data Management*, June 1969, p. 26.
16. D. F. Heany, *Development of Information Systems* (New York: The Ronald Press Company, 1968), p. 390.
17. In a 1966 survey of American Association of Collegiate Schools of Business members, 97 percent of the respondents endorsed education in computer technology. A survey of this effort in colleges of business is described in Daniel Couger, "Educating Potential Managers About Computers," *California Management Review*, Fall 1968.
18. See Robert G. Murdick and Joel E. Ross, "The Need for Systems Education" (three-part series), *Journal of Systems Management*, July, August, and September, 1969.

19. For an in-depth study of the need for training managers and systems analysts, and the recommended curricula, see Joel E. Ross, *The Relationship of ADP Training Curriculum and Methodology in the Federal Government* (Washington, D.C.: Association for Educational Data Systems, 1967), a report prepared under the sponsorship of the U.S. Department of Health, Education and Welfare.
20. Herbert A. Simon, "Will the Corporation be Managed by Machines?" in *The Shape of Automation* (New York: Harper & Row, Publishers, 1965), p. 49.
21. James E. Webb, *Space Age Management* (New York: McGraw-Hill Book Company, 1969), p. 146.
22. Philip H. Thurston, "Who Should Control Information Systems?" *Harvard Business Review,* November–December 1962, p. 135.
23. John T. Garrity, "Top Management and Computer Profits," *Harvard Business Review,* July–August 1963, p. 6.
24. Donald F. Cox and Robert E. Good, "How to Build a Marketing Information System," *Harvard Business Review,* May–June 1967.
25. John Diebold, "Bad Decisions on Computer Use," *Harvard Business Review,* January–February 1969, p. 16.
26. National Bureau of Standards, *Training for Automation and Information Processing in the Federal Service* (Washington, D.C.: U.S. National Bureau of Standards, 1966).
27. Churchill, *Computer-Based Information Systems for Management,* p. 141.

index

Ackoff, Russell, 48
Activity design form, 479
Adaptive systems, defined, 281
Administration, basic elements of, 36
Age of Synthesis, 5–6
Alphanumeric code, 325
Alternatives, determining and evaluating, 118
Analog models, characteristics of, 380
Andrews, Kenneth, 57
Argyris, Chris, 41, 44–45, 77–79, 82, 93
Authority:
   chain of command and, 37, 49, 53, 54
   organizing and delegation of, 124–25
   responsibility and, 37
   sources of, 87–89
   (*see also* Leadership)
Automation (*see* Computer-based information systems; Computers)

Bakke, E. Wright, 50
Balance, as integrating process, 107
Batch processing system, 156*n*, 161, 227–28
Behavioral school, 43–45
Bennis, Warren, 41, 134, 550
Binary representation, defined, 207
Black box concept, 387–90
Blake, R. R., 50, 97
Block diagram models, 387–90
Blumenthal, S. C., 324
Bottom-up approach, 437
Boulding, Kenneth E., 290
Budgeting of MIS planning, 437
Business organization system, defined, 8

Caplow, Theodore, 87
Central processing unit (CPU), 205
Centralization:
   computer technology and, 249
   of control, 133
   Fayol and, 37
Chain of command (scalar principle), 37, 49, 53, 54
Channels of communication:
   defined, 329
   network of, 333, 335
Classical theory of organization, 52–54
   assumptions of, 77–78
   cornerstone of, 119
   span of management in, 123
   systems approach and, 9–10
   tenets of, 53–54
Classification:
   of data, 316
   of information, 323–26
Closed systems, defined, 281
Collegial style of leadership, 94–96
Communication, 327–39
   barriers to, 331–33
   concepts of, 328–30
   described, 69, 327
   importance of, 314
   in informal groups, 85–87
   as integrating process, 107
   interpersonal, 330–33
   network of, 333–36
   redundancy in, 3, 18
   (*see also* Data; Information)

Competitive information, types of, 169
Computer-based information systems:
    components of, 201–11
    conversion from manual to, 212–21
    documentation of, 522
    MARIS as, 284–87
    (see also Data-bank concept: Feedback; Management information systems; Programmed decision systems)
Computers:
    assembly of, 217
    dehumanizing effect of, 21
    growth of market for, 185
    importance of, 39–40
    information best suited for, 177
    programs for, 217–19
    replacing middle management, 249
    speed of, 238
Concept generation, defined, 328
Concepts:
    black box, 387–90
    dynamic systems, 104
    generation of, 328
    immaturity–maturity, 79
    (see also Data-bank concept)
Conceptual systems, defined, 279
Constraints:
    defined, 118
    in MIS gross design, 450–53
    policies as, 120
Control, 125–30
    defined, 49, 110
    of detailed design project, 477
    in feedback, 135–36, 292, 298, 300–301
    of financial plan, 302
    integration of, 258
        integration of planning and, 128–30
    MIS and, 164–65
        control of MIS planning, 163, 438–39, 523
        operational control, 425–26
    operational, 128, 255, 425–26
    through standards of performance, 125–27
    systems approach to, 134–36
Control information, types of, 172–73
Conversion of data, 316
Coordination, as function of top management, 255
Coordination principle, defined, 49
Cordiner, Ralph, 453
Cost:
    as constraint, 451
    of information, 228, 320, 325
    of MIS, 161–62, 507
    of modeling, 386
    as standard of performance, 125–26
CPU (central processing unit), 205
Creative systems approach, defined, 12
Cultural factors:
    in communication, 331
    in decision making, 363–64
Customer departmentation, defined, 120
Cutover, described, 520–21
Cyert, Richard M., 46

Dale, Ernest, 42, 46, 123
Dalton, Melville, 41, 69, 91
Data:
    forms for collection of, 516–17
    life cycle of, 315–17
    meaning of, 314–15
    population of, defined, 327
    storage of, 316, 325
Data-bank concept, 221–32
Data bases, 517
    defined, 323
    of detailed design, 488–89
    growth of, 555
Data processing:
    electronic (see Electronic data processing)
    elements of, 198
    integrated, 256
Davis, Keith, 44, 95–96
Dean, Joel, 47
Dearden, John, 177, 256
Decision-assisting information system, 243–45
Decision centers in communication network, 333, 334
Decision making, 355–73
    anatomy of, 365–68
    empirical information for, 24
    as integrating process, 107–8
    MIS in (see Management information systems)
    nonprogrammed, 356–58
    process of, 360–65
    programmed (see Programmed decision systems)
    rational, 25
    techniques for, 244
    (see also Problem solving)
Decision rules, 20, 185, 240, 241, 377
Decision theory school, 46–47
Departmentation, 120–22
Descriptive models, characteristics of, 379
Design:
    file, 215–16
    of MIS (see Detailed design; Gross design)
Detailed design, 474–503
    aim of, 475–76
    data base of, 488–89
    documenting, 496
    information formats for, 493–94
    levels of automation in, 487–88
    performance criteria of, 477–78
    quantitative modeling of, 489–92
    subsystems of, 478–85
    testing of, 494–95
Deterministic information, defined, 319–20
Deterministic models, characteristics of, 381
Dewey, John, 358
Dewey Decimal System, 325
Diebold, John, 185
Differentiation, defined, 73–74
Directing:
    defined, 49, 110
    integration of, 257
Discipline:
    defined, 37
    in informal groups, 87

Dissemination of information, 326
Drucker, Peter, 32, 355
Dubin, R., 41
Dynamic information, defined, 320–21
Dynamic models, characteristics of, 380

Economic trends, as environmental information, 169
EDP (*see* Electronic data processing)
Effectiveness:
 defined, 93
 of information storage, 326–27
Efficiency:
 defined, 94
 in transmission, 329–30
Eisenhower, Dwight D., 123
Electronic data processing (EDP), 195–97
 clerical applications of, 247
 defined, 201, 211
 effects of, on structure of management, 249
 inputs in, 202–3
 storage in, 205–10
Empirical school, 45–46
Empirical systems, defined, 12, 279
Environment:
 in classification of information systems, 270–72
 information search in, defined, 322–23
 organizational information needs and, 455–56
 as part of systems approach, 107
Environmental information, types of, 168–69
Etzioni, Amitai, 92
Evaluation of data, 317
External constraints, types of, 452–53
External storage:
 in EDP, 211
 in manual information system, 200

Facilities network, 269
Fayol, Henri, 34, 36–38, 48, 49, 59
Feedback, 292–301
 control and, 135–36, 292, 298, 300–301
 defined, 110, 298–99
 elements and operation of, 292–99
 self-correction of systems through, 301
 theory of, 19
 use of models in, 390–93
Files:
 design, of, 215–16
 for implementation of MIS, 517–18
 master, defined, 517
Financial information systems, 175–77
Financial plan:
 outputs and control of, 302
 planning and, 170
 standards of performance for, 126
Flowcharts:
 general system, 463–64
 for inventory control system, 220
 program, 216–17
 types of, in detailed design, 485–87
Follet, Mary Parker, 59, 89

Formal organizational system, described, 68–69
Forms:
 activity design, 479
 data collection, 516–17
Forrester, Jay W., 46
Function models, types of, 379
Functional departmentation, defined, 120
Functional principle, defined, 49
Functional system, described, 70
Fusion process, defined, 50

Gaming, 20, 47, 381
Gantt chart, 437
Garrity, John T., 558
General models, characteristics of, 381
General system flowchart, 463–64
Generality models, types of, 381
Generation of data, 315–16
Gilbreth, Lillian M., 47
Government controls, 72, 168, 452
Graicunas, V. A., 123
Grapevine patterns of communication network, 333
Gross design, 446–47
 constraints in, 450–53
 developing alternative, 461–62
 documenting, 462–67
 fundamental ideas of, 446
 information needs and sources for, 453–61
 need to define problem in, 446–47
 report of, 467–68
 setting objectives for, 447–49
Group dynamics, defined, 83
Gulick, L., 49, 53

Hall, A. D., 328
Hawthorne experiments, 38–39, 44, 54, 59
Herzberg, Frederick, 44, 45, 79–81, 94–95
Heuristics 47
Hierarchical classification of information, 323–24
Hitch, Charles, 47
Homans, G. C., 41
Horizontal integration of resources, 260–61
Human behavior school, 43–44
Human relations:
 in informal groups, 85
 neoclassical organization theory, 54–56
 productivity and, 38–39

Iconic models, characteristics of, 380
IDP (integrated data processing), 256
Immaturity–maturity concept, 79
Incentives:
 needs and, 75
 noneconomic and economic, 83
 wage, 36
Independent variables in model construction, 400
Inductive approach, systems approach vs., 13–16
Informal organization, 55, 83–91
 conflict and cooperation in, 91

Informal organization (*cont.*)
  described, 69
  nature and formation of, 83–86
  as part of system, 106
  power and authority in, 87–90
  standards and norms of, 87
Information:
  best suited for computer use, 177
  characteristics of, 317–21
    as catalyst, 154
    as resource, 159–60
  control and, 172
  defined, 314–15
  organizing and, 171
  in planning, 166–70
  provided by MIS, 160–61
  search for, 322–23
  sources, 457–58
  storage of (*see* Storage)
  (*see also* Data)
Information flows:
  in communication network, 333, 335
  in detailed design, 485–87
Information network, 269–70
Information systems (*see* Batch processing system; Computer-based information systems; Feedback; Major information systems; Management information systems; Manual information system; Real-time information systems)
Input documents, purpose of, 213–15
Input/output analysis in gross design, 458–59
Input/output devices, need to improve, 555
Inputs:
  in block diagram model, 388
  in EDP, 202–3
  in feedback, 293, 300
  gross design, 464
  in manual information system, 199
  in MARIS, 284
Intangible standards of performance, defined, 126
Integrated data processing (IDP), 256
Internal constraints, types of, 451–52
Internal information, types of, 170
Internal storage:
  in EDP, 205–9
  in manual information system, 200
Inventory accounting system, 163
Inventory control system:
  comparison between manual and computer-based, 211–12
  in gross design concept, 465–67
  test rules for, 489, 491
Isolates, defined, 85

Keating, S. F., 550
Kettering, Charles, 17
Knowledge:
  as criterion of professionalism, 58
  as prerequisite for MIS, 159
Koontz, Harold, 49, 117
Korzybsky, Alfred, 291

Leadership, 91–99
  nature of, 92
  situational approach to, 92–93
  styles of, 93–97
Learned, Edward P., 46
Leavitt, Harold J., 21, 248–49
Lewin, Kurt, 83
Likert, Rensis, 41, 50

McDonough, A. M., 325, 549
McFarlan, F. Warren, 177
McFarland, Dalton E., 49
McGregor, Douglas, 41, 44, 50, 77, 79, 105
Machine systems, defined, 280
Machines, information for, 320–21
McNamara, Robert S., 22
Major information systems, 176, 264
Man–machine interfaces, 330, 555
Man–machine systems, 280, 288–89, 317–20
Man-made systems, defined, 280
Management:
  characterized, 56–59
  functions of, 48–49
    (*see also* Control; Decision making; Directing; Organizing; Planning; Staffing)
  general principles of, 36–38
  McNamara's definition of, 22
  programmed decision systems and levels of (*see* Programmed decision systems)
  as science (*see* Management science)
  as system, 136–41
  theories of (*see* Management theory)
  (*see also* Managers)
Management control, defined, 128
Management information systems (MIS), 175–87, 422–43, 506–63
  basic, 175–84
    financial, 175–77
    marketing, 178–79
    personnel, 179–83
    production/operations, 177–78, 180
    purchasing, 184
  classification of, 263–75, 283–84
  decision-assisting, 243–45
  defined, 7, 69, 292
  elements of, 160–62
  as empirical systems, 279
  evolution of, 154–58
  function of, 138–40
  future of, 548–63
  implementation of, 506–43
    data collection for, 516–17
    documenting, 521–22
    files for, 517–18
    plans for, 507–11
    procedures for, 513–14
    testing of, 518–20
  integration of, 256–57
  operation of, 162–66
  planning of, 422–43
    need for, 423–26
    objectives, 426–28
    project, 429–33
    reporting and controlling, 163, 438–39, 523

Management information systems (MIS) (*cont.*)
  techniques, 434–37
  prerequisites for, 159–60
  (*see also* Computer-based information systems; Manual information system)
Management operating systems, defined, 264
Management process school, 48–49
Management reporting systems, defined, 264
Management science, 376–417
  defined, 20–21, 377–78
  models and (*see* Models)
  in programmed decision system, 240, 243
  requirements of, 376
  techniques of, 20–21
Management theory, 32–51
  development of, 32–40
  schools of, 41–51
  systems approach to (*see* Systems approach)
  (*see also* Modern organization theory)
Managerial grid, uses of, 97
Managers:
  future, 23–25
  MIS and, 158, 462–67, 557–62
  overall functions of, 35, 108
  technicians compared with, 447
Manpower information systems, 182–83
Manual information system:
  conversion of, 212–21
  documenting, 521–22
March, James G., 33, 41, 45, 46, 107
MARIS (computer-based marketing information system):
  components of, 286
  inputs and outputs in, 284
  parameters in, 285
  structure of, 287
Market, as control information, 172
Marketing information system, 178–79
  (*see also* MARIS)
Markov-process state-descriptions, 394–95
Marshall, Alfred G., 33
Maslow, A. H., 44, 75, 79
Master classification plan, 265
Master file, defined, 517
Master Program Schedule (MPS), 437
Master Project Network Plan, 437
Material control system, objectives of, 449
Material logistics system, described, 70
Materials network, 268–69
Mathematical data transmission theory, 327–30
Matrix state-descriptions, 395–96
Mayo, Elton, 44, 54 ,59
Mechanistic approach, 24–25
Medium-range plans, defined, 116
Memory, computer, 205–9
Middle management:
  information needs of, 455–56
  integration of, 262–63
  programmed decision making and, 248–54
Military, the:
  as pioneer in management, 33
  structured approach to decision making, 46

The Military (*cont.*)
  view of, on information systems, 256–57
Minor information systems, defined, 264
Models, 133, 378–402
  block diagram, 387–90
  gaming, 9, 20, 47, 381
  quantitative, in detailed design, 489–92
  (*see also* Simulation)
Modern organization theory:
  characteristics of, 40–41
  systems approach to, 105–8
  (*see also* Informal organization; Leadership; Motivation)
Modules:
  basic, in block diagram concept, 388–90
  complete systems, 299
  defined, 259
Money networks, 269
Monte Carlo methods, 20, 47
Mooney, James D., 49, 53
Moore, Franklin G., 49
Morris, William T., 366–68
Motivation:
  differentiation in, 73–74
  frustration and, 82
  hygiene factors and, 79
  needs and, 74–77
  organizational control and, 77–79
  Theories X and Y of, 44, 50, 77, 78
Motivators, positive, 79–82, 95
Mouton, Jane S., 50, 97
MPS (Master Program Schedule) 437
Multidimensional flow technique, 458

Natural systems, defined, 279
Needs, 74–81
  basic, 75–77
  hierarchy of, 44
Negative feedback, defined, 391
Neoclassical organization theory (human relations approach), 54–56
Network flows (resource flows), 104, 136, 138–39, 267–70
Networks:
  communication, 333–36
  facilities, 269
  information, 269–70
  materials, 268–69
  money and order, 269
Newman, William H., 49
Noise, minimization of, 329
Nonadaptive systems, defined, 281
Nonlinear information, defined, 321
Nonstationary systems, defined, 282
Normative models, characteristics of, 379

Objectives:
  defined, 113
  of MIS gross design, 447–49
  of MIS planning, 425–28, 431–32
  of programmed decision systems, 256–61
  setting, 117
O'Donnell, Cyril, 49, 117
Open systems, defined, 280–81
Operating systems, 8

570 index

Operational control, 128, 255, 425–26
Optner, Stanford L., 282
Orders network, 269
Organistic approach, defined, 24
Organizational specialization, 54–55
Organizational systems, classified, 283
Organizations:
  cybernetic concept of, 135, 139, 141
  defined, 40
  effects of computers on, 249
  future, 22–23
  informal (*see* Informal organization)
  information systems compared with, 8
  integration of, 258–59
  interests served by, 71–73
  modern, complexity of, 4, 16–19
  network of communication in, 333–36
  as system, 136–41, 299–302
  systems approach to (*see* Systems approach)
  (*see also* Management)
Organizing, 118–25
  defined, 48
  delegation of authority in, 124–25
  departmentation and, 120–23
  implementation of MIS, 512
  information and, 171
  integrating with planning and control, 128–30
  span of management and, 123–24
  systems approach to, 133–34
Orlicky, Joseph, 428
Output documents, purpose of, 215
Outputs:
  in block diagram model, 388
  in electronic data processing, 211
  in feedback, 293, 300–301
  of financial plan, 302
  gross design, 464–66
  in manual information system, 201
  in MARIS, 284

Parameters:
  of models, 393
  system, defined, 285
Parsons, Talcott, 52
P/C/T (performance/cost/time), 438–39
Performance:
  measuring, 127–28
  of MIS, 161
  standards of, 125–27
  trade-off criteria, 477–78
Permanent systems, defined, 281
Personnel:
  as control information, 173
  in MIS, 162, 514–15
  planning of, 255
  records of, 183
Personnel information system, 179–83
PERT (*see* Program Evaluation Review Technique)
Physical standards of performance, defined, 126
Planning, 108–18
  defined, 48

Planning (*cont.*)
  dimensions and types of, 111-16
  information and, 166–70
  integration of, 257
    integration of control and, 128–30
  iterative nature of, 110
  labor, 255–56
  MIS for, 164–65
  of MIS implementation, 507–11
  process of, 116–18
  production, 247
  sequence, 436
  systems approach to, 131–33
  (*see also* Systems approach)
Planning analysis and control component, 165
Planning information system, described, 171
Policies:
  as constraints to planning, 170
  defined, 114–15
Population of data, defined, 327
Positive motivators, 79–82, 95
Power, defined, 89
Power subsystems, 90
Power systems, described, 69–70
PPBS (Program Planning and Budgeting Systems), 133
Pragmatic approach, 12–13
  to problem solving, 350
Predictive models, characteristics of, 379
Probabilistic information, 319–20
Probabilistic models, characteristics of, 381
Probability theory, 20
Problem boundaries, defined, 450
Problem solving, 342–54
  defined, 342
  formulation and nature of problems in, 344–48
  process of, 348–54
  systems approach to, 9–11
    (*see also* Systems approach)
  (*see also* Decision making)
Process departmentation, defined, 123
Processors:
  in block diagram model, 388
  central, in electronic data processing, 203–5
  complexity of, 296–98
  in feedback, 293
  in manual information system, 200
Product changes, causes of, 18
Product departmentation, defined, 120
Product planning, defined, 255
Production, factors of, 169
Production/operations information systems, 177–78, 180
Production planning, 247
Productivity, 36, 38–39
Professionalism, criteria of, 57–58
Program Evaluation Review Technique (PERT), 133, 184, 476
  PER/COST, 184
  PERT/CPM (Critical Path), 184, 257, 437
  PERT/LOB (Line of Balance) and PERT/TIME, 184
Program flowchart, purpose of, 216–17

Program Planning and Budgeting Systems (PPBS), 133
Programmed decision systems, 20, 39, 185–87, 229–32, 238–75
 classification of information systems for, 263–75, 283–84
 decision-assisting information systems and, 243–45
 integration as objective of, 256–61
 levels of management and, 245–56, 270–71
 nature of process of, 239–43
Project departmentation, defined, 123
Project planning of MIS detailed design, 476–77
Project proposal outline, MIS, 433
Projects, defined, 429
Psychological factors:
 in communication, 331
 in decision making, 362–63
Purchasing information system, 184

Quality, as standard of peformance, 125
Quantitative school, 47–48
Queuing theory, 20, 47

R&D (research and development), 17, 173
Rational factors in decision making, 362
Real-time information systems, 161
 defined, 156, 228–29
 growth of, 552–53
Receivers in communication system, 330
Records:
 internal and external, 457
 personnel, 183
Recruitment, function of, 183
Redundancy in communication process, 3, 18
Reiley, Allan C., 49
Reliability of information, 320
Reports:
 of gross design, 467–68
 on MIS planning, 438–39
 on P/C/T, 438–39
Reproduction of data, 316
Research and development (R&D), 17, 173, 184
Resource flows (network flows), 104, 136, 138–39, 267–70
Resource planning, defined 256
Resources:
 defined 104
 information as, 159–60
 integration of, 259–62
Retrieval of information, 323–27
Revenue, as standard of performance, 126
Roethlisberger, Fritz, 44
Roman Catholic Church, and management, 33
Roy, Donald F., 86

SAGE (Semi-Automatic Ground Environment) 229
Sales forecast, planning and, 170
Sampling of information, 458
Scalar principle (chain of command), 39, 49, 53, 54

Schlaifer, Robert O., 48
Schmidt, Warren H., 92
Schools of management theory, 41–51
Scott, William G., 40, 55, 105, 107–8
Search, information, 322–23
Self-control, as criterion of professionalism, 58
Semi-Automatic Ground Environment (SAGE), 229
Sensors in MIS, 163, 165
Sequence planning, 436
Service systems, 553–54
Shannon, Claude, 319
Short-term plans, defined, 116
Sign, defined, 314
Simon, Herbert, 41, 44–46, 52, 107, 238, 363, 548, 557
Simulation, 20, 47
 described, 20–21, 397–99
 as information system, 184
 possibilities offered by, 230–32
 to test detailed design, 494–95
Smith, Adam, 33, 54
Social factors:
 in communication, 331
 in decision making, 363
Social responsibility, as criterion of professionalism, 58
Social system school, 44–45
Social systems:
 defined, 280
 informal organization as, 83–91
Social trends, as environmental information, 168–69
Source documents, internal and external, 484
Space layouts for implementing MIS, 511–12
Specialization:
 of labor, 33, 37, 119
 organizational, 54–55
Specialized models, characteristics of, 381
Staff principle, 49
Staffing, defined, 48–49
Standards of performance, 125–27
 in information feedback, 300–301
State-descriptive models of systems, 392–96
Static models, characteristics of, 380
Stationary systems, defined, 282
Status symbols, 83, 84
Steady-state information, defined, 320–21
Steiner, George A., 11–12, 115, 162
Storage:
 of data, 316, 325
 in EDP, 205–10
 information:
  important aspects of, 325–27
  in manual information system, 200, 222–27
  types of classification used, 323–24
Strategic planning, 112–15
 as function of top management, 255
Strategy, defined, 115
Structure models, types of, 380
Subsystems:
 defined, 282
 of detailed design, 478–85
 defining, 482–83

Subsystems (*cont.*)
  sketch of, 485–87
  sources of information for, 483–85
  examples of, 15
  power, 90
Supersystems, defined, 282
Supply factors, planning and, 170
Symbolic models, characteristics of, 380
Synergism, defined, 9, 23
Systems, 278–89, 386–89
  boundaries of, 287–88
  characteristics of, 288–89
    holistic nature of, 25
  classification of, 279–84
  components of, 285–86
  defined, 7–8
  modeling of (*see* Models)
  organization as, 136–41, 299–302
    (*see also* Organizations)
  (*see also* Systems approach; Systems theory; *and specific systems; for example*: Computer-based information systems; Management information systems)
Systems analysis, defined, 105, 132
  (*see also* Models)
Systems approach, 4–29, 104–8, 13–37
  basic purpose of, 104–5
  characteristics of, 8–9, 11–13
  to control, 134–36
    (*see also* Control)
  future of, 21–26
  importance of, 5
  inductive approach vs., 13–16
  need to develop, 6
  to organizing, 133–34
    (*see also* Organizing)
  parts of, 105–8, 136–37
  philosophy of, 10–11
  to planning, 131–33
    (*see also* Planning)
  reasons for, 16–21
Systems theory, 289–92

Tactical planning, defined, 112–13
Tannenbaum, Robert, 92
Task-force meetings, as source of information, 483
Task-solving patterns of communication network, 333, 335
Taylor, Frederick W., 34–36, 38, 47, 53, 54, 59
Technological revolution 16–17
Temporary systems, defined, 134, 281–82
Territory departmentation, defined, 120
Terry, George, 39, 49
Test rules for inventory management (TRIM), 489, 491
Theoretical systems approach, defined, 12
Theories:
  feedback theory, 19
  mathematical data transmission theory, 327–30
  neoclassical organization theory, 54–56

Theories (*cont.*)
  probability theory, 20
  queuing theory, 20, 47
  systems theory, 289–92
  X and Y, 44, 50, 77, 78
  (*see also* Classical theory of organization; Management theory; Modern organization theory)
Theory X and theory Y, 44, 50, 77, 78
Thome, P. G., 10
Time, as standard of performance, 125
Time-and-motion study, 35
Time reference models, types of, 380
Time sharing, 553
Top management:
  information needs of, 455–56
  integration of, 262–63
  programmed decision system and, 254–56
Total organization, informal, defined, 83
Total systems approach:
  defined, 8
  information network as linkage in, 270
  of MIS, 256
  Optner on, 282
Townsend, Robert, 82
Training and development, 183, 514–15, 555–56
Transfer function, 287, 389
Transmission:
  of data, 315–16
    mathematical theory of, 327–30
  efficiency of, 329–30
  of information, rate and frequency, 319
Transmitters in communication, 328
Transportation of data, 316
Tree diagrams, 396
TRIM (test rules for inventory management), 489, 491

Uncertainty reference models, types of, 381
Uniterm index method of storage, 324
Unity of command, 37, 53–55
Uris, Auren, 23
Urwick, Lyndall, 49, 53
Users of information:
  identifying, 325
  interest profiles of, 326

Value of information, 320
Vertical integration of resources, 260–61
Von Neumann, John, 47

Ways, Max, 32
Webb, James E., 557
Weber, Max, 51, 52, 88
Whisler, Thomas L., 21, 248–49 548
Wiener, Norbert, 154
Willard, R. G., 10
Work breakdown structure (WBS) in MIS planning, 434–36
Work package information checklist, 436
Work sampling, 458
Working conditions, productivity and, 38